Speech and Voice Science

THIRD EDITION

Speech and Voice Science

THIRD EDITION

Alison Behrman, PhD, CCC-SLP

With Contributions By Donald Finan, PhD

5521 Ruffin Road
San Diego, CA 92123

e-mail: info@pluralpublishing.com
Website: http://www.pluralpublishing.com

Library of Congress Cataloging-in-Publication Data

Names: Behrman, Alison, author. | Finan, Donald, author.
Title: Speech and voice science / Alison Behrman with contributions by Donald Finan.
Description: Third edition. | San Diego, CA : Plural, [2018] | Includes bibliographical references and index.
Identifiers: LCCN 2017030922| ISBN 9781597569354 (alk. paper) | ISBN 1597569356 (alk. paper)
Subjects: | MESH: Speech—physiology | Voice—physiology | Case Reports
Classification: LCC QP306 | NLM WV 501 | DDC 612.7/8—dc23
LC record available at https://lccn.loc.gov/2017030922

Contents

Preface to the Third Edition

I have three distinct, yet interwoven, professional roles: teacher, research scientist, and clinician. This book grew out of my clinical practice. How odd, you might think, for this book is a basic science textbook written primarily for students of speech-language pathology. The role of teacher or research scientist would appear to be a more likely candidate as motivation for this book. Yet I have been struck constantly by the realization of principles of physics and physiology in my interactions with my patients. In truth, the answers for many of the clinical questions raised by speech-language pathologists can be found in the science of voice and speech production and perception. How does one address a deficit in a voice- or speech-disordered individual? Why does a therapeutic technique work for one patient and not for another?

In sum, a solid grounding in speech science makes a speech-language pathologist a better clinician. This book was motivated by my desire to provide students of speech-language pathology with a strong fund of knowledge in speech science—so that they would have this part of the necessary tools with which to become outstanding clinicians and so that they, too, could experience the delightful process of clinical inquiry, problem solving, and, yes, clinical *creativity*. For it is only with a fund of knowledge larger than the moment—greater than one accesses on a day-to-day basis—that one can truly have the freedom to be creative in therapeutic approaches and techniques.

This book is intended primarily for undergraduate and graduate students in speech-language pathology. It should also be of interest to doctoral students and to research scientists as a basic reference text. It is my hope that seasoned clinicians, too, will find this book valuable as a reference source when they encounter patients with speech and voice disorders that present therapeutic challenges.

This book addresses the physics, acoustics, and physiology of voice and speech production. An effort is made to provide a sense of history (remote and recent) and, thereby, a sense of the future direction of the field. I have tried to incorporate some interesting and even amusing notes in the shorter side boxes to help lighten some of the admittedly dense material. Other side boxes are central to understanding the content of the chapter. Printed textbooks remain quite linear in their presentation of material. Most college students, however, have become acclimated to the nonlinear information-gathering style of the Internet, and so I suspect that they will enjoy the side boxes without finding them distracting.

New to the Third Edition

Some exciting new changes have been made to this third edition. Clinical cases, with discussion questions, have been added at the beginning of Chapters 4, 5, 7, 8, and 9 and two more at the end of Chapters 7 and 8. These cases serve to emphasize to the student the clinical utility of speech and voice science and to stimulate thinking and, hopefully, some lively classroom (in-person or virtual) discussions. Discussion questions are provided at the end of each clinical case. Although each clinical case focuses upon the content of the chapter in which it occurs, information is also drawn from other chapters, with some of the discussion questions addressing topics of other chapters. Thus, instructors may find it useful to help the students reexamine each clinical case in subsequent chapters.

Two new chapters have been added to this third edition. Don Finan has provided a much-needed chapter on instrumentation (Chapter 12). It covers basic information about digital signal processing, the instrumental array, consideration of instrumental specifications, and how to obtain valid and reliable acoustic and biophysical data. It demystifies the data acquisition process while, hopefully, stimulating students to try their hand at data gathering themselves.

A new chapter on prosody (Chapter 9) has been added in response to growing interest in prosodic differences among speakers with different native language backgrounds, as well as prosodic disturbances associated with disease processes. Some of the information contained in that chapter had previously been located at the end of the chapter on consonants. Now in its own chapter, coverage of prosody has been expanded to include the acoustic properties that contribute to stress, prominence, and speech rhythm, and its clinical relevance is highlighted.

New to this third edition is the use of the PluralPlus companion website. For students, material includes study aids such as key terms and review questions for each chapter (except for Chapter 1) and a speech science version of a game called Taboo—a lighthearted way to help students study. After all, speech science should be fun (at least a little). For instructors, suggestions for classroom learning activities and lab assignments using free, downloadable acoustic analysis software are offered to provide more effective learning experiences for both undergraduate and graduate students. Revised and updated slides are provided for traditional classroom lectures, and responses to the clinical case questions are provided to help guide classroom discussions or testing.

Reorganization of the introductory material provides a new chapter (Chapter 2) on the physics of motion. This chapter appeared in the first edition and then mysteriously disappeared in the second addition. It has been brought back due to popular demand.

How to Use This Book

The curriculum for speech and voice science varies considerably at the undergraduate and graduate levels across university programs. As such, this book offers some flexibility for faculty. The order of the chapters is organized for a full course in undergraduate speech science. The basic physics of sound (Chapters 2 and 3) lays the groundwork for the students' understanding of speech and voice production. Subsequent chapters mirror somewhat the process of speech production—the respiratory, phonatory, resonatory, and articulatory subsystems (Chapters 3 through 8)—and the interplay of those subsystems in prosody (Chapter 9). Once the students have that basic understanding of speech and voice production, they are ready to ponder the theories of speech production and perception (Chapters 10 and 11).

The chapters on voice production (Chapter 5 and 6) are quite in-depth, and the content may be beyond what some instructors need for (or have time in) an undergraduate course in speech science. The chapters are designed such that the more advanced information on phonatory biomechanics and measurement can easily be omitted. And these two chapters work well as part of the curriculum of a graduate-level course in voice disorders.

Don Finan's excellent new chapter on instrumentation (Chapter 12) can be used in several ways. Some instructors may want to cover this chapter early in the semester, after Chapters 2 and 3, to prepare students for discussion of the instrumentation sections at the end of Chapters 4 through 8. Other instructors may prefer to address the topic in the order in which it is presented in the book, so that students have a basic knowledge of speech and voice production within which to explore the gathering of instrumental data. The chapter was written to work well with either of these approaches. The chapter also stands well on its own as a reference for graduate- and doctoral-level students who are conducting research.

Chapters 4, 5, 7, and 8 each contain a short review of the relevant anatomy. It is presumed that students will have taken a course in anatomy and physiology of the speech mechanism or are taking that course concomitant with speech science. Therefore, here, the anatomy is presented as a refresher for students and for easy reference, rather than at a level of detail expected for novel learning of the material. The anatomy sections also serve to highlight some important anatomical features that prepare the students for the subsequent speech and voice science topics.

For Chapters 1 through 11, I have used "we" throughout this book in lieu of "I" even though the chapters were largely sole authored. The reason for the plural pronoun is that the knowledge and authority with which I wrote those chapters is drawn from a legion of speech and voice scientists who have contributed the vast amount of data upon which this book is based. They have done all the good cooking. I am just carrying it to the table.

As always, I welcome comments, criticisms, and suggestions for changes to future editions to keep this textbook as useful as possible for instructors and students. You can find me at Alison.Behrman@lehman.cuny.edu

Acknowledgments

Many individuals contributed to the creation of the three editions of this textbook, and without them this project would never have come to fruition. I am quite indebted to the following people:

To Donald Finan, who contributed a fabulous chapter on instrumentation to this third edition.

To Maury Aaseng, whose delightful illustrations bring alive the book.

To Andrew Pancila, who revised the spectrograms in Chapter 8 to make them more legible for this third edition.

To Karen J. Kushla, who provided helpful editing on some of the hearing science topics in Chapters 3 and 11.

To Philip Doyle, James and Zaida McDonough, and Sarah Sheridan, whose thoughtful commentary on the first edition made this book more readable.

To my students across the years, who inspire and teach me, perhaps more than I teach them.

And a large thank you to the Plural Publishing family (some of whom, sadly, are no longer with us): Angie and Sadanand Singh, Sandy Doyle, Valerie Johns, Kalie Koscielak, and Linda Shapiro.

About the Contributor

Donald Finan, PhD, is a Professor in the Audiology and Speech-Language Sciences program at the University of Northern Colorado. He is a speech scientist with a background that encompasses speech-language pathology and audiology, speech physiology, neuroscience, and instrumentation. His research interests include the measurement of noise in relation to auditory exposure, normal speech motor control over the lifespan, the use of technology in clinical and research settings, and the development of original tools and pedagogies for speech science instruction. Dr. Finan is the co-developer of the innovative course Musical Acoustics and Health Issues taught at the University of Northern Colorado. In this course, students explore acoustics by constructing cigar box guitars and PVC pipe didgeridoos, among other hands-on projects related to the speech and hearing sciences. Dr. Finan is the inaugural Coordinator of ASHA's Special Interest Group 19, Speech Science, and he moderates the Facebook page "Speech Science Toolbox" (https://www.facebook.com/SpeechScienceToolbox/) where resources for teaching speech science are shared.

About the Illustrator

Maury Aaseng received his degree in Graphic Design from the University of Minnesota, Duluth, with an emphasis on illustration in design. Before graduation, a semester in Australia allowed him to focus on exotic wildlife illustration. He now lives in San Diego, where he illustrates full time. He has created images for a variety of book topics, such as diseases, nature, inventors, forensics, and speech pathology*. In addition to book illustration, he makes custom paintings and is a member of the Southern California Cartoonists Society. His many trips to the San Diego Zoo have been the inspiration behind his zoo-themed comic strip, Nolan's Ark.

Aaseng enjoys spending his time outdoors, and is an enthusiastic naturalist. Drawing and a love of animals developed into passions during his childhood in Wisconsin. Frequent camping trips into the California countryside have continued to fuel both interests. His other hobbies include SCUBA and snorkeling, bowling, reading, and biking.

*Note: This is definitely the first book he's illustrated such complex ideas as a punk rocker's tongue, a pig talking on a cell phone, and the uncontrollable, maddening craving for toast.

1

Introduction

Figure 1–1

I'm scared of this course. I've heard speech science is really hard!

—Unidentified panicking undergraduate student

1.1 The Clinical Usefulness of Speech and Voice Science

Let us right away get to the heart of the question. Why do speech-language pathologists need to study speech science? Certainly, if a student intends to become a research scientist, so the argument goes, then such knowledge is important. But most students of speech-language pathology do not become research scientists. Most students become clinicians who work with, for example, children who have articulation or fluency problems or with adults who have aphasia, voice, or motor speech disorders. Certainly, the study of speech science is not particularly relevant to those students. Or so the argument goes.

Can we understand communication problems, abnormal communicative processes, without understanding the way in which communication is supposed to work typically? No. Thus, we study first the typical processes upon which communication is based. The communication problems that we encounter as speech-language pathologists can be divided broadly into deficits in language and deficits in speech. (Interplay between the two areas occurs, of course, and this fact is addressed intermittently throughout the book.) To address language deficits, we need a strong knowledge base in linguistic rules and the formulation of language. To address speech and voice deficits, we are concerned with the production and perception of speech sounds and the voice source signal. If we do not understand the basics of sound production and of sound perception, then how are we to be effective clinicians? The act of speaking, for all its ordinariness, is remarkably complex. Without this knowledge, we conduct therapy as if wearing blinders, limited in our ability to understand what our client is doing and what we need to do to help the client achieve the goals of therapy. Consider the following scenarios.

Scenario 1

You are asked to evaluate the speech of a 15-year-old girl who is having difficulty being understood in class. Her teachers report that her voice sounds very nasal, she does not speak loud enough to be heard easily, and she does not seem to pronounce her words very clearly. The teachers wonder whether she has some type of structural deformity and, in addition, whether she has an attitude or emotional problem, or whether again she does not try hard enough, or is just a bit lazy in her speech. You quickly determine that she does indeed have an excessive nasal quality to her speech. Her parents report that it has been a problem since she had her tonsils and adenoids removed 6 months earlier. You are aware that, in a small percentage of children, this surgical procedure can result in excessively nasal speech, and you suspect problems with her velopharyngeal port. As part of your diagnostic testing, you select certain words and phrases for her to produce that are likely to be particularly revealing of velopharyngeal port incompetence. The pressure characteristics of the phonemes contained within the speaking test you give her will help you to make your diagnosis. How do you know which words and phrases to select? You assess her articulation and it is clear to you that she does not have an articulation problem, but, rather, the excessive nasality is interfering with the production of certain phonemes. Features of these phonemes reveal problems with the ways in which she regulates airflow and air pressure within her vocal tract. How do you know this? And, finally, you must explain to her teachers why the student is unable to generate sufficient intensity to be heard clearly and how this is a direct result of hypernasality. What is your explanation? In this case, your knowledge of speech science has enabled you to conduct an evaluation and to address the concerns of the teachers, and has helped to prevent teachers from forming inaccurate assumptions about the student. (To find out the answers to these questions, you'll need to read Chapters 7 and 8, and parts of Chapters 4 and 5. And to understand completely what you read, you'll need some of the information in Chapters 2 and 3 as well.)

Scenario 2

You work with an individual for whom American English is not his native language. He knows that his accent is making it difficult for colleagues to understand him easily, and he is concerned that it may limit his career growth. He does not want to lose his native cultural identity but would like to make himself more easily understood. Your evaluation reveals that he has difficulty with some of the vowels of English. You note that his vowels tend to be shorter in duration than those of most Americans, he uses almost no diphthongs, and he often rounds his lips when we do not and fails to round them when we do for some of the back vowels in particular. In this case, your knowledge of the acoustics of vowel production helps you know what to listen for in his speech and what features to identify that are calling attention to themselves as different from those of a native speaker of American English. You can explain to your client about these differences, thereby helping him to understand what needs to be addressed in therapy. In this case, your knowledge of speech science has contributed to increasing the sensitivity of your ear to important features of his speech by providing a conceptual framework to help you organize what you hear. In other words, your studies in speech science help you to know what to listen for!

Scenario 3

In February, one of the elementary school teachers at the school where you work comes to see you about her voice. She reports that since she began teaching second grade the previous September, her voice has become progressively worse. It cracks, sounds very hoarse, and her throat hurts when she speaks. By the end of each week, she can barely get a sound out, and it only gets a little better as she rests it on the weekends. Her ear, nose, and throat physician has told her that she has nodules, noncancerous abnormalities of her vocal folds that are caused by incorrect and excessive voice use. You know that teachers are particularly susceptible to voice problems because of the speaking demands of their job. You also know that you cannot tell her simply to speak less or to speak more quietly, because she teaches second grade! Despite using a microphone and nonverbal strategies to

get the children's attention, her symptoms persist, and she must be able to use her voice every day for long periods of time, sometimes loudly. You know that by creating the right relationship between the air pressure above her glottis and the air pressure between her vocal folds, she will be able to gain greater intensity more easily and gently. You give her exercises that will help create this appropriate interaction. From where does your understanding of vocal fold vibration and vocal tract pressure waves arise? In this case, your knowledge of speech science allows you to understand the mechanisms that have caused your client to develop a voice problem, and this same knowledge enables you to develop therapeutic exercises to help your client overcome the problem.

All the above scenarios are real. And they emphasize that speech science provides a knowledge base that enables you, the clinician, to solve problems and to be *creative* in your therapies. What do we mean by creative? A common cry by novice clinicians is, "I don't know what to do in therapy with this client." A common response by the seasoned clinician is "I can't give you a cookbook of therapy techniques. Each client is different, and *you* must determine what your client needs." And a chasm seems to appear between the two sides, with the novice clinician feeling that, somehow, the more experienced clinician is "holding back" and not sharing the secrets of clinical speech pathology. The creativity comes from understanding the speech production system and being able to solve problems within the diagnostic and therapeutic processes.

1.2 Defining Speech Science

Speech production is the generation of airflow and the creation of air pressures by the displacement (movement) of bodily structures, which, taken together, cause the disturbances of air that constitute phonemes, the smallest meaningful units of sound. Thus, the science of speech production must include the study of the movement of the relevant body structures and the air particles. Therefore, **speech science** includes the study of aerodynamics, the movement of air and the forces used to generate the movements. Speech science also includes the study of **acoustics**, a branch of physics devoted to the study of sound: its production, transmission, and effects. And speech science includes the study of kinematics and dynamics. **Kinematics** is the study of motion, the positions, velocities, and acceleration of body parts. Whereas kinematics is concerned with movements without regard to the forces that cause the movements, **dynamics** is concerned with the forces that cause the movements. Speech science must also include the study of **psychoacoustics**, an interdisciplinary field of psychology and acoustics that addresses the relationship between the physical properties of a phenomenon and our perception of these properties.

What is the distinction between speech and voice? The *Oxford English Dictionary* provides the following definition of voice: "sound formed in or emitted from the human larynx in speaking, singing, or other utterance." Speech is defined as "the natural exercise of the vocal organs; the utterance of words or sentences; oral expression of thought or feeling." Narrowly, we can define voice as the production of sound waves by vibration of the vocal folds, whereas speech refers to the production of phonemes by structures of the vocal tract above the larynx, particularly the oral cavity. Yet, in later chapters of this book, we will discuss voice production as depending on characteristics of the vocal tract, and so it is not confined only to the larynx. And the presence or absence of voicing is an important feature of phonemes, so that speech production includes the activity of the larynx. Sometimes we will use the general term *speech science* for economy of words instead of saying voice and speech science.

As you progress through your study of speech science, you will learn that speech and voice production is a complex neuromechanical activity that requires coordination of the breathing, phonatory, and resonatory/articulatory subsystems. Neuromechanical means that speech production is regulated by both the neurologic system and the physical properties of the structures that it governs. In Chapters 4, 5, and 6, you will learn that the breathing subsystem provides the aerodynamic power that drives the vibration of the vocal folds to produce the source of the voiced sound. In Chapter 7, you will learn that the resonatory/articulatory subsystem functions as a dynamic (active and changeable) acoustic filter. And in Chapter 8, you will learn that articulation, particularly the movement of the structures of the mouth, alters the spatial configuration of the vocal tract in a specific time-ordered fashion. These dynamic changes to the spatiotemporal configuration of the vocal tract result in changes to its acoustic resonant properties. (By spatiotemporal, we mean a given posture or positioning of the vocal tract as a function of time.) The articulatory subsystem acts not only as an acoustic resonator but also as a sound source separate from the phonatory source. Together, the phonatory sound source, the acoustic filtering, and the articulatory sound sources yield the various speech sounds of our language. If all of this is a bit confusing to you, the student, don't worry. It will become clearer over the course of the following chapters.

An effort has been made throughout all the chapters to emphasize the dynamic nature of speech science. Facts are revisable data about the world. That is, facts originate through scientific study and, as new knowledge is gained, the "facts" can change. The data upon which our knowledge of speech science is based come from experimentation, and the information in this book comes from research studies by many voice and speech scientists. These experiments include observing and measuring how the speech production system functions during routine speaking situations and under a variety of different conditions, such as sustained vowel phonation, running speech, producing loud or soft speech and high and low pitches, or when the speech production system is constrained (restricted) in some unusual way. In addition, much information about speech function has been gained by observing what happens when a structure is damaged, through disease or trauma. Although certain facts about the speech production system have changed little since they were first discovered, others are continually being revised. And much remains unknown, yet to be discovered.

We discover new information about the speech production system through observation and often with the help of instrumentation. Some instrumentation is so complicated and expensive that its use is reserved only for research purposes. Other instrumentation is used commonly in routine clinical practice during evaluation and sometimes during therapy. Instrumentation serves both to expand and to limit the possibilities for physiologic research. That is, instrumentation helps us measure what we cannot measure with our own unaided senses alone, and in that sense, it serves to expand our possibilities for gaining knowledge about the speech production system. Yet all instrumentation imposes certain restrictions upon the individual—perhaps the speaker must remain immobile while being tested, or only certain types of movements can be measured accurately, or events that occur very rapidly cannot be measured at all. All instrumentation has strengths and limitations. A wide selection of speech instrumentation, some reserved for research purposes only and some also used in clinical application, is discussed at the end of Chapters 4 through 8, and Chapter 11 is devoted to the explanation of instrumental arrays and how they influence the data we obtain.

Do you apply every bit of speech science to every client? Of course, you do *not*. Similarly, the physician does not apply all that she has learned in medical school to every patient. But that does not mean that the speech-language pathologist or the physician should study only those areas most relevant to clinical practice. In later chapters, we will learn about the concept of nonlinearity, which means broadly that the relationship between the cause and the effect is not direct or, more colloquially, that the whole is greater than the sum of its individual parts. The various topics contained in this textbook that comprise an introduction to speech and voice science serve as a broad fund of knowledge that, in a cumulative sense, will provide you with a strong understanding of speech production and enable you to solve problems and to be creative in your clinical practice. So, in response to the questions, "Why do we have to know this? When will I ever *use* this? This has nothing to do with speech disorders!" you can respond, "This information is part of the larger base upon which I practice the clinical skills of speech pathology." It has *everything* to do with clinical practice.

Gardeners are fond of saying that one should place a 50-cent plant in a five-dollar hole. In other words, the plant has a better chance of reaching its fullest potential with an investment of time and effort into preparation of the foundation. This text offers the five-dollar hole—a foundation in the science of voice and speech production, upon which to build excellent clinical skills.

1.3 Advice for Students on Effective Study Techniques

"I don't understand. I studied so hard—how did I get such a low grade on the test?"

"I know the material. It's just the way she words the questions on the test that really confuses me."

"I'm so upset. I spent all week studying, and still I did poorly on the exam."

"I know the material. I just get so nervous during the test that I can't think."

"I thought I knew the material, but then I realized when I took the test that I studied the wrong things."

"I really need an A in this course."

Sound familiar? There's an adage: *If you always do what you've always done, then you'll always get what you've always got.* If you aren't earning the grade you want, then it's time to do something different. Here are some suggestions that have worked for my students.

Study as Though You Are Having a Test Every Week

The course for which you are using this book is dense with facts and conceptually complex, and the information is often not at all intuitive. For most students, waiting until the week (or weekend) before a test and then studying intensively is not a good strategy. If, at the time of the test, you find yourself unable to recall information that you thought you knew, or confused by the way a question is worded, it is likely that you tried to memorize too much information too quickly. You didn't give yourself time to learn it—to understand it and apply it in different situations (e.g., different types of questions).

The solution is to pretend that you will have a test during the first class of each week, and the test will include all the information covered during the prior week. Study seriously for the imaginary test. Four things will happen because of this tactic. First, you will become aware of what you don't understand, and you will have an opportunity to ask your professor in class (or during office hours or via email) well before the real test. Second, you will learn more during class. A great deal of the information in speech and voice science builds on previously learned facts and concepts. When you are well grounded in the prior information, the new class material makes much more sense and becomes easier to acquire. Third, you will be able to answer correctly different types of questions, even when the questions approach the information in a different way than you studied, such as the ability to draw inferences. The reason is that you will have given yourself more time overall to learn the information. Rather than only memorizing facts, you will *understand* the information. Fourth, you will enter the test feeling more confident and, therefore, more calm, which will enable you to think more clearly and access the information you know more readily.

A common objection to this advice to study each week is lack of time. You have other demanding courses that you are taking this semester. If you spend so much time studying for this course each week, you will have no time to do your other work. Or so you say. That's not true. Let's say that the course for which you are using this textbook is 3 credits, and your semester load is 15 credits. You should be spending about 2 to 3 hours per week for every credit hour. Let's take the higher number, so we'll say that you should

be spending 9 hours studying every week for every course, for a total of 45 hours (3 hours × 15 credits or, similarly, 9 hours × 5 courses). Add the 45 hours to your in-class hours, and you come out with a workweek of about 60 hours. That's typical for many adults in the workforce (including, ahem, your professors). (Ask your parents how many hours a week they put in at their jobs.) A 60-hour workweek gives you plenty of time to be with your friends, in person and through social media. Do the math on your own workweek currently. Be honest. It's probably well below 60 hours. If, truly, you are putting in the hours but you're not getting the results (grades) you want, another possibility is that your study time is not effective. So here's another tip.

Study With a Partner or Group

Take 2 of the 9 study hours per week and devote them to partner or group sessions. Don't wait until the week before the test to form a group. Do it the first week of class and work together consistently throughout the semester. Quiz each other. Explain concepts and define vocabulary words to each other. Compare notes. Explaining a concept to another person is one of the best ways to learn it. You may have a misconception about something and not even realize it. You may have missed something in class or in your reading. You may have written something in your notes that is incorrect. Your partner or group will help reveal those errors. Yes, it can be challenging to find a common time when a group of students is available. But you can do it. If your schedule is that difficult, then find a partner rather than a group, or use Skype or Google Hangouts or another online meeting application.

Reach Beyond Memorization to Understand the Material

Often, when a student shows up in my office seeking advice on how to improve her grade, I start by asking, "How are you studying currently?"

Typically, the student tells me that she rewrites her notes and highlights information to study, or she makes study note cards of key facts and quizzes herself. Well, that's fine, but it's insufficient. What if you forgot to include certain information on your study note cards? What happens when the test requires that you access that information differently from how you studied it? More often than not, you will be unsuccessful.

Here are some examples of how to memorize *and understand*. Let's say you are studying respiration, and you need to learn about Boyle's law. Memorize the law. But then reread the relevant sections of the text and study your class notes to understand the relevance of Boyle's law to breathing and the physiologic mechanisms by which Boyle's law is maintained. This type of studying gives you a deeper understanding of the material beyond memorization and enables you to answer test questions that require you to draw connections between concepts. To help guide you in drawing connections, work with the Study Guide questions found in the Plural-Plus website that accompanies this textbook (More on that in a moment).

Create Quizzes and Tests and Give Them to Yourself

Frequently, students say that they test themselves on material. But often, they test themselves using flashcards, for example, and if the answer doesn't readily come to them, they look at the answer. Try a different method. Write out a quiz or a test (depending on the amount of material you are studying). You may even want to create the test using your study partner or group, so that you are not familiar with the questions. Then, take the test but simulate true test conditions. Give yourself an appropriate amount of time, as you would have in class. Then, take the test. Do not check answers until you have completed the test. Allowing yourself to struggle to recall correct answers, as you might during the actual test, will let you know what confusion you have and what you need to study more. And practice will help build your confidence to manage test anxiety.

Stay Mindfully Present in Class

Do not fall into the habit of being a mindless note taker. Taking notes in class without thinking, with the expectation that you can study the information later, is an inefficient use of class time. It creates more work for you outside of class. Instead, commit to being mindfully present in class. Listen to the lecture, participate in discussion, think about the material on which you are taking notes, try to relate the information to prior facts that you have learned in class, and interject questions when you don't understand. You will find that class goes by more quickly and enjoyably, and you will have learned some of the material along the way!

Read Assignments Before *and* After Class

Use part of your out-of-class study time to read the assigned portion of the text before the class in which the material is covered. By reading the material before it is discussed in class, you will have a conceptual framework of and a familiarity with the material, which will make you better prepared to learn in class. You will know what material you need help understanding. You might even say to your professor just before class that you found a specific topic very confusing and you need help understanding it. Although, most likely, your professor has anticipated what material will be particularly difficult for students to learn, by pointing out your confusion, you help your professor tailor the lesson more specifically to your needs. It is quite likely that material you find confusing is also problematic for your fellow students.

Then, reread the assigned material after that class and before the next class. Refer to your class notes as you read. Use this time to actively process the information. Write down the key ideas. Write down your own paraphrase of the ideas. If practical, draw a picture or set of symbols that helps you remember the key idea. Try to connect something you have observed in life with the key idea. Are there still areas of confusion for you? Reach out to your professor during office hours or during the next class. By staying on top of any confusion you may have, rather than letting it build and surprise you a week before an exam, you will have a significantly easier time studying for a test and greater confidence during the test.

One last word on reading: Be judicious with your highlighter when reading. If an entire paragraph or three quarters of a page is highlighted, what help is that to your studying? In dense textbooks such as this one, highlight not what you need to know but a key or summarizing statement that draws information together, or a critical piece of information.

Use the Study Aids

Within each chapter are section study questions. Sometimes they occur after major sections. Other times, when the reading is particularly dense, they occur after minor sections too. Section study questions are generally quite broad. Their purpose is to help you focus on the key concepts and to assess your learning. You will likely need to reread sections and review the figures to answer the questions. If you are willing to spend time working through the answers and provide thorough answers, you will achieve a deeper understanding of the material that will enable you to answer exam questions more easily. Answers are not provided for these questions, because they address information in the paragraphs immediately preceding their location. The hard work of checking on your answers by rereading sections is part of studying the material and preparing for tests. Note that the text provided in the gray boxes is not included in the section study review questions. That information is typically supplemental and sometimes provides interesting side notes. Check with your professor for each chapter to determine which note boxes contain required information. Make sure to use the PluralPlus companion website designed for students. It contains key words and review questions for each chapter (except Chapter 1) that test your knowledge of specific details addressed in the chapter. (And yes, an answer key is provided for these review questions!)

In sum, use multiple methods of studying, and give yourself ample time to learn the material. Your efforts are likely to be rewarded.

2

Describing and Explaining Motion

Figure 2–1. Early experimental devices used to explore the nature of vibration. From *Dynamics: The Geometry of Behavior* (2nd ed., p. 115), by R. H. Abraham and C. D. Shaw, 1992, Redwood City, CA: Addison-Wesley Publishing Company. Reprinted with permission of R. H. Abraham.

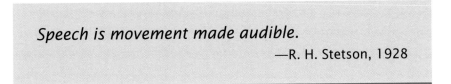

Speech is movement made audible.

—R. H. Stetson, 1928

In clinical speech pathology, it is often the case that the patient must be taught certain underlying skills before his or her communication deficit can be addressed directly. Such skills may include a preschool child discriminating between the concepts of hard and soft onset before learning how to produce light articulatory contacts to reduce his stuttering. Or it may include teaching an adult recovering from neck cancer surgery about the mechanics of tongue movement in the production of phonemes so that the patient is better able to learn compensatory strategies for articulation. Basic skills are the building blocks upon which these therapies are based. The process of learning any new skill typically rests upon some set of underlying basic skills or knowledge. The acquisition of knowledge about speech and voice science is no different. Before we study the movement of the vocal folds or the tongue, we must understand how and why these structures move the way they do. Without movement, we have no speech communication. In this chapter, we learn how to talk about motion and the rules that govern motion.

2.1 Systems of Measurement

Frequently, speech-language pathologists measure quantities. We count the number of syllables per minute to assess speaking rate. We measure the average rate of vibration of the vocal folds. We assess the peak rate of air flowing through the vocal tract during sustained sound production. All these measurements require units to make them meaningful. (If someone asked you how far away you lived, and you said six, that would be meaningless without units. Six minutes away by car? Six miles away? Six blocks away?) In general, certain units of measurement are used together in what is called a system of units. Most countries around the world use the metric system. The United States is one of the last countries to use the English system. The metric system, however, is used in science worldwide, even in the United States, and therefore students of speech-language pathology should become comfortable with it. The metric system is known as the International System (abbreviated SI for

History of Measurement

Standardization of measurements arose from the need to have agreement on weights and measures in everyday commerce. Merchants (and buyers) needed to know that the food and other goods they sold were getting a fair price compared to that sold by other vendors. During the Middle Ages in Europe, each town or other political division maintained its own standards. Large, traveling trade fairs pushed for standardization of measures. The Keeper of the Faire in Champagne, France, for example, kept an iron bar against which (and against copies made from which) all bolts of cloth were measured for sale. In 1215, King John of England signed the Magna Carta, which required, among other things, that "there shall be standard measures of wine, ale, and wheat throughout the kingdom." The English system based upon the standardization of the foot for length (derived from the length of the king's foot outside of church on a given day), the pound for weights, and the second for speed, eventually developed from this document. In 1799, at the end of the French Revolution, the French Academy declared that the standard for distance would be one ten-millionth of the distance on the Earth's surface between the equator and the North Pole at the longitude of Paris, and thus the meter was developed. The Academy also declared that the gram would be used for weights and that it would be defined as the mass of a cubic centimeter of water at 4 degrees centigrade (approximately 39 degrees Fahrenheit). It would seem, then, that the influence of politics is everywhere, including the measurement of speech and voice production.

the French Système International). In the metric system, sometimes called the MKS system, distance is measured in meters, volume is measured in liters and the unit of mass is kilograms, and time is measured in seconds (hence, MKS for meter, kilogram, second). The older metric system is the CGS system, which uses smaller units, the centimeter, gram, and second. (There are a few other differences that will be addressed when we talk about pressure.) In the United States (English system), distances are measured in feet. A kilometer (1,000 meters) is close to two thirds of a mile. A centimeter (1/100th of a meter) is a bit less than half an inch. (See the conversion tables in Appendix A.) Although the U.S. system measures solid volume in cubic feet, liquids are generally measured in gallons (3.785 liters), quarts, and pints. The liter is becoming a more common measure of drinks, such as soft drinks.

2.2 Describing Motion: Speed, Velocity, Acceleration, and Deceleration

The movements of speech are achieved by the management of forces. Everyone is generally familiar with the concept of force—a push or a pull. We do not see forces, just as we do not see wind, but we see the effect of forces on objects, including ourselves. When an object, or part of our body, behaves in a certain way, we infer that it is the result of one or more forces. If you doze off in class and your jaw drops down so that your mouth is agape, your classmates know that the force of gravity has pulled your mandible downward. If you slide your book across the floor, you know that it will come to a stop because of the force of friction that opposes the sliding motion (or because it hits something like a desk or door). A force can be identified and measured by the effect it has on an object.

Speed describes the relationship of distance and time. It is defined as the distance an object travels in a given unit of time. In daily life, we might express the speed of a car in miles per hour. As speech-language pathologists, we might measure the speed of talking (speech rate) in syllables per minute. Velocity has the same numerical value as speed, but it also contains information about the direction of movement. The velocity of a car might be 60 miles per hour due west. The speed is known as the magnitude of the velocity. The symbol for the magnitude of the velocity is v. In speech-language pathology, there is no direction of speech rate, so we would not describe speaking rate in terms of velocity. However, we may conduct research on the velocity of lip movement for production of /p/ and measure the peak velocity of downward movement of the jaw in milliseconds.

When the speed of an object is unchanging, or when it is constant in a single direction, we say that the object is in uniform motion. Movement does not always occur at a steady pace, however. Objects can speed up or slow down as they travel. Acceleration is the change in velocity as a function of time. For example, the car traveling on a flat surface at 60 mph may accelerate (speed up) at a rate of 100 feet per second for each second it travels downhill. Its acceleration would then be expressed as feet per second per second, or feet per second squared. When the car slows down, that is, when the change in velocity is negative, the object has decreasing velocity; it is decelerating.

Relationship of Space and Time

A tourist stops by a small country farm stand to get some fresh vegetables. As the tourist is admiring the countryside, the farmer offers to show the tourist around the farmer's small family farm. During the tour, the tourist cannot resist bragging a bit about his own country estate back home. He says to the farmer, "My estate is so large that it takes me an hour to drive from one end of it to the other." The farmer thought for a moment and then replied, "I used to have a car like that once."

2.3 Newton's Laws Explain Motion

The modern science of mechanics was begun by Sir Isaac Newton (1642–1727). Among his many contributions that are relevant to the study of voice and speech are his laws of motion. These three laws describe how any object behaves when acted upon by an outside force. Remember that a force is a phenomenon that can produce a change in an object's state of activity.

The First Law of Motion

Newton's first law of motion states that a moving object will continue moving in a straight line at a constant speed and a stationary object will remain at rest, unless acted upon by an outside force. Said another way, an object will accelerate or decelerate only if acted upon by an outside force. Therefore, change in the velocity of an object means that some outside force acted upon the object. More specifically, an *unbalanced* force acting upon an object results in movement. If two forces are acting equally upon an object, one pushing and the other pulling, then no change in motion will result. Do not confuse "no change in motion" with "lack of motion." If the push and pull forces are balanced to keep an object moving, then no acceleration or deceleration will occur. Although no change in motion occurs, the object will continue to move at a steady speed. The unbalanced force is often referred to as the net force. The first law of motion is sometimes called the law of inertia. Inertia is the tendency for an object to resist change in its state of motion. (Inertia is an important concept in the transmission of sound waves.)

The Second Law of Motion

Newton's second law states the following. When a net force acts on an object, the object accelerates in the same direction as the force. The acceleration is directly proportional to the net force and inversely proportional to the mass of

---

Newton's Second Law of Motion

In words: The net force of an object is equal to its mass times its acceleration and points in the direction of the acceleration.

The equation using words: Net force = mass times acceleration.

The equation using symbols: $F = ma$ where the symbol m stands for mass.

---

the object. (By inverse, we mean the opposite direction.) Put more simply, the larger the force, the greater the acceleration, and the larger the mass, the smaller the acceleration. The **mass** of an object is the amount of matter it contains. A ball thrown by a man will accelerate faster than one thrown by a child, because the man can generate greater force. A woman can lift up the child more easily than she can lift up the man, because the child has less mass than the man. The greater the mass, the more force is exerted by gravity, so the heavier the object. Therefore, the greater the mass, the more force must be exerted upon it to achieve a given acceleration. Throw a baseball and a medicine ball with the same force. The baseball will accelerate faster and go farther than the greater mass of the medicine ball. The unit of force is called, appropriately enough, the newton (abbreviated N). A newton is defined as the force that accelerates a 1-kilogram mass at the rate of 1 meter per second per second (1 kg-m/s^2).

The Third Law of Motion

Newton's third law of motion states that for every action (force), there is an equal and opposite reaction (force). Whenever a force is exerted upon an object, the object simultaneously exerts an equal and opposite force on whatever is applying the initial force (Figure 2–2). A subtle but important point is that the third law is not about cause and effect but about action and reaction of forces. The action and reaction act

Figure 2–2. Newton's third law of motion.

2.4 Momentum and Energy

Momentum

Our everyday experience tells us that very large objects can be difficult to stop, even if they are moving slowly. Every driver knows that it is a very bad idea to cut sharply in front of a large tractor-trailer truck, even one going slowly. The large mass of the truck prevents it from stopping (or even slowing) very quickly. And we know that if the truck is traveling at a high speed, it takes even longer to stop. We also know, however, that very small objects can also be difficult to stop. A bullet shot from a gun is one such example. From these examples, we can intuit that the greater either the mass or the speed of an object, the more difficult it is to stop or to change its direction. The momentum of an object is the product of its mass and velocity. Therefore, an increase in either mass or velocity will increase momentum proportionally. Just like velocity, momentum has both a magnitude and a direction. There is no special unit of measurement for momentum as there is for force. The units of measurement for momentum are those for mass times velocity, or kg-m/s.

We often use scientific terms in a nonscientific, looser fashion, which usually only adds to the confusion of students trying to learn the more exact meaning. However, in the case of momentum, the way in which we use the word in everyday language is quite close to the scientific meaning. In speech therapy, we might tell a patient that it is better to have regular weekly therapy appointments rather than inconsistent attendance every few weeks, to avoid losing momentum in the therapeutic process. By this we imply that once a patient starts moving forward (making improvements) in therapy, it is easier to continue to improve. Whereas if the patient stops attending sessions, it becomes more difficult to resume the forward progress. This statement is accurate if we think about momentum as the product of an object's mass and velocity. The greater the velocity, given a constant mass, the greater the momentum. Inertia, the tendency for

as a pair, but they act on different objects. It may help to understand this third law if you think about knocking into someone while skating (rollerblades or ice skates). After you knock into someone, you will glide backward because of the force acting against you in reaction to the force you initially exerted against the other person.

Study Questions

1. Define force, speed, velocity, and momentum.

2. For each of Newton's three laws of motion, provide the definition in words, and write the equation and definition of the symbols used in each equation.

an object to resist movement, must be overcome to achieve forward (or backward) momentum. When we discuss vocal fold vibration in Chapter 5, we will see how we must expend greater force to start our vocal folds vibrating than to maintain them in vibration.

Energy

We talk about energy in communication when we say that someone is an energetic speaker or, conversely, lacks energy. In fact, speech production is all about the transfer of energy—from the air in the lungs to the vocal folds to the air in the vocal tract to the articulatory structures and ultimately to the radiated aerodynamic energy that strikes the eardrum of the listener. Individuals with voice and speech disorders may complain of speech requiring too great an expenditure of energy. Speech pathologists may plan their therapies to target increased energy efficiency when talking. The management of energy in the vocal tract is a critical factor in the treatment of voice and speech problems.

Energy, Work, and Power

A patient with a speech disorder may report that speaking feels like a lot of work. Work is per-formed whenever a force is exerted over some distance. Do not confuse the scientific term work, as used in physics, and the lay term. If you push the tip of your tongue hard against your alveolar ridge behind the front teeth or clamp your jaws together tightly, you may be expending considerable energy and applying a large force, but no work is performed. No distance has been traveled by the tongue or jaw. However, if you produce the word "top," your tongue tip travels downward for the /t/ and the jaw displaces downward for the vowel, and thus both movements have performed actual work. If there is no motion, or if the force is perpendicular to the motion, the work is zero. The metric unit of measurement for work is newton-meters, defined as joules (abbreviated J and pronounced /dzul/, which rhymes with "fool"). The name comes from the English scientist James Prescott Joule (1818–1889), who explored the properties of energy. One joule is the amount of work done when you exert a force of 1 newton through a distance of 1 meter. Energy is closely related to work. Energy is defined as the ability to do work. A system must have energy to exert a force over a distance. Power is the rate at which work is done. Equivalently, power can be defined as the rate at which energy is expended. The unit of power is the watt, named after the Scottish inventor James Watt (1736–1819) who

Clinical Assessment of Speaking Effort

As speech pathologists, we contend often with patients who have to expend more energy to speak than most other people. The cause may be structural deformity or disease, in which case the patient must compensate for the abnormality to communicate clearly. In other cases, the extra work is simply a habit, such as people who are used to speaking too loudly or who tend to hold their breath when talking. Assessment of the patient's perception of the level of energy or effort required for speech is important. The information can contribute to planning therapeutic goals, and it can be used as a measure of treatment outcome. But how does one assess this information in routine clinical practice? One common method is to use a visual analog scale: a line 10 cm long with end-anchors describing the sensation of effort, such as "no effort" and "100% effort." Patients are asked to put an X on the line that represents their perception of the average level of effort required for speech. Then, the speech-language pathologist measures where the X falls on the line, and that number (in cm) becomes the "effort score." A goal of therapy would be to decrease the effort score.

developed the steam engine that facilitated the Industrial Revolution. The watt is defined as the expenditure of 1 joule of energy in 1 second.

Work Defined

In words: Work is done whenever a force is exerted over a distance (or, equivalently, when something is displaced). The amount of work done is proportional to both the force and the distance, or displacement.

The equation using words: Work (in joules) equals Force (in newtons) times Displacement (in meters).

The equation using symbols: $W = F \times d$.

Power Defined

In words: Power is the amount of work done divided by the time it takes to do it. Power is the energy expended divided by the time it takes to expend it.

The equation using words: Power (in watts) equals Work (in joules) divided by Time (in seconds).

Or equivalently: Power (in watts) equals Energy (in joules) divided by Time (in seconds).

We know that work is equal to force times displacement. Thus, we can rewrite the expression for power as:

Power = Work / Time

= (Force x Displacement) / Time

= Force x (Displacement / Time)

We know that displacement divided by time equals velocity, so finally, we can express power as:

Power = Force x Velocity

When we change the light bulb in a lamp, the wattage rating, perhaps 60, 75, or 100 watts, lets us know the amount of energy the light bulb will consume. It is not directly a measure of the brightness of the light the bulb will give off, although all things being equal, bulbs of higher wattage give off more light.

Kinetic and Potential Energy

It is helpful in our discussions of speech and voice production to understand two types of energy: kinetic and potential. Kinetic energy is associated with moving objects. It is the most obvious form of energy—the energy of motion. The mass and the speed of an object govern its kinetic energy. Greater mass and greater speed yield greater kinetic energy. Momentum and kinetic energy are closely related. Potential energy, on the other hand, is waiting to be released. It is the energy that could result in the exertion of a force over a distance but is not doing so at the present moment. If a quantity in nature is not changed, it is said to be conserved. For a given system, if we ignore friction, the relative

Horses and Horsepower

James Watt came up with the term "horsepower" as a unit of measurement to more easily sell his invention, the steam engine. Steam engines were purchased initially for use in the mines as a replacement for horses to drive the pumps that removed water. The best sales pitch was to tell potential buyers how many horses could be replaced by the purchase of a steam engine. He conducted a series of experiments and found that on average, a horse could do 550 ft–lb of work every second over an average working day. (Either he had tireless horses, or he was being a bit optimistic in his calculations!) He named this unit 1 horsepower. Curiously, we still use horsepower to rate the power of car engines, although few of us consider the car a replacement for our horse.

amounts of kinetic and potential energy can change, but the total amount of energy cannot change (Figure 2–3). Consider the situation in which, frustrated after hours of studying speech science, you want to shove your textbook off the desk and into the garbage can. The book's potential energy equals the kinetic energy of the fall that it *might* experience. Potential refers to the future, and so the potential energy equals the kinetic energy that the object is capable of experiencing next. Potential energy varies with the mass of the object and with the distance traversed. Ignoring friction, the overall energy of the book is conserved.

Study Questions

3. How are momentum, deceleration, and acceleration related to Newton's three laws of motion?

4. Define energy and distinguish between kinetic and potential energy.

5. Provide the formulas for work and power.

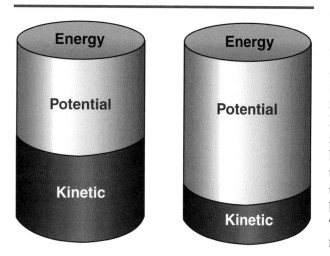

Figure 2–3. For a given system, if we ignore friction, the relative amounts of kinetic and potential energy can change, but the total amount of energy cannot change.

2.5 Three States of Matter

The state of a medium—solid, liquid, or gas—refers to the way in which the molecules are arranged in a given material. The effectiveness of the forces that hold the molecules together defines the state. A material is identified as a solid if it holds its shape and volume (at a given temperature; most solids expand as they get warmer) independent of its container. A solid is sufficiently rigid to counteract outside force that is imposed upon it. A liquid, similar to a solid, maintains a constant volume (at a given temperature), but unlike a solid, it assumes the shape of its container. Water and mercury are among the few materials that occur naturally in their liquid state at typical values of atmospheric pressure and temperature. The molecules of liquids have more kinetic energy than those of solids. Unlike solids, the molecules of liquids do not remain in place but slide freely over one another (Figure 2–4).

Visualize the grains of sand in a partially filled clear plastic container with the lid closed. Turn the container on its side and the grains of sand slide over one another. Of course, each grain of sand is a solid. But as they shift and slide, these grains of sand function as a visible kind of analogy for the shifting (which we cannot see with our naked eye) of the molecules of liquid. This ability to slide freely is critical to the efficient production of voice, as we shall later learn. Another property of liquids that is important for efficient vibration of the vocal folds is surface tension. All molecules in a liquid have a weak attraction to one another, so each molecule has forces pulling at it from above, below, and adjacent to it. But the molecules on the surface of the liquid have no molecules of the liquid above them, only adjacent molecules beside them and those below them (Figure 2–5). Thus, the surface molecules experience a net force pulling them downward. Although this is not a very large force, it is sufficient to support a very light insect striding across the surface of a still pond. It is sufficient to allow the water

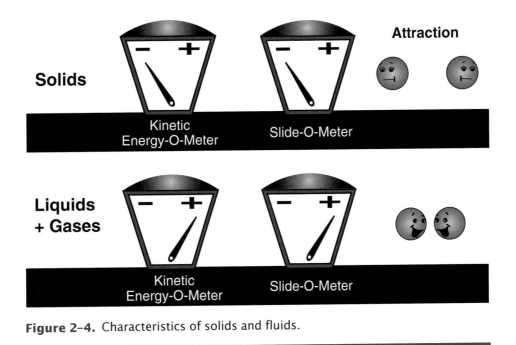

Figure 2-4. Characteristics of solids and fluids.

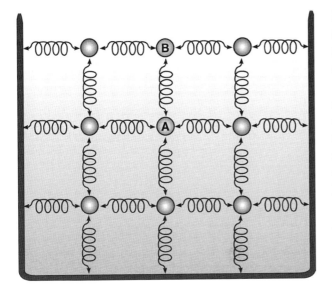

Figure 2–5. Surface tension. Molecule A, equally attracted in all directions, will move in any direction given a slight imbalance in force. For molecule B, on the other hand, the forces exerted in the horizontal plane yield a surface tension, like a tightly fitted sheet. Adapted from *The Respiratory System* (p. 168), by A. Davies and C. Moore, 2003, Edinburgh: Churchill Livingstone, an imprint of Elsevier Science, Ltd. Reprinted with permission from Elsevier.

level in a glass to rise just fractionally above the surface of the glass without spilling over. Surface tension plays a critical role in human physiology, as we shall learn in Chapters 4 and 5.

When material is in the gaseous state, it retains neither its shape nor its volume but rather expands to fill the container in which it is located (Figure 2–6). The expandability is limited, but for purposes of speech science and our consideration of the vocal tract, we can ignore those limits. The molecules of a gas interact primarily by colliding with one another (Figure 2–7). Although at first glance this may not appear terribly important for voice and speech production, it is a fundamental property and bears closer examination. The air molecules in the vocal tract are colliding not only with one another but also with the structures of the vocal tract, which are, in effect, the temporary container of the air molecules. Newton's first law of motion tells us that when an air molecule bounces off the wall of the vocal tract, the wall must have exerted a force back onto the molecule in the air. Remember that this law tells us that if a mass accelerates

Figure 2–6. When material is in the gaseous state, it retains neither its shape nor its volume but rather expands to fill the container in which it is located.

(such as in the case of an air molecule changing direction), then a force must have been applied to it. At the same time, Newton's third law tells us that the molecule is exerting an equal and opposite force against the wall. The collision of countless molecules against the walls of the vocal tract, as well as other structures such as the vocal folds and articulators, is perceived by the speaker as air pressure, a phenomenon we shall explore soon at greater length.

It is sometimes helpful to talk about both liquids and gases together because they often behave similarly. We can use the term *fluid* to refer to both liquids and gases because the collection of molecules that forms the body of the liquid or gas can change shape freely. The study of the aerodynamics of the vocal tract is the study of fluid in motion.

Density

The property of matter that indicates the amount of material packed into a given volume is called density. Density is a function of the mass of the atoms that comprise the material, and more relevant to our studies, it is also dependent upon the arrangement of the atoms. Those materials

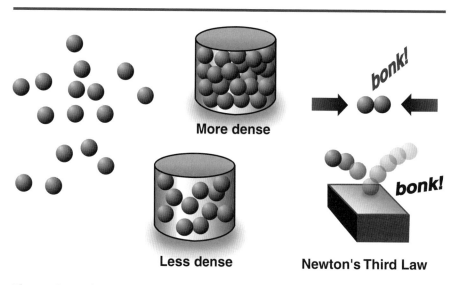

More dense

Less dense

Newton's Third Law

Figure 2–7. The molecules of a fluid such as air interact primarily by colliding with one another and with the walls of their container.

in which the atoms are more closely packed together, such as lead, iron, and diamond, are denser than materials that have looser structure, such as bone, wood, and water. Density is measured in units of grams per cubic centimeter (g/cm³), or equivalently, kilograms per cubic meter. A cubic centimeter of water at 4 degrees centigrade (approximately 39 degrees Fahrenheit) has a mass of 1 gram, so its density equals 1 g/cm³. In this system of measurement, the density of any material tells you how dense it is relative to the same volume of water. But do not confuse density with weight, or with the volume of a material. The density of a small chip of a bar of pure gold is the same as the density of the entire bar of gold. To obtain the density of a given material, its mass is divided by its volume (see Density Defined). See Table 2–1 for the densities of some common biological and nonbiological materials.

Density Defined

In words: Density depends upon the structure of the atoms from which the material is made and how closely together the atoms are packed.

The equation using words: Density equals mass divided by volume.

The equation using symbols: $\rho = m/V$ where the Greek letter ρ (rho) is used to denote density.

Elasticity and Stiffness

Stiffness is the degree to which an object resists being deformed. **Elasticity** is the ability of an object to spring back to its resting shape when

---

Archimedes

Archimedes was an ancient Greek mathematician and inventor who was born in Syracuse, Sicily, when it was a Greek city. As the story goes, he was friendly with Hieron II, king of Syracuse and the surrounding area. Hieron had given a metalsmith pure gold and pure silver of known weights to make him a wreath-shaped crown. When he received the crown from the smith, it indeed weighed exactly the weight of the gold and silver added together that he had supplied. Then he challenged Archimedes to determine whether the smith had used some other, less precious metals in the crown and kept some of the gold and silver for himself. (In our terms, was the crown pure gold, or was it only gold-plated?) It would have been easy to cut through the crown and see, for example, whether it had some lead in the inside. However, the catch was that Archimedes was not supposed to damage the crown not even to scratch it.

He thought and thought but got nowhere.

So, he decided to take a break and relax in a nice bath. He filled his bathtub close to full and stepped into it. Some water spilled over the edge of the tub. That gave Archimedes the solution he was looking for. Fill a container to the top with water. Slowly and gently (so as not to splash) he put the crown into the container. Then he caught and measured the water that spilled. That amount of spilled water had to be the same as the exact volume of the crown. He compared it to the volume of the gold and silver that the king had given to the smith. If the volume of the crown, as measured by the volume of the spilled water, was not the same as the volume of the metal that the king supplied, then the smith used some other material inside the crown. Archimedes was so excited at his discovery that he ran through the streets shouting *Eureka*, Greek for "I have found [it]," or, more precisely, "I found [it] and still have [it]." He didn't even notice that he was still naked!

Table 2–1. Relative Densities of Common Solids and Liquids

Material[a]	Density (g/cm³)
Air	0.001293
Ethyl alcohol	0.8
Water (4° C)	1.0
Blood	1.05
Bone	1.08
Concrete	2.3
Diamond	3.5
Iron	7.9
Silver	10.5
Lead	11.3
Gold	19.3
Mercury	13.6

[a]At 39° Fahrenheit at sea level (unless otherwise noted).

deforming forces are removed. Stiffness and elasticity characterize the way in which materials change shape when acted upon by an external force (Figure 2–8). The bonds between mole-cules of the material elongate and the material gets longer when a pulling force is applied to it. This stretching response of material is explained by Hooke's law, named after the English scientist Robert Hooke (1635–1702). Hooke's law states that the change in length of a material is proportional to the force applied to it. In other words, the harder you pull on something, the more it stretches. A common example of Hooke's law involves the elastic or rubber band. If you pull on a rubber band, it stretches. Pull harder and it stretches longer. The stretch response to the force of the pulling tells us that the rubber band is not very stiff at all. If you let go of the rubber band after stretching it, it will snap back to its original shape. That response of the rubber band tells us that it is elastic. Rubber bands are constructed to have a low stiffness and a high elasticity, so they stretch easily—but only to a point. If you pull too much, the rubber band will snap. The elastic limit of the material has been reached, and the bonds between the molecules are permanently altered.

Steel is an example of a stiff yet elastic medium. The George Washington Bridge is a suspension bridge over the Hudson River, thus connecting New York City with New Jersey. The

Osteoporosis

Bone density is an important factor in the health of bones. In general, when we talk about bone density, we are referring to bone mineral density (BMD), which is the measure of the amount of calcium in a specific region of bone and is measured in g/cm². From this information, an estimate of the strength of the bones can be made. BMD can be used to predict the risk of fracturing bone. BMD is measured with a specialized type of x-ray technique called quantitative computed tomography or dual-energy x-ray absorptiometry. Average BMD is about 3.9 g/cm² in adult men and 2.9 g/cm² in adult women. As we age, we lose BMD naturally, and so our risk of fracture increases. The bad news is that our ability to repair tissue damage decreases with age, making fractures particularly dangerous for older persons. If your BMD is lower than 1.0 g/cm², you are considered to have a bone density disease such as osteoporosis. Women are at higher risk of osteoporosis, the most common bone disease, than are men, due to hormonal changes associated with menopause. Osteoporosis affects half of all women over the age of 45 and can result commonly in wrist, hip, and spine fractures. Many women are advised to take calcium supplements as part of their daily diet and to participate regularly in weight-bearing exercises to slow down the process of decreasing bone mineral density (Woolf, 1988).

Stiffness

Elasticity

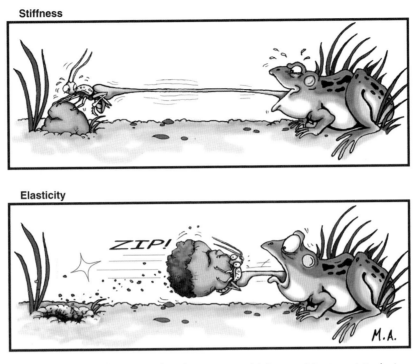

ZIP!

M.A.

Figure 2–8. Stiffness is the degree to which an object resists being deformed. Elasticity is the ability of an object to spring back to its resting shape when deforming forces are removed.

cables sway in high winds and with the flow of heavy traffic, all without breaking, a fact that should be comforting to most commuters but can sometimes feel a bit disconcerting. The properties of stiffness and elasticity are quite important to speech and voice production, as we shall soon discover.

Pressure

The force exerted by the collision of air molecules against the sides of a container and the resulting opposite force exerted by the container wall is perceived as pressure. In general, when we talk about pressure, we are talking about two pressures—one outward and one inward. Picturing an inflated balloon may help clarify this concept. The air molecules inside the balloon are colliding with one another and the inner wall of the balloon, and exerting an outward force, or pressure. The air outside of the balloon—the

atmosphere—is exerting an inward pressure against the outer wall of the balloon. As you blow more air into the balloon, the number of molecules increases, causing an increase in the amount of collisions, thus raising the pressure exerting an outward force. If the force exerted becomes too great compared to the inward force exerted by the atmosphere, the balloon pops. It is important to emphasize that everywhere inside the balloon the pressure is equal. (In reality, situations might arise in which the pressure is not equal everywhere inside the balloon, particularly when considering temperature. However, the purpose of this discussion is to lay the foundation for the following chapters, in which the aerodynamic forces in the lungs and vocal tract are addressed. Therefore, we shall keep things relatively simple here.) Remember that pressure is related to collisions of molecules in a fluid. The molecules move in all directions, colliding with one another and with the walls of the container. The forces exerted on the molecules and on the walls of the container are equal. Unless the force or the area changes, the pressure is the same everywhere inside the fluid.

Units of Measurement of Pressure

Measurement of pressure is quite important in speech and voice science. Speech production is, after all, the manipulation of airflows and air pressures. The unfortunate truth, however, is that pressure is measured using a host of different units, depending upon the normal range of pressure one would expect for a given situation (and depending a bit on conventional habits and historical politics and oddities; see the side box on History of Measurement). In the English system of measurement, pressure is measured in pounds per square inch. This might be familiar to those who inflate car or bicycle tires. In SI, using the MKS system—meter, kilogram, second—the unit of measurement for pressure is the pascal (Pa), named in honor of Blaise Pascal (1623–1662), a French scientist and philosopher who pioneered the field of fluid mechanics. One **pascal** is equal to the force of one newton exerted over an area of 1 square meter. The pascal was added to the units of measurement in 1971. Before that, pressure in SI was expressed in units of newtons per meter squared (N/m^2). In the SI CGS system, however (remember—centimeter, gram, second), instead of the pascal, the microbar is used to measure pressure. A microbar is equivalent to 1 $dyne/cm^2$. (Dynes are still used in sometimes hearing science.)

To complicate matters further, medicine and physiology traditionally use measures based upon manometry, a system employing its own special instruments for measuring pressure. In this system, the pressure is measured by the force required to displace a column of some liquid in a tube. Blood pressure is still measured in millimeters of mercury. Lung pressure (most relevant for aerodynamic measures of speech) was and still is, to some extent, measured in cm H_2O. For example, if you blow into a tube containing a column of water, the force required to elevate the column of water by 5 cm would be considered 5 cm H_2O pressure. (The instrument used to measure pressure in this way is called a U-tube manometer, because the tube of water is shaped like the letter U.) Weather pressure was traditionally measured by the force required to move a column of mercury in an instrument called a barometer. If the mercury is rising, it signifies that the atmospheric pressure is increasing, and conversely, falling mercury means the barometric pressure is decreasing.

Understandably, the multitude of terms is enough to make any student of speech science a bit frustrated! Although air pressure in the vocal tract traditionally has been measured in cm H_2O, currently it is increasingly being measured in kilopascals. The amount of pressure represented by 1 pascal is too small to be of much practical use for speech production, however, and so we use the kilopascal (kPa). See Table 2–2 for the conversions. Of some interest, the kilopascal is a convenient measure in regard to conversions. One kPa is equal to 10 cm H_2O, and normal barometric pressure at sea level is approximately 100 kPa.

Pressure Defined

In words: Pressure is a force divided by the area over which the force is exerted.

The equation using words: Pressure equals force divided by area.

The equation using symbols: P = F/A.

Study Questions

6. Explain the concepts of stiffness and elasticity.

7. Define pressure and discuss the different methods of measuring pressure. What methods make most practical sense for measuring pressures relative to speech production?

Table 2–2. Conversion of Pressure Measurements

1 kilopascal (kPa) = 10.197 cm H_2O = 10^4 dyn/cm^2 (microbars)

1 dyn/cm^2 (microbar) = 1.0×10^{-4} kPa = 1.0197×10^{-3} cm H_2O

1 cm H_2O = 0.098 kPa = 980.68 dyn/cm^2 (microbar)

References

Abraham, R. H., & Shaw, C. D. (1992). *Dynamics: The geometry of behavior* (2nd ed.). Redwood City, CA: Addison-Wesley.

Davies, A., & Moore, C. (2003). *The respiratory system.* Edinburgh, UK: Elsevier Science.

Stetson, R. H. (1928). Motor phonetics. *Archives Néerlandaises de Phonétique Expérimentale. 3,* 1–216. (Reprinted in: J. A. S. Kelso & K. G. Munhall (Eds.) (1988), *R. H. Stetson's motor phonetics.* Boston, MA: Little, Brown.)

Woolf, A. D. (1988). *Osteoporosis: A clinical guide.* Philadelphia, PA: Lippincott.

3

Sound Waves

If a tree falls in a forest and no one is around to hear it fall, does it make a sound?

Figure 3–1. If a tree falls in a forest and no one is around to hear it fall, does it make a sound?

Mr. Watson - come here - I want to see you.
The first audible words spoken over the telephone.

—Alexander Graham Bell, Scottish Inventor of the
telephone and audiometer, among many
other inventions (1847–1922)

Does a tree falling in the forest create a sound if no one is around to hear it fall? We shall leave that oft-debated question to the philosophy classes; however, as speech-language pathologists, we will define sound as a pressure wave that is audible to the human ear with normal auditory sensitivity. The nature of that pressure wave, its production and perception, are the heart of the content of this textbook and, indeed, the heart of clinical speech-language pathology. And so the sound wave bears closer examination.

3.1 Vibration

What is vibration? At its most simple, **vibration (oscillation)** is a back-and-forth motion. Pretend you have a small ball attached to a spring suspended from a bar. The ball has a certain mass (a measure of the quantity of its matter), and we refer to this setup as a mass-spring system. Initially, the ball will stretch the spring to a point where it will sit quietly at rest, suspended on the spring. The ball-spring system is then said to be at **equilibrium**. When not disturbed by an outside force, the ball will maintain this rest position. We know this fact because Newton's first law of motion tells us so. If the spring is distorted by some agent pulling it downward and then releasing it, the mass and spring will immediately recoil upward. Why? Because Newton's third law of motion tells us that a force will act upon the system equally and opposite to the initial downward distortion. The potential energy that is built up in the system by the downward pull will be released as kinetic energy in the upward movement. The force that causes the mass-spring system to be restored to its prior, undistorted position is called a **restorative force**. The initial force that caused the mass-spring system to move from its position of equilibrium can be referred to as a **displacement force**. When the system is undisturbed at rest, it is at equilibrium, which means that the net restoring forces acting upon it are zero. The greater the displacement force, the greater proportionately the restorative force. Stretch the spring a little and the force that acts to restore the mass to equilibrium is small. Displace the spring a great deal, and the restorative force is large. (Displace the mass too much and the spring breaks—a special situation we will ignore.)

Now we know that if the mass is displaced by pulling on the spring, it will not simply move back to its initial rest position and stop. If an object is distorted and then released, elastic restorative forces accelerate the mass upward toward its equilibrium position (Figure 3–2). As the mass approaches equilibrium, the net restoring force decreases, and eventually when the mass reaches equilibrium, the net restoring force is zero. But why does the mass not stop at that point? Why does it maintain its upward trajectory? Inertial forces cause the mass to continue moving upward. Remember that inertia is the tendency of an object to resist change in movement. And we know that the momentum of an object is a product of its mass and acceleration. Thus, inertia causes the mass to overshoot the equilibrium position and continue moving upward. As the mass continues to overshoot equilibrium (that is, the negative displacement is increasing), the restorative force increases. The increasing restorative force acts to slow the upward movement of the mass—the restorative force acts to decelerate the mass. Finally, it stops at its topmost point and is pulled back toward equilibrium. However, the inertia of the displaced mass causes it to overshoot the rest position and distort in the opposite direction. Again, elastic restorative forces cause the mass to return to its original position. And again, the inertia of this second displacement causes the object to overshoot the rest position and distort in the initial direction. This cycle of vibration continues to repeat itself. However, frictional forces (forces that oppose movement) will cause the vibration to lose energy with each cycle, unless an outside force provides energy, and eventually the mass will stay in its rest position (Figure 3–3).

3.2 The Nature of Waves

Speech is composed of sound waves, which is why we spend so much time studying waves.

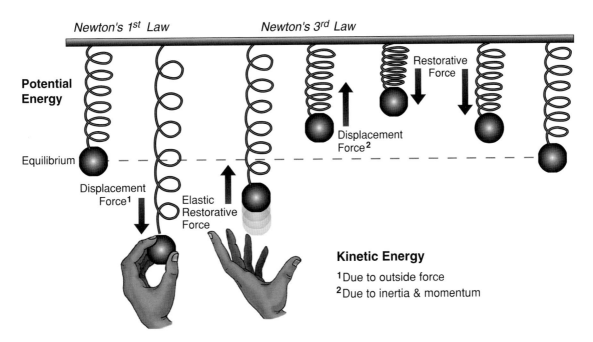

Figure 3–2. A description of vibration.

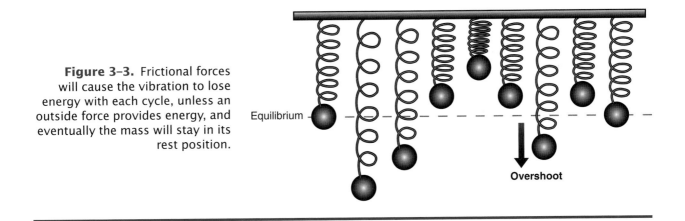

Figure 3–3. Frictional forces will cause the vibration to lose energy with each cycle, unless an outside force provides energy, and eventually the mass will stay in its rest position.

Waves are all around us, more ubiquitous probably than most people realize. Waves are composed of vibrations that move energy from Point A to Point B without actually moving an object or material from A to B. How is this so?

Waves are created by a disturbance. A wave is a disturbance that travels through a medium, transporting energy from one location to another. The medium is the material through which the wave passes; it is that which carries or transports the wave. Throwing a stone into a pond causes waves. The stone (and the force with which it has been thrown) is the disturbance, and the

medium that transports the disturbance is water. The medium is simply a series of interconnected particles that interact with one another. The particles of the water wave are the water molecules. Say hello to your friend and your friend hears you because of the sound wave you produced. Your vocal folds created the disturbance (much more about that later). The medium that transports the disturbance is air. The particles of air that interact with one another to carry the energy of your "hello" to your friend are the air molecules. In old-time western movies, the cowboy would put his ear against the railroad track to feel for vibrations alerting him that a train was approaching. The train creates a disturbance and the metal railroad track is the medium. The molecules of metal are the particles that interact with one another and the resulting vibrations through the train track are felt by the cowboy. The examples of waves in the pond, the air, and the train track are all examples of **mechanical waves**, which require a medium to transport energy from one point to another. Energy transfer of mechanical waves cannot occur in a vacuum. (Other waves, such as light and electromagnetic waves, are not mechanical, but they are generally not considered for study in speech-language pathology.)

Pulse Waves

The simplest wave is a **pulse wave**, in which a single disturbance travels through a medium. Set up a row of dominoes, standing on end and not touching at a distance less than their height. Knock over the first one. The first domino will knock over the next one, and this disturbance will travel down the row of dominoes in a single pulse wave. Hold a jump rope at one end and have your friend hold the other end. Abruptly raise your hand up and down once. This disturbance causes the rope at your end to move up and down. The single upward and downward movement travels along the rope to your friend in a single pulse wave. Think of a line of cars driving along a road. Pretend each car is driving at a steady 30 mph. A bit of road is broken, requiring the cars to slow down. Thus, each car decelerates as it nears the broken area and then accelerates back to 30 mph after passing over the broken road. When viewed from a traffic helicopter above, the disturbance of the broken road causes a pulse wave of momentary slowing down. The stone thrown into the pond sends out a single pulse wave in all directions. A single clap of the hands transmits a pulse sound wave. Speech contains many examples of pulsed sounds, such as the phonemes /t/ and /k/, or the tongue click contained in certain African languages. We will explore the characteristics of pulse speech sound waves in detail in a later chapter.

Longitudinal Pressure Waves

Unlike a pulse, most waves are characterized by repeated disturbances over some period of time. **Sound waves** consist of a series of pressure disturbances. Consider a vibrating tuning fork (Figure 3–4). When the tuning fork is struck with a mallet, the tines vibrate back and forth (Figure 3–5). As they vibrate, the tines push on the air particles surrounding them. The forward motion of the tines pushes the air molecules forward. Let us pretend that we can see the individual air particles moving. Examining a single air molecule, the force of the tine moving forward causes Particle A to collide with Particle B. This collision causes Particle A to be pushed back into its rest position (an equal and opposite force, remember), while displacing Particle B forward, which in turn collides with Particle C. Due to momentum, however, Particle A overshoots rest position and moves farther away from Particle B. The collisions of air molecules result in regions of increased density and air pressure called **compressions**. The restorative force and momentum cause the air particles to separate, resulting in regions of decreased density and air pressure, called **rarefactions**. The alternating compressions and rarefactions of air molecules are the traveling sound wave. Because

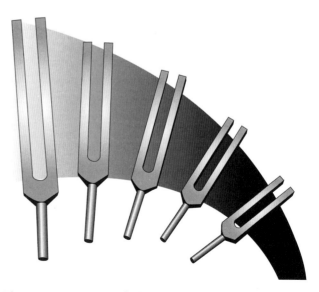

Figure 3–4. Tuning forks of different sizes.

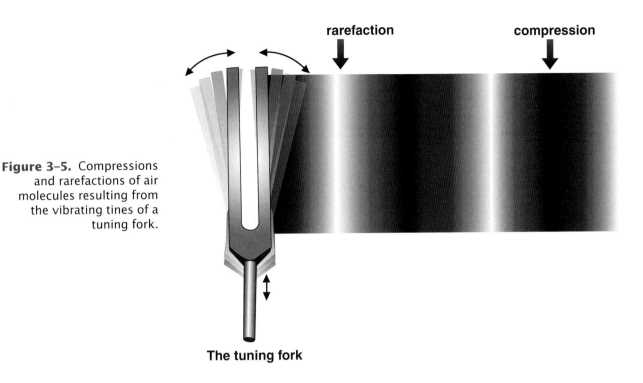

rarefaction   compression

Figure 3–5. Compressions and rarefactions of air molecules resulting from the vibrating tines of a tuning fork.

The tuning fork

Tuning Fork

A tuning fork is a deceptively simple instrument in which two tines (prongs) form a U-shape (see Figure 3–5). The tuning fork is deceptive because it is made of elastic steel that is designed to vibrate at a single frequency, producing a pure tone (see section on Pure Tones later in this chapter). The tuning fork was invented in 1711 by John Shore, the trumpet player to the British court of George I (born in 1660, became king in 1714, and died in 1727). Tuning forks are commonly used to tune musical instruments because they produce a "pure" vibration (more about that soon). One "plays" a tuning fork by striking it gently against a hard surface. The result-ing sound pressure wave is generally of low amplitude, yielding a soft sound (we discuss soon the relationship of amplitude and sound). Therefore, tuning forks often are heard most easily by being struck and then being placed on a solid surface that resonates (more on that later in the chapter) with greater amplitude. You can see in Figure 3–4 that tuning forks are made in different lengths. The length of the tines determines the frequency at which the tuning fork will vibrate. We will learn about the relationship of length and frequency in the Resonance and Standing Waves sections and in our discussion of vocal fold vibration in Chapter 5.

the sound wave is composed of a repeating pattern of regions of high pressure and low pressure moving through a medium, a sound wave is sometimes referred to as a pressure wave.

Sound pressure waves are longitudinal waves. In **longitudinal waves**, the particles of the medium move parallel to the direction of the wave (see Transverse Waves on page 31 for more information about different types of waves). Said another way, particle motion is parallel to wave motion. As the sound wave moves from the speaker's lips to the listener's ears, the particles of air vibrate backward and forward parallel to the direction in which the wave energy is transported. Regardless of the source (vocal folds, clapping hands, tuning fork), sound is always a longitudinal wave. The distinguishing feature of a longitudinal wave is that the particles of the medium move in a direction parallel to the direction of energy transport.

3.3 Transfer of Energy in Waves

Sound waves are mechanisms of energy transfer. Energy can be carried by the particles or by the wave itself. Suppose that you have a row of dominoes that are lined up, each standing on end very close to the next but not touching. If you tap the first domino so that it falls over onto the second domino, that domino will in turn fall onto the third domino, which will knock over the fourth domino. This will continue until all the dominoes have been knocked over. In this example, the energy has been transferred from your finger tap to the final domino. The falling pattern of the dominos was a wave of

movement of each individual particle (domino). The individual particles did not move forward from beginning to end with the wave; they only moved slightly in place (falling over). The wave, however, traveled from the first to the last domino. (Hence, the term "domino effect" to describe a cascade of events that starts with a single initial event.) The motion of the wave was not the same as the motion of the individual particles. In contrast, let's say that you take the first domino and throw it at another domino. In this case, the kinetic energy of the thrown domino is imparted directly to the next domino. The thrown domino travels in an arc but it is not a wave motion. The particle, not the wave, carries the energy to another particle. (See Figure 3–6 for examples of the methods of energy transfer just discussed.)

Think back to the displacement of air molecules as the result of the vibrating tuning fork. As the first particle is displaced, it pushes on the second particle, which displaces that second particle from its equilibrium position. As the second particle is displaced, it in turn displaces the third particle, and so on. In this way, the disturbance itself is traveling through the particles. But the particles themselves do not travel

Figure 3–6. Transfer of energy can be represented by (**A**) throwing the object or (**B**) collision of a series of objects—a wave.

beyond their own area of disturbance. Think of the particles as being interconnected by springs, like a child's Slinky toy (Figures 3–7 and 3–8). The springs transmit the displacement from one particle to the next. Any point on the coiled toy moves back and forth a small distance, but the disturbance itself is transmitted along the length of the entire toy.

Figure 3–7. Particle movement in a longitudinal pressure wave is represented by balls attached to the individual coils of a child's Slinky toy. The energy is transmitted in a wave from one vibrating (back and forth) particle to the next.

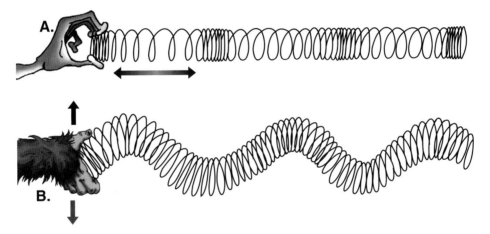

Figure 3–8. A. A longitudinal wave is represented by the horizontal motion of individual coils of a child's Slinky toy, which are parallel to the horizontal motion of the wave along the entire length of the toy. **B.** A transverse wave is represented by the vertical motion of the individual coils, which is perpendicular to the horizontal motion of the wave along the entire length of the toy.

Transverse Waves

One of the most common types of waves that can be visualized easily is the ocean wave, or the ripples in water created by throwing a stone into a pond. Be careful, however, not to get confused. Although there are similarities between these types of waves and sound waves, their properties are different. Ocean waves and pond ripples are examples of a combination of longitudinal and transverse waves. In a longitudinal wave, the vibration of the medium is parallel to the motion of the wave, such as the wave created with the Slinky toy in Figure 3–8A. In the motion of transverse waves, the vibration is perpendicular to the motion of the wave. In a transverse wave, instead of compressions, there are high points (crests), and in place of rarefactions, there are low points (troughs) (Figure 3–8B).

Transverse waves typically occur in more rigid mediums. For example, in our earlier example of a pulse wave traveling along a jump rope, the single upward and downward movement of the vibration is an example of a transverse wave. Gravity helps the particles in a transverse wave return to equilibrium. Transverse waves cannot exist by themselves in a fluid because the molecules would simply slip by one another rather than being pushed upward or downward. However, water waves are a combination of transverse and longitudinal waves. The transverse characteristic (crests and troughs) dominates visually, but the individual water molecules follow an elliptical path, therefore combining motions that are both perpendicular and parallel to the motion of the wave. Sound waves do not have crests and troughs.

Sound waves are longitudinal, with parallel compressions and rarefactions of molecules. Note, however, that our previous discussion of energy transfer applies to both transverse and longitudinal waves. An individual point in the transverse wave moves up and down but not forward. An individual point in the longitudinal wave moves forward and backward around a central point, but it does not travel forward down the length of the toy. A fun example of a transverse wave is the stadium wave performed by the fans (Figure 3–9). Each individual stands up and sweeps his hands up over his head and then brings his arms down as he sits down. When this activity is performed by each person sequentially, the visual effect is a giant wave sweeping around the stadium. Each person rises and falls, as in a crest and a trough, but everyone remains in the same position relative to the entire stadium. The movement of the individual "particles" is not the same as the movement of the wave. Could you change the stadium wave to a longitudinal wave, like a sound wave? Sure. Instead of standing up and sitting down, an individual could lean quickly to the right to bonk into the next person (compression), then sit back erect (rarefaction) as the next person moves quickly to the right. Such a longitudinal stadium wave probably would not look as impressive from the air, however!

Figure 3–9. A stadium wave is an example of a transverse wave.

3.4 Visualizing a Sound Wave

In our example of simple vibration of the mass-spring system, we noted a repetition of a pattern: the repeated upward compression and down-

ward extension of the mass and spring. If we ignore frictional forces, we could say that this upward and downward oscillation continues unchanged through each cycle of vibration. This movement is an example of **simple harmonic motion**, also called projected uniform circular motion. Figure 3–10 shows a waveform of simple harmonic motion. A waveform is a graphic representation of the change of some phenomenon (a vibration in this case) as a function of time. The waveform of simple harmonic motion is a projection of circular motion at constant speed onto one axis in a plane. Figure 3–10 is the projection of the arc of the upward and downward movement of the mass-spring unit drawn onto the white background. If we could scroll the white background forward at a steady rate, we would see that the projection of the uniform up and down movement is circular; hence, the name uniform circular motion. By convention, a waveform is drawn with time on the *x*-axis oriented horizontally. This representation of uniform circular motion is also called a **sinusoidal wave**, or **sine wave** for short, because circular motion can be represented mathematically by the sine and cosine of an angle.

Just as we represent uniform circular motion as a waveform, we can display a sound wave graphically by representing the areas of high pressure (compressed air molecules) and

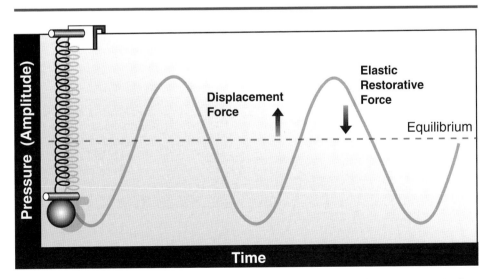

Figure 3–10. A waveform of uniform circular motion (simple harmonic motion).

low pressure (rarefied air molecules) with the upward and downward curves of the waveform (Figure 3–11). The horizontal *x*-axis represents time going forward and the vertical *y*-axis represents the amplitude of the pressure.

3.5 Properties of Sound Waves

We describe the objects around us by their distinguishing characteristics—size, weight, color, shape, for example. We can also describe sound waves by their distinguishing characteristics.

Frequency

The **frequency** of a sound wave is the rate at which the particles vibrate back and forth each second. It answers the question of how often the air molecules vibrate or, said another way, how often the pattern of compressions and rarefactions repeats itself. The unit of measurement for frequency is the hertz, using the symbol Hz (note that no period is used after the symbol). In case you are wondering, the measurement unit is named after Heinrich Rudolf Hertz (1857–1894), who was the first to transmit and receive radio

waves. Before the unit of measurement was designated the hertz, frequency was measured in cycles per second, which is equivalent to hertz. One cycle is equal to one complete repetition of a pattern. In our sound pressure wave, one cycle represents one unit of alternating compression and rarefaction of air molecules. It is important to note that, for purposes of calculating the frequency, the beginning point of the cycle can be designated anywhere on the waveform if the end point of the cycle follows after one complete pattern repetition. The point in the cycle at which the waveform begins is referred to as the **phase**. Phase is not critical for calculation of frequency, but it shall become relevant later in our discussion of resonance.

If a wave is composed of particles that vibrate 100 times every second, then we say that its frequency is 100 Hz. It is important to know that each particle in the medium vibrates at the same frequency. This makes sense if we consider for a moment how the particles are set into motion. In the simplest example, a single particle is disturbed by some mechanical force. This disturbance causes it to collide with its neighbor, which in turn causes the second particle to collide with its neighbor. Each collision sets off the vibration of another particle and also causes the particle before it to move back toward rest posi-

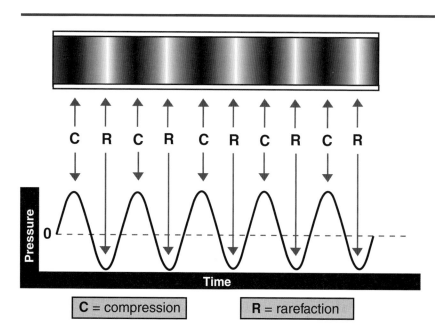

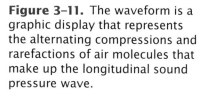

Figure 3–11. The waveform is a graphic display that represents the alternating compressions and rarefactions of air molecules that make up the longitudinal sound pressure wave.

tion. Because each particle is composed of the same matter, each particle vibrates in the same way, so all particles are moving (vibrating) at the same frequency. Everywhere the motion is at the same rate. The rate at which the source of the sound vibrates is the rate of the vibration of the sound wave. If the first particle is set into motion at a rate of vibration of 210 Hz (210 cycles of alternating compressions and rarefac-

tions per second), then every other particle in the wave is set into vibration at 210 Hz. (See Table 3–1 for some interesting facts about frequencies.) Specifically, each cycle, or repeating pattern, is composed of 210 alternating rarefactions and compressions of air molecules.

In Figure 3–12, two waveforms are displayed, one corresponding to a low frequency and the other to a higher frequency. Both plots represent

Table 3–1. Amusing Frequency Statistics

Frequency	Description
10 Hz	Typical car engine (equivalent to 600 revolutions per minute)
50 Hz	European standard alternating current (AC)
60 Hz	American electrical AC
100 Hz	Typical car engine "redlining" (equivalent to 6,000 rpm)
261.6 Hz	Musical tone C4: middle "C" on the piano
440 Hz	Musical tone A4 (A above middle C): "concert pitch"
740 kHz	The clock speed of the Intel 4004, in the mid-1970s, the very first commercial microprocessor
3–73 GHz	The clock speed of the 2005 Pentium 4 microprocessor
30–300 MHz	(Electromagnetic waves) TV broadcast signals
88–108 MHz	(Electromagnetic wave) FM radio broadcast signals

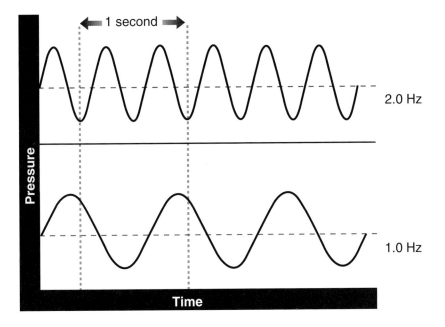

Figure 3–12. Two sine waves of different frequencies.

one second of each wave. Note that in the higher frequency wave, the fluctuations in sound pressure occur closer together, or more rapidly, than in the lower frequency wave. In the same amount of time (1 second), there are more compressions and rarefactions of air molecules in the higher frequency wave than in the lower frequency wave.

Period

If we look at the waveforms in Figures 3–13 and 3–14, we see the change in pressure as a function of time (that is, the wave's frequency). But what if we want to measure how long it takes to go through just one cycle of compression and rarefaction? The time between successive points of low or high pressure is called the **period**, and is the reciprocal of the frequency. This means that a sound wave with a high frequency will have a small period, and a sound wave with a low frequency will have a large period. Think about it: The longer the duration of the period, the more time it takes to complete one cycle

of compression and rarefaction, so there are fewer cycles per second, and the frequency is lower. The shorter the duration of the period, the less time it takes to complete once cycle, so the higher the number of cycles per second, or the higher the frequency.

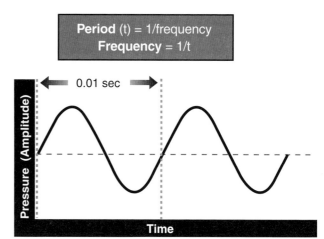

Period (t) = 1/frequency
Frequency = 1/t

Figure 3–13. The time between a successive alternating compression and rarefaction is called the period.

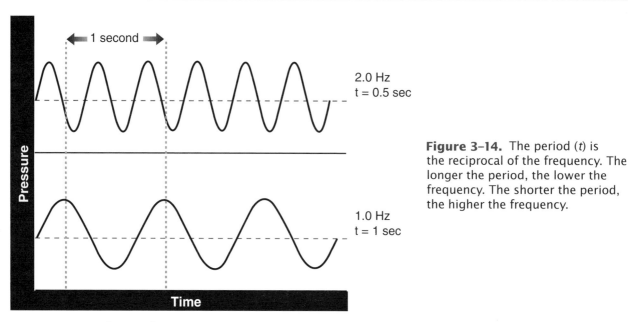

2.0 Hz
t = 0.5 sec

1.0 Hz
t = 1 sec

Figure 3–14. The period (t) is the reciprocal of the frequency. The longer the period, the lower the frequency. The shorter the period, the higher the frequency.

Relationship of Frequency and Period Defined

The words: The longer the period, the lower the frequency. The shorter the period, the higher the frequency.

The equations using words: Period = 1/frequency and Frequency = 1/period.

The equation using symbols: $t = 1/f$ and $f = 1/t$.

Study Questions

6. Without referring to Figures 3–10 and 3–11, can you draw a waveform that represents simple harmonic motion? Label the x- and y-axes. Draw and label the line of equilibrium. Indicate a point of compression and one of rarefaction. Where does the displacement force occur? The elastic restorative force?

7. Define frequency and period, and explain the relationship between the two measures.

8. Calculate the period of a 220-Hz sound wave to the nearest tenth.

9. Calculate the frequency of a sound wave with a period of 6.5 ms. (*Hint:* 6.5 ms = .0065 s)

Intensity

Every sound wave has a characteristic amount of energy. What do we mean by this? When we talk about a sound pressure wave, we can think of the energy in that wave as a measure of its power. Remember that the pressure wave is initiated by a disturbance—let's say a guitar string that is vibrating back and forth. It disturbs the air molecules immediately adjacent to it, a disturbance that then causes those particles to disturb the next adjacent molecules, and so on. The disturbance, which carries energy, travels from one air molecule to the next. The amount of energy, or power, that is transferred from one particle to the next depends on the **amplitude** of vibrations of the guitar string. If the guitar string is plucked strongly (more work is done to displace the string from its position of equilibrium, or rest), then the string vibrates with wider amplitude. The wider the amplitude of vibration, the greater the displacement of the string; the greater the displacement of the adjacent air particles from rest position, the more power is imparted.

Intensity is the power per unit area and is expressed in units of measurement called watts (W). By convention, the area of measurement is the square meter (m^2), and so intensity is expressed as W/m^2. In Figure 3–15, we see that the power of the sound wave is represented by its amplitude. The greater the power of the sound wave, the greater its amplitude. Although amplitude of the sound pressure wave and its power or intensity are directly related, the intensity increases more rapidly than does the amplitude. In fact, intensity or power increases as the square of the amplitude of the sound pressure. For example, for a doubling of amplitude, the increase of intensity will be quadrupled (2^2). When the amplitude is increased by a factor of 6, the intensity will be increased by a factor of 36 (6^2).

The inverse is also true; when the amplitude is halved, the intensity is decreased by four times. This information becomes important for classrooms, as the students sitting in the back row hear the instructor at a much lower intensity than the students sitting in the front row. If a student sitting in the back row has hearing loss, the instructor may not be heard, especially if the amplitude of noise surrounding the student is greater than the amplitude of the instructor's voice. As the sound pressure wave is carried through a medium, its intensity diminishes with increasing distance from the source. This decrease is due to the outward propagation of the sound wave, spreading out over a progressively larger surface area. As energy is always conserved in nature, and the area through which the sound wave propagates increases, the power must decrease. (Remember, the power is measured on a per-area basis.) This relationship between intensity and distance from the source is called the inverse square relationship (Figure 3–16). That is, the intensity varies inversely with the distance from the source. Remember that the inverse relationship means that as one quantity increases, the other quantity decreases. The **inverse square relationship** means that whatever factor by which the distance is increased, the intensity is decreased by a factor equal to the square of the distance change factor. For example, if the distance from the source is increased by a factor of 2 (doubled), the intensity is reduced by a factor of 4 (quartered), because the square of 2 is 4.

Unlike frequency, we do not measure the absolute value of intensity of sound. Rather, we measure intensity as the relative power of one sound to another. The relative measurement of intensity is not unlike identifying height as tall or short; these descriptors imply that an individual is tall or short relative to other individuals. Speech intensity is measured in decibels of sound pressure level (dB SPL). Let's take a moment to explore this measure.

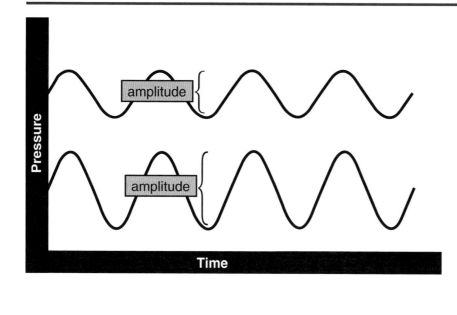

Figure 3–15. The peak-to-peak height of the pressure wave represents its power. Although the amplitude of the sound pressure wave and its power or intensity are directly related, the intensity increases more rapidly than does the amplitude.

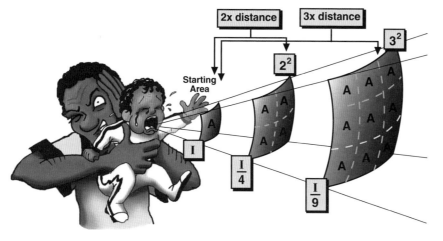

Figure 3–16. The inverse square relationship means that whatever factor by which the distance is increased, the intensity is decreased by a factor equal to the square of the distance change factor.

Hearing Thresholds

The faintest detectable sound is called the threshold of human hearing. The average person with normal hearing sensitivity can detect a sound that has an intensity of 1×10^{-12} W/m². This level corresponds to a pressure wave in which the compressions of air particles have only 0.3 billionths of an atmosphere pressure greater than the surrounding air. It also means that the air particles are displaced by only a billionth of a centimeter. The loudest sound that can be detected without damaging the structures of the ear is more intense than one billion times the threshold of hearing!

Table 3–2. Hearing Thresholds

Frequency Range	Animal
20 Hz–20 kHz	Human beings
50 Hz–45 kHz	Dogs
100 Hz–65 kHz	Cats
1 kHz–100 kHz	Bats
1 kHz–150 kHz	Dolphins
200 Hz–90 kHz	Rats
5 Hz–10 kHz	Elephants

The range of intensities that can be detected by the human ear is very large (see Hearing Thresholds above and Table 3–2). Therefore, the scale commonly used to measure intensity is based upon multiples of 10. Such scales are called **logarithmic scales** and allow us to manage large ranges of numbers more easily. A well-known logarithmic scale is the scale used to measure earthquake magnitude. An earthquake of magnitude 5 releases 10 times as much energy as a quake of magnitude 4. (By the way, the earthquake is a pressure wave, not unlike sound waves. However, the frequency of earthquake pressure waves is on the order of 1 Hz, well below the threshold of hearing. Therefore, seismologists, rather than acousticians, "listen" to earthquakes!) The logarithmic scale used to measure intensity is the decibel (dB) scale. A **decibel** is one tenth of a Bel, a unit named after the Scottish American scientist Alexander Graham Bell (1847–1922), inventor of the telephone. (We shall bump into the Bell family again in Chapter 7, where we will find that his father also had some interest in speech production.) The decibel unit describes the relative intensity of a sound wave. The threshold of hearing at 1000 Hz (1×10^{12} W/m² or equivalently, 20 µPa) is assigned a sound level of 0 dB. A sound wave that is 10 times as intense (1×10^{11} W/m²) is assigned a sound level of 10 dB. A sound wave that is 100 (10×10) times as intense (1×10^{10} W/m²) as the threshold of hearing corresponds to 20 dB. A sound wave that is 1,000 ($10 \times 10 \times 10$) times as intense as the threshold of hearing corresponds to 30 dB. A 50-dB sound wave would have an intensity that is ($10 \times 10 \times 10 \times 10 \times 10$) times as intense ($1 \times 10^7$ W/m²) as the threshold of hearing. You can quickly see that using a logarithmic scale allows us to talk about sound intensity more easily than the nonlogarithmic notation of watts/m². (See Table 3–3 for relative intensity levels of common events.)

Intensity of speech, then, is a ratio of acoustic powers expressed in logarithms. Because we said that speech creates a pressure wave in air, we measure intensity of speech in units of dB sound pressure level (dB SPL). The sound pressure level (SPL) is the difference in decibels (dB) between a pressure of interest and the standard reference pressure of 0.0002 dyne per square centimeter, or more currently but equivalently under the newer MKS measurement system, 1×10^{12} W/m² (or its equivalent, 20 µPa). To compare the relative intensities of two sounds, the following formula is used:

$$dB\ SPL = 20 \log_{10} (P_m/P_r)$$

in which P_m is the sound you want to measure and P_r is the reference sound (the one you use

Table 3–3. Relative Intensity Levels

Sound Source	Decibels	Energy Relative to Threshold	Physical Sensation
	0	1	Threshold of hearing
Quiet breathing	10	10	Just audible
Voiced whisper	30	1,000	
Soft speech	40	10,000	
Typical conversation	60	1 million	
Normal street traffic	70	10 million	
Screaming baby	90	1 billion	Threshold for endangering hearing
Power leaf blowers	100	10 billion	
Loud music concert	120	1 trillion	Threshold of pain
Construction jackhammer	130	10 trillion	
Jet taking off nearby	150	1 quadrillion	Threshold over which total deafness may occur

for comparison). We can calculate the intensity in dB SPL of a certain sound if we know how much greater its sound pressure wave is compared to the reference pressure. For example, we are told that a very soft whisper is produced with 10 times as much sound pressure as a sound produced at hearing threshold (barely audible). In other words, P_m/P_r is equal to 10. The log of 10 equals 1 (that is, $10^1 = 1 \times 10$) and $20 \times 1 = 20$. Therefore, we would say that the very soft whisper is produced at 20 dB SPL.

$$P_m/P_r = 10$$

$$dB\ SPL = 20\ \log_{10}(10)$$

$$dB\ SPL = 20 \times 1 = 20$$

We also can compute in the opposite direction and calculate the relationship of one sound pressure to the other if we know both intensity levels. For example, we are told that the intensity of a moderately soft conversation is produced at 60 dB SPL.

$$60\ dB\ SPL\ 20\ \log_{10}(P_m/P_r)$$

Substitute X for $\log_{10}(P_m/P_r)$ to get
$$60\ dB\ SPL = 20X$$

Now solve for X by dividing each side by 20:
$$60/20 = 20/20X$$

$$X = 3 = \log_{10}(P_m/P_r),\ so$$
$$\log_{10} 3 = 10 \times 10 \times 10 = 10^3 = 1,000$$

We learned that a sound wave that is 1,000 (= $10 \times 10 \times 10$) times as intense as the threshold of hearing corresponds to 30 dB (in units of power, W/m^2). Since power = pressure × pressure, for every 10-fold increase in intensity (in units of power), there is a 20-fold increase in intensity (in units of dB SPL). Therefore, speech that is 1,000 times as intense as the threshold of hearing is equal to 60 dB SPL.

Another important concept to know about decibels is how to interpret values of different decibels relative to each other. Using the equation

$$dB\ SPL = 20 \log_{10} (P_m/P_r)$$

and if $P_m/P_r = 2$ (i.e., measured pressure = 2× the reference pressure)

we can determine that $\log_{10} 2 = 0.3$
(that is, $10^{0.3} = 2$)

$$20 \times 0.3 = 6\ dB\ SPL$$

A 6-dB increase is equivalent to a doubling of sound pressure, and conversely, a 6-dB decrease is equivalent to a halving of sound pressure.

Wavelength

Wavelength is the distance traveled by one cycle of vibration (one cycle of alternating compression and rarefaction of air molecules). The symbol for wavelength is the Greek letter lambda (λ). In Figure 3–17, it is evident that the wavelength and period (and, therefore, frequency) are related. Wavelength refers to cycle distance, and frequency and period refer to aspects of cycle time. Wavelength also depends upon the

speed of sound. The speed of sound traveling through the atmosphere is, in turn, dependent mainly on altitude (density of air molecules) and temperature (speed of movement of the molecules) (more on the speed of sound below). The standard reference is 59°F at sea level, at which the velocity of sound is 340 meters/s (761 mph). Therefore, the wavelength of a sound wave is calculated as the speed of sound divided by the frequency of the wave.

As an example, let's say that a man says "hi" at a steady frequency of 120 Hz. (The frequency is common for men, as we shall learn in Chapter 4, but saying "hi" at a steady frequency is unlikely, as we shall learn in Chapter 7!) Let us also assume that a woman produces the same greeting but at a steady frequency of 220 Hz (a common frequency at which women speak). Using the standard reference for the speed of sound, the sound wave of the man's greeting has a wavelength of 2.8 m/s, whereas the sound wave of the woman's greeting has a wavelength of approximately 1.6 m/s. From the equation for wavelength and these examples, we can see that frequency and wavelength are inversely related. (Recall that an inverse relationship simply means that as one quantity is increased, the other will decrease.) Higher frequency sounds correspond to shorter wavelengths, and lower frequency sounds correspond to longer wavelengths.

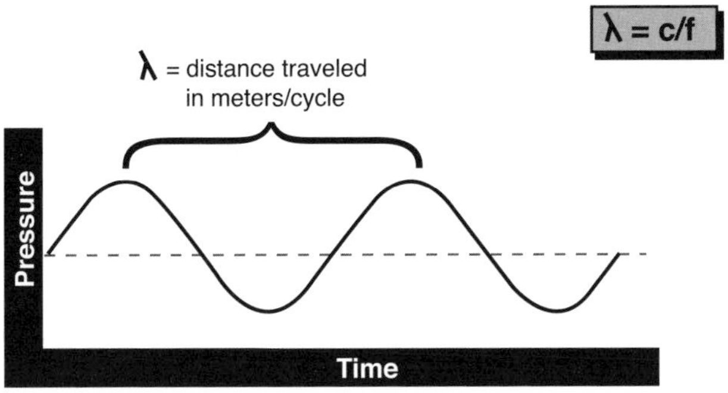

Figure 3–17. Wavelength is the distance traveled by one cycle of vibration (one cycle of alternating compressions and rarefactions of air molecules).

Wavelength Defined

The words: An inverse relationship exists between wavelength and frequency.

The equation using words: Wavelengths (in m) = velocity of sound (in m/s) / frequency (in Hz)

The equation using symbols: $\lambda = c/f$ where λ is the symbol for wavelength and c is the symbol for the velocity of sound.

Speed of Sound

The speed of sound refers to the rate at which the pressure disturbance is transmitted from one particle to the next. Do not confuse speed and frequency and wavelength. Frequency of a sound wave refers to the number of cycles of compressions and rarefactions per second, and answers the question "how often?" Wavelength is the distance traveled per cycle of compression and rarefaction, and answers the question "how far?" Speed, however, characterizes the distance per unit of time. The speed of a sound wave is the distance that a compression or rarefaction travels per second, so speed answers the question "how fast?" Speed is usually expressed as distance divided by time. The unit of measurement is meters/second (m/s). We know that a car traveling down the road will cover more distance the faster it goes. Similarly, the faster a sound wave travels, the more distance it will cover per unit of time.

The speed of a sound wave is determined by the properties of the medium through which it travels. The greater the density of a mass, the greater the inertia and the slower the interaction between neighboring molecules. Hence, all other things being equal, sound travels faster through less dense material. Air is three times as dense as helium, and so sound waves travel three times as fast through helium as through the normal atmosphere (see Donald Duck in Chapter 7). However, another important characteristic that determines the speed of a sound wave is the state of the medium (solid, liquid, gas). Solid materials generally have the strongest bond between molecules of the three states, followed by liquids, with gases having the weakest bonds. The strong bonds allow the particles to interact with one another more easily than weaker bonds. For this reason, sound waves travel faster in solids than in liquids, and they travel faster in liquids than in gases. Therefore, even though inertial factors would seem to favor gases, the strong bonds between molecules of certain solids outweigh the inertia.

The temperature and pressure of the air also influence the speed of sound. The pressure influences the density of the air, because greater pressure results in increased density of particles. The temperature influences the strength of the interaction between the particles. At a given air pressure, the higher temperature causes the interactions between particles to become more elastic. That is, the particles are more easily separated. The medium therefore has less resistance to being deformed (changing shape). When the temperature is 68°F at sea level pressure, sound travels at 343 meters/second (equal to 750 mph).

Sometimes, speed of sound is referred to as the velocity of sound. Velocity is speed in a given direction. Sound pressure waves, however, generally radiate outward in all directions, and therefore, for our purposes, we use speed and velocity equivalently in this specific instance.

In summary, the speed of a sound wave is not dependent upon its frequency or wavelength. (Remember the inverse relationship of frequency and wavelength: As one quantity increases, the other quantity must decrease.) The speed of a sound wave can be altered only by the properties of the medium through which it travels.

Study Questions

10. Define intensity. How are pressure and amplitude of vibration related to intensity?

11. What is meant by the inverse square relationship?

12. How do we measure intensity? Why is a logarithmic scale used? (*Hint*: how much energy is in an extremely loud sound compared to one that is just barely perceptible to us?)

13. Define wavelength.

14. What factors can influence the speed of a sound wave? What properties of sound waves do not affect the speed?

Turn Down the Music!

The wavelength of a sound wave and the material through which it travels affect us daily. Have you ever sat next to someone listening to music through headphones? Chances are, if the music was turned up sufficiently loudly or the earpieces were sitting loosely, you could hear the bass but little else. Low-frequency, long-wavelength sounds spread out more than do high-frequency, short-wavelength sound pressure waves. The longer wavelengths bend around objects and propagate through solids more easily, whereas the short-wavelength sounds are highly directive and do not escape easily around and through objects. We shall learn in later chapters that the frequencies of speech sounds are generally high frequency. Therefore, the low bass sounds escape the music lover's earphones more easily than do the higher frequency sounds of speech as well as other musical instruments such as the flute.

Why Do Sounds Travel Farther at Night?

It is easier to hear faraway sounds in the evening than in the daytime. This effect is due to air temperature and a phenomenon called *refraction*. In general, during the daytime, the air nearer to the ground is warmer than the air higher up away from the ground. The sound wave travels more easily in the warmer temperatures and gets slowed down by the cooler temperatures. This difference in velocity causes refraction, a bending upward of the sound waves toward the slower moving, cooler air. At night, the opposite occurs. The sound waves bend downward toward the cooler air along the ground. Thus, the sounds waves appear to be traveling farther, as they stay closer to the ground across a greater distance.

3.6 Pure and Complex Tones

An object that vibrates with energy at a single frequency is said to produce a pure tone. **A pure tone** is the audible result of simple harmonic motion and its graphic representation, the sine wave. The tuning fork produces a pure tone. A mass-spring system or a pendulum is a good example of an object undergoing simple harmonic motion (although the amplitude and frequency are not sufficient to generate sound on its own).

Let's say that we strike two tuning forks simultaneously, one vibrating at 100 Hz and the other vibrating at 500 Hz, both with equal energy (Figure 3–18, middle and lower panels, respectively). If we combine these two sinusoid waves together, we obtain the complex waveform shown at the top of Figure 3–18. Immediately we can see that it appears more complex than a simple sine wave. It represents a **complex sound**, being made up of two or more sine waves of different frequency. Now let us suppose that we strike both tuning forks again, but one with a slight force and the second with a greater force, so that the resulting sound pressure waves differ in both frequency and intensity (Figure 3–19). The 500-Hz tone (bottom panel) has half the sound pressure level of the 100-Hz tone (middle panel). If we combine these two sine waves (top panel), again we obtain a complex sinusoid. Compare the shapes of the complex waveforms of Figures 3–18 and 3–19. The patterns of each cycle are the same because the frequencies of the sine waves that make up the waveforms are the same. Only the amplitudes are different. In Figure 3–20, we see three sine waves of different

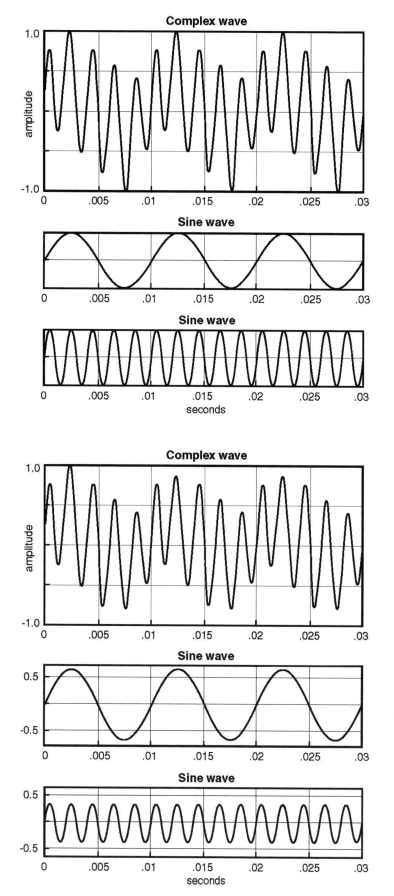

Figure 3–18. The complex wave (*top panel*) is composed of two sine waves of similar amplitude and different frequencies, one at 100 Hz (*middle panel*) and one at 500 Hz (*bottom panel*). Note that the f_o of the complex waveform is equal to the f_o of the lowest component sine wave.

Figure 3–19. The complex wave (*top panel*) is composed of two sine waves, one at 100 Hz (*middle panel*) and one at a lesser amplitude but a higher frequency of 500 Hz (*bottom panel*). Note that the f_o of the complex waveform is equal to the f_o of the lowest component sine wave.

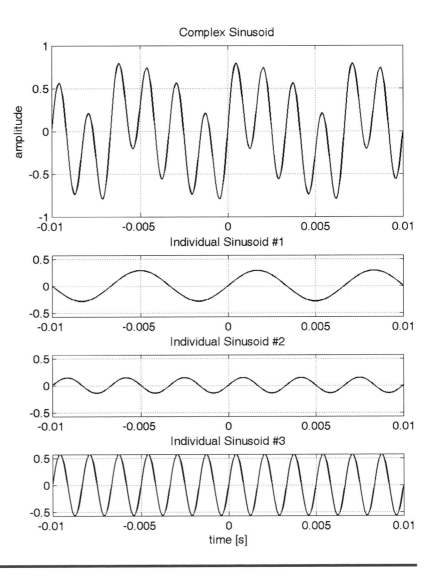

Figure 3–20. A complex wave (*top panel*) having three sine wave components of 250 Hz, 500 Hz, and 750 Hz, all with different amplitudes. Note that the f_o of the complex wave is equal to the f_o of the lowest frequency component.

frequencies and amplitudes combine to form yet another complex wave. Here we obtain a different pattern of the complex wave than those of Figures 3–18 and 3–19 because the component sine waves are of different frequencies.

Three features of the complex waves are important to understand. Note that the frequency of the complex wave in all three figures is equal to the frequency of the lowest component sine wave. In Figures 3–18 and 3–19, the complex pattern repeats with the same period as the 100-Hz tone. In Figure 3–20, the complex wave repeats each cycle at the same frequency as the 250-Hz tone. The period of any complex wave is always equal to the highest period of the component sine waves. Said another way, the frequency of the complex wave is equal to the frequency of the lowest (frequency) component sine wave. This frequency, which represents the repetition frequency of the complex pattern, is called the **fundamental frequency** (f_o). The f_o is the lowest frequency of a complex periodic tone. As we will learn in Chapter 5, f_o is an important feature of voice production.

The second feature of the complex waves is the arithmetic relationship of the sine waves to each other. In Figure 3–20, the second sine wave of 500 Hz is an integer multiple of the f_o

(250 × 2), and the third sine wave of 750 Hz is also an integer multiple of the f_o (250 Hz × 3). A complex sound wave in which the component sine waves all have a mathematical relationship between them is said to be a complex **periodic** sound. Although few sounds in nature are pure tones, many are periodic complex waves, including musical instruments such as the violin, piano, or horn, and, most relevant for speech-language pathologist, the sound of the human voice. (As we will learn in Chapter 5, voice is not exactly periodic. All human function has a small amount of inherent variability . . . hence the expression, we're *only* human.) Voice is considered **nearly periodic** or, equivalently, **quasiperiodic**. But for now, we can treat the voice as a complex periodic wave. Complex tones are perceived as richer sounding than the pure tone of a vibrating tuning fork. But, in general, both the pure and complex tones will be perceived as pleasant.

The third important feature of complex waves is the repetition of the same pattern of the waveform in each cycle of vibration. In a complex periodic wave, the successive disturbances (compressions and rarefactions of air molecules) are equally spaced and have a constant shape. This repetition of the same pattern in each cycle is a hallmark of periodicity and is a result of the integer relationship of the component sine waves comprising the complex wave. Why is it that an arithmetic relationship between the f_o

and the higher-frequency component sine waves exists? To answer that question, we need a bit more background about the behavior of sound waves, but we will return to this question and its answer in the section on Standing Waves.

Power Spectra

The waveform is only one way in which we can graphically represent pure and complex tones. We also can use a **power spectrum**, a plot of the power (energy per unit of time) of given frequencies of the sound (Figure 3–21). Power spectra (the plural of spectrum) answer the question "which frequencies contain the sound's power?" The power spectrum is a frequency domain plot, whereas the waveform is a time domain plot. We shall learn in Chapters 7

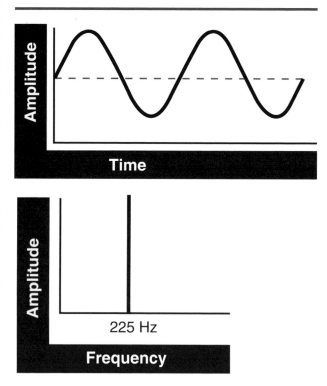

Figure 3–21. The acoustic waveform (*top*) is a plot of the change in amplitude of the pressure wave over time. The power spectrum (*bottom*) is a "snapshot" of the energy of each frequency component of the pressure wave.

and 8 that we can examine the microphone signal (time domain) in the frequency domain (called a spectrogram) and thereby obtain different and important information about speech sounds. The speech-language pathologist must be able to analyze both types of signals. In Figure 3–21, a 225-Hz sine wave and its corresponding power spectrum are presented. Frequency is represented along the horizontal x-axis, and the power, or amplitude, is represented along the vertical y-axis. Time is not specifically represented in the power spectrum. Rather, think of the power spectrum as a snapshot of the waveform. We can look at the power spectrum of different time portions of the waveform. However, at least one complete cycle of vibration must be represented in the power spectrum. The duration of the waveform included in the power spectrum is often called the "window" of time represented. Eventually, when we consider power spectra of speech waveforms, the portion of the waveform selected for power-spectrum analysis will become important but not for the waveforms we are considering at present.

So far, we have taken a series of known sine waves of different frequencies and intensities and combined them into a complex tone. We also can go in the opposite direction, however,

and take a complex sound and break it down into its component sine waves. This analytic process of decomposing a complex wave into its separate sine waves most commonly is accomplished by Fourier analysis (developed in 1807 by Baron Jean Baptiste Joseph Fourier [1768–1830], a French mathematician). **Fourier analysis** is a highly complex mathematical process that has been made accessible to all of us nonmathematical types thanks to high-speed digital processing. Fourier theorem states that all periodic waveforms can be decomposed as the sum of a series of sine waves with frequencies in a harmonic series at specific phase relationships to one another. (Decomposing a waveform refers to simplifying the waveform into its component parts.)

In Figure 3–22, we see three sine waves on the left, each of different frequency and amplitude. These sine waves combine to produce the complex periodic waveform shown in the upper right corner. We may decompose the waveform into its component sine waves, as shown in the power spectrum in the lower right corner. Note that the three vertical lines are located at 100 Hz, 200 Hz, and 400 Hz, which correspond to the frequencies of the sine waves on the left. Therefore, we can refer to this spectrum as a **line spectrum**. Note also, in the power spectrum, that the

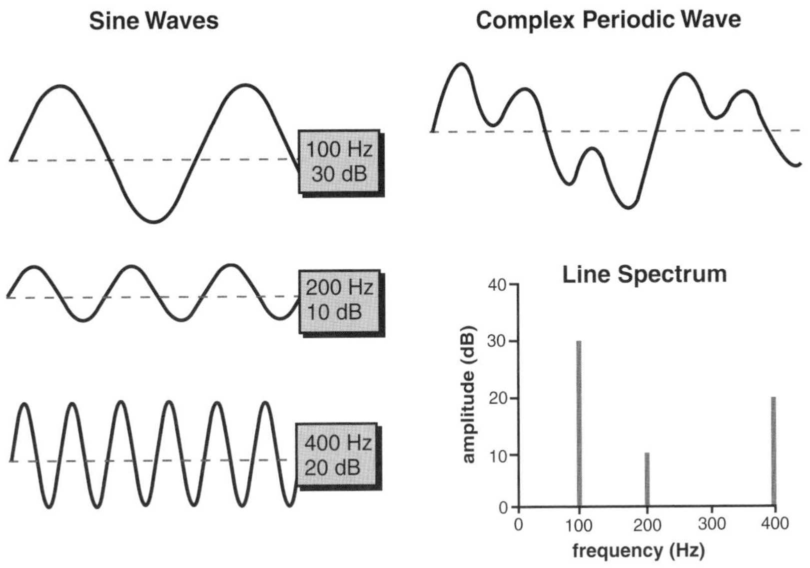

Figure 3–22. The power spectrum (*lower right*) shows that the complex periodic wave (*upper right*) is composed of three sine waves (*left*), each of different frequency and amplitude. The power spectrum is called a line spectrum because it contains energy at discrete frequencies.

100-Hz line has the greatest amplitude, extending to 30 dB; the 400-Hz line has somewhat lower amplitude, extending to 20 dB; and the 200-Hz line has the lowest amplitude, extending only to 10 dB. The amplitude of these lines corresponds to the amplitude of their respective sine waves. In other words, the power spectrum contains the complete information about the components of the complex periodic wave.

Noise

Up to this point, we have been talking about complex periodic sound waves. The great majority of sounds that occur in nature, however, are complex **aperiodic** sounds. The pressure wave of an aperiodic sound consists of sine waves that do not have an orderly arithmetic relationship to one another. Such sounds are not perceived as having a distinctive frequency, generally. Create some noise—perhaps rustle a piece of crumpled paper. Try to hum the sound of the noise by matching its pitch. Can't do it? That's because noise has no dominant frequency. Examples of complex aperiodic pressure waves are many; some are continuous sounds such as the sound produced by the ocean waves, the wind, or the rustle of leaves. Other aperiodic sounds are transient in nature, such as the clapping of hands (a repeated series of transient sounds), the beat of a snare drum, or the snap of a twig. And some aperiodic sounds are a combination of transient and continuous sounds, such as the sound of street traffic. All these sounds, technically, are referred to as noise, although certainly not all noise is perceived as unpleasant.

An example of noise (created by rustling leaves) is illustrated in Figure 3–23. Note that the cycles in the waveform are not equally spaced in time and are not of constant shape. The lack of consistent repetition of a pattern of each cycle is a hallmark of aperiodicity and is the result of the lack of multiple integer relationships among the component sine waves. Examine the power spectrum corresponding to this

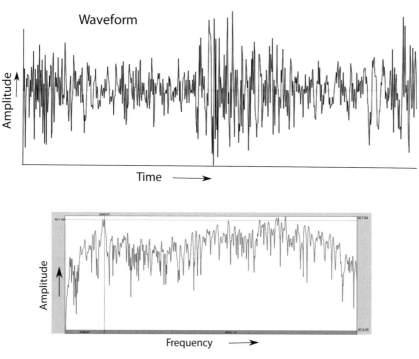

Figure 3–23. A waveform of noise (*top*) and it's corresponding continuous power spectrum (*bottom*).

noise (shown below the waveform). If we tried to draw a vertical line representing the energy at each frequency, as we did for the complex periodic waveform, we would end up with a solid black area, because the noise contains energy at almost every frequency, although not all at equal amplitude. Therefore, instead of drawing a line at every frequency, by convention, only the spectral **envelope** (upper border or outline) is shown, and instead of calling it a line spectrum, it is referred to as a **continuous spectrum**.

Although noise has no dominant frequency, it does not necessarily have equal energy at all frequencies. You can see that the spectral envelope in Figure 3–23 is not a flat line. The line moves up and down to represent greater and lesser energy at each frequency. However, on average, you can observe that no single frequency or narrow range of frequencies dominates to enable the human ear to perceive a dominant frequency. Yet, noise can be perceived as higher or lower pitched relative to other noises. In Chapter 8, we will learn that many speech sounds are not at all periodic and that the range of frequencies of the noise is an important acoustic cue to accurate perception of the sound.

Periodicity is a very important concept in speech and voice science. When we examine voice production in Chapters 5 and 6, we will learn that the human voice is almost but not quite periodic. Individuals with voice problems frequently have voices that are highly disturbed in their periodicity. And measurement of the amount of noise in their voices, as described in Chapter 6, is one measure obtained in a speech-voice evaluation.

Study Questions

15. Define complex wave.

16. What is the f_o of a complex wave composed of the following three frequencies: 100 Hz, 350 Hz, and 500 Hz?

17. What defines a complex wave as periodic? Nearly periodic?

18. Define the appearance of a periodic waveform. (*Hint*: Compare the appearance of one cycle to another.)

19. What is a power spectrum? Without referring to textbook figures, can you draw the power spectrum (with appropriately labeled axes) for a sine wave of 220 Hz? For a complex wave containing energy at 200 Hz and twice the energy at 400 Hz?

20. Line and continuous spectra represent what types of sounds, respectively?

3.7 Behavior of Sound Waves

The way sound waves interact with each other, the tissues of the vocal tract, and the surfaces and environment surrounding the speaker and listener are important features of communication. They influence how we produce and perceive sound.

Interference

Although two objects cannot occupy the same space at the same time, two (or more) sound waves can and do occupy the same place at the same time. Our world is filled with a multitude of sounds that reach our ears simultaneously. When two or more sound waves meet, the result is wave interference. Remember that as a compression passes through a medium, it pulls the particles together into a small region of space, creating a high-pressure region. A rarefaction, on the other hand, pushes particles apart, creating a lower pressure region. If an area of rarefaction of a wave meets the area of rarefaction of another wave, the net effect is to amplify the rarefaction. If an area of compression of a wave meets the area of compression of another wave, the net effect is to amplify the compression. These net effects are examples of **constructive interference**.

In Figure 3–24, two sets of sine waves are superimposed on each other, represented graphically as transverse waveforms in A and C, and as alternating compressions and rarefactions in B and D. The top waveforms in columns A and B each are completely in phase with the waveform in the row immediately below (the middle row). The phase describes where in its cycle a periodic waveform is at any given time. When each pair of waves is superimposed upon the other, that is, interfere with each other (the bottom row), the compressions occur at the same location in each wave at the same time, and similarly, the rarefactions in each wave occur at the same location at the same time. The net effect of the interference is a *reinforcement* of the compressions and rarefactions. The reinforcement results in higher pressure of the compressions and lower pressure of the rarefactions, as represented by higher

and lower peaks in the transverse waveform and greater contrast of the light and dark gray of the longitudinal wave in the bottom row. These large amplitude oscillations in sound pressure result in a sound wave that has greater intensity than either wave individually.

On the other hand, if a wave interferes with another wave such that a compression of one wave meets a rarefaction of the other wave, **destructive interference** has occurred. The top waveforms in columns C and D of Figure 3–24 are each completely out of phase with the waveforms immediately below (in the middle row). This time, when each pair of waveforms is superimposed on one another, the compressions of one wave occur at the same location as the rarefactions of the other wave (bottom row). The net effect of the interference is a *cancellation* of the compressions and rarefactions. The cancellation

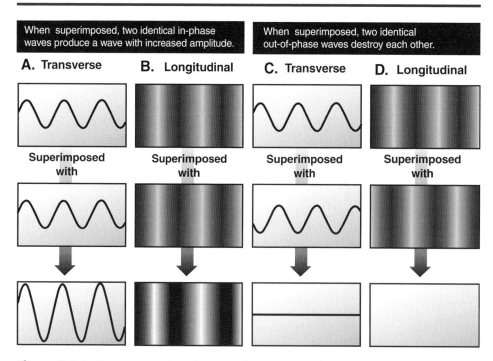

Figure 3–24. Constructive interference of two waves, shown as a waveform (**A**), and as a series of alternating compressions and rarefactions (**B**). The waves are completely in phase with each other. The resultant wave has increased amplitude. Destructive interference of two waves, shown as a waveform (**C**) and as a series of alternating compressions and rarefactions (**D**). The waves are completely out of phase with each other. The result is complete cancellation of the wave.

results in no compressions or rarefactions, that is, a lack of sound. No upward or downward deflections in the resulting transverse wave are present, and no distinct changes in gray scale are noted in the resulting longitudinal wave.

In Figure 3–25, we see an example of two waves of equivalent frequency and amplitude, but the waves are neither completely in phase nor completely out of phase. (If we were more mathematically inclined, we would specify the degree to which they are in phase using the degrees of a circle. For our purposes, we say that the waveforms are not completely in or out of phase.) Although the compressions and rarefactions of these two waves do not "line up" completely, they are close to each other. That is, when the waves are superimposed on each other, the compressions of one wave occur close to the compressions of the other wave. And the rarefactions of one wave occur close to the rarefactions of the other wave. The net effect is a mixed or complex interference. The waves do not completely reinforce one another, but

some reinforcement occurs. The result is a small increase in intensity of the sound wave. If the phase relationship of the waves is such that the compressions of one wave are closer to the rarefactions of the other wave (instead of closer to the compressions of the second wave), the net effect is a small decrease in intensity. In complex interference, the effect on the intensity of the resultant sound wave depends on the degree to which the two interfering waves are in or out of phase. The more in phase the two waves, the greater the reinforcement and increased intensity. The more out of phase the two waves, the greater the cancellation and decreased intensity.

Boundaries

As a sound wave travels through a medium, typically, it encounters some object that obstructs its forward movement. The obstruction can

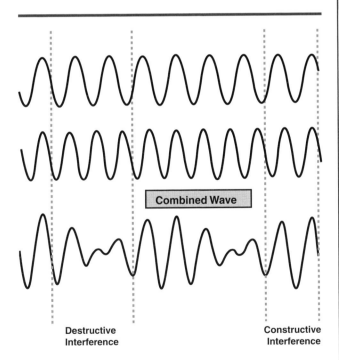

Figure 3–25. Mixed, or complex, interference results when two waveforms are not completely in phase or completely out of phase.

> **Beat Tones**
>
> When two sound waves of almost the same frequency interfere with one another, an interesting perceptual phenomenon can occur that is referred to as a beat tone. The two sound waves can start out interfering constructively with each other. But because they are just a little bit different in frequency, one wave will begin to lag behind the other, and the two waves will begin to interfere destructively with each other. But that relationship shifts again soon, because of the slight difference in frequencies. The successive increases and decreases of intensity from the alternating constructive and destructive interferences result in a pulsing sound called beats. The beat frequency is the difference of the higher frequency wave minus the lower frequency wave. Orchestral musicians are careful to avoid the audience-annoying sound of beat frequencies by carefully tuning their instruments to one another.

be thought of simply as another medium. The interface between the two mediums is called the **boundary**, and the way in which the sound wave is altered at that boundary is called the boundary behavior. Three possible boundary behaviors can occur when a sound wave encounters a change in the medium: **reflection** (bouncing backward off a boundary), **diffraction** (bending around an obstacle without going through a boundary), and **transmission** (going through a boundary). Diffraction is not so much a concern of the vocal tract as it is a concern of room acoustics, especially in concert halls and opera houses.

Reflection

When a sound wave encounters a boundary, a portion of the energy in the wave is reflected back toward the origin. The original sound wave emanating from the vibration source is called the **incident wave**. The portion of the energy that returns back is called the **reflected wave**. Another portion of the energy is transmitted across the boundary into the new medium. The amount of energy that is reflected back depends on the similarity of the two mediums. The greater the similarity, the less reflection occurs and the greater the transmission. The greater the dissimilarity, the more the energy is reflected and the less the energy is transmitted. When the sound wave is traveling through the air of the vocal tract and encounters the hard palate, for example, one would expect greater reflection than transmission of energy, because air is unlike tissue.

The vocal tract, from the vocal folds up to the lips, can be conceptualized as a cylindrical tube, closed at one end (the vocal folds) and open at the other (the lips). We will learn that the vocal folds oscillate open and closed during vibration, and the lips open and close during speech to form various phonemes. For our purposes, we can simplify our model of the vocal tract as a tube with one open and one closed end, like a test tube. Each end of the tube represents a boundary. As the sound wave comes to the end of the tube (the lips), the meeting of the enclosed air of the tube (the vocal tract) and the open expanse of the atmosphere beyond

the mouth represents a boundary. A portion of the air will be transmitted out, and another portion will be reflected back into the vocal tract and travel in the direction opposite to the initial sound wave. The reflection of sound waves at boundaries is quite relevant to speech production, as we will soon learn.

Study Questions

21. Define constructive and destructive interference.

22. Look at Figure 3–24. Can you describe the events in A, B, C, and D without reading the caption?

23. Describe the two types of behaviors that can occur when a sound wave meets a boundary within the vocal tract.

3.8 Resonance

Nearly every object can be set into vibration, and each of those objects can be considered a medium through which a pressure wave can travel. When the pressure wave reaches the boundary between the object and the atmosphere, the vibrating object causes the air particles to be set into vibration. Some objects can be set into vibration more easily than others. A tuning fork, for example, is designed specifically to be set into vibration quite easily. Air molecules vibrate very easily, although you may not perceive that pressure wave as sound unless the amplitude is sufficiently large and the frequency is sufficiently fast (to reach our hearing threshold of intensity and frequency). The wall of your living room, however, is not set into vibration very easily. If you bang your fist on the wall, it will not vibrate very much. If your next-door neighbor plays music very loudly, however, the bass in the music will likely set your wall into vibration and you will hear it. How difficult is it to cause an object to vibrate, and what would be the frequency and amplitude of the resulting vibration? The answer to these questions lies in a phenomenon called **resonance**.

Natural Resonant Frequency

To understand resonance, take a few moments to think about a child on a swing. We consider the swing and the child to be an oscillatory system. We know that the oscillation of the swing behaves in the same way as the earlier example of the mass-spring system. When the swing is hanging straight down, it is at the equilibrium point. The displacement of the swing results in a buildup of a restorative force, with an overshoot of equilibrium due to inertia. If there is no one to push the child on the swing, and the child does not "pump" her legs, then friction will overcome the displacement and restorative forces, the arc (amplitude) of the swing will slowly decrease, and eventually the swing will come to rest.

There are two ways to put energy into the swing oscillatory system (Figure 3–26). An adult can come along and push the child. Alternatively, the child can pump her legs out and lean back as she moves from the equilibrium position forward to the top of the arc. Then as the restorative force overcomes the swing and it accelerates back toward equilibrium, the child can tuck her legs in and lean forward a bit. In both cases, an outside force (the adult's push or the child's pumping movement) results in a large increase in the amplitude of the vibration. And in both cases, a harder push by the adult or greater pumping effort on the part of the child will not increase the frequency of the swing (the velocity with which it travels through its arc). Why is that? The critical factor is the timing of the outside force. If energy is supplied to the swing with appropriate timing in its movement through an arc, the amplitude of its movement will increase. Specifically, if the energy is supplied to a vibration at the same frequency (or very close to the frequency) of the vibration, it will increase the amplitude, or energy of the vibration. If the adult tries to push the swing forward as it is still moving backward in its arc, little energy will be imparted to the swing. Indeed, the swing may be jerked to a halt. What has occurred is that energy was imparted to a swing at a frequency other than the resonant frequency of the swing. It is important to note that the amplitude is independent of the frequency. Push the swing harder and it will not make the swing travel faster, but only in a larger arc. The phenomenon of matching energy input to a system and the frequency of vibration of the system is called resonance.

We can define resonance as a large increase in the amplitude of a vibration when a force is applied at a natural frequency of an object or

Figure 3–26. If energy is supplied to the swing (by pumping one's legs or by getting a push from Mom) at or very close to the natural resonant frequency of the swing, the amplitude of the resulting vibration (the arc of the swing) will be large.

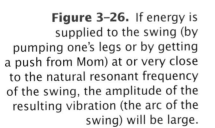

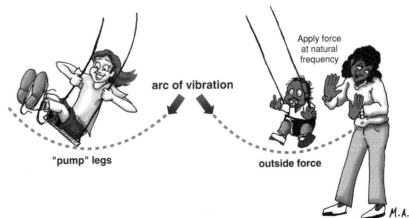

arc of vibration

"pump" legs

Apply force at natural frequency

outside force

M.A.

medium. Virtually any object can be disturbed by dropping, striking, strumming, or some other means. If the amplitude of the resulting vibrations is sufficiently large, and the resulting frequency of vibrations is within the range of human hearing, then the sound wave will be heard. When set into motion, the rate at which the object vibrates is called its natural frequency. It is the frequency, or set of frequencies, at which the object vibrates most easily and with the largest amplitude. Said another way, it is the frequency or set of frequencies that is "most preferred" by an object or medium when set into vibration.

Tuning forks, when set into motion, vibrate at a single frequency and produce a pure tone. Most objects or mediums have natural frequencies that vibrate at more than a single frequency and, hence, produce complex tones. What determines the frequency of the pure tone or set of frequencies of the complex tone? The frequency at which the object will be set into vibration depends upon the speed and the wavelength of the pressure wave. Recall in the section on Wavelength, we noted that wavelength is calculated as the speed of sound divided by the frequency of the sound wave. We can restate that relationship as follows:

Frequency = speed/wavelength

Furthermore, recall in the section on Speed of Sound, that the speed and wavelength of the pressure wave are dependent on the properties of the medium. The different strings on a guitar or notes of a piano have different tensions (tightness of the strings) and densities (mass per unit volume) and length. These properties determine the speed and wavelength of the pressure wave of the medium when it is set into vibration. The natural or resonant frequency of a vibrating object depends upon what the object is made of (influencing the speed of the sound wave) and the length of the object (influencing the wavelength of the sound wave).

What determines the rate of vibration of the mass-spring system and the child's swing? Consider first the mass-spring system. The mass attached to a spring is suspended so that it rests at its equilibrium point. The stiffness of the spring and the size of the mass determine the frequency. Stiffness refers to the amount of force required to displace (stretch or compress) the spring. The greater the stiffness, the greater the displacement force required to move the mass from equilibrium and, therefore, the greater the restorative force and quicker return toward equilibrium (Figure 3–27). We would expect that increased stiffness would result in faster movement, or higher frequency. In regard to the effect of the mass on frequency, we know that the greater the mass, the greater the inertial forces, and, therefore, the greater the mass, the slower the motion. Greater stiffness causes higher frequency and greater mass causes lower frequency.

Consider now the child's swing. Imagine a child's toy swing, one designed for a dollhouse. Would the doll's swing move faster or more slowly than the real swing with the child? The doll's swing would travel much faster than the full-sized swing, not because it is lighter but because it is smaller. Now imagine that there

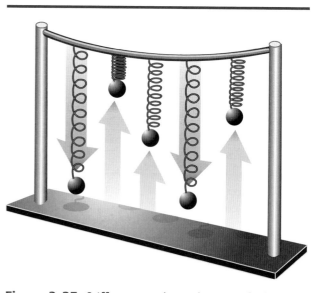

Figure 3–27. Stiffness regulates the rate of vibration. Assuming that all the springs are of the same length when not acted upon by an outside force (a push or a pull), and assuming that all the balls at the end of each spring are of similar mass, the springs of similar stiffness will bounce up and down (oscillate) together at approximately the same frequency. Springs of dissimilar stiffness will oscillate at different frequencies.

are two full-sized swings side by side, identical in every way except for the length of the ropes suspending each swing. One swing is suspended by ropes that are twice as long as those attached to the other swing. Which swing travels (vibrates) faster? The swing with the shorter length ropes. (Recall Tuning Fork on page 29 and Figure 3–4 that different lengths of tines of tuning forks specified the frequency of the sine wave they produced.) Length, then—or more generally size—in addition to stiffness and mass, determines the rate of vibration of the natural frequency of an object or material (Figure 3–28). These characteristics are highly relevant to speech and voice production, as we shall soon discuss.

Standing Wave Patterns

Recall that we identified an incident wave as one that originates from the vibration sound source and the reflected wave as the sound pressure wave that is reflected back by an obstruction. Generally, the interference pattern that results is complex, with only small amplitude increases occurring at intermittent locations. However, certain frequencies of vibration, when reflected

back, will produce an interference pattern that appears to stand still, and for that reason, the pattern is called a **standing wave** (Figure 3–29).

Figure 3–29. The superposition of two or more waves within a confined space may result in a standing wave, so called because the interference pattern appears to be standing still. Standing waves are created in the vocal tract and are important features of vocal tract resonance.

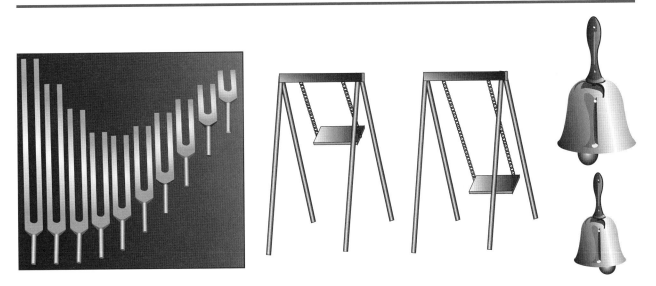

Figure 3–28. Length, or size, regulates the rate of vibration. A tuning fork with short tines, when struck, will produce a higher frequency sound wave than a tuning fork with long tines. A swing with short rope will oscillate back and forth faster than a swing with long rope. A small bell will ring at a higher frequency than a larger bell.

Standing waves depend on two or more waves being superimposed on one another. This superposition occurs when waves meet a boundary. Therefore, we generally speak about standing wave patterns in confined spaces. The vocal tract is a confined space, and, therefore, the concept of standing waves is important to the understanding of speech production.

Standing waves are resonant patterns, just as constructive and destructive interference that we discussed earlier are also types of resonant patterns. The interference patterns we discussed previously originated from waves of different sources; therefore, the two waves could easily have different frequencies. In the vocal tract, the standing wave is a result of interference of the incident wave (produced by the vocal folds) and its own reflected wave. Therefore, the incident and the reflected wave both have the same frequency. The reflected wave moves back through the incident wave in such a way as to produce stable regions of constructive and destructive interference.

One way to understand the mechanics of a standing wave is with a jump rope. Let's say that you are holding a long jump rope with the other end tied to a post (Figure 3–30). You move the jump rope up and down, which causes a wave pulse to travel the length of the rope. (This maneuver is different from swinging the rope in a circle to allow someone to jump in time to the swing. In this experiment, we are just shaking the rope vertically.) Part of the energy will be absorbed by the post, but a portion will be reflected back along the rope. The waves resulting from your movement will interfere with the waves reflected back from the post. If you are careful about how you time your hand movements, you will create a distinctive pattern of movement of the jump rope called a standing wave. It is called a standing wave because the pattern of waves does not appear to move but rather seems to stand in place.

Rules Governing Standing Waves

Some rules govern the behavior of standing waves. The longest standing wave achievable is

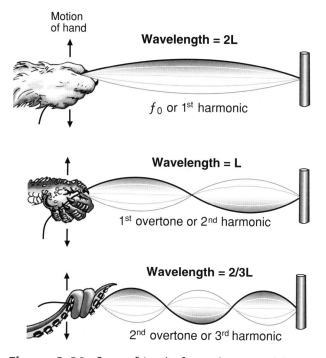

Figure 3–30. Some friends from the animal kingdom help demonstrate the creation of standing waves using a rope fixed at one end to a pole. We consider the other end to be fixed as well, because a hand (or paw or tentacle) holds the rope. Adapted from J. Trefil and R. M. Hazen, *Physics Matters: An Introduction to Conceptual Physics*, 2004, Copyright Wiley & Sons, Inc. Adapted with permission.

twice the length of the rope. If we represent a given wavelength as L, then the longest wave has a wavelength of 2L, where half the cycle is achieved between your hand moving up and down and the fixed point of the post. The reason becomes clear if you think of the pattern with the longest cycle you can achieve while shaking a rope up and down. Note that one-half wavelength is equal to the length of the rope. The longest wavelength has the lowest frequency, that is, it is the fundamental frequency. Different patterns can be created, however. If you move your hand up and down exactly twice as fast, you can achieve a standing wave of wavelength L. This new resonant frequency has twice the frequency of the fundamental and is called a **harmonic** of the fundamental. It is usually called the second harmonic (the first harmonic being equal to the fundamental frequency) or, in music, the first **overtone**. If you shake the rope faster still, you will achieve the third longest wave, of wavelength two-thirds L. This wave is the third harmonic (or second overtone) and has three times the frequency of the fundamental. We can continue shaking the rope faster and creating successively higher harmonics. Not only is each harmonic a multiple of the fundamental frequency, but, in fact, each harmonic is an integer multiple of the fundamental. Remember previously in the discussion of complex tones, we said that a complex sound wave consists of a set of frequencies, all of which have a whole number (integer) mathematical relationship between them. We see now that this relationship is a function of the wavelength of the vibration. As we noted in our discussion of complex wave spectra, successively higher harmonics tend to have less energy as the frequency increases, largely because the amplitude of displacement is not as great.

You may have observed in Figure 3–30 that along the wave, there appear one or more points of low amplitude and one or more points of high amplitude. In the standing wave of the longest length, the lowest points of amplitude are at either end, and the highest point of amplitude is in the center. These are the **nodes** and **antinodes**, respectively (Figure 3–31). The particles located at the nodes have the smallest amplitude. They are barely moving at all. The particles located at the antinodes have the largest amplitude of movement. In the pattern of L, there are three nodes (at either end and in the center) and two antinodes. In the pattern of two-thirds L, there are four nodes and three antinodes. Why are we worrying about nodes and antinodes? Because they contribute to meaningful differences among vowel sounds, which we will discuss in Chapter 7.

Now let us reexamine the definition of a standing wave in light of the rules we have just discussed. When a medium vibrates at its resonant

Notation for Harmonic Frequencies

Titze et al. (2015) have recommended the following notation for designating harmonic frequencies: $2f_o$ for the second harmonic, $3f_o$ for the third harmonic, and so on. The fundamental frequency, or f_o, is presumed to be the first harmonic $(1)f_o$, although the "1" is presumed and would never be indicated, so it is written in parentheses here. By referring to the second harmonic as "two ef-oh," it reminds us that the second harmonic is twice the fundamental, and $3f_o$ ("three ef-oh") is three times the fundamental, and so on. Furthermore, use of this notation avoids confusion with formant frequencies (a quantity to be described in Chapter 7).

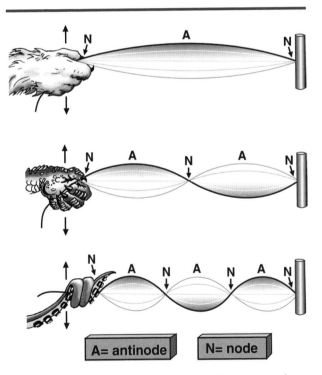

Figure 3–31. Locations along a standing wave where no amplitude of vibration appears to occur are called nodes. Nodes are regions of minimal energy. Locations where the largest amplitude of the wave appears to be "frozen" motionless are called antinodes. Antinodes are regions of maximal energy.

frequency, it vibrates in such a way that a standing wave is formed. Each of the natural frequencies at which an object vibrates is associated with a standing wave pattern. At a frequency other than a harmonic, the interference of the reflected and incident wave results in a disturbance that is irregular and nonrepeating. Therefore, the natural frequencies of an object or medium are simply the harmonic frequencies at which standing wave patterns are established.

A note of caution should be interjected at this point to avoid confusion. The figures use a rope to represent standing wave patterns. We know that the upward and downward movement of the wave pattern generated by the rope is a transverse pressure wave, and sound is a longitudinal pressure wave. However, to diagram standing waves using a pressure wave tends to get a little confusing visually and so we cheat a bit and use a rope!

A medium can vibrate at almost a limitless number of frequencies, not only at its natural resonant frequency. It can be very difficult to force a medium into vibration at some frequencies, whereas it is easiest to force a medium into vibration at its natural resonant frequencies. Said another way, it can take a large amount of energy to force a vibration at certain frequencies, whereas it takes less energy to force the medium into vibration at its resonant frequencies. In fact, the standing waves represent the vibration patterns with the lowest energy because the compressions and rarefactions cancel each other out. In other words, the standing wave patterns represent the lowest vibration or resonant modes of the medium. **Modes** are patterns of **vibration**, each associated with its own frequency. We say that an object or medium favors only a few specific modes or patterns of vibration, those that result in the highest amplitude of vibration with the least input of energy. Therefore, objects are forced most easily into resonant vibrations when disturbed at frequencies natural to them.

Standing waves and the production of integer harmonic multiples of the fundamental resonant frequency occur in the vocal tract much the same way that they occurred in our description of the vibrating rope. An important differ-

ence is that the confined space of the vocal tract behaves as a tube that is closed at one end (the larynx) and open at the other (the mouth). At the open end (the mouth) is a maximum vibration, an antinode, unlike the jump rope, which had a minimum vibration (node) at both ends. The closed end of the vocal tract (the larynx, which we will discuss in Chapter 5) represents a node. This arrangement contributes to the production of vowels as we will study in Chapter 7.

Study Questions

24. Explain the concept of natural resonant frequency. Use a child's swing as an example. Can you think of another example in everyday life of something that is set into vibration?

25. How is the natural resonant frequency of an object affected by its stiffness, mass, and length?

26. What is a standing wave?

27. Cover up all the labels in Figure 3–30. Can you explain the rules governing standing waves by describing the three harmonics?

28. What are nodes and antinodes? Cover up the labels in Figure 3–31 and label the nodes and antinodes.

Forced Vibration

Vibration may be free or forced. **Free vibration** occurs when an object or medium is allowed to vibrate freely after an initial disturbance. The tuning forks that we have been tapping during this chapter are good examples of free vibration. Once disturbed, they vibrate freely at a frequency specified by their size and stiffness. For **forced vibration** to occur, the medium or object must be driven by an outside source that is itself an oscillator (Titze, 1994, p. 83). (Actually, self-sustaining oscillation is a third type of vibration and highly relevant to voice production. We will discuss that concept further in Chapter 5.) The input of energy from plucking a string or hitting a tuning fork disturbs the particles and forces the object into vibration at its natural resonant frequency. Remember we said that when a pressure wave encounters a change in medium—a boundary—some of the energy is transmitted to the new medium. The tendency of one medium to set an adjoining or interconnected medium into vibration is called forced vibration. The object or medium that is set into vibration is called a resonator. A cell phone that is set to announce a call by vibration is an example of forced vibration.

Suppose you have two tuning forks very close to each other (but not touching), both free to vibrate (Figure 3–32). Let's say that the resonant frequency of both tuning forks is 440 Hz. Strike a tine of one of the tuning forks with a mallet. This will cause the tuning fork to vibrate at 440 Hz. The air surrounding the tuning fork similarly will be set into vibration by the pressure wave transmitted from the tuning fork, also at 440 Hz. Anyone standing close by will hear this sound. If you reach out and hold the first tuning fork, dampening (stopping) its vibrations, it will cease producing sound. But the 440-Hz tone will still be heard. The pressure wave transmitted through the air from the first tuning fork *forced* the second tuning fork into vibration. The two tuning forks are connected by air particles. The sound waves traveling from the first tuning fork share the same natural frequency as the second tuning fork, thus causing the second tuning fork to be set into vibration very easily. We can say that the energy carried by the sound wave through the air from the first tuning fork *is tuned* to the frequency of the second tuning fork. This scenario is an example of resonance. Resonance occurs when one object vibrating at the same resonant or natural frequency of a second object forces the second object into vibration. The result of resonance is always a large vibration. In our earlier example of the adult pushing the child on a swing (see Figure 3–26), the adult doing the pushing is "tuning" his or her pushes to the resonant frequency of the swing to gain maximal amplitude of swing vibration.

But now suppose that a third tuning fork was also set near the first two instruments (see

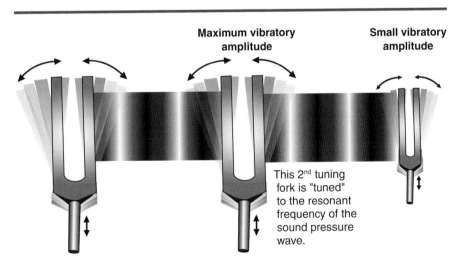

Maximum vibratory amplitude

Small vibratory amplitude

This 2nd tuning fork is "tuned" to the resonant frequency of the sound pressure wave.

Figure 3–32. The tuning forks on the left and in the middle are both of similar size, and therefore they both have similar resonant frequencies. The smaller tuning fork on the right, however, has a different resonant frequency. The vibrations from the tuning fork on the left will set the middle instrument into full vibration, but the tuning fork on the right will respond with much smaller amplitude vibration.

Figure 3–32). Only this third tuning fork is much smaller than the other two. We have learned that size affects the rate of vibration of an object. When we hit the tines of the first tuning fork, would it force this third, smaller tuning fork into vibration, as it did the second, similarly sized tuning fork into vibration? Not exactly. We would expect that the smaller tuning fork would have a different natural resonant frequency because it is smaller than the other two instruments. It may well be forced into vibration, but the amplitude of vibration will be smaller: that is, it will have less energy. When a vibrating object forces another, interconnected object into vibration, the

Breaking Glass With Sound

We are all familiar with the cartoon of the opera singer producing a very high note that breaks glass. In the cartoon, we "know" that the glass is broken because of the terrible screech of the singer (Figure 3–33). Can this really happen, and does it mean that the singer is very bad? We can answer that question now, at least in part, with our knowledge of resonance and

Figure 3–33. Can an opera singer really break a glass with her voice? Possibly, if several conditions are met.

sound waves. Glass, like any other material, has a natural resonance, one or more frequencies at which it will vibrate easily with large amplitude. Under certain conditions, it might be possible to break glass with a sound wave produced by a singer. One condition that could make this scenario possible is if the glass has a very strong resonance. That means it vibrates very easily. We know that some glasses (and especially crystals) can be tapped to produce a clear "ring," which is the sound produced by the vibration of the glass in its natural resonance. Other glasses do not ring as easily. It depends upon the structure of the glass. Another condition is that the glass must be fixed to the table. Otherwise, the energy of the vibrations would be used to move the glass along the table rather than to stretch the bonds of the molecules in the glass itself toward breaking. The glass would also have to contain tiny areas of weaknesses—smaller than could be detected without a magnifying lens—to make it more susceptible to breaking. And finally, the note produced by the opera singer would have to be at a frequency very close to the natural resonant frequency of the glass in order to produce the maximal vibration, and at a very great intensity, to make the vibration strong enough to break the molecular bonds. So, could it be done? Probably, if all these conditions were met. Would it mean, as the cartoon implies, that the singer is so bad that she breaks glass? On the contrary—the singer would have to be quite good to produce a sufficiently loud and clear tone!

second object will vibrate even if it is not tuned to the first object. It will be set into vibration even if its natural resonant frequency is different from that of the first object. However, the resulting amplitude of vibration will be much less than in the case of an object that is tuned to the vibration of the first object. Let us add one more concept, that of acoustic resonators, and we have the foundation for exploring speech production.

Acoustic Resonators

We know that violins and guitars and pianos are all instruments that are set into vibration by hitting or stroking or plucking their respective strings. But we also know that the shape and size of the instruments affect their sound. Why is that? And we know that wind instruments have no strings, yet their size and shape affect the sound produced by blowing into them through their respective mouthpieces. Why is that? The answers lie in the air contained within each of these instruments. The air inside each musical instrument is set into vibration by the vibrating strings (in the case of the string instruments) or by the musician blowing into (or across, as with flutes) the mouthpiece (in the case of the wind instruments). Recall that a resonator is an object or medium that is set into vibration. When the air inside a partially or completely enclosed container is set into vibration, we say that the container is an **acoustic resonator** (Figure 3–34). (The tuning fork and many of the other objects that we have set into vibration throughout this chapter are examples of **mechanical resonators**.) Just as the length of the pendulum or the swing dictates the resonant frequency of those objects, so too the size of the resonating cavity (the partially enclosed space of the instrument) determines the resonant frequency of the vibration.

When the cover ("skin") of a drum is struck with a stick, the cover is set into vibration at a resonant frequency determined by its size (specifying the wavelength) and tension (specifying the speed). The energy of the vibrating drum cover is transmitted to the air space inside the drum, forcing the air column into vibration at

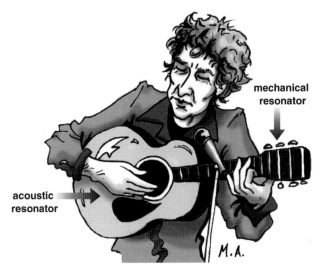

Figure 3–34. An acoustic guitar is an acoustic resonator.

a resonant frequency specified by the size of the air space. Consider an electric guitar that is unplugged. Remember that the electric guitar has no acoustic resonating space. Pluck one of its strings and the resulting pressure wave will not be heard well. The sound board of the electric guitar will be forced into vibration. But the combined energy of the vibrating string and soundboard do not transmit the energy into the surrounding air very well. The instrument is designed to be played with electric amplification of the strings' vibrations. If that guitar string is attached to an acoustic resonator (an acoustic guitar body), however, the vibrating string forces the air into vibration and the resulting sound is considerably louder. The entire system (string, wood of the guitar body, air inside the guitar) vibrates with considerable energy and forces the air surrounding the guitar into vibration. The amplitude of the pressure wave, the energy carried by the alternating compressions and rarefactions, creates a sound with greater intensity than that of the unplugged electric guitar. Forced vibration allows a sound to be amplified by taking advantage of the resonant frequencies of an adjoining or interconnected medium.

Acoustic resonators play a featured role in voice and speech production, for the column of air in the vocal tract is an acoustic resonator.

Recalling our discussion about different-sized tuning forks (see Figure 3–32), the proximity of the frequency at which a column of air is set into vibration to the natural resonant frequency of the acoustic resonator is a key concept in the description of speech sound production. And that fact brings us to a discussion of the physiology and biomechanics of the source of the column of air—the lungs.

Study Questions

29. Explain the difference between free and forced vibration.

30. Under what conditions would you expect the vibration of one object to result in a strong (large amplitude) vibration of a second object? Under what conditions would you expect a weak (small amplitude) vibration to result?

31. What is the difference between a mechanical and an acoustic resonator? Which type of resonator is the vocal tract?

Recommended Internet Sites for Further Learning

http://www.acs.psu.edu/drussell/Demos.html
The Penn State Acoustics and Vibrations Animations by Dan Russell, PhD

This website contains numerous animations and explanations of a variety of acoustic phenomena covered in the chapter. It will help you visualize and understand just about every concept covered in this chapter. I recommend it highly.

http://www.acs.psu.edu/users/sparrow/animations.html
Animations for Acoustics Education by Vic Sparrow, Pennsylvania State University

This website contains animations for some of the concepts discussed in the chapter. Much of the content is above the level of this book, but some animations are quite helpful.

http://www.animations.physics.unsw.edu.au/waves-sound/
Animations from University of New South Wales, School of Physics in Sydney, Australia, provide wonderful visuals for oscillations, traveling waves, sound waves, standing waves, and more.

http://www.phon.ucl.ac.uk/resource/software.php
Mark Huckvale, from the University College London, provides software programs, including Esynth for synthesizing complex waves, and Esystem, a web-based program used to create signals and filters.

References

Titze, I. R. (1994). *Principles of voice production.* Englewood Cliffs, NJ: Prentice Hall.

Titze, I. R., Baken, R. J., Bozeman, K. W., Granqvist, S., Henrich, N., Herbst, C., . . . Wolfe, J. (2015). Toward a consensus on symbolic notation of harmonics, resonances, and formants in vocalization. *Journal of the Acoustical Society of America, 137,* 3005–3007.

Breathing

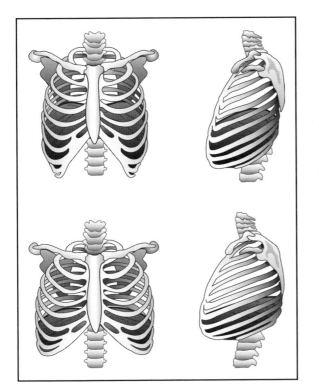

Figure 4–1. The diaphragm is, perhaps, the most important muscle of breathing. The diaphragm and rib cage are positioned at the end of tidal exhalation (*top panel*) and at the end of deep inhalation (*bottom panel*).

An air-stream or moving current of air, provided by the action of some of the organs of speech, makes audible the movements of other organs. An air-stream, as far as we know, is the basis of the whole of the sound, in all its variety, of human speech. An air-stream is produced by an air-stream mechanism.

—Abercrombie and Dixon (1965, p. 24)

Clinical Case 1: Breath-Holding Speech

Clinical cases are based upon real patients whom the author has treated. Evaluation and treatment information has been edited to focus upon specific features related to the chapters. Note that clinical cases incorporate information that is covered in this and other chapters (and some information about diagnosis and therapy that you will learn in future courses). You are encouraged to review this case before you begin your study of this chapter and once again after you have completed the chapter. You may also want to revisit this case later in the semester.

Seleena was a 36-year-old bilingual (Spanish-English) woman attending school to become a social worker. She worked part-time as a medical receptionist. She came for a voice and speech evaluation with the main concerns of often not being understood and of having to work too hard to talk. She said that at her work, which was in a noisy, hospital-based medical office, and in her clinical internship at school, people often asked her to repeat herself. She was concerned that, when she spoke in English, her Spanish accent was "too strong." She also stated that she found it physically tiring to talk with people for an extended time and that her throat and shoulders ached at the end of the day. She said that her friends told her that it was more work to talk in her second language—English. She said that it was often difficult for people to hear her in class. She attributed her soft voice to her self-consciousness about her Spanish accent. (However, upon further questioning, she did admit that she also spoke softly in Spanish.) She described herself as very shy and said that although she enjoyed being around people and looked forward to helping people as a social worker, she did not like being "the center of attention." Her medical history was unremarkable (that is, she was healthy).

A speech-language evaluation revealed good English language skills with a mild Spanish accent. Vocal quality was within normal limits but speech was moderately soft. Mean speaking intensity (assessed during a reading task) was below normal limits, but mean speaking fundamental frequency was normal. Mean airflow and maximum sustained phonation during sustained "ah" were also both below normal limits. During reading and conversation, she was observed to hold her upper body rigidly, with her shoulders mildly elevated. Overall, her posture was "closed"—that is, during speaking she kept her arms close to her body, using small gestures and opening her mouth minimally while speaking.

The initial clinical hypothesis was that Seleena was breath-holding during speech. That is, it appeared that she was using excessive inspiratory checking to minimize airflow. Thus, intensity was significantly decreased. Decreased range of motion of the oral articulators appeared to be exacerbating the decreased intensity and reducing clarity of phoneme production. Stimulability testing was conducted to test that hypothesis. Use of exaggerated speech breathing (deeper and lower inhalations, increased breathiness of speech to use greater expiratory airflow), more upright and open posture, and exaggerated oral articulation resulted in significantly increased intensity and speech clarity. And Seleena reported that it was easier to speak, although she did comment that it sounded as though she were now shouting.

Seleena's Spanish-accented English was not a factor in her communication problem. The breath-holding was making Seleena feel out of breath (despite having too much air maintained in her lungs) and the extra muscular work was fatiguing. A maladaptive compensatory behavior (that is, doing something to try to solve the problem when, in fact, that "something" was making the problem worse) was increased muscular effort. Seleena was not using *insufficient* breath support. Instead, she was using an *inefficient* speech breathing pattern.

Therapy goals included improved coordination of breathing with speech production, improved posture, greater relaxation of the upper thoracic and neck muscles, and increased freedom of movement of the oral articulators. Additional therapy goals included educating Seleena about speech breathing and speech production so that she understood the nature of the problem and the rationale for the therapy goals. Counseling goals included self-discovery of how her speech reflected her self-perceptions and recalibration of her perception of her speech intensity (that is, helping her to judge her new conversational intensity as being appropriate and not being too loud). As Seleena became successful in using these new speech skills in her everyday communication, she found that people understood her easily. She realized that her Spanish accent was not a deterrent to listener comprehension, and thus, she became more comfortable with the sound of her speech.

Clinical Case Discussion Questions

1. What is inspiratory checking? What muscles was Seleena engaging to achieve inspiratory checking? Why would it become fatiguing to use checking action excessively?

2. Why would decreased airflow result in decreased intensity? What is the relationship between intensity and loudness? (Review Chapter 3)

3. Examine Figures 4–14 and 4–15. Where would Seleena's speech fall on the relaxation curve?

4. Examine Figure 4–16. Can you draw the change in lung volume that would represent Seleena's characteristic lung volumes during speech? (*Hint*: Does Selena exhale down to resting lung volume at the end of a phrase group?)

4.1 Introduction

Speech breathing is the regulation of breathing for voice and speech production. A substantial portion of many voice and speech therapies is directed toward management of speech breathing, and with good reason, for speech is the product of the regulation of airflow and air pressure. Some speakers, despite a normal respiratory system, do not coordinate speech breathing with muscular activity of the larynx and upper vocal tract. This impaired coordination may occur because of habit or significant speech demands. Other speakers do have structural abnormality or disease of the respiratory system and need to learn speech breathing strategies that compensate for limitations in their ability to regulate air pressure and airflow. Speech pathologists who are knowledgeable about the physiology and biomechanics of speech breathing are better prepared to develop effective therapy for these groups of patients.

There are several terms associated with breathing with which the speech pathologist should become familiar. We use the term breathing as a global descriptor for the processes of **inhalation**, or **inspiration**, the movement of air into our upper and lower airways, and **exhalation**, or **expiration**, the movement of air out of the lower and upper airways. (By convention, the lower airway is below the larynx, the upper airway is from the larynx up through the mouth, nose, and sinuses.) Breathing is the most relevant term for speech pathologists because we are concerned primarily with the ways in which we generate and propagate the air pressure disturbances that comprise speech sounds. However, the regulation of the movement of air molecules is governed not only by linguistic needs but also by physiologic needs, specifically respiratory demands. We make a distinction between respiration and breathing. Respiration is the process of gas exchange. In the narrowest biological meaning, it refers to gas exchange at the level of the cell. It is the biological basis for breathing. Ventilation, a term used by physiologists, is the processes of moving air into and out of the lower airway to enable gas exchange.

Overview of Neuroanatomic Terms and Organization

The central nervous system refers to the nerve cells, also called neurons. Nerves are bundles of nerve fibers, which by themselves are processes of neurons covered with membranes. Nerves are the basic structural and functional elements of the nervous system. This system includes all neural structures of the body, structures that enable the organism to perceive environmental and internal stimuli, to integrate them, and to respond to them. The central nervous system consists of the brain and spinal nerves and ganglia associated with them. The vast bulk of the peripheral nervous system consists of membrane-covered processes of neurons, although the bodies (perikarya) of these neurons are in the brain or the spinal cord. The peripheral nerves that extend from the brainstem to the organs outside the central nervous system are called the cranial nerves. The peripheral nerves that originate in the spinal cord and travel to other organs are called the spinal nerves. Nerves may be associated with motor function, sensory function, or both. The motor, or efferent, system carries information from the central nervous system to the periphery, and the sensory, or afferent, system carries information from the periphery back to the central nervous system. (Although the distinction between afferent and efferent neurons is generally clear within the peripheral nervous system, it is much less clear and more complicated within the central nervous system.) All neurons have cell bodies. Clusters of cell bodies within the central nervous system are referred to as nuclei, and cell body clusters in the peripheral nervous system are called ganglia. (The singular of "ganglia" is "ganglion.") (Exceptions to this naming system exist, perhaps to confuse students! For example, one cluster of cell bodies within the brain is called the basal ganglia.) Bundles of nerve fibers in the central nervous system that form an anatomic or functional unit are called pathways or tracts. These tracts or pathways transmit neural impulses to other neurons. In the peripheral nervous system, the nerves transmit impulses to muscle or sensory organs. Peripheral nerves also may be categorized as somatic or visceral. Somatic generally includes the motor and sensory nerves that supply the skeletal muscles for volitional movement, as well as skin sensation, vision, and hearing. The visceral system includes the sensory and motor neurons that serve automatic functions, such as the digestive and cardiovascular system, as well as taste and smell. Unfortunately, the somatic-visceral system is based upon embryologic development, and therefore it does not make sense completely when applied to the adult. And of some importance to the speech-language pathologist, the muscles of the face and larynx and some of the pharyngeal muscles are classified as visceral.

Another commonly discussed functional subdivision is the autonomic nervous system, which consists of the motor neurons that innervate smooth muscle, cardiac muscle, and glands, all of which are involved in non-volitional, reflexive functions. The autonomic nervous system is further subdivided into the sympathetic and parasympathetic systems. The sympathetic system is usually described as functioning to prepare the body for emergency activity, such as escaping injury quickly ("fight or flight" response). The parasympathetic system functions to conserve visceral function ("rest and digest" response).

Neurons transmit sensory or motor information by way of electrical activity conducted along the length of the nerve. The information is transmitted from one neuron to the next and between neurons and muscle fibers by way of synapses. Synapses consist of chemicals called neurotransmitters, which enable the electrical activity to pass from one cell to the next. The information transmitted across a synapse is either excitatory or inhibitory. An excitatory impulse facilitates firing of the connecting neuron or muscle fiber. Inhibitory impulses act to hold back or suppress activity of the connecting neuron or muscle fiber. The axon is the extension of the neuron cell body that forms a synapse with another neuron or muscle fiber. Each axon branches repeatedly, forming up to 10,000 synapses, allowing each cell body to receive information from up to 1,000 other neurons (Duffy, 2005). The important point to understand is the following. The ultimate response of a neuron or muscle fiber is the result of the summation of information received from hundreds of other neurons.

Conceptual organization of the motor system by its various functions can help us to understand the purpose of the different anatomic parts. Four major functional subdivisions of the motor system, based upon Benarroch, Westmoreland, Daube, Reagan, and Sandok (1999) and further discussed in Duffy (2005, p. 35), are the direct activation pathway, the indirect activation pathway, the control circuits, and the final common pathway. The final common pathway or, equivalently, the lower motor neurons, consists of the cranial and spinal nerves, through which all muscle activity is mediated. (See Motor Units and Muscle Activity on p. 73 for more information on how this mediation occurs.) The direct activation pathway is also called the direct motor system or the pyramidal tract. It is divided into the corticobulbar and corticospinal tracts, which provide motor information to the cranial and spinal nerves, respectively. The direct activation pathway directly links the cerebral cortex to the final common pathway, sending primarily excitatory information. In other words, the corticospinal and corticobulbar tracts generate muscle contraction, rather than inhibition of movement, for the fine motor control of the voice and speech production system. The indirect activation pathway is also called the indirect motor system or extrapyramidal tract. It consists of multiple connections that are generally much shorter than those of the direct activation pathway. A major function of the indirect activation pathway is to connect the cerebral cortex and the reticular formation, a diffuse area of neurons in the medulla, pons, and midbrain that form the central core of the brainstem. The reticular formation is involved in motor, sensory, visceral, and conscious functions, particularly arousal, attention, and awareness regulation (Jürgens, 2002). Through the indirect activation pathway, it contributes both excitatory and inhibitory impulses to the final common pathway, thus contributing substantially to the regulation of muscle tone. Through unconscious regulation of muscle tone and posture, the indirect activation pathway provides a framework upon which purposeful and complex fine motor activity of speech production can take place (Duffy, 2005).

The control circuits do not have direct connection with the final common pathway but rather coordinate and integrate the excitatory and inhibitory impulses from the direct and indirect activation pathways. The two major control circuits are the basal ganglia and the cerebellum. It should be noted that many neuroanatomy texts consider the basal ganglia as part of the extrapyramidal tract. Here we follow the organizational schema explained in Duffy (2005). The basal ganglia are a collection of cell nuclei deep within the brain that contribute to regulation of muscle tone and stabilization of posture during fine and gross motor movements and particularly may regulate motor planning and motor learning, including initiation, amplitude, and velocity of purposeful movements. (The name is somewhat confusing, because as we noted earlier, the term ganglia generally refers to cell bodies outside the central nervous system.) The output of the basal ganglia is inhibitory. The cerebellum lies under the cerebrum and participates in coordination of movement, comparing motor planning information from the cortex with the peripheral sensory feedback information about what happened. In this way, the cerebellum contributes to motor learning and control. The output of the cerebellum is excitatory. The motor cortex sends impulses to both the basal ganglia and the cerebellum, which, in turn send information back to the cortex via the thalamus. The balance of excitatory and inhibitory inputs to the cortex is essential for smooth and coordinated movements of speech production.

4.2 Respiration

In brief, our breathing is driven by the need to remove carbon dioxide (CO_2) and obtain oxygen (O_2). The air we inhale is rich in oxygen. (Air contains approximately 21% oxygen and the remainder is largely nitrogen.) Our circulating blood carries the oxygen, necessary to sustain life, to our tissues. Upon its return to the lungs, the blood's oxygen supply is depleted, but it is rich in carbon dioxide, an acidic gas and the major waste product of cellular metabolism. (The word oxygen is derived from the Greek *oxy-*, meaning "sharp" or "acid," and *-gen*, meaning to "produce.") The oxygen and carbon dioxide are exchanged across the extraordinarily thin membranes separating the lungs and tiny blood vessels, the capillaries, by a process called diffusion. Diffusion is the process of movement of molecules of a fluid from regions of high concentration to regions of low concentration. Once the oxygen diffuses across the membrane into the blood, the now oxygen-rich blood circulates to the rest of the body, and the carbon dioxide is exhaled from the lungs. The constant circulation of air into and out of the lungs is essential to this life-sustaining process. It is fortunate that the structures of the breathing mechanism are exquisitely designed to capitalize on the laws of physics for optimizing breathing for respiratory function and for speech breathing.

4.3 Balloons or Boyle's Law?

How do we breathe? More specifically, how do we pull air into our lungs and expel it outward?

Often, people have a vague idea that we expand our lungs to breathe in and contract our lungs to breathe out, but the biomechanics and physiology of breathing remain a mystery. A common misconception is that the mechanics of breathing are like blowing up a balloon. A balloon is a highly elastic material. Apply a force to the balloon and it elongates easily. The force applied is an increase in air pressure inside the balloon, which is achieved by blowing air into it. The increased air pressure stretches the elastic material, and the volume of the balloon increases. Breathing is not at all like blowing up a balloon (Figure 4–2). Instead of forcing the expansion of the container (the lungs) to accommodate an increase in the volume of air, the biomechanics of breathing are such that the size of the container is increased, causing a pressure drop, resulting

Figure 4–2. The mechanics of breathing are *not* similar to inflating a balloon!

in an inward rush of air. Further understanding of the biomechanics of breathing requires exploration of the relationship of volume and pressure and airflow, and the structures involved in breathing and their movements in relation to one another.

The relationship of volume and pressure is best explained by **Boyle's law**, named after Robert Boyle (1627–1691), a British scientist, born in Ireland, who is sometimes referred to as the "father of modern chemistry" because of his publications on the scientific method in regard to chemical experimentation. Boyle's law tells us that if the volume of a gas is increased, given a constant temperature, the pressure will decrease. And conversely, if the volume of a gas is decreased, the pressure will increase. (History tells us that, in a bit of controversy, this relationship was discovered by Boyle's student, Robert Hooke, and that this relationship of volume and pressure should be credited to him. We leave the argument of credit to the scientific historians.) Boyle's law specifies an inverse relationship between the volume and the pressure of a gas, under circumstances of a constant temperature (Figure 4–3). This inverse relationship makes sense given what we know about the movement of gases. The molecules of a gas are always in motion, moving randomly and bumping into one another and the walls of their container, thereby exerting a force on one another and on the walls of the container. The smaller the volume in which the gas is contained, the more often the molecules will bump into one another, or exert a force on one another, during their random movements. At a constant temperature, the pressure of a gas can be increased by introducing more molecules into a given container or decreasing the volume of the container. In either condition, the effect is the same: The density of molecules increases, causing an increase in the number of molecule collisions, thereby resulting in an increase in pressure.

The breathing mechanism is designed specifically to take advantage of Boyle's law. Fluid flows as a result of differences in pressure. This pressure differential is a requisite condition for fluid flow, be it liquid or gas. The pressure difference may be caused by gravity, for example, exerting a pull on water in an overturned glass. Alternatively, the pressure difference may be the result of a change in the volume of the container in which a gas is enclosed, such as occurs in breathing. We do not force air into our lungs when we inhale, and the incoming air does not force the lungs to make room by expanding, such as occurs when blowing up a balloon. On the contrary, we expand the volume of the lungs in three directions: anteroposteriorly (front to back), inferiorly-superiorly (lower to higher), and laterally (sideways). This expansion causes a drop in the air pressure within our lungs. When this drop in pressure occurs, the pressure in the lungs is said to be negative relative to the pressure outside the lungs, the atmospheric pressure. Negative pressure simply means that the pressure is lower than atmospheric pressure. This pressure differential between the atmosphere and the lungs causes the air to flow into our lungs. When a difference in pressure between two adjacent and connected areas occurs, the air (or any fluid) will flow from the higher pressure to the lower pressure until it is equalized (Figure 4–4). It follows from this that to exhale, the pressure difference must be such that a positive pressure exists within the lungs relative to

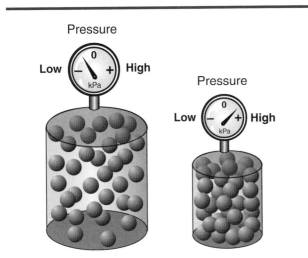

Figure 4–3. Boyle's law tells us that an inverse relationship exists between the volume and the pressure of a gas, under circumstances of a constant temperature.

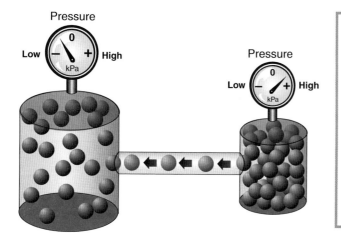

Figure 4–4. Fluids (including the air in our lungs and vocal tract) flow from higher to lower pressures.

Study Questions

1. Define speech breathing, inhalation/ inspiration, and exhalation/expiration.

2. What is respiration?

3. Define Boyle's law.

4. What is the difference between the mechanics of blowing up a balloon and how we breathe?

the atmosphere. That is, to move air out of the lungs, the pressure inside the lungs must be greater than atmospheric pressure. To achieve a positive lung pressure, the lung volume must contract. It would seem, then, that changing lung volume is critical to breathing. And that is so. The implications of this are quite important to speech pathologists. It means that the efficiency with which an individual expands and contracts the volume of the lungs directly influences the efficiency of breathing. Said another way, if you work hard to expand the lungs (which occurs indirectly, as we shall soon learn), you work hard to breathe. Speech breathing under these circumstances sometimes becomes effortful, a fact that impairs voice and speech production.

Let us examine how we expand the lungs efficiently to inhale and decrease lung volume to exhale. We turn to the structures and function of the lower airway to better understand the physiology of breathing. A brief review of the structures of the breathing mechanism is integrated into the following discussion. But you are urged to access one of the many excellent texts of anatomy and neuroanatomy of the speech production system for a more detailed explanation.

4.4 Anatomy of the Lower Airway

Gas exchange and movement of air into and out of the vocal tract is achieved by the pulmonary system, which is composed of the trachea ("windpipe"), the bronchial tree, and the lungs. (*Tracheia* is Greek for "rough" with "artery" understood, a term coined when the Greeks wrongly thought that the arteries carried air.) The lungs are a smooth, shiny, spongy organ divided into the left and right lung. The right lung has three lobes, with two on the left (the heart occupies some space on the left side of the chest). It may surprise you to learn that the lungs contain no muscle. The lungs are composed of approximately 90% air and only 10% solid tissue. The tissues include blood vessels, connective tissues (such as collagen and elastin fibers), respiratory tissue specialized for the exchange of gases, and the bronchial tree passageway, the latter of which originates with the trachea.

The pulmonary system is enclosed within the thorax, or thoracic cavity, which is made up of the ribcage, the spinal vertebrae posteriorly (in the back), and the sternum, or breastbone anteriorly (in the front), the shoulder (composed of the clavicle and scapula bones) superiorly (above), and the pelvis inferiorly (below). A large muscle, the diaphragm, forms the floor of the thoracic cavity and at the same time the roof of the abdominal cavity. Twelve sets of bony and cartilaginous ribs encircle the thoracic cavity. The first seven sets of ribs (the "true" ribs) are connected directly to the sternum by cartilaginous segments. The next three sets (the "false" ribs") are connected to each other anteriorly by cartilaginous segments that are connected to the lower part of the sternum. The lowest two sets (the "floating" ribs) do not extend completely around to the front and remain unattached at their anterior end. All cartilage and bones (except the hyoid bone, to be discussed in Chapter 5) abut another cartilage or bone by means of a joint. The joints allow these skeletal elements to articulate (meet) but still enable some freedom of movement.

Joints may be structured in several different ways, each of which allows a variable amount of freedom of movement. However, common to all joint movement is that the frictional force, arising from skeletal elements moving against one another, is minimized by synovial fluid, a highly viscous fluid within the joint. The ribs articulate with the spinal cord posteriorly in such a way that a small amount of upward gliding movement is possible during respiration. At rest, the posterior end of each rib, where it attaches to the spine, is slightly higher than the anterior end of each rib, so that the ribs slant downward, traversing from back to front. In addition, most of the ribs undergo a slight twist from their posterior to anterior ends. Near the spine, the outer surface of the rib is angled slightly upward, whereas in the front, the outer surface is more vertical. The biomechanical significance of these attachments is threefold: The ribs move in unison, they move upward as well as outward, and the movement is not confined to the front of the body, but rather expansion is achieved laterally and even posteriorly.

The trachea is the flexible passageway extending inferiorly from the larynx. It divides into the left and right bronchial tubes and then divides again multiple times within the left and right lungs. Descriptively named the bronchial tree, each subdivision or branching yields smaller tubes with successively smaller diameters. Over a million smaller airways, called bronchioles, are

present in the adult lungs. Each branching is called a "generation," and there are 38 generations in the bronchial tree from the trachea to the smallest tube called the terminal bronchiole. At the end of each terminal bronchiole are clusters of microscopic sacs called alveoli (Figure 4–5). The alveoli are surrounded by tiny blood vessels called capillaries (all parts of the body have capillaries, of course, not only the lungs), which carry blood to and from the lungs and the heart. The exchange of gases occurs by diffusion, the chemical exchange of molecules across the membranes separating the capillaries and the alveoli.

The biology of breathing specifies that diffusion must occur quickly. (The brain demands a constant and rapid source of oxygen). To achieve diffusion quickly, three features must be present: a large surface area, a thin and permeable membrane, and a high concentration gradient. The number of alveoli within the adult lung is estimated at approximately 7 million (Zemlin, 1998, p. 38), providing a total surface area of approximately 70 m^2, almost a quarter the size of a tennis court. (The standard tennis court has an area of about 260 m^2.) The alveolar and capillary membranes are each only one cell thick. A high concentration gradient, with respect to lung physiology, means that much more oxygen

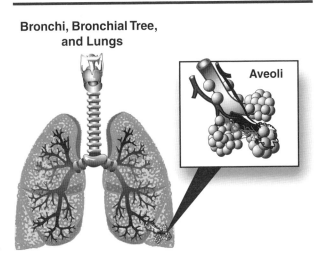

Bronchi, Bronchial Tree, and Lungs

Figure 4–5. The exchange of gases occurs between the tiny blood vessels and the alveoli.

is present in the alveoli than in the blood within the capillaries surrounding the alveoli. The high concentration gradient is achieved by continual ventilation on the alveolar side of the membrane and continual blood flow on the capillary side of the membrane. The alveoli are constantly moistened with water from cells in which the oxygen is dissolved before diffusing into the blood. The tiny alveoli, perhaps 0.25 mm in diameter, are highly elastic. They would collapse if not kept open by the outward force of the thoracic cavity. In fact, they are so small and elastic that the surface tension of the water inside the alveolar sacs could cause the sacs to be in danger of collapsing were it not for a fluid (referred to often as a soapy surfactant) that helps reduce surface tension of the water. The expanded alveoli contribute to the sponginess of the lungs, and that is how we can say that the lungs are composed largely of air. Not all the air in the lower airway participates in gas exchange. Dead space may be defined as the portion of the volume of air in any cycle of breathing that does not participate in gas exchange. It is, in effect, "wasted" air from the respiratory viewpoint. Upon inhalation, the air from the nose and mouth extending down to the first nine generations of the bronchial tree is anatomic dead space. No gas exchange occurs within these levels and the air is largely exhaled unaltered.

Lung Pressure

The pressure within the alveoli is called alveolar pressure. Alveolar pressure is equivalent to the pressure elsewhere in the lungs. **Pascal's law** tells us that a change in pressure is rapidly transmitted everywhere in an enclosed space and is not diminished as it is transmitted. Therefore, we can use the terms "lung pressure" and "alveolar pressure" synonymously. Furthermore, we shall learn in Chapter 5 that the space between the open vocal folds in the larynx is called the glottis. In discussion of voice production, the lung pressure is often referred to as subglottal pressure, the air pressure below the glottis. Just as lung pressure and alveolar pressure are equivalent, so too are lung pressure and **subglottal pressure**. Lung (or alveolar or subglottal) pressure is traditionally measured in cm of H_2O. It is a relative pressure, defined relative to the atmospheric pressure, which by convention is always set to zero. So, if the alveolar or lung pressure is higher than the atmosphere, we say it is positive. If the lung pressure is lower than atmospheric pressure, we say that the lung pressure is negative. A lung pressure of 1 cm of H_2O would mean that the pressure within the lungs is 1 cm of H_2O pressure less than the atmospheric pressure. Pascal's law, like many of the laws of physics, is an ideal law and can be applied to the complex human body only with some adjustments. As you read the chapter, it will become clear that internal forces generated by the elasticity of the lungs and chest wall strongly influence transmission of lung pressure.

Yawns

Yawning is a strange phenomenon indeed. It is a semiautomatic reflex that occurs throughout the animal kingdom (especially in cats). Did you know that we start yawning at approximately the third week of gestation, before we are even born? We all know that yawns are contagious. Even just reading about yawns will make you want to yawn! We become susceptible to the suggestion of yawning before we are 2 years old. The average yawn lasts about 6 seconds and that remains constant throughout life. The neurobiology of yawning is not understood clearly. The hypothalamus plays an important role in the regulation of yawning (Argiolas & Melis, 1998). Although it has long been believed that yawning occurs most frequently when we are tired or bored, more current research suggests that it may also be a mechanism for regulating temperature, by drawing cooler air into the body (Gallup & Eldakar, 2011). Other research suggests that yawning may be more related to stretching (Provine, Hammernik, & Curchack, 1987). An older, more common theory is that yawning occurs because we have a buildup of CO_2 in our bloodstream. As your breathing slows down, less oxygen moves into the lungs and across the alveolar membrane into the bloodstream. The resulting buildup of CO_2 can be lowered by taking in a deeper breath. (Recall that the air in the first nine generations of the bronchial tree does not participate in gas exchange.) In shallow breathing, it may be that insufficient movement of air occurs in the lower bronchioles and alveoli. Although this theory is now disputed by more current research, the mechanisms of yawning remain uncertain.

Motor Units and Muscle Activity

All motor neurons branch several times as they enter a muscle, and each of these branches innervates many muscle fibers (supplies the tissue with nerves). Each branch terminates in microscopic end plates within a muscle. The combination of a single motor neuron branch and the muscle fibers it innervates is called a motor unit. Motor units are the smallest functional neuromuscular unit, meaning that the brain can activate individual motor units of a single neuron. However, once activated, all muscle fibers of a given motor unit are stimulated. So the brain cannot stimulate an individual muscle fiber, but it can stimulate a group of muscle fibers. The size of a motor unit varies depending upon the function of the muscle. Large muscles that are involved in high force and large motor movements, such as the large muscles of the leg, may have as many as 2,000 fibers per motor unit. Very small muscles that do not bear heavy loads but control precise, fine movement, such as the eye muscles, may have only 10 fibers per motor unit. Some of the muscles that connect the cartilages of the larynx (the intrinsic muscles, as we will learn in Chapter 5) have motor units of approximately 100 muscle fibers (Faaborg-Andersen, 1957). In general, the slower a movement and the less weight borne by the muscle, the fewer the motor units activated. As the movement becomes faster and/or the weight becomes greater, more motor units within the muscle are activated. To sustain muscle contraction, the motor units must be activated repeatedly.

The Work of Muscles

Muscle movement is an extraordinarily complex activity, particularly for the fine motor coordination required for voice and speech production. However, the general principles of muscle movement can be applied in a straightforward manner. Muscles are contractile tissues, meaning that muscle fibers (generally long and slender) contract when stimulated by nerve impulses. Muscles can shorten by as much as 50% of their initial resting length, but in general, they function within 10% of their resting length (Lieber, 2002). In fact, contraction is the only active movement that a muscle can perform. On relaxation, the muscle returns passively to its original resting tone, and it can be stretched passively beyond its resting length (soon to be explained). Muscle tone can be thought of as a low level of muscle activity when the muscle is not intentionally contracted to do work. It is the natural resting tension of a muscle. Tone characterizes the muscle's readiness to work.

The skeletal elements are the bones and cartilages. They move by action around a joint, and that movement is a result of forces acting upon them. When a muscle contracts and it is unopposed, the muscle fibers shorten. This change of length in the muscle is referred to as isotonic. When isotonic contraction results in shortening of the muscle and movement of a skeletal element, we say that the muscle action is concentric. When the muscle contraction is opposed by another muscle, so that no movement occurs, and the muscle is not shortened, the contraction is called isometric. When the muscle contraction is partially opposed, so that movement is slowed but not completely inhibited, we say that the contraction is eccentric. See Table 4–1 for a summary of these movements.

When a muscle contracts, the amount of work achievable depends on the load of the muscle. The load is defined by the internal and external body forces. Internal forces include the weight of the body parts involved in the movement and the opposing pull of other muscles (to be explained further below). External forces act against a muscle from the outside. Gravity is an external force. If you lift this textbook up, the primary muscle movement is one of concentric action. Hold the textbook aloft, and the muscle activity is isometric, resisting the forces of gravity acting on the mass of the textbook (and your arm) without moving. Slowly lower the textbook onto the table, and you have achieved eccentric action.

Agonist-Antagonist Pairs

Most muscles work in pairs, called agonists and antagonists. The muscle that contracts to achieve a given movement is the **agonist**. A muscle that opposes contraction of another muscle is called an **antagonist**. Recall that muscles can contract and relax, but they cannot elongate and stretch by themselves. The antagonist muscle is stretched by the contraction of the agonist. The antagonist muscle is responsible for opposing movement. A muscle acts as an agonist in one action and as an antagonist in the opposite action. An example of agonist-antagonist muscle groups can be observed in shoulder movement. To elevate the shoulders, as in a shrug, the muscles of the neck (agonists in this movement)

Table 4–1. Types of Muscle Movement

Tension–Load Relationship	Muscle Length	Action
Tension greater than load	Muscle shortens	Concentric
Tension equal to load	Length remains unchanged	Isometric
Tension less than load	Muscle lengthens	Eccentric

must contract, passively stretching the muscles of the back (antagonists). To depress the shoulders, the muscles of the upper back (now acting as the agonists) must contract to achieve the downward pull on the shoulders, whereas the neck muscles (now the antagonists) must relax and allow themselves to be stretched passively. In our discussion of thoracic muscle activity during speech, we will see that the muscles that expand and shrink the volume of the thoracic cavity work as agonist-antagonist pairs.

For any given movement, two categories of agonist muscles can be identified: the prime mover and the synergist. The prime mover is the muscle that is primarily responsible for a given movement. That is, its contraction generates the bulk of the force in the direction of the target movement. The agonist synergists are muscles that assist the prime movers. Usually they do not contribute as much force but often provide additional control of the movement. Sometimes, there is ancillary movement of another skeletal element that is not the primary target. The synergistic muscle activity can stabilize the other skeletal elements and help to prevent unwanted movement. A familiar example that is easy to visualize is leg movement. Standing on one foot, swing your other leg front to back. Numerous muscles of the hips, back, and shoulders work synergistically to stabilize the torso and prevent unwanted upper body movement that could result in loss of balance. This concept of synergistic muscle activity is highly important to the discussion of muscle activation in breathing. Although we may talk about one or another muscle being a prime mover in inhalation or exhalation, it should be emphasized that numerous other muscles work synchronously and synergistically to achieve the target goal. The abdominal muscles, as we will discuss later, participate in this synergism as a stabilizing element for activity of the ribcage muscles.

Muscles and Levers

When muscles contract, they apply force to one or more skeletal elements. The resulting movement is achieved through the joints that connect skeletal elements to one another. The muscle-joint-skeletal element unit can be characterized as a lever, a rigid bar that rotates about a fixed point, called a fulcrum. A child's seesaw (or teeter-totter, depending on your geographic dialect) is a good example of a lever with the fulcrum in the center. Without too much effort, a child at one end of the seesaw can exert a force (push off the ground with her legs) and lower the child at the other end. In levers, rotational forces are created about the fulcrum, which accomplish work. We can think of the joints as fulcrums and the bones or cartilage as the (more or less) rigid bar. The muscles are how the force is exerted. We can characterize the movement in terms of velocity and force. How rapidly does a movement occur in a given direction, and with what force does the movement occur? A trade-off exists between the velocity and force in any lever system. The lever system, composed of the muscle and skeletal element, can maximize the advantage of either the velocity or the force but not both at the same time. Velocity and force have an inverse relationship. That is, if velocity is maximized (increased), force is minimized. If force is maximized, velocity is minimized. To achieve a very rapid movement, the force must be limited. And to achieve a very forceful movement, the speed will not be as great.

Although a seesaw always has the fulcrum in the middle, most of the muscle/skeletal element levers are designed with the fulcrum at one end. The muscles attach to the skeletal element close to the joint and far from the load at the other end. Think of the biceps, the muscle in the front of the upper arm that bulges when lifting a weight. The biceps inserts very close to the elbow joint. Yet the weight to be lifted is in the hand, at the other end of the lever. This lever arrangement would appear to provide a mechanical "disadvantage" to the operation of the arm. However, remember that we said, in typical use, muscle contracts approximately 15% to 20% of its resting length. Most muscles can exert the greatest tension when at their resting length, not when at their shortest length (and that concept will become important when we discuss control of fundamental frequency of vocal fold vibration in Chapter 5). The biceps needs to shorten only a very small amount to produce a correspondingly large motion of the hand. (Think about a toothpick lying on the table. Press down on one end. The movement at the end on which you press down is very small, but the corresponding upward movement of the free end of the toothpick is proportionately quite large.) By shortening only a small degree, a maximal amount of tension is created for a relatively small amount of work—an energy-efficient design relative to speed.

The Muscles of Breathing

We noted earlier that lung expansion occurs in three dimensions: anteroposteriorly, inferiorly-superiorly, and laterally. To achieve this three-dimensional expansion, many muscles are involved in breathing, depending on the level and type of activity in which one is engaged (and we include speaking in those activities). We will not address each muscle, as a comprehensive presentation of anatomy is not the purpose of this textbook, and numerous excellent anatomy texts in our field are available for reference. Muscles may be described by their principal location, including those of the neck, thorax, back, and abdominal wall. Functionally, the muscles can be divided into those that primarily control inhalation and those that are involved dominantly in exhalation. The major muscles of the lower airway that function in inspiration during all types of breathing, including when sitting quietly at rest, are the diaphragm and the external intercostals. The major lower airway muscles of exhalation are the internal intercostals. The diaphragm is generally considered the primary muscle of inspiration. It separates the thoracic and abdominal cavities (see Figure 4–1). It is attached to the spinal column and the lower border of the rib cage. The center of the diaphragm is composed of the central tendon. At rest, the diaphragm is convex shaped, with the dome oriented upward toward the lungs. Upon contraction, the muscle flattens

downward and spreads outward and slightly anteriorly. Although the abdominal contents are not considered part of the breathing system per se, it should be noted that the contraction and relaxation of the diaphragm causes cyclic compression of the abdominal viscera (organs of the abdomen). Furthermore, we will learn that the abdominal contents exert an important downward pull on the lungs that helps increase the efficiency with which the thoracic muscles can exert their forces.

The rostral (toward the front, from Latin *rostrum*, a bird's "beak," a ship's "beak" or "prow") external intercostal muscles are active primarily during inspiration. The external intercostal (Figure 4–6) muscles are not a single muscle but rather a series of short-fibered muscles that extend from the lower aspect of one rib to the upper aspect of the adjacent rib below it. The fibers of the muscles are oriented so that they angle inferiorly and anteriorly; that is, the upper end of the muscle fibers attaches more posteriorly than the lower end. Upon contraction, the rostral external intercostal muscles result in two types of movement that elevate the ribcage. One type of movement is often likened to the action of a pump handle, in which the anterior portion of each rib is elevated, like the action of an old-fashioned pump handle. The other movement is likened to the action of a bucket handle, referring to the upward and outward expan-

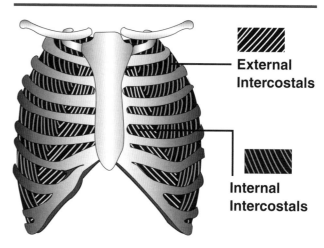

Figure 4–6. The internal and external intercostals.

sion of the ribs on each side. Upon contraction of the rostral external intercostal muscles, the greatest distance in the resulting ribcage movement is anterior (toward the front), not superior (upward). Watch the breathing of someone who is sitting quietly. As the individual inhales, his or her chest moves upward slightly, but the dominant movement is outward. Only the rostral portion of the external intercostal muscles has the mechanical advantage of ribcage expansion for inspiration (Wilson, Legrand, Gevenois, & De Troyer, 2001). The more caudally located (toward the back, from the Latin *cauda*, meaning "tail") external intercostals likely are active during expiration.

The internal intercostal muscles are primarily active during expiration (see Figure 4–6). They connect each rib to the adjacent rib below, deep to (further inside than) the external intercostals. Like the external intercostal muscles, the bulk of the fibers of the internal intercostals also lies at an angle, but inferior and posterior. That is, the upper end of the muscle fibers attaches more anteriorly than the lower end. On contraction, the bulk of the internal intercostal muscles cause the ribs to descend and draw inward. Recall that, in our discussion of the external intercostals, we noted that the rostral portions were active during inspiration, but the more caudal fibers were active during expiration. Similarly, the more rostral fibers of the internal intercostal muscles have the mechanical advantage to lower the rib cage and therefore are considered expiratory muscles. The more caudally located fibers of the internal intercostal muscles, however, are mechanically positioned to elevate the rib cage and therefore more likely to be active during inspiration.

Synergistic contraction of many of the other muscles of the neck, chest, back, and the abdominal wall contributes to the expansion and contraction of the thoracic cavity as well as provides stabilization for optimizing the activity of the primary movers of the thorax (Figure 4–7). It is important to emphasize that all muscles engaged in breathing act not only to change the volume of the lungs and thoracic cavity but also to stabilize posture to varying degrees. The activity of these muscles may depend upon the breath support requirements of the individual—quiet breathing at rest, breathing during physical exertion, speech breathing at soft or loud levels, and even combining loud speech with great physical exertion, as when a parent lifts up a small child in play while singing "whee!" The engagement of these muscles may also depend upon the motor strategy used by an individual. The term **motor equivalence** refers to the phenomenon in which individuals demonstrate different motor behaviors in response to the same stimulus (Gracco & Abbs, 1986; Hughes & Abbs, 1976). When applied to breathing, motor equivalence means that individuals may achieve the same task, such as breath support for speech or physical activity, using different strategies of muscle activation. The variability within and across speakers can make it a bit more difficult for the student of speech-language pathology to understand how we breathe for speech. But we are thankful that variability also provides the flexibility for the wide range of speaking demands integrated with numerous levels of physical activity. Throughout the chapter, as we discuss the biomechanics of breathing under different conditions, we shall note the relevant muscles that play a synergistic role in breathing.

Study Questions

5. Identify the structures through which air passes as we breathe.

6. How does gas exchange occur?

7. Describe muscle movement in general.

8. Explain the terms agonist and antagonist with regard to muscle contraction.

9. How does a lever system facilitate efficiency of muscle contraction?

10. Identify the major muscles of inhalation and exhalation and their effect on the ribcage upon contraction.

11. Define motor equivalence.

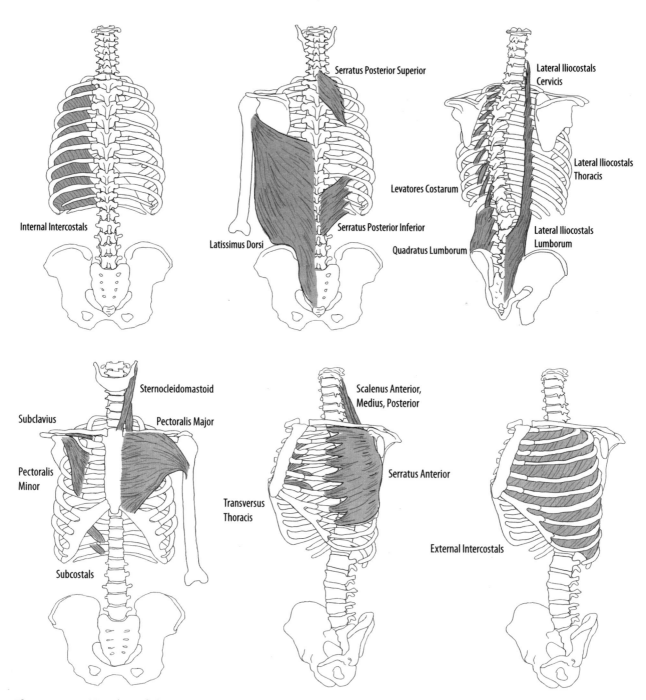

Figure 4–7. Muscles of the rib cage. From *Evaluation and Management of Speech Breathing Disorders: Principles and Methods* (pp. 19–20), by T. J. Hixon and J. D. Hoit, 2005, Tucson: AZ: Redington Brown. Reprinted with permission.

4.5 The Biomechanics of Breathing

The Biomechanics of Tidal Breathing

And so, we return to the question, how do we breathe? Let us first consider quiet breathing at rest, called quiet tidal breathing. It is the type of breathing you have been doing as you read this chapter. (Unless you have been reading this textbook while exercising on a stationary bicycle at the gym, in which case your breathing is different. We consider breathing under exertion in a subsequent section of this chapter.)

Recall that lungs contain no muscle. The tissue does not contract and relax in the same way that a muscle changes length. The two factors that enable lung volume changes are the linkage between the lungs and the thoracic cavity, and the restorative forces of the lung tissues. First we will consider the linkage. Encasing the outside of each lung is a membrane called the visceral pleura. Attached to the inner lining of

the thoracic cavity is a similar membrane called the parietal pleura (from Latin *paries parietis*, a wall of a house). These membranes are very thin, fibrous, and elastic and lie almost against each other. They are separated only by a viscous mucous fluid, called the pleural fluid. This fluid-filled separation often is referred to as the pleural space. (The area between the pleural membranes is called a potential space because it is not an air-filled space, let alone a vacuum. This narrow area is filled with a thin sheet of pleural fluid.) The pleural fluid causes the two membranes to adhere to each other. The exact mechanism of adhesion is not known. Surface tension of the fluid contributes to the adhesion, but the surface tension of the thick fluid is not sufficient to account entirely for the adhesion. Of critical importance, the pleural fluid also acts to reduce frictional forces that arise from inhalation and exhalation, allowing for increased ease of movement. Therefore, if the thorax expands or contracts to stretch or shrink the pleural sac, the pleural linkage dictates that the lungs must stretch or shrink accordingly (Figure 4–8).

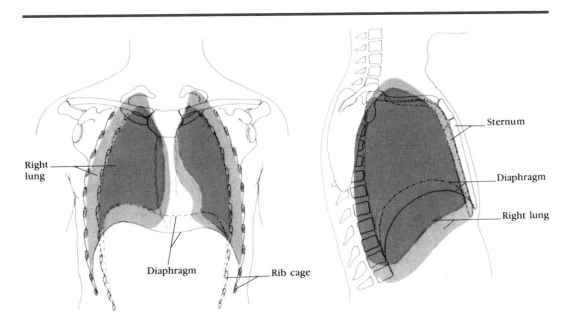

Figure 4–8. Anterior (**A**) and lateral (**B**) views of the change in thoracic cavity volume during inspiration (*light gray*) and exhalation (*dark gray*). From *Anatomical and Physiological Bases of Speech,* by D. R. Dickson and W. Maue-Dickson, 1996, Butterworth-Heinemann. Reprinted with permission from Elsevier.

Recall that a negative pressure is said to exist when the pressure in an enclosed space is lower than the atmospheric pressure. The intrapleural pressure (pressure of the potential space between the pleura) has been estimated to be approximately 5 cm of H_2O during quiet breathing, that is, 5 cm of H_2O lower than atmospheric pressure (Davies & Moore, 2003). (The pressure varies a bit depending upon where it is measured along the length of the lungs. Due to gravity, the negative pressure is greater at the top of the lungs than at its base when standing up.)

The restorative forces of the tissues are the other factor-enabling changes in lung volume. These are forces, not due to muscle contraction, but rather to **elastic recoil forces** acting upon the lungs and thorax to return them to their resting state on being stretched. If the thorax was not linked to the lungs by the pleural lining but rather was free to move on its own, the thorax would expand. In fact, it would expand to a size equal to the expansion of the chest when the lungs are filled to approximately 60% of their vital capacity (the total volume of air that can be exchanged during a single maximal

breathing cycle) or 75% of their total capacity (Davies & Moore, 2003). The lungs, similarly freed, would contract (Figure 4–9). Said another way, the natural volume of the lungs at rest is considerably smaller than the natural volume of the thoracic cavity at rest. During quiet breathing, the moment of equilibrium occurs at the end of the exhalation, just before inhalation begins. This point is the moment when the forces pulling at the thorax to expand the rib cage are balanced with the forces pulling the lungs to contract. You can think of the thorax as a slightly compressed spring and the lungs as a slightly extended spring. The restorative forces are a buildup of potential energy as it interacts with the elasticity of the tissue. For this reason, the restorative forces also are called the elastic recoil forces. With no other forces acting upon it, the compressed spring of the thorax would expand, and the extended spring of the lungs would contract. Linked together, however, the lungs and the thorax exert opposite pulling forces upon each other. At the end of an exhalation during quiet breathing, these forces are balanced (in equilibrium), and the breathing system is at rest-

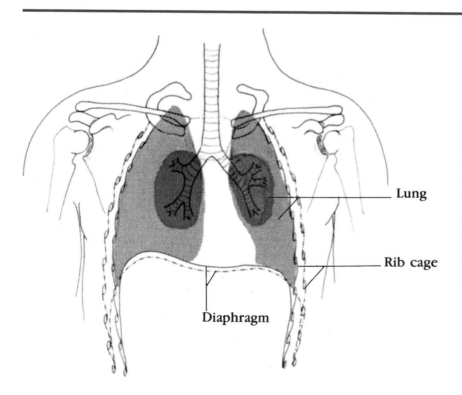

Figure 4–9. Lung volume at rest (*light gray*) and upon opening pleural spaces to atmospheric pressure (*dark gray*). From *Anatomical and Physiological Bases of Speech* (p. 83), by D. R. Dickson and W. Maue-Dickson, 1996, Butterworth-Heinemann. Reprinted with permission from Elsevier.

Lung

Rib cage

Diaphragm

Pneumothorax

A pneumothorax, or "collapsed lung," results from rupture of the pleural linkage, usually due to trauma, such as a broken rib piercing the pleural membrane or a stab or gunshot wound. In such a case, the air inside the lung leaks into the pleural space, and the expansion of the ribcage does not expand the lung, because the mechanical linkage of the lung to the chest wall has been compromised. Thus, it becomes quite difficult to draw air into the lung. Patients report that it feels like an elephant is sitting on their chest or that they are trying to breathe through a covering over their mouth. (The other lung is still able to fully expand.) In rare cases, the rupture is so great that the lung collapses entirely. More commonly, the lung still has some limited capability of expansion. Treatment may involve removal of the air that has leaked into the plural space. Often, the rupture heals on its own.

in the syringe (the intrapleural pressure) must remain at a stable negative pressure. To enlarge the volume of the balloon and further inflate it, as the plunger is drawn outward, the negative pressure in the syringe must increase.

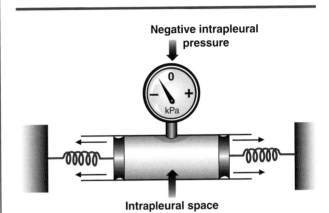

Figure 4–10. Creating negative intrapleural pressure. Adapted from *The Respiratory System* (p. 33), by A. Davies and C. Moore, 2003, Edinburgh: Churchill Livingstone, an imprint of Elsevier Science Ltd. Reprinted with permission from Elsevier.

ing expiratory level. (Caution: Equilibrium does not mean that the muscles are not contracted. On the contrary, they are actively engaged. Rather, at equilibrium, the forces are balanced.) The volume in the lungs at this point of equilibrium is called resting lung volume, or resting expiratory level.

Knowing that the elastic recoil forces of the lungs and the chest wall act in opposition, an easy way to understand the negative intrapleural pressure is shown in Figure 4–10. The two plungers represent the lungs and chest wall, and the space in between is the pleural space. You can see how drawing the plungers outward (the elastic recoil forces of the lungs are inward and those of the chest wall are outward) lowers the pressure in the enclosed intrapleural space. If we change the analogy just a bit, it will show how the intrapleural pressure changes depending upon the lung volume. Pretend that we have a very large syringe. Place a partially inflated balloon inside the syringe (Figure 4–11). To maintain the volume of the balloon, the pressure

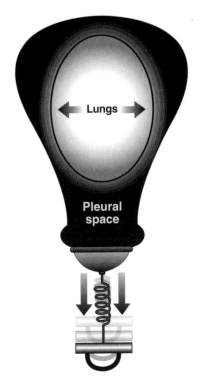

Figure 4–11. Decreasing the intrapleural pressure causes the lung volume to expand.

And so, during quiet breathing, we start the cycle at resting lung volume (resting expiratory level), the equilibrium point of the opposing restorative forces of the lungs and the thorax. To initiate inhalation, the diaphragm contracts, flattening downward. (Only some of the muscle fibers contract with each inspiration, and different fibers contract during different inspiratory cycles. This alternation of contracted fibers may contribute to the fatigue-resistance of the diaphragm.) Because it is connected to the lungs via the pleural membranes, the downward pull of the diaphragm stretches the pleural membranes, causing a drop in the intrapleural pressure. The lowered position of the diaphragm increases pressure on the abdominal structures immediately below it. Thus, the abdomen pulls downward and pushes outward (if one does not "hold in the stomach" with abdominal muscles). The outward movement of the abdomen helps to pull outward on the lower ribs, thus increasing the transverse dimension of the thoracic cavity. A portion of the external intercostal muscles contracts slightly. Their contraction may help to elevate the ribs outwardly and increase the anteroposterior (transverse) dimension of the lungs. However, in quiet tidal breathing, the main purpose of the contraction of the external intercostal muscles is to stiffen the wall of the thorax (Hixon & Hoit, 2005, p. 51). The muscle contraction helps to increase the efficiency of the diaphragmatic contraction in expanding lung volume. The increased volume results in a decrease in the pressure of the air within the bronchi by approximately 1 cm of H_2O below atmospheric pressure, resulting in an inward flow to equalize the pressure (Boyle's law). Upon equalization of pressures, the inward flow stops. At this point, the restorative force of the lungs is greater than the force causing the lung tissue to contract, and exhalation begins. In exhalation, the diaphragm relaxes passively and curves upward. (In speech, it does not relax completely but maintains a slight contraction, or tone or tension, to respond more quickly to the ongoing demands of speech.) During quiet **tidal breathing**, on average, the diaphragm moves approximately 1 cm up and down. On average, we take approximately 12 to 15 breaths per minute. The external intercostal muscles relax, drawing the ribs downward and inward. These actions cause the volume of the thorax to decrease, which in turn decreases the volume of the lungs and alveoli. The decreased volume results in an increase in air pressure in the lungs so that their pressure is greater than atmospheric pressure, which causes the air to flow out of the lungs to equalize pressure with the atmosphere (Boyle's law again). This represents one cycle of quiet tidal breathing. The volume of air that is exchanged during any particular cycle of inhalation/exhalation is called the tidal volume. When it occurs at rest, the cycle is referred to as quiet tidal breathing. An important feature to note about quiet tidal breathing is that the exhalation phase is achieved without active muscle contraction. It is simply a passive response to the elastic recoil force of the lungs.

Lung Elasticity

The ability of the lungs to expand and contract is due to their elasticity. The elastic properties of the lungs derive from two sources. Approximately half comes from the presence of millions of alveoli that make up the lungs. The other half of the elastic property of the lungs comes from the tissue fibers that make up the walls of the alveoli. About half of these fibers are elastin, the same type of fibers that contribute to the elasticity of other tissues, including the vocal folds. The way in which elastin fibers expand is often likened to the stretch of pantyhose (Figure 4–12). The fibers are linked together and kinked. Upon expansion, the kinks unbend. But the other half of the elasticity comes from collagen fibers, which do not stretch as much. These fibers act to limit lung expansion and prevent overexpansion.

Figure 4–12. Elastin fibers in the lung tissue behave similarly to a nylon stocking when stretched. Unstretched (**A**) and stretched (**B**). Adapted from *The Respiratory System* (p. 35), by A. Davies and C. Moore, 2003, Edinburgh: Churchill Livingstone, an imprint of Elsevier Science Ltd. Reprinted with permission from Elsevier.

Lung Volumes and Capacities

Breathing function often is discussed relative to specific subdivisions of the volume of air in the lungs and the capacities of the lungs. These subdivisions will be helpful in our discussion of speech breathing. Reference to Figure 4–13 will help you quickly understand the relationship among the four lung volumes and four lung capacities. Each volume is distinct, with no overlap. The lung capacities describe two or more lung volumes. We have already identified the tidal volume as the volume of air exchanged during a single cycle of breathing. Tidal volume will vary, depending upon the respiratory needs of the individual at any given moment. In quiet tidal breathing, the tidal volume is approximately 15% of the vital capacity. The total lung capacity is the maximum volume of air that the lungs can hold. However, not all the total lung capacity is available for exhalation. After a maximal exhalation, a volume of air remains in the lungs,

called the residual volume, up to approximately 25% of the total lung capacity (Zemlin, 1998, p. 79). The remaining portion of the total lung capacity is the vital capacity, the total volume of air that can be exchanged during a single maximal inhalation and exhalation cycle. You know from personal experience that the lungs could still expand considerably to take in more air at the end of the inhalation during tidal breathing. Similarly, the lungs could contract more to expel a greater volume of air at the end of a tidal exhalation. The amount of air that could still be inhaled is called the inspiratory reserve volume. The amount of air that still could be exhaled is called the expiratory reserve volume. At resting lung volume, the tendency for the lungs to recoil inward is balanced by the tendency for the chest wall to spring outward. This point at which the elastic recoil forces of the lungs and thorax are balanced generally occurs at approximately 38% to 40% of vital capacity (Zemlin, 1998). Quiet tidal breathing begins and ends each cycle at

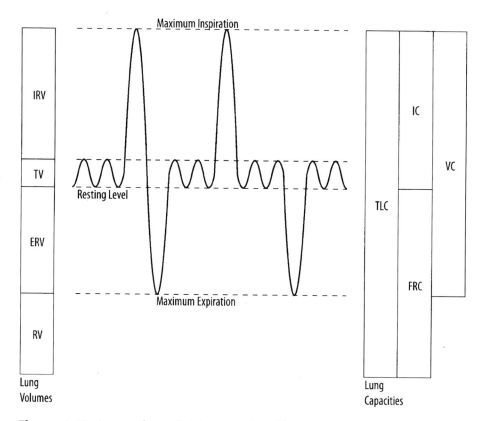

Figure 4–13. Lung volume divisions consist of inspiratory reserve volume (*IRV*), tidal volume (*TV*), expiratory reserve volume (*ERV*), and residual volume (*RV*). Lung capacity divisions are total lung capacity (*TLC*), inspiratory capacity (*IC*), functional residual capacity (*FRC*), and vital capacity (*VC*). From *Evaluation and Management of Speech Breathing Disorders: Principles and Methods* (p. 36), by T. J. Hixon and J. D. Hoit, 2005, Tucson, AZ: Redington Brown. Reprinted with permission.

resting lung volume. We said earlier that tidal volume of the lungs is approximately 15% of vital capacity. Therefore, at the end of a quiet inhalation, the volume of air in the lungs is approximately 55% of vital capacity (the volume for tidal breathing and approximately 40% volume at resting expiratory level).

The total amount of air remaining in the lungs when the recoil forces are balanced is called functional residual capacity. Several factors can influence the various lung divisions. Individuals with larger body size will have larger lung volumes, so in general men will have larger lung volumes than women. Children have smaller lung volumes than adults, in part due to their smaller body size. In the elderly, degenerative changes result in decreased vital capacity and increased residual volume.

Speaking on "Residual Volume"

A word of caution: Do not confuse residual volume with functional residual capacity. A common mistake is to say that someone is "speaking on residual volume" when they speak for a prolonged period below resting lung volume. See Clinical Case 2 in Chapter 5, "Running Out of Breath."

The Biomechanics of Forced Inhalation and Exhalation

The level of breathing activity is increased during physical exertion. **Forced inhalation** occurs when a greater volume of air is inspired than during tidal breathing. Forced inhalation occurs at volumes above approximately 60% of vital capacity, generally to support a greater level of physical activity or effortful speech. To achieve forced inhalation, we employ greater contraction of the muscles of inspiration—the diaphragm and external intercostals, as well as engaging many other muscles that contribute to expanding the rib cage, that act on the neck, shoulders, spine, abdomen, and pelvis. **Forced exhalation** occurs when the volume of air in the lungs is moved out at a rate faster than during tidal breathing and/or a greater volume of air is exhaled than during tidal breathing (below resting expiratory level). In forced exhalation, the internal intercostal muscles contract (as well as numerous other muscles), exerting a downward and inward pull on the rib cage, causing the ribs to move faster (and to a greater extent) than relaxation of the external intercostals alone. That is, forced exhalation is an active process, in contrast to exhalation during tidal breathing, which occurs by the passive force of relaxation pressure. In tidal breathing, exhalation is passive. In forced inspiration and exhalation, inhalation engages more muscles, and exhalation is active.

In forced inhalation, several muscles may contribute to expansion of the thoracic cavity, in addition to the external intercostals and the diaphragm. Evidence reviewed by Dickson and Maue-Dickson (1996, p. 128) suggests that in the anterior thorax, a portion of the internal intercostals, called the interchondral portion, may elevate the ribs. (Elevation is the opposite action of most the fibers of the internal intercostals muscles, which depress the ribs and facilitate exhalation.) In addition, other muscles may be active in high-effort inhalation, including the scalene muscles in the anterior neck, the sternocleidomastoid and the trapezius muscles of the neck, the pectoralis major and minor of the chest, the abdominal muscles, and possibly the levator costarum muscles and the serratus posterior superior muscles of the back.

In forced exhalation, in addition to the contraction of the internal intercostal muscles, contraction of abdominal muscles is highly important, contributing to rapid upward movement of the diaphragm. The upward and downward movement of the diaphragm can approach 10 cm (Davies & Moore, 2003) with assistance from the forceful upward thrust of the abdominal structures. Other muscles contribute to contraction of the thoracic cavity, in addition to the internal intercostals, thereby lowering lung volume in effortful breathing and possibly within some speech conditions. In the anterior thorax, the transverse thoracic may assist the internal intercostal muscles and depress the ribs. Contraction of the external abdominal obliques may contribute to elevating the diaphragm and stabilizing the vertebral column. Other muscles, particularly those of the back, such as the serratus posterior inferior, subcostal, innermost intercostal muscles, and latissimus dorsi, have the potential to pull the ribs downward or stabilize the spine. However, their specific contributions to forced exhalation are unknown.

Study Questions

12. Define tidal breathing.

13. What are the pleural linings and what is their critical contribution to breathing mechanics?

14. What is the significance of resting lung volume?

15. Identify and define: the four lung volumes and four lung capacities.

16. Define forced inhalation and exhalation.

4.6 The Biomechanics of Speech Breathing

It is evident that multiple forces act upon the breathing system. These forces can be characterized as active and passive. The passive forces include gravity, elastic recoil forces of the ribcage and lungs, and the surface tension of the alveoli. Together they represent the **relaxation pressure** acting to return the breathing system to resting expiratory level, the point of equilibrium. A critical concept to recognize is that relaxation pressure is *positive* when it acts to *decrease* lung volume and *negative* when the pressure acts to *expand* lung volume. Therefore, the relaxation pressure is positive at lung volumes above resting lung volume and negative at volumes below resting lung volume. The active forces of breathing are muscle contractions. Although the lung volume dictates the level of relaxation pressure, at any point during the breathing cycle, these active forces can be used to counteract the relaxation forces. It will become evident in our discussion of speech breathing that the degree of passive elastic recoil forces and active forces of muscle contraction are related to each other and depend upon the level of breathing activity.

The elastic recoil forces are commonly summarized in a graphic representation called a relaxation curve (Figure 4–14), first diagrammed by Rahn, Otis, Chadwick, and Fenn (1946) and Campbell (1958). The relaxation curve charts the pressure generated by the elastic recoil forces at different percentages of vital capacity. By way of introduction to the relaxation curve, try the following exercise. First, recall that the thorax is like a compressed spring, and its elastic recoil exerts an expansion force. The lungs are like a stretched spring, with the elastic recoil exerting a compression force. Now, inhale deeply and then hold your breath for a moment before you let the air out. Note how much pressure you feel against your chest during the breath-holding. Now inhale less deeply and again hold your breath before exhaling. And repeat the gesture with an even shallower inhalation. Note

the decrease in pressure sensation against your chest during each breath-holding maneuver as you inhale less deeply. Charting the pressure at each of those points would yield the portion of the curve above resting lung volume. Now explore the bottom part of the curve. Starting at resting expiratory level (the end of a cycle of quiet tidal breathing before you begin to inhale anew), exhale just a bit more air and then hold your breath. Note the sensation of pressure in your chest. Return to resting lung volume and exhale even more air, again noting the sensation of chest pressure. Charting the pressures at each of these moments of exhalation at different lung volumes would yield the portion of the curve below resting lung volume.

Some key points to observe about the relaxation curve warrant discussion. The difference in the pressure between the alveoli and the atmosphere is called the **transthoracic pressure**. It represents the amount of pressure needed to expand or contract the lungs and chest wall simultaneously. If the transthoracic pressure is negative, that means the pressure in the alveoli is lower than the atmospheric pressure, and the relaxation pressures act to expand the lungs and thoracic wall to cause inhalation. If the transthoracic pressure is positive, that means the pressure in the alveoli is higher than the atmospheric pressure, and the relaxation pressures act to contract the lungs and thoracic wall to cause exhalation. At resting expiratory level, the inward elastic recoil forces of the lungs are balanced by the outward elastic recoil forces of the thorax, and so an equilibrium point exists. Note that resting lung volume is located at approximately 38% of total lung capacity.

Another point to emphasize is that the curve above resting lung volume represents the relaxation pressures working to decrease lung volume. The curve below resting lung volume represents the relaxation pressures working to increase lung volume. Even at residual volume, the lungs are distended (expanded), and the elastic recoil forces, left unopposed, would cause the lungs to contract. (Recall that the lungs are always distended. Only in the case of a com-

Relaxation Curve

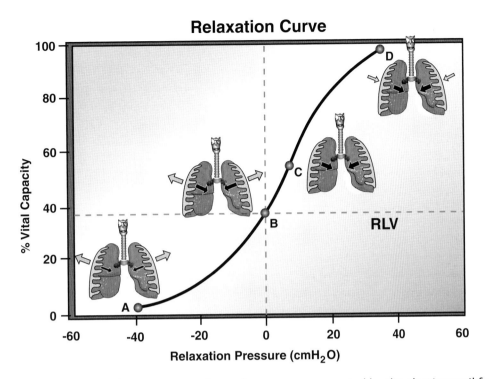

Figure 4–14. The relaxation curve charts the pressure generated by the elastic recoil forces at different percentages of vital capacity. Each of the points on the curve (A–D) and their accompanying pair of lungs represent the balance of the elastic recoil force of the lungs (*black arrows*) and the rib cage (*gray arrows*). *A.* At the bottom of vital capacity, the elastic recoil forces acting upon the lungs to decrease their overall volume are minimal (*represented by very small black arrows pointing inward*). However, the elastic recoil forces acting upon the chest wall to expand it outward are quite large (represented by thicker gray arrows pointing outward). *B.* At resting lung volume (RLV), the relaxation pressure is balanced, such that the elastic recoil forces acting to expand the chest wall are equal to the forces acting to decrease the lung volume. *C.* As vital capacity increases, a point is reached in which the chest wall is at its resting size. *D.* At maximal vital capacity, the elastic recoil forces of the chest wall and lungs are acting to decrease overall volume. Note that the relaxation pressure acting upon the lungs is always inward, to decrease lung volume, whereas the direction of the relaxation pressure acting upon the chest wall depends upon the vital capacity.

plete rupture of the pleural membranes would the lungs collapse.)

In healthy lungs at low volume, relatively little pressure differential is required to distend the lungs. At higher lung volumes, however, when there is greater stretch of the lung tissue and greater elastic recoil force, relatively greater pressure must be applied to get the same increase in volume compared to the lower lung volume. That is, the lungs become stiffer at higher volumes.

Relaxation Curve and Phonation

The relaxation curve can help us understand how the passive and active forces of breathing are managed to accommodate the demands of speech production. Let us consider first the demands of sustained vowel phonation (making a prolonged vowel sound), superimposed upon the relaxation curve in Figure 4–15. For sustained vowel phonation, we target a constant and stable lung pressure throughout the phonation

Relaxation Curve

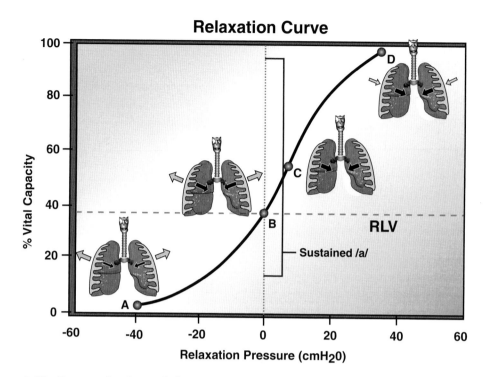

Figure 4–15. For sustained vowel phonation, we target a constant and stable lung pressure throughout the phonation across all lung volumes. The portion of the figure above resting expiratory level (RLV) represents positive relaxation pressure, which means that the net elastic recoil forces are acting to compress the combined lungs and chest wall. The portion of the figure below RLV represents negative relaxation pressure, meaning that the net forces are acting to expand the combined lungs and chest wall. (Although the elastic recoil forces of the lungs in *A* are inward, the net relaxation pressure of the combined lungs and chest wall is outward.) Exhalation from Point *D* to *C* to *B* can be achieved with passive relaxation pressure alone. Exhalation from *B* to *A* can only be achieved using active muscle contraction. Therefore, speaking below RLV requires more work than speaking above RLV.

across all lung volumes. (Lung pressure remains quite stable during speech, except as modified for frequency, intensity, and linguistic demands, as we shall discuss in Chapter 5.) A lung pressure of approximately 7 cm of H_2O is used in this example. (We shall learn in Chapter 5 that lung pressures of 2 to 3 cm of H_2O are sufficient to maintain soft phonation, and lung pressures of 15 cm of H_2O and beyond will generate loud speech.) Note that the relaxation curve intercepts the pressure used for phonation at approximately 60% of vital capacity. This intercept signifies that relaxation pressures are sufficient to sustain phonation at lung volumes above approximately 60% of vital capacity. Below that level (where the relaxation curve crosses the line representing phonation pressure), relax-

ation pressures are insufficient to sustain phonation. Between 38 and 60% of vital capacity (38% being resting expiratory level), expiratory muscle activity is required to supplement relaxation pressures to maintain the requisite alveolar pressure for speech. Below resting expiratory level, expiratory muscle activity must be used not only to maintain sufficient alveolar pressure for phonation but also to overcome the passive elastic recoil forces of the lungs and thorax (and of course, to keep oxygenating one's blood while speaking). Therefore, the first clinical implication to be highlighted in Figure 4–15 is that, in general, phonation is more efficient (less work) when it occurs above resting expiratory level. We can see that even for a relatively simple speech task such as sustained vowel phonation requiring an average level of lung pressure, the passive and active forces of the breathing system must be managed in a complex fashion.

Examine once more the portion of the relaxation curve above 60% of vital capacity, where the relaxation pressure is sufficient to generate the required alveolar pressure for phonation. In fact, note that relaxation pressure is in excess of that required for phonation. At 100% of vital capacity, the relaxation pressure is generating a lung pressure of approximately 40 cm of H_2O, well beyond the requirements of our speaker (and anyone else talking at typical conversational intensity). If one were to allow the passive forces to act upon the lungs wholly unchecked, a sustained phonation would not be produced; rather, a sound more like a voiced sigh would be produced. Try it. Take a comfortably deep breath, begin to phonate any vowel, and then allow the lungs and chest wall to relax wholly. (Admittedly, allowing one's breathing system to completely relax is very difficult. But you get the idea.) The rapid decrease in lung pressure does not allow for a sustained sound. To sustain phonation, the inspiratory thoracic muscles must be engaged to hold the elastic recoil forces in check. This braking activity, called **inspiratory checking action**, counteracts the relaxation pressures and promotes the steady lung pressure necessary for phonation. Inspiratory checking is used only when the pressure generated by the lung volume is greater than would be necessary to sustain phonation, so the second clinical implication of Figure 4–15 is the inefficiency of taking a breath much deeper than is necessary to sustain phonation. The greater the relaxation pressure above that which is necessary to sustain phonation, the greater the inspiratory checking required for control of that pressure. We should note here that, of some interest, the abdominal muscles participate in inspiratory checking (Hixon, Mead, & Goldman, 1976). Although the abdominals are considered primarily expiratory muscles, Hixon and colleagues hypothesize that their activity helps to stabilize chest wall movement, thereby providing greater thoracic control during inspiratory checking at higher lung volumes.

Study Questions

17. Define relaxation pressure. Explain the three passive forces that comprise relaxation pressure.

18. (Try not to refer to the text diagrams as you complete the following tasks.) Draw the relaxation curve: Label the x- and y-axes. Mark four points on your relaxation curve: the bottommost point, the topmost point, the intersection of 0 on the x-axis and 38% on the y-axis, and the intersection of 7 cm H_2O on the x-axis and 55% on the y-axis. For each of the four points, explain the pressures acting upon the volumes of the lungs and chest wall.

19. Define inspiratory checking action and explain when it would be used.

20. Referring to the relaxation curve in Figure 4–15, explain why initiating speech at Points A, B, C, and D would be efficient or inefficient.

Running Speech

Figure 4–15 addresses the balance of passive and active forces for sustained phonation. However, sustained phonation is a special case of speech breathing, used during singing or speech-pathology evaluation. The demands of speech breathing for typical speaking (often called running speech) are more complex than for sustained phonation. Unless specifically noted, the term speech breathing refers to the breathing demands for running speech. The average rate of quiet breathing (12 to 20 breaths per minute) is generally like the rate of breathing during running speech. But the timing of the inspiratory and expiratory phases, the volumes of air inhaled and exhaled, and the muscular activity are all quite different during speech breathing compared to breathing at rest or during exertion in the absence of speech.

Figure 4–16 shows a simulation of what speech breathing might look like as a function of lung volume, compared to quiet tidal breathing and forced inhalation and exhalation. Note that speech generally occurs at lung volumes above resting expiratory level. Speech is generally initiated at lung volumes equal to the peak of tidal breathing up to twice its depth. The lung volumes used for soft to normal conversation are, on average, only slightly different from quiet tidal breathing. Speech produced at greater intensity will be initiated at higher lung volumes, because greater air pressure is required to achieve greater intensity of speech. Most running speech occupies the area between approximately 35 and 60% of vital capacity (Hixon, Goldman, & Mead, 1973), which overlaps generally with quiet tidal breathing.

Phrase Breath Groups

The timing of the breathing phases is quite different in speech breathing compared to nonspeech breathing. In tidal breathing, the inspiratory phase occupies approximately 40%

of the total breathing cycle, whereas the expiratory phase occupies approximately 60% of the total cycle. In speech breathing, the inspiratory phase is shortened and the expiratory phase is lengthened. The relationship may be closer to 10% inspiration and 90% exhalation. However, linguistic rules constrain the duration of the breathing cycle by the length of the phrase breath group. The **phrase breath group** is the number of words or syllables that are spoken on one exhalation. The length of the phrase breath group is determined by linguistic content and personal habit. If you say the short sentence, "I'm going home," it would sound odd to take a breath within the sentence. Such a pause, even very rapid, would likely convey linguistic meaning. (Try this. Say the sentence on one exhalation. Then take a short, rapid breath before the word "home." How is the possible meaning of the sentence altered by that pause?) Now say a more complex sentence, such as, "I'm going home even though I haven't been home in years and I really have a lot of trepidation about that trip in the middle of the summer." This can be uttered as one phrase breath group. But to do so requires a substantially greater inhalation than was required for the first utterance. Most people

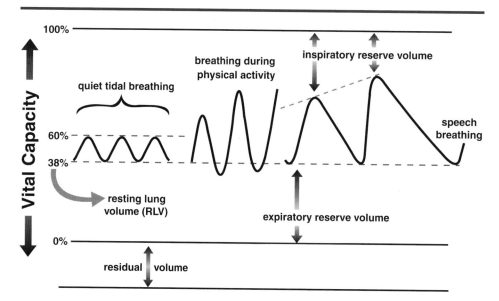

Figure 4–16. Changes in lung volume change during quiet tidal breathing, physical activity, and moderately loud running speech.

would be well advised to divide the sentence into two phrase breath groups, using a short inhalation perhaps between the words "years" and "and." The length of the phrase breath group is closely related to the lung pressure used to drive vocal fold vibration. We shall examine additional aspects of linguistic effect upon speech breathing shortly. And we will return to the relationship of lung pressure and its effect upon speech production in Chapter 5 when we examine vocal fold vibration.

In a seminal study of the contribution of active muscle force to speech breathing, Hixon et al. (1976) provide data that help to explain the complexity of balancing the active and passive forces in the regulation of lung volume and pressure. Four points about their data are particularly important. First, passive relaxation pressure alone is never the solitary force managing speech breathing. Active force (muscle contraction) is always contributing to management of lung volume, albeit in varying degrees, throughout all phases of speech breathing. As soon as the inspiratory muscles relax, the expiratory muscles take over.

Second, the diaphragm, the ribcage inspiratory muscles, and the abdominal muscles are all active to varying degrees at the beginning of an utterance. The exact time at which thoracic and abdominal muscles activate for the onset of loud speech varies across individuals (Draper, Ladefoged, & Whitteridge, 1959). However, at all intensity levels, the abdominal muscles are quite active. In fact, they are more continuously active in speech breathing than during tidal breathing or even forced inhalation and exhalation (Draper et al., 1959; Estenne, Zocchi, Warl, & Macklem, 1990; Newsom Davis & Sears, 1970). The abdominal wall activity contributes to the efficiency of lung volume changes achieved by the diaphragm and by the chest wall muscles, providing a platform against which the diaphragm and chest wall muscles can exert their forces (Hixon & Hoit, 2005).

The third important point from the Hixon et al. (1976) data to be emphasized is that the magnitude of the inspiratory muscle force is directly related to lung volume, and the magni-

tude of the expiratory muscle force is inversely related to lung volume. That is, inspiratory muscle force gradually decreases over the course of the breath group as lung volume decreases, whereas expiratory muscle force gradually increases over the course of the breath group as lung volume decreases.

Fourth, recall that at the beginning of the utterance, the relaxation pressure exceeds the lung pressure necessary to generate a moderate intensity level of speech (refer to Figure 4–15). Nevertheless, diaphragmatic muscle contraction abates substantially in the early part of the utterance. The inspiratory muscles of the rib cage provide the checking action to limit the relaxation pressure. The authors explain that the reason for this arrangement is associated with the downward pull of the abdominal contents upon the diaphragm (and hence a similar downward force upon the rib cage and lungs). The

Posture of Breathing

The posture of a patient is addressed often in speech-voice therapy in regard to optimal breath support for voice and speech production. A simple exercise will make the importance of posture very clear. Sit down and allow the spine to curve outward into a "C" and let your chin hang down a bit. Count to 10. Sit upright (but don't arch your back) and elongate the spine, as though a string was connected to the top of your head and it was pulling you up straight. Count to 10 again. Now lie down flat on your back and count to 10 once more. Likely, you found it most effortless to count when sitting upright. Curving forward inhibits the ability of the thoracic cavity to expand. Gravity, too, is an important factor in thoracic expansion. When lying prone, the abdominal contents are forced back and expand toward the head, putting pressure on the diaphragm and therefore reducing the resting volume of the lungs.

intrapleural pressure decreases as lung volume decreases, which in return releases the upward pull on the abdominal contents. In this way, the abdomen replaces the force exerted by the diaphragm to stabilize the chest wall and provide a force against which the thoracic muscles can exert their pull.

Adaptation of Speech Breathing to Variable Internal and External Demands

The system controlling speech breathing must be highly adaptable to the changeable internal demands of our bodies and the equally changeable external demands of our communication. Hixon and Hoit (2005, p. 67) apply the concept of "adaptive control" to speech breathing: the necessary changes that must occur when critical variables are altered. As a mundane example, if you bang your knee on the kitchen table, you may favor the other leg throughout the day, resulting in a slight alteration of your gait. You may do this on purpose, to limit the amount and duration of weight that the sore knee must bear during ambulation. However, you may not even realize you are favoring the good knee until a colleague asks you why you are limping. Adaptive control of speech breathing may similarly be achieved overtly as a conscious act or unconsciously. If you read a story about lions aloud to children, you may (or may not) purposely take a deep breath and begin a phrase at a higher lung volume to simulate a loud and long roar of a lion. In that case, you are adapting the percentage of vital capacity at which you initiate speech to plan for the longer or louder phrase (and hence, greater portion of vital capacity to be consumed). On the other hand, perhaps you are exercising on the treadmill and you talk to the person running in place next to you. Most likely, you do not plan how to accommodate increased ventilatory needs by altering your speech breathing, but you are likely aware that your speech is more effortful and clearly altered. Many variables have the potential to affect speech breathing, including body type, cognitive-linguistic factors, style of

breathing, and respiratory demands. We shall briefly examine each of these in turn.

Body Type

We have learned that **elastic resistance** is a factor that controls airflow, and we know from our study of forces in Chapter 2 that the mass of an object interacts with acceleration to define force. Therefore, it is reasonable to presume that the degree of muscle development and excess adipose (fatty) tissue in an individual could affect the biomechanics of speech breathing. And indeed, Hoit and Hixon (1986) found clear differences in speech breathing as a function of body type. Overweight subjects used greater abdominal wall activity over that of the rib cage as compared to thin subjects, among other differences. The authors hypothesized that this strategy was associated with diaphragmatic positioning. In the heavier speaker, the additional mass could exert a pull (flattening effect) upon the diaphragm, inhibiting its ability to produce the rapid changes in lung volume required for the inspiratory phase during speech.

Of some interest, despite the differences in lung volumes and capacities between men and women, data suggest that most of the movements of the ribcage and abdomen during speech breathing, as well as syllables per breath group, when normalized (expressed as a percentage of vital capacity), are not sex dependent (Hodge & Rochet, 1989; Hoit, Hixon, Altman, & Morgan, 1989).

Cognitive-Linguistic Variables

Speech is a communication act, and so, the motor activity that results in the speech sound wave is modulated by the variable cognitive and linguistic demands of the communicative context (that is, by what you are thinking, what you are trying to communicate, and what emotion if any you wish to communicate to the person with whom you are speaking). The cognitive-linguistic variables do not alter the basic biomechanics of speech breathing (Hixon et al., 1973; Hodge & Rochet, 1989; Hoit et al., 1989). However, the timing of the inspiratory and expiratory events is affected significantly by such variables. For example, inspiration occurs most frequently at grammatical and semantic boundaries, such as before and after clauses and at the end of sentences (Bailey & Hoit, 2002; Winkworth, Davis, Adams, & Ellis, 1995), suggesting that linguistic features have a regulatory effect upon speech breathing.

Indeed, as listeners, we are so accustomed to inspiratory pauses at linguistically appropriate points that such pauses call attention to themselves when they occur at semantically inappropriate points. In addition, deeper inhalations generally occur prior to longer phrases, as compared with shorter preparatory inhalations before shorter phrases (Winkworth et al., 1995), giving evidence of the effect of cognitive planning on speech breathing. Cognitive load is well known to alter timing of the breathing cycle. Alterations in fluency such as silent pauses (during the expiratory phase when speech would normally occur) are common when formulating thoughts during speech (Greene & Cappella, 1986). Interestingly, the percent of vital capacity at which the utterance occurs is generally independent of cognitive-linguistic load (Mitchell, Hoit, & Watson, 1996). Yet the words per breath group decrease due to the use of silent pauses and slower speech rate. Although this suggests air wastage and therefore inefficiency, one could also interpret this feature as evidence of the constancy or stability of the biomechanics of speech breathing.

Speech Breathing Personality

The specific characteristics of the speech breathing pattern may vary across individuals, and these differences may be quite stable (Benchetrit et al., 1989). These patterns are sometimes called ventilatory or respiratory personality (Dejours, 1996; Shea & Guz, 1992), and we shall refer to this unique pattern as **speech breathing personality**, as that is our particular interest.

Several different speech breathing personalities have been discussed in the literature, such as clavicular, chest, and diaphragmatic breathing.

The focus of these different speech breathing personalities is the relative contribution of the thoracic and the abdominal cavities in support of speech. Much of the research into different breathing strategies originated with Bouhuys, Proctor, and Mead (1966), who explored these styles relative to the demands of singing. Here we restrict our discussion, however, to speech production.

Clavicular breathing is described as over-activity of the pectoral muscles of the upper chest, marked by distinct upward movement of the shoulders, or clavicle. The sternocleidomastoid muscle would be particularly active in this type of breathing. Individuals who have neurologic or lung disease may use this adaptive strategy to compensate for impaired function. It is, however, a highly inefficient means of achieving lung expansion in a healthy individual. Sometimes, clavicular breathing is also referred to as paradoxical breathing because of the tendency for the abdomen to be drawn inward during inspiration, instead of distended slightly outward.

In chest or "high" breathing (Figure 4–17), the abdominal muscles are active, restricting the compression of the abdominal contents as the diaphragm contracts during inhalation (for example, holding in one's stomach). This abdominal muscle activity would be expected to inhibit flattening of the diaphragm and therefore to limit the vertical expansion of the lungs. In theory, limiting vertical expansion would force the thoracic muscles to be engaged more actively, so that the ribs could be elevated. Rib elevation would allow greater expansion in the anteroposterior plane, supposedly in compensation for the limited diaphragmatic lowering. Some evidence during exercise, however (Estenne et al., 1990), suggests that the increased expansion of the thoracic cavity exerts a lateral pull on the diaphragm, resulting in flattening of the diaphragm and vertical expansion of the lungs. This type of breathing style, therefore, may be advantageous in vocal tasks demanding increased breath support, such as singing.

Diaphragmatic breathing, sometimes also referred to as abdominal or "low" breathing, is

Figure 4–17. Patterns of chest and abdominal muscle activity during breathing may vary across individuals as well as activity. Chest or "high" breathing is sometimes referred to as "pear-shaped up," and abdominal or "low" breathing is sometimes referred to as "pear-shaped down." No one style of breathing is correct for everyone in all situations.

Research Methods

How do researchers study changes in speech breathing under different metabolic demands? Two primary methods are used to alter the body's demand for oxygen. One method is to have the subjects increase their level of physical activity while speaking, such as walking or running on a treadmill. The other method is to alter the gas mixture of the inhaled air. The oxygen level is decreased slightly and the carbon dioxide level is increased. Of course, those experiments are performed very carefully and the gas mixture is never altered so much that any subject incurs more than mild risk. In fact, many times the change in gas mixture is equivalent to that which is inhaled when vacationing at a ski resort at 8,000 feet (and the subjects don't have to pay the price of a lift ticket).

regarded as the optimal style, the target pattern, in speech and voice therapy (see Figure 4–17). The abdominal muscles remain engaged, but not to the extent of contraction of chest breathing. As a result, the abdominal contents are distended outward, offering less resistance to the diaphragm, which is allowed to contract and flatten easily. Antagonistic muscle contraction of the thorax is minimized (except for postural stabilization) to keep the chest wall free to expand fully.

Unfortunately, these categories are misleading in their oversimplification, and little empirical evidence exists to support the complete mechanical advantage or disadvantage of these strategies. Furthermore, it is likely that even within one speech breathing personality, the specific demands of a given speech act will result in engagement of different muscles. For example, the sternocleidomastoid and scalene muscles of the neck and the upper trapezius muscles of the back are engaged more actively during speech production that requires extremes of frequency and dynamic range (Pettersen, Bjorkoy, Torp, &

Westgaard, 2005). In addition, some evidence suggests that breathing pattern strategy may be gender based. McCoy (2005) found that trained female singers use more abdominal activity than do trained male singers, although both used thoracic muscle activity quite heavily. Demands of singing, however, are quite different from those of running speech. Nevertheless, it is likely that no single pattern of breathing is optimal for speech.

Respiratory Demands

Our bodies must somehow integrate the demands of speech production with the metabolic or respiratory demands of gas exchange, of getting oxygen into our blood so we stay alive. The exact means by which this balance is achieved are not known for certain. Most of us, however, have had the experience that talking while jogging or working out at the gym causes changes in speech: Breath groups shorten, voice quality becomes breathier and weaker, and loudness control is impaired. Although as speech-language pathologists, we are concerned with the breathing system primarily as a power source for voice and speech production, the metabolic ventilatory demands of the body supersede its communicative function. Too much oxygen (and too little CO_2) in the blood ("overbreathing," or hyperventilation) can result in dizziness, blurred vision, numbness, and tingling. Too little oxygen and too much CO_2 (hypoventilation) can cause impaired cellular respiration, tissue damage, and, ultimately, death.

In a landmark study, Bunn and Mead (1971) assessed speech breathing and respiratory demands during quiet tidal breathing and during reading aloud. They found that ventilation rates were higher during speech breathing than tidal breathing. In fact, these and other speech scientists (Abel, Mottau, Klubendorf, & Koepchen, 1987; Hoit & Lohmeier, 2000) found that speaking is associated with slight hypoventilation. Tidal breathing immediately upon cessation of speaking was found to be variable for a short period, with some speakers demonstrating brief breath-holding to reestablish balanced gas exchange.

Speech breathing during exercise or in a less rich oxygen atmosphere (see Research Methods) will be altered due to the increased ventilatory demands (Bailey & Hoit, 2002; Bunn & Mead, 1971; Doust & Patrick, 1981; Otis & Clark, 1968). Overall, as ventilatory demands increase, the length of the phrase breath group decreases, the expiratory time decreases, and larger lung volumes are used. Rate of speech, however, is unaltered. Bailey and Hoit (2002) note that these adaptations allow a large volume of air to be moved out of the lungs quickly, as would be required in the presence of greater metabolic demand.

Interestingly, adaptation of speech breathing occurs not only in the speaker but also in the listener. In a unique study of conversational

Circular Breathing

Musicians who play wind instruments such as the oboe or clarinet are often required to sustain a note for considerably longer than is possible from using expiratory airflow on a single breath alone. Talented musicians overcome this problem by using a strategy called **circular breathing**, which enables the individual to replenish the volume of air in his or her lungs by inhaling, all the while continuing to blow air out of the mouth and into the wind instrument, thereby breathing and maintaining the musical note simultaneously! How do they accomplish this feat? The oral cavity is used to impound air by using the cheeks as a bellows. As the musician sustains the tone and the lung volume decreases well below resting expiratory level, he (or she) puffs out the cheeks. The resulting increased volume of the oral cavity captures additional air. Try this for yourself. Close your lips, puff out your cheeks, and maintain the posture while you breathe in and out through your nose. Shift the air from one side of your mouth to the other as you continue to breathe. You are adjusting the distribution of the volume of air in your mouth by using your cheek muscles, breathing all the while through the nasal passages by way of the open velopharyngeal port. You are able to maintain your breathing by lowering the velopharyngeal port, thereby sealing off the oral cavity from the rest of the vocal tract. Musicians use their cheek muscles to squeeze the impounded air out of their mouth and through the instrument. After inhalation and subsequent increase in lung volume, the velopharyngeal port is raised and the air is once more exhaled through the oral cavity into the instrument. The back-and-forth shift between nasal airflow plus impounded oral air, and oral airflow while maintaining the appropriate musical note, is quite tricky and requires training.

dyads (partners), McFarland (2001) found that the breathing pattern of the listener approximated that of the speaker, rather than that of quiet tidal breathing. That is, the inspiratory phase shortened and the expiratory phase lengthened. This finding suggests that cognitive-linguistic load on speech breathing is increased not only during speaking but also in processing spoken language. Hixon and Hoit (2005, p. 92) remark that this feature may be characteristic of a larger biological phenomenon in which physiologic systems become coupled (synchronized rhythmically) (Thaut, 2003). Many speakers who are participating in voice therapy due to certain types of voice disorders are often noted to breath-hold while awaiting their turn to speak within a conversation (author's unpublished data). Other linguistic factors may be influencing that behavior, different from the observations of McFarland (2001) but still representative of coupling of the two speech systems. In a different context, a common clinical event is to experience sympathetic breath-holding and other disruptions in breathing when listening to a speaker with a significant fluency or voice problem (also an example of coupling). Exploration of the breathing behavior of listeners who are not conversational partners (such as audience members at a lecture) might reveal interesting information that could contribute to our understanding of the synchronization of speech breathing in different communicative contexts.

Study Questions

21. How is the cycle of inhalation/exhalation altered for running speech, as compared to tidal breathing?

22. Define phase breath group.

23. What are the four important concepts to be learned from the Hixon et al. (1976) study?

24. How might carrying significant excess weight influence speech breathing?

25. How do linguistic factors influence speech breathing?

26. How does cognitive load influence speech breathing?

27. Define speech breathing personality.

28. Provide two examples of different styles of speech breathing and describe how they differ.

29. What is the effect of increased respiratory demands upon phrase breath group length, expiratory time, lung volume, and rate of speech?

4.7 The Work of Breathing

We are concerned with the flow of air in the lungs and vocal tract. Relative to these confined spaces, airflow is the volume of air moving through a given cross section of a tube per unit of time. Recall, at the beginning of this chapter, we noted that air flows because of a pressure difference between two points, moving from greater pressure to lesser pressure. The difference in pressure between the two points is called the **driving pressure**, for it is this difference that causes the volume of air to move (Figure 4–18). Assuming no change in resistance (which will be explained soon), the airflow is directly proportional to the driving pressure, so that if the pressure is doubled, the rate of the flow will double. If the driving pressure is halved, the flow rate will be reduced by half.

Airway Resistance

Recall that work is defined as the product of a force and displacement. Breathing requires work to generate the airflows necessary for voice and speech production. The work performed is largely to overcome resistance to the airflow. **Resistance** is the opposition to movement. The

Figure 4–18. Driving pressure, the difference in pressure between two locations, causes movement of a volume of air.

types of resistance that concern us in regard to breathing are airway resistance, elastic resistance, and viscosity. Airway resistance is examined first. **Airway resistance** is due mainly to the diameter of the airways. The narrower a tube, the more resistance the tube offers to the airflow. (Think about how much work it is to blow through a narrow straw compared to blowing out a puff of air without anything at your lips.) Earlier we stated that airflow is directly proportional to the driving pressure, given no change in resistance. Airflow is inversely proportional to resistance. So accounting for resistance, we can say that the airflow is determined by the ratio of the change in air pressure to resistance. In fact, the lumen (width) of the tube has an extraordinarily large effect on the resistance. If the diameter of the tube is doubled, resistance will be lowered by a factor of 16. If the diameter of the tube is halved, resistance will be raised by a factor of 16. Lung volume influences airway resistance. As lung volume increases (during inhalation), airway resistance decreases because the airways distend (enlarge), so the larger radius lowers the resistance.

The relationship of airway diameter to resistance has significant implications for the path taken by air as we inhale. Almost half of the total resistance of the airway is in the upper airway, specifically the nose, pharynx, and larynx (Baier, Wanner, Zarzecki, & Sackner, 1977; Davis, Bartlett, & Luschei, 1993). The nose extends from the nostrils, or external nares, to the choanae, the internal nares. The choanae empty into the nasopharynx (the nasal part of the pharynx). Each nostril narrows to form a nasal valve. The

total cross-sectional area of the nasal airway at this point is approximately 30 mm^2, narrower than at any other point in the upper airway. The inward airflow must then make a sharp turn as it enters the wider part of the nose (approximately 140 mm^2 lumen) in the area of the turbinates (see Airway Humidification below). The nasal passages represent a tube with a smaller radius compared to the mouth, so they offer greater resistance to the airflow than does the mouth. You would expect, therefore, that the resistance would be increased as the lumen of the air passages in the lungs gets smaller. Approximately 80% of the total airway resistance below the larynx resides in the trachea and the bronchi. Little resistance is offered by the bronchioles and alveoli. This fact may seem in contradiction to our earlier statement that resistance is inversely related to the diameter of the airway. But the air can enter many bronchioles simultaneously (the bronchioles are "in parallel"), so that the resistance is quite low.

The nervous system also regulates airway resistance. Specifically, the autonomic nervous system controls airway constriction. Recall from Overview of Neuroanatomic Terms and Organization on page 66 that the autonomic nervous system is composed of the sympathetic and parasympathetic systems. The sympathetic system, designed to prepare the body for emergency activity, dilates or widens the airways, which lowers resistance and eases the work of breathing. The parasympathetic system, designed to conserve visceral function, constricts airways, which increases resistance.

Airway Humidification

The major purpose of the upper airway, beyond serving as a transport system to move air into the lower airway, is to condition the air —add humidification and remove pollutants. The turbinates are folds of tissue within the nose, covering a large surface area (150 cm²). The vascular mucosal erectile tissue that covers the turbinates is important in conditioning the air we breathe in. Unfortunately, the mucosal tissue covering the turbinates has the potential to swell substantially when irritated by colds or allergies. However, the turbinate mucosa swells normally during breathing, but in an asymmetric fashion, so that one nostril offers more resistance to the airflow than the other. When we breathe through our nose, we alternate breathing through one nostril dominantly for a few hours and then cycle to the other nostril. Transit time for the air during nasal breathing is less than 0.1 second, during which time, in room-temperature breathing, the air is raised from 68°F to 88°F. When the air enters the trachea, it is a toasty 95°F. In addition to being warmed, the air is also humidified, reaching almost the point of saturation by the time it enters the trachea. Contrary to popular belief, it is not necessary to breathe through the nose to humidify the air. The mouth humidifies the air well but does not provide the initial filtering capabilities that the nose can provide. Most of the particles we inhale are trapped in the sticky mucus along the walls of the nasal cavity, which is then moved into the pharynx by the beating cilia (tiny hairs) and ultimately swallowed. (Dog lovers take note. The cilia in a dog's nose beat in the opposite direction, causing the mucus to exit the nose. Hence the dog's perpetually wet nose.) Despite the ability of the oral cavity to humidify inspired air, persistent oral breathing may dehydrate the superficial lining of the mucosa of the airway and vocal folds (Sivasankar & Fisher, 2002).

Laminar and Turbulent Airflow

We have assumed throughout our discussion so far that the airflow is smooth, orderly, straight, and uninterrupted. Such flow is called laminar. When air flows at high velocity, particularly through an airway that has irregular walls, the flow is not laminar, but disorganized, with the tendency to form little circular whirlpools, called eddies. This type of flow is called turbulent (Figure 4–19) and is found mainly in the largest airways, such as the trachea. In **turbulent flow**, a large portion of the movement of the air is not parallel to the axis of the tube. Instead, the fluid flows at all angles, even backward. To sustain turbulent flow, a larger driving pressure is required compared to **laminar flow**. The relationship of airway resistance to flow rate when the airflow is turbulent is considerably more complex. No

Figure 4–19. Laminar airflow is smooth and orderly. Turbulent airflow is disorderly and forms circular whirlpools. A larger driving pressure is required to sustain turbulent airflow than to sustain laminar airflow.

easily defined proportional relationship exists between resistance, flow, and driving pressure for turbulent flow. During quiet tidal breathing, laminar flow exists in the lower bronchi and bronchioles. Transitional flow, which is partly laminar and partly turbulent, exists in between the trachea and the lower bronchii. During forced inspiration, the trachea expands to assist in lowering resistance to the flow and increasing volume to lower air pressure.

Elastic Resistance

In addition to airway resistance, the work of breathing arises from the need to overcome elastic resistance. **Elastic resistance** refers to the work required to prevent tissue from springing back to its original shape, once deformed, in order to change the volume of the thoracic cavity and lungs. The relaxation curve discussed earlier describes the forces relative to elastic resistance. During quiet breathing, the work of breathing represents a bit less than 5% of our total metabolic rate. Deep, slow breathing requires the most work to be done against the elastic resistance of the tissues, whereas rapid shallow breathing requires the most work to be done against the resistance of the airways. In the deeper breathing required for prolonged speech utterances or loud speech, maintaining appropriate posture helps to minimize the additional work done against the elastic resistance of the lungs and thorax.

Dyspnea

The term dyspnea refers to the sensation of work to breathe. It is a highly complex perception that is not completely understood. A variety of situations can cause one to feel "out of breath" or that breathing is effortful or "hard work." Dyspnea can be experienced when the breathing rate is elevated, the load opposing muscle contraction is increased (cocontraction of antagonist muscles, for example), or when the muscles are weakened, such as in certain diseases (Ripamonti & Bruera, 1997). When we "underbreathe" or "overbreathe," we may perceive dyspnea, as the level of inappropriate breathing corresponds proportionately to the level of dyspnea perceived.

Smoking and Breathing

It is evident that the elasticity of the lungs is a critical feature of normal breathing function. Diseases of the lungs affect the elasticity in different ways. In medicine, the elasticity of the lungs usually is expressed in terms of compliance. **Compliance** is the change in the volume of a container produced by a change in the pressure across the walls of the container. It reflects the ease with which the lungs or chest wall are stretched. In diseases that cause lowered compliance, more work is required to inhale. In diseases that cause abnormally high compliance, more work is required to exhale. Emphysema is a lung disease caused predominately by smoking. It causes the walls between the alveoli to break down. The radii of the alveoli are therefore enlarged, reducing the inward pressure, making it easier to expand the lungs. In other words, the lungs have a greater compliance. But there is a loss of elastic recoil, and it is more difficult to compress the lungs and therefore exhale. People with advanced emphysema have a barrel-shaped chest. The more expanded lungs generate less of an elastic recoil force on the thoracic cavity, and therefore the ribcage is allowed to expand more than when coupled to a pair of healthy lungs. No cure for emphysema exists. Quitting smoking and some medical treatments can help slow down its progress. Smoking causes death through lung cancer and emphysema. Smoking is an incredibly foolish habit to start and a terrifically difficult habit to stop.

Viscosity

Viscosity is a measure of the internal friction of a fluid. **Friction** is a force that results in a drag on an object, slowing it down (Figure 4–20). We are familiar with the force of friction in everyday life. We may not think about friction within a fluid quite as readily, however. Perhaps the easiest way to understand viscosity is to pour some different fluids. Water, which has a low viscosity, spills out of its container very easily. Maple syrup has a high viscosity and pours more slowly. Honey, even more viscous, pours more slowly still. Honey is more viscous than maple syrup, and both are more viscous than water. Most of us have experienced walking through water, such as in a pool or lake. We know that it is more difficult than walking on dry land, because water is more viscous than air. The water offers greater resistance to our body than does the air. Similarly, if you have ever been in a sauna, perhaps you may have felt that it was a bit more difficult to breathe. That is because the extra moisture adds to the overall viscosity of the air.

Study Questions

30. Define airway resistance.

31. How does the structural design of the airway system affect resistance? Include specifically the nasal and oral portions of the airway and the bronchial trees.

32. How does the nervous system regulate airway resistance?

33. Define turbulent and laminar airflow.

34. What is the relationship of airway resistance and type of airflow?

35. Define elastic resistance.

36. Define viscosity and friction.

4.8 Instrumentation for Measuring Breathing Kinematics

We address only a small portion of the instrumentation available for conducting research on speech breathing. Much of the information about speech breathing behaviors is based on research that has assessed muscle activity using electromyography. (In fact, as we shall discover in Chapter 5, a considerable amount of information about phonation also is based on electromyographic studies.) Movement of large groups of muscles that change lung volume and the relative size of the chest and abdomen is based on another type of instrumentation, called noninductive plethysmography. We reserve our discussion of instrumentation and measures of aerodynamics for Chapters 6 and beyond, after we have addressed laryngeal and articulatory biomechanics.

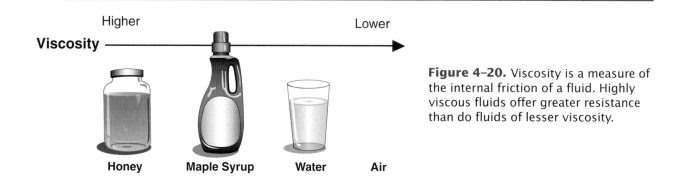

Figure 4–20. Viscosity is a measure of the internal friction of a fluid. Highly viscous fluids offer greater resistance than do fluids of lesser viscosity.

Electromyography (EMG)

Electromyography is the study of the electrical activity of muscles (Basmajian & Deluca, 1985). When a motor neuron fires, it sends an electrical signal, called an action potential, to the muscle fibers. The action potential causes a change in the chemical balance of the muscle fibers, called depolarization. This electrical activity results in a muscle twitch (contraction). The depolarization generates an electrical field around the muscle fibers, called a muscle fiber action potential. The motor neuron together with all the muscle fibers that it innervates (provides neural input to) is called a motor unit. The muscle fiber action potentials from all the muscle fibers of a single motor unit are called the motor unit action potential (MUAP). Motor unit action potentials can be detected and measured by electrodes, sensors designed to measure electrical activity.

EMG electrodes are of three types: surface, needle, and hooked-wire. Surface electrodes can detect the change in muscle electrical activity on the surface of the skin covering the muscle. However, often the muscle is not close to the skin or is surrounded by other active muscles, making it difficult for the surface electrode to "hear" the activity of a specific muscle, or to distinguish among different muscle contractions.

Needle and hooked-wire electrodes are inserted directly into the muscle and more accurately can detect and identify action potentials. Needle electrodes are used in very small muscles only because large muscle movement can displace the needle, resulting in erroneous readings for the researcher and increased discomfort for the subject. The procedure is usually only mildly uncomfortable, depending upon the muscles being assessed, but nevertheless the procedure is invasive, and some muscles can be difficult to access. Hooked-wire electrodes are placed more securely within the muscle and are less likely to be displaced by large movements.

The strong advantage of EMG technology is the ability to measure muscle activity quantitatively, particularly the activity of different muscles for the same event (such as an inhalation or vocalization). Disadvantages of EMG, in addition to physical discomfort, include the difficulty that can arise in making sure that the target muscle under study is indeed the muscle that is being measured. Furthermore, because different motor unit action potentials within the same muscle may be activated differently, the exact placement of the needle or hooked-wire electrode can be of critical importance. The output of the EMG, called an electromyogram (Figure 4–21), shows the electrical activity of an entire muscle, called the interference pattern.

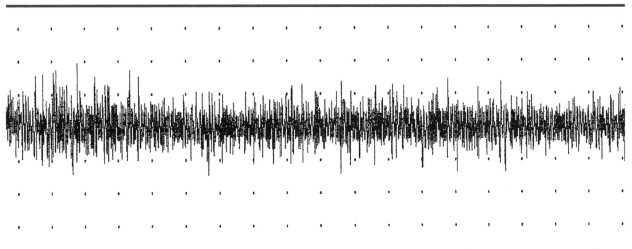

Figure 4–21. Recording of the electrical activity of the left thyroarytenoid muscle (the muscle of the vocal folds) during phonation. Each horizontal division represents 200 milliseconds.

Kotby et al. (1992) provide a historical review of electromyography. They note that laryngeal electromyography (LEMG) began with Weddell, Feinstein, and Pattle (1944) using electrodes inserted from within the throat. Fink, Basch, and Epanchin (1956) began to use percutaneous insertion (through the skin from the outside of the body). In Chapter 5, we will find that EMG has been used heavily to determine the activity of the laryngeal muscles in control of fundamental frequency and intensity. And in Chapter 7, we will note the application of EMG to articulatory muscle activity. The application of EMG to speech breathing is not as common, largely due to the difficulty of accessing the deep muscles, such as the diaphragm. EMG has been used, however, to explore chest wall movements during speech breathing in healthy speakers (Estenne et al., 1990; Hoit, Plassman, Lansing, & Hixon, 1988) and in speakers who stutter (Denny & Smith, 2000). Surface electrodes, despite their disadvantages as described above, have been used to explore respiratory muscle activity during speech (McFarland & Smith, 1989), and when used in clinical application for patient feedback during therapy, their noninvasiveness outweighs their lack of precision (Hixon & Hoit, 2005). Hixon, Siebens, and Minifie (1969) did, however, conduct EMG investigation of the diaphragm with specially designed surface electrodes. EMG research in speech breathing, voice, and speech production has a long and rich history (Hirose, 1971).

Respiratory Inductance Plethysmography

Inductance plethysmography measures the change in lung volume during breathing and the relative contributions of the abdomen and rib cage. A wire coil, arranged in a zigzag pattern, is attached to a band that is wrapped around the chest. A second band is wrapped around the abdomen. As the chest wall and abdomen expand and contract during breathing, the coils similarly expand and contract. Stone (1996) explains the mechanism of inductance plethysmography as follows. As the length of the coils within the bands

change, the ratio of the diameter of the band to the length changes, which results in a change in the inductance. Inductance is the opposition to change in the flow of an electrical current. A magnetic field is created by current flow through the wire, and conversely, a magnetic field can create current flow. The current created by the magnetic field (the induced current) flows in the direction opposite to and out of phase with the original current flow, resulting in interference, called *reactance*, which acts to slow down or speed up the flow of the original current. The strength of the magnetic field is proportional to the current flow. The inductance properties (the changes in the current) depend upon the diameter-to-length ratio. Therefore, as the wire stretches with lung volume changes, the inductance properties change. The appropriate transducers and circuitry measure the inductance changes proportional to the lung volume changes during breathing.

Hoit and Hixon (1987) established procedures for making chest wall kinematic observations. Commercial units such as the Inductotrace (formerly, Respitrace: Ambulatory Monitoring, Ardsley, NY) and the Respigraph (Non-Invasive Monitoring Systems, Miami Beach, FL) have been widely available, and as a result, inductance plethysmography has been widely used in the study of chest wall kinematics in normal and abnormal speech breathing (Sperry, Hillman, & Perkell, 1994; Warren, Morr, Rochet, & Dalston, 1989; Winkworth et al., 1995).

Study Questions

37. What is electromyography (EMG)? Include a description of the three types of electrodes that may be used with EMG.

38. What are the advantages and disadvantages of using EMG?

39. What does inductance plethysmography measure, and how does it work?

Recommended Internet Sites for Further Learning

http://academicearth.org/courses/human-anatomy-dissection

University of Michigan Human Anatomy dissection. Videos of anatomic dissection of different parts of the body.

http://oac.med.jhmi.edu/res_phys/Tutorial-Menu.html

Johns Hopkins School of Medicine's tutorials in respiration. Provides nice, short tutorials in many of the topics covered in this chapter.

http://www.acbrown.com/lung/index.htm

Professor A. C. Brown Physiology and Neuroscience websites. Provides tutorials, quizzes, and references on respiratory topics.

References

Abel, H., Mottau, B., Klubendorf, D., & Koepchen, H. (1987). Pattern of different components of the respiratory cycle and autonomic parameters during speech. In G. Sieck, S. Gandevia, & W. Cameron (Eds.), *Respiratory muscles and their neuromotor control* (pp. 109–113). New York, NY: Alan R. Liss.

Abercrombie, D., & Dixon, A. St. J. (1965). *Studies in phonetics and linguistics*. London, UK: Oxford University Press.

Argiolas, A., & Melis, M. R. (1998). The neuropharmacology of yawning. *European Journal of Pharmacology, 34*, 1–16.

Baier, H., Wanner, A., Zarzecki, S., & Sackner, M. A. (1977). Relationships among glottis opening, respiratory flow, and upper airway resistance in humans. *Journal of Applied Physiology, 43*, 603–611.

Bailey, E., & Hoit, J. (2002). Speaking and breathing in high respiratory drive. *Journal of Speech, Language, and Hearing Research, 45*, 89–99.

Basmajian, J. V., & Deluca, C. J. (1985). *Muscles alive: Their functions revealed by electromyography*. Baltimore, MD: Williams & Wilkins.

Benarroch, E. E., Westmoreland, B. F., Daube, J. R., Reagan, T. J., & Sandok, B. A. (1999). *Medical neurosciences: An approach to anatomy, pathology, and physiology by systems and levels* (4th ed.). Philadelphia, PA: Lippincott-Raven.

Benchetrit, G., Shea, S., Pham, Dinh, T., Bodocco, S., Baconnier, P., & Guz, A. (1989). Individuality of breathing patterns in adults assessed over time. *Respiration Physiology, 75*, 199–210.

Bouhuys, A., Proctor, D., & Mead, J. (1966). Kinetic aspects of singing. *Journal of Applied Physiology, 31*, 870–872.

Bunn, J., & Mead, J. (1971). Control of ventilation during speech. *Journal of Applied Physiology, 31*, 870–872.

Campbell, E. (1958). *The respiratory muscles and the mechanics of breathing*. Chicago, IL: Yearbook Medical.

Davies, A., & Moore, C. (2003). *The respiratory system*. Edinburgh, UK: Churchill Livingstone.

Davis, P. J., Bartlett, D. A., Jr., & Luschei, E. S. (1993). Coordination of the respiratory and laryngeal systems in breathing and vocalization. In I. R Titze (Ed.), *Vocal fold physiology: Frontiers in basic science* (pp. 189–226). San Diego, CA: Singular.

Dejours, P. (1996). *Respiration*. New York, NY: Oxford University Press.

Denny, M., & Smith, A. (2000). Respiratory control in stuttering speakers: Evidence from respiratory highfrequency oscillations. *Journal of Speech, Language, and Hearing Research, 43*, 1024–1037.

Dickson, D. R., & Maue-Dickson, W. (1996). *Anatomical and physiological bases of speech*. Boston, MA: Butterworth-Heinemann.

Doust, J., & Patrick, J. (1981). The limitation of exercise ventilation during speech. *Respiration Physiology, 46*, 137–147.

Draper, M. H., Ladefoged, P., & Whitteridge, D. (1959). Respiratory muscles in speech. *Journal of Speech and Hearing Research, 2*, 16–27.

Duffy, J. R. (2005). *Motor speech disorders: Substrates, differential diagnosis and management* (2nd ed.). St. Louis, MO: Mosby.

Estenne, M., Zocchi, I., Warl, M., & Macklem, P. T. (1990). Chest wall motion and expiratory muscle use during phonation in normal humans. *Journal of Applied Physiology, 68*, 2075–2082.

Faaborg-Andersen, K. (1957). Electromyographic investigation of intrinsic laryngeal muscles in humans. *Acta Physiologica Scandinavia, 41*, 1–147.

Fink, B. R., Basch, M., & Epanchin, V. (1956). The mechanism of opening of the human larynx. *Laryngoscope, 66*, 410–425.

Gallup, A. C., & Eldakar, O. T. (2011). Contagious yawning and seasonal climate variation. *Frontiers in Evolutionary Neuroscience, 22,* doi:10.3389/fnevo.2011. 00003

Gracco, V. L., & Abbs, J. H. (1986). Variant and invariant characteristics of speech movements. *Experimental Brain Research, 65,* 156–166.

Greene, J., & Cappella, J. (1986). Cognition and talk: The relationship of semantic units to temporal patterns of fluency in spontaneous speech. *Language and Speech, 29,* 141–157.

Hirose, H. (1971). Electromyography of articulatory muscles: Current instrumentation and technique. *Haskings Labs Status Reports, 25/26,* 73–86.

Hixon, T. J., Goldman, M. D., & Mead, J. (1973). Kinematics of the chest wall during speech production. *Journal of Speech and Hearing Research, 16,* 78–115.

Hixon, T. J., & Hoit, J. D. (2005). *Evaluation and management of speech breathing disorders: Principles and methods.* Tucson, AZ: Redington Brown.

Hixon, T. J., Mead, J., & Goldman, M. D. (1976). Dynamics of the chest wall during speech production: Function of the thorax, rib cage, diaphragm, and abdomen. *Journal of Speech and Hearing Research, 19,* 297–356.

Hixon, T. J., Siebens, A. A., & Minifie, F. D. (1969). An EMG electrode for the diaphragm. *Journal of the Acoustical Society of America, 46,* 1588–1590.

Hodge, M., & Rochet, A. (1989). Characteristics of speech breathing in young women. *Journal of Speech and Hearing Research, 32,* 466–480.

Hoit, J. D., & Hixon, T. (1986). Body type and speech breathing. *Journal of Speech and Hearing Research, 29,* 313–324.

Hoit, J. D., & Hixon, T. (1987). *Evaluation and management of speech breathing disorders: Principles and methods.* Tucson, AZ: Redington Brown.

Hoit, J., Hixon, T., Altman, M., & Morgan, W. (1989). Speech breathing in women. *Journal of Speech and Hearing Research, 32,* 353–365.

Hoit, J., Hixon, T. J., Watson, P. J., & Morgan, W. J. (1990). Speech breathing in children and adolescents. *Journal of Speech and Hearing Research, 33,* 51–69.

Hoit, J., & Lohmeier, H. (2000). Influence of continuous speaking on ventilation. *Journal of Speech, Language, and Hearing Research, 43,* 1240–1251.

Hoit, J. D., Plassman, B. L., Lansing, R. W., & Hixon, T. J. (1988). Abdominal muscle activity during speech production. *Journal of Applied Physiology, 65,* 2656–2664.

Hughes, O. M., & Abbs, J. H. (1976). Labial-mandibular coordination in the production of speech: Implications for the operation of motor equivalence. *Phonetica, 33,* 199–221.

Isshiki, N. (1964). Regulatory mechanism of voice intensity variation. *Journal of Speech and Hearing Research, 7,* 17–29.

Jürgens, U. (2002). Neural pathways underlying vocal control. *Neuroscience and Biobehavioral Reviews, 26,* 235–258.

Kotby, M. N., Fadley, E., Madkour, O., Barakah M., Khidr, A., Alloush, T., & Saleh, M. (1992). Electromyography and neurography in neurolaryngology. *Journal of Voice, 6,* 159–187.

Lieber, R. L. (2002). *Skeletal muscle structure, function and plasticity: The physiological basis of rehabilitation.* Philadelphia, PA: Lippincott Williams & Wilkins.

McCoy, S. (2005). Breath management: Gender-based differences in classical singers. *Folia Phoniatrica et Logopedica, 57,* 246–254.

McFarland, D. (2001). Respiratory markers of conversational interaction. *Journal of Speech, Language, and Hearing Research, 44,* 128–143.

McFarland, D. H., & Smith, A. (1989). Surface recordings of respiratory muscle activity during speech: Some preliminary findings. *Journal of Speech and Hearing Research, 32,* 657–667.

Mitchell, H., Hoit, J., & Watson, P. (1996). Cognitive-linguistic demands and speech breathing. *Journal of Speech and Hearing Research, 39,* 93–104.

Moore, C. A., Caulfield, T. J., & Green, J. R. (2001). Relative kinematics of the rib cage and abdomen during speech and nonspeech behaviors of 15-month-old children. *Journal of Speech, Language, and Hearing Research, 44,* 80–94.

Nakazawa, K., Shiba, K., Satoh, I., Yoshida, K., Nakajima, Y., & Konno, A. (1997). Role of pulmonary afferent inputs in vocal on-switch in the cat. *Neuroscience Research, 29,* 49–54.

Newsom Davis, J., & Sears, T. A. (1970). The proprioceptive reflex control of the intercostal muscles during their voluntary activation. *Journal of Physiology, 209,* 711–738.

Otis, A., & Clark, R. (1968). Ventilatory implications of phonation and phonatory implications of ventilation. In A. Bouhuys (Ed.), *Speech production in man* (pp. 122–128). New York, NY: Annals of the New York Academy of Sciences.

Pettersen, V., Bjorkoy, K., Torp, H., & Westgaard, R. H. (2005). Neck and shoulder muscle activity and thorax movement in singing tasks with variation in vocal loudness and pitch. *Journal of Voice, 19,* 623–634.

Provine, R. R., Hammernik, H. B., & Curchack, B. B. (1987). Yawning relation to sleeping and stretching in humans. *Ethology, 76,* 152–160.

Rahn, H. A., Otis, L. E., Chadwick, & Fenn, W. (1946). The pressure-volume diagram of the thorax and lung. *American Journal of Physiology, 146,* 161–178.

Reilly, K. J., & Moore, C. A. (2003). Respiratory sinus arrhythmia during speech production. *Journal of Speech, Language, and Hearing Research, 46,* 164–177.

Ripamonti, C., & Bruera, E. (1997). Dyspnea: Pathophysiology and assessment. *Journal of Pain and Symptom Management, 13,* 220-232.

Shea, S., & Guz, A. (1992). Personnalite ventiltoire: An overview. *Respiration Physiology, 52,* 275–291.

Sivasankar, M., & Fisher, K. V. (2002). Oral breathing increases Pth and vocal effort by superficial drying of vocal fold mucosa. *Journal of Voice, 16,* 172–181.

Sperry, E. E., Hillman, R. E., & Perkell, J. S. (1994). The use of inductance plethysmography to assess respiratory function in a patient with vocal nodules. *Journal of Medical Speech-Language Pathology, 2,* 137–145.

Stone, M. (1996). Instrumentation for the study of speech physiology. In N. J. Lass (Ed.), *Principles of experimental phonetics* (pp. 495–524). St. Louis, MO: Mosby.

Thaut, M. H. (2003). Neural basis of rhythmic timing networks in the human brain. *Annals of the New York Academy of Sciences, 999,* 364–373.

Warren, R. H., Morr, K., Rochet, A., & Daltson, R. (1989). Respiratory response to a decrease in velopharyngeal resistance. *Journal of the Acoustical Society of America, 86,* 917–924.

Weddell, G., Feinstein, B., & Pattle, R. E. (1944). The electrical activity of voluntary muscle in man under normal and pathological conditions. *Brain, 67,* 178–257.

Wilson, T. A., Legrand, A., Gevenois, P. A., & De Troyer, A. (2001). Respiratory effects of the external and internal intercostal muscles in humans. *Journal of Physiology, 530,* 319–330.

Winkworth, A. L., Davis, P. J., Adams, R. D., & Ellis, E. (1995). Breathing patterns during spontaneous speech. *Journal of Speech and Hearing Research, 38,* 124–144.

Zemlin, W. R. (1998). *Speech and hearing science: Anatomy and physiology* (4th ed.). Needham Heights, MA: Allyn & Bacon.

5

Phonation I:
Basic Voice Science

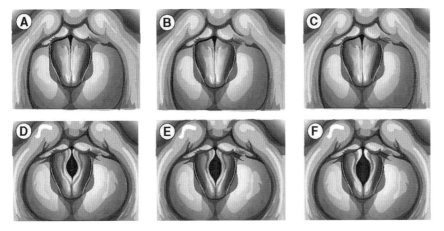

Figure 5–1. Vocal fold vibration captured with high-speed digital imaging. From "Analysis of Vocal Fold Vibrations From High Speed Laryngeal Images Using Hilbert Transform-Based Methodology," by Y. Yan, K. Ahmad, M. Kunduk, and D. Bless, 2005, *Journal of Voice, 19*, p. 163. Reprinted with permission from the Voice Foundation.

A voice is such a deep, personal reflection of character.

—Sir Daniel Day-Lewis, English Actor (1957–)

Clinical Case 2: Running Out of Breath

Clinical cases are based upon real patients whom the author has treated. Evaluation and treatment information has been edited to focus upon specific features related to the chapters. Note that clinical cases incorporate information that is covered in this and other chapters (and some information about diagnosis and therapy that you will learn in future courses). You are encouraged to review this case before you begin your study of this chapter and once again after you have completed the chapter. You may also want to revisit this case later in the semester after you have covered additional chapters.

Christine was a 29-year-old marketing assistant for a startup technology firm. The company was young and small, and every employee handled multiple jobs. But Christine loved her work and didn't mind the long hours and the hectic pace. However, since recovering from the flu a couple of months prior, in which she had a persistent cough (but went to work anyway!), she found that her voice would get hoarse and fatigued toward the end of the day. By the end of the week, it was a tremendous effort to get any sound out at all. She was otherwise quite healthy, and her otolaryngology visit revealed normal vocal folds. Significant squeezing of the larynx was noted upon endoscopic examination. She was given a diagnosis of muscle tension dysphonia (MTD)—a voice disorder in the absence of any laryngeal pathology characterized by use of excessive muscular effort during phonation—and voice therapy was recommended.

At her voice evaluation, vocal quality was mildly hoarse and moderately strained (that is, it sounded as though voice production was effortful). Christine's self-assessment of her voice disorder (using the Voice Handicap Index—a survey of questions designed to assess patients' perception of their voice problem) was a score of 45, suggesting the perception of a moderate vocal handicap. (People

without dysphonia generally score between 0 and 11, approximately.) Jitter and shimmer values were elevated, but H:N was within normal limits. Of note, she was observed to speak using excessively long phrase groups prior to pausing to inhale. Her phrase endings typically were produced with vocal fry and significantly reduced loudness. Overall, her rate of speech sounded quite rapid. She was also noted to use a forward head posture—as though she were jutting her jaw forward and trying to make a strong impact upon the listener with her words.

It was hypothesized that her MTD was associated with use of excessive laryngeal and upper thoracic tension. The tension appeared to arise from long phrase breath groups, which in turn was caused by the rapid rate of speech and the effort to maintain adequate lung pressure for phonation as her lung volume decreased below resting expiratory level. Simply put, she was not pausing to inhale! The flu and persistent cough were likely the precipitating factor for the MTD. While Christine was using *insufficient* breath support at the end of her phrases, her speech breathing pattern is better characterized as *inefficient*, because she starts out each phrase with sufficient lung pressure.

To test this hypothesis, stimulability testing was conducted using a reading task marked for places to pause and inhale. Christine was guided to shorten her breath groups and pause to inhale briefly after each breath group. Vocal quality improved markedly. Voice therapy was initiated. The major therapy goal was to maximize coordination of breathing with phonation by shortening phrase breath groups and increasing use of short inhalations (catch-breaths) to replenish lung volume. Although Christine reported that she found this new style of speech breathing to be less fatiguing and it resulted in a more pleasant voice, she expressed concern that talking "so slowly" at her fast-paced job would result in her getting cut off by others and her opinions not being heard. Video feedback of her new speaking style helped her to recognize that her speech was not too slow, and the positive feedback she received at work further served to reinforce use of her new speech breathing pattern.

Clinical Case Discussion Questions

1. What is the relationship between lung pressure and phrase breath groups? Revisit Figures 4–14 and 4–15 and relate Christine's speech breathing habits to the relaxation pressure curve.

2. Why would Christine demonstrate vocal fry and decreased intensity at phrase endings? (*Hint*: What is the relationship between lung pressure and vocal fold stiffness and vocal fry?)

3. Compare Clinical Case 1 from Chapter 4 with this clinical case. How do the inefficient speech breathing patterns compare?

4. How is the acoustic theory of speech production (see Chapter 7) relevant to Christine's speech-voice deficit?

5.1 Overview

Phonation is the generation of sound by means of vocal fold vibration. The vocal folds, a pair of multilayered folds of tissues situated in the larynx, convert the aerodynamic energy generated by the lungs into acoustic energy in the form of sound waves. Unlike musical instruments—such as a violin with its oscillating strings or a flute with its vibrating column of air—the vocal folds vibrate rapidly open and closed to produce puffs of air consisting of oscillating air molecules. The oscillating puffs of air travel up the vocal tract and out the mouth and nose. Audible perceptual characteristics of the voice—the pitch, loudness, and quality—are defined by the air pressure from the lungs, the forces of the muscles within and external to the larynx, the biomechanical properties of the vocal folds, and the shape of the vocal tract above the vocal folds.

5.2 Anatomy of the Larynx

Only a very brief presentation of the laryngeal structures is provided here. You are strongly encouraged to refer to one of the many excellent anatomy texts for more in-depth presentation.

Structural Framework

The vocal folds are housed within the larynx, a structure composed of multiple cartilages connected by ligaments, membranes, and muscles (Figure 5–2). (Ligaments are ropelike structures, whereas membranes are sheet-like, flat structures.) The larynx extends from the root of the

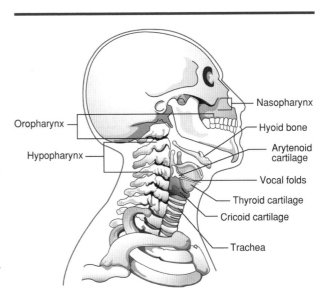

Figure 5–2. Laryngeal cartilaginous structures in anatomic relationship. Adapted from *The Larynx: A Multidisciplinary Approach* (2nd ed., p. 34), by M. P. Fried, 1996, Mosby.

tongue to the top of the trachea in the anterior of the neck or throat at the level of cervical vertebrae four, five, and six. Anteriorly, the larynx is covered by skin, fascia, and muscle. The pharynx is lateral and posterior to the larynx. The hypopharynx is the space just below the pharynx.

Three paired and three unpaired cartilages comprise the larynx (Figures 5–3 and 5–4). The cartilages are connected by ligaments and lined with mucous membranes. The unpaired cartilages are the cricoid, thyroid, and epiglottis. The paired cartilages are the arytenoids, corniculate, and cuneiform. (The cuneiform cartilages do not play a substantial role in voice production, so we will ignore them here.) The cricoid cartilage, often likened to a signet ring (*krikos* means "ring" in Greek) in shape with a broader back than front, is the lowermost cartilage, connected to the trachea by a fibroelastic membrane. The largest cartilage, the thyroid, immediately superior to (just above) the cricoid cartilage, articulates with the cricoid via paired processes (a prominent or projecting part of a structure) that comprise the cricothyroid joint, allowing the larynx to rock back and forth. (The "Adam's apple," usually more prominent in men, is the notch of the thyroid cartilage.) The paired arytenoid cartilages ride atop the back of the cricoid cartilage, articulating by means of the cricoarytenoid joints. The corniculate cartilages sit on the

uppermost surface of the arytenoid cartilages, raising the height of the arytenoid complexes. The epiglottis, often described as leaf-like in

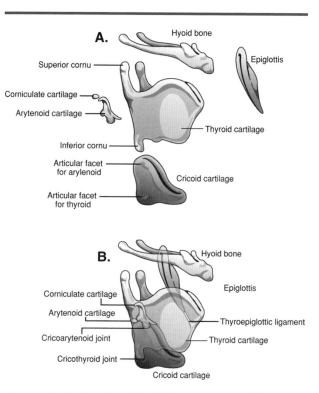

Figure 5–3. Disarticulated (**A**) and normal (**B**) larynx side views. Adapted from *The Larynx: A Multidisciplinary Approach* (2nd ed., p. 35), by M. P. Fried, 1996, Mosby.

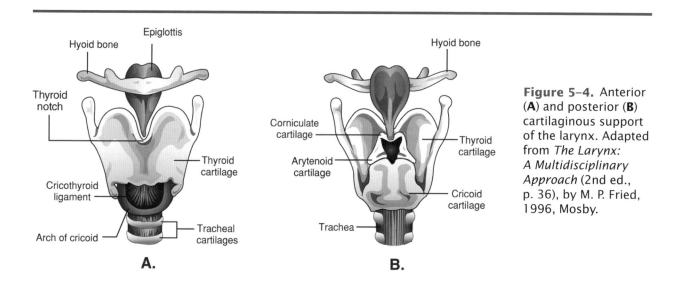

A.

B.

Figure 5–4. Anterior (**A**) and posterior (**B**) cartilaginous support of the larynx. Adapted from *The Larynx: A Multidisciplinary Approach* (2nd ed., p. 36), by M. P. Fried, 1996, Mosby.

shape, sits immediately inside the anterior surface of the thyroid cartilage, attached only at its inferior end to the inner thyroid cartilage by ligaments. The cricoid, thyroid, and most of the arytenoid cartilages are all composed of hyaline cartilage, which tends to ossify (harden into bone) within the sixth decade of life. The epiglottis and corniculate cartilages, as well as the portion of the arytenoid cartilages to which the vocal folds attach, are composed of elastic cartilage and therefore do not ossify but remain flexible through life. The average length of the larynx is 44 mm in men, with a diameter of 43 mm. Length and diameter of the larynx in women are, on average, 36 mm and 41 mm, respectively.

One more anatomic structure should be described in connection with the larynx: the hyoid bone. The hyoid bone is an unpaired, slightly horseshoe-shaped structure, located just above the thyroid cartilage in the anterior wall of the hypopharynx. Ossification of the hyoid occurs early in life. The hyoid is the only bone in the body that does not articulate directly with another bone. Although not strictly part of the larynx, it is often considered part of the larger laryngeal framework because of its role in supporting the larynx. The hyoid bone articulates with the left and right superior processes of the

thyroid cartilage by means of an extrinsic ligament, the thyrohyoid membrane. It attaches to the base of the tongue superiorly via the glossoepiglottic ligaments and therefore serves the important function of connecting tongue movement to laryngeal and supraglottal movement. The hyoid functions as an anchor point for numerous muscles. The glossoepiglottic ligaments and their overlying mucous membranes form the right and left valleculae, small wells on either side of the posterior larynx.

Laryngeal Membranes and Cavities

The extrinsic ligaments attach the larynx to the hyoid bone superiorly and to the trachea inferiorly (Figures 5–5, 5–6, 5–7, and 5–8). They consist of the thyrohyoid membrane, the cricothyroid membrane, and the thyroepiglottic, hyoepiglottic, and cricotracheal ligaments (Figure 5–9).

The cartilages of the larynx, together with the hyoid bone, are interconnected by a fibroelastic membrane, which is composed of individual intrinsic ligaments. The inside, or cavity, of the larynx forms a tube continuous with the lower airway (the trachea and the lungs) and the upper airway (the pharynx, nose, and mouth). The fibroelastic membrane is covered by a mucous membrane, which forms a wet and relatively smooth lining of the cavity that helps to maximize its aerodynamic properties, as we discuss later in the chapter. The intrinsic ligaments are composed of the quadrangular membranes, and aryepiglottic folds, both located above the vocal folds, the vocal ligament within the vocal folds, and the conus elasticus below the vocal folds. The quadrangular membranes extend from the arytenoids and the inner thyroid cartilage to the epiglottis, forming the ventricular folds. The upper lateral edge of the quadrangular membrane covers the aryepiglottic muscles, which run from the apex of the arytenoid cartilages to the sides of the epiglottis, forming the aryepiglottic folds. The conus elasticus makes up the upper walls of the trachea immediately below the vocal folds. The uppermost border of the conus elasticus comprises the vocal ligament,

Clinical Assessment of the Thyrohyoid Membrane

One type of voice disorder is called muscle tension dysphonia (MTD). MTD is generally believed to be characterized by excessive contraction of the intrinsic and extrinsic laryngeal muscles, or cocontraction of agonist and antagonist muscles. One of the components of the diagnostic workup for a patient suspected of having MTD is palpation (manipulation with the hand on the neck) of the thyrohyoid space. If the thyrohyoid space is foreshortened or asymmetric (one side more contracted than the other), MTD is often suspected.

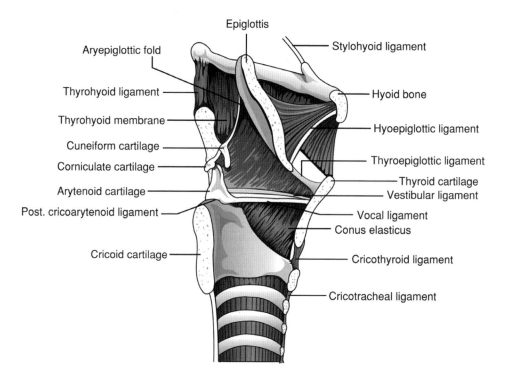

Figure 5-5. Suspensory ligaments of the larynx. Adapted from *The Larynx: A Multidisciplinary Approach* (2nd ed., p. 37), by M. P. Fried, 1996, Mosby.

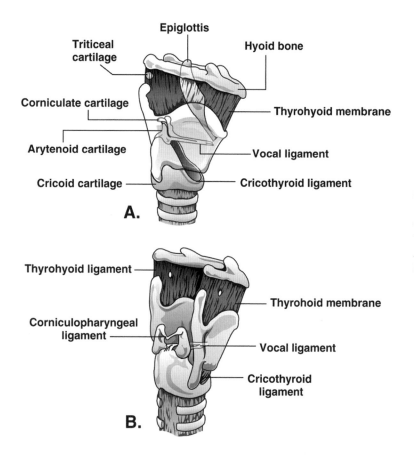

Figure 5-6. Intrinsic laryngeal ligaments viewed laterally (**A**) and obliquely (**B**) (from posterior). Adapted from *The Larynx: A Multidisciplinary Approach* (2nd ed., p. 38), by M. P. Fried, 1996, Mosby.

112

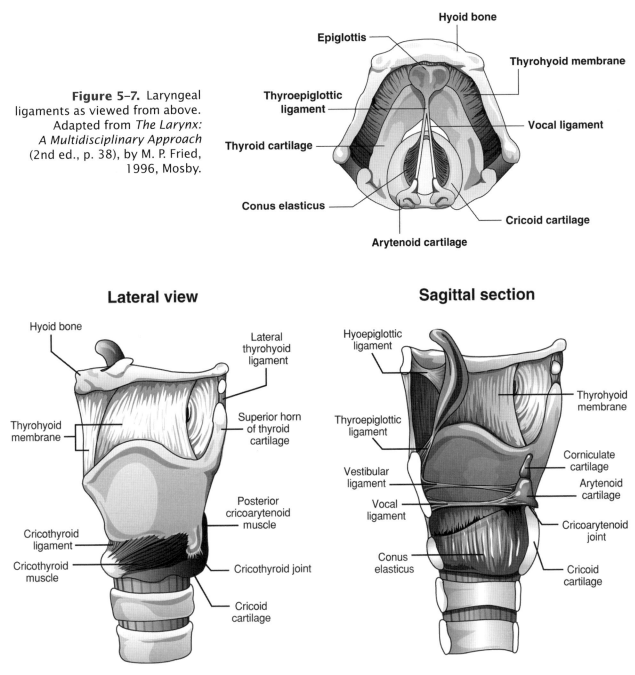

Figure 5–7. Laryngeal ligaments as viewed from above. Adapted from *The Larynx: A Multidisciplinary Approach* (2nd ed., p. 38), by M. P. Fried, 1996, Mosby.

Figure 5–8. Lateral view (*left*) and sagittal section (*right*) of laryngeal ligaments.

which is described in the section on the lamina propria. The conus elasticus is lined with mucous-secreting glands that lubricate the airway.

The uppermost cavity of the larynx, termed the vestibule, is enclosed by the epiglottis anteriorly, the aryepiglottic folds superiorly, the ven-tricular folds laterally, and the arytenoid mounds posteriorly. The vestibule also is generally referred to as the supraglottic space. The shape of this cavity may make an important contribution to voice production, as we discuss further on. The ventricular folds, also called the false

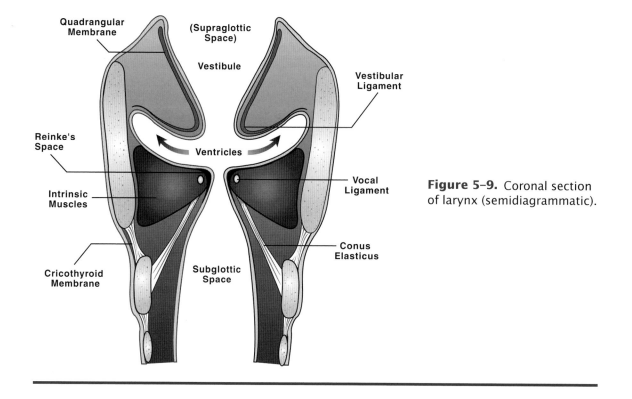

Figure 5–9. Coronal section of larynx (semidiagrammatic).

vocal folds, are composed of mucous membrane covering the fibrous vestibular ligament. Although it was generally believed that the vestibular folds contained no muscle, more recent evidence (Kotby, Kirchner, Kahane, Basiouny, & el-Samaa, 1991) documents the presence of a ventricular muscle and suggests that part of the thyroarytenoid muscle of the true vocal folds (to be discussed below) does extend superiorly into the ventricular folds. The space between the ventricular vocal folds and the true vocal folds is called the laryngeal ventricle. Within the left and right laryngeal ventricles are 60 mucous-secreting glands, which lubricate the vocal folds. The quadrangular membrane and aryepiglottic folds help to protect the airway from saliva and

Ventricular Phonation

The ventricular folds are not used in human phonation. (They are, however, used by cats to producing purring!) Neither their mass nor their stiffness promotes self-oscillation in the same way as the true vocal folds. In extraordinary cases of laryngeal pathology, the ventricular folds can be set into motion, producing a very low-frequency pulsing sound due to their large mass. In general, however, the voice disorder known as ventricular phonation refers not to actual vibration of the ventricular folds but to medial squeezing of the false vocal folds into the airway, so that they impede vibration of the true vocal folds and absorb acoustic energy of the glottal wave. The exact mechanism by which the ventricular folds are medialized is unknown. Reidenbach (1998) and Sanders, Wu, Mu, Li, and Biller (1993) found that muscle activity in the ventricular folds persists in the case of recurrent laryngeal nerve paralysis, suggesting that the superior laryngeal nerve may contribute innervation to the ventricular folds.

food, which may accumulate in the right and left valleculae immediately anterior to the epiglottis.

Three Functions of the Larynx

In the study of speech and voice science, we tend to focus on the phonatory function of the larynx. However, the primary purpose of the larynx is to protect the lungs from a foreign body, whether an errant piece of food or one's own saliva. The ability of the vocal folds to close rapidly provides an excellent seal to prevent such intrusions. Indeed, only one of the intrinsic muscles of the larynx, the posterior cricoarytenoid, functions to abduct (open) the vocal folds, whereas all the other intrinsic muscles assist in adduction (vocal fold closure). The larynx is surrounded laterally and posteriorly by the lower pharynx. At approximately the level at which the larynx opens into the airway of the trachea, the posterior pharynx empties into the esophagus. At the sides of the larynx, the pharyngeal space forms deep wells called piriform fossa, also known as piriform sinuses.

Because the phonatory and swallowing functions share common structures and spaces, the possibility exists for a bit of food or drop of liquid to make its way onto or past the vocal folds. The presentation of something other than air to the larynx stimulates a cough. The vocal folds adduct rapidly, and the lungs are compressed to increase the air pressure. The larynx elevates, the vocal folds are abducted (moved apart), and the continued and rapid compression of the lungs causes a high pressure jet of air to be released, one hopes thus ejecting the foreign object along with it. Throat clearing is closely related to coughing. The vocal folds are drawn together, the larynx is lowered, and the lungs are compressed to increase lung pressure. The vocal folds are momentarily opened and air is forcefully expelled. Frequently, the throat-clear is a rhythmic and rapid two-beat opening and closing.

In the first stage of the cough or throat-clear, the lungs are forcefully compressed while the airway is sealed at the level of the vocal folds. As a result, the air pressure below the vocal folds increases. This series of events is called a **Valsalva maneuver** (named for Antonio Maria Valsalva, an Italian anatomist and physician [1666–1723]). The Valsalva maneuver is used in medicine to evaluate cardiac function, because a sustained Valsalva raises intrapleural pressure, which impedes blood flow to the heart temporarily. Although both coughing and throat-clearing are efficient means of clearing saliva, mucus, and sometimes foreign bodies from the airway, the

Laryngopharyngeal Reflux and Voice Problems

Laryngopharyngeal reflux (LPR) is a medical problem experienced by many people. The contents of the stomach, which are highly acidic, travel back up from the stomach, referred to as retrograde movement, beyond the ring of muscle at the top of the esophagus, known as the esophageal sphincter. (A sphincter is a band of muscle that encircles the opening of a tube in the human body, like the esophagus. The sphincter, through muscular contraction, closes in a circular fashion like a purse string.) The acidic mucus can irritate the posterior larynx, particularly the tissues covering the arytenoid cartilages, as well as the vocal folds themselves. The epithelium lining the pharynx and larynx does not withstand the acid as well as the esophagus itself and can become sufficiently irritated to cause discomfort such as a burning sensation or dryness of the throat, sensation of a foreign body in the airway, and production of excessive mucus. Voice production can become impaired due to both the irritation of the mucosal covering of the vocal folds, as well as maladaptive motor strategies used to compensate for the irritation.

maneuvers are potentially phonotraumatic to the vocal folds. **Phonotrauma** is defined as those voice use patterns leading to traumatic tissue changes of the vocal folds (Verdolini, 1998).

The valving action of the vocal folds also participates in breathing. During breathing, a phasic inward and outward movement of the vocal folds occurs (Brancatisano, Dodd, & Engel, 1991; Kuna, Insalaco, & Woodson, 1988). During inspiration, the vocal folds move outward slightly; during exhalation, they move inward slightly. The outward movement serves to widen the lumen (opening) of the airway to decrease resistance to the airflow and ease inhalation. Slight medial movement of the vocal folds during exhalation increases resistance to the airflow and may help to slow the rate of airflow and increase gaseous exchange at the level of the alveoli. During deep inhalation, extrinsic laryngeal muscles abduct the vocal folds wider than during quiet tidal breathing to widen further the glottal lumen and decrease resistance to the airflow (Davis, Bartlett, & Luschei, 1993; McCaffrey & Kern, 1980; Suzuki & Kirschner, 1969).

In addition to airway protection and phonation, the valving action of the larynx also functions to stabilize the upper body during certain maneuvers, such as lifting a heavy object, running upstairs, and "pushing" for defecation and childbirth. The stabilization maneuver begins similarly to that of a cough or throat-clear; after inhalation, the vocal folds are adducted to seal the airway. By sealing the airway, the thoracic cavity becomes rather fixed in size, or rigid. This posture allows the lower body to more efficiently generate the necessary forces for movements such as heavy lifting or running, for example, rather than allowing the forces to be partially dissipated to movement of the chest wall.

Laryngeal Muscles

The muscles of the larynx are identified as being intrinsic and extrinsic. Intrinsic muscles are those that interconnect the laryngeal cartilages, whereas extrinsic muscles extend from a laryngeal cartilage to an external point of attachment.

(See Tables 5–1 and 5–2 for summary information on the intrinsic and the extrinsic muscles, respectively.)

Intrinsic Muscles

The intrinsic muscles are responsible for vocal fold movement and the fine motor control required for regulation of f_o, intensity and tonal quality of the voice, in conjunction with aerodynamic regulation (Figures 5–10 through 5–12).

The intrinsic laryngeal muscles often have been categorized by their primary function relative to the vocal folds (Figure 5–13). **Abduction** refers to the opening, or outward (lateral) movement, of the vocal folds. **Adduction** refers to the inward (medial) or closing movement. Muscles that function to adduct the vocal folds include the lateral cricoarytenoid, the transverse arytenoid, and the oblique arytenoid muscles. The only intrinsic muscle that functions to abduct the vocal folds is the posterior cricoarytenoid. The thyromuscularis is categorized as a relaxer of the vocal folds. This muscle is the lateral portion of the thyroarytenoid muscle, part of the vocal folds themselves. Two muscles are considered tensors of the vocal folds, the thyrovocalis and the cricothyroid muscles. The thyrovocalis is the medial portion of the thyroarytenoid muscle. The cricothyroid muscle is the only intrinsic muscle that does not attach to the arytenoid cartilages. The cricothyroid, as its name suggests, connects the cricoid and thyroid cartilages. It elongates the vocal folds and is the primary regulator of f_o, discussed later in the chapter. Both the laryngeal functions of airway protection and voice production require rapid and precise movements of the vocal folds. These functions are served well by the intrinsic laryngeal muscles, which are among the fastest in the human body (second only to the eye muscles) (Faaborg-Andersen, 1957; Mårtensson, 1968). These muscles contain fibers that control fine movements over relatively long periods of time, and fibers that allow for rapid buildup of tension (Cooper, Partridge, & Alipour-Haghighi, 1993). Both functions are necessary for the many intricate and coordinated movements required for speaking.

Table 5–1. Intrinsic Muscles of the Larynx

Muscle	Origin	Attachment	Function	Innervation
Abductor				
Posterior cricoarytenoid	Posterior surface of cricoid cartilage	Muscular process of arytenoid cartilages	Rotate vocal process of arytenoid laterally	Recurrent laryngeal nerve
Adductors				
Cricothyroid	Anterior and lateral surface of cricoid cartilage	Pars recta: Lower surface of thyroid cartilage Pars oblique: Thyroid cartilage between lamina and inferior horns	Pars recta: Pulls thyroid cartilage down Pars oblique: Draws thyroid cartilage forward	Superior laryngeal branch of CN X
Interarytenoids	Arytenoid cartilage	Opposite arytenoid cartilage Transverse = unpaired Oblique = paired, X-shaped	Oblique: Pulls apex of arytenoids medially Transverse: Glides arytenoids (and vocal folds) together (no rotation)[a]	Recurrent laryngeal nerve
Lateral cricoarytenoids	Arch of cricoid	Muscular process of arytenoid	Rotate muscular process forward and inward (adducting vocal folds)	Recurrent laryngeal nerve
Tensors and Relaxers				
Thyroarytenoid: Thyromuscularis (lateral fibers) (slightly inferior to thyrovocalis)	Thyroid angle	Anterolateral surface of arytenoid and muscular process[b]	Pulls arytenoids forward (releasing tension on thyrovocalis and vocal ligament to laxen vocal folds). Possibly also sphincter function working in conjunction with other adductory muscles	Recurrent laryngeal nerve
Thyrovocalis (medial fibers) (slightly superior to thyromuscularis) Also tensors: see cricothyroid and posterior cricoarytenoid	Posterior surface of angle of thyroid	Vocal process and lateral surface of arytenoid	Tenses vocal fold	Recurrent laryngeal nerve

[a]The adductory function of the interarytenoid muscles is assisted by the lateral and posterior cricoarytenoid muscles. In the absence of cricoarytenoid assistance, the interarytenoid muscles would act as abductors of the vocal folds because they would cause the vocal processes of the arytenoids to rotate laterally.

[b]Some of the fibers of the thyromuscularis course upward from the angle of the thyroid cartilage and attach to the lateral margin of the epiglottis as the thyroepiglottic muscle. Other fibers course along the lateral margin of the ventricle and attach to the lateral margin of the epiglottis as the ventricular muscle.

Table 5–2. Extrinsic Muscles of the Larynx

Muscle	Origin	Attachment	Function	Innervation
Elevators				
Digastric	Mastoid, inner mandible surface	Hyoid	Elevates hyoid (and moves it anteriorly)	CN V (anterior belly) CN VII (posterior belly)
Geniohyoid	Inner surface of mandible at chin	Anterior surface of hyoid bone	Draws tongue and hyoid bone forward	CN XII
Mylohyoid	Mylohyoid line from mandibular symphysis to last molar	Median raphe from mental symphysis to hyoid bone	Elevates hyoid or depresses mandible (also helps in swallowing)	CN V
Stylohyoid	Styloid of temporal bone	Greater cornu of hyoid	Elevates and retracts hyoid	CN VII
Thyrohyoid	Thyroid cartilage	Hyoid bone	Depresses hyoid bone or elevates thyroid cartilage	CN XII
Depressors				
Sternohyoid	Medial portion of clavicle and sternum	Inferior surface of hyoid bone	Depresses hyoid bone	CN XII
Sternothyroid	Sternum and first costal cartilage	Thyroid cartilage	Depresses thyroid cartilage	CN XII
Omohyoid	Superior margin of scapula	Inferior border of hyoid bone	Depresses and retracts hyoid bone	CN XII

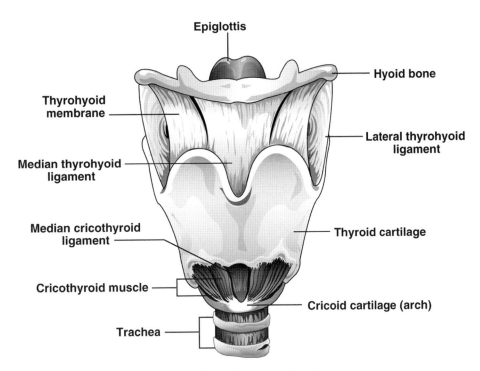

Figure 5–10. Intrinsic laryngeal muscles, anterior view.

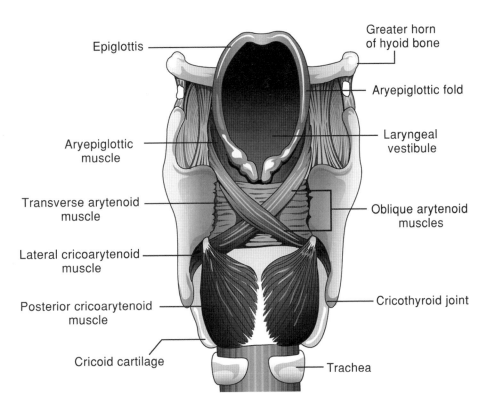

Figure 5–11. Intrinsic laryngeal muscles, posterior view.

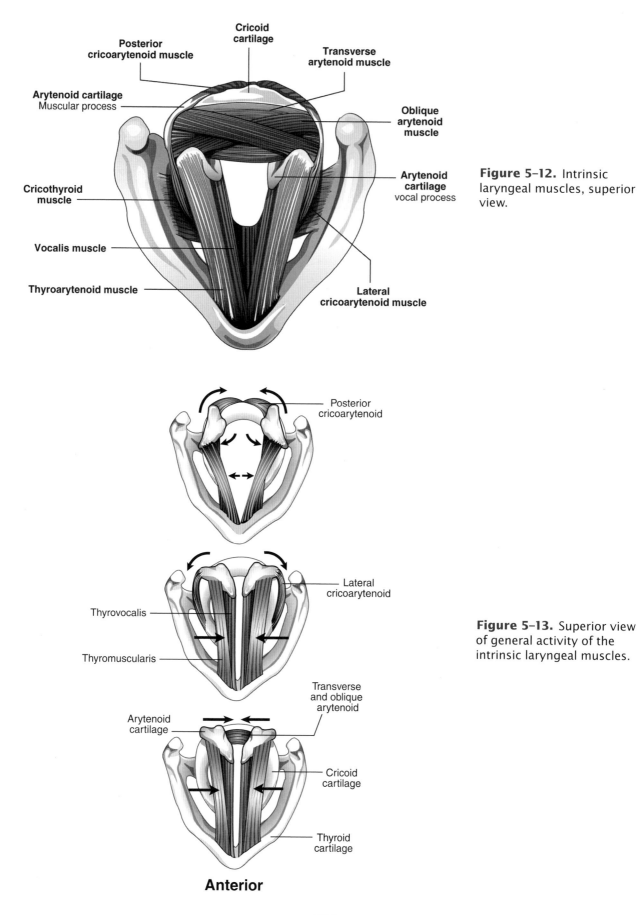

Figure 5–12. Intrinsic laryngeal muscles, superior view.

Figure 5–13. Superior view of general activity of the intrinsic laryngeal muscles.

120

Although it is tempting to assign such straightforward functions to each of the intrinsic muscles, you are cautioned not to be lulled by such simplicity. The muscles act together, both as synergists and as agonist-antagonists, to provide the vast range of pitch and intensity combinations of which we know the human voice is capable. Furthermore, as discussed in Chapter 4, motor equivalence means that speakers use a variety of motor strategies to achieve a vocal target. It is interesting to note that variability among individuals exists. Poletto, Verdun, Strominger, and Ludlow (2004) found that only the activity of the posterior cricoarytenoid muscle consistently produced a single result, vocal fold abduction. The cricothyroid and thyroarytenoid muscles were active in varying degrees during both abduction and adduction, and these actions varied among individuals. Although identified primarily as a tensor of the vocal folds in its lengthening action, the cricothyroid may have other effects on the vocal folds depending upon the activity of the other laryngeal muscles. During inhalation and sniffing, the cricothyroid muscle is active, contributing to vocal fold abduction (Kuna & Vanoye, 1994; Poletto et al., 2004). In truth, a great deal is yet to be learned about the net forces generated by simultaneous muscle activation and the resulting biomechanical effects upon the vocal folds (Ludlow, 2005).

Extrinsic Muscles

The extrinsic laryngeal muscles include many of the muscles of the jaw and strap muscles (large shoulder and neck muscles) (Figure 5–14). They serve to adjust the overall position of the larynx within the neck and help to stabilize the laryngeal position, particularly so that the intrinsic muscles can exert their forces (Jürgens, 2002). Although the larynx is attached inferiorly to the trachea by the cricotracheal ligament, it is suspended superiorly from multiple extrinsic muscles. The extrinsic muscles of the larynx are

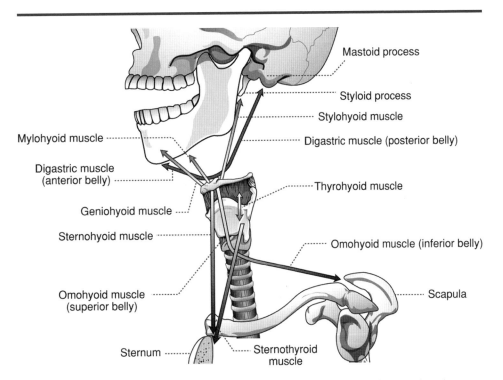

Figure 5–14. Schematic of activity of the extrinsic laryngeal (infrahyoid and suprahyoid) muscles.

all infrahyoid muscles ("below" the hyoid). Most attach from the hyoid bone inferiorly to the larynx. The extrinsic laryngeal infrahyoid muscles include the sternothyroid (connecting the thyroid cartilage with the sternum), the sternohyoid (connecting the sternum with the hyoid bone), and the thyrohyoid muscle (connecting the thyroid cartilage with the hyoid bone). (The omohyoid and inferior pharyngeal constrictor are also considered infrahyoid muscles, but they are not generally considered extrinsic laryngeal muscles.) Muscles that attach from the hyoid bone to structures above it are called the suprahyoid ("above" the hyoid) muscles. These include the stylohyoid, mylohyoid, geniohyoid, and digastric muscles, and sometimes the middle pharyngeal constrictor is also included as a suprahyoid muscle (Dickson & Maue-Dickson, 1996). Although suprahyoid muscles are not considered extrinsic laryngeal muscles, they do move and stabilize

the mobile hyoid bone (Hirano, Koike, & von Leden, 1967). When the hyoid bone is displaced, the movement acts upon the extrinsic laryngeal muscles, which in turn affect the larynx and the position of the vocal folds and the supraglottal vocal tract (Figure 5–15).

To understand more fully the role of the extrinsic laryngeal muscles in phonation, think of the entire laryngeal framework as a highly flexible tube that can be raised and lowered as well as moved laterally. Place your hand over your larynx and swallow and you can feel the larynx raise and lower. With your hand still lightly placed over the larynx, sing from a very low to a very high pitch. Most likely, you will feel the laryngeal framework elevate as you raise your pitch. (More about laryngeal position and pitch change later!) Now, with your hand, gently rock the larynx side to side. You should feel it move freely and perhaps you even can hear

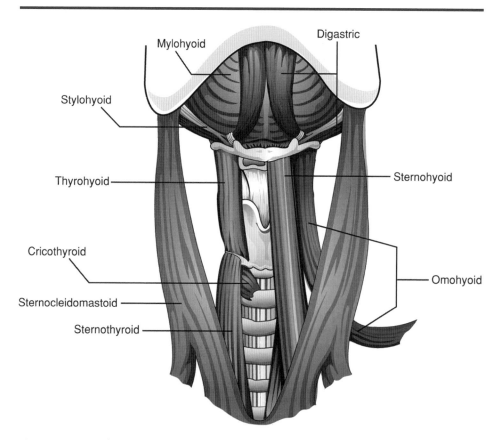

Figure 5–15. The strap muscles, anterior view.

or feel a bit of "crackling" as the larynx moves. That crackling is called **crepitus** (Latin: a rattling, creaking, crackling), and it is produced by the cartilages moving against one another. Although it may not be a good sign to hear crepitus in the knee, it is a normal sign of a healthy and mobile larynx!

Study Questions

1. Identify the three paired and three unpaired laryngeal cartilages.

2. Cover up the labels in Figures 5–4 through 5–9 and identify all the structures.

3. Describe the three functions of the larynx.

4. Describe separately the general functions of the intrinsic and extrinsic laryngeal muscles.

5. To what do the terms abduction and adduction refer? What muscles control these actions?

6. Cover up the labels in Figures 5–10 through 5–12 and identify all the muscles, ligaments, and membranes.

7. Identify the supra- and infrahyoid muscles and their functions.

The Vocal Folds

Structural Overview

The vocal folds are a paired structure that attaches anteriorly inside the thyroid cartilage at the level of the thyroid notch. They are sometimes referred to as the true vocal folds, to distinguish them from the ventricular or false vocal folds. (Although the true vocal folds usually are referred to simply as the vocal folds, the false vocal folds are always identified with the modifier "ventricular" or "false.") The left and right vocal folds attach posteriorly to the left and right arytenoid cartilages, respectively. When completely adducted, the vocal folds seal the airway, allowing no escape of air into or out of the lungs. When the vocal folds are abducted (open), the space that is formed between them is called the **glottis**, or **glottal opening** (Figure 5–16). The airway below the vocal folds is called the **subglottis**, and the airway above the vocal folds is called the **supraglottis**. In any discussion of the dynamics of phonation and speech, the aerodynamic activity within the vocal tract is typically referred to as subglottal and supraglottal pressures and flows. The anterior commissure defines the glottal opening in the anterior portion of the vocal folds, and the posterior commissure describes the glottal opening between the arytenoid cartilages. In adult men during quiet breathing, the length of the glottis is approximately 20 mm (approximately

---

Phonation   **Inspiration**

Figure 5–16. Vocal folds adducted (*closed*) on left and abducted (*open*) on right. **A.** True vocal fold. **B.** Ventricular fold. **C.** Aryepiglottic fold. **D.** Arytenoid complex. **E.** Glottis.

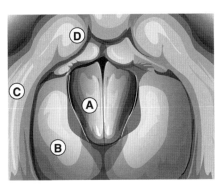

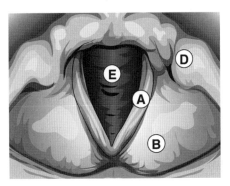

0.8 in.) from the anterior to posterior commissure and approximately 8 mm (approximately 0.3 in.) wide at the posterior commissure. Of course, the width of the glottal opening is variable depending upon the position of the vocal folds during breathing, phonation, or other physical activity.

The medial edge of each vocal fold that borders the glottis often is referred to as the free margin. The posterior two-fifths of each vocal fold, from 4 to 8 mm in length (approximately 0.2 to 0.3 in.), depending on gender and age, is sometimes called the cartilaginous vocal folds (and the space between them, the cartilaginous glottis). Here the vocal folds attach to the arytenoid cartilages at the vocal processes, the portion of the cartilages that project anteriorly toward the thyroid notch. The anterior three-fifths of each vocal fold is sometimes referred to as the membranous vocal folds (and the space between them, the membranous glottis). Approximately 15 mm (approximately 0.6 in.) in length in men and 12 mm (approximately 0.5 in.) in length in women, the membranous vocal folds vibrate to produce the acoustic pressure wave that provides the source signal of the voice. The cartilaginous portion of each of the vocal folds does not vibrate.

The thyroarytenoid is the muscle of the vocal folds, attaching anteriorly at the inside of the thyroid cartilage at the thyroid notch and posteriorly to the arytenoid cartilages. The medial portion of the thyroarytenoid is the thyrovocalis muscle, often referred to as the vocalis. It represents the larger mass of the thyroarytenoid muscle. The fibers of the vocalis muscle attach posteriorly to the vocal process of the left and right arytenoid cartilages. Recall that the thyromuscularis muscle is the lateral portion of the thyroarytenoid, the fibers of which attach to the muscular processes of the arytenoid cartilages. The fibers are somewhat inferior to those of the thyrovocalis. Some controversy exists regarding the anatomic differentiation of these two muscles. However, evidence for the functional distinction between these two muscles is clear (von Leden, 1961).

Lamina Propria

Hirano (1974, 1977) and Fujimura (1981) described the vocal folds as multilayered folds of tissue, with each layer having a different histology, which in turn gives rise to unique biomechanical properties (Figure 5–17). The outermost (superficial) layer of the vocal folds, the epithelium, is quite thin (less than 0.1 mm thick). In the mid–vocal fold region, the cells are stratified squamous-type epithelium, which is particularly well suited for the friction and collision forces encountered during vocal fold vibration (Hirano, 1977). The epithelial layer forms ridges (plicae). No mucous secreting glands are found on the medial margins of the vocal folds. The epithelial layer contains no cilia (hair cells). Ciliated, columnar epithelium is found above and below the vocal folds. The epithelium overlays the lamina propria, approximately 1.2 mm thick (Hirano, 1977), which consists of three layers and is of critical important to vocal fold vibration. The most **superficial layer of the lamina propria** (approximately 0.5 mm thick) is composed of loosely arranged elastin fibers and a cellular matrix. Elastin fibers are highly elastic and therefore easily stretched. This layer is thinly populated with fibers, and the fibers are randomly arranged. The consistency of this superficial layer is like gelatin. It is often called **Reinke's space**. A few capillaries are found in Reinke's space, but no lymphatics. The low density of connective tissue fibers in Reinke's space results in a highly mobile layer of tissue. The **intermediate layer of lamina propria**, 1 to 2 mm thick, immediately below the superficial layer, is also composed of **elastin fibers**, but these are more densely distributed and interwoven and organized to lie parallel to the free edge of the vocal folds. Some collagen fibers are also present in this intermediate layer. Collagen is often likened to thick cotton threads. **The deep layer of the lamina propria**, also 1 to 2 mm thick, is composed heavily of collagen fibers, which, like the elastin fibers of the intermediate layer, are tightly packed and lie parallel to the length of the vocal folds. Although the division between

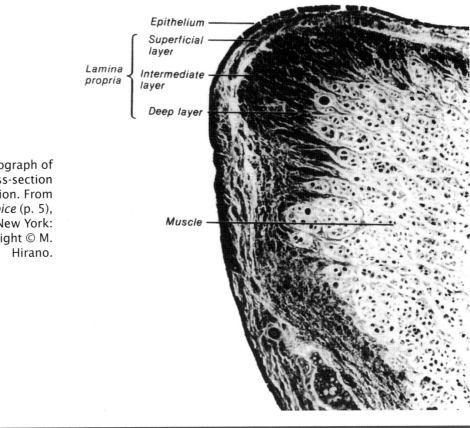

Epithelium

Superficial
layer

Lamina
propria

Intermediate
layer

Deep layer

Muscle

Figure 5–17. Photomicrograph of adult male vocal fold cross-section through the mid-portion. From *Clinical Examination of Voice* (p. 5), by M. Hirano, 1981, New York: Springer-Verlag. Copyright © M. Hirano.

the superficial and intermediate layers is quite distinct, the separation between the intermediate and deep layers is not so distinct, and many of the connective tissue fibers appear to be interwoven. Immediately deep to the lamina propria is the thyroarytenoid muscle, which forms the bulk of the vocal folds. The muscle courses in an anterior-posterior direction in each vocal fold, parallel to the elastin fibers of the intermediate lamina propria, and the collagen fibers of the deep lamina propria. The **mucoserous blanket**, an additional layer above the epithelium, is a cover of mucous secretions that originate from glands below the vocal folds and within the vestibule. This mucous blanket is important to vocal fold vibration (Hirano & Kakita, 1985). It helps protect the epithelium and likely functions to maintain adequate hydration (Gray, 2000).

Proceeding from superficial to deep, the layers of the vocal folds gradually become increasingly stiff. The epithelium and Reinke's space are highly pliable layers. The thyroarytenoid muscle is relatively stiff. The epithelium is attached to the superficial layer of the lamina propria by the **basement membrane zone** (Figure 5–18), traditionally not considered a distinct separate layer of the vocal folds but rather a zone of complex protein bonds that is designed to withstand the vibratory forces and maintain the integrity of the epithelial layer protecting the lamina propria (Gray, 2000).

Mechanical Layers

Table 5–3 presents the different schemata for organizing the histologic layers of the vocal folds into biomechanical functional units. The **body-cover model** (Fujimura, 1981; Hirano, 1977) groups the muscle and deep layer of lamina

Figure 5–18. Structure of the basement membrane zone of the vocal folds. From "Basement Membrane Zone Injury in Vocal Nodules," by S. D. Gray, 1991, in *Vocal Fold Physiology*, J. Gauffin and B. Hammarberg (Eds.). Reprinted with permission of John Wiley & Sons Limited.

Table 5–3. Mechanical Organization of the Histological Layers of the Vocal Folds[a]

Three-Layer Model	Body-Cover Model
Mucosa	Cover
Epithelium	Epithelium
SLLP	SLLP
	ILLP
Ligament	Body
ILLP	DLLP
DLLP	Muscle
Muscle	

[a]SLLP, ILLP, and DLLP refer to superficial, intermediate, and deep layers of the lamina propria, respectively.

propria together, and the remainder of the lamina propria is grouped in turn with the epithelium as the cover layer. Alternatively, the five histologic layers can be reclassified into three mechanical layers, consisting of the epithelium and Reinke's space (referred to as the **mucosa**), the **transition (vocal ligament)**, and the **body** (thyroarytenoid muscle). The vocal ligament, the intermediate and deep layers of lamina propria, is the uppermost portion of the conus elasticus. The functional significance of these biomechani-

cal schemata is considerable. We shall learn that distinct biomechanical properties of the different layers allow the vocal folds to vibrate and allow for changes in pitch and loudness. Before concluding our initial discussion of the histological and biomechanical layering of the vocal folds, it should be noted that since Hirano's (1974, 1977) work, it has become evident that the concentrations of other important proteins in the lamina propria do not conform to the three-layer schema (Pawlak, Hammond, Hammond, & Gray,

Vocal Cords to Vocal Folds

Historical reviews of voice production are recounted by van den Berg (1958) and later more fully by von Leden (1996), starting with the ancient scientist Galen, who considered the trachea and not the larynx to be the voice source, with sound produced like the tones of a flute. Anatomic drawings in the Renaissance period provided detailed depictions of the larynx, including, most famously, those of Leonardo de Vinci in his *De Corpore Humano* in the 1500s. In the 1700s, Dodart, a Parisian physician, theorized that the larynx and not the trachea was the organ of voice production. He identified the "lips" in the larynx as being responsible for controlling the size of the glottal opening, which in turn regulated the pitch of the voice. This valving action was likened to a horn, and the laryngeal lips controlled the airflow just as the airflow through the horn is controlled by the lips of the musician. The contribution of vocal fold vibration to voice production was finally demonstrated in 1741 by Antoine Ferrein (1693–1769), a French anatomist and surgeon, in what is believed to be the first recorded experimentation using canine larynges. He likened the vibration to the strings of a musical instrument. From Ferrein's work came the term vocal cords, used for more than two centuries as the descriptor of the vibrating masses that produce voice.

The word cord implies a ropelike structure, which in turn conjures up images of a vibration like the jump-rope waves we explored in earlier chapters.

Ferrein's experiments led most scientists to abandon the concept of voice as produced by a wind instrument in favor of the stringed instrument. Subsequent physiologists studied the larynges of animal and human cadavers and concluded that the voice was produced more similarly to a reed instrument. In 1863, Hermann von Helmholtz (1821–1894), a German physiologist, physicist, and mathematician, demonstrated that voice was the result of puffs of air escaping through the glottis up the vocal tract. Although we now know that the vocal folds do not behave like a vibrating string, some of the properties of vibrating strings do accurately describe the vibration of the vocal folds. We will examine those properties in greater detail in our discussion of frequency control, and we shall return to Helmholtz and his puffs of air in Chapter 7. The date at which scientists began to refer to the paired vibratory structures as vocal folds is unclear. Farnsworth (1940) referred to them as both cords and folds in his treatise on high-speed filming of laryngeal dynamics, and now, the term **vocal folds** is the standard and correct nomenclature.

1996). The exact role of these other proteins in the biomechanical properties of the vocal folds, however, remains unclear. (See Genomics and Proteomics in Chapter 6).

Cricothyroid Joints

The cricothyroid muscle regulates the angle of the thyroid cartilage with respect to the cricoid cartilage by rotating the thyroid cartilage forward and downward around the axis of the cri-

cothyroid joints (Figure 5–19). These joints are formed by the inner surface of the inferior horns of the thyroid cartilage and the side of the cricoid cartilage. They are plane synovial joints, meaning that they are formed by relatively flat surfaces that move over one another, lubricated with synovial fluid to reduce friction and, therefore, ease movement and limit wear and tear on the cartilages. Each joint is held together by a cricothyroid ligament. The articular surfaces of the joints and their ligament attachments limit the movement of the joints, precluding sliding

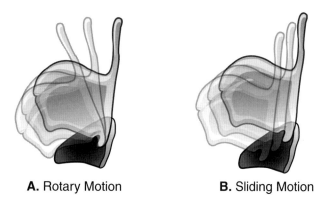

A. Rotary Motion   **B.** Sliding Motion

Figure 5–19. Movement of the cricothyroid joint includes rotary (**A**) and sliding (**B**) motions.

of the entire thyroid cartilage upward or downward. The joint only permits rotation such that when the cricothyroid muscle contracts, it rotates the thyroid cartilage downward and anteriorly. The cricothyroid muscle is the largest of the intrinsic laryngeal muscles and has two anatomic subdivisions, the pars recta (the anterior portion) and the pars oblique (the posterior portion) (Honda, 1995; Hong et al., 1998). The pars recta consists of those fibers located most medially, coursing upward and slightly posteriorly. The fibers of the pars oblique are located more laterally and their course is more oblique (angling posteriorly). Due to their different positions, contraction of the pars recta will rotate the thyroid cartilage downward, and contraction of the pars oblique, while also rotating the thyroid cartilage downward, will pull the thyroid cartilage forward. Recall that the vocal folds are fixed to the inner anterior surface of the thyroid cartilage and attach to the arytenoid cartilages posteriorly. Therefore, if the arytenoids are held so that they are not pulled forward, both actions of the pars recta and pars oblique will result in an elongation of the vocal folds. The forward gliding motion of the thyroid cartilage upon contraction of the pars oblique may be responsible for up to 30% to 40% of the potential elongation of the vocal folds and it contributes to vocal fold adduction (Arnold, 1961; Vilkman, 1987). The maximal length change may be as great as 25% of the total vocal fold resting length (Dick-

son & Maue-Dickson, 1996, p. 51). As we shall soon learn, elongation of the vocal folds plays a critical role in the tension on the vocal folds, which regulates fundamental frequency (f_o) and contributes to intensity control as well.

Cricoarytenoid Joints

The cricoarytenoid joints, formed by the articular facets of the arytenoid and cricoid cartilages and the paired cricoarytenoid ligament, are bilateral (right and left) symmetric joints. They allow the arytenoid cartilages to rock (the predominant movement) and glide, enabling the vocal folds to adduct and abduct. Due to their role in opening and closing the vocal folds, these joints play a central role in the preservation of the airway for breathing as well as in vocal fold movement for phonation. For this reason perhaps, the cricoarytenoid joints have been the subject of numerous research studies (Cérat, Charlin, Brazeau-Lamontagne, & Mongeau, 1988; Paulsen & Tillmann, 1999; Sellars & Sellars, 1983; von Leden & Moore, 1961). Joint movement has been analyzed using cadaver larynges and computational modeling (Berry, Montequin, Chan, Titze, & Hoffman, 2003; Hunter, Titze, & Alipour, 2004; Selbie, Zhang, Levine, & Ludlow, 1998; Wang, 1998). Dickson and Maue-Dickson (1996, p. 156) summarize the movements of these joints based upon the research: A limited amount of sliding along the surface of the cricoid cartilage is permitted, with a rocking motion being the dominant movement with the greatest range of motion. The lateral cricoarytenoid (an adductor) and posterior cricoarytenoid (the abductor) are antagonists, having opposite actions on the vocal folds. Both muscles attach to the muscular process of the arytenoid cartilages, and so their action upon the cricoarytenoid joint depends upon the relative activity of the two muscles. Upon vocal fold abduction, the tip of the medial edge of the vocal process moves from a medial inferior to a lateral superior position (Figure 5–20). The vocalis, therefore, which attaches to this medial portion of the vocal process, both lengthens and elevates the vocal folds as they are

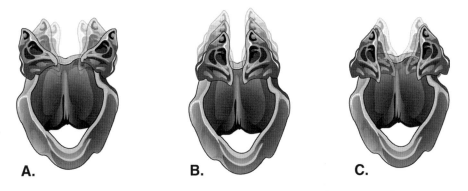

Figure 5–20. Movements of the bilateral cricoarytenoid joints. **A.** The primary movement is achieved through rocking in anterior, posterior, medial, and lateral directions, enabling abduction and adduction of the vocal folds. **B.** A small amount of sliding also occurs, contributing to change in longitudinal tension of the vocal folds. **C.** A minor amount of rotation is possible.

abducted. Normal aging causes changes to the cricoarytenoid joints (Casiano, Ruiz, & Goldstein, 1994; Dedivitis, Abrahao, de Jesus Simoes, Mora, & Cervantes, 2001; Kahane & Hammons, 1987).

Blood Supply to the Larynx and Lymphatic Drainage

Oxygen-rich blood travels to the larynx via the arteries and leaves by way of the veins or lymph system. The arteries that supply the larynx form a complex network and often anastomose (join together by forming an open mouth between two parts) with one another. The laryngeal muscles, mucous membranes, and glands receive their blood supply from arteries that branch from the common carotid artery, which arises from the aorta. The laryngeal veins, which carry blood depleted of oxygen back to the lungs to get a new supply of oxygen, are a complex network that drains into the jugular vein.

All tissues leak some fluid into their extracellular (also called interstitial) spaces. This fluid cannot be allowed to build up but rather must be drained away. The lymphatic system defends the body against disease and acts as a drainage system to move the interstitial fluid into the bloodstream so that it can be carried away. The lymphatic system in the neck and larynx drains into the internal jugular vein. Interestingly, the vocal folds have minimal lymphatic drainage. This lack of lymphatic drainage may contribute to the formation of edema (swelling) and benign lesions when the vocal folds are exposed to prolonged phonotrauma (voice use behaviors such as screaming that can cause damage to the vocal fold mucosa).

Study Questions

8. Define glottis, subglottis, and supraglottis.

9. Identify the three layers of the lamina propria and describe their composition.

10. Define Reinke's space.

11. Describe the body-cover mechanical model of the vocal folds.

12. Describe the three-layer mechanical model of the vocal folds.

13. What is the function of the cricothyroid joint, and what effect does movement of the joint have on the vocal folds?

14. What types of movements are made by the cricoarytenoid joints and what is the result of those movements?

5.3 Neural Control of Phonation

Central Motor Control

Neurologic control of phonation is highly complex, and only an overview is provided here. An excellent in-depth discussion is presented in Jürgens (2002), Ludlow (2005), Larson (1988), and Yoshida, Tanaka, Saito, Shimazaki, and Hirano (1992), as well as in the anatomy and physiology texts for speech-language pathologists (Dickson & Maue-Dickson, 1996, for example). Motor commands originate in the cerebral cortex of the brain, largely in the areas called the inferior precentral gyrus and the supplementary motor area. The nerve fibers descend in a bundle called the corticobulbar tract, passing through the internal capsule to the brainstem. (Recall from Chapter 4 that the corticobulbar tract is the bundle of nerve fibers in the direct-activation pathway that provides motor information to the cranial nerves.) Within the brainstem at the junction of the pons and medulla, most of the fibers cross over to the opposite side. The fibers of the corticobulbar tract that innervate the larynx synapse at the nucleus ambiguus, the main nucleus of the vagus. Therefore, most (but not all) of the neural signal that ultimately travels to the right side of the larynx originates from the left side of the brain, and the innervation to the left side of the larynx originates from the right side of the brain. The basal ganglia also contribute to motor control of the larynx.

Peripheral Motor Neural Control and Brainstem Nuclei

All the intrinsic laryngeal muscles receive efferent (motor) innervation from cranial nerve X, the vagus (Latin for *wandering*), a peripheral motor neuron that arises from the nucleus ambiguus of the medulla oblongata in the brainstem (Figures 5–21 and 5–22). Cranial nerve X divides into three major branches, the pharyngeal branch and the recurrent and superior laryngeal nerves. The superior laryngeal nerve descends laterally to the pharynx and divides into an internal and external branch. The internal branch carries

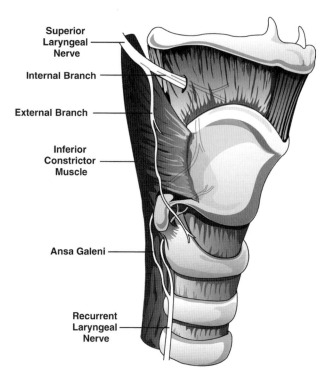

Figure 5–21. Laryngeal nerve supply.

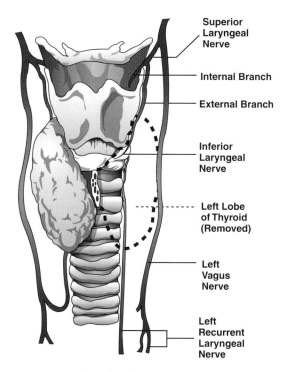

Figure 5–22. The left and right superior and recurrent laryngeal nerves. Adapted from *Professional Voice: The Science and Art of Clinical Care* (3rd ed., p. 160), by R. T. Sataloff (Ed.), San Diego: Plural Publishing, Inc., 2005. Adapted with permission.

afferent (sensory) fibers, which are discussed later in this chapter. The external branch of the superior laryngeal nerve travels to the crico-thyroid muscle, which it innervates. The other branch of the vagus, the recurrent laryngeal nerve, innervates all the other intrinsic laryngeal muscles. The recurrent branch travels a long and circuitous path to reach the larynx, and the path differs on the right and left sides of the body. The left recurrent laryngeal nerve descends in the neck and separates from the vagus at the aortic arch and loops under the arch from back to front. The nerve enters the groove between the esophagus and the trachea as it ascends to the larynx. The right recurrent laryngeal nerve separates from the vagus to loop under the right subclavian artery and then it too ascends to the larynx in the groove between the esophagus and trachea. Upon ascending back up to the larynx, these nerves are called the right and left inferior laryngeal nerves and enter the larynx just poste-rior to the cricothyroid joint.

Whereas the intrinsic laryngeal muscles are innervated by the vagus, the extrinsic laryngeal muscles receive motor innervation from other cranial nerves (see Tables 5–1 and 5–2). The ansa cervicalis is a loop of nerves in the neck formed by the junction of hypoglossal nerve (cranial nerve XII) and the second and third cervical spinal nerves. Branches of the ansa cervicalis, together with the first cervical spinal nerve, innervate the infrahyoids: the thyrohyoid, sternohyoid, and sternothyroid muscles and the inferior belly of the omohyoid muscle. The ansa cervicalis originates in the nucleus ambiguus in the brainstem, and the first cervical spinal nerve originates in the spinal cord.

Recall from Chapter 4 that the motor unit is the smallest functional neuromuscular unit controlled by the brain. Motor units that con-tain a small number of muscle fibers provide greater control of muscle contraction, whereas

Why Do I Get a Lump in My Throat When I Am About to Cry?

Emotional sounds, such as laughter and cry-ing, are likely controlled by regions of the brain distinct from those that control voli-tional speech. The anterior cingulate cortex, the periaqueductal gray, the nucleus ret-roambiguus, and the nucleus ambiguus may all be involved in emotional expression. In certain neurological diseases, such as spas-modic dysphonia, in which the speaking voice is disturbed by uncontrolled spasms of the vocal folds, individuals can laugh, cry, and shout normally (Brin, Blitzer, & Stewart, 1998; Izdebski, Dedo, & Boles, 1984).

Neuromodulation and Neural Plasticity

Neuromodulation is the immediate change in the activity of one or more neurons. It is achieved through either enhancement of excitatory neurons or suppression of inhibi-tory neurons. Neuromodulation characterizes the moment-to-moment activity of the ner-vous system. It represents the balance of the excitatory and inhibitory influences upon the motor neuron. Neuroplasticity describes a per-manent change in neural activity patterns for a given motor activity. Synapses are dynamic: They change depending on their level of activity. The connectivity between neurons is enhanced with use. It is helpful to conceptual-ize phonatory (and speech) neural control not as separate circuits but rather as overlapping circuits that are activated in different ways. You are cautioned against thinking that only one or two muscles are active at any time for a given phonatory gesture. Rather, it is prefera-ble to think about all the muscles being active to some extent, with certain muscle activity greater than others.

the strength of the contraction is regulated by the number of motor units that are recruited (activated). Intrinsic laryngeal muscles have a small innervation ratio, meaning that the motor units each contain a small number of muscle fibers (Faaborg-Andersen, 1957).

Voice Disorders Arising From Trauma to the Recurrent Laryngeal Nerve (RLN)

The aorta is the largest vessel in the arterial system, which carries oxygenated blood from the heart to the rest of the body. The left RLN travels beneath the aorta and then ascends to innervate the larynx. Certain types of vascular disease will affect the left RLN, such as enlargement (aneurysm) of the aorta or subclavian artery, which can press on the RLN and cause it to stop functioning correctly. Sometimes, neurologic damage can occur during surgery, because of the proximity of the nerves to the surgical site. Thyroid gland surgery is one such example, as the thyroid gland is attached to and covers the lateral walls of the thyroid cartilage where the superior laryngeal nerve is located. If that nerve is damaged only on one side, the symptoms are generally not very noticeable (unless the patient is a singer or actor). Bilateral damage to the superior laryngeal never, however, will result in severe limitations of pitch range, because that nerve controls contraction of the cricothyroid muscle, which in turn controls elongation of the vocal folds and, hence, f_o. If the recurrent laryngeal nerve is damaged on either the right or left side of the neck, the result will be a vocal fold that has decreased mobility (paresis) or, in severe cases, complete paralysis (lack of movement). If both the right and left RLN are damaged, the paresis or paralysis is bilateral. Bilateral vocal fold immobility can be life threatening if the immobile vocal folds are positioned close together, providing too narrow an airway for safe breathing. If the vocal folds are immobile and positioned laterally, breathing is safe but phonation is nearly impossible.

Why Don't We Cough Every Time We Speak?

Laryngeal muscle control includes volitional input from the cerebral cortex and reflexive control in the periaqueductal gray and nucleus retroambiguus, located in the midbrain (Zhang, Bandler, & Davis, 1995). The interaction between the volitional control for voice production from the higher cortical areas and the reflexive action of the lower subcortical areas is not completely understood. The anterior cingulate gyrus may contribute to volitional control of intonation (variations in pitch and loudness) (Jürgens, 2002). Experiments that have stimulated the limbic system in monkeys have produced reflexive vocalizations, suggesting that this area of the brain may contribute to control of emotional speech (Jürgens, 2002). Most of the laryngeal reflexes are controlled by stimulation of the sensory fibers of the superior laryngeal nerve and, to a lesser extent, by sensory fibers of the recurrent laryngeal nerve (Ludlow, 2005). These fibers terminate in cell bodies in the nodose ganglion of the nucleus solitarius. Ludlow, Van Pelt, and Koda (1992) found that administering a brief puff of air to the vocal fold mucosa elicits electrical activity of the superior laryngeal nerve. They found that rapid (within 100 ms), repeated stimulation decreases the response of the neurons, suggesting that the central nervous system may inhibit cough/closure response during speech.

Peripheral Sensory Control and Brainstem Nuclei

We began our discussion of motor innervation at the highest level, the cerebral cortex, because motor commands travel from the cortex down through the central nervous system to the peripheral nerves and then to the muscles for activation of contraction. Sensory information, however, travels in the opposite direction, from the periphery to the central nervous system. Mechanoreceptors sensitive to tactile and aerodynamic pressures generate sensory signals from the mucous membranes of the epiglottis, base of the tongue, aryepiglottic folds, and the upper larynx via the internal branch of the superior laryngeal nerve, which exits the larynx through the thyrohyoid membrane. Afferent information below the vocal folds is transmitted by the left and right recurrent laryngeal nerves. Sensory information is then transmitted from the internal and recurrent laryngeal nerves of the vagus to reach the inferior vagal ganglion, one of the sensory ganglia of the vagus. The afferent neurons then enter the brainstem and terminate in the nucleus solitarius. In addition to tactile sensation, the vagus also carries information from sensory endings in the joint capsules to provide proprioception (awareness of location or position of one's body within space) and pressure changes through baroreceptors located in the mucosa of the larynx. The cough reflex, discussed earlier in reaction to a foreign body, is mediated by the visceral afferent (sensory) portion of the vagus. Autonomic fibers of the vagus control dilation of the blood vessels and the extent of laryngeal secretions.

Muscle spindles, sensory receptors located within the muscle, provide sensory information regarding muscle fiber stretch. The prevalence of muscle spindles in the intrinsic laryngeal muscles is uncertain (Keene, 1961). Spindles may occur in the interarytenoid and lateral cricoarytenoid muscles but may not be present in the other intrinsic muscles (Ludlow, 2005). Evidence for proprioceptive feedback from stretch receptors in laryngeal muscles is provided by Kirchner and Wyke (1965) and Wyke (1974). Mechano-

receptors in the vocal fold mucosa are important for feedback control regulating movement (Adzaku & Wyke, 1979), and sensory receptors in the cricoarytenoid and cricothyroid joints provide feedback on the relative movement of the cartilages comprising the joints (Wyke, 1969). Sensory feedback from the larynx is relayed to the nucleus tractus solitarius and, secondarily, from the nucleus parabrachialis.

Study Questions

15. Identify the cranial nerve that supplies neural input to the larynx.

16. Which muscles are innervated by the recurrent branch of that nerve?

17. Which muscle is innervated by the superior laryngeal branch?

5.4 Theories of Voice Production

Our current understanding of the biomechanics of vocal fold vibration and voice production is the result of centuries of work by scientists from diverse fields (medicine, physics, linguistics, speech-language pathology, and singing, to name a few) developing theories, conducting experiments to test those theories, and then refining the theories and conducting more experiments! Our current knowledge and understanding are as much the result of successful experiments as of rejected hypotheses. Zemlin (1998, p. 178) and von Leden (1996), in an historical overview of the development of theories of voice production, report that in 1843, Johannes Peter Müller (1801–1858, German anatomist, physiologist, and pathologist) first proposed the **myoelastic-aerodynamic theory** of voice production, a theory that forms the basis of our current understanding of how voice is produced. Müller set the vocal folds of an excised larynx into vibration by sending a jet of air upward through the glottis and manipulating the longitudinal tension of the vocal folds by exerting a pulling force on them. In this way, Müller demonstrated two phenomena: First, adducting the vocal folds and thereby moving them directly into the airstream causes them to vibrate, and, second, increasing the tension of the vocal folds causes the rate of vibration to increase. Of considerable importance, he noted that the vibration of the tissue itself was passive, being controlled by the airstream. In 1958, van den Berg published a detailed explanation of Müller's theory, "postulating that the vocal folds are actuated by the stream of air delivered by the lungs and trachea" (van den Berg, 1958, p. 242). His explanation was so thorough that the concept became known as "van den Berg's myoelastic-aerodynamic theory," despite its initial development by Müller. The

Theory Rejected

In 1950, a physicist and voice scientist named Raul Husson proposed the **neurochronaxic theory** as an alternative to the myoelastic-aerodynamic conceptualization of voice production. Husson proposed that neural input, not aerodynamic forces, caused the muscles of the vocal folds to pulsate, which then modified the airstream to produce the sound wave. Zemlin (1998, p. 182) points out that, for Husson's theory to be accurate, two alterations in the anatomy and physiology of the larynx would have to occur. First, the fibers of the vocalis muscle would have to course oblique to the glottis so that muscular contraction could cause the vocal folds to be pulled laterally, opening the glottis. We know, of course, that the vocalis muscle courses in an antero-posterior direction. Second, because the neurochronaxic theory specifies that each cycle of vibration is achieved by a neural pulse, the recurrent laryngeal nerve would have to fire at a physiologically impossible rate to sustain the frequencies of vibration commonly achieved during speech.

Experimentation With the Excised Larynx and Computational Models

Numerous researchers have conducted important experiments using excised larynges. What is an excised larynx, and why is it used in voice research? An **excised larynx** is one that has been removed from a human cadaver or from an animal that has been sacrificed for experimentation. The larynx is preserved in a chemical formulation so that the tissues do not break down. The organ is set on a support frame and an air supply is situated below the vocal folds to simulate air exhaled from the lungs. Force can be applied to selected isolated intrinsic muscles, and airflow and air pressure can be finely manipulated to calculate precise effects of such manipulation on voice production. Such precise manipulation of isolated factors cannot be achieved in the in vivo (living) larynx. Experimentation that would be too dangerous or physically uncomfortable can be performed readily on the excised larynx, yielding a great wealth of information.

Another way to learn about vocal dynamics is through using software simulations of the larynx and vocal tract, called computational models. Such simulations consist of dozens of mathematical formulas specifying aerodynamic and viscoelastic forces. Early models, such as those of Titze and Talkin (1979), explored the effect of manipulating muscle activity on f_0 and intensity. These models form the basis for our current understanding of voice production.

basis of this theory is that the elasticity of the vocal folds allows them to be set into vibration by aerodynamic forces, specifically a phenomenon known as the Bernoulli (Daniel Bernoulli, 1700–1782) effect. Van den Berg (1958) reports that Tonndorf (1925) was the first scientist to relate the Bernoulli effect to aerodynamics of the glottis. Although our current knowledge of voice production has modified the role played by the Bernoulli effect, this aerodynamic force remains a central factor in voice production, and so we examine it closely before continuing our exploration of vocal fold vibration.

The Bernoulli Effect

Fluids in motion behave differently, in some respects, than static (still) fluids. The major difference between static and dynamic (moving) fluids can be summarized as follows: In a fluid under movement, the pressure exerted by a fluid on a surface decreases as the velocity of the fluid across the surface increases. This is Bernoulli's force, often known as the **Bernoulli effect**. It is an expression of the conservation of energy for a moving fluid. The Bernoulli effect has a critical role in vocal fold vibration and, hence, in voice production, and so we will examine several examples of this phenomenon. A common example familiar to many people is the flight of an airplane. Although airplanes are certainly heavier than air, the Bernoulli effect contributes to the plane's ability to fly. You may have seen that the upper surface of the wings of the plane

is more curved than their under surface. This shape is called an "airfoil." Of course, we know that the shortest distance between two points is a straight line. As the plane gathers speed moving down the runway, the air must travel farther over the top of the wings than past the underside of the wings. Therefore, the air over the top of the wings must travel faster to "keep up" with the air moving along the underside of the wings. The Bernoulli effect tells us that the faster velocity results in lower pressure over the top of the wings, thus producing a net upward force (called "lift"). When the plane gets moving fast enough, the lift helps the plane to rise.

We can think of the Bernoulli effect in another situation that is particularly relevant for voice production. Suppose that we have air flowing through a tube that has a narrow section in the middle of it (Figure 5–23). The walls of the tube are rigid so that, unlike a balloon, they cannot expand. Therefore, if we blow 100 mL of air into the tube per second, 100 mL of air per second must exit the tube. If we placed pressure gauges along the length of the tube, we would find that the pressure is lower in the narrower part of the tube as compared to the two wider ends. Why is that? The fluid must flow faster through the narrower region of the tube. The same amount of fluid must pass by every point along the tube as it flows from one end to the other. Otherwise, fluid would back up in one part of the tube. Therefore, in the narrower region of the tube, the individual particles (molecules) must move faster in this region. The Bernoulli principle, said another way, tells us the

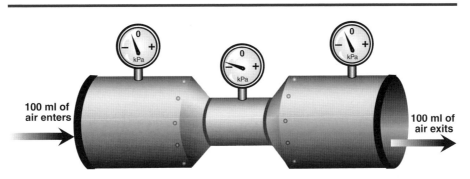

Figure 5–23. The Bernoulli effect.

following: The pressure in a fluid decreases as its velocity increases.

Students can sometimes be confused about the Bernoulli effect because of the stipulation that fluid cannot back up but must flow everywhere at the same rate. When we consider the effect of the Bernoulli force, we must allow that fluid (air, in the case of the vocal tract) cannot be compressed around the narrowed tube; that is, it cannot be allowed to "back up." (The reasons for this are considerably beyond the scope of this textbook.) The following two examples will help to clarify this concept.

You are traveling along a particularly busy section of highway during the afternoon rush hour. There are two lanes of traffic in each direction, and all the cars are going 60 miles an hour. A car has broken down in the right-hand lane up ahead, so all cars must merge into the left lane to get around the stalled car. What happens? First, cars slow down as they drive by the stalled vehicle, to get a look at what is going on ("rubbernecking"—we are a curious species). Cars also slow down because they must merge together into one lane. So, there is a bottleneck. Cars back up behind the stalled vehicle. The road beyond the stalled vehicle is only sparsely populated with cars, as each car is released slowly from the bottleneck and accelerates to resume travel. Consider the cars to be molecules of air. Consider the highway to be a tube that is narrowed in the middle (at the location of the stalled vehicle). The cars are not obeying the laws of physics in this regard but rather the laws of human nature (slow down in a merge and check out the stalled vehicle). To prevent a backup of cars behind the area of constriction (narrowing), the cars would have to speed up as they merge and pass by the stalled vehicle. This would not be particularly safe, but it would certainly obey the Bernoulli effect and prevent a traffic jam!

Consider another example: a large parade containing many marching bands, floats, and clowns. A college marching band is currently passing by you, consisting of 10 band members abreast in each of 12 rows (Figure 5–24). The area of the block at which you are standing to watch the parade is narrower than the rest of

Figure 5–24. The "Bernoulli High School" marching band!

the route due to the construction site across from you, which has equipment placed out in the street partially obstructing the flow of traffic. Because of the equipment, only 5 band members can fit abreast, not the full 10. The band members cannot squeeze closer together, because of their instruments, so they must form extra rows to allow everyone to pass through the narrowed area. But all the band members must continue marching at the same pace, or else the bands and floats will get backed up behind them, and the parade will look terrible. What to do? The solution is to have the band members march double time past the narrowed area, as only half as many members can pass by at once. That will preserve the overall rate of flow of the marching band and the entire parade. Consider the band members to be molecules of air. The molecules speed up through the narrowed area, and therefore the overall rate of flow is maintained.

There are numerous examples of the Bernoulli force in everyday life. If you have ever gone boating on a lake, you may have experienced another example of the Bernoulli effect. Imagine two canoes or rowboats sitting quietly side by side in the water. If they are very close to each other, the boats will repeatedly "bonk" together—hit each other and bounce off, only to be drawn together and bonk again, repeating this cycle over and over again. What is occurring? The water flowing between the boats is effectively flowing through a narrowed tube. Therefore, the rate of flow must be increased, and the Bernoulli effect shows us that the pressure within the flow must be decreased. The greater pressure of the water flowing on the opposite side of the boats together with the lesser pressure of the water between the boats will effectively draw the boats together.

Daniel Bernoulli (1700–1782)

Bernoulli was a Swiss physicist who determined that Newton's second law of motion (force is equal to mass times acceleration) applied to atoms and molecules. That is, if the number of air molecules is doubled, the rate of collision between the molecules and the container walls must double, and so the resulting air pressure must be doubled as well. Similarly, decrease the number of air molecules by one-half, and the rate of collisions will be halved, leading to a halving of the air pressure. Daniel Bernoulli was born in Groningen, the Netherlands, where 250 years later, one of the world's leading voice science laboratories would be located. (See the discussion of van den Berg earlier in this chapter.) Daniel Bernoulli was a member of a brilliant but contentious family of scientists, and he achieved a great place in scientific history for his advances in hydrodynamics.

Venturi Effect

Named after the Italian scientist, Giovanni Battista Venturi (1746–1822), who first described this effect, the **Venturi effect** is another aerodynamic phenomenon that occurs within the vocal tract. Quite simply, the Venturi effect is the acceleration of fluid, like air, through a narrowed area. You have experienced the Venturi effect if you have walked between two high-rise buildings on a windy day. As you proceed between the buildings, the wind velocity increases. The air accelerates through the narrow opening between the buildings. The Venturi effect also occurs in the capillaries, in that the blood flow accelerates when flowing from a larger to a smaller blood vessel. Imagine a garden hose with water flowing easily from the nozzle. Place an imaginary finger over the nozzle so that it partially occludes the opening of the garden hose. What happens? The water accelerates out of the hose with greater force and arcs away across the garden to a greater distance (Walker, 1987). The acceleration is the result of the Venturi effect. The Venturi effect is not a fundamental principle governing the totality of this strange human phenomenon we call voice production, but it does occur. It occurs because the lung pressure is greater than the supraglottal pressure, and so the airflow is driven under pressure from the lungs upward through the narrowed opening of the glottis, causing the airstream to accelerate upward out of the glottis during part of the vibratory cycle. The effect of this acceleration is important to the modulation of the acoustic signal in the vocal tract, and we will return to it in Chapter 7 when we address vocal tract resonance.

The Myoelastic-Aerodynamic Theory

Now with a good understanding of the Bernoulli effect, we can explore the myoelastic-aerodynamic theory of voice production. Originated by Müller and further expanded upon and credited to van den Berg, the theory emphasized the interdependent relationship of the Bernoulli effect and certain physical properties of the vocal folds, particularly their tension, mass per unit of length, and elasticity. The prefix *myo* means muscle. Recall from Chapter 2 that elasticity is the ability of an object to return to its original shape after outside forces (a push or a pull) stop causing the deformation. Tension is the force used to stretch or elongate the vocal folds. Tension is the result of the interaction of the pulling force exerted on the vocal folds and the resistance to the force (stiffness) offered by the vocal folds. The myoelastic component of the theory specifies that these physical properties of the vocal folds and the degree of vocal fold adduction in preparation for phonation are under active neuromuscular control. The aerodynamic component is the Bernoulli force that draws the vocal folds into vibration.

The strength of the myoelastic-aerodynamic theory is that it identifies the self-oscillating nature of the vocal folds. Recall in Chapter 3 that we defined free and forced vibration. Self-oscillation is a third type of vibration. Self-oscillation means that the vibration is not dependent upon neural input (see the description of the neurochronaxic theory in Theory Rejected) but rather a steady, external oscillating driving source (Titze, 1994a, p. 83). That external driving source identified in the myoelastic-aerodynamic theory is the airflow from the lungs. Self-oscillation also requires a nonlinear interaction among the components of the system, which was not clearly identified in this early theory of phonation. We shall return to this essential nonlinear component in the following section on the Biomechanics of Vocal Fold Vibration. The myoelastic-aerodynamic theory emphasizes that vocal fold vibration is a passive event that results from an interaction or coupling of the glottal opening, the physical properties of the vocal folds, and the lung pressure. (The terms lung pressure and subglottal pressure are used equivalently. Now that we are familiar with the structures of the larynx and particularly the glottis, we will use the term lung pressure.) A major weakness of the myoelastic-aerodynamic theory as it was initially proposed, however, as discussed by Titze (1980), is the overstatement of the contribution of the Bernoulli effect, which by itself cannot sustain self-oscillation of the vocal folds. Let us examine a cycle of vibration using a currently revised myoelastic-aerodynamic theory.

5.5 Biomechanics of Vocal Fold Vibration

Let us consider a cycle of vibration. The cycle as described is depicted graphically in Figures 5–25, 5–26, and 5–27. Throughout this section, unless otherwise noted, letters A through L refer to

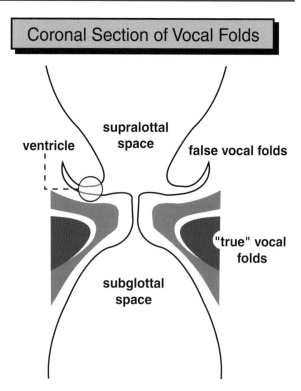

Figure 5–25. Schematic of coronal section of vocal folds.

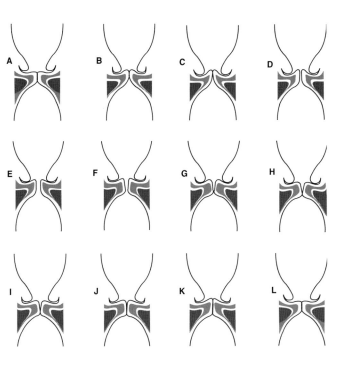

Figure 5–26. Schematic of coronal view of vocal fold vibratory motion. Note that this sequence is meant to represent vibratory behavior in a very general fashion and does not imply the relative duration of the opening and closing phases of vibration.

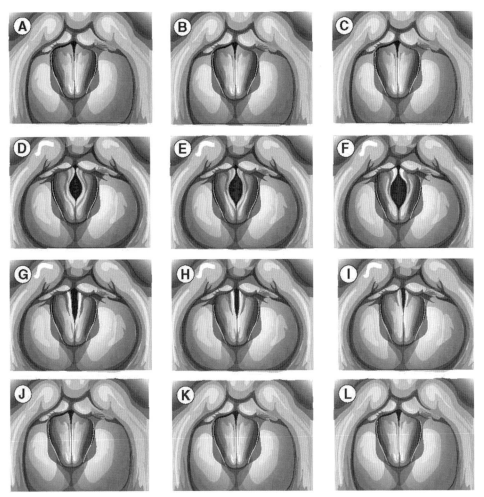

Figure 5–27. Schematic of superior view of vocal fold vibratory motion.

both Figures 5–26 and 5–27. For purposes of this explanation, let us assume that at the onset of phonation, the arytenoid cartilages rock inward to adduct the vocal folds lightly, in this way closing the glottis partially or completely (A). The medial, or adductory, movement of the vocal folds is sometimes referred to as approximation. Closely approximated vocal folds are almost but not quite touching, whereas completely approximated vocal folds seal the glottis closed. (Differences in the **prephonatory phase** will be explained further under Phonation Onset, and the relationship of medial compression and lung pressure is explored further in Phonation Threshold Pressure.)

As the thoracic cavity is compressed to exhale (for voice production occurs on exhalation), the lung pressure increases below the glottis as the airflow meets the resistance of the closed vocal folds. The increased lung pressure pushes against the pliable and elastic vocal folds. When the lung pressure is great enough to overcome vocal fold resistance, the folds are pushed laterally to open the glottis. Note in B that the inferior (lower) border of the vocal folds separates before the superior (upper) border (sometimes referred to as the lower and upper lips or margins of the vocal folds, respectively). Although the lower margin has separated, the glottis is still closed because the upper margin remains in contact. The shape of the glottis as viewed from below is triangular with the wider base below and the point of the triangle formed by the upper margins of the vocal folds. This configuration is referred to as a **convergent-shaped glottis** (Titze, 1994a, p. 95). The convergent glottis is like a pyramid, with the upper margin of the vocal folds forming the apex of the pyramid and the lower margin and conus elasticus forming the wider base. The convergent shape does not require the upper edge of the vocal folds to be closed. The convergent shape facilitates a relatively high lung pressure that forces the vocal folds laterally.

In C, we observe that the upper margins of the vocal folds have separated, opening the glottis to allow airflow upward through the glottis. The upper margins separate due to the force of

the air pressure and the lateral pull of the elastic tissue. In effect, the upper margin is dragged along, albeit somewhat delayed, by the lateral movement of the lower margin. In D, we see the maximal opening of the glottis. The upper and lower borders of the vocal folds appear in parallel, but they are moving in opposite directions. The lower border is reaching its maximum lateral excursion while the upper border continues to open. For confirmation, when we look ahead at E, we note that the lower border of the vocal folds is already returning to midline.

When the glottis opens (C), airflow commences. The lung pressure is greater than the pressure immediately above the glottis, causing a pressure drop across the vocal folds. Recalling that fluid flows from greater pressure to lesser pressure, the airflow is drawn upward through the vocal folds. A jet stream of air flows upward through the narrow chink of the glottal opening (see The Venturi Effect on p. 137).

In E and F, as the lower border of the vocal folds is returning to midline, we see that the shape of the glottis is now that of an inverted triangle, with the base at the top and the point at the bottom, formed by the adducting lower margin of the vocal folds. This glottal configuration (Figure 5–28A) is called a **divergent-shaped glottis** (Titze, 1994a, p. 95). In the divergent

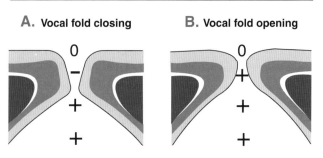

A. Vocal fold closing   **B.** Vocal fold opening

Figure 5–28. Divergent (**A**) and convergent (**B**) shaped glottis. All the signs are relative to supraglottal pressure. (Supraglottal pressure is not zero, but because we are comparing subglottal and intraglottal pressures *relative* to the supraglottal pressure, we identify the latter as zero.) The negative intraglottal pressure in **A** simply means that the pressure is lower than supraglottal pressure. And the subglottal plus signs in **A** and **B** represent pressures higher than those supraglottally.

Janwillem van den Berg and the Groningen Voice Laboratory

Dr. van den Berg was one of the founders of modern voice science. The son of a butcher, he was born in Akkrum, the Netherlands, and went to Amsterdam to study physics. His introduction to voice production came in a class taught by Louise Kaiser, the first professor in phonetics in Amsterdam. van den Berg's training as a physicist made him doubtful of the then current explanation that the voice worked on the same basis as Savart's explanation of the hunting whistle. He began conducting research into alternative theories of voice production. During World War II, van den Berg took shelter in Groningen to avoid possible transportation to Germany as a war worker.

Eventually, he secured a position as physicist in the Physiologic Laboratory in Groningen, where he had an opportunity to perform these experiments. In those years, the French physicist Husson had developed an alternative theory to explain the vibrations of the vocal folds, the neurochronaxic theory, which van den Berg refuted through his experimentation and writings. He published his initial thesis in 1953. van den Berg died in 1985. The Groningen Voice Laboratory, under the direction of Dr. Harm Schutte, a disciple of van den Berg, continued to be a valuable source of experimental data on many aspects of voice and singing production for many years.

glottis, the shape is an inverted pyramid, with the lower margins of the vocal folds placed more medially than the upper margins. This shape results in the Bernoulli effect, causing a lowering of the transglottal pressure and an inward pull of the lower margin of the vocal folds. In G, we see the contact of the lower margin of the vocal folds, effectively closing the glottis and the moment of cessation of airflow. In G and H, the upper border of the vocal folds is returning to midline, being pulled by and lagging behind the lower border. In I, full contact of the vocal folds is established.

A concept that sometimes confuses students is the difference between opening and closing of the vocal folds during vibration and the abduction and adduction of the vocal folds. Note that we began our discussion of phonation by identifying the prephonatory positioning of the vocal folds (A). The vocal folds are abducted during breathing, and by movement of the arytenoid cartilages via the cricoarytenoid joint, the vocal folds are adducted to initiate phonation. The opening and closing of the vocal folds during phonation occur through the coupling of the aerodynamic forces and the biomechanical properties of the tissues as a passive event. Dur-

ing vocal fold vibration, the arytenoid cartilages do not rock the vocal folds open and closed. When phonation is stopped, the vocal folds are then abducted by movement of the arytenoid cartilages and breathing resumes.

Viscoelastic Component

The elasticity of the vocal fold tissues determines their ability to spring back to their original shape after being deformed by both aerodynamic forces and the collision of the tissues at midline. Viscosity, as you may recall from Chapter 3, is a measure of internal friction and tells us how well a fluid flows. The superficial layer of lamina propria has a low viscosity and flows easily. Imagine fluids of different compositions layered one atop the other with little mixing of the two (such as oil and water). Viscosity tells us about the relative ease with which layers of tissue slide over one another in response to a shear force. The force that contributes to the upheaval of tissue described as the mucosal wave (see below) is a **shear force**, defined as one that acts parallel to a surface. **Viscoelasticity**, therefore, references both the elastic resistance of the vocal fold tissues and the ease with which the vocal folds return to their original shape and position. Recall our discussion in Chapter 4 about the elastic restorative forces that contribute to the recoil of the lungs and chest wall during exhalation. These same forces are at work in the vocal folds during phonation. When the rush of air through the glottis forces the vocal folds apart, momentum helps them stretch laterally beyond their resting position, and they build up restorative forces, which ultimately cause them to snap back to midline and collide into each other.

Vertical Phase Difference: The Mucosal Wave

In discussing phonatory biomechanics, it is often helpful to divide the cycle into opening (see Figures 5–26 and 5–27 A–E) and closing (see Figures 5–26 and 5–27 F–L) phases. We can also identify an open (D through F) and closed (A through C and H through L) phase. The opening and closing phases are component parts of the open phase. Air flows through the glottis during the open phase, but the airway is sealed during the closed phase so that no air escapes through the glottis.

Note that in the closing phase of the cycle (F through L), the inferior (lower) border of the vocal folds is contacting before the superior (upper) border. This phenomenon was remarked upon as the **vertical phasing** or **out-of-phase movement**, described by Titze and Strong (1975) as "the movement of different vertical portions of the glottal edge of the [vocal folds] in opposite directions at a given point in time" (p. 740). Farnsworth (1940) described this out-of-phase movement as "a wave-like motion or ripple is seen to pass over the top surface from the glottis toward the walls of the larynx" (p. 207). The mucosal movements of the lower and upper margins are said to be out of phase with each other because, during the early part of the closing phase, the lower border is adducting, or moving medially, while the superior margin is still moving laterally, or abducting (F). Similarly, during the early portion of the opening phase,

the inferior border is abducting while the superior border is still adducting. Both the opening and closing phases of vibration proceed from the lower margin first, followed by the upper margin. We identify this difference in vertical phase as the **mucosal wave**, which describes the traveling wave of mucosa from the inferior to superior margin and continuing laterally toward the boundary between the vocal folds and the laryngeal ventricle. (See Figure 5–29 for a schematic model of this motion.) As we will learn in Chapter 6, considerable effort has been focused on developing instrumentation that can image and measure the mucosal wave.

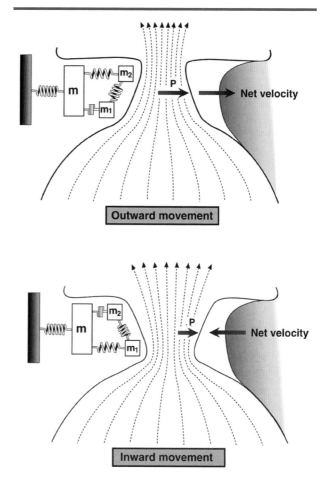

Figure 5–29. Vocal fold vibration modeled as three connected masses showing vertical phase difference. Adapted from *Principles of Voice Production* (p. 95), by I. R. Titze, 1994, Englewood Cliffs, NJ: Prentice-Hall. Adapted with permission.

A critical concept to be emphasized is the necessity of a pressure difference across the vocal folds. The lung pressure must be greater than the supraglottal pressure (the pressure just above the vocal folds) for airflow to occur. (Recall that air flows from greater pressure to lesser pressure.) Transglottal pressure is the relative difference between the pressure just below and just above the vocal folds. The **transglottal pressure** often is referred to as the **driving pressure** in that this difference in air pressures is the driving force that sets the vocal folds into vibration.

We have noted that the original myoelastic-aerodynamic theory overemphasized the role of the Bernoulli effect. Our present understanding of vibratory dynamics identifies two features of the aerodynamic component that differ from the initial theory. First, the aerodynamic forces, both the lung pressure and the Bernoulli effect, work primarily upon the lower margins of the vocal folds due to the convergent and divergent shapes of the glottis during vibration (Gauffin, Binh, Ananthapadmanabha, & Fant, 1983). The movement of the upper margins of the vocal folds is due primarily to the viscoelastic properties of the vocal folds, and we have already discussed how they are dragged along by the movement of the lower margins. Thus, we see that the original myoelastic-aerodynamic theory of voice production did not account for the fact that the Bernoulli effect by itself does not differentiate between opening and closing movements of the vocal folds. Instead, we see that the aerodynamic force must be raised during vocal fold opening and lowered during closing to maintain vibration. The lung pressure plays an important role in pushing the vocal folds apart, and this is independent of the Bernoulli effect.

In addition, the original myoelastic-aerodynamic theory, with its emphasis on the Bernoulli effect, depended upon complete glottal closure. For if the vocal folds are slightly abducted, according to the original theory, the narrowed glottal channel would result in a lowering of intraglottal pressure and the vocal folds would be pulled together. Yet we know that, in some cases, the vocal folds remain slightly separated during vibration (and we will explore this style

of phonation in our discussion of Phonation Onset later in this chapter).

It should also be noted that, in addition to a difference in vertical phase, a difference in **anterior-posterior phase** occurs (Childers & Krishnamurthy, 1985). The vocal folds open and close in a zipperlike fashion, starting anteriorly and proceeding posteriorly. This is due to the fixed attachment of the vocal folds at the thyroid cartilage and the movable points of attachment of the vocal folds posteriorly at the vocal processes of the arytenoid cartilages.

Study Questions

18. Describe the Bernoulli effect.

19. Describe a cycle of vocal fold vibration using the updated myoelastic-aerodynamic theory. Importantly, include the contribution of the physical properties of the vocal folds and the aerodynamic forces.

20. What is the relevance of the convergent- and divergent-shaped glottis during phonation?

21. How do the restorative forces of the vocal fold tissues contribute to vibration?

22. Define shear force.

23. Define viscoelasticity.

24. Explain the out-of-phase movement of the mucosal wave.

25. Why is the transglottal pressure often referred to as the driving pressure of vibration?

The Importance of Vocal Fold Closure

Another critical concept to emphasize is the importance of phonatory glottal closure to voice production. At the moment of closure of the vocal folds, the airflow through the glottis is rapidly halted. The supraglottal airflow, however, briefly continues its upward trajectory (due to momentum). With no air mass to follow behind it, the pressure immediately above the vocal folds drops, pulling back the upward column of air. A collision of air molecules occurs as the air column compresses backward. We know from our discussion in Chapter 3 that restorative forces will cause this compression of air molecules to expand and then to compress again, continuing in a cycle of compressions and rarefactions. The compressions and rarefactions of air molecules caused by the sudden closure of the vocal folds are referred to as the excitation of the supraglottal air mass. Every time the vocal folds open and then close, a pulse of excited air is sent up the vocal tract, like a shock wave of sound. When the vocal folds are open during quiet breathing, the air flows relatively undisturbed up the vocal tract. When the vocal folds vibrate open and closed, the air becomes chopped into pulses of alternating compressions and rarefactions, each traveling up the vocal tract as an acoustic shock wave. Glottal closure, therefore, is the event that results in acoustic excitation of the air in the vocal tract. In Chapter 7, we will examine more closely the nature of acoustic excitation. For now, let us consider that it represents the imparting of energy to the air by causing rapid alternating compressions and rarefactions of the air molecules.

Upon opening of the vocal folds, the sound energy may travel from the glottis upward through the vocal tract or downward from the glottis into the trachea and lungs. Sound energy that travels subglottally is completely lost to the listener. Do not get confused between sound energy and the direction of the airflow. As you phonate, your breath travels from the lungs upward through the vocal tract. Although the dominant direction of the sound energy is upward from the vocal folds, some of the sound energy also disperses downward in the opposite direction. On a windy day, you can talk to a person who is standing upwind from you. If the wind is very strong, the sound energy from your vocal tract gets dispersed quickly, so that it does not carry as well

upstream. But it still does radiate through the air against the current of the wind.

Glottal Volume Velocity

Strictly speaking, the glottis is the space between the vocal folds. The term is used as a modifier, however, to identify events associated with the vibration of the vocal folds. For example, glottal vibrations may be used to refer to the mucosal wave of the vocal folds. And as we will discuss later in the chapter, glottal attack refers to a type of initiation of vocal fold vibration, and glottal resistance describes the degree to which the vocal folds impede airflow through the glottis. The **glottal volume velocity** (also called **transglottal airflow**) is the volume of air flowing through the glottis as a function of time during phonation. The **glottal waveform** is a plot of the glottal volume velocity (Figure 5–30). Time is plotted on the horizontal x-axis, and increasing volume of airflow is plotted upward along the vertical y-axis. Each cycle of the glottal volume velocity corresponds to one opening and closing cycle of vibration. The flat, horizontal line portion of the waveform represents a lack of glottal flow. In other words, the vocal folds are adducted and the glottis is closed. The upward deflection of the waveform represents airflow through the glottis. The downward deflection represents a decrease in glottal volume velocity as the vocal folds are adducting. The peaks of the waveform represent maximum volume velocity, corresponding to maximum glottal opening. Note that the airflow increases from zero somewhat gradually compared to the shutoff of the airflow, which occurs more rapidly. We will learn in Control of Intensity that the rapidity of the cessation of airflow is of critical importance to the intensity of the sound (Hollien, 1974; Monsen & Engebretson, 1977).

Laryngeal Airway Resistance

The vocal folds are a variable impediment to the airflow. When completely abducted during inhalation, the vocal folds impede the airflow

**Glottal Volume
Velocity**

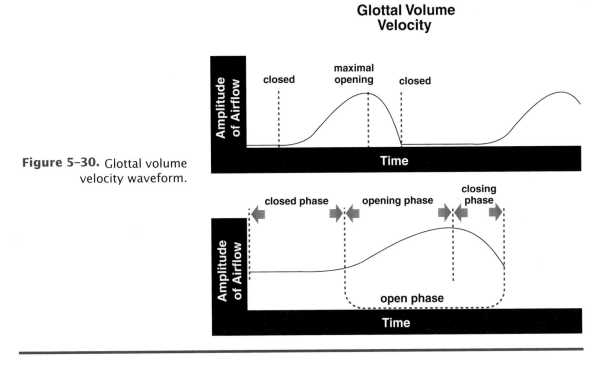

Figure 5–30. Glottal volume
velocity waveform.

minimally. When fully adducted, their resistance is complete, for no air flows through the glottis. At all other moments throughout the vibratory cycle, the vocal folds offer partial resistance to the airflow, depending on the phase of the mucosal wave. **Glottal resistance**, also called **laryngeal airway resistance**, is a measure of the amount of resistance the vocal folds offer to the airflow. Although the resistance changes from moment to moment throughout the vibratory cycle, glottal (or laryngeal airway) resistance generally refers to the average resistance across many vibratory cycles. It is quantified as the ratio of the transglottal pressure to the transglottal flow. Transglottal pressure is exceedingly difficult to measure. We can, however, estimate resistance in the following ways. We will learn in Chapter 7 that vowels are produced with a relatively nonconstricted vocal tract. So, we can assume that the supraglottal pressure is basically equivalent to atmospheric pressure because of this open communication with the air outside the body during vowel production. With the supraglottal air pressure equal to atmospheric pressure, the **lung pressure** becomes the effective driving pressure for the airflow. Therefore,

glottal resistance can be measured as the ratio of the lung pressure to the glottal volume velocity (Smitheran & Hixon, 1981). As it is a measure of the ratio of pressure to flow, the units of measurement for glottal resistance is cm of $H_2O/L/s$, with cm of H_2O for pressure and liters per second for flow. An off-the-shelf instrumentation system for assessing voice and speech by Kay/Pentax (Lincoln Park, NJ), popularly used in clinical research, uses the MKS system, measuring pressure in newtons and flow in s/m^6, so that the units of measurement for glottal resistance is newtons-s/m^6. In the CGS system, pressure is measured in dynes and flow in s/cm^5, so the unit of measurement for glottal resistance becomes dynes-s/cm^5, a common unit used in the research literature (Hirano, 1981).

Phonation Threshold Pressure

Phonation threshold pressure is the minimal lung pressure required for phonation. Phonation threshold pressure at phonation onset, the lung pressure level required to initiate phonation, is greater than phonation threshold pressure at phonation offset, the lung pressure below which phonation cannot be sustained. Recall from Chapter 2 that inertia is the tendency for a mass at rest to remain at rest. To initiate vibration, the lung pressure must overcome the inertia of the vocal folds. Once in vibration, the momentum of the vocal folds contributes energy to drive the vibration, and therefore less lung pressure is required to maintain phonation. In general, a minimum lung pressure between 0.3 and 0.5 kPA (3 to 5 cm of H_2O) is required to initiate phonation, but 0.1 to 0.2 kPa less is required, at a minimum, to sustain phonation (Draper, Ladefoged, & Whitteridge; 1960; Lieberman, Knudson, & Mead, 1969). Many factors affect the value of the phonation threshold pressure. Phonation threshold pressure varies indirectly with vocal fold thickness, and it varies directly with f_o, vocal fold viscosity, mucosal wave velocity, separation of the vocal folds in the prephonatory stage (Finkelhor, Titze, & Durham, 1988; Gramming, 1989; Plant, Freed, & Plant, 2004; Verdolini-Marston, Titze, & Drucker, 1990), and with dehydration of the tissue (Verdolini-Marston et al., 1990). Some evidence suggests that an individual's perception of level of phonatory effort is correlated directly with phonation threshold pressure (Chang & Karnell, 2004). Phonation threshold pressure is variable within an individual and across individuals because of its dependence on frequency, intensity, and laryngeal airway resistance (Plant et al., 2004) as well as the manner of phonation onset.

Phonation Onset

Earlier, we alluded to the possibility of more than one positioning of the vocal folds in the prephonatory, or phonation-ready, phase of the vibratory cycle. The initiation of phonation, referred to as the onset of phonation, is often divided into three categories: simultaneous (gentle), breathy, and glottal attack (Moore, 1938). Phonation onset was explored in early high-speed laryngeal imaging (to be discussed further on) (Faaborg-Andersen, 1957; Moore, 1938; Werner-Kekuk & von Leden, 1970), in acoustic studies (Koike, 1967), and in electromyography (Hirose & Gay, 1973; Koike, 1967). Together,

those studies provide the following information. In **simultaneous (gentle) onset**, also referred to as soft onset, as its name implies, phonation is initiated by simultaneous exhalation and adduction of the vocal folds at midline. In **breathy onset**, also called aspirate onset, the exhalation and airflow through the glottis is initiated before the vocal folds are adducted. The amount of air released before onset of phonation can be quite variable, ranging from minimal to significant air wastage. In **glottal attack**, also called hard onset of phonation, the vocal folds are firmly approximated prior to initiating phonation. Hard onset involves significant medial compression of the vocal folds, allowing a buildup of lung pressure. When the vocal folds are released, the vocal folds are blown apart in an "explosive nature" (Zemlin, 1998, p. 147). Therefore, one would expect that phonation threshold pressure for the onset of phonation in hard glottal attack would be greater than for that of soft or aspirate onset. All three types of phonation onset require coordinated adjustments among the intrinsic laryngeal muscles and initiation of airflow.

Vocal rise time is a helpful parameter with which to assess phonation onset. **Vocal rise time** is the duration from the onset of sound to the moment at which the amplitude of the acoustic sound pressure wave reaches a steady state (Figure 5–31). Vocal rise time decreases from breathy to gentle to hard onset. The different characteristics of the three styles of phonation onset are summarized in Table 5–4.

Gentle (simultaneous) phonatory onset generally is considered the optimal means of initia-

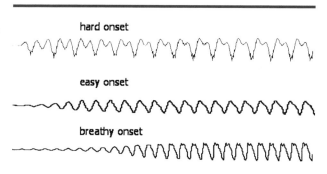

Figure 5–31. These waveforms of the acoustic signal show the progressive increase in vocal rise time from hard to easy to breathy onsets.

Table 5–4. Summary of Characteristics of Phonation Onset[a]

	Soft (Gentle, Easy, Simultaneous)	Breathy (Aspirate)	Hard (Glottal Attack)
Vocal rise time[b] (ms)	120 (SD 25.2, range 60–120)	190 (SD 31.5, range 100–190)	23 (SD 10.2, range 18–42)
Initial movement of vocal folds	Medial	Medial	Lateral
Onset of airflow and vocal fold vibration	Airflow simultaneous with vibration	Airflow prior to vibration	Airflow simultaneous with vibration
Medial compression of vocal folds	Lightly adducted	Closely approximated but not completely adducted	Significant medial compression
Activity of posterior cricoarytenoid muscle before initiation of vibration	Suppressed throughout prephonatory period	Active throughout prephonatory period	Decreases well before onset of voicing
Lateral cricoarytenoid, cricothyroid, interarytenoid, and thyroarytenoid	Gradual increase before voicing	Gradual increase before voicing	Active well before onset of voicing

Sources:

[a]Data (except where noted) from: Koike, Y. (1967) Experimental studies on vocal attack. *Oto-rhino-laryngol Clinics Kyoto, 60,* 663–688 and Hirose, H., & Gay, T. (1973). Laryngeal control in vocal attack. An electromyographic study. *Folia Phonatirica, 25,* 203–213.

[b]Unpublished data from Behrman.

tion of phonation. Hard onset is often associated with voice disorders (Koike, 1967) hypothesized to cause phonotrauma due to the increased forces generated within the vocal folds. For this reason, in the treatment of individuals with voice disorders, the reduction of hard phonatory onset is often a therapeutic goal. Perhaps the most common therapeutic strategy, developed by one of the great singing teachers, William Vennard (1967), is to have the individual place an "h" before words starting with a vowel. In Chapter 7, we will learn about the manner of production of sounds like those represented by the letter "h." Suffice it to say for now that insertion of this sound prior to a vowel forces the initiation of airflow prior to vibration, so that the first movement of the vocal folds is inward, as in soft or breathy onset. In this way, the potential trauma to the vocal folds is minimized by reducing the contact force of the vocal folds. We will examine the forces acting upon the vocal folds that are necessary to phonation but, in excess, may contribute substantially to vocal problems.

Study Questions

26. Explain why vocal fold closure is important.

27. Define glottal volume velocity and glottal waveform.

28. Define glottal resistance and provide a synonym.

29. What is phonation threshold pressure, and what is an average value for it?

30. Name and describe the three types of phonation onset.

31. What is vocal rise-time?

5.6 Biomechanical Stress-Strain Properties of Vocal Fold Tissues

The control of f_o and intensity requires variable stiffness of the biomechanical layers of the vocal folds. Changes in stiffness are obtained actively and passively. Passive changes can be understood using a stress-strain plot. From a biological perspective, stress is the sum of the biological reactions of an organism to internal or external adverse stimuli (physical or cognitive). Becoming ill from working too hard (too little sleep, poor nutrition) is a common reaction to stress. The definition we will use, however, is a biomechanical one. **Stress** is the force divided by the cross-sectional area perpendicular to the direction of the force. In other words, stress is the force per unit area. It can be thought of as the opposite of relaxation. Stress is a measure of the internal distribution of force per unit area within a material. It is the internal force that results in a change in the volume or shape of a material

after the material has been subjected to external forces. Stress tends to displace (move) the material. **Strain** is the length of the change of the tissue in the direction of the force divided by its resting length. That is, when the vocal folds are stretched long or contracted short, the force acting upon them is called strain. Tension on the vocal folds represents the tautness of the tissue, the pulling force exerted on them. The stress and strain placed upon the vocal folds can be viewed in terms of the tension placed on them. As the vocal folds are placed under tension and stretched (elongated), the stress increases with increasing strain. Figure 5–32 shows a stress-strain curve, a graph of the elongation of the thyroarytenoid muscle and mucosal cover of a dog as a function of the force (stretch) exerted upon them. The greater the force, the greater the tension placed on the tissue.

Canine vocal folds often are used in research on vocal fold physiology because of their similarity to human vocal folds. (Similar, but not the same. A significant difference between dogs and

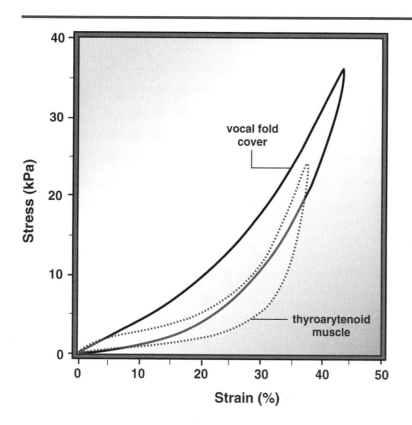

Figure 5–32. Force-elongation curves for vocal fold cover (*solid lines*) and muscle (*dashed lines*), based on excised canine larynx. Adapted from *Principles of Voice Production* (p. 39), by I. R. Titze, 1994, Englewood Cliffs, NJ: Prentice-Hall. Adapted with permission.

human beings is the lack of a vocal ligament in dog vocal folds. The crucial role of the vocal ligament is discussed as we explore f_o control later in the chapter.) Recall from Chapter 4 that muscles can contract and relax, but they cannot elongate and stretch by themselves. The antagonist muscle is stretched by the contraction of the agonist. Therefore, the stretch-strain curve describes what occurs when a muscle is passively stretched by another active muscle. Although in the case of Figure 5–32, the curves represent ex vivo (out of the living body) stretching of the canine thyroarytenoid muscle and cover by a mechanical force mechanism designed in a laboratory, the curve likely simulates the passive stretch and release of the thyroarytenoid muscle in the human body as acted upon by cricothyroid muscle contraction and release.

Alipour-Haghighi and Titze (1991) and Titze (1994a, p. 39) identify some properties of the canine stress-strain curve that are notable. First, the plot is curved rather than straight. Recall from Chapter 2 that Hooke's law states that the change in length of a material is proportional to the force applied to it. In other words, the harder you pull on something, the more it stretches. That is true for the vocal folds, but the relationship is not completely linear.

Linearity simply means that the output is directly proportional to the input; the reaction to a force is directly proportional to the force applied. In a linear system, a small force will result in a small reaction, and incrementally larger forces will result in proportionally larger responses. Figure 5–33 shows that, in a linear

system, a plot of the reaction as a function of the input force will result in a straight line. The stress-strain plot of the vocal folds (see Figure 5–32) shows that the vocal folds do not completely adhere to Hooke's law; that is, they do not react linearly when stretched. At the beginning of the stretch, an increase in 10 or 20% strain produces a disproportionately small amount of stress. But as the stretch progresses, at 30 or 35% strain, one obtains the opposite effect, a disproportionately large increase in stress. Said another way, with increased length, the muscles become stiffer. Thus, with successive force placed upon them, the tissue does not stretch as much. This nonlinearity occurs because of muscle physiology. Myofilaments, small threadlike components of the muscle fibers, are overlapping when at rest. In the early part of the stretch, the overlapping decreases, allowing the muscle to elongate easily. Once the myofilaments are no longer overlapping, increased stretch begins to pull at the molecular bonds of the myofilaments, causing increased resistance to the stretch and greater stiffness (Matthews, 2003).

A second notable feature of the stress-strain curves is that the upward slope of the curve upon stretch of the muscle is different from the downward slope of the curve as the muscle is released and allowed to contract back to resting length. Note, for example, that when the muscle is stretched to 20% of its resting length (20% strain), the stress built up in the muscle is a little bit over 5 kPA, yet as the muscle is being relaxed and decreases to 20% strain, the stress within the muscle is approximately 2 kPA. You can experience this phenomenon yourself. Stand upright, then bend over from the waist and with your legs straight, place your hands at the level of your calves. As you stretch downward, the leg muscles are being placed under increasing strain as they are stretched. You feel the stress placed on the muscles as a tightness. Now slide your hands down to the floor (or close to it!) and release to come back to your calves. The stress that you experience now is likely less than that experienced on the downward movement. The reason for this difference is that some of the molecular bonds within the muscle fibers are

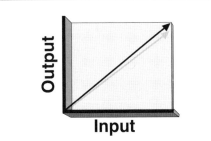

Figure 5–33. Linearity refers to the degree to which the output of a system follows a straight line.

released under the initial strain as you stretched to the floor. Then, as you slide back to your calves, these bonds, which contribute to the stress when the muscle is stretched, have already been partially released (Matthews, 2003).

Note in Figure 5–32 that the stress-strain relationship of the mucosal cover is a bit more linear than that of the muscle, in that the stretch-response lines are straighter. Less connective tissue in the mucosal cover results in a more proportional response, so that at progressive elongations, the cover increases in stiffness at a steadier rate than does the muscle. Note, however, that upon elongation compared to relaxation, a difference exists in the stress-strain relationship for the mucosal cover, just as we observed earlier with the muscle.

Study Questions

32. Define stress and strain.

33. Define linearity.

34. Explain two notable features of the stress-strain curve as they relate to vocal fold vibration.

5.7 Physiology of Phonatory Control

Fundamental Frequency (f_o)

What specifies the f_o, or rate of vibration of the vocal folds? Our understanding of the control of f_o derives from Müller's experimentation over 150 years ago in altering the frequency of vibration of his excised larynx model by exerting a pull on the vocal folds, and van den Berg's 1958 treatise on the physics of this phenomenon. More recently, Titze (1991) has described the biomechanical result from the coordinated activity of the cricothyroid and thyroarytenoid muscles, together with the contribution of lung

pressure. In our physiologic overview, primary control of f_o is achieved by the cricothyroid muscle, secondary control by the thyroarytenoid muscles, and additional control by the lung pressure. (Activity of the extrinsic laryngeal muscles also plays a role in f_o control, but this activity is related to articulatory gestures and will be addressed in Chapter 7.) In general, contraction of cricothyroid increases f_o. Contraction of the thyroarytenoid muscle may either increase or decrease f_o, depending on several variables to be discussed. Increased lung pressure raises f_o. In our biomechanical overview, f_o is controlled by the length of the vocal folds and the tension exerted upon their mass per unit length, and their stiffness. (See Table 5–5 for normative data of f_o in men, women, and children and Figure 5–34 for a lighter view.)

Natural Resonance of the Vocal Folds

Students of speech science often find it helpful, in their quest to understand f_o control, to liken the action of the vocal folds to the strings of a musical instrument. Our experience tells us that larger musical instruments produce lower tones than smaller instruments. Recall from Chapter 3 that the frequency at which a string vibrates depends on its tension, density (mass per unit volume), and length. In a musical stringed instrument, tension, density, and length can be independent of one another. We know that a bass cello has very long strings that vibrate more slowly (and hence produce a lower sound) than do the shorter strings of a violin, which vibrate faster and produce a higher tone. In summary, the shorter the string, or the smaller the mass or the greater the tension, the higher the f_o. Therefore, we would assume that longer and thicker vocal folds would vibrate more slowly than those that are shorter and thinner. We know that women, in general, speak at a higher pitch than do men and that the voices of young children are even higher pitched than those of adult women. The reason for these gender and age differences is associated with the overall mass and length of the vocal folds. On average, men have longer and thicker vocal folds than do women, and

Table 5–5. Normative Data for Fundamental Frequency

Habitual mean speaking F_0 (reading)

Men = 115 Hz[a]

Women = 215 Hz[b,c]

Children (picture description)

Boys
Mean age 5.6 years = 240 Hz[d]
Mean age 10.5 years = 220 Hz[e]

Girls
Mean age 5.6 years = 243 Hz[d]
Mean age 11.2 years = 238 Hz[f] (reading)

These data are provided as general guidelines only. All values are approximate. The reader is encouraged to examine the original sources for specific means, ranges, and standard deviations.

Sources:

[a]Hollien, H., & Shipp, T. (1972). Speaking fundamental frequency and chronologic age in males. *Journal of Speech and Hearing Research, 15,* 155–159.

[b]Stoicheff, M. I. (1981). Speaking fundamental frequency characteristics of nonsmoking female adults. *Journal of Speech and Hearing Research, 24,* 437–441.

[c]Saxman, J. H., & Burk, K. W. (1967). Speaking frequency characteristics of middle-aged females. *Folia Phoniatrica, 19,* 167–172.

[d]Awan, S. N., & Mueller, P. B. (1996). Speaking fundamental frequency characteristics of White, African American, and Hispanic kindergartners. *Journal of Speech and Hearing Research, 39,* 573–577.

[e]Morris, R. J. (1997). Speaking fundamental frequency characteristics of 8- through 10-year old white- and African-American boys. *Journal of Communication Disorders, 30,* 101–116.

[f]Horii, Y. (1983). Some acoustic characteristics of oral reading by ten- to twelve-year-old children. *Journal of Communication Disorders, 16,* 257–267.

Figure 5–34. An amusing and musical look at the effect of length and mass per unit of length on f_o. Adapted from *Principles of Voice Production* (p. 186), by I. R. Titze, 1994, Englewood Cliffs, NJ: Prentice-Hall. Adapted with permission.

young children have very short vocal folds of relatively little mass. We know that the slower the rate of vibration, the lower the perceived pitch produced from that vibration. Although helpful, the comparison of vocal folds to stringed instruments has the potential to unleash considerable confusion because vocal fold vibration does not behave wholly like a string. The analogy weakens when we consider change in f_o. We know that the vocal folds can produce many frequencies, and it is this adjustment in vibratory rate that we now examine.

When we consider the control of f_o, we find that the vocal folds behave partly like a string and partly like a spring (Titze, 1994a, p. 193). The principal biomechanical factor in the regulation of f_o is vocal fold tension, which in turn regulates the stiffness of the layers of tissue of the vocal folds (Honda, 1995). The **tension of the vocal folds** is regulated by their length, which we learned earlier is regulated by the movement of the cricothyroid joint. Unlike the strings of musical instruments, **vocal fold stiffness** is regulated predominantly by vocal fold length (Titze, 1994a, p. 194), and the tension, mass per unit volume, and length interact with one another to achieve the target frequency of vibration.

It may be that students often become confused about the control of f_o because they try to consider all cases at once. To help keep things clear, let us consider the following examples separately: soft phonation at low and mid-speaking range of pitch, high-pitched phonation, and loud phonation.

Cover-Dominant Vibration

In general, only the vocal fold cover (the epithelium and the superficial and intermediate layers of the lamina propria) vibrates during soft and high-frequency phonation and not the body (the deep layer of the lamina propria and the thyroarytenoid muscle). Let us first consider f_o change during this situation, in soft or high-pitched phonation. The cricothyroid muscle contracts, largely unopposed by its antagonist, the thyroarytenoid muscle. The resulting anterior movement of the thyroid cartilage causes the vocal folds to lengthen. All the layers of the vocal folds increase in stiffness, but we will focus particularly on the cover, the layers that vibrate in our current example. The cover of the vocal folds increases in stiffness in response to the increased tension exerted by the pull on the vocal folds induced by cricothyroid contraction. Recall from our discussion in Chapter 3 about a mass-spring oscillator that the stiffness of the spring and the size of the mass determine the frequency. Stiffness refers to the amount of force required to displace (stretch or compress) the spring. The greater the stiffness, the greater the displacement force required to move the mass from equilibrium, and therefore the greater the restorative force and quicker return toward equilibrium. So, we would expect that increased stiffness would result in faster movement or higher frequency. And indeed, in our example of high-pitched phonation, the increased stiffness results in a higher rate of vibration.

A second factor that contributes to the increase in frequency in our example is the change in mass per unit of length. As the vocal folds are elongated under the increased tension, their mass per unit of length decreases. (Think of a rubber band that becomes thinned in the process of stretching.) In our discussion of the mass-spring oscillator in Chapter 3, we learned that the greater the mass, the greater the inertial forces, and therefore the slower the motion: so greater mass per unit of length results in lower frequency. In our example of high-pitched phonation, although the overall mass of the vocal folds has not changed, the mass per unit of length has decreased, resulting in an increased rate of vibration. The analogy with a stringed instrument is related but dissimilar. The longitudinal tension of the guitar string can be increased, with a resulting decrease in mass per unit of length, by turning the peg to which the string is attached. The overall length of the string, however, remains constant. In the vocal folds, the tension and length covary, but in the musical instrument, that is not always the case.

It is important to note that the increased stiffness of the vocal folds (cover and body) occurs passively. Recall that the histology of the epithelium, superficial and intermediate layers of the lamina propria, specifies their inherent biomechanical properties, including stiffness. The increase in stiffness occurs because of the longitudinal tension placed on the tissues by the pull on the thyroarytenoid muscle (to which the cover is attached) by the contraction of the cricothyroid muscle. The rate-increasing effect of the increased stiffness of the cover overcomes the rate-lowering effect of the lengthened vocal folds, causing an overall increase in vibratory rate.

Let us now relate the biomechanical properties of the tissues of the vocal folds, discussed earlier, to the movement of the vocal folds upon change in f_o. The rate of vibration of the string of a violin or guitar can be altered by a slight turn of the peg to which the string is attached. (Think of the subtle adjustments made by the musician to alter the pitch of a string when tuning his instrument.) The very small adjustments to tension result in a large change in vibratory rate because the strings of musical instruments are quite stiff. Said another way, a large increase in the stress of the string of a musical instrument can be achieved with a small increase in tension (Titze, 1994a, p, 201). The vocal folds, however, as with all human tissue, are much less stiff than the strings of a musical instrument. As we learned earlier, the different layers of the vocal folds have different stress-strain properties, with the elastin fibers like rubber bands and the collagen fibers like cotton threads. Overall, however, the vocal folds respond to stress more like a rubber band than like a guitar string. Therefore, a large increase in length is required to achieve an increase in stress. However, from our earlier examination of the stress-strain curve, we know that the vocal folds behave in a nonlinear fashion. Therefore, as the vocal folds increase in length and become stiffer, smaller incremental changes in length can achieve proportionately greater increases in f_o (until the upper limits of frequency are reached).

Recall that fibers of the deep layer of the lamina propria, part of the vocal ligament, intertwine with muscle fibers of the thyroarytenoid.

The vocal ligament may assume much of the stiffness at levels of high strain, particularly when the thyroarytenoid is not contracted, as would be achieved during high sustained phonation. Alipour-Haghighi and Titze (1991) hypothesize that not only does this leave the mucosal cover sufficiently loose to vibrate well, but it may also explain why dogs cannot produce sustained phonation at a high pitch very well!

Body Plus Cover Vibration

Now let us consider the slightly more complicated cases of phonation at low frequency or with moderate to high intensity. We have seen the effect of increased stiffness through passive stretch of the vocal folds, as exemplified by the stress-strain curve. However, in low-frequency phonation, the thyroarytenoid muscle often is involved in vibration, which brings about active stress through muscle contraction. (Of course, the passive stretch of the vocal folds is achieved with active contraction of the cricothyroid muscle. However, when we refer to active and passive stress characteristics of the vocal folds, we restrict our discussion to the vocal folds themselves.) In voice production of moderate to high intensity at all pitches, the thyroarytenoid muscle always participates in vibration. Recall that the thyroarytenoid and the cricothyroid muscles are antagonists. When unopposed by the cricothyroid, contraction of the thyroarytenoid muscle will result in a decrease in overall length of the vocal folds by pulling the arytenoid cartilages forward. The shortening of the thyroarytenoid muscle decreases the tension on the cover of the vocal folds, causing the cover to slacken (Hirano, 1974). Reducing the tension on the mucosal cover causes a thickening, or increase in mass per unit of length. We know that an increase in mass will result in a decrease in vibratory rate, and so we would predict that unopposed contraction of thyroarytenoid muscle would result in lowered pitch.

Predicting frequency change based on muscle contraction can get tricky, however. Recall that stiffness, in addition to mass per unit of length, is a variable that controls rate of vibration. The stiffness of a muscle increases upon contraction. If the thyroarytenoid is involved in vibration, as in a moderately loud voice, then the effective stiffness of the vocal folds (the overall resulting stiffness when accounting for all factors) would be increased. Increased stiffness results in a faster rate of vibration. So, in our example of unopposed contraction of thyroarytenoid muscle, what factor dominates the effect upon vibratory rate; the decreased stiffness and increased mass per unit of length of the mucosal cover or the increased stiffness of the body? The answer is—it depends! It depends on the degree to which the body is involved in phonation (Titze, Jiang, & Drucker, 1988; Titze, Luschei, & Hirano, 1989). At low- and mid-frequency phonation, the thyroarytenoid muscle contributes the dominant longitudinal stress, allowing the lamina propria to remain lax to participate in large-amplitude mucosal wave vibration. With increased intensity, however, the increased stiffness of the muscle may become more dominant, causing a rise in f_o.

Control of f_o is closely related to control of intensity, and typically these two dimensions will covary. Exploration of this covariance begins with a discussion of the contribution of lung pressure to f_o control.

Lung Pressure in the Regulation of f_o

Up to this point, discussion of the control of f_o has focused on the dynamic balance of the agonist-antagonist pair of the cricothyroid and the thyroarytenoid muscles. Lung pressure, however, may also help control f_o (Ttize, 1989). Lung pressure may affect the amplitude of lateral movement of the vocal folds. The greater the lung pressure, the greater the vibrational amplitude, or lateral stretch of the vocal folds. This stretch results in a dynamic elongation of the vocal folds. The resulting transitory increase in the strain of the vocal folds would be expected to increase tissue stress, which would increase the elastic recoil force, and so the vocal folds would snap back faster, raising f_o. The increased elastic recoil force would be expected to cause the vocal folds to overshoot the midline, colliding with each other with greater force as the mucosal cover is forced upward and laterally in a mucosal wave. If the lung pressure is not maintained at the higher level, however, inertia would overcome the increased amplitude of vibration, causing it to damp out (lose energy) and return to equilibrium. Explore this phenomenon by saying "hey!" at a moderately soft level, and then say it again loudly. Most likely, you will hear a higher pitch with increased loudness, followed by a fall in pitch as the loudness decreases at the end of the word. (The relationship between pitch and loudness is explored further in the Voice Range Profile in Chapters 6 and 7.) If no attempt is made to control f_o with activation of the thyroarytenoid or the cricothyroid muscle, and f_o is allowed to vary freely, research shows that an increase of approximately 20 Hz per kPa can be achieved (Titze, 1995) or even higher, up to 30 to 40 Hz per kPa (Hixon, Klatt, & Mead, 1971; Lieberman et al., 1969; Titze, 1989). The extent of the contribution of lung pressure to f_o regulation during running speech is uncertain. Although not as substantial a regulator as the contraction of the cricothyroid and the thy-

Ingo Titze and the National Center for Voice and Speech

The National Center for Voice and Speech (NCVS), organized in 1990 with support by the National Institute on Deafness and Other Communicative Disorders of the National Institutes of Health (NIDCD/NIH), is a consortium of institutions dedicated to research, clinical, and educational endeavors in many areas of voice and speech. Under the leadership of Ingo Titze, a physicist and engineer, an influential body of research data has been produced in areas of phonation, acoustic phonetics, voice disorders, singing, and computer simulations.

roarytenoid muscles, at certain frequency and intensity levels, lung pressure likely plays a role (Atkinson, 1978). The role of lung pressure in f_o regulation may be less substantial in running speech than in singing, in which much higher levels of lung pressure are used, and precise pitch control is essential.

Differential Control of f_o: Evidence From EMG Data

In Chapter 4, we learned that electromyographic (EMG) studies have contributed to our knowledge of patterns of muscle activity in breathing. EMG also has been used to elucidate the activity of the laryngeal muscles. (Surface EMG, however, is not particularly valuable, as the intrinsic muscles cannot be distinguished from the larger infrahyoid muscles. Needle or hooked-wire electrodes must be used instead.) A substantial body of research describing muscle activity is derived from EMG studies, stemming from the pioneering EMG work in laryngeal physiology by Faaborg-Anderson (1957). EMG data provide evidence of the correlation of activity of the cricothyroid muscle with change in f_o (Arnold, 1961; Atkinson, 1978; Baer, Gay, & Niimi, 1976; Hirano, Ohala, & Vennard, 1969; Shipp, Doherty, & Morrissey, 1979; Shipp & McGlone, 1971). McHenry, Kuna, Minton, Vanoye, and Calhoun (1997) found that the fibers of the pars recta and the pars oblique of the cricothyroid muscle are differentially activated in f_o change. Many of the same studies, however, found considerable activity of other intrinsic muscles, including particularly the thyroarytenoid and the lateral cricoarytenoid (Honda, 1985) and even the posterior cricoarytenoid muscle (Hollien, 1983). Evidence from other studies (Honda, 1995) shows that activity of the extrinsic laryngeal muscles is also involved in f_o regulation (Erickson, Baer, & Harris, 1983; Sonninen, 1968). Vertical laryngeal movement with change in f_o is a well-observed phenomenon. (Stand in front of a mirror and raise your pitch very high, then descend low. Unless you are a trained singer, you most likely will see an upward movement of the larynx

with increased pitch and a downward laryngeal movement with decreasing pitch. Although muscle activity is not consistent for all individuals, Honda (1995) demonstrated that the sternothyroid, in addition to the cricothyroid, participates in change of f_o. Contraction of the sternothyroid lowers the larynx, which reduces the anterior-inferior pull of the thyroid cartilage. This action causes the vocal folds to shorten and thicken, resulting in a decrease in f_o. Contraction of the sternohyoid causes the hyoid bone to descend and possibly has the same effect upon the larynx and vocal folds as contraction of the sternothyroid. Thyrohyoid contraction may draw the larynx upward, or the hyoid bone and larynx downward, depending upon the activity of the suprahyoid antagonist muscles. The geniohyoid, a suprahyoid muscle, has been correlated with increased f_o (Erickson et al., 1983) by action of an upward pull of the laryngeal hyoid complex. These EMG studies contribute evidence that strategies of muscle activation differ across individuals for the same vocal target.

Fundamental frequency varies considerably in running speech. The changes of pitch in our voice signal a statement (downward) or question (upward) and are used to add emphasis and alter meaning of an utterance. (We will return to this discussion in more detail in Chapter 9 as we address prosody.) Atkinson (1976, 1978) gathered EMG data to show that the cricothyroid and the thyroarytenoid are used synergistically but that specific patterns of muscle activation vary considerably across individuals. Ludlow (2005) notes that interspeaker variation in air pressure and airflow is likely a factor in this variability. As with all laryngeal adjustments, muscle activity must be coordinated with aerodynamic activity.

Study Questions

35. Define fundamental frequency, provide its symbol, and give average values for adult men and women and children.

36. What factors regulate the natural resonance of the vocal folds?

37. What factors regulate change in fundamental frequency?

38. Under what circumstances does the body of the vocal folds vibrate along with the cover?

39. What is the contribution of lung pressure to the control of fundamental frequency?

40. What information have EMG data contributed to our understanding of fundamental frequency control?

Control of Intensity

Recall from Chapter 3 that the amplitude of a sound pressure wave represents the amount of power in the wave. Intensity is the power per unit of area, and it increases as the square of the amplitude of the sound pressure wave. The major determinants of the amplitude of the wave and, hence, vocal intensity are the lung pressure, the closure of the vocal folds, and other adjustments of the vocal tract. We will consider the first two in turn, and reserve consideration of the vocal tract for Chapter 7. (See Table 5–6 for normative data on intensity in men, women, and children.)

Lung pressure is the major regulator of intensity (Isshiki, 1964, 1965; Ladefoged & McKinney, 1963). Recall that lung pressure is the force of the air from the lungs exerted on the vocal folds from below. In general, increasing the lung pressure causes a larger amplitude of mucosal wave vibration and a greater amount of air to escape through the vocal folds during the open phase of vibration. Quite simply, a large volume of air speeding through the open glottis contains more air molecules than a small volume of air (Figure 5–35). Therefore, the excitation of the larger volume of air will generate greater acoustic power than the smaller air volume. On average, sound pressure level (SPL) is proportional to the square of the lung pressure (Ladefoged & McKinney, 1963). As a general approximate rule, an 8- to 12-dB SPL increase can be achieved with a doubling of lung pressure (Titze, 1994a, p. 230). This rule is generally true, but particularly for the lower frequencies typically used in speech. Increases in lung pressure appear to have a greater effect upon intensity at a lower f_o than at a higher f_o (Isshiki, 1964). The reason for this dependence upon f_o has to do with glottal resistance. Recall that glottal resistance is the ratio of air pressure to airflow at the level of the glottis. It is defined as the lung pressure divided by the airflow rate. The vocal folds present a variable obstruction to the airflow. When they are completely adducted, the vocal folds offer complete resistance to the airflow. If the vocal folds are placed under increased tension by elongation due to contraction of the cricothyroid, for example, one could imagine that it would require a great deal of lung pressure to force them apart. In this situation, the vocal folds are offering considerable resistance to the airflow. Now imagine very lax vocal folds, as would occur at low f_o. In this case, the vocal folds may well require less lung pressure to separate. If the lung pressure is increased at the low f_o, the lax vocal folds would be pushed wide apart. And, in fact, we have noted already that amplitude of mucosal wave vibration is greater at low f_o as compared to high f_o.

At high frequencies, the vocal folds are already under considerable tension and offer substantial resistance to the airflow. Therefore, resistance cannot be increased easily. The important point to understand here is that lung pressure is the major regulator of intensity, particularly at lower f_o. At higher f_o, both lung pressure and airflow regulate intensity, depending on the tension of the vocal folds, and hence their resistance to the airflow.

Lung pressure during speech typically averages approximately 0.7 kPa, with average ranges between 0.3 and 1.2 kPa. Moderately loud speech is achieved with lung pressures of

Table 5-6. Normative Data for Intensity

Habitual (Moderate) Intensity
Reading (at habitual speaking F_0) = 70 dB SPL[a,b]
Sustained vowel (at habitual speaking F_0) = 75 dB SPL[c]
Minimum Intensity
Sustained vowel (at 10% of frequency range, average of male and female values) = 49 db SPL[d]
Maximum Intensity
Sustained vowel (at 90% of frequency range, average of male and female values) = 102 dB SPL[d]
Intensity (Dynamic) Range

Sustained vowel (averaged across the entire frequency range)
  Women = 51–104 dB SPL[d]
  Men = 47–100 dB SPL[d]

These data are provided as general guidelines only. All values are approximate. The reader is encouraged to examine the original sources for specific means, ranges, standard deviations, and mouth-to-microphone distances.

Sources:

[a]Awan, S. N. (1993). Superimposition of speaking voice characteristics and phonetograms in untrained and trained vocal groups. *Journal of Voice, 7,* 30–37.

[b]Gelfer, M. P., Andrews, M. L., & Schmidt, C. P. (1991). Effects of prolonged loud reading on selected measures of vocal function in trained and untrained singers. *Journal of Voice, 5,* 158–267.

[c]Gelfer, M. P., & Young, S. R. (1997). Comparisons of intensity measures and their stability in male and female speakers. *Journal of Voice, 11,* 178–186.

[d]Sulter, A. M., Schutte, J. K., & Miller, D. G. (1995). Differences in phonetogram features between male and female subjects with and without vocal training. *Journal of Voice, 9,* 363–377.

Figure 5–35. Lung pressure is the major regulator of intensity. In general, increasing the lung pressure causes a greater volume of air to escape upward through the vocal folds during vibration.

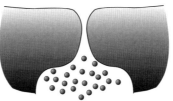

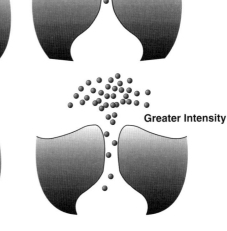

Lower Intensity

Lower P_{sub}

Greater Intensity

Greater P_{sub}

Life Span and Control of Intensity

Aging may have some limiting effect on maximal intensity (Ptacek, Sander, Maloney, & Jackson, 1966). Given that intensity control arises from aerodynamic, laryngeal, and supraglottal vocal tract adjustments, it is reasonable to ask which factors are responsible for age-related changes in intensity. Some reduction in lung capacities and the force generated by the breathing muscles (Hoit & Hixon, 1987; Kahane, 1981; Sperry & Klich, 1992) may cause limitations in control of intensity in the aged. Most data do not show reduced lung pressures generated for loud speech in older individuals (Baker et al., 2001; Holmes, Leeper, & Nich-olson, 1994; Melcon, Hoit, & Hixon, 1989), although some evidence does suggest reduced lung pressure in older men (Higgins & Saxman, 1991). Senescent changes in the tissues of the vocal folds, however, have been heavily documented in the research literature, and those changes typically cause reduced closure of the vocal folds during phonation (Honjo & Isshiki, 1980; Linville, 1992; Tanaka, Hirano, & Chijwa, 1994). It is likely that changes in phonatory glottal closure are responsible for reduced intensity with increasing age, but more research is necessary to explain the role of the breathing system to age-related changes in voice.

approximately 1.0 kPa. Up to 3 kPa is typical for loud speech. (See Tables 5–7 and 5–8 for normative data on lung pressure and airflow at different intensities.)

Earlier we discussed the fact that the closure of the vocal folds is the event that results in excitation of the supraglottal air mass. Therefore, closure of the vocal folds is also a critical factor in regulation of intensity. Three features of the closure are particularly important to note: the duration, the speed, and the degree of the closure. First, the duration of the closed phase increases with greater intensity, which permits an increase in the lung pressure level. Further-

Table 5–7. Normative Data for Subglottal Pressure at Different Intensities in Adults

Volume	Mean P_{sub} (cm of H_2O)	Range (cm of H_2O)
Soft		
Men	3.8	2.3–5.7
Women	4.1	2.6–6.3
Normal		
Men	7.8	4.5–12.8
Women	10.2	3.8–12.6
Loud		
Men	14.9	7.3–24.4
Women	19.8	9.1–27.7

Source: Data from Wilson, J. V., & Leeper, H. A. (1992). Changes in laryngeal airway resistance in young adult men and women as a function of vocal sound pressure level and syllable context. *Journal of Voice, 6,* 235–245.

Table 5–8. Normative Data for Mean Airflow During Sustained Vowel Phonation

	Mean Age (y)	Mean Airflow (mL/s)	Range (mL/s)
Children[a]			
Boys	10	218	—
Girls	10	180	—
Adults[b]			
Men	—	141	109–182
Women	—	119	76–172

Sources:
[a]Trullinger, R. W., & Emanuel, F. W. (1989). Airflow, volume, and duration characteristics of sustained vowel phonation in normal-speaking children. *Folia Phoniatrica, 41,* 297–307.
[b]Isshiki, N., & von Leden, H. (1964). Hoarseness: Aerodynamic studies. *Archives of Otolaryngology, 80,* 206–213.

more, as the closed portion of the vibratory cycle increases, less sound energy is lost in the subglottal space, allowing more of the sound energy to be transmitted outward to the listener. Second, the faster the vocal folds close, that is, the sharper the cutoff of the air flowing through the glottis, the more energy is transmitted to the air mass above the vocal folds (Gauffin & Sundberg, 1989; Holmberg, Hillman, & Perkell, 1988).

And finally, the third feature of the closure of the vocal folds that influences intensity is the degree of the closure. Incomplete closure can limit the buildup of lung pressure, and it can allow loss of acoustic energy in the subglottal direction. Furthermore, the incomplete closure allows some of the airflow to leak through the glottal gap. That continuous airflow is not modulated by the closure of the vocal folds. That is, the air that leaks through the gap does not participate in the forceful backward compression against the vocal folds. Therefore, the air contains little acoustic energy.

Recall in Chapter 4 that *motor equivalence* refers to the tendency of individuals to use different patterns of muscle activation for the same reaction to a stimulus (Abbs, 1979; Hughes & Abbs, 1976). Baker et al. (2001) provide interesting data to show considerable variability among individuals for intensity regulation, with variable increased levels of activation for activity of the thyroarytenoid muscle and lateral cricoarytenoid and cricothyroid muscles as coregulators

of increased intensity. These actions would be expected to increase closure and tension of the vocal folds, providing increased resistance to the higher levels of lung pressure required for more intense speech.

On average, men can produce greater vocal intensity than women. Most likely, their larger vocal tract and greater lung capacity (on average) are the reasons for this sex difference. As a result, men can generate greater air pressure and airflow. Figure 5–36 displays glottal closure during phonation in a man (left) and woman (right). Note that there is a posterior glottal gap visible in the illustration of the woman's vocal folds. Such a gap is not uncommon in women. The open communication between the sub- and supraglottal vocal tracts may contribute to the lesser intensity achievable by women as compared with men.

In summary, intensity is a complex interplay between lung pressure and tension of the vocal folds (Baker et al., 2001). We know from Chapter 4 that lung pressure can be elevated by increasing the volume of air contained within the lungs (breathing in more deeply) and by activating the expiratory muscles to reduce the overall volume of the thoracic cavity. It should be no surprise, therefore, that ribcage movements are greater at higher intensity for men and women as compared with lower intensity (Stathopoulos & Sapienza, 1993). Activity of the extrinsic laryngeal muscles may also increase with greater intensity

Figure 5–36. Vocal fold closure during phonation in a normal healthy man (*left*) and woman (*right*). Many women have a posterior glottal gap during closure, which may contribute to a slightly breathier and softer voice as compared to the voices of men.

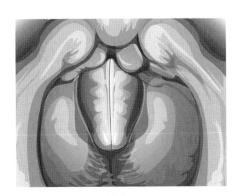

A. Male

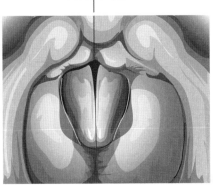

Posterior gap

B. Female

(Hirano et al., 1967). Contraction of the cricothyroid muscle may contribute to intensity regulation through adductory action of the vocal folds (Tanaka & Tanabe, 1986). Two important points should be emphasized regarding control of intensity. First, changes in lung pressure cannot occur without many other changes to the voice production system. Second, the specific motor strategies used to alter intensity as well as f_o will vary slightly across individuals. See Table 5–9 for a summary of the effects of changes in f_o and intensity on the mucosal wave and phonatory glottal closure.

Auditory Feedback of Control of f_o and Intensity

Auditory feedback plays an important role in the control of f_o (Sapir, McClean, & Luschei, 1983). The **Lombard effect**, first described by Etienne Lombard in 1911, is the tendency for individuals to increase their vocal intensity within high ambient noise levels. Although this effect may be associated with awareness that speech needs to be louder for the listener to hear the speaker clearly within background noise (Lane & Tranel, 1971), the Lombard effect is quite a stable automatic response and requires training to suppress (Pick, Siegel, Fox, Garber, & Kearney, 1989). The response has been replicated in several studies (Ferrand, 2006; Winkworth & Davis, 1997). It is equally robust in children and adults (Amazi & Garber, 1982).

Ludlow (2005) points out that congenitally deaf children and adults with acquired severe hearing loss have difficulties with f_o control, despite training. The behavior of our voice production system suggests that the auditory and phonatory systems have interrelated reflex circuits in the brain (Sapir, McClean, & Larson, 1983). For example, f_o often is raised in response to auditory feedback in which the frequency has been altered. This response is not always consistent because intensity is also sensitive to auditory feedback, and f_o and intensity are related (see further discussion on this relationship in the sections on Voice Range Profile in Chapters 6 and 7.) Burnett, Freedland, Larson, and Hain (1998) found that when individuals were presented with auditory feedback of lowered pitch, the speakers rapidly adjusted their pitch upward. The importance of auditory feedback in the control of f_o has been shown in experiments using auditory masking. Auditory masking is the presentation of white noise (noise that contains equal energy at all frequencies) through headphones while an individual is speaking, so that the individual cannot hear his or her own voice. Mallard, Ringel, and Horii (1978) found that subjects with auditory masking had greater difficulty maintaining their f_o than did subjects who had afferent nerve blocks. Similarly, Larson, Burnett, Kiran, and Hain (2000) showed that disturbances in auditory feedback can have an immediate effect on pitch control. Auditory feedback is just one important sensory feedback system that contributes to f_o and intensity control. Variations in air pressure around the glottis are registered by pressure receptors, and changes in the length of the vocal folds are monitored by stretch receptors (Garrett & Luschei, 1987; Keene, 1961; Suzuki & Sasaki, 1977). Perhaps these sensory receptors interact with auditory

Table 5–9. Summary of Vocal Fold Vibratory Dynamics

	Lower F$_0$s	Higher F$_0$s	Lower dB SPL	Higher dB SPL
Amplitude of mucosal wave	Increased	Decreased	Decreased	Increased
Duration of glottal closure	Increased	Decreased	Decreased	Increased

feedback to modulate and stabilize changes in f_o and intensity (Ferrand, 2006).

Biomechanical Forces During Phonation

Sonninen, Damsté, Jol, and Fokkens (1972) discussed the types of mechanical loads and deformations occurring in the vocal folds during phonation. Titze (1994b) summarized six different types and amounts of mechanical stress to which the vocal folds are subject, including tensile, contractile, impact, aerodynamic, interarytenoid, and shear stress. **Tensile stress** is the greatest force per unit of area of the vocal folds. This stress is a longitudinal force applied in the anterior-to-posterior direction, parallel to the fibers of the lamina propria and muscle. Tensile stress is due to contraction of the cricothyroid. In this sense, tensile stress is a passive force exerted upon the vocal folds. The vocal folds of a female singer who sustains a high C (440 Hz) may experience tensile stress of 500 kPa (Titze, 1994b), or approximately 70 lbs per square inch! (One kPa is equal to 0.145 lbs per square inch.) **Contractile stress** is an active stress, which was discussed above relative to the stress-strain curve; we know that the contractile stress is a function of the elongation (strain) of the vocal folds. Contractile stress in canine vocal folds has been found to range from 30 to 115 kPa (Alipour-Haghighi, Titze, & Perlman, 1989, 1991).

Impact stress (also called collision stress) occurs from the impact of the vocal folds at midline. Upon impact of the vocal folds, the velocity decreases quite rapidly. Impact stress has been measured in human beings (Gunter, Howe, Zeitels, Kobler, & Hillman, 2005; Hess, Verdolini, Bierhals, Mansmann, & Gross, 1998; Yamana & Kitajima, 2000), although it is difficult for individuals to tolerate the placement of a pressure sensor between the vocal folds. The collision force is greater with increasing lung pressure (Jiang & Titze, 1994). We learned that increases in lung pressure cause wider amplitude of vibration. And we know that the increased amplitude

of vibration causes an increase in the restorative forces, resulting in greater force with which the vibrating mass returns to midline. The collision force may increase with f_o, but that depends on the degree of closure of the vocal folds. We have learned that, at high pitches, the vocal folds may not completely approximate. Over the surface of the contact, however, the collision force would be increased because of the increased velocity of the tissue. Research suggests collision stress of 0.5 to 5.0 kPa may be achieved at habitual speaking f_os (Jiang & Titze, 1994). When incomplete contact of the vocal folds occurs during vibration, although the collision stress may be reduced, the vocal folds are subject to inertial stress. Recall from Chapter 2, Newton's first law of motion defines inertia as the tendency for an object to resist change in its state of motion. The greater the f_o, the greater the momentum of the vocal folds, which must overcome the inertia. Like collision stress, **inertial stress** occurs from the acceleration and deceleration of the vocal folds but does not include the stress arising from impact. Inertial stress is increased at greater f_os. **Inertial stress** is less than collision stress, approximately 1 to 2 kPa during typical speech frequencies and intensities (Titze, 1994b). The impact stress between the arytenoid cartilages, called arytenoid contact stress to distinguish it from stress arising from the impact of the vocal folds, is estimated at 1 to 5 kPa (Scherer, Cooper, Alipour-Haghighi, & Titze, 1985). Although not a direct function of vibration of the vocal folds, interarytenoid contact stress may be increased to gain more effortful closure of the vocal folds.

Aerodynamic stress is the air pressure within the glottis during the open phase of phonation. At high intensity, aerodynamic stress may reach as high as 5 to 6 kPa (Schutte, 1980) but typically will be minimal during conversational speech intensities.

The final stress that Titze (1994b) considers, shear stress, may be of considerable importance, particularly in the formation of benign pathology of the vocal folds. **Shear stress** is a force applied parallel to the surface of the vocal folds, as compared to collision force, which is applied perpendicularly to the tissue surface (Figure 5–37). The shear stress exerted on the vocal folds during phonation is due to the upheaval of tissue that forms the mucosal wave. Its value is difficult to estimate but will increase with greater amplitude of vibration, as would be achieved in low f_os or increased intensity. Shear stress will decrease with increasing length of the vocal folds, as would be achieved in higher f_os. Figure 5–38 summarizes the relative magnitude of the various mechanical stresses, with shear stress omitted.

5.8 Voice Quality

Voice quality is a perceptual attribute that describes the sound of the voice beyond its pitch and loudness. Hundreds of adjectives can be used when discussing voice quality. Descriptors traditionally used by speech pathologists to characterize voice quality include many adjectives with negative connotations, such as rough, breathy, harsh, strident, strained, pressed, and nasal. Somewhat curiously, only a few descriptors are associated with positive features, and these are heavily borrowed from singers, including brightness and ring. The perception of voice quality is a subjective phenomenon influenced by a host of factors, not the least of which is personal preferences. However, voice quality may be predicted in part by laryngeal dynamics and described, again only partially, by its acoustic features.

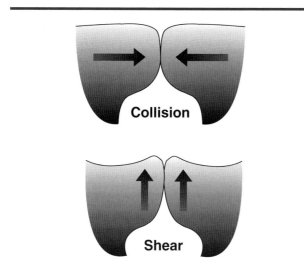

Figure 5–37. Collision force is applied perpendicular to the surfaces of the vocal folds. Shear stress is a force applied parallel to their surfaces.

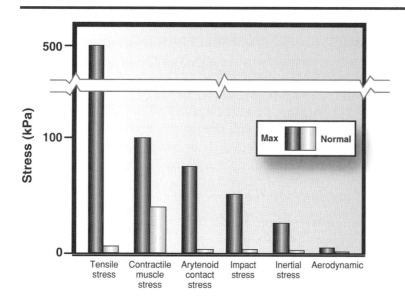
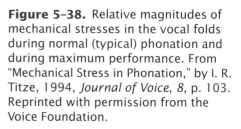

Figure 5–38. Relative magnitudes of mechanical stresses in the vocal folds during normal (typical) phonation and during maximum performance. From "Mechanical Stress in Phonation," by I. R. Titze, 1994, *Journal of Voice, 8,* p. 103. Reprinted with permission from the Voice Foundation.

In Chapter 6, we will study the interactive relationship between the resonant characteristics of the vocal tract with the acoustic characteristics of the source signal (the glottal volume velocity). We shall learn that voice quality, the listener's perception of the voice, is the complex sum of both laryngeal influences and influences arising from the rest of the vocal tract. For now, we shall briefly examine the laryngeal contribution to voice quality. In Chapter 6, we will expand upon this topic.

Breathy voice quality is associated with incomplete glottal closure during the closed phase of vibration. A portion of the glottal airflow escapes through the glottis during what should otherwise be fully adducted vocal folds. This airflow is turbulent and contributes noise to the vocal signal, rather than harmonic structure, and intensity is diminished. At the other end of the vocal spectrum is pressed voice, in which the open phase is reduced. Although the biomechanics of pressed voice are not known precisely, it may be achieved by increasing contraction of the thyroarytenoid muscle, and hence its stiffness, thereby achieving faster and more prolonged closure of the vocal folds.

We have already discussed the fact that the vocal folds do not move as a uniform block of tissue but rather exhibit both a difference in vertical phase and a zipper-like opening and closing motion. **Mode of vibration** refers to nonuniform tissue movement (Titze, 1994a, p. 94). The mode of vibration of the vocal folds contributes to voice quality. Normal modes of vibration include different registers (to be discussed in Chapter 6). Abnormal modes of vibration are generally caused by pathology of the vocal folds and result in an impaired vocal quality. Often, this altered voice quality is described as hoarse, which generally consists of a breathy and a rough component. The breathy component we have already identified as arising from incomplete glottal closure. The rough component is due to irregular mucosal wave movement. Breathy, rough, and pressed voice, as well as some of the other descriptors of vocal quality, can be described by their acoustic characteris-

tics. We shall reserve the discussion of acoustic characteristics of the speech signal for Chapter 7.

Study Questions

41. How is intensity regulated?

42. Provide average values of intensity for habitual speaking, soft, and loud phonation.

43. Define the Lombard effect.

44. Define the six different types of mechanical stress to which the vocal folds are subjected: tensile, contractile, impact, inertial, aerodynamic, and shear.

45. Define voice quality.

Recommended Internet Sites for Further Learning

http://www.voiceproblem.org/introduction/index.php
The Washington Voice Consortium, a nonprofit educational website, provides information about abnormal voice production.

http://www.ncvs.org/products_tutorial.html
Voice Production Tutorials of The National Center for Voice and Speech provides excellent tutorials on many of the scientific concepts of voice production.

References

Abbs, J. H. (1979). Speech motor equivalence: The need for a multi-level control model. In *Proceedings of the Ninth International Congress of Phonetic Sciences* (Vol. 2). Copenhagen, Denmark: Institute of Phonetics.

Adzaku, F. K., & Wyke, B. (1979). Innervation of the subglottic mucosa of the larynx, and its significance. *Folia Phoniatrica, 31,* 271–283.

Alipour-Haghighi, F., & Titze, I. R. (1991). Elastic models of vocal fold tissues. *Journal of the Acoustical Society of America, 90,* 1326–1331.

Alipour-Haghighi, F., Titze, I. R., & Perlman, A. (1989). Tetanic contraction in vocal fold muscle. *Journal of Speech and Hearing Research, 32,* 226–231.

Alipour-Haghighi, F., Titze, I. R., & Perlman, A. (1991). Tetanic response of the cricothyroid muscle. *Annals of Otology, Rhinology, and Laryngology, 100,* 626–631.

Amazi, D. K., & Garber, S. R. (1982). The Lombard sign as a function of age and task. *Journal of Speech and Hearing Research, 25,* 581–585.

Arnold, G. E. (1961). Physiology and pathology of the cricothyroid muscle. *Laryngoscope, 71,* 687–753.

Atkinson, J. E. (1976). Inter and intraspeaker variability in fundamental voice frequency. *Journal of the Acoustical Society of America, 60,* 440–446.

Atkinson, J. E. (1978). Correlation analysis of the physiological factors controlling fundamental voice frequency. *Journal of the Acoustical Society of America, 63,* 221–222.

Baer, T., Gay, T., & Niimi, S. (1976). Control of fundamental frequency, intensity, and register of phonation. *Haskins Laboratories: Status Report on Speech Research, SR-45/45,* 175–185.

Baker, K. K., Ramig, L. O., Sapir, S., Luschei, E. S., & Smith, M. E. (2001). Control of vocal loudness in young and old adults. *Journal of Speech, Language, and Hearing Research, 44,* 297–305.

Berry, D. A., Montequin, D. W., Chan, R. W., Titze, I. R., & Hoffman, H. T. (2003). An investigation of cricoarytenoid joint mechanics using simulated muscle forces. *Journal of Voice, 17,* 47–62.

Brancatisano, A., Dodd, D. S., & Engel, L. A. (1991). Posterior cricoarytenoid activity and glottic size during hyperapnea in humans. *Journal of Applied Physiology, 71,* 977–982.

Brin, M., Blitzer, A., & Stewart, C. (1998). Laryngeal dystonia (spasmodic dysphonia): observations of 901 patients and treatment with botulinum toxin. *Advances in Neurology, 78,* 237–252.

Burnett, T. A., Freedland, M. B., Larson, C. R., & Hain, T. C. (1998). Voice F0 responses to manipulations in pitch feedback. *Journal of the Acoustical Society of America, 103,* 3153–3161.

Casiano, R. R., Ruiz, P. J., & Goldstein, W. (1994). Histopathological changes in the aging human cricoarytenoid joint. *Laryngoscope, 104,* 533–538.

Cérat, J., Charlin, B., Brazeau-Lamontagne, L., & Mongeau, C. J. (1988). Assessment of the cricoarytenoid joint high-resolution CT scan study with histoanatomical correlation. *Journal of Otolaryngology, 17,* 65–67.

Chang, A., & Karnell, M. P. (2004). Perceived phonatory effort and phonation threshold pressure across a prolonged voice loading task: A study of vocal fatigue. *Journal of Voice, 18,* 454–466.

Childers, D. G., & Krishnamurthy, A. K. (1985). A critical review of electroglottography. *CRC Critical Reviews in Biomedical Engineering, 12,* 131–161.

Cooper, D. S., Partridge, L. D., & Alipour-Haghighi, F. (1993). Muscle energetics, vocal efficiency, and laryngeal biomechanics. In I. R. Titze (Ed.), *Vocal fold physiology: Frontiers in basic science* (pp. 37–92). San Diego, CA: Singular.

Davis, P. J., Bartlett, D. A., Jr., & Luschei, E. S. (1993). Coordination of the respiratory and laryngeal systems in breathing and vocalization. In I. R. Titze (Ed.), *Vocal fold physiology: Frontiers in basic science* (pp. 189–226). San Diego, CA: Singular.

Dedivitis, R. A., Abrahao, M., de Jesus Simoes, M., Mora, O. A., & Cervantes, O. (2001). Cricoarytenoid joint: Histological changes during aging. *São Paulo Medical Journal-Revista Paulista de Medicina, 119,* 89–90.

Dickson, D. R., & Maue-Dickson, W. (1996). *Anatomical and physiological bases of speech.* Boston, MA: Butterworth-Heinemann.

Draper, M. H., Ladefoged, P., & Whitteridge, D. (1960). Expiratory pressures and air flow during speech. *British Medical Journal, 18,* 1837–1843.

Erickson, D., Baer, T., & Harris, K. S. (1983). The role of the strap muscles in pitch lowering. In D. M. Bless, & H. J. Abbs (Eds.), *Vocal fold physiology* (pp. 281–285). San Diego, CA: College-Hill Press.

Faaborg-Andersen, K. (1957). Electromyographic investigation of intrinsic laryngeal muscles in humans. *Acta Physiologica Scandinavica, 41*(Suppl. 140), 1–150.

Farnsworth, D. W. (1940). High-speed motion pictures of the human vocal cords. *Bell Laboratories Record, 18,* 203–206.

Ferrand, C. T. (2006). Relationship between masking levels and phonatory stability in normal-speaking women. *Journal of Voice, 20,* 223–228.

Finkelhor, B. K., Titze, I. R., & Durham, P. K. (1988). The effect of viscosity changes in the vocal folds on the range of oscillation. *Journal of Voice, 1,* 320–325.

Fujimura, O. (1981). Body-cover theory of the vocal fold and its phonetic implications. In K. Stevens, & M. Hirano (Eds.), *Vocal fold physiology* (pp. 271–281). Tokyo, Japan: University of Tokyo Press.

Garrett, D., & Luschei, E. (1987). Subglottic pressure modulation during evoked phonation in the anesthetized cat. In T. Baer, C. Sasaki, & K. Harris (Eds.), *Laryngeal function in phonation and respiration* (pp. 139–153). San Diego, CA: College-Hill Press.

Gauffin, J., Binh, N., Ananthapadmanabha, T. V., & Fant, G. (1983). Glottal geometry and volume velocity waveform. In D. M. Bless & J. H. Abbs (Eds.), *Vocal fold physiology: Contemporary research and clinical issues* (pp. 194–201). San Diego, CA: College-Hill Press.

Gauffin, J., & Sundberg, J. (1989). Spectral correlates of glottal voice source waveform characteristics. *Journal of Speech and Hearing Research, 32,* 556–565.

Gramming, P. (1989). Non-organic dysphonia: A comparison of subglottal pressures in normal and pathological voices. *Acta Oto-Laryngologica, 107,* 156–160.

Gray, S. D. (2000). Cellular physiology of the vocal folds. In C. Rosen & T. Murry (Eds.), *Otolaryngologic Clinics of North America: Voice disorders and phonosurgery I* (pp. 679–699). Philadelphia, PA: W. B. Saunders.

Gunter, H. E., Howe, R. D., Zeitels, S. M., Kobler, J. B., & Hillman, R. E. (2005). Measurement of vocal fold collision forces during phonation: Methods and preliminary data. *Journal of Speech, Language, and Hearing Research, 48,* 567–576.

Hess, M. M., Verdolini, K., Bierhals, W., Mansmann, U., & Gross, M. (1998). Endolaryngeal contact pressures. *Journal of Voice, 12,* 50–67.

Higgins, M. B., & Saxman, J. H. (1991). A comparison of selected phonatory behaviors of healthy aged and young adults. *Journal of Speech and Hearing Research, 34,* 1000–1010.

Hirano, M. (1974). Morphological structure of the vocal cord as a vibrator and its variation. *Folia Phoniatrica, 26,* 89–94.

Hirano, M. (1977). Structure and vibratory behavior of the vocal folds: Current results, emerging problems, and new instrumentation. In M. Sawashima & F. S. Cooper (Eds.), *Dynamic aspects of speech production* (pp. 13-30). Tokyo, Japan: University of Tokyo Press.

Hirano, M. (1981). *Clinical examination of voice.* New York, NY: Springer-Verlag.

Hirano, M., & Kakita, Y. (1985). Cover-body theory of vocal fold vibration. In R. G. Daniloff (Ed.), *Speech science* (pp. 1–46). San Diego, CA: College-Hill Press.

Hirano, M., Koike, Y., & von Leden, H. (1967). The sternohyoid muscle during phonation. *Acta Oto-Laryngologica, 64,* 500–507.

Hirano, M., Ohala, J., & Vennard, W. (1969). The function of the laryngeal muscles in regulating fundamental frequency and intensity of phonation. *Journal of Speech and Hearing Research, 12,* 616–628.

Hirose, H., & Gay, T. (1973). Laryngeal control in vocal attack: An electromyographic study. *Folia Phonatirica, 25,* 203–213.

Hixon, T. J., Klatt, D. H., & Mead, J. (1971). Influence of forced transglottal pressure on fundamental frequency. *Journal of the Acoustical Society of America, 49,* 105(A).

Hoit, J. D., & Hixon, T. J. (1987). Age and speech breathing. *Journal of Speech and Hearing Research, 30,* 351–366.

Hollien, H. (1974). On vocal registers. *Journal of Phonetics, 2,* 125–143.

Hollien, H. (1983). In search of vocal frequency control mechanisms. In D. M. Bless & H. J. Abbs (Eds.), *Vocal fold physiology* (pp. 286–297). San Diego, CA: College-Hill Press.

Holmberg, E. B., Hillman, R. E. & Perkell, J. S. (1988). Glottal airflow and transglottal air pressure measurement for male and female speakers in soft, normal, and loud voice. *Journal of the Acoustical Society of America, 84,* 511–529.

Holmes, L. C., Leeper, H. A., & Nicholson, I. R. (1994). Laryngeal airway resistance of older men and women as a function of vocal sound pressure level. *Journal of Speech and Hearing Research, 37,* 789–799.

Honda, K. (1985). Variability analysis of laryngeal muscle activities. In I. Titze & R. Scherer (Eds.), *Vocal fold physiology: Biomechanics, acoustics, and phonatory control* (pp. 127–137). Denver, CO: The Denver Center for the Performing Arts.

Honda, K. (1995). Laryngeal and extra-laryngeal mechanisms of F0 control. In F. Bell-Berti & L. J. Raphael (Eds.), *Producing speech: Contemporary issues, for Katherine Safford Harris* (pp. 215–232). New York, NY: American Institute of Physics.

Hong, K. H., Ye, M., Kim, Y.M., Kevorkian, K. F., Kreiman, J., & Berke, G. S. (1998). Functional differences between the two bellies of the cricothyroid muscle. *Otolaryngology-Head and Neck Surgery, 118*, 714–722.

Honjo, I., & Isshiki, N. (1980). Laryngoscopic and voice characteristics of aged persons. *Archives of Otolaryngology, 106*, 149–150.

Hughes, O. M., & Abbs, J. H. (1976). Labial-mandibular coordination in the production of speech: Implications for the operation of motor equivalence. *Phonetica, 33*, 191–221.

Hunter, E. J., Titze, I. R., & Alipour, F. (2004). A three-dimensional model of vocal fold abduction/adduction. *Journal of the Acoustical Society of America, 115*, 1747–1759.

Isshiki, N. (1964). Regulatory mechanism of voice intensity variation. *Journal of Speech and Hearing Research, 7*, 17–29.

Isshiki, N. (1965). Vocal intensity and air flow rate. *Folia Phoniatrica, 17*, 92–104.

Izdebski, K., Dedo, H. H., & Boles, L. (1984). Spastic dysphonia: A patient profile of 200 cases. *American Journal of Otolaryngology, 5*, 7–14.

Jiang, J., & Titze, I. R. (1994). Measurement of vocal fold intraglottal pressure and impact stress. *Journal of Voice, 8*, 132–144.

Jürgens, U. (2002). Neural pathways underlying vocal control. *Neuroscience and Biobehavioral Reviews, 26*, 235–258.

Kahane, J. C. (1981). Anatomic and physiologic changes in the aging peripheral speech mechanism. In D. S. Beasley & G. S. David (Eds.), *Aging: Communication processes and disorders* (pp. 21–46). New York, NY: Grune & Stratton.

Kahane, J. C., & Hammons, J.-A. (1987). Developmental changes in the articular cartilage of the human cricoarytenoid joint. In T. Baer, C. Sasaki, & K. S. Harris (Eds.), *Laryngeal function in phonation and respiration* (pp. 14–28). Boston, MA: College-Hill Press.

Keene, J. F. L. (1961). Muscle spindles in human laryngeal muscles. *Journal of Anatomy, 95*, 25–29.

Kirchner, J. A., & Wyke, B. (1965). Articular reflex mechanisms in the larynx. *Annals of Otology, Rhinology, and Laryngology, 74*, 749–769.

Koike, Y. (1967) Experimental studies on vocal attack. *Oto-rhino-laryngol Clinics Kyoto, 60*, 663–688.

Kotby, M. N., Kirchner, J. A., Kahane, J. C., Basiouny, S. E., & el-Samaa, M. (1991). Histo-anatomical structure of the human laryngeal ventricle. *Acta Oto-Laryngologica, 111*, 396–402.

Kuna, S. T., Insalaco, G., & Woodson, G. E. (1988). Thyroarytenoid muscle activity during wakefulness and sleep in normal adult humans. *Journal of Applied Physiology, 65*, 1332–1339.

Kuna, S. T., & Vanoye, C. R. (1994). Laryngeal response during forced vital capacity maneuvers in normal adult humans. *American Journal of Respiratory Critical Care Medicine, 150*, 729–734.

Ladefoged, P., & McKinney, N. P. (1963). Loudness, sound pressure, and subglottal pressure in speech. *Journal of the Acoustical Society of America, 35*, 454–460.

Lane, H., & Tranel, B. (1971). The Lombard sign and the role of hearing in speech. *Journal of Speech and Hearing Research, 14*, 677–709.

Larson, C. (1988). Brain mechanisms involved in the control of vocalization. *Journal of Voice, 2*, 301–311.

Larson, C. R., Burnett, T. A., Kiran, S., & Hain, T. C. (2000). Effects of pitch-shift velocity on voice F0 responses. *Journal of the Acoustical Society of America, 107*, 559–564.

Lieberman, P., Knudson, R., & Mead, J. (1969). Determination of the rate of change of fundamental frequency with respect to subglottal air pressure during sustained phonation. *Journal of the Acoustical Society of America, 45*, 1537–1543.

Linville, S. E. (1992). Glottal gap configuration in two aged groups of women. *Journal of Speech and Hearing Research, 35*, 1209–1215.

Ludlow, C. L. (2005). Central nervous system control of the laryngeal muscles in humans. *Respiratory Physiology and Neurobiology, 147*, 205–222.

Ludlow, C. L., Van Pelt, F., & Koda, J. (1992). Characteristics of late responses to superior laryngeal nerve stimulation in humans. *Annals of Otology, Rhinology, and Laryngology, 101*, 127–134.

Mallard, A. R., Ringel, R. L., & Horii, Y. (1978). Sensory contributions to control of fundamental frequency of phonation. *Folia Phoniatrica (Basel), 30*, 199–213.

Mårtensson, A. (1968). The functional organization of the intrinsic laryngeal muscles. *Annals of the New York Academy of Sciences, 155*, 91–97.

Matthews, G. G. (2003). *Cellular physiology of nerve and muscle* (4th ed.). Malden, MA: Blackwell.

McCaffrey, T. V., & Kern, E. B. (1980). Laryngeal regulation of airway resistance: 1. Chemoreceptor reflexes. *Annals of Otology, Rhinology, and Laryngology, 89*, 209–214.

McHenry, M. A., Kuna, S. T., Minton, J. T., Vanoye, C. R., & Calhoun, K. (1997). Differential activity of the pars recta and pars oblique in fundamental frequency control. *Journal of Voice, 11,* 48–58.

Melcon, M. C., Hoit, J. D., & Hixon, T. J. (1989). Age and laryngeal airway resistance during vowel production. *Journal of Speech and Hearing Disorders, 54,* 282–286.

Monoson, P., & Zemlin, W. (1984). Quantitative study of a whisper. *Folia Phoniatrica, 36,* 53–65.

Monsen, R., & Engebretsen, M. (1977). Study of variations in the male and female glottal wave. *Journal of the Acoustical Society of America, 62,* 981–993.

Moore, P. (1938). Motion picture studies of the vocal folds and vocal attack. *Journal of Speech and Hearing Disorders, 3,* 235–238.

Paulsen, F., & Tillmann, B. N. (1999). Composition of the extracellular matrix in human cricoarytenoid joint articular cartilage. *Archives of Histology and Cytology, 62,* 149–163.

Pawlak, A. S., Hammond, T., Hammond, E., & Gray, S. D. (1996). Immunocytochemical study of proteoglycans in the vocal folds. *Annals of Otology, Rhinology, and Laryngology, 105,* 6–11.

Pick, H. L., Jr., Siegel, G. M., Fox, P. W., Garber, S. R., & Kearney, J. K. (1989). Inhibiting the Lombard effect. *Journal of the Acoustical Society of America, 85,* 894–900.

Plant, R. L., Freed, G. L., & Plant, R. E. (2004). Direct measurement of onset and offset phonation threshold pressure in normal subjects. *Journal of the Acoustical Society of America, 116,* 3640–3646.

Poletto, C. J., Verdun, L. P., Strominger, R., & Ludlow, C. L. (2004). Correspondence between laryngeal vocal fold movement and muscle activity during speech and nonspeech gestures. *Journal of Applied Physiology, 97,* 858–866.

Ptacek, P. H., Sander, E. K., Maloney, W. H., & Jackson, C. C. R. (1966). Phonatory and related changes with advanced age. *Journal of Speech and Hearing Research, 9,* 353–360.

Reidenbach, M. M. (1998). The muscular tissue of the vestibular folds of the larynx. *European Archives of Otorhinolaryngology, 255,* 365–367.

Sanders, I., Wu, B. L., Mu, L., Li, Y., & Biller, H. F. (1993). The innervation of the human larynx. *Archives of Otolaryngology-Head and Neck Surgery, 119,* 934–939.

Sapir, S., McClean, M. D., & Larson, C. R. (1983). Human laryngeal responses to auditory stimuli. *Journal of the Acoustical Society of America, 73,* 315–321.

Sapir, S., McClean, M. D., & Luschei, E. S. (1983). Effects of frequency-modulated auditory tones on the voice fundamental frequency in humans. *Journal of the Acoustical Society of America, 73,* 1070–1073.

Scherer, R. C., Cooper, D. S., Alipour-Haghighi, F., & Titze, I. R. (1985). Contact pressure between the vocal processes of an excised bovine larynx. In I. R. Titze & R. Scherer (Eds.), *Vocal fold physiology: Biomechanics, acoustics, and phonatory control* (pp. 292–303). Denver, CO: Denver Center for the Performing Arts.

Schutte, H. K. (1980). *The efficiency of voice production.* Groningen, Netherlands: Kemper.

Selbie, W. S., Zhang, L., Levine, W. S., & Ludlow, C. L. (1998). Using joint geometry to determine the motion of the cricoarytenoid joint. *Journal of the Acoustical Society of America, 103,* 1115–1127.

Sellars, I., & Sellars, S. (1983). Cricoarytenoid joint structure and function. *Journal of Laryngology and Otology, 97,* 1027–1034.

Shipp, T., Doherty, E. T., & Morrissey, P. (1979). Predicting vocal frequency from selected physiological measures. *Journal of the Acoustic Society of America, 66,* 678–684.

Shipp, T., & McGlone, R. (1971). Laryngeal dynamics associated with voice frequency change. *Journal of Speech and Hearing Research, 14,* 761–768.

Smitheran, J., & Hixon, T. (1981). A clinical method for estimating laryngeal airway resistance during vowel production. *Journal of Speech and Hearing Disorders, 46,* 138–146.

Solomon, N. P., McCall, G. N., Trosset, M. W., & Gray, W. C. (1989). Laryngeal configuration and constriction during two types of whispering. *Journal of Speech and Hearing Research, 32,* 161–174.

Sonninen, A. (1968). The external frame function in the control of pitch in the human voice. *Annals of the New York Academy of Sciences, 155,* 68–90.

Sonninen, A, Damsté, P. H., Jol, J., & Fokkens, J. (1972). On vocal strain. *Folia Phoniatrica (Basel), 24,* 321–336.

Sperry, E. L., & Klich, R. J. (1992). Speech breathing in senescent and younger women during oral reading. *Journal of Speech and Hearing Research, 35,* 1246–1255.

Stathopoulos, E. T., & Sapienza, C. (1993). Respiratory and laryngeal measures of children during vocal intensity variation. *Journal of the Acoustical Society of America, 94,* 2531–2543.

Suzuki, M., & Kirschner, J. A. (1969). The posterior cricoarytenoid as an inspiratory muscle. *Annals of Otology, Rhinology, and Laryngology, 78,* 849–864.

Suzuki, M., & Sasaki, C. (1977). Effect of various sensory stimuli on reflex laryngeal adduction. *Annals of Otolaryngology, 86,* 30–36.

Tanaka, S., Hirano, M., & Chijiwa, K. (1994). Some aspects of vocal fold bowing. *Annals of Otology, Rhinology, and Laryngology, 103,* 357–362.

Tanaka, S., & Tanabe, M. (1986). Glottal adjustment for regulating vocal intensity: An experimental study. *Acta Oto-Laryngologica, 102,* 315–324.

Titze, I. R. (1980). Comments on the myoelastic-aerodynamic theory of phonation. *Journal of Speech and Hearing Research, 23,* 495–510.

Titze, I. R. (1989). On the relation between subglottal pressure and fundamental frequency in phonation. *Journal of the Acoustical Society of America, 85,* 901–906.

Titze, I. R. (1991). Mechanisms underlying the control of fundamental frequency. In J. Gaufffin & B. Hammarberg (Eds.), *Vocal fold physiology: Acoustic, perceptual and physiologic aspects of vocal mechanisms* (pp. 129–138). San Diego, CA: Singular.

Titze, I. R. (1994a). *Principles of voice production.* Englewood Cliffs, NJ: Prentice-Hall.

Titze, I. R. (1994b). Mechanical stress in phonation. *Journal of Voice, 8,* 99–105.

Titze, I. R. (1995). Motor and sensory components of a feedback-control model of fundamental frequency. In F. Bell-Berti & L. W. Raphael (Eds.), *Producing speech: Contemporary issues for Katherine Safford Harris* (pp. 309–318). New York, NY: American Institute of Physics.

Titze, I. R., Jiang, J., & Drucker, D. (1988). Preliminaries to the body-cover theory of pitch control. *Journal of Voice, 1,* 314–319.

Titze, I. R., Luschei, E., & Hirano, M. (1989). The role of the thyroarytenoid muscle in regulation of fundamental frequency. *Journal of Voice, 3,* 213–224.

Titze, I. R., & Talkin, D. T. (1979). A theoretical study of the effects of various laryngeal configurations on the acoustics of phonation. *Journal of the Acoustical Society of America, 66,* 60–74.

Tonndorf, W. (1925). Die Mechanik bei der Stimmlippenschwingungen und beim Schnarchen. (The mechanisms of vocal fold vibration and snoring.) *Zeitschrift für Hals-Nasen-Ohrenheilkunde, 12,* 241–245.

van den Berg, J. (1958). Myoelastic-aerodynamic theory of voice production. *Journal of Speech and Hearing Research, 1,* 227–244.

Vennard, W. (1967). *Singing: The mechanism and the technique* (4th ed.). New York, NY: Carl Fischer.

Verdolini, K. (1998). The language we use in clinical practice. *Newsletter, Special Interest Division 3: Voice and Voice Disorders, 8,* 3–4.

Verdolini-Marston, K., Titze, I. R., & Drucker, D. G. (1990). Changes in phonation threshold pressure with induced conditions of hydration. *Journal of Voice, 4,* 142–151.

Vilkman, E. (1987). An apparatus for studying the role of cricothyroid articulation in the voice production of excised human larynges. *Folia Phoniatrica (Basel), 39,* 169–177.

von Leden, H. (1961). The mechanism of phonation. *Archives of Otolaryngology, 74,* 660–676.

von Leden, H. (1996). A cultural history of the human voice. In R. T. Sataloff (Ed.), *Professional voice: The art and science of clinical care* (3rd ed., pp. 9–88). San Diego, CA: Singular.

von Leden, H., & Moore, P. (1961). The mechanics of the cricoarytenoid joint. *Archives of Otolaryngology, 73,* 541–550.

Walker, J. (1987). Why a fluid flows faster when the tub is pinched. *Scientific American, 257,* 104–107.

Wang, R. C. (1998). Three-dimensional analysis of cricoarytenoid joint motion. *Laryngoscope, 108,* 1–17.

Werner-Kukuk, E., & von Leden, J. (1970). Vocal initiation. *Folia Phonatirica, 22,* 107–116.

Winkworth, A. L., & Davis, P. J. (1997). Speech breathing and the Lombard effect. *Journal of Speech, Language, and Hearing Research, 40,* 159–169.

Wyke, B. D. (1969). Deus ex machina vocis: An analysis of the laryngeal reflex mechanisms of speech. *British Journal of Disorders of Communication, 4,* 3–25.

Wyke, B. D. (1974). Laryngeal myotactic reflexes and phonation. *Folia Phoniatrica, 26,* 249–264.

Yamana, T., & Kitajima, K. (2000). Laryngeal closure pressure during phonation in humans. *Journal of Voice, 14,* 1–7.

Yoshida, Y., Tanaka, Y., Saito, T., Shimazaki, T., & Hirano, M. (1992). Peripheral nervous system in the larynx: An anatomical study on the motor, sen-

sory and autonomic nerve fibers. *Folia Phoniatrica, 44,* 194–219.

Zemlin, W. R. (1998). *Speech and hearing science:
Anatomy and physiology* (4th ed.). Needham Heights,
MA: Allyn & Bacon.

Zhang, S. P., Bandler, R., & Davis. P. J. (1995). Brainstem integration of vocalization: Role of the nucleus
retroambigualis. *Journal of Neurophysiology, 74,*
2500–2512.

Phonation II: Measurement and Instrumentation

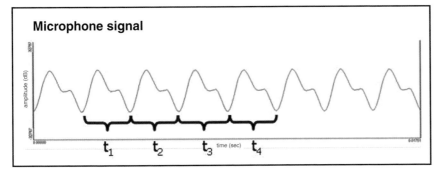

Figure 6–1. Short-term perturbation of the f_o, called jitter, can be calculated using several different formulas, all of which average the cycle-to-cycle variability in the frequency (or period) of the waveform.

The heart of science is measurement.
—Erik Bruinjolfsson, American Academic (1962–)

In this chapter, we explore many different methods for assessing the dynamics of vocal fold vibration. (Chapter 12 provides critical information on how to acquire digital information. Here, we focus upon that information we might want to acquire.) We group our discussion into measurement of f_o and intensity using the voice range profile, quantitative measures of phonatory aerodynamics, and an exploration of common research and clinical instrumentation. Additional quantitative measures of phonation that are important for both clinical and research purposes include the long-term average spectrum, the harmonics-to-noise ratio, and cepstral measures. Discussion of these measures, however, is reserved for Chapter 7 because they require knowledge of the filter characteristics of the vocal tract, which are discussed in that chapter. In Chapter 7, we shall revisit the voice range profile for similar reasons. Also included in this chapter is a discussion of vocal registers. Although registers are a feature of phonation and not a measurement, the topic is included here because an understanding of one instrument, the electroglottograph, is quite helpful in understanding and visualizing registers.

6.1 Measurement of f_o and Intensity

Measurement of f_o and intensity for clinical and research purposes can be divided generally into three categories of measurement: levels of habitual use of the voice, levels of maximum performance, and degree of regularity. Measurement of habitual use of the voice answers the question, "What is the performance of the vocal system of this individual under routine use?" Data on tasks requiring maximum performance answer the questions, "What is the performance of the system under mechanical stress? What are the physiologic limits of the system?" Assessment of regularity answers the question, "How stable is the voice production system?" These categories have parallels in testing other physiologic systems, particularly pulmonary function and cardiac

performance. To assess completely a physiologic system, we need to know how it performs routinely on a habitual basis, how it performs under stress or at its maximum capabilities, and the consistency or regularity of its output. We will examine each of these categories in turn.

f_o Measures

Daily, we all tend to anchor our f_o around a common range. The average f_o at which we speak is called the mean speaking f_o, and the range within which we typically speak is called the mean speaking f_o range. The mean speaking f_o and its range are considerably influenced by linguistic factors such as the speech content. A highly emotional topic might cause us to speak at a different f_o than a bland topic. Lack of familiarity or a context that causes us to be nervous might likewise influence the average f_o. Commonly, the mean speaking f_o and its range are assessed during sustained vowel phonation, reading, or a spontaneous speaking task. Some evidence does suggest that the task influences the frequency values obtained (Zraick, Birdwell, & Smith-Olinde, 2004). Reading tasks often consist of a series of sentences or passages. Some commonly used passages to assess mean speaking f_o are provided in Appendix B. Considerable variation in mean speaking f_o is found within individual subjects, averaging approximately three semitones across multiple readings (Coleman & Markham, 1991).

Maximum performance tests provide information about the physiologic capabilities of the voice production system (Kent, Kent, & Rosenbek, 1987). A woman's average habitual speaking f_o may be 230 Hz, for example, but that tells us nothing about how high or low she can phonate. **Maximum frequency range of phonation** represents the span from lowest to highest frequency of which the individual is physiologically capable. It can be elicited by having an individual phonate from lowest to highest pitch at a self-selected comfortable loudness level. Maximum range of phonational frequency also can be elicited as part of a frequency-intensity task called the voice range profile, discussed further on.

Table 5–5 provided normative data on f_o values for men, women, and children. It is important to note that the voice is capable of a much wider range of frequencies than are habitually used. We tend to use a relatively small range of frequencies toward the lower end of our range. During typical speech, men will most commonly use f_o values between 80 and 150 Hz and women between 150 and 250 Hz.

The third broad measurement category is the regularity of frequency and intensity. We learned in Chapter 5 that the vibration of the vocal folds is not exactly a complex periodic sound pressure wave but rather a nearly periodic or quasiperiodic function. A small amount of cycle-to-cycle variability is inherent in the human body. Too much variability, however, and the sound produced is abnormal. Therefore, measurement of the regularity of the vibration is an important characterization of the health of the laryngeal system. **Perturbation** is the variability or irregularity in a system (Titze, 1994). Short-term f_o perturbation, called **jitter**, represents the nonvolitional variability in the f_o as measured during sustained vowel phonation (see Figure 6–1). (It can also be measured from a vowel extracted from a word within running speech, but the clinician must be careful that it be a steady portion of a vowel and not during a volitional change in frequency.) Short-term perturbation refers to the cycle-to-cycle variability of the duration of the period. It is important to note that jitter is characterized as a short-term perturbation and it is not measured over the duration of a word or phrase. We will learn in Chapters 7 and 8 that f_o is affected by production of consonants and, to a lesser extent, by change in vowels. We will also explore the purposeful f_o changes that occur over the course of a phrase to signal linguistic intent, such as a rising f_o to signal a question. For these reasons, jitter is only measured during steady-state phonation (sustained vowel at a single pitch or from within the vowel extracted from a word embedded in running speech). Jitter exists at a low level in all vibrations of the vocal

folds, for no physiologic system is completely periodic.

Jitter can be measured using several different formulas. One of the more common methods is **jitter ratio**. In this measure, the difference in period of each adjacent pair of cycles is averaged to yield a mean difference in period for the waveform. This mean difference is then divided by the average period duration to yield a ratio of average period difference to average period. Dividing the average difference in periods by the average period helps to remove the effect of f_o from the jitter calculation. Accounting for the frequency is important because the magnitude of the jitter is dependent upon the frequency at which the speaker is phonating (Lieberman, 1963). The ratio of the average cycle-to-cycle pitch variability to the average period also can be expressed as a percentage, in which case it is called the **jitter percent**. Another method of calculating jitter, the **jitter factor**, simply uses the jitter ratio method but replaces the period with the frequency. That is, the average cycle-to-cycle difference in frequency is divided by the average frequency of the sample. **Relative average perturbation** (Koike, Takahashi, & Calcaterra, 1977) is a third common method of calculating jitter. Also called the **frequency perturbation quotient**, this method takes the average difference in periods between each three adjacent cycles and divides it by the average period. (Alternatively, five cycles can be averaged together, in which case it is called the **pitch perturbation quotient**.) In this way, the relative average perturbation largely removes any slow shift in frequency that may occur during normal sustained phonation. (Even the steadiest voice will contain a bit of frequency shift over the course of the sustained phonation. Perturbation is aimed at identifying the cycle-to-cycle variability, not the longer term frequency trend.) Which measure is best to use? No single measure is preferable. But it is important to specify which measure is used in any written documentation, such as evaluative report, and to use the correct norms for comparison. Normative data for jitter are provided in Table 6–1.

Table 6–1. Normative Data for Jitter

	f_o	Men	f_o	Women
Jitter ratio[a]	110 Hz	0.042 ms	—	—
Jitter factor[b]	102 Hz	0.48 ms	—	—
Relative average perturbation[c]	112 Hz	0.21 ms	221 Hz	0.28

Sources: Data from

[a]Orlikoff, R. F. (1990). Heartbeat-related fundamental frequency and amplitude variations in healthy young and elderly male voices. *Journal of Voice, 4,* 322–328.

[b]Hollien, H., Michel, J., & Doherty, E. T. (1973). A method for analyzing vocal jitter in sustained phonation. *Journal of Phonetics, 1,* 85–91.

[c]Till, J. A., Jafari, M., Crumley, R. L., & Law-Till, C. B. (1992). Effects of initial consonant, pneumotachographic mask, and oral pressure tube on vocal perturbation, harmonics-to-noise, and intensity measurements. *Journal of Voice, 6,* 217–223.

A large body of research literature has shown that normal vibration of the vocal folds should have a low level of jitter and that pathologic (abnormal) voices frequently have high levels of jitter (Horii, 1979; Lieberman, 1963; Scherer, Gould, Titze, Meyers, & Sataloff, 1988). As a cautionary note, however, some evidence suggests that jitter is not always sensitive to improvement in voice after treatment of voice therapy or surgery (Carding et al., 2004), and jitter is not appropriate as a screening measure to distinguish normal from abnormal voices (Ludlow, Bassich, Connor, Coulter, & Lee, 1987).

Intensity Measures

In addition to f_o, the habitual intensity level and the physiologic range from softest to loudest (without incurring physical strain) are important parameters of considerable interest in research and clinical practice. In elicitation of any intensity values, the distance from the speaker's mouth to the microphone is of critical importance. (Recall that intensity diminishes as the distance from the sound source increases.) Although no standard exists for mouth-to-microphone distance, a common distance is 12 inches (30 cm), although it depends upon the type of microphone used. (See the discussion of microphone type and

positioning in Chapter 12.) Most important, one should document the distance and use the same distance for all measurements when comparisons are to be made. (Table 5–6 provided normative data for intensity levels.)

Not only does the level of f_o perturbation provide us with information about the stability of laryngeal dynamics, but the perturbation of the amplitude of the sound pressure wave can also tell us about laryngeal stability (Horii, 1980). Recall that the amplitude of the acoustic waveform indicates the amount of energy in the pressure wave and that intensity is a measure of the power per unit area. **Shimmer** is the short-term variability in the amplitude of the acoustic waveform (Figure 6–2). Like jitter, we do not want to measure amplitude perturbation over the course of a word or phrase, because of the effect of consonants on intensity and volitional changes in dynamic (intensity) range that may occur. Therefore, like jitter, shimmer is measured from the steady-state portion of a vowel, and it can be measured using a variety of formulas. One of the more common measures is shimmer in dB, which is the ratio of the amplitudes of two adjacent cycles averaged over the length of the sample. That is, every pair of adjacent cycles within the sample is compared and then the ratios of each comparison are averaged to provide a mean value of the differences in adjacent cycle amplitudes. The cycle-to-cycle variability also can be expressed as a percentage of the mean amplitude value, and the result would be called **shimmer percent**. Another popular method for measuring shimmer is the **amplitude perturbation quotient**. This measure is comparable to the jitter measure of relative amplitude perturbation, in that it averages the amplitude over a longer number of cycles, 11 as originally devised by Koike and von Leden (1969). That is, the amplitude of 11 adjacent cycles is averaged. Then shift over one cycle and average another 11 adjacent cycles. Shift over a cycle and compute another 11-cycle average, and so all cycles in the sample have been included in at least one average. Then all of those averages are themselves averaged together. As with jitter measures, the different shimmer measures will yield slightly different values, and therefore it is important to be aware of which formula is being used when comparing data to norms. (See Table 6–2 for shimmer norms.)

Shimmer level often is used as a diagnostic criterion for abnormal voice and then as a measure of treatment outcome. A note of caution, however, should be mentioned regarding perception of jitter and shimmer. Although these measures often correspond to the level of vocal disturbance, typically we cannot discriminate between jitter and shimmer perceptually (Krieman & Gerratt, 2005). A direct correlation between jitter or shimmer and degree of voice impairment does not exist. Furthermore, as with jitter, shimmer values cannot be used as a screening measure to differentiate between normal and abnormal voice, although shimmer may be a more powerful measure of treatment outcome than jitter (Ludlow et al., 1987).

Voice Range Profile (VRP)

Given that the balance of vocal fold tension and lung pressure contribute to both f_o and intensity

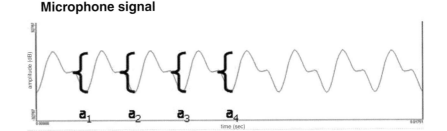

Figure 6–2. Short-term perturbation of the amplitude of the acoustic signal, shimmer, can be calculated using several different formulas, all of which average the cycle-to-cycle variability in the amplitude of the waveform.

Table 6–2. Normative Data for Shimmer

	F_0	Men	F_0	Women
Shimmer in dB[a]	—	0.37	—	0.23
Amplitude perturbation quotient[b]	108 HZ	0.00403	206 Hz	0.00329

Sources: Data from

[a]Horii, Y. (1980). Vocal shimmer in sustained phonation. *Journal of Speech and Hearing Research, 23*, 202–209.

[b]Takahashi, H., & Koike, Y. (1975). Some perceptual dimensions and acoustical correlates of pathologic voices. *Acta Oto-Laryngologica, Supplement, 338*, 1–24.

control, it should be no surprise that a close relationship exists between f_o and intensity. This relationship is shown easily in a graphic display called a **voice range profile** (VRP) (Figure 6–3). The horizontal x-axis represents f_o and the vertical y-axis represents dB SPL. The speech-language pathologist produces a tone (using a piano, computer tone-generator, or pitch pipe, for example) that is used for pitch-matching. The person being tested produces a vowel (/a/ or /i/ usually) at the selected pitch as softly and then as loudly as possible. The intensity levels of the soft and loud phonation trials are recorded and plotted at the phonated frequency. The clinician can read the intensity level from a sound-level meter and plot the appropriate point with pencil and paper (using her ear to judge whether the patient matched the target pitch closely), or a computer equipped with a microphone can be used to register and graph the results automatically. The procedure is then repeated at selected frequencies across the person's entire frequency range (Pabon & Plomp, 1988; Schutte & Seidner, 1983). Several technical factors are relevant to the valid elicitation of a voice range profile, including the mouth-to-microphone distance and the order in which the minimum and maximum intensities at selected frequencies are elicited. These factors have been discussed, and standardization recommendations have been made by Schutte and Seidner (1983) and the International Association of Logopedics and Phoniatrics (1992).

Upon completion of the voice range profile, the upper contour represents the maximum intensity at each frequency and the lower contour represents the minimum intensity at each frequency. In the plot shown in Figure 6–3, the solid lines represent an average voice range profile for men, whereas the dashed lines represent an average plot for a woman. It should be kept in mind, of course, that these values are averages, and not only will they vary among individuals, but an individual's results will vary from day to day as well (Gramming & Akerlund, 1988; Gramming, Sundberg, & Akerlund, 1991).

In the research literature, the voice range profile is also called the phonogram (Komiyama, Watanabe, & Ryu, 1984), phonetogram (Damste, 1970; Schutte & Seidner, 1983), and f_o-SPL profile (Coleman, Mabis, & Hinson, 1977). From the earliest investigations of Wolfe, Stanley, and Sette (1935) and Stout (1938) through the resurgence of interest in the VRP that began with Damste (1970), the voice range profile has been used to explore differences in phonatory function of men and women (Coleman et al., 1977), adults and children (Hacki & Heitmuller, 1999; Heylen et al., 1998), and singers and untrained speakers (Awan, 1991). The voice range profile has been used to assess frequency and intensity limitations in patients with voice disorders (Behrman, Agresti, Blumstein, & Sharma, 1996; Hacki, 1996) and to assess outcome of treatment for voice disorders (Dejonckere, van Wijck, & Speyer, 2003; Gramming & Ackerlund, 1988).

Various methods of quantifying the shape and area enclosed by the frequency-intensity borders have been used to analyze the voice range

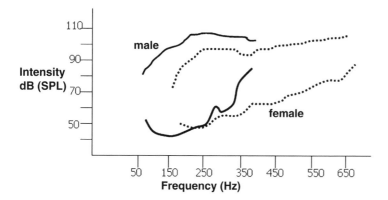

Figure 6–3. A voice range profile elicited from an adult male (*solid lines*) and female (*dotted lines*) phonating the vowel /ɑ/ (unpublished data from the author).

profile (Airainer & Klingholz, 1993; Heylen et al., 1998; Ikeda et al., 1999; Sulter, Wit, Schutte, & Miller, 1994). However, simple visual inspection of the upper and lower contours provides considerable insight into phonatory control when we consider the underlying physiology (Gramming & Sundberg, 1988; Titze, 1992). Several features of the voice range profile are notable. The first characteristic we note is the overall area enclosed by the upper and lower contours. The wider the area (the higher the upper contour, the lower the lower contour, and the greater length of both contours), the more flexible the voice, in that both the dynamic (intensity) and pitch ranges are large.

Another feature one readily notes is that the dynamic range is reduced at the upper and lower extremes, and widest around the mid-frequency range. At the lowest frequencies, it is difficult to achieve significantly increased intensity because the vocal fold cover must remain lax to achieve the slow rate of vibration. Yet the overall resistance to the airflow must be increased to withstand the increased lung pressure necessary for increased intensity. In summary, these two factors constrain dynamic energy at the lowest frequencies. At the highest frequencies, a similar relationship exists in balancing lung pressure with vocal fold tension. To achieve high-frequency phonation, we know that the vocal folds must be quite tense, which would then increase their resistance to the airflow, which would in turn require high lung pressure to maintain phonation. Such high levels of lung pressure would, of course, result in greater intensity.

And finally, both the upper and lower contours tilt upward in the higher frequencies. That is, both the average man and woman can phonate more softly in middle frequencies than in the highest frequencies. And both men and women can phonate more loudly at the higher frequencies than at the low and mid-frequency range. The reason is that the high lung pressure required for greater intensity also requires that the vocal folds are able to withstand the greater pressures. In general, that increased resistance is achieved with greater vocal fold stiffness, which in turn raises f_0. Factors relating to the resonant characteristics of the vocal tract also have a significant effect upon the shape of the voice range profile, and we shall examine those factors in the next chapter. Although the voice range profile gives us considerable information about the relationship of frequency and intensity, it tells us little about voice quality, although some authors have elicited voice range profiles restricted to specific vocal quality of the individual (Pabon & Plomp, 1988).

Genomics and Proteomics

We only have to listen to the voices of family members to know that genetic factors influence the sound of our voices. Part of the reason for this relationship is the similarity in structure of the vocal tract among family members. But we also know that certain diseases are familial, passed down through generations. Chromosomes, threadlike structures found in the nuclei of each cell, contain genes, which are composed of deoxyribonucleic acid (DNA) connected in a specific sequence. The genetic basis for voice has been recognized and studied for many years (Luchsinger & Arnold, 1965).

Recently, however, significant advances in gene mapping and technologic capabilities have heightened the research activity as applied to normal and abnormal voice production. The DNA contains the total genetic information present in the cell—the genome, and the study of genomes is called **genomics**. Gene expression refers to the activity level of a gene above baseline, as measured by the quantity of proteins being produced. ("Expression" means "squeezing or pressing out.") Cells accomplish their functions through proteins, oxygen, and carbohydrates and trace elements.

Proteomics is the field of study of proteins. The fields of genomics and proteomics are in their infancy in regard to voice science. Currently, scientists are studying three factors that may influence the expression of specific genes in the vocal folds: microenvironment, soluble factors, and mechanical forces (Gray, Thibeault, & Ylitalo, 2005). The microenvironment of the vocal folds can include changes in humidity, airborne pollutants, and gastric acid reflux from the stomach. Soluble factors include hormones and medications. And certainly, we have explored throughout this chapter the considerable mechanical forces that arise on and within the vocal fold tissues during phonation. As with most aspects of human physiology and health, researchers are finding that voice production is a function of both genes and environment (Gray et al., 2005). Environmental factors may be negative, such as cigarette smoke or phonotraumatic voice use, but they can also be positive, such as professional singing and learning to use a different style of speaking, as might occur in voice therapy (Gray, Hammond, & Hanson, 1995). In the larger field of genetics, gene mapping has helped identify specific genes that are responsible for a given trait or disease.

Unfortunately, genetic mapping has not proved to have much clinical application to the process of voice production and vocal fold abnormalities yet. However, a recent technologic advance called microarray processing has enabled scientists to explore thousands of genes simultaneously to examine potential gene expression under various conditions. For example, it has long been held that a common, benign vocal fold lesion (mucosal irregularity) called nodules is due to phonotraumatic voice use. Examining vocal fold tissue in individuals with nodules using microarray processing, Gray et al. (1995) found in the lamina propria evidence of increased production of two proteins, fibronectin and collagen type IV, both of which may contribute to scarring. The data suggest that genetic expression is altered in the presence of such lesions.

The challenge for future research is to determine whether a genetic predisposition for certain vocal fold pathologies may exist, for that would then open the door for more finely focused approaches to prevention and treatment. Gray et al. (2005) include among the possible clinical applications of research in "voice biology" in the coming decades, medications that, at the molecular level, are tailored to a disease process in a specific individual and voice therapy validated through clinical trials to achieve improvement in the protein structure of the vocal folds to facilitate improved vibration. Major hurdles in methodology have yet to be overcome, and years of painstaking research need to be conducted to achieve these goals. Yet genomics and proteomics hold tremendous promise for increased understanding of voice and laryngeal disorders and diseases and their treatment.

Study Questions

1. Measurement of f_o and intensity can be divided into three categories. Name them.

2. Define mean speaking f_o and mean speaking f_o range.

3. Define perturbation, jitter, and shimmer.

4. What is a voice range profile?

5. What is the general difference between voice range profiles elicited from men and women?

6. What physiologic factors contribute to the general shape of the voice range profile? (For example, why does the lower contour curve upward with increasing frequency?)

6.2 Measurement of Phonatory Aerodynamics

Voice and speech production are aerodynamic phenomena, and therefore assessment of air pressures and airflows often provides meaningful information about an individual's phonatory system. Here we examine some common measures of voice aerodynamics used in research and clinical applications. In Chapter 7, we will explore the measurement of aerodynamics of the upper vocal tract in regard to articulatory dynamics.

Airflow and Lung Pressure

Mean airflow is measured as it exits the oral and nasal cavities. It is measured as the volume of air that passes a given point (the instrumentation measuring the airflow) in milliliters per second. An anesthesia-type face mask is commonly used to collect the airflow. The mask is connected to an electronic sensor, an airflow transducer, called a **pneumotachograph**. Alternatively, the face mask can be designed with special screens across which the airflow is registered using specialized electronic circuitry (Rothenberg, 1977). Although the measurement of airflow is not particularly difficult, it does require an excellent understanding of the instrumentation, as well as of the physiology. For additional information on the instrumental array, see Baken and Orlikoff (2000). In Chapter 5, Table 5–8 (mean airflow norms) displays normative data for mean airflow during sustained vowel phonation. (Production of consonants alters mean airflow, and therefore measures of peak airflow for consonant production and during running speech are addressed in Chapter 8.) We have learned that the airflow can be altered by an interaction of the air pressure, glottal resistance, amplitude of mucosal wave vibration, and longitudinal tension of the vocal folds. Therefore, mean airflow must always be assessed with consideration of the f_o and intensity at which the person is producing voice. Table 5–8 (airflow norms) reflects that, even given a steady frequency and intensity, normal values vary widely among individuals. For this reason, by itself, the mean airflow does not tell us much about the functioning of the system and certainly it is not diagnostic by itself of the specific nature of a vocal abnormality (Schutte, 1980). However, taken together with other measures of lung pressure and glottal resistance, as well as frequency and intensity data, the mean airflow can be highly useful in assessment of effectiveness of treatment for voice problems (Holmberg, Doyle, Perkell, Hammarberg, & Hillman, 2003).

Lung pressure is a key variable in regulation of intensity and contributes to f_o control, and therefore its measurement is important in the study of normal and abnormal voice production. Direct measurement of lung pressure is achieved by inserting a hypodermic needle through the cricothyroid membrane just below the vocal folds (Plant & Hillel, 1998; Plant & Younger, 2000). Air flows from the trachea through the needle to a pressure sensor. The disadvantage of this procedure is that it must be performed by a physician and can be uncomfortable for the research subject. The advantage, however, is that one obtains an accurate measure of lung pressure and, importantly, lung pressure can be measured during running speech.

A highly common method of measurement of lung pressure, and one that is more "clinically friendly," is the estimation of lung pressure from **intraoral pressure** (Figure 6–4) (Löfqvist, Carlborg, & Kitzing, 1982; Smitheran & Hixon, 1981). When the vocal folds are open so that air can flow through the glottis, and no air can flow out

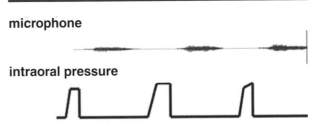

Figure 6–4. Three repetitions of /pae/ shown in the microphone signal (*top panel*) and a smoothed intraoral pressure signal (*bottom panel*). Note that the intraoral pressure is highest during the closed portion of the /p/ and immediately decreases upon release of the plosive.

the nose, and the lips are sealed, the pressure everywhere in the vocal tract is equal. This equal pressure situation occurs during production of the phoneme /p/. When the /p/ is produced and then immediately released into a vowel, the pressure as measured in the mouth (the intraoral air pressure) during the /p/ is assumed to be equal to the lung pressure produced during the adjacent vowel. It is critical, however, for both sounds to be produced at a steady f_o and intensity (as we have learned, lung pressure may vary with both f_o and intensity). Therefore, the task generally consists of multiple repetitions of the /p/ plus vowel combination all linked together, with instructions to maintain a steady pitch and loudness. Intraoral pressure can be measured with a pressure transducer connected to a small plastic tube that is inserted into the mouth. The method provides results that are comparable to the more direct tracheal puncture method except at the extremes of f_o and intensity (Plant & Younger, 2000). The disadvantages of this method are that the speech context is artificial and an intraoral pressure probe may further constrain the speaker so that values may not be reflective of actual, habitual speech in every speaker. Furthermore, lung pressure during running speech cannot be measured, because of the specific consonant-vowel task necessary. A strong advantage of this method is its ease of use and noninvasive nature. Table 5–7 provided normative data for lung pressure under various phonatory conditions.

Another indirect and noninvasive measure of lung pressure is the **airway interruption method** (Jiang, O'Mara, Conley, & Hanson, 1999; Makiyama, Yoshihashi, Mogitate, & Kida, 2005). Like the method described above, the airway interruption method estimates lung pressure from the intraoral pressure. In this case, instead of using the /p/ to block the airflow, an external valve connected to a mouthpiece or face mask is used to rapidly block the airflow during sustained vowel phonation. Measurement of intraoral pressure is made immediately after the external valve cuts off airflow. This pressure is assumed to be equal everywhere in the vocal tract, like the occurrence of equal pressure dur-

ing the production of /p/. Other, less commonly used but excellent methods of measurement of lung pressure, both direct and indirect, have been used in the research literature, as discussed in Baken and Orlikoff (2000).

Vocal Efficiency

Vocal efficiency is a highly relevant concept in the treatment of voice disorders, so we will spend a bit of time examining it. We are familiar with the concept of efficiency in everyday life. Any process that consumes energy can be judged by its efficiency. We try to buy fuel-efficient vehicles so that we get high mileage from a tank full of gasoline. When lifting a heavy weight, we may try to place our body in an optimal position to maximize the efficiency of our arm and leg joints to balance the weight (recall our discussion of joints and fulcrums in Chapter 2). Efficiency can be defined most simply as the ratio of the output of a system to the input, sometimes expressed as a percentage. It would seem that a highly efficient voice production system would be desirable. It would be quite tiresome to expend a great deal of lung power for very little sound power. (And indeed, some voice-disordered patients seek the help of laryngologists and speech-language pathologists for that very complaint—too much effort to speak!) The effectiveness with which this process occurs is quantified (characterized numerically) by a vocal efficiency measure.

If we are going to quantify vocal efficiency, we must select the input energy and the output energy to be compared. Voice production involves the process of converting aerodynamic power (lung pressure times airflow rate) to acoustic power. Therefore, a true measure of the efficiency of energy conversion by the vocal folds would assess the ratio of aerodynamic power to acoustic power at the level of the glottis, which we would call **glottal efficiency**. Acoustic power is measured in watts, the SI unit (see History of Measurement in Chapter 2) of measurement for power. Acoustic power, or intensity at the level of the glottis, is not the same as intensity of the sound pressure wave as it is radiated from the

How Efficient Are We?

Isshiki (1981) notes that, from a physiologic energy consumption (and highly impractical) viewpoint, vocal efficiency might capture the amount of energy used by the body for producing a certain unit of voice. Although not a realistic way to consider efficiency, Titze (1992, p. 242) has done some calculations to determine just how efficient we can be when considering the fuel we take in and the mechanical work we can produce. We measure our fuel in kilocalories. (By convention, the term calorie is commonly used and shows up on the sides of cereal boxes, but the correct nutritional term is kilocalorie.) A kilocalorie (or calorie if you really prefer) represents the amount of energy required to raise the temperature of a liter of water 1 degree Celsius at sea level. Let us assume that the average person consumes 2,000 (kilo) calories per day. Twenty-four hours contains 86,400 seconds. One (kilo)calorie is equal to 4.189 joules of energy. Divide the consumption of kilocalories by seconds, and you have an energy input rate of 100 joules per second, which is equivalent to 100 watts. (Remember, in Chapter 2, we said that 1 watt equals the expenditure of one joule of energy in 1 second.) Therefore, if we are 100% efficient in converting chemical energy (our food) into mechanical energy (muscle movement), we could turn an old-fashioned hand-crank generator to illuminate continuously a 100-watt light bulb. The human body cannot achieve 100% efficiency for a given output because too many other systems require energy simultaneously. However, if we were operating at 10% efficiency (closer to reality), we could crank the generator continuously to maintain illumination of a very dim 10-watt light bulb.

Now let us return to considering vocal efficiency as physiologic energy consumption for voice production (Isshiki, 1981). How much of our metabolism is used for voice production? Titze (1992) provides these calculations. Let us assume that the average individual could generate a lung pressure of 2 kPa (20 cm of H_2O) for maximum vocal intensity. Furthermore, the mean flow rate would be approximately 0.5 liters per second (equal to .0005 m^3 per second). We know that aerodynamic power (in watts) is the product of lung pressure and mean flow rate. So the maximum aerodynamic power for voice production would be approximately 1 watt. Recall from the light bulb generator that our maximum energy consumption is 100 watts. So even using our maximum aerodynamic power to produce voice, we are using only about 1% of our total metabolic power. No wonder we can talk and do so many other activities at the same time!

speaker's mouth. (The reason why the glottal acoustic power is not the same as that radiated from the lips has to do with the resonance of the vocal tract, to be discussed in Chapter 7.) Instead, we measure vocal efficiency and calculate it as the acoustic power as it radiates from the mouth (not the glottis) (Tanaka & Gould, 1983). In summary, therefore, vocal efficiency is defined as the ratio of the radiated acoustic power to the aerodynamic power. Aerodynamic power equals mean lung pressure times mean glottal flow.

Vocal efficiency is greater in adults than in young children (Tang & Stathopoulos, 1995). Voice disorders tend to create an inefficient larynx. For example, Jiang, Stern, Chen, and Solomon (2004) found vocal efficiency to be reduced in patients with benign lesions of the vocal fold (in which a noncancerous growth protrudes from the free margin of the vocal fold). Individuals with unilateral vocal fold paralysis (one vocal fold cannot adduct properly to initiate normal phonation) also have reduced vocal efficiency (Hartl, Hans, Vaissiere, Riquet, & Brasnu, 2001).

Why do such voice disorders cause poorer vocal efficiency? Tanaka and Gould (1985) found that with voice-disordered individuals, the lower efficiency values were associated with higher airflow rates, generally due to incomplete glottal closure. This finding is consistent with our knowledge that closure of the vocal folds is the event that results in excitation of the column of air in the vocal tract. Because improved vocal efficiency may reflect positive change in phonatory function after treatment (Zeitels, Hillman, Franco, & Bunting, 2002), vocal efficiency can be used to document the effect of treatment.

Vocal efficiency is not just about getting the most output for the least input. Titze (1992) notes that the concept of efficiency becomes a bit more complicated when the system in question has more than one output. He has us consider the light bulb, an energy conversion system in which electrical energy is converted into light energy. However, light is not the only output. On a hot summer day, the heat generated from the light bulb can be so noticeable as to make you want to turn the light off. Both heat and light are the output, yet light is the only desirable output, and so heat is considered a nonuseful byproduct that decreases the overall efficiency of the bulb. When we consider the efficiency of the vocal folds, we are concerned with the vocal output. We must also consider the preservation and longevity of the system (Cooper, Partridge, & Alipour-Haghighi, 1993; Titze, 1992). Although our bodies are, in general, designed to be highly efficient, our parts eventually wear out with extended use, and most are not replaceable, unfortunately. Hence, we do not want to achieve a high level of vocal efficiency at the cost of tissue damage. In some types of voice disorders, excessively forceful contraction of the intrinsic laryngeal muscles can result in a great deal of acoustic power relative to the lung pressure, but that acoustic power is achieved with excessive collision and shear forces to the vocal folds. Often, the goal of voice therapy is to achieve a somewhat decreased efficiency to gain increased vocal longevity. In other words, we temper the vocal efficiency with vocal economy (Titze, 1992).

S/Z Ratio

The s/z ratio (Eckel & Boone, 1981) is a maximum performance task that requires nothing more than a stopwatch for instrumentation. It has, therefore, enjoyed some longstanding popularity. The s/z ratio is used to assess the integrity of phonatory glottal closure. It is a statistic of the relative durations of maximum phonation of the phonemes /s/ and /z/. The s/z ratio has no units of measurement. In Chapter 7, we will learn that both the /s/ and /z/ consonants are produced in the same place in the oral cavity and in the same manner. That is, the tongue is in contact with the hard palate just behind the upper front teeth, with a narrow channel or groove left open between the tongue and the palate to allow the outflow of air. The narrow constriction produces turbulent airflow, which is the sole source of the sound for the /s/. To produce /z/, the vocal folds vibrate to produce a glottal acoustic wave, the sound of which is added to the turbulent airflow in the mouth. In sum, the only difference between the two sounds is the vibration of the vocal folds. Increased laryngeal resistance should occur with production of /z/ compared to /s/, because the glottis is wide open for the /s/ (minimal resistance) and vibrating open and closed for the /z/ (greater resistance). For a speaker with normal vibratory dynamics, it is hypothesized that an individual should be able to sustain the /s/ and the /z/ for equal durations, yielding an s/z ratio of 1. In cases of incomplete glottal closure during phonation, the glottal resistance would be lowered, allowing greater escape of air, and the /z/ would be sustained for shorter duration, yielding a ratio greater than 1.

An advantage of this measure is the ease with which it can be obtained, and some data suggest that ratios will differ between those with normal and abnormal voices (Eckel & Boone, 1981; Schneider, Denk, & Bigenzahn, 2003). However, attempts to establish normative data have met with difficulties, particularly due to inconsistent elicitation procedures and wide variability of results, weakening its use as a screening measure for voice problems (Mueller, Larson, & Summers, 1993; Soman, 1997; Trudeau

& Forrest, 1997). For example, Gelfer and Pazera (2006) found that the intensity at which the /s/ and /z/ are produced would be expected to affect ratio values significantly. Furthermore, they found that, in young adults with healthy voices, some individuals routinely tend to hold one consonant longer than the other.

Despite the popularity of the s/z ratio, some data do not necessarily support the assumption that /s/ and /z/ should be able to be sustained for equal durations (Kent, Kent, & Rosenbek, 1987; Tait, Michel, & Carpenter, 1980; Trudeau & Forrest, 1997). It may be that the target s/z ratio could be less than 1, because the /z/ might normally be sustained for greater duration than the /s/ due to the increased resistance to the airflow associated with vibration of the vocal folds (Tait et al., 1980). The validity of the s/z ratio is questioned for several reasons, largely because several compensatory behavioral maneuvers can be used to achieve normal or near-normal values. Some of these compensations are beneficial and, in fact, compensatory behaviors form the basis for much of voice therapy. For example, excessive inspiratory checking (maintenance of excessive contraction of the inspiratory muscles while phonating) can be used to maintain lung expansion, decreasing expiratory flow (in lieu of the resistance to the airflow that would be offered by the adducted vocal folds in normal phonation) and thereby helping to maintain longer voicing.

However, some of the behavioral maneuvers used to achieve normal values for the s/z ratio are maladaptive for speech production. For example, excessive constriction of the supraglottal musculature, particularly the ventricular folds, can help to achieve increased resistance to the airflow, again slowing down rate of egressive flow and helping to maintain longer phonation.

Maximum Phonation Time

Maximum phonation time (MPT) (Ptacek & Sander, 1963), as the name implies, measures the duration of a maximally sustained vowel, and for reasons similar to the s/z ratio, it ought to be sensitive to impaired phonatory glottal clo-

sure. The **maximum phonation time** is elicited by asking the individual to take a deep breath and sustain a vowel at comfortable pitch and loudness for as long as possible. The duration is then measured. It requires no sophisticated instrumentation—only a watch with a second hand. Like the s/z ratio, maximum phonation time is used to assess the integrity of phonatory glottal closure. Men produce greater maximum phonation time than women in general, due to their greater lung volume (Yanagihara, Koike, & von Leden, 1966). Normative data for maximum phonation time are presented in Table 6–3. Concerns about the validity of maximum phonation time (Solomon, Garlitz, & Milbrath, 2000) are similar to those explained above for s/z ratio. Use of compensatory strategies (both positive and negative) may strongly influence the phonatory duration. Furthermore, a learning effect can strongly influence this measure. That is, second and third trials by an individual produce improvement due to practice. This practice effect strongly limits the utility of maximum phonation time as a measure of the effectiveness of voice therapy or other treatment for voice disorders. In addition, the method of elicitation is critical.

Table 6–3. Maximum Phonation Time (MPT)

	Mean Age (y)	MPT (s)
Children[a]		
Boys	6	10.4
	10	22.2
	15	20.7
Girls	6	10.6
	10	15.9
	15	19.5
Adults[b]		
Men	17–41	24.9
Women	18–40	17.9

Sources: Data from
[a]Finnegan, D. E. (1988). Maximum phonation time for children with normal voices. *Folia Phoniatrica, 37,* 209–215.
[b]Ptacek, P. H., & Sander, E. K. (1963). Maximum duration of phonation. *Journal of Speech and Hearing Disorders, 28,* 171–182.

The speech-language pathologist must strongly encourage the patient continually during the task to produce a maximally sustained phonation, so that a true representative sample is obtained. Furthermore, the relationship of MPT to normal phonatory function is unclear. The fact that normal-voiced individuals can produce sustained /a/ for 20 seconds on average, for example, does not mean that it is a requisite behavior for speech. Nevertheless, maximum phonation time is a popular measure, particularly as part of a battery of tests to assess treatment for vocal pathology that results in incomplete glottal closure (Hughes & Morrison, 2005; Lim, Choi, Kim, & Choi, 2006).

Phonation Quotient

The **phonation quotient**, related to maximum phonation time, is the vital capacity divided by the maximum phonation time, measured in milliliters per second (Hirano, Koike, & von Leden, 1968). Phonation quotient is a good measure of the volume of air used as a function of sustained phonation, when aerodynamic measures such as mean flow are unavailable (Hirano, 1989). Normative data for phonation quotient ratio are presented in Table 6–4. A weakness of phonation quotient as a diagnostic tool, however, is that the vital capacity measure is obtained in a nonspeech maneuver and therefore does not necessarily reflect the air usage during phonation. It should also be noted that the phonation quotient uses a maximally sustained vowel. Thus, it is subject to the same weaknesses as the maximum phonation time task. The mean airflow rate during sustained phonation is a stronger measure of air usage during voice production.

Table 6–4. Phonation Quotient (PQ) Norms

	PQ
Adults	
Men	145
Women	137

Source: Data from Rau, D., & Beckett, R. L. (1984). Aerodynamic assessment of vocal function using hand-held spirometers. *Journal of Speech and Hearing Disorders, 49,* 183–188.

Study Questions

7. In general, how is mean airflow measured?

8. How can lung pressure be measured from intraoral pressure?

9. Define vocal efficiency and glottal efficiency.

10. What factors can affect vocal efficiency?

11. Explain the s/z ratio. What are some threats to the validity of this measure?

12. Define maximum phonation time and provide average values for children, men, and women.

13. How do practice effects and elicitation methods influence values of maximum phonation time?

14. Define phonation quotient.

6.3 Instrumentation for Exploring the Dynamics of the Vocal Folds

Mucosal wave vibration and phonatory glottal closure are critical determinants of the acoustic characteristics of the voice. Therefore, considerable effort has been applied to developing instrumentation for exploration of these features, for both research and clinical purposes. **Glottography** refers to the analysis of vibratory movements of the vocal folds during phonation using any one or a combination of measures, including photoglottography, electroglottography, ultrasound glottography, and inverse filtering (Kitzing, 1986). These methods provide waveforms corresponding to various aspects of the phonatory behavior of the vocal folds. The waveforms are called time varying, in that they depict specific aspects of the vibration of the vocal folds over time, the unit of which may range from as short as a small number of vibratory cycles to lengthier sustained vowel phonation or running speech. Glottographic waveforms supplement more direct methods of visualizing tissue movement, including stroboscopy, high-speed video, and videokymography. We begin our discussion of instrumentation with these three methods of directly viewing the vibration of the vocal folds, and then we will examine some of the glottographic waveforms, reserving inverse filtering for Chapter 8. We will learn that all methods have strengths and weakness, and unfortunately, no single method provides all the information needed to understand vibratory behavior fully. For an in-depth examination of instrumentation relating to physiology of the vocal folds, you are referred to Baken and Orlikoff (2000).

Stroboscopy

We start with the instrumentation that is, by far, the most commonly used clinical method of visualization of the vocal folds. **Stroboscopy** is the process of using a pulsing light to simulate movement at a rate slower than the actual rate of movement of the object being imaged (Figure 6–5). The word is derived from the Greek *strobos*, "a swirling" and *skopien* "to observe." Vocal fold vibration is too rapid for the eye to process clearly, even at the slowest rate of vibration (the very lowest male pitch). (Think of visualizing the spokes of a bicycle wheel while someone is riding the bicycle quickly. The individual spokes blur together.) Stroboscopy, particularly when connected to video recording equipment, provides the viewer with the ability to visualize mucosal wave vibration—not the actual vibration, but a visual estimate of the vibration. This concept of a visual estimate will be further explained below.

Stroboscopy works because of two visual perceptual features. First, the image must be illuminated uniformly without perception of variation (e.g., flicker). Second, motion is perceived

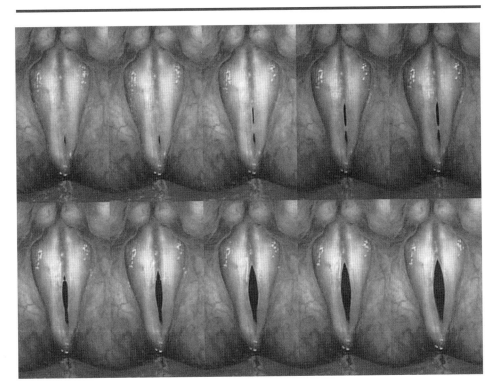

Figure 6–5. A sequence of stroboscopic images of vocal fold vibration showing the opening phase of vibration (*proceeding from upper left to upper right and lower left to lower right*). Courtesy of Kay/Pentax (Lincoln Park, NJ).

The History of Stroboscopy

Overviews of the historical development of stroboscopy and some of its strengths and weaknesses are provided by Faure and Müller (1992); Hanson, Gerratt, and Berke (1990); and Wendler (1992). Simon Stampfer (1792–1864), an Austrian professor at the Technical College of Vienna, and Joseph Plateau (1801–1883), a scientist from Brussels, each developed the earliest stroboscopes in 1832, instruments for creating the illusion of motion from a series of still images. Called the stroboscope by Stampfer, the device consisted of a flat disk with a series of evenly spaced holes around the rim, and on one side were an equal number of hand-drawn figures representing a sequence of movements. If one held the stroboscope with the figures facing the mirror and spun the disk while looking through the holes, the images would appear to move. A more elaborate version, called the zoetrope, became quite popular as a parlor game among the wealthy in the early 20th century. (Perhaps we can consider it the very earliest version of renting movies for home viewing.) Unfortunately, both men damaged their eyes from staring into the sun during their experiments. In 1878, a physician named Oertel applied the stroboscopic technology of the time to laryngeal examination of his patients. Since that time, many physicians and scientists have contributed to the evolution of stroboscopic instrumentation and have applied stroboscopy as both a clinical diagnostic and a research tool. van den Berg (1958) described the use of stroboscopy in his exposition on the myoelastic-aerodynamic theory of voice production. Seminal papers on normal and abnormal vibratory dynamics of the vocal folds were written by Smith (1954) and Timcke, von Leden, and Moore (1958, 1959). von Leden (1961) developed the first stroboscope electronically synchronized to vibration of the vocal folds, thus allowing its use in routine medical examination of patients with voice disorders.

Early Laryngology

von Leden (1996) recounts the story of the first visual examination of the vocal folds, actually a self-examination. Manuel García (1805–1906) was the son of a famous singer who in turn sang opera in New York City in his early 20s. Perhaps he did not have the technical expertise or talent of his father, for he soon developed voice problems and stopped performing. To the benefit of the future singing and voice therapy community, however, he did devote the remainder of his life to the pursuit of the teaching of singing. The story is told that while walking through the Tulleries in Paris in 1854, his own reflection, produced by the sun shining upon a window, gave him the idea of examining his own larynx with a dental mirror and the light of a candle.

from sampling (illuminating briefly) images at specific points in time (Mehta, Deliyski, & Hillman, 2010). Current technology uses a xenon bulb to generate a very brief and intense pulse of light. Because the strobe light is the only source of illumination in an otherwise dark vocal tract, we can see the vocal folds only when they are illuminated by the brief light pulse. The flash of the light is triggered by the fundamental frequency as measured by a microphone (or an electroglottograph, as described below). Using electronic circuitry, the bulb can be set to flash at the same rate as the f_o. What would be observed in this case? Let us consider what is happening. The flash illuminates the vocal folds at a moment in time in the vibratory cycle. The next flash again illuminates the vocal folds at another moment in time. But because the flash rate is equivalent to the rate of vibration of the vocal folds, the vocal folds will be illuminated at the same point in each vibratory cycle. If the vibration is completely periodic (without variation in f_o), then the vocal folds will appear to be not moving at all (Figure 6–6B).

Typically, however, the rate of the flashes is set to slightly lower than the actual rate of vibration of the vocal folds (by approximately 2 Hz). In this case, the repeated flashes illuminate the vocal folds briefly at different points in each cycle. If one observes the vocal folds during this series of brief illuminations, the vocal folds appear to change position only at those brief moments (Figure 6–6A). The brain interprets this series of slightly altered images by filling in the gaps between the images to yield an illusion of smoothly continuous motion. In this way, the strobe light "samples" images of the vocal folds from sequential moments across multiple cycles, and the brain strings them together into a continuous image of one complete vibration. The sequential stroboscopic images appear to be a slow-motion video of the vibration of the vocal folds. It should be noted that the instrument used to shine the light on the vocal folds and to carry back the image of the vocal folds (called an endoscope) can be placed through either the mouth or the nose. If placed through the mouth, the individual is limited to sustaining a vowel. If the endoscope is placed through the nose, the individual can speak as he or she would normally.

If vibration of the vocal folds was perfectly periodic, the stroboscopic images would be completely true to the actual vibration. Vocal fold vibration is not perfectly periodic, however. Small irregularities exist in the rate of vibration and in movement of the tissue from cycle to cycle, and so the sampling of images obtained by the strobe as blended together by the observer's brain is less than a perfect representation of the true vibration. Keep in mind that stroboscopic imaging is composed of very brief glimpses of moments selected from different glottal cycles. The more irregular the actual vibration of the vocal folds, the less accurate the representation by the stroboscopic images. In fact, with many voice disorders, it is not unusual for the stroboscopic images to be somewhat blurry or "jittery" because of the irregularity of the vibration and resulting difficulty in synchronizing the rate of

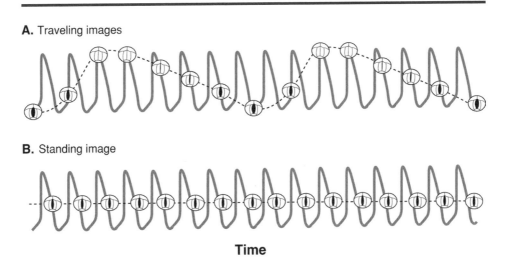

A. Traveling images

B. Standing image

Time

Figure 6–6. "Still" (**A**) and "traveling" (**B**) stroboscopic images. Adapted from *The Larynx: A Multidisciplinary Approach* (2nd ed., pp. 82–83), by M. P. Fried, 1996, Mosby.

strobe-light pulses to the rate of the vibrating vocal folds.

The clinical use of stroboscopy is described well in Hirano (1981) and Hirano and Bless (1993). Physiologically relevant features of the vibration, including extent of phonatory glottal closure and the presence or absence and regularity of the mucosal wave vibration of the vocal folds, are recorded in a somewhat standardized fashion.

Some clinical researchers (including the author) have attempted to gather quantitative measures of the glottal area, from digitized images extracted from the stroboscopic examination (Bloch & Behrman, 2001; Omori, Kacker, Slavit, & Blaugund, 1996; Schneider, Wendler, & Seidner, 2002; Yumoto, 2004). Although such measures can contribute information on vibratory dynamics, the fact that the sequential strobe images do not represent true vibratory behavior limits their validity.

High-Speed Laryngeal Imaging

In 1940, D. W. Farnsworth, an engineer for Bell Telephone Laboratories, reported the development of high-speed motion picture photography of the vibration of the vocal folds. With his colleagues, he acquired images of the vocal folds at rates up to 4,000 frames per second, with each exposure lasting 1/10,000th of a second. These images were then displayed at 16 frames per second, so that a fundamental frequency of 250 Hz appeared to be vibrating at one cycle per second, certainly giving the viewer ample time to analyze the vibration. Current **high-speed laryngeal imaging** produces superior resolution at imaging rates from 2 to 4 kHz (Hertegård, Larsson, & Wittenberg, 2003; Schuberth, Hoppe, Döllinger, Lohscheller, & Eysholdt, 2001; Yan, Ahmad, Kunduk, & Bless, 2005) (or up to 8 kHz for black and white images). The strong advantage of this technology is the accuracy with which even highly irregular vibration of the vocal folds can be imaged. Unlike stroboscopy, which combines select images from different sequential cycles, high-speed technology images vibration at 20 to 30 times the fundamental frequency. However, the sharpness of the images is still below that of stroboscopy, and the cost of a high-speech camera remains out of the reach of many clinical settings. Furthermore, the vast number of images obtained from even a short video of vibration can be cumbersome to analyze. These disadvantages mean that the technology remains restricted to large medical and academic institutions.

Videokymography (VKG)

Like high-speed imaging, **videokymography** (from Greek *kuma*, a wave) is based on acquisition of images at a very rapid rate. Unlike high-speed imaging, however, videokymography does not image the entire area of the vocal folds. Developed by Svec and Schutte (1996), videokymography uses a modified video camera that records images at approximately 8000 Hz from a single line that runs through the vocal folds (Figure 6–7). Typically, the middle of the vocal folds, where vibratory amplitude is widest, is selected for scanning. Successive line images are then displayed in real time with time presented on the vertical y-axis. Videokymography has been used to assess vibratory irregularities in cases of vocal fold pathology (Schutte, Svec, & Sram, 1998) and in exploration of quantitative measures of vibratory dynamics, including amplitude of mucosal wave movement, from excised canine larynges (Jiang, Chang, et al., 2000). The advantages of such a system, like high-speed video, are a true cycle-to-cycle imaging of vocal fold vibration, such that irregularities in the periodicity can be visualized clearly. Furthermore, the videokymography instrumentation is considerably less expensive than high-speed cameras, making it quite practical for clinical application. However, unlike high-speed video, the visual image that is displayed by videokymography is not at all intuitive (see Figure 6–7). A further disadvantage of the technology is that the images are in black and white. In addition, videokymography must be coupled with either stroboscopy or high-speed video to obtain complete visualization of the vocal folds.

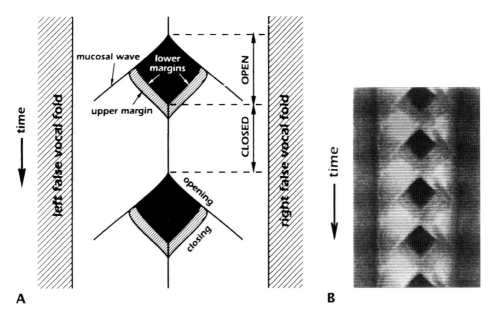

Figure 6–7. Imaging vocal fold vibrating using videokymography. **A.** Schematic of the line-imaging mode of the vocal folds used to build the videokymography image. **B.** The videokymographic image. The active imaging line is positioned at the mid–vocal fold level. A slight asymmetry in vibration is observed between the left and right vocal fold. The left and right vocal folds are shown on the left and right side of the image, respectively. Unlike waveforms, in which time proceeds forward from left to right, in the kymogram, time advances forward from the top to the bottom of the image (4.5 glottal cycles within the time segment of 18.4 ms). From "Videokymography: High-speed line scanning of vocal fold vibration," by J. G. Svec and H. K. Schutte, 1996, *Journal of Voice, 10,* p. 203. Reprinted with permission of the Voice Foundation.

Photoglottography (PGG)

We have learned that closure of the glottis is a critical component of voice production and that the persistence of even a relatively small glottal gap during the closed phase of vibration can result in unwanted voice changes. Therefore, the ability to examine the pattern of glottal closure, usually with simultaneous acquisition of other acoustic, aerodynamic, or vibratory measures, can help us to learn more about normal and abnormal voice production. **Photoglottography** (PGG) provides information about the relative size of the glottal opening. PGG is a technique that measures the amount of light passing through the vocal folds during each vibratory cycle (Figure 6–8). In theory, the amount of light shining through the glottis is proportional to the amount of opening of the vocal folds, which of course is variable as they oscillate open and closed. Therefore, PGG provides an approximation of the variable cross-sectional area of the glottis during phonation (Baer, Löfqvist, & McGarr, 1983; Berke et al., 1987).

First used by Sonesson (1959), PGG generally involves shining a light through the glottis and then recording the amount of light that escapes through the glottis during phonation using some type of light sensor connected to a recording device. The waveform one obtains corresponds to the opening, closing, and closed phases of vibration. The instrumentation can be arranged in a variety of ways but generally consists of a light source that is suspended above the vocal folds (using the light from a fiberoptic endoscope or separate light emitting source)

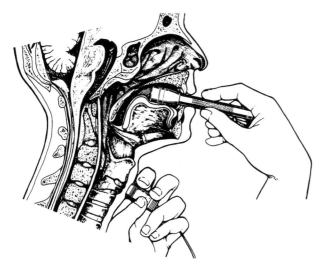

Figure 6–8. Photoglottography measures the relative glottal opening by determining the amount of light passing through the glottis during each vibratory cycle. From "Photoglottography: A clinical synopsis," by B. R. Gerratt, D. G. Hanson, G. S. Berke, and K. Precoda, 1991, *Journal of Voice, 5,* p. 101. Reprinted with permission of the Voice Foundation.

and a light sensor that is placed externally on the neck just below the level of the vocal folds (Lisker, Abramson, Cooper, & Schvey 1969). (Yes, if the light source is sufficiently bright, enough light will filter through the neck tissues for recording by the external sensor.) Alternatively, the light source can be directed through the glottis from above by inserting it through the mouth (Doyle & Fraser, 1993). Importantly, PGG provides information only about the relative glottal area, not about the absolute or true area. That is, we cannot know whether the maximum glottal opening in each cycle is 3 cm wide or that the mid-portion of the cycle has an opening of 1 cm. But we could know that the mid-cycle glottal opening is 33% of the maximum, for example.

Gerratt, Hanson, Berke, and Precoda (1991) provide an extensive review of the potential clinical application of PGG. It has been used in clinical research of voice disorders, particularly in examination of phonatory glottal closure in

New Methods of Visualizing the Larynx

We have learned that the histology of the vocal folds specifies their biomechanical properties. In addition, analysis of the ultrastructure of the tissues of the vocal folds (the microscopic details of the cells) can be essential for diagnosis of disease. Stroboscopy and high-speed imaging provide information about the surface features of the tissue. Generally, computed tomography (CT), magnetic resonance imaging (MRI), x-ray imaging, and biopsy (removing a piece of tissue and examining it under the microscope) have been the only way to examine the histologic structure of the vocal folds. CT and MRI, however, are limited in their resolution. That is, their ability to show the details of the cellular structure is limited. Biopsy requires cutting into the vocal folds, which can cause scarring and disrupt normal mucosal wave movement. New imaging technology, however, is making it possible to examine the inner tissues of the vocal folds without slicing into the tissue and risking damage to healthy tissue. Within the past decade, a

new noninvasive imaging method, called optical coherence tomography (OCT), has been developed, which offers very high-resolution cross-sectional imaging of human tissue 2 to 3 mm deep into the tissue. OCT uses light to identify different tissue structures. The magnitude and phase of the light reflected from the different tissue structures provide information about the structures of the tissues. The detail provided is greater than 10 times that of ultrasound (Bibas et al., 2005). (Ultrasound imaging is discussed in Chapter 7.) OCT was used first in ophthalmology because the eye, like the vocal folds, is highly sensitive to potential scarring from invasive imaging methods. OCT has been investigated in human and animal vocal fold tissue (Nassif, Armstrong, de Boer, & Wong, 2005), particularly in identifying different types of tissue pathology (Wong et al., 2005). Future technology may address increasing the depth of tissue that can be analyzed and improving the ease of use of the instrumentation for routine clinical application.

the case of unilateral vocal fold paralysis (lack of abductory or adductory movement of one vocal fold) (Hanson, Gerratt, Karin, & Berke, 1988; Jiang, Lin, & Hanson, 2000; Slavit & Maragos, 1994) and the neurologic disorder Parkinson disease (Gerratt et al., 1991; Lin, Jiang, Hone, & Hanson, 1999), as a measure of treatment outcome after voice therapy (Kitzing & Löfqvist, 1979), and in children (Doyle & Fraser, 1993). Overall, however, its clinical application has been somewhat limited, in large part due to the lack of easily accessible commercial instrumentation.

PGG does have limitations (Coleman & Wendahl, 1968; Gerratt et al., 1991), only a few of which we will mention here. First, it is invasive, in that it requires either the light source or the light sensor to be placed within the vocal tract. Many speech pathologists may not be comfortable with or able to accomplish this part of the procedure, particularly if they are not employed within a hospital or other type of health care setting. Second, the lack of an absolute reference confounds interpretation of the waveform. That is, the PGG signal only provides information about the relative, not actual, amount of light passing through the vocal folds. And so the lowest amount of light recorded by the PGG instrumentation does not necessarily mean that the glottis is completely sealed but only that the glottis is the most closed relative to other points in the vibratory cycle. If one acquired high-speed video at the same time as the PGG signal, however, the respective points on the waveform could be corroborated with the video image, providing at least a partial solution to the problem. A third weakness of the PGG method is that the light sensor, whether placed below or above the vocal folds, may not accurately register the light transmitted through the glottis due to vocal tract movement. Supraglottal squeezing of the ventricular folds, for example, may block part of the light reaching the sensor, causing the resulting waveform to suggest greater glottal closure than is occurring.

Electroglottography (EGG)

Whereas PGG provides information about the relative changes in glottal opening, **electroglot**tography (EGG) provides a waveform that has been shown to correspond to the relative contact of the vocal folds during vibration (Childers & Krishnamurthy, 1985; Colton & Conture, 1990; Scherer, Drucker, & Titze, 1988). (A note of caution to the student: Do not misread EGG as EEG. The former represents electroglottography. The latter represents electroencephalography, a method of assessing brain activity.) The electroglottograph, the instrument that produces the EGG waveform, consists of a pair of surface electrodes that are placed on the outside of the neck over the left and right sides of the thyroid cartilage. The electrodes are connected to a signal generator that supplies a very high-frequency (300 kHz to 5 MHz), low-voltage (approximately 0.5 V) current through the electrodes. The electrical current that flows across the neck from one electrode to the other does not harm the tissue and is not felt by the individual being tested, because of the combination of very high frequency and very low voltage of the signal. Tissue is generally an excellent conductor of electricity, whereas air is a very poor conductor of electricity. If the vocal folds are open, the air gap across the glottis offers considerable resistance to the flow of electricity. If the vocal folds are in contact, then the resistance to the electrical flow across the electrodes is quite low. The resistance varies as a function of the degree of contact of the vocal folds. That is, within the closing phase, during which vocal fold contact is increasing, the resistance to the electrical current is decreasing. Similarly, within the opening phase, as vocal fold contact decreases, the resistance to the current increases. When connected to an output device such as a computer with the appropriate display software, the resulting waveform depicts the change in resistance across the two electrodes, which corresponds to the relative contact of the vocal folds.

In Figure 6–9, we see the correspondence of the vibratory events to the shape of the EGG waveform. These schemata have been depicted by many scientists: Rothenberg (1981) used images of vocal fold vibration; Lecluse, Brocaar, and Verschuure (1975) used seven stroboscopic images correlated with the phase of vocal fold contact; and Childers and Krisnamurthy (1985)

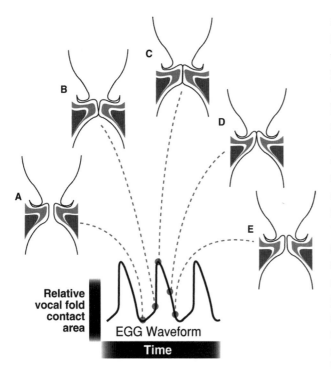

Figure 6–9. The relative positions of the vocal folds as they correspond to approximate points on the EGG waveform.

used a graphic of relative phases of the opening of a zipper. As depicted in Figure 6–9 and by convention, moving upward on the vertical *y*-axis corresponds to decreasing resistance (and hence to increasing relative vocal fold contact). This often-depicted ideal EGG waveform is elicited during sustained vowel phonation within the range of typical speaking f_o. Observe that the portion of the waveform depicting decreasing vocal fold contact (and therefore corresponding to increasing glottal opening) is more abrupt than the increasing contact (closing phase) of the vocal folds. Note also the brief duration of the maximal relative contact of the vocal folds (corresponding in the normal larynx to glottal closure). Recall that the opening phase is of greater duration than the closing phase, and the closed phase occupies the shortest duration of the vibratory cycle within the range of typical speaking f_o for men and women.

Childers and Krishnamurthy (1985) and Colton and Conture (1990) provide an overview

of the history of the EGG, recounting that it was introduced by Fabre in 1957 (at the same time van den Berg was reporting on the myoelastic-aerodynamic theory of voice production). It was not until the 1970s, however, that the EGG became more commonly used, due to increased availability of off-the-shelf EGG instrumentation. Fourcin and Abberton developed a commercial EGG, which they called the laryngograph (Fourcin & Abberton, 1977). Since that time, others have developed commercial instruments (Rothenberg, 2002; Rothenberg & Mahshie, 1988), and considerable exploration of the EGG signal has been pursued. Owing to both the easy availability and completely noninvasive nature of the instrumentation, the EGG became very popular in clinical research, with well over 200 research publications since the 1970s by many different authors. In-depth analysis of the instrumentation, an exhaustive review of the research literature relating to the EGG instrumentation, and interpretation of EGG waveforms and their clinical use in interpretation of voice disorders are available in the literature (Children & Krishnamurthy, 1985; Colton & Conture, 1990; Kitzing, 1990; Titze, 1990).

The advantages of electroglottography are its ease of use, the relatively inexpensive and readily available commercial instrumentation, and its noninvasive nature. In addition, calculating the f_o from the EGG signal is relatively easy compared to its calculation from the acoustic waveform: One can see readily that demarcation of individual vibratory cycles is much clearer in the EGG signal. (The acoustic reasons for the complexity of the microphone signal are addressed in Chapter 7.) The disadvantages of the EGG, however, are many and serious. Poor signal quality is common in individuals with small larynges, particularly women and children, for whom the change in resistance due to vocal fold contact or absence of contact is quite small. A similar difficulty in obtaining adequate signal strength is common for individuals with thick necks (due either to heavy musculature or fat), because the signal becomes dispersed.

The most serious problem with the EGG, however, is interpretation of the waveform, particularly in people with voice disorders. The presence of strands of mucus across the vocal folds can change the nature of the resistance to the electrical current between the two electrodes, confounding interpretation of true contact of the vocal folds. Muscular hyperfunction (excessive contraction of the intrinsic and extrinsic laryngeal muscles) can change the nature of the resistance, altering the shape of the waveform and further complicating interpretation. Unfortunately, one can obtain normal-appearing waveforms from individuals with vocal pathology and perceptually impaired voice. Despite the common illustrations of ideal waveforms in publications of EGG research, the clinical reality is that variability in waveform shape is obtained across normal and disordered voices. The vertical phase difference and the antero-posterior, zipper-like opening and closing of the vocal folds can make identification of the moment of opening quite difficult (Childers & Krishnamurthy, 1985). Furthermore, waveforms from normal-voiced individuals may not yield such distinct phase points (Painter, 1988). Colton and Conture (1990) comment that "although the EGG reproduces the appropriate phases of the vibratory cycle, it does so in an imprecise manner" (p. 17). The imprecision is often sufficient to limit application to clinical research significantly. For these reasons, beyond use as an f_o tracking device with which to synchronize the stroboscopic light to the vibrations of the vocal folds, its routine clinical use in diagnosis of voice disorders is rare (Behrman, 2005). Its use is more favored in research, particularly when coupled with simultaneous acquisition of other glottographic signals, such as that obtained from photoglottography (Gerratt et al., 1991).

Each method of exploring vibration of the vocal folds has its strengths and weaknesses, as we have seen. For this reason, clinical scientists often gather simultaneously two or more different types of signals (Baer et al., 1983; Gerratt et al., 1991; Habermann, Jiang, Lin, & Hanson, 2000; Hess & Ludwigs, 2000) with each method serving to complement the others' shortcomings. The PGG waveform shows changes in glottal area and defines the open and closed phases (assuming complete phonatory glottal closure) and relative durations of the opening and closing phases of the open period. But PGG tells us little when the vocal folds are in contact. In contrast, the EGG waveform shows changes in the area of vocal fold contact when the vocal folds are in contact with one another, including the separation of the vocal folds from below during the closed phase and the return of contact from below after closing. But EGG tells us little when the vocal folds are completely separated (Hanson, Jiang, D'Agostino, & Herzon, 1995). The EGG waveform identifies portions of the vocal fold vibratory cycle in terms of relative vocal fold contact, whereas the PGG signal identifies the same waveform segments in terms of relative glottal opening. The two are related but not synonymous. The closing phase of the PGG cycle and the increasing contact phase of the EGG cycle are equivalent in the normal larynx in which we have visual confirmation that the vocal folds are closing normally and fully, and the EGG waveform is free of aberrations.

Open Quotient (OQ), Speed Quotient (SQ), and Contact Quotient (CQ)

The open phase describes the time when the vocal folds are not completely closed and, hence, air flows through the glottis. The opening phase describes the time from separation of the upper margin of the vocal folds until the point of maximum opening (when the vocal folds are maximally abducted). The closing phase describes the time from peak opening until the point when the inferior margins of the vocal folds contact (closing the glottis). The closed phase is the time when the vocal folds are completely adducted and air does not flow through the glottis.

Three quantitative measures from the glottographic waveforms are helpful for summarizing the changes in glottal opening and vocal fold contact during phonation. The **open quotient** is the ratio of the open phase of vocal fold vibration to the entire duration of the glottal cycle (Tarnoczy, 1951). The **speed quotient** is the ratio of the duration of the opening phase of the vocal folds to the duration of the closing phase (Timcke et al., 1959). The **contact quotient** (sometimes referred to as the closed quotient) is the ratio of the period during which the vocal folds are in contact to the entire glottal cycle (Hacki, 1996; Orlikoff, 1991).

Open quotient tends to increase with increasing f_o (Kitzing & Sonesson, 1974; Timcke et al., 1958). At normal conversational frequency and intensity, the closed quotient varies between 32% and 60% of the entire cycle (Higgins & Saxman, 1991; Howard, Lindsey, & Allen, 1990; Orlikoff, 1991). The closed phase represents a smaller percentage of the entire cycle as f_o increases. In the low- and middle-frequency ranges, the duration of the closed phase increases with increasing intensity. Speed quotient, however, appears to be more independent of f_o (Hanson et al., 1990; Timcke et al., 1958). The open phase portion of the cycle, the open quotient, increases with rising f_o in the lower and middle frequency ranges and decreases with greater intensity (Hildebrand, 1976, as reported by Hanson et al., 1990; Sonesson, 1959; Stathopoulos & Sapienza, 1993). In parallel fashion, the closed portion of the cycle would therefore be decreased in these circumstances. In fact, for many women, the vocal folds may not close completely at higher frequencies (Sonneson, 1959). Although Timcke et al. (1958) found the speed quotient to be more independent of f_o, Hildenbrand (1976) reported that speed quotient decreased significantly in the lower and middle f_o ranges. The open quotient varies inversely with intensity, and the speed quotient varies directly with intensity (Murty, Carding, Kelly, & Lancaster, 1991; Stathopoulos & Sapienza, 1993). It should be noted that open- and speed quotient values may differ depending on whether they are derived from the glottal volume velocity waveform or the EGG waveform, as these each represent different phenomena (Sapienza, Stathopoulos, & Dromey, 1998). Given the disadvantages of the EGG signal as discussed earlier, these ratios are likely to be more valid when derived from the glottal volume velocity waveform.

We can relate the value of these ratios to the physiology of vocal fold vibration. The vocal folds are thicker when an individual is speaking at lower f_os, as compared to when that individual is speaking at higher f_os, during which time the vocal folds are stretched more thinly. During vibration, a greater phase lag between the lower and upper margins of the vocal folds should occur with thick compared to thin vocal folds. The greater phase lag should, in turn, result in a longer closed phase than with thinned folds (Sundberg, Faahlstedt, & Morell, 2005).

These ratios allow for quantitative analysis of vibratory behavior of the vocal folds, which can be valuable both for understanding the wide range of normal and disordered vocal behaviors and for contributing to measurement of treatment outcome in the case of a voice disorder. However, in discussing these ratios, a few notes of caution are warranted. First, the exact points on the waveform that correspond to vibratory events such as open and closed are estimates and therefore can vary from one study to the next and affect ratio values (Sapienza et al., 1998). Second, the clinical utility of these measures for voice disordered individuals continues to remain relatively unexplored. Although one would expect the ratios to be different for patients with different types of pathology (Hanson et al., 1988), the derivation of these measures can be problematic in abnormal voices, largely due to the cycle-to-cycle variability of the vibration of the vocal folds, which can be substantial.

In a third note of caution, although closed quotient has been calculated from the EGG signal, it is not recommended. Why? Because the EGG signal does not tell us anything about the glottis. The peak of the EGG signal does not necessarily represent glottal closure but rather the maximal relative closure of the glottis. One assumes that, in a normal healthy larynx, the peak represents complete closure of the glottis. But to be certain that the peak of the EGG waveform represents a closed glottis, one needs simultaneously to gather another signal that provides that information, such as high-speed photography or photoglottography. Visual information from stroboscopy, obtained in synchrony with the EGG signal, also has been used to facilitate interpretation of the EGG waveform (Karnell, 1989). Caution should be used in such interpretations, however, due to the lack of individual cycle information provided by stroboscopy.

Study Questions

15. Explain stroboscopy: the instrumentation used, how it works, and what type of image it provides.

16. What is a weakness of stroboscopy with respect to aperiodic vibration?

17. How is high-speed laryngeal imaging different from stroboscopy?

18. Define videokymography.

19. Define photoglottography and explain its limitations.

20. Explain the instrumentation of electroglottography and the concept of how it works.

21. In Figure 6–9, cover up the five images of the vocal folds, and see if you can explain the theoretical vocal fold positions at each of the five marked points on the waveform.

22. What are the advantages and weaknesses of electroglottography?

23. Define open, speed, and contact quotients.

6.4 Vocal Registers

In our discussion of voice quality, we noted that the normal modes of vibration include registers. A voice **register** is a series of consecutive f_o values of approximately equivalent vocal qual-

ity (Hollien, 1974). Register refers to particular modes of vibration of the vocal folds (Laver, 1980, p. 93). Three basic speaking registers are commonly accepted: pulse (also called glottal fry), modal (sometimes called chest), and falsetto (sometimes called loft, although in singing, falsetto and loft are often identified as distinct registers) (Colton & Hollien, 1972). These divisions apply to the postpubescent voice only (McAllister, Sederholm, & Sundberg, 2000). Conceptually, registration (consideration of the different registers) is a highly controversial area for discussion. How to define and distinguish among the different registers, and even what to call them, is the subject of frequent debate among scientists and teachers and clinicians in speech and singing. Laver (1980, p. 93) tells us that Mörner, Fransson, and Fant (1963) characterize the discussion of registers by noting that registration "suffers from an abundance of terms and an ambiguity of their use" (p. 18). We will identify four factors as the source of the confusion, starting with the fact that registration is a *psychoacoustic* phenomenon. Recall from Chapter 1 that we defined the term "psychoacoustic" as the perception of an acoustic event. Much of the identification of registers is based on perceptual judgments, and all the difficulties surrounding perception of vocal attributes apply to registration.

A second factor contributing to the confusion is that the physiology and acoustics underlying the different registers are incompletely understood. Third, register is sometimes used to refer to the voice quality change due to f_o change alone and not the quality change associated with different modes of vocal fold vibration (Laver, 1980). Fourth, the registers identified in singing are different from those for speaking, but the terms overlap. And finally, the fifth source of confusion relates to the distinction between normal and abnormal modes of vocal fold vibration. Abnormal vibratory modes result in a variety of vocal qualities, as discussed earlier. When we speak of registers, however, most commonly we restrict ourselves to the different qualities achieved by normal modes of vibration.

The boundary between two registers, called a transition, is perceived as an abrupt change in voice quality. The register transition is abrupt, but the underlying physiologic and acoustic variables that control the transition vary continuously (Titze, 1994, p. 253). The concept of an abrupt change caused by a continuously changing variable is important in psychoacoustics and will be particularly relevant when we discuss vowel production in Chapter 7, consonant production in Chapter 8, and models of speech perception in Chapter 10. To understand this concept more clearly, let us consider ambulation, a less abstract phenomenon than registration. Typically, walking is characterized by contact of at least one foot with the ground at all times. You lift your right foot to step forward while your left foot is on the ground. Only after the right foot makes contact with the surface does the left foot completely lose contact with the ground. Running (or even easy jogging) is characterized by loss of contact of both feet from the ground for a moment—a little jump, if you will. Consider speed as the variable that causes change from walking to running. As you move from slow to fast walking to running, your rate of movement is continuously varying, accelerating in this case. Yet the transition from walk to run occurs abruptly (Figure 6–10). The abrupt transition from one state to another due to a continuously changing variable is called a **quantal change** (Stevens, 1972). Register transitions are quantal changes. The underlying, continuously altered variables are f_o and other vocal fold vibratory characteristics, which we shall now examine.

Modal Register

Most speech by men and women occurs within **modal register**. The span of frequencies in modal register is approximately 90 to 450 Hz for men and 150 to 520 Hz for women. Singers may divide the modal register into **chest voice** (lower-pitched and heavier sound) and head voice (higher-pitched and lighter sound) or, alternatively, low, mid, and high voice (Cleveland, 1994). Most of this chapter, and indeed the bulk of this book, addresses the production of voice and speech in modal register.

Vocal Fry

In **vocal fry** phonation, the cricothyroid muscle is relaxed so that there is minimal tension on the

Figure 6–10. The transition from walking to running is a quantal change.

vocal folds. (Other terms synonymous with vocal fry include glottal fry and pulse phonation, and linguists, in particular, may use creak, creaky voice, laryngealized voice, or glottalization.) The vocal folds are shortened and thickened, with increased mass per unit length and a lax mucosal cover. Because of this glottal configuration, four major features characterize vocal fry, all of which strongly affect the sound produced in this register. First, the f_o is quite low, approximately 35 to 50 Hz, and, somewhat remarkably, this range is the same for both men and women (Sorensen & Horii, 1984). A second feature is prolonged duration of the closed phase. Third, the mean airflow and lung pressure produced in this register are considerably lower than in modal voice (Blomgren, Chen, Ng, & Gilbert, 1998). The fourth major feature of this register is a double closure pattern for each cycle. Although a single, prolonged phase of vocal fold contact can occur during pulse phonation (Whitehead, Metz, & Whitehead, 1984) or even a triple closure pattern (Blomgren et al., 1998), the double closure pattern is more commonly cited (Monsen & Engebretson, 1977) and may be more common in men than in women (Chen, Robb, & Gilbert, 2002).

In Figure 6–11, the EGG waveform, together with a simultaneously obtained microphone signal, shows dramatically the different mode of phonation in vocal fry. One can typically see double excitations, called **dichrotic phonation** (Childers & Larar, 1984; Kitzing & Löfqvist,

1979). What is meant by double excitations? Recall that the closure of the vocal folds is the moment of excitation of the air in the vocal tract. If, within a single cycle, the vocal folds were to close, bounce open, and then rapidly close again before finally opening to complete the cycle, one would obtain two moments of acoustic excitation. The perception of this double excitation is typically described as dichrotic, or creaky, and, hence, the use of the term fry (imagine the crackling sound of frying food). The neural-auditory system processes information such that auditory stimuli presented at a rate faster than approximately 70 Hz will be heard as a single continuous sound. In modal and falsetto registers, the pulses of acoustic energy follow much more closely, one after the next, and so the perception is a continuous sustained tone. At the lower frequencies of vocal fry, however, the individual pulses are perceived distinctly.

The slow rate of vibration in vocal fry is attributed to the shortened and thickened vocal folds (Hollien, Girard, & Coleman, 1977), an accompanying decrease in vocal fold stiffness (Whitehead et al., 1984), and decreased lung pressure and airflow (McGlone & Shipp, 1971). These factors result in reduction of the elastic restoring force of the vocal folds, yielding a slower rate of vibration. The speed quotient, based on the EGG signal, is increased in vocal fry compared to modal register, indicating longer duration of the opening phase, which is likely due to the lowered lung pressure (Chen, Robb, &

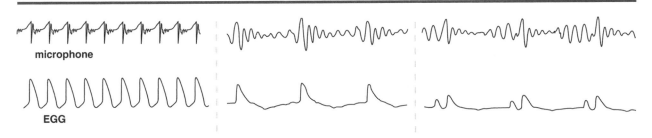

Figure 6–11. Modal phonation (*left*) and two patterns of glottal fry (*middle and right*), characterized by greater duration of each cycle and (*right*) dichrotic vibration. Adapted from "Acoustic, Aerodynamic, Physiologic, and Perceptual Properties of Modal and Vocal Fry Registers," by M. Blomgren, Y. Chen, M. L. Ng, and H. R. Gilbert, 1998, *Journal of the Acoustical Society of America, 103*, 26–54. Adapted with permission of the Acoustical Society of America.

Gilbert, 2002). It should be noted that, although vocal fry is considered a normal mode of vibration, voice therapists usually consider excessive use of this register to be potentially harmful to the vocal fold mucosa (Ylitalo & Hammarberg, 2000). However, the connection between use of vocal fry and dysphonia remains uncertain (Behrman & Akhund, 2016).

Falsetto

The **falsetto** voice occupies the frequencies above modal register. This register is most easily recognized in the male voice at a very high pitch. The mechanism of frequency change in falsetto occurs by contraction of cricothy-

roid, unopposed by thyroarytenoid. The vocal folds elongate and their mass per unit length decreases. This action results in a substantial amount of tension on the vocal folds and increased stiffness. The frequency-raising effect of the decrease in thickness of the vocal fold cover overcomes the frequency-lowering effect due to any increase in overall vocal fold length, resulting in a faster rate of vibration. The high level of tension causes increased buildup of elastic recoil of the vocal folds, reduced amplitude of mucosal wave vibration, and shortened closed phase of the vibratory cycle. Sometimes, a complete lack of closed phase results. These features of reduced amplitude of mucosal wave oscillation and decreased glottal closure have been observed in high-speed films (Farnsworth,

Whispering

Whispering is not a mode of phonation but rather a means of communicating in the absence of vocal fold vibration. Two predominant laryngeal configurations have been observed in whisper. In one type, the vocal folds are in a Y configuration with the anterior portion of the vocal folds toed in and the remainder of the vocal folds abducted widely (Solomon, McCall, Trosset, & Gray, 1989). In another common configuration, the vocal folds are abducted widely in the more typical V-shape. Whisper can sound either quiet (low airflow) or forced (high airflow with increased turbulence). Interestingly, the laryngeal configuration appears to be independent of type of whisper. Whisper is characterized by increased peak flow rates (Monoson & Zemlin, 1984). Airflow rates can be twice as great in quiet whisper and three times as great in forced whisper compared to typical speech. In general, when comparing whisper to soft speech, whisper employs lower lung volumes, greater airflow, lower laryngeal airway resistance, and fewer syllables per breath group (Stathopoulos, Hoit, Hixon, Watson, & Solomon, 1991). The fewer syllables are likely due to the higher airflow. The lower laryngeal airway resistance is likely due to the wide open glottis, which offers little resistance to the airflow. Is whispering bad for the voice? Conventional wisdom holds that whispering as a strategy to decrease phonotrauma to the vocal folds is ill-advised for individuals with voice disorders (Rubin, Praneetvatakul, Gherson, Moyer, & Sataloff, 2006). Yet others have found it a potentially therapeutic strategy (Hufnagle & Hufnagle, 1983). Whispering may promote excessive muscle contraction in the larynx and vocal tract (Rubin et al., 2006). And the increased airflow may be a factor in drying the vocal fold mucosa, although there is no specific evidence to support the drying effect. Furthermore, because the vocal folds must be held abducted under tension (whether in the Y or V posture), it is possible that this tension results in constriction of the tiny blood vessels of the vocal folds.

1940) and stroboscopy (Timcke et al., 1959). The EGG waveform also reflects these changes. The EGG waveform peak is more pointed, corresponding to a much shorter duration of maximum relative vocal fold contact or even lack of complete closure. Furthermore, the opening and closing phases appear more symmetric (Kitzing, 1990). The falsetto voice is perceived as quite high pitched, of course, due to the elevated f_o. This register also is perceived as being lighter and breathier due to the reduced amplitude of mucosal wave vibration and the reduced duration or even complete lack of vocal fold closure.

Study Questions

24. What is register? Why is it conceptually controversial?

25. What is the relevance of the term "quantal change" to register?

26. Explain modal register, vocal fry, and falsetto, and provide a synonym for each. Include average f_o values for each register.

27. In addition to rate, how does vocal fold vibration differ in glottal fry and falsetto as compared to modal register?

Recommended Internet Sites for Further Learning

http://www.ims.uni-stuttgart.de/phonetik/ EGG/ page13a.htm

University of Stuttgart Experimental Phonetics Group demonstration of different instrumentation used to examine the larynx.

http://voiceresearch.free.fr/

A French website on voice research, with good diagrams and explanation of electroglottography.

References

Airainer, R., & Klingholz, F. (1993). Quantitative evaluation of phonetograms in the case of functional dysphonia. *Journal of Voice, 7*, 136–141.

Awan, S. N. (1991). Phonetographic profiles and F0-SPL characteristics of untrained versus trained vocal groups. *Journal of Voice, 5*, 41–50.

Baer, T., Löfqvist, A., & McGarr, N. (1983). Laryngeal vibrations: A comparison between high-speed filming and glottographic techniques. *Journal of the Acoustical Society of America, 73*, 1304–1307.

Baken, R. J., & Orlikoff, R. F. (2000). *Clinical measurement of speech and voice* (2nd ed.). San Diego, CA: Singular Thomson Learning.

Behrman, A. (2005). Common practices of voice therapists in the evaluation of patients. *Journal of Voice, 19*, 454–469.

Behrman, A., Agresti, C. J., Blumstein, E., & Sharma, G. (1996). Meaningful features of voice range profiles from patients with organic vocal fold pathology: A preliminary study. *Journal of Voice, 10*, 269–283.

Behrman, A., & Akhund, A. (2016). The effect of loud voice and clear speech on the use of vocal fry in women. *Folia Phoniatrica et Logopaedica, 68*, 159–166.

Berke, G. S., Moore, D., Hanke, D., Hanson, D. G., Gerratt, B. R., & Burstein, F. (1987). Laryngeal modeling: Theoretical, in vitro, in vivo. *Laryngoscope, 97*, 871–881.

Bibas, A. G., Podoleanu, A. G., Cucu, R. G., Bonmarin, M., Dobre, G. M., Ward, V. M., . . . Jackson, D. A. (2005). 3-D optical coherence tomography of the laryngeal mucosa. *Clinical Otolaryngology and Allied Sciences, 29*, 713–720.

Bloch, I., & Behrman, A. (2001). Quantitative analysis of videostroboscopic images in presbylarynges. *Laryngoscope, 111*, 2022–2027.

Blomgren, M., Chen, Y., Ng, M. L., & Gilbert, H. R. (1998). Acoustic, aerodynamic, physiologic, and perceptual properties of modal and vocal fry registers. *Journal of the Acoustical Society of America, 103*, 2649–2658.

Carding, P. N., Steen, I. N., Webb, A., MacKenzie, K., Deary, I. J., & Wilson, J. A. (2004). The reliability and sensitivity to change of acoustic measures of voice quality. *Clinical Otolaryngology and Allied Sciences, 29*, 538–544.

Chen, Y., Robb, M. P., & Gilbert, H. R. (2002). Electroglottographic evaluation of gender and vowel effects during modal and vocal fry phonation. *Journal of Speech, Language, and Hearing Research, 45*, 821–829.

Childers, D. G., & Krishnamurthy, A. K. (1985). A critical review of electroglottography. *CRC Critical Reviews in Biomedical Engineering, 12*, 131–161.

Childers, D. G., & Larar, J. N. (1984). Electroglottography for laryngeal function assessment and speech analysis. *IEEE Transactions in Biomedical Engineering, 31*, 807–817.

Cleveland, T. F. (1994). A clearer view of singing voice production: 25 years of progress. *Journal of Voice, 8*, 18–23.

Coleman, R., Mabis, J., & Hinson, J. (1977). Fundamental frequency sound pressure level profiles of adult male and female voices. *Journal of Speech and Hearing Research, 20*, 197–204.

Coleman, R. F., & Markham, I. W. (1991). Normal variations in habitual pitch. *Journal of Voice, 5*, 173–177.

Coleman, R. F., & Wendahl, R. W. (1968). On the validity of laryngeal photosensor monitoring. *Journal of the Acoustical Society of America, 44*, 1733–1735.

Colton, R. H., & Conture, E. G. (1990). Problems and pitfalls of electroglottography. *Journal of Voice, 4*, 10–24.

Colton, R. H., & Hollien, R. (1972). Phonational range in modal and falsetto registers. *Journal of Speech and Hearing Research, 15*, 708–713.

Cooper, D. S., Partridge, L. D., & Alipour-Haghighi, F. (1993). Muscle energetics, vocal efficiency, and laryngeal biomechanics. In I. R. Titze (Ed.), *Vocal fold physiology: Frontiers in basic science* (pp. 37–92). San Diego, CA: Singular.

Damste, P. H. (1970). The phonetogram. *Practica OtoRhino-Laryngologica, 32*, 185–187.

Dejonckere, P. H., van Wijck, I., & Speyer, R. (2003). Efficacy of voice therapy assessed with the voice range profile (phonetogram). *Revue de Laryngologie Otologie, Rhinologie, 124*, 285–289.

Doyle, P. C., & Fraser, S. C. (1993). A simplified clinical procedure for the acquisition of photoglottographic waveforms from children and adults. *American Journal of Speech-Language Pathology, 2*, 36–40.

Eckel, F. C., & Boone, D. R. (1981). The s/z ratio as an indicator of laryngeal pathology. *Journal of Speech and Hearing Disorders, 46*, 147–149.

Farnsworth, D. W. (1940). High-speed motion pictures of the human vocal cords. *Bell Laboratories Record, 18*, 203–206.

Faure, M.-A., & Müller, A. (1992). Stroboscopy. *Journal of Voice, 6*, 139–148.

Fourcin, A. J., & Abberton, E. (1977). Laryngograph studies of vocal fold vibration. *Phonetica, 34*, 313–315.

Gelfer, M. P., & Pazera, J. F. (2006). Maximum duration of sustained /s/ and /z/ and the s/z ratio with controlled intensity. *Journal of Voice, 20*(3), 369–379.

Gerratt, B. R., Hanson, D. G., Berke, G. S., & Precoda, K. (1991). Photoglottography: A clinical synopsis. *Journal of Voice, 5*, 98–105.

Gramming, P., & Akerlund, L. (1988). Non-organic dysphonia: Phonetograms for normal and pathological voices. *Acta Oto-Laryngologica (Stockholm), 106*, 468–476.

Gramming, P., & Sundberg, J. (1988). Spectrum factors relevant to phonetogram measurement. *Journal of the Acoustical Society of America, 83*, 2352–2360.

Gramming, P., Sundberg, J., & Akerlund, L. (1991). Variability of phonetograms. *Folia Phoniatrica, 43*, 79–92.

Gray, S. D., Hammond, E., & Hanson, D. F. (1995). Benign pathologic response of the larynx. *Annals of Otology, Rhinology, and Laryngology, 104*, 13–18.

Gray, S. D., Thibeault, S. L., & Ylitalo, R. (2005). Genomics and proteomics in voice. In R. T. Sataloff (Ed.), *Professional voice: The science and art of clinical care* (pp. 117–124). San Diego, CA: Plural.

Habermann, W., Jiang, J., Lin, E., & Hanson, D. G. (2000). Correlation between glottal area and photoglottographic signal in normal subjects. *Acta Oto-Laryngologica, 120*, 778–782.

Hacki, T. (1996). Comparative speaking, shouting and singing voice range profile measurement: Physiological and pathological aspects. *Logopedics, Phoniatrica, Vocology, 21*, 123–129.

Hacki, T., & Heitmuller, S. (1999). Development of the child's voice: Permutation, mutation. *International Journal of Pediatric Otorhinolaryngology, 49* (Suppl. 1), S141–S144.

Hanson, D. G., Gerratt, B. R., & Berke, G. S. (1990). Frequency, intensity, and target matching effects on photoglottographic measures of open quotient and speed quotient. *Journal of Speech and Hearing Research, 33*, 45–50.

Hanson, D. G., Gerratt, B. R., Karin, R. R., & Berke, G. S. (1988). Glottographic measures of vocal fold vibration: An examination of laryngeal paralysis. *Laryngoscope, 98,* 541–549.

Hanson, D. G., Jiang, J., D'Agostino, M., & Herzon, G. (1995). Clinical measurement of mucosal wave velocity using simultaneous photoglottography and laryngostroboscopy. *Annals of Otology, Rhinology, and Laryngology, 104,* 340–349.

Hartl, D. M., Hans, S., Vaissiere, J., Riquet, M., & Brasnu, D. F. (2001). Objective voice quality analysis before and after onset of unilateral vocal fold paralysis. *Journal of Voice, 15,* 351–361.

Hertegård, S., Larsson, H., & Wittenberg, T. (2003). High-speed imaging: Applications and development. *Logopedics, Phoniatrics, Vocology, 28,* 133–139.

Hess, M. M., & Ludwigs, M. (2000). Strobophotoglottographic transillumination as a method for the analysis of vocal fold vibration patterns. *Journal of Voice, 14,* 255–271.

Heylen, L., Wuyts, F. L., Mertens, F., De Bodt, M., Pattyn, J., Croux, C., & Van de Heyning, P. H. (1998). Evaluation of the vocal performance of children using the voice range profile index. *Journal of Speech, Language, and Hearing Research, 41,* 232–238.

Higgins, M. B., & Saxman, J. H. (1991). A comparison of selected phonatory behaviors of healthy aged and young adults. *Journal of Speech and Hearing Research, 34,* 1000–1010.

Hildebrand, B. H. (1976). *Vibratory patterns of the human vocal cords during variations in frequency and intensity* (Doctoral dissertation). University of Michigan, University Microfilms International.

Hirano, M. (1981). *Clinical examination of voice.* New York, NY: Springer-Verlag.

Hirano, M. (1989). Objective evaluation of the human voice: Clinical aspects. *Folia Phoniatrica, 41,* 89–144.

Hirano, M., & Bless, D. M. (1993). *Videostroboscopic examination of the larynx.* San Diego, CA: Singular.

Hirano, M., Koike, Y., & von Leden, H. (1968). Maximum phonation time and air usage during phonation. *Folia Phoniatrica, 20,* 185–201.

Hollien, H. (1974). On vocal registers. *Journal of Phonetics, 2,* 125–143.

Hollien, H., Girard, G., & Coleman, R. (1977). Vocal fold vibratory patterns of pulse register phonation. *Folia Phoniatrica, 29,* 200–205.

Holmberg, E. V., Doyle, P., Perkell, J. S., Hammarberg, B., & Hillman, R. E. (2003). Aerodynamic and acoustic voice measurements of patients with vocal nodules: Variation in baseline and changes across voice therapy. *Journal of Voice, 17,* 269–282.

Horii, Y. (1979). Fundamental frequency perturbation observed in sustained phonation. *Journal of Speech and Hearing Research, 22,* 5–19.

Horii, Y. (1980). Vocal shimmer in sustained phonation. *Journal of Speech and Hearing Research, 23,* 202–209.

Howard, D. M., Lindsey, G. A., & Allen, B. (1990). Towards the quantification of vocal efficiency. *Journal of Voice, 4,* 205–212.

Hufnagle, J., & Hufnagle, K. (1983). Is quiet whisper harmful to the vocal mechanism? A research note. *Perceptual Motor Skills, 57,* 735–737.

Hughes, R. G., & Morrison, M. (2005). Vocal cord medialization by transcutaneous injection of calcium hydroxylapatite. *Journal of Voice, 19,* 674–678.

Ikeda, Y., Masuda, T., Manako, H., Yamashita, H., Yamamoto, T., & Komiyama, S. (1999). Quantitative evaluation of the voice range profile in patients with voice disorder. *European Archives of Otolaryngology, 256*(Suppl. 1), S51–S55.

International Association of Logopedics and Phoniatrics (IALP) Voice Committee. (1992). Discussion of assessment topics. *Journal of Voice, 6,* 196–198.

Isshiki, N. (1981). Vocal efficiency index. In K. N. Stevens & M. Hirano (Eds.), *Vocal fold physiology* (pp. 193–207). Tokyo, Japan: University of Tokyo Press.

Jiang, J. J., Chang, C. I., Raviv, J. R., Gupta, S., Banzali, F. M., Jr., & Hanson, D. G. (2000). Quantitative study of mucosal wave via videokymography in canine larynges. *Laryngoscope, 110,* 1567–1573.

Jiang, J., Lin, E., & Hanson, D. G. (2000). Glottographic phase difference in recurrent nerve paralysis. *Annals of Otology, Rhinology, and Laryngology, 109,* 287–293.

Jiang, J., O'Mara, T., Conley, D., & Hanson, D. (1999). Phonation threshold pressure measurements during phonation by airflow interruption. *Laryngoscope, 109,* 425–432.

Jiang, J., Stern, J., Chen, H. J., & Solomon, N. P. (2004). Vocal efficiency measurements in subjects with vocal polyps and nodules: A preliminary report. *Annals of Otology, Rhinology, and Laryngology, 113,* 277–282.

Karnell, M. P. (1989). Synchronized videostroboscopy and electroglottography. *Journal of Voice, 3,* 68–75.

Kent, R. D., Kent, J., & Rosenbek, J. (1987). Maximum performance tests of speech production. *Journal of Speech and Hearing Research, 52,* 367–387.

Kitzing, P. (1986). Glottography, the electrophysiological investigation of phonatory biomechanics. *Acta OtoRhino-Laryngologica Belgica, 40,* 863–878.

Kitzing, P. (1990). Clinical applications of electroglottography. *Journal of Voice, 4,* 238–249.

Kitzing, P., & Löfqvist, A. (1979). Evaluation of voice therapy by means of photoglottography. *Folia Phoniatrica, 3,* 103–109.

Kitzing, P., & Sonesson, B. (1974). A photoglottographical study of the female vocal folds during phonation. *Folia Phoniatrica, 26,* 138–149.

Koike, Y., Takahashi, J., & Calcaterra, T. C. (1977). Acoustic measures for detecting laryngeal pathology. *Acta Oto-Laryngologica, 84,* 105–117.

Koike, Y., & von Leden, H. (1969). Pathologic vocal initiation. *Annals of Otology, Rhinology, and Laryngology, 78,* 138–147.

Komiyama, S., Watanabe, H., & Ryu, S. (1984). Phonographic relationship between pitch and intensity of human voice. *Folia Phoniatrica, 26,* 1–7.

Kreiman, J., & Gerratt, B. R. (2005). Perception of aperiodicity in pathological voice. *Journal of the Acoustical Society of America, 117,* 2201–2211.

Laver, J. (1980). *The phonetic description of voice quality.* Cambridge, UK: Cambridge University Press.

Lecluse, F. L. E., Brocaar, M. P., & Verschuure, J. (1975). The electroglottography and its relation to glottal activity. *Folia Phoniatrica, 27,* 215–224.

Lieberman, P. (1963). Some acoustic measures of the fundamental periodicity of normal and pathologic larynges. *Journal of the Acoustical Society of America, 35,* 344–353.

Lim, J. Y., Choi, J. N., Kim, K. M., & Choi, H. S. (2006). Voice analysis of patients with diverse types of Reinke's edema and clinical use of electroglottographic measurements. *Acta Oto-Laryngologica, 126,* 62–69.

Lin, E., Jiang, J., Hone, S., & Hanson, D. G. (1999). Photoglottographic measures in Parkinson's disease. *Journal of Voice, 13,* 25–35.

Lisker, L., Abramson, A. S., Cooper, F. S., & Schvey, M. H. (1969). Transillumination of the larynx in running speech. *Journal of the Acoustical Society of America, 45,* 1544–1546.

Löfqvist, A., Carlborg, B., & Kitzing, P. (1982). Initial validation of an indirect measure of subglottal pressure during vowels. *Journal of the Acoustical Society of America, 72,* 633–635.

Luchsinger, R., & Arnold, G. E. (1965). *Voice-speech language: Clinical communicology, its physiology and pathology.* Belmont, CA: Wadsworth.

Ludlow, C. L., Bassich, C. J., Connor, N. P., Coulter, D. C., & Lee, Y. J. (1987). The validity of using phonatory jitter and shimmer to detect laryngeal pathology. In T. Baer, C. Sasaki, & K. S. Harris (Eds.), *Laryngeal function in phonation and respiration* (pp. 492–509). Boston, MA: Little, Brown.

Makiyama, K., Yoshihashi, H., Mogitate, M., & Kida, A. (2005). The role of adjustment of expiratory effort in the control of vocal intensity: Clinical assessment of phonatory function. *Otolaryngology-Head and Neck Surgery, 132,* 641–646.

McAllister, A., Sederholm, E., & Sundberg, J. (2000). Perceptual and acoustic analysis of vocal registers in 10-year-old children. *Logopedics, Phoniatrics, Vocology, 25,* 63–71.

McGlone, R., & Shipp, T. (1971). Some physiologic correlates of vocal fry phonation. *Journal of Speech and Hearing Research, 14,* 769–775.

Mehta, D. D., Deliyski, D. D., & Hillman, R. E. (2010). Commentary on why laryngeal stroboscopy really works: Clarifying misconceptions surrounding Talbot's law and the persistence of vision [Letter to the editor]. *Journal of Speech, Language, and Hearing Research, 53,* 1263–1267.

Monoson, P., & Zemlin, W. (1984). Quantitative study of a whisper. *Folia Phoniatrica, 36,* 53–65.

Monsen, R., & Engebretsen, M. (1977). Study of variations in the male and female glottal wave. *Journal of the Acoustical Society of America, 62,* 981–993.

Mörner, M., Fransson, F., & Fant, G. (1963). Voice register terminology and standard pitch. *Quarterly Progress and Status Report, 4,* 17–23.

Mueller, P., Larson, G. W., & Summers, P. A. (1993). Letter to the editor. *Language, Speech, and Hearing Services in Schools, 24,* 177–178.

Murty, G. E., Carding, P. N., Kelly, P. J., & Lancaster, P. (1991). The effect of intensity on combined glottography. *Clinical Otolaryngology and Allied Sciences, 16,* 399–400.

Nassif, N. A., Armstrong, W. B., de Boer, J. F., & Wong, B. J. (2005). Measurement of morphologic changes induced by trauma with the use of coherence tomography in porcine vocal cords. *Otolaryngology-Head and Neck Surgery, 133,* 845–850.

Omori, K., Kacker, A., Slavit, D. H. & Blaugrund, S. M. (1996). Quantitative videostroboscopic measurement of glottal gap and vocal function: An analysis of thyroplasty type 1. *Annals of Otology, Rhinology, and Laryngology, 105,* 280–285.

Orlikoff, R. F. (1991). Assessment of the dynamics of vocal fold contact from the electroglottogram: Data from normal male subjects. *Journal of Speech and Hearing Research, 34,* 1066–1072.

Pabon, J. P. H., & Plomp, R. (1988). Automatic phonetogram recording supplemented with acoustical voice-quality parameters. *Journal of Speech and Hearing Research, 31,* 710–722.

Painter, C. (1988). Electroglottogram waveform types. *Archives of Oto-Rhino-Laryngology, 245,* 116–121.

Plant, R. L., & Hillel, A. D. (1998). Direct measurement of subglottic pressure and laryngeal resistance in normal subjects and in spasmodic dysphonia. *Journal of Voice, 12,* 300–314.

Plant, R. L., & Younger, R. M. (2000). The interrelationship of subglottic air pressure, fundamental frequency, and vocal intensity during speech. *Journal of Voice, 14,* 170–177.

Ptacek, P. H., & Sander, E. K. (1963). Breathiness and phonation length. *Journal of Speech and Hearing Disorders, 28,* 171–182.

Rothenberg, M. (1977). Measurement of airflow in speech. *Journal of Speech and Hearing Research, 20,* 155–176.

Rothenberg, M. (1981). Some relations between glottal airflow and vocal fold contact area. *ASHA Reports, 11,* 88–96.

Rothenberg, M. (2002). Correcting low-frequency phase distortion in electroglottograph waveforms. *Journal of Voice, 16,* 32–36.

Rothenberg, M., & Mahshie, J. J. (1988). Monitoring vocal fold abduction through vocal fold contact area. *Journal of Speech and Hearing Research, 31,* 338–351.

Rubin, A. D., Praneetvatakul, V., Gherson, S., Moyer, C. A., & Sataloff, R. T. (2006). Laryngeal hyperfunction during whispering: Reality or myth? *Journal of Voice, 20,* 121–127.

Sapienza, C. M., Stathopoulos, E. T., & Dromey, C. (1998). Approximations of open quotient and speed quotient from glottal airflow and EGG waveforms: Effects of measurement criteria and sound pressure level. *Journal of Voice, 12,* 31–43.

Scherer, R. C., Drucker, D. G., & Titze, I. R. (1988). Electroglottography and direct measurement of vocal fold contact area. In O. Fujimura (Ed.), *Vocal fold physiology: Voice production, mechanisms, and functions* (pp. 279–291). New York, NY: Raven.

Scherer, R., Gould, W., Titze, I., Meyers, A., & Sataloff, R. (1988). Preliminary evaluation of selected acoustic and glottographic measures for clinical phonatory function analysis. *Journal of Voice, 2,* 230–244.

Schneider, B., Denk, D. M., & Bigenzahn, W. (2003). Functional results after external vocal fold medialization thyroplasty with the titanium vocal fold implant. *Laryngoscope, 113,* 628–634.

Schneider, B., Wendler, J., & Seidner, W. (2002). The relevance of stroboscopy in functional dysphonias. *Folia Phoniatrica et Logopedica, 54,* 44–54.

Schuberth, S., Hoppe, U., Döllinger, M., Lohscheller, J., & Eysholdt, U. (2001). High-precision measurement of the vocal fold length and vibratory amplitudes. *Laryngoscope, 112,* 1043–1049.

Schutte, H. K. (1980). *The efficiency of voice production.* Groningen, Netherlands: Kemper.

Schutte, H., & Seidner, W. (1983). Recommendations by the Union of European Phoniatricians (UEP): Standardizing voice area measurement/phonetography. *Folia Phoniatrica (Basel), 35,* 286–288.

Schutte, H. K., Svec, J. G., Sram, F. (1998). First results of clinical application of videokymography. *Laryngoscope, 108,* 1206–1210.

Slavit, D. H., & Maragos, N. E. (1994). Arytenoid adduction and type I thyroplasty in the treatment of aphonia. *Journal of Voice, 8,* 89–91.

Smith, S. (1954). Remarks on the physiology of the vibrations of the vocal cords. *Folia Phoniatrica, 6,* 166–178.

Smitheran, J., & Hixon, T. (1981). A clinical method for estimating laryngeal airway resistance during vowel production. *Journal of Speech and Hearing Disorders, 46,* 138–146.

Solomon, N. P., Garlitz, S. J., & Milbrath, R. L. (2000). Respiratory and laryngeal contributions to maximum phonation time. *Journal of Voice, 14,* 331–340.

Solomon, N. P., McCall, G. N., Trosset, M. W., & Gray, W. C. (1989). Laryngeal configuration and constriction during two types of whispering. *Journal of Speech and Hearing Research, 32,* 161–174.

Soman, B. (1997). The effect of variations in method of elicitation on maximum sustained phoneme duration. *Journal of Voice, 11,* 285–294.

Sonesson, B. (1959). A method for studying the vibratory movement of the vocal folds. *Journal of Laryngology and Otology, 73,* 732–737.

Sorensen, D., & Horii, Y. (1984). Frequency characteristics of male and female speakers in the pulse register. *Journal of Communication Disorders, 17,* 65–73.

Stathopoulos, E. T., Hoit, J. D., Hixon, T. J., Watson, P. J., & Solomon, N. P. (1991). Respiratory and laryngeal function during whispering. *Journal of Speech and Hearing Research, 34,* 761–767.

Stathopoulos, E. T., & Sapienza, C. (1993). Respiratory and laryngeal function of women and men during vocal intensity variation. *Journal of Speech and Hearing Research, 36,* 64–75.

Stevens, K. N. (1972). The quantal nature of speech: Evidence from articulatory-acoustic data. In E. E. David & P. B. Denes (Eds.), *Human communication: A unified view* (pp. 51–66). New York, NY: McGraw-Hill.

Stout, B. (1938). The harmonic structure of vowels in singing in relation to pitch and intensity. *Journal of the Acoustical Society of America, 10,* 137–146.

Sulter, A. M., Wit, H. P., Schutte, H. K., & Miller, D. G. (1994). A structured approach to voice range profile (phonetogram) analysis. *Journal of Speech and Hearing Research, 37,* 1076–1085.

Sundberg, J., Fahlstedt, E., & Morell, A. (2005). Effects on the glottal voice source of vocal loudness variation in untrained female and male voices. *Journal of the Acoustical Society of America, 117,* 879–885.

Svec, J. G., & Schutte, H. K. (1996). Videokymography: High-speed line scanning of vocal fold vibration. *Journal of Voice, 10,* 201–205.

Tait, N. A., Michel, J. F., & Carpenter, M. A. (1980). Maximum duration of sustained /s/ and /z/ in children. *Journal of Speech and Hearing Disorders, 45,* 239–246.

Tanaka, S., & Gould, W. J. (1983). Relationships between vocal intensity and noninvasively obtained aerodynamic parameters in normal subjects. *Journal of the Acoustical Society of America, 73,* 1316–1321.

Tanaka, S., & Gould, W. J. (1985). Vocal efficiency and aerodynamic aspects in voice disorders. *Annals of Otology, Rhinology, and Laryngology, 94,* 29–33.

Tang, J., & Stathopoulos, E. T. (1995). Vocal efficiency as a function of vocal intensity: A study of children, women, and men. *Journal of the Acoustical Society of America, 97,* 1885–1892.

Tarnoczy, T. (1951). The opening time and opening-quotient of the vocal cords during phonation. *Journal of the Acoustical Society of America, 23,* 42–44.

Timcke, R., von Leden, H., & Moore, P. (1958). Laryngeal vibrations: Measurements of the glottic wave, Part 1: The normal vibratory cycle. *Archives of Otolaryngology, 68,* 1–9.

Timcke, R., von Leden, H., & Moore, P. (1959). Laryngeal vibrations: Measurements of the glottic wave, Part 2: Physiologic variations. *Archives of Otolaryngology, 69,* 438–444.

Titze, I. R. (1990). Interpretation of the electroglottographic signal. *Journal of Voice, 4,* 1–9.

Titze, I. R. (1992). Acoustic interpretation of the voice range profile (phonetogram). *Journal of Speech and Hearing Research, 35,* 21–34.

Titze, I. R. (1994). *Principles of voice production.* Englewood Cliffs, NJ: Prentice-Hall.

Trudeau, M. D., & Forrest, L. A. (1997). The contributions of phonatory volume and transglottal airflow to the s/z ratio. *American Journal of Speech-Language Pathology, 6,* 65–69.

van den Berg, J. (1958). Myoelastic-aerodynamic theory of voice production. *Journal of Speech and Hearing Research, 1,* 227–244.

von Leden, H. (1961). The electronic synchron-stroboscope. *Annals of Otology, Rhinology, Laryngology, 70,* 881–893.

von Leden, H. (1996). A cultural history of the human voice. In R. T. Sataloff (Ed.), *The art and science of clinical care* (pp. 9–88). San Diego, CA: Singular.

Wendler, J. (1992). Stroboscopy. *Journal of Voice, 6,* 149–154.

Whitehead, R., Metz, D., & Whitehead, G. (1984). Vibratory patterns of the vocal folds during pulse register phonation. *Journal of the Acoustical Society of America, 75,* 1293–1297.

Wolfe, S. K., Stanley, D. & Sette, W. J. (1935). Quantitative studies on the singing voice. *Journal of the Acoustical Society of America, 6,* 255–266.

Wong, B. J., Jackson, R. P., Guo, S., Ridgway, J. M., Mahmood, U., Su, J., . . . Chen, Z. (2005). In vivo optical coherence tomography of the human larynx: Normative and benign pathology in 82 patients. *Laryngoscope, 115,* 1904–1911.

Yan, Y., Ahmad, K., Kunduk, M., & Bless, D. (2005). Analysis of vocal-fold vibrations from high-speed laryngeal images using a Hilbert transform-based methodology. *Journal of Voice, 19,* 161–175.

Yanagihara, N., Koike, Y., & von Leden, H. (1966). Phonation and respiration: Function study in normal subjects. *Folia Phoniatrica, 18,* 323–340.

Ylitalo, R., & Hammarberg, B. (2000). Voice characteristics, effects of voice therapy, and long-term follow-up of contact granuloma patients. *Journal of Voice, 14,* 557–566.

Yumoto, E. (2004). Aerodynamics, voice quality, and laryngeal image analysis of normal and pathologic voices. *Current Opinion in Otolaryngology and Head and Neck Surgery, 12,* 166–173.

Zeitels, S. M., Hillman, R. E., Franco, R. A., & Bunting, G. W. (2002). Voice and treatment outcome from phonosurgical management of early glottic cancer. *Annals of Otology, Rhinology, and Laryngology Supplement, 190*, 3–20.

Zraick, R. I., Birdwell, K. Y., & Smith-Olinde, L. (2004). The effect of speaking sample duration on determination of habitual pitch. *Journal of Voice, 19*, 197–201.

7

The Production and Perception of Vowels

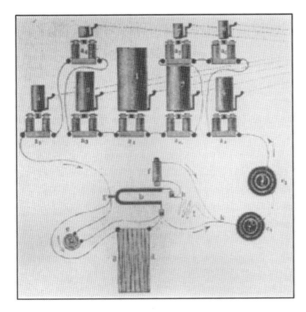

Figure 7–1. Helmholtz's instrumental array for analysis of the acoustics of vowels. From "A Cultural History of the Larynx and Voice," by H. von Leden, (p. 86), in R. T. Sataloff (Ed.), *Professional Voice: The Science and Art of Clinical Care* (Vol. I, 3rd ed.). 2005, San Diego, CA: Plural Publishing, Inc. Reprinted with permission.

The filling of a very deepe flagon with a constant streame of beere or water sounds ye vowells in order.

—Sir Isaac Newton (1642–1727), about 1665

Clinical Case 3: Accent Management

Clinical cases are based upon real patients whom the author has treated. Evaluation and treatment information has been edited to focus upon specific features related to this and other chapters. Note that clinical cases incorporate information that is covered in the chapters (and some information about diagnosis and therapy that you will learn in future courses). You are encouraged to review this case before you begin your study of this chapter and once again after you have completed the chapter. You may also want to revisit this case later in the semester after you have covered additional chapters.

Jaime is a 29-year-old man who was born and raised in the Dominican Republic. His native language is Spanish. He moved to the United States when he was 26 and began to study English. Although he was taking courses in English as a second language, he went to a speech-language pathologist (SLP) to improve his pronunciation in English so that he would be better understood.

The SLP who conducted the evaluation prepared for the evaluation by researching the Spanish language—especially the phonetic inventory, syllable structure, and prosody patterns. She learned that the Spanish inventory of vowels consists of /i, e, a, o, u/ (although many dialectical differences exist). Thus, Spanish has a much smaller inventory of vowels than does English, which contains seven tense vowels (/i, e, æ, ɑ, ɔ, o, u/ and four lax vowels /ɪ, ɛ, ʌ, ʊ/), although again with many dialectical variations. She also learned that Spanish vowels are generally pure monophthongs, while in American English dialects, /i, e, o, u/ are often diphthongized. The SLP also learned that, in Spanish, syllables often end in a vowel, and fewer consonant clusters are allowed in Spanish than in English. She learned that vowel reduction in Spanish is much less common than in English and that syllables tend to be pronounced with equal stress.

The SLP conducted an evaluation of Jaime's pronunciation and prosody, using single words, phrases, reading, and conversation. She judged his intelligibility overall to be moderately decreased. She noted that he pronounced the American lax vowels /ɪ, ɛ/ as the tense vowels /i, e/, respectively. She found that he frequently omitted final consonants, particularly when they occurred in clusters. This omission was particularly problematic for omission of /s/ in words that ended in consonants, because the omitted /s/ was an important morpheme signifying possession or pluralization. She also observed that Jaime used nasal coarticulation in place of nasal phoneme production: He often omitted the nasal consonant and, instead, heavily nasalized the preceding vowel. And she noted that he reduced many clusters to singleton consonants or inserted a vowel between consonants in a cluster.

The SLP developed an accent management strategy with Jaime to address tense-lax vowel differences, final consonants, and production of unstressed-stressed syllable differences. She knew that the tense-lax vowel continuum and the difference between unstressed and stressed syllables incorporated both vowel duration and spectral cues. Thus, she planned to use both types of cues to help Jaime change his articulation. Despite her unfamiliarity with Spanish, the SLP relied upon her knowledge of acoustic cues of phonemes (Chapters 7 and 8) and features of prosody (see Chapter 9) and was confident in her ability to conduct an appropriate evaluation and proceed with an intervention plan.

Clinical Case Discussion Questions

1. What are the major acoustic cues that predict vowel identity in English? How might you expect these cues to differ in Spanish?
2. How do articulatory movements correspond to spectral cues of vowels?

3. The SLP used spectrographic analysis to help her identify differences between vowel targets and Jaime's actual vowel production. What filter setting would be most appropriate for the SLP to use, and how might the spectrograms show such differences?

4. Once you have studied Chapter 8 (consonants), return to this clinical case and discuss how nasal coarticulation occurs and how the SLP might help Jaime distinguish between nasalized vowels and production of the nasal consonant.

5. Once you have studied Chapter 9 (prosody), return to this clinical case and discuss how the SLP might use both duration and spectral cues to help Jaime produce a greater distinction between unstressed and stressed syllables.

6. How is the acoustic theory of speech production relevant to Jaime's case?

Phonemes

Phonemes are sounds that can differentiate between words. So the vowels in *cat* and *cut* are phonemically distinct. We know that the spelling of a word does not necessarily identify phonemic differences. The vowels in the words *light* and *lit* are phonemically distinct but represented with the same orthographic symbol. Some sounds, however, are not produced the same but they are not phonemically distinct. The consonant /l/ provides such an example in the words *leak* and *color*. Say each of these words slowly and feel the location of your tongue. The /l/ in *leak* is produced with a more anterior tongue position than the /l/ in *color*. Yet the two /l/ productions would never, by themselves, differentiate between words in American English, and so they are the same phonemes. A phoneme, therefore, is not a single sound but a group of sounds. A phoneme consists of all the variations in production of a given sound that do not cause the sound to change the meaning of a word. Phonemes are groups or units of sounds that provide the foundation upon which languages can be written down in a systematic and unambiguous fashion (Ladefoged, 2006, p. 33).

It follows, then, that **phonemic transcription** is a method of writing sounds that results in a difference in meaning. In contrast, **phonetic transcription** is a method of writing sounds that includes the differences in pronunciation within a phonemic class. Both phonemic and phonetic transcription of American English vowels are often not straightforward, largely because of the many regional differences in pronunciation. In addition, differences of opinion among phoneticians further confound transcription. A phonetician is an individual who studies the mechanisms of speech perception and production within a language or across different languages. Part of the disagreement arises from the fact that the sounds of any language, including American English, are dynamic, or changeable, both over the long and short term. Sounds evolve slowly over time because of geopolitical and sociologic forces. Over the short term, sounds change depending upon the phonetic context in which they occur in a given utterance. The rules that describe these short-term or context-dependent changes are referred to as the phonology of a language.

Phonetic transcription includes the effect of the phonologic rules. That is, phonetic transcription represents the actual pronunciation (more or less, in its general outlines). In contrast, phonemic transcriptions provide the basic underlying pronunciation but do not include the details provided by the phonologic rules. Phonetic transcription is often identified as being *narrower* than phonemic transcription or, conversely, phonemic transcription is *broader* than phonetic transcription. Phonetic transcription uses brackets ([ ]) around each group of International Phonetic Association (IPA) symbols that comprise a phonetic segment and includes diacritic markers, symbols that provide additional information about the context-specific pronunciation of the phoneme. Phonemic transcription uses forward slashes (/ /) around each group of sounds. For example, the word *sip* would be transcribed phonemically as /sɪp/ and phonetically as [sɪpˈ], where the latter includes the diacritic to show that the final /p/ is unreleased. The various (nonmeaningful) pronunciations of the sounds that make up a phoneme are called allophones. **Allophones** are variations in the production of a phoneme due to individual speaker variability and phonetic context (the influence of the neighboring phonemes). But the allophonic variations do not change the meaning of the words. So [p] and [pˈ] are allophones. Similarly, we could say that the [pˈ] is an allophonic variation of [p]. The allophones are a result of the phonologic rules that specify the context-dependent pronunciation of phonemes.

7.1 Introduction

Up to now, we have addressed only the **voice source**, the sound pressure wave generated by the vibrating vocal folds. If you could hear the phonatory signal without the vocal tract attached, it would sound like the sound produced by a bilabial voiced trill, or *raspberry*, also called a *Bronx cheer* in the author's hometown. (You can hear the sound of laryngeal phonation by listening to the electroglottographic signal.) Just as the sound of a vibrating string is dependent on the acoustic resonator (be it a guitar or a piano), so too the sound produced when we say "ah" is dependent on the resonating characteristics of the vocal tract.

This chapter is dedicated to the description of vowels, so we had better define vowels right up front. Zemlin (1998) defines a **vowel** as a vocal sound produced by relatively free passage of the airstream through the larynx and oral cavity (p. 582). In contrast, a **consonant** is a speech sound produced with one or more areas of the

---

The International Phonetic Association

The International Phonetic Association—founded in Paris in 1886 by a group of phoneticians from Britain, Denmark, France, and Germany—seeks to promote the scientific study of phonetics and its many practical applications. Toward this goal, the IPA provides to all academic communities throughout the world a standardized notation for representing the phonetic system of all languages, the International Phonetic Alphabet. The International Phonetic Alphabet is updated as needed with new symbols (see Appendix D). The newest symbol added in 2005, is the labiodental flap, represented by the "right-hook v" symbol.

Why can't we use the conventional American English alphabet and orthography (spelling) to represent the vowels and consonants? For one thing, they don't provide sufficient detail for representing all the phonemes of our language in a unique and consistent way. For example, the words *light*, *height*, and *site* rhyme. Only the initial sounds differ. But the three words are spelled differently. How can we represent the way our client produces sounds if the letters used to represent the sounds vary from word to word? We need a system such that each symbol always represents one sound.

vocal tract narrowed by some degree of constriction (partial or transiently complete). We will learn in Chapter 8 that this division between consonants and vowels does not always work, and some sounds are classified as consonants but act more like vowels. In English, however, one major difference between consonants and vowels is that vowels form the nucleus of the syllable. Additionally, vowels are always produced with vocal fold vibration, whereas consonants may have an alternative sound source. In this and subsequent chapters, specific sounds are often represented with IPA phonetic symbols of American English. See Appendix D to reference the IPA chart.

7.2 Acoustic Theory of Speech Production

Exploration of the production of vowels began long ago, evident by the quote of Sir Isaac Newton at the start of this chapter. In the mid-18th century, soon after Antoine Ferrein (1693–1769) identified the vocal cords as the string-like vibrators that produced human voice, a Swiss physiologist, Albrecht von Haller (1708–1777), wrote about vocal resonance, noting that it was related in some way to the cavities of the nose, throat, and sinuses (von Leden, 1996). A German physiologist, Hermann von Helmholtz (1821–1894), pioneered experimentation in acoustics using excised larynges. His observations laid the groundwork for the next century of research in resonance and acoustics (von Leden, 1996). In the mid-19th century, Johannes Müller, the scientist who first pioneered the myoelastic-aerodynamic theory of voice production, presented early concepts of the relative contributions of the vocal folds and the vocal tract to the formation of the acoustic pressure wave. We owe much of our current understanding of the vocal tract, however, to the works of Gunnar Fant (1960, 1980) and Stevens and House (1955, 1961).

In 1960, Fant published his *Acoustic Theory of Speech Production*, which established the foundation upon which our current knowledge of acoustic phonetics is based. The **acoustic theory of speech production** tells us two important fundamental characteristics of speech sound production. First, the theory tells us that the features of the vocal tract can be inferred from its acoustic output. In other words, specific articulatory postures produce specific sounds. Recall from our exploration of acoustic resonators that the characteristics of vibration are specified by the size and shape of the acoustic resonating space. If we consider the supraglottal vocal tract as an acoustic resonator, then we can imagine that different articulatory postures would change the shape of the acoustic resonator and hence the characteristics of the output sound pressure wave.

The second important point explained by Fant's acoustic theory is that the speech production system may be broken down into two major components, the sound source and the filter, or resonator. For this reason, in fact, the acoustic theory of voice production is also called the **source filter theory**. The source creates the sound rich in harmonic structure. The filter selects a portion of the harmonic frequencies to be radiated out of the mouth. In Chapter 5, we learned about the vocal signal produced by the vibration of the vocal folds. All speech sounds that are *voiced* contain the sound pressure wave produced by vocal fold vibration, which includes all vowels and many consonants in American English. As mentioned above, the vocal folds are not the only speech sound source. They are, however, the only sound source of phonation, or voiced sounds. The sound source provides the input to the vocal tract, and the resonator filters, or modulates, the sound. Recall that a resonator is an object or medium that is set into vibration. When the air inside a partially or completely enclosed container is set into vibration, we say that the container is an **acoustic resonator**. The vocal tract is an acoustic resonator.

Let us use a common kitchen food strainer as an analogy for the vocal tract filter, or resonator. Cook up a pot of spaghetti, and then pour the contents of the pot into the strainer to filter the spaghetti from the cooking water. The way in which the strainer works is size dependent. Water

Source Filter (Acoustic) Theory of Speech Production

The words: The speech sound pressure wave is a result of the resonant characteristics of the vocal tract acting upon the source characteristics of the phonatory signal that is generated by the vibrating vocal folds.

The equation in words: The spectrum of the sound pressure wave at some distance from the lips is a product of the spectral characteristics of the glottal volume velocity, the vocal tract transfer function, and the radiation characteristics of the oral cavity opening at the lips.

The equation in symbols:

$$P(f) = U(f) \cdot T(f) \cdot R(f) \text{ where}$$

P = spectrum of the sound pressure wave exiting the lips

U = glottal volume velocity

T = vocal tract transfer function

R = radiation characteristics of the lips

The (f) indicates that all parameters are expressed as a function of frequency. So, for example, U(f) would be represented by a line spectrum of the glottal volume velocity. We could also consider the glottal volume velocity as a function of time, U(t), in which case it would be represented by the glottal volume velocity waveform (as we saw in Chapter 5).

Linearity and Time Invariance

The relationship between vocal tract posture and speech sound output, and hence the acoustic theory of vowel production, rests upon two assumptions: linearity and time invariance. Recall that in Chapter 5, we said that linearity occurs when the output of a system is directly proportional to the input. In a linear system, a plot of the output as a function of the input will result in a straight line. Therefore, in a nonlinear system, the input may result in a disproportionately large output. If the speech production system is linear with respect to its acoustic output, then multiple inputs to the system will result in an output that is simply the sum of those inputs. Time invariance means that as the input is time delayed or time advanced, the output will be similarly time delayed or time advanced. As discussed in earlier chapters, the human body does not always adhere completely to underlying theories of the behavior of physical phenomena. In truth, the voice production system is nonlinear and not time invariant. But for most purposes (including studying speech and voice science), we can make the assumptions of linearity and time invariance.

can escape through the holes in the strainer, but spaghetti is too large and remains captured in the strainer. Other features of the spaghetti, such as its color, are irrelevant to the operation of the strainer. The vocal tract resonator, or filter, is frequency dependent. In other words, the way in which the vocal tract acts upon or resonates the vocal sound source is dependent on the frequency components of the source. Recall that the vocal sound source is a complex nearly periodic pressure wave composed of a fundamental frequency and harmonics. The harmonics are integer multiples of the fundamental frequency, which will be further explained as we progress in this discussion. The vocal tract resonates the source signal by allowing certain frequencies to pass through the filter with greater amplitude than other frequencies. The characteristic resonances of the vocal tract are those frequencies that are selected for radiating out of the mouth. The characteristic resonances are called **formants** (so named by Hermann von Helmholtz [1821–1894], the 19th-century acoustician, mathematician, and physicist).

Acoustic Characteristics of the Source

The equation in the section on source filter theory is an expression of Fant's acoustic theory (Figure 7–2). Let us begin our exploration of the

acoustic theory with examination of the spectral characteristics of the source.

It is easiest to start with an idealized waveform, rather than a glottal waveform that could be produced by a human larynx. The waveform in Figure 7–3 is a triangular wave, so named because of its shape. It contains, in theory, an infinite number of harmonics, each of which is an odd-numbered multiple of the fundamental frequency. (Recall, when we discussed the phonatory system, that we defined that glottal volume velocity as the volume of air flowing through the glottis as a function of time. Also recall, in our discussion of sound waves, that a Fourier transformation decomposes the nearly periodic complex wave into its spectral components, the f_o and its harmonics.) As you go up in harmonic frequency, each harmonic decreases in amplitude at a rate that is proportional to the inverse square of the harmonic number. The decrease in harmonic amplitude with increasing frequency of the harmonic is referred to as the roll-off characteristic of the spectrum. In this idealized triangular wave, the roll-off is 12 dB per octave (doubling of harmonic frequency). When we discuss the source filter theory in general terms, we identify the **spectral roll-off** of the sound source as 12 dB per octave. However, the spectral roll-off of an actual glottal waveform may be similar to the triangular wave, or it could be very different. It is important to note, however, that the roll-off of the source spectrum, that is, the decrease in amplitude of successively higher harmonics of the phonatory signal, will always decrease uniformly. The rate

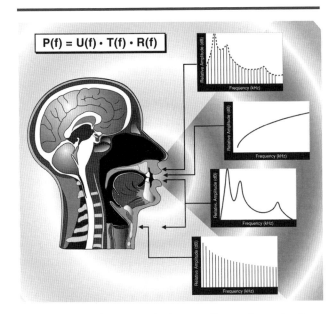

Figure 7–2. The acoustic theory of speech production.

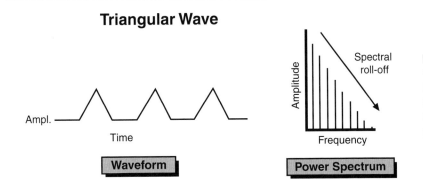

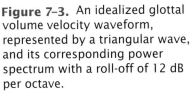

Figure 7–3. An idealized glottal volume velocity waveform, represented by a triangular wave, and its corresponding power spectrum with a roll-off of 12 dB per octave.

of the uniform decrease, however, depends upon several factors. (The reason we used a triangular wave with odd multiples of the fundamental will become clearer as we discuss vocal tract resonances further on.)

What specifies the shape of the glottal volume velocity waveform and its corresponding spectral contents? Recall from Chapter 5 that the closure of the vocal folds during vibration is critical to the production of the sound pressure wave. Phonatory glottal closure contributes substantially to the spectral characteristics of the glottal volume velocity. In general, the faster the cutoff of the airflow, corresponding to faster vocal fold closure, the greater the excitation of the column of air in the vocal tract, and therefore the greater the energy in the higher frequency harmonics. We would expect the energy roll-off of the power spectrum to be quite gradual in this case (Figure 7–4). However, if phonatory glottal closure was incomplete, so that some air flowed turbulently through the open glottis even during the closed phase, one would expect much less energy in the higher harmonics. The weaker harmonic structure would be perceived as being breathy, and the spectral roll-off would be quite steep. In this way, the amplitude of the harmonics affects the voice quality. Although the actual relationship among the harmonic amplitudes will vary, the lower frequency harmonics will generally dominate. That is, the glottal volume velocity waveform contains a large amount of energy in the lower frequency harmonics.

The **source spectrum** is the input energy, the raw material if you will, for the acoustic reso-

nator, the vocal tract. The rate at which the column of air is set into vibration is defined by the rate of vocal fold vibration. A sustained vowel of 100 Hz means that the vocal folds are vibrating open and closed 100 times a second, and therefore 100 puffs of air per second are propelled upward from the glottis. The rate at which the column of air in the vocal tract is set into vibration is the major determinant of pitch. The frequencies at which the column of air resonates, however, is determined by the size and shape of the vocal tract. Said another way, the rate of vibration determines the fundamental frequency and the harmonic frequencies of the alternating compressions and rarefactions of each puff of air. But the way in which the harmonics are filtered depends upon the resonant characteristics of the vocal tract. The resonant frequencies of the vocal tract determine the vowel that is produced and contribute to the quality of the sound.

Study Questions

1. What are the two major components of speech sound production explicated by Fant's (1960) acoustic theory of speech production?

2. Why is the acoustic theory of speech production also referred to as the source filter theory?

Glottal Volume Velocity

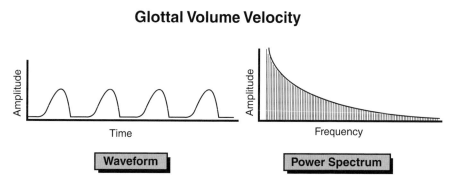

Figure 7–4. A more realistic glottal volume velocity waveform and corresponding power spectrum.

3. The vocal tract filter responds to what feature of the glottal source spectrum (the sound wave emanating up from the vocal folds)?

4. Define formant.

5. Define spectral roll-off and give an average value per octave in an idealized wave.

6. What specifies the shape of the glottal volume velocity waveform and its corresponding spectral content?

The Vocal Tract Transfer Function

A formant is a concentration of energy around a particular frequency in the acoustic wave. Formants are very important, because they shape our perception of vowels. We'll explore this concept further in this chapter. Let's start by exploring what specifies the frequency of a given formant.

The length and cross section of the vocal tract define its resonance characteristics. Let us begin with our examination of the resonance characteristics of the vocal tract (the **transfer function**) by simplifying the vocal tract into a uniform tube that is closed at one end (the vibrating vocal folds) and open at the other (the lips) (Figure 7–5). If we produce the neutral vowel /ə/, called a schwa, the cross-sectional area of the vocal tract is fairly uniform along its length, which is on average approximately 17.5 cm in adult males (14.7 cm in adult females and 8.75 cm in small children) (Zemlin, 1998, p. 297). The bend in the vocal tract at the back of the mouth does not affect the resonant characteristics. For this vocal tract tube with a uniform diameter that is closed at one end and open at the other, the resonances are a function of the length of the tube (Figure 7–6). The tube will resonate energy best at a frequency that has a wavelength four times the length of the tube.

Recall that in Chapter 3 we learned that an inverse relationship exists between wavelength and frequency, such that the wavelength of a sound pressure wave is equal to the velocity of

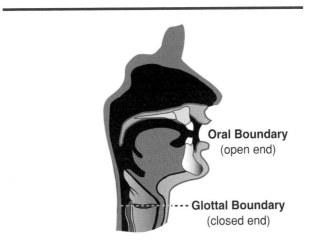

Figure 7–5. The acoustics of the vocal tract can be modeled with an open boundary at the lips and a closed boundary at the glottis.

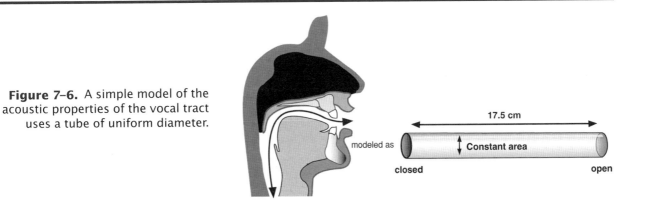

Figure 7–6. A simple model of the acoustic properties of the vocal tract uses a tube of uniform diameter.

sound divided by the frequency ($\lambda = c/f$). We can rearrange the equation:

$$f = c/\lambda$$

and find that frequency is equal to the speed of sound divided by the wavelength. The velocity of sound is approximately 340 meters per second (34,000 cm/s). So, for our average adult male vocal tract of 17.5 cm in length, we know that the wavelength of the first resonant frequency is 70 cm (17.5 × 4). We can then calculate its frequency as follows:

$$F = \frac{34{,}000 \text{ cm/s}}{70 \text{ cm}}$$

$$= 485.7 \text{ Hz}$$

We have now found the first resonant frequency, or formant, of the vocal tract. The vocal tract acts like a tube closed at one end and open at the other, so it will resonate only odd-numbered multiples of the lowest frequency. Therefore, the second formant frequency will be located at 485.7 × 3 (1,457 Hz), and the third formant frequency will be located at 485.7 × 5 (2,428 Hz). In theory, the vocal tract has an infinite number of resonant frequencies, or formants. However, only the first four or five formants are relevant for speech perception and production, and, for specification of a given *vowel*, only the first three formants are required. See the Odd-Quarter Wavelength Relationship on page 217 for more discussion of the relationship of formant frequency and vocal tract length. The formula is equivalent to the one presented above.

What can change the location of the formant frequencies? The overall length of the vocal tract will have a dramatic effect upon the frequency location of the formants. Let us assume a vocal tract length is shorter, approximately 15 cm. Then we know that the wavelength of the lowest resonant frequency is 60 cm (15 × 4). Following the formula above, 34,000/60 = 566.67 Hz. The second formant frequency would be located at 1700 Hz (566.67 × 3). (Recall that characteristic resonances of the vocal tract are located at odd multiples of the lowest resonant frequency.)

The third formant frequency would be located at 2833 Hz (566.67 × 5). And finally, let us assume a child's vocal tract length of 9 cm. For this short vocal tract, the wavelength of the lowest resonant frequency would be 36 cm (9 × 4). Again, using the same formula, 34000/36 = 944.44 Hz. F2 would be located at 2833 Hz (944.44 × 3) and F3 would be located at 4722 Hz (944.44 × 5).

Thus, we can see that shortening the vocal tract will raise the formant frequencies, and conversely, elongating the vocal tract will lower the formant frequencies. Figure 7–7 illustrates this phenomenon with a series of three resonance curves. These curves display amplitude on the vertical *y*-axis and frequency on the horizontal *x*-axis. The peaks of the curves represent the spectral peaks, or formants of the vocal tract. Given the difference in resonance curves of the three vocal tract lengths, we would assume that the formant frequencies of a woman's vocal tract would be higher than those of a man, and in general, the formant frequencies of a child's vocal tract would be much higher than that of an adult. And we shall learn a bit further on in the chapter that this is indeed true. A note of caution: Do not confuse formants and harmonics! In Chapter 5, we learned that the *higher* the f_o, the *wider* the spacing between the harmonics. Formants are resonating characteristics of the vocal tract and describe the acoustic filter. Harmonics are multiples of the f_o and describe the sound source.

Differences in vocal tract length exist among individuals, but within an individual, the vocal tract length can also vary. Protruding the lips, as in the production of the vowel /u/, lengthens the vocal tract just a bit, but sufficiently to lower the formant frequencies. In Chapter 5, we learned that the larynx is a mobile structure that can be raised and lowered by the muscles of the neck. Raising the larynx upward in the neck shortens the vocal tract, and lowering the larynx elongates the vocal tract. These laryngeal movements raise and lower formant frequencies, respectively. Lip movements are critical to the production of speech sounds, whereas control of laryngeal height is more important in singing than in speech (Sundberg, 1987).

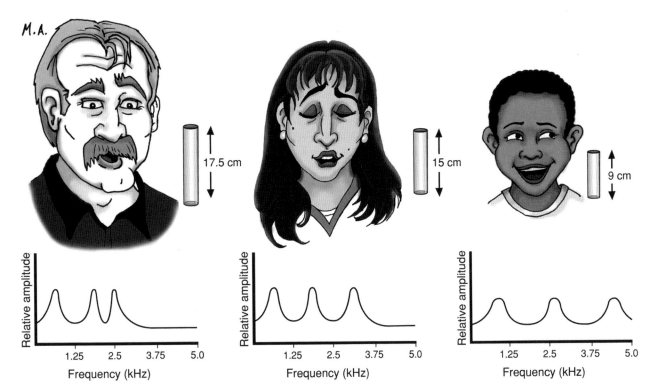

Figure 7–7. Theoretical resonance curves for a man, woman, and child.

Formant Frequency (Odd-Quarter Wavelength Relationship)

The words: In the simplest case of vowel production in which the vocal tract has a uniform cross-sectional area throughout its length, the formant frequencies of the vocal tract are defined only by the length of the tube according to the odd-quarter wavelength relationship.

The equation in words: Selecting only odd-numbered frequencies, the formant frequency is determined by the velocity of sound divided by four times the length of the vocal tract.

The equation in symbols:

$$F_n = (2n - 1)(c/4L) \text{ where}$$

F_n = Formant number (*n* can be any positive integer)

c = velocity of sound (at room temperature) = 340 meters per second

L = vocal tract length, the standard of which is assumed to be 17.5 cm (adult male)

The portion of the equation $(2n - 1)$ results in the selection of the odd-numbered integers only.

Acoustic Characteristics of Lip Radiation

If we refer back to the equation that represents the acoustic theory of speech production, presented in the source filter equation on page 212, and its schematic description, presented in Figure 7–2, we note that the mouth opening plays a critical role in the speech sound pressure wave. Recall from Chapter 3 in our discussion of boundary conditions that an acoustic wave is altered when it encounters a change in the medium through which it is traveling. The mouth opening represents a boundary, a change from the vocal tract tube to the atmosphere. The characteristics of this boundary are such that when the sound pressure wave exits the oral cavity, the higher frequency harmonics are resonated more than the lower frequency harmonics. Why is that? Recall from our earliest discussions of sound pressure waves in Chapter 3 that the greater the energy, the greater the displacement of air particles. Therefore, air particle displacement is greatest at frequencies that have the greatest intensity. The source spectrum has a 12-dB per octave energy roll-off, which means that the f_o and lower harmonics have greater intensity than the higher harmonics. At the boundary between the lips and the atmosphere, the atmosphere offers greater resistance to the lower frequencies, associated with larger particle displacements, than the resistance offered to the higher frequencies with their smaller particle displacement. In other words, the radiation characteristics at the lips *favor* the high-frequency components.

In the case of our ideal triangular wave of Figure 7–3, the radiated power is proportional to the square of the frequency, so that for every octave (doubling of frequency), the acoustic power increases by a factor of four, or equivalently, 6 dB ($10 \log_{10} 4 = 6$). Therefore, a maximum gain (increase) of 6 dB per octave can be achieved at the mouth opening. Combine this lip radiation filter function with the triangular wave source spectrum of 12 dB per octave roll-off, and we find a net output of 6 dB per octave roll-off of the sound pressure spectrum that radiates out into the atmosphere (and presumably to the ear of a listener).

Study Questions

7. Explain how one might calculate the value of the first resonant frequency, or formant, of the vocal tract for an average adult male.

8. What can change the location (frequency) of the formant frequencies?

9. Why do the acoustic radiation characteristics of the lips favor the high-frequency components by up to 6 dB per octave?

Resonance and Standing Waves

Why does the vocal tract resonate best at a frequency that is four times the length of the tube and at odd integer multiples of the lowest resonant frequency? Recall from Chapter 3 that standing waves are the result of constructive interference of an incident and reflected wave. We identified standing waves as a resonant pattern of the vocal tract. The pressure wave generated by the vocal folds travels up the vocal tract, and when it reaches the lips and the sudden and dramatic increase in expanse of the atmosphere, a portion of the wave is reflected back into the vocal tract. When the reflected wave reaches the glottis (the closed end of the tube), it is reflected back up the vocal tract. The resulting interference patterns of the incident and reflected waves result in a standing wave, in which areas of air particles vibrate with maximum or minimum amplitude. At the closed end of the tube (the vocal folds), the pressure will be greatest and the volume velocity will be at a minimum (the velocity is maximally constrained). At the open end of the tube (the lips), the volume velocity will be greatest because it is minimally constrained, and the pressure therefore will be at a minimum. Said another way, air particles vibrate most effectively at the open end of the tube and least effectively at the closed end of the tube. Vibration will be reinforced or transmitted most effectively if the wavelength of the vibration *matches* the resonance characteristics of the tube. Therefore, frequencies at which the wavelengths have a maximum velocity at the tube opening, or equivalently, a minimum pressure, will be transmitted most effectively.

Figure 7–8A shows a pressure wave within a tube that is closed at one end and open at the other. The wave is artificially extended beyond the "mouth" opening to assist in visualization of the following concept. The longest possible wavelength that provides a velocity maximum (pressure minimum) at the opening of the tube is one-quarter the length of the tube. In Figure 7–8B, we see that a wavelength that is three-quarters the length of the tube also provides a volume velocity maximum at the open end. And similarly, in Figure 7–8C, five-quarters of the wavelength (one full cycle plus a quarter) also adheres to the goal of providing a pressure minimum (velocity maximum) at the open end of the tube. Note that each progressively higher frequency wavelength is an odd-multiple integer of the lowest frequency, which could progress upward, in theory infinitely (1/4, 3/4, 5/4, 7/4, 9/4, etc.).

In Figures 7–9 and 7–10, we see the same principle at work within the vocal tract. The nodes are regions of volume velocity minimum, where particle vibration is at its minimum (and pressure is at its maximum). The antinodes are regions of volume velocity maximum, where particle vibration is at its maximum (and pressure is at its minimum). Therefore, we see that an antinode is located at the oral cavity opening to the atmosphere, and a node is located at the

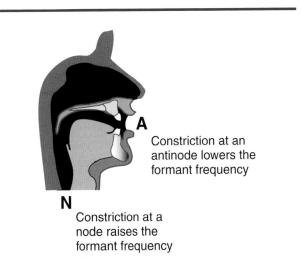

Figure 7–9. Antinode and node locations at vocal tract boundaries.

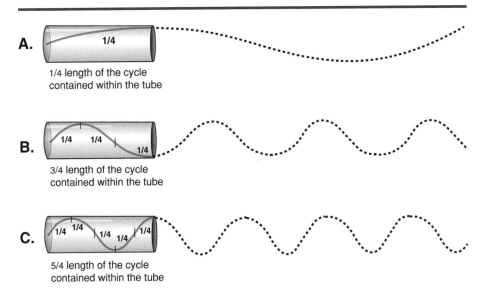

Figure 7–8. A. The longest possible wavelength that provides a velocity maximum (pressure minimum) at the opening of the tube is one-quarter the length of the tube. **B.** A wavelength that is three-quarters the length of the tube also provides a volume velocity maximum at the open end. **C.** Five-quarters of the wavelength (one full cycle plus a quarter) also adheres to the goal of providing a pressure minimum (velocity maximum) at the open end of the tube.

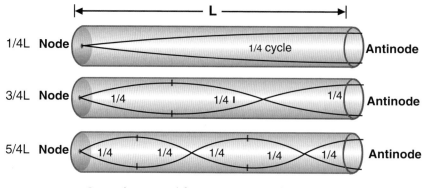

Figure 7–10. One-, three-, and five-quarter wavelengths of a tube open at one end.

glottis (the closed end of the tube). F1, the lowest resonant frequency of the vocal tract, has a wavelength that is four times the length of the vocal tract and contains one node (at the glottis) and one antinode (at the lips). F2, the first odd multiple of the lowest formant frequency, has a wavelength that is three-quarters the length of the vocal tract. F3, the second odd multiple of the lowest formant frequency, has a wavelength that is five-quarters the length of the vocal tract.

A critical point to emphasize is that vocal tract formants represent *potential* resonances of the vocal tract. The vocal tract can only filter the energy with which it is supplied. Place your mouth into the shape of /ɑ/ but do not voice the vowel. Now say the vowel aloud. The formants of the vocal tract are located at the same frequencies whether you provide energy from the glottal sound source or not. Now use a voiceless whisper to produce vowel /ɑ/ and then the vowel /i/. You can hear the difference between the two sounds even though you have only supplied the vocal tract with turbulent, aperiodic airflow instead of complex harmonic structure. Changes to the spectral characteristics of the source do not change the characteristics of the vocal tract transfer function. The vocal tract does not add energy; that is, it does not increase the amplitude of any specific harmonic. It only selectively allows a greater or lesser amount of the energy of each harmonic to be radiated out of the vocal tract.

Study Questions

10. Why does the vocal tract resonate best at a frequency that is four times its length and at odd integer multiples of the lowest resonant frequency?

11. Can you explain Figures 7–8 and 7–10 without looking at the captions?

7.3 Vowels

At the beginning of this chapter, we defined vowels as those sounds containing a glottal source spectrum and resonating with a relatively non-constricted vocal tract. We also defined vowels as the nucleus of syllables. Although the vocal tract is open relative to the production of consonants, some constriction does occur. In fact, a small degree of vocal tract constriction at various locations along the vocal tract must occur in order to specify a given vowel. The location of the relative constrictions and the degree of the constrictions can be used to predict, or specify, the acoustic output of all vowels of American English. Constrictions of the vocal tract are achieved by movement of the tongue, jaw, and lips, and, to a lesser extent in English, contraction of the muscles of the pharyngeal wall. First, we look at the general effect of constrictions on the first three formants. Then we examine more closely vocal tract postures and their acoustic output for each vowel.

Vocal Tract Constrictions and Formant Frequencies

Up to this point, we have focused on the overall length of the vocal tract tube, and we have learned that increasing the length of the tube lowers formant frequencies. Our discussion has considered the vocal tract to be a tube with a uniform cross-sectional area. Of course, this is not actually true. Recall that the length and the cross section define the resonant characteristics (formants) of a tube. In fact, changes in the cross-sectional area of the vocal tract along its length are critical to defining vocal tract resonance and, hence, the speech sounds that are produced. Different vocal tract postures are defined by select degrees of constrictions located at a variety of points along the vocal tract due to movement of the **articulators** (lips, tongue, mandible, and pharyngeal muscles). A constriction in the vocal tract at or near a node or antinode for a particular formant changes the frequency of the formant. In physics, the term **perturbation** is used to mean disturbance. Relative to voice source characteristics, a perturbation is an irregularity of frequency (jitter) or amplitude (shimmer), as discussed in Chapter 6. Relative to the vocal tract transfer

function, perturbation is used as a synonym for constriction because it is, indeed, a perturbation of the standing wave created in the vocal tract.

Two rules govern the relationship between formant frequency and perturbation. First, a constriction at or near an antinode, at which point the volume velocity is at a maximum and the pressure is at a minimum, lowers the frequency of the formant. Second, a constriction at or near a node, at which point the volume velocity is at a minimum and the pressure is at a maximum, raises the frequency of the formant. From these two rules of perturbation we can specify general relationships of vocal tract posture and formant frequencies. Recall from the discussion of standing waves that an antinode is always located at the opening of the lips. Therefore, all formants are lowered by labial constriction. Conversely, formants tend to be raised by lowering of the mandible (increasing mouth opening). As stated earlier, the first three formants are the most important for vowel production. Applying the two rules mentioned above regarding formant frequency and perturbation (constriction), the following general effects of vocal tract configuration on the first three formants may be stated and are summarized in Table 7–1.

First Formant Frequency (F1)

F1 is influenced by oral cavity opening and by constriction in the lower pharynx, just above the glottis. (Lowering of the mandible tends to naturally constrict the hypopharynx.) Specifically, F1

Table 7–1. General Effect of Vocal Tract Lengthening and Constriction on Format Frequency

Formant Frequency	Increased Vocal Tract Length	Location of Constriction (Perturbation)					
		Hypo-pharynx	Pharynx	Oro-pharynx	Mid-Oral Cavity (Palate)	Anterior Oral Cavity (Alveolar Ridge)	Lips
F1	Lowered	Raised	Raised			Lowered	Lowered
F2	Lowered	Raised		Lowered		Raised	Lowered
F3	Lowered	Raised	Lowered	Raised	Lowered	Raised	Lowered

is lowered by a constriction in the oral cavity near the point of maximum volume velocity. F1 is raised by constriction in the pharynx. The tracings in Figures 7–11 and 7–12 show that the constrictions of the anterior oral cavity occur during lip rounding for /u/ and the lingual-palatal constriction for /i/, and that the posterior-inferior constriction occurs during production of the vowel /ɑ/.

Second Formant Frequency (F2)

F2 is most influenced by the shape of the posterior portion of the tongue. Specifically, F2 is lowered by a constriction in the area of the lips or at the back of the oral cavity in the oropharynx, as in the production of /u/ (see Figure 7–12). F2 is raised by a constriction in the anterior oral cavity behind the lips, as in the production of /i/.

Third Formant Frequency (F3)

F3 is most influenced by the position of the tip of the tongue. Specifically, F3 is lowered by constriction at the lips and in the middle of the mouth, as in production of the r-colored vowel /ɝ/ (Kent, Dembowski, & Lass, 1996). F3 is raised by a constriction in the oropharynx, as in the production of the vowel /ɑ/ and by constriction in the anterior mouth as in the production of the semivowel /j/.

Study Questions

12. What are the two rules that govern the relationship between formant frequency and perturbation?

13. What is the effect of labial constriction on all formants?

14. Identify the effect of articulatory constriction at different points in the supraglottal vocal tract on the frequency of the first, second, and third formant frequencies.

The Traditional Vowel Quadrilateral

For over 100 years (Ladefoged, 2006, p. 177), vowels have been classified by three dimensions

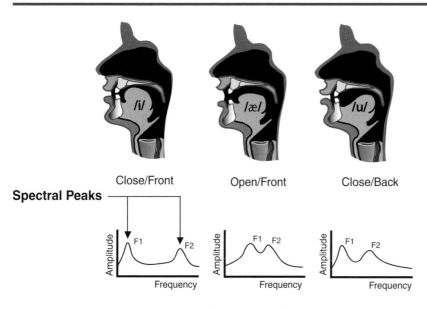

Figure 7–11. Idealized resonance curves corresponding to vocal tract shapes for three vowels.

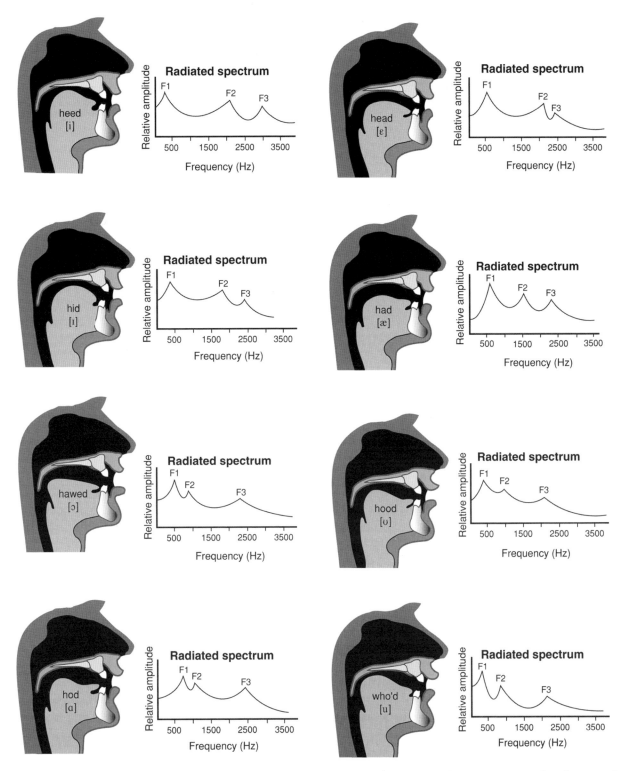

Figure 7–12. Vocal tract posture, corresponding resonance curves, and actual power spectra for the vowels extracted from the words *heed, hid, head, had, hod, hawed, hood,* and *who'd*, based on partial tracing of x-ray images. We tend to identify the spectral peaks as formants. Formants are resonance properties of the vocal tract. The resonance peaks in the spectrum of the radiated acoustic pressure wave characterize the effect of the interaction of the formants and the glottal sound source spectrum. The resonance spectra were obtained using LPC (*linear predictive coding*) from corresponding sustained vowel phonation by an adult female. Adapted from *Speech and Hearing Science: Anatomy and Physiology*, 4th ed., p. 299, by W. R. Zemlin, 1998, Needham Heights, MA: Allyn & Bacon.

of their vocal tract articulatory posture, tongue height (high, mid, or low), tongue advancement (front or back), and lip rounding. The vowels corresponding to the articulatory posture can then be plotted in a corresponding fashion, organized in a chart as depicted in Figure 7–13. The vertical axis represents tongue height, and the horizontal axis represents tongue advancement. Note the vowels on the corners of the chart. The most extreme high vowels are /i/ and /u/. The lowest vowels are /æ/ and /ɑ/. The most front vowels are /i/ and /æ/, and the most back vowels are /u/ and /ɑ/. These four vowels are often referred to as the **corner vowels**, precisely because of their locations on the vowel chart. The five front vowels (Table 7–2), moving from high to low tongue position, are /i/, /æ/, /e/, /ɛ /, and /æ/. The five back vowels (Table 7–3), again moving from high to low tongue position, are /u/, /ʊ/, /o/, /ɔ/, and /ɑ/. Tongue height can also be described as close or open. The vowel /i/ is an example of a **close vowel**, /æ/ is an example of an **open vowel**, and /e/ would be a mid-vowel, all corresponding to oral cavity opening. Note also the shape of the chart is that of a quadrilateral, and, hence, it is called the vowel quadrilateral.

Table 7–2. Front Vowels

	Word Position		
	Initial	**Medial**	**Final**
/i/	east	meat	funny
/ɪ/	is	stick	(not found)
/e/	eight	berate	heresay[a]
/ɛ/	edge	head	(not found)
/æ/	aggravate	back	(not found)

[a]The /e/ is considered by some linguists to always represents a diphthong.

Table 7–3. Back Vowels

	Word Position		
	Initial	**Medial**	**Final**
/u/	ooze	hoot	blue
/ʊ/	(not found)	should	(not found)
/o/	omit	motor	tango
/ɔ/	awesome	daunting	paw
/ɑ/ or /a/	ogle	father	spa

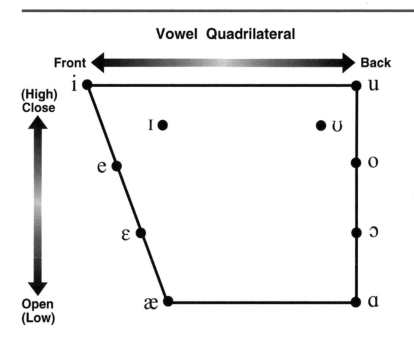

Vowel Quadrilateral

Figure 7–13. A plot of the vowels corresponding to traditional descriptors of hypothesized articulatory posture, in which the vertical axis represents tongue height and the horizontal axis represents tongue advancement.

Within the approximate center of the **vowel quadrilateral** are found the central vowels (Figure 7–14). **Central vowels** are those that are neither front nor back but are produced with the tongue position considered to be dominantly in the middle of the oral cavity (Table 7–4). Central vowels are often said to have a *reduced* vowel quality. These vowels are so described in part because of their more neutral vocal tract posture, as compared to the other vowels. Recall from our introductory discussion of the acoustic theory of vowel production that the neutral schwa vowel /ə/ was modeled as a tube of uniform cross-sectional area (see Figure 7–6). In this way, the more active tongue positions can be thought of as reduced to a central position. Reduction also refers to vowel perception. The vowels on the outer border of the quadrilateral chart have greater auditory distinction from one another than the more central vowels. Examples of reduction of vowels from a stressed to an unstressed syllable include the /ɔ/ in the second syllable of *confront* moving to the /ə/ in first syllable of *umbrella*.

Vowel Quality and Articulatory Posture

Vowels are more difficult to categorize than consonants. We will learn in Chapter 8 that consonants have a relatively distinct articulatory configuration compared to vowels. A moment's exploration will reveal the difficulties inherent in describing vowels. Produce the high front corner vowel /i/ and then slide slowly to the low front corner vowel /æ/ in the same breath group.

Table 7–4. Central Vowels and Rhotics

	Word Position		
	Initial	**Medial**	**Final**
/ə/	about	deny	stoma
/ʌ/	ugly	shut	(not found)
/ɚ/	urbane	terrain	mother
/ɝ/	urban	hurt	whir

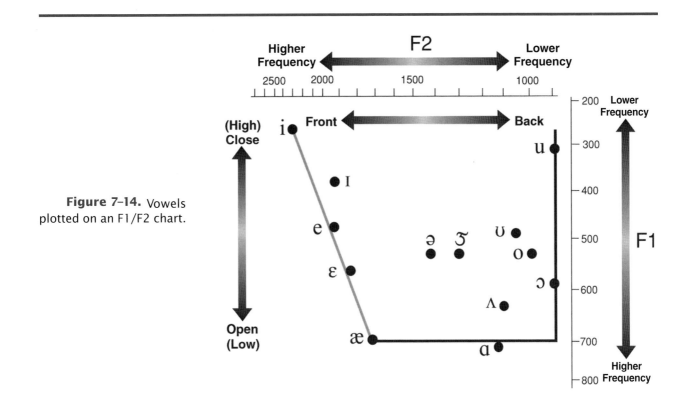

Figure 7–14. Vowels plotted on an F1/F2 chart.

According to the traditional vowel quadrilateral, we are told that the tongue remains advanced but moves from the highest to the lowest position in the oral cavity. Listen to the sound of the vowel change as you alter the articulatory posture. Note that the vowels lie on a continuum of sound and articulatory movement. When exactly does one vowel become the next? Exactly how is the tongue shaped in the mouth for each sound? The answers to these questions are difficult to obtain. In fact, what we know now is that the dimensions of tongue height and tongue advancement are not, in fact, strictly accurate descriptors of tongue position. Rather, these dimensions are descriptors of how the *vowels are perceived relative to one another.* Just as we describe features of the source signal as vocal quality, we can describe the features of vocal tract resonance.

Produce the vowel /i/ again. Most probably, you can feel the body of your tongue raised up high in the mouth. The tongue tip is anterior in the mouth. Now start with /i/ once more and move to /u/ in the same breath group. Two events occur: The lips round and the tongue retracts. So the high (or close) unrounded front vowel /i/ moved to the low (or open) rounded back vowel. But how much does your tongue retract? For many people, the tongue tip remains quite forward. We believe that the vowel is a back vowel because we are told it is so. Our auditory perception of the vowel, that is, the vowel quality, tells us that the sound is back, and not our sense of tongue position within our mouth. What, then, is directing our perception of vowel quality? The answer lies in the acoustic representation of the vowels. We have learned that the articulatory configuration of the vocal tract, that is, the vocal tract posture, specifies the formant frequencies. And we will learn that the relationship among the formant frequencies provides the acoustic representation of the vowel. But the vocal tract posture is substantially more complex than a simple description of tongue height and tongue advancement. We can begin to answer our question by asking another question. What is the relationship of formant frequency to the classic dimensions of tongue height, tongue advancement, and lip rounding?

Acoustic Representation of Vowel Quality

Figure 7–14 plots the vowels on a grid in which the vertical *y*-axis is the frequency of the first formant, and the horizontal *x*-axis is the frequency of the second formant. A few features are immediately apparent. First, the vowels form an approximate shape of the quadrilateral, similar to Figure 7–13. And so we know that the vowels do have, in general, the relationship described in the traditional vowel quadrilateral, as specified by F1 and F2 (Ladefoged, Harshman, Goldstein, & Rice, 1978).

The second feature we note is that specifying vowels in terms of tongue height and advancement is not completely accurate. Despite the arrangement of the vowels in the quadrilateral, these dimensions are not uniformly presented throughout the chart. The highest front and back vowels, /i/ and /u/, respectively, are not produced with equal tongue height. The back vowel /u/ is lower than /i/. In addition, the back vowels are all produced with variable degrees of "backness."

If the specification of vowel quality using tongue height and advancement is flawed, then why does this traditional method persist? The simple answer is because it is somewhat accurate and a better method has not been found. With the caution in mind that the descriptors of tongue position should be interpreted loosely, we can explore further the effect of the articulator movement upon the formant frequencies as summarized in Table 7–1. Rather than tongue height and advancement, we shall use the more appropriate descriptors of **vowel height** and vowel advancement. In Figure 7–14, note that, in general, the frequency of the first formant appears to have an inverse relationship with vowel height. That is, as the vowel becomes lower or more open, F1 increases. This relationship holds for both the front and back vowels. We state, therefore, that the frequency of the first formant inversely influences the perception of vowel height. The relationship of F2 and vowel height is less certain. For the front vowels, F2 decreases as the vowel becomes more open. For the back vowels, no clear relationship is apparent.

The perception of **vowel advancement** is less straightforward. As the vowels move from back to front, F2 increases generally but not consistently. And as we stated earlier, lip rounding tends to lower the frequency of all formants. It is most likely that the perception of vowel advancement is a function of both F1 and F2 (Ladefoged, 2006, p. 188). As the first and second formant frequencies move closer together, the perception of back vowel quality increases.

The pattern of formant frequencies can be visualized more easily by representing the formant as a line plotted on a graph in which the *x*-axis represents time, and the *y*-axis represents frequency. Such a plot is a stylized adaptation

of a sound spectrogram, discussed in detail further in this chapter under Instrumentation. In Figure 7–15, it is immediately evident, as we move around the vowel quadrilateral from front to back, that a generally systematic relationship exists between the relative location of the first formants and the articulatory posture of the vocal tract. Two features are emphasized.

First, for the front vowels, the frequency locations of the first and second formants are generally spaced rather far apart, whereas the frequencies of the second and third formants are generally located close to each other. Focusing on the vowel quality, we can say that as the vowel quality moves forward, F1 and F2 become more separated. Focusing on resonance cavity, we can say that as the anterior space in the oral cavity becomes smaller, and the resonance space of the posterior oral cavity widens, F1 and F2 become more separated. As we move to the back vowels, we note that F1 and F2 are located close

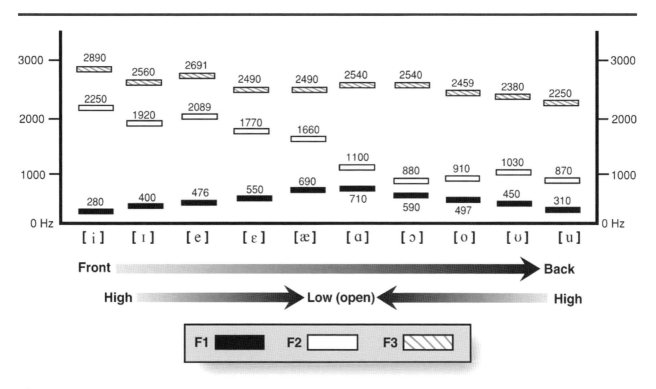

Figure 7–15. A stylized spectrogram, in which the formant frequencies for each vowel are plotted on a graph in which the *x*-axis represents time and the *y*-axis represents frequency. Note that as the vowel quality moves from high to low front, F2 lowers, drawing F1 and F2 progressively closer together. Note also that for the back vowels, F2 and F3 are spaced relatively far apart.

to each other, whereas the frequencies of the second and third formants are generally located farther apart from each other. In fact, the perceptual vowel quality of backness is a function of the relationship of F1 and F2.

The second feature to note is that, for both the front and back vowels, F1 varies inversely with vowel height, as stated earlier. In general, vowel height decreases and F1 increases as we move from the high (close) front vowel /i/ to the low (open) front vowel /æ/.

Resonating Cavities of the Vocal Tract

The traditional emphasis on tongue position, particularly anterior tongue position, as the major descriptor of vowel production is not difficult to understand. The vowel quadrilateral and the corresponding movements of the articulators were developed before instrumentation allowed easy access to acoustic analysis. Therefore, the focus of early explorations of vowel production was on the movements that could be observed or felt. We are in the habit of thinking about articulation as a phenomenon of the oral cavity, defined by the movement of the lips, mandible, and anterior tongue. The tongue, however, is a very large muscle, connected at its base to the hyoid bone. (See the overview of Tongue Anatomy later in this chapter.) The tongue is also an incompressible structure, which means that retracting the tongue tip, for example, will cause the portion of the tongue in the oropharynx to be affected as well. Movements of the mandible similarly will affect the base of the tongue. And movement of the base of the tongue will influence the relative constriction of the pharynx, which has an effect upon the acoustic representation of a vowel. Furthermore, although the tongue and mandible often move together, they also can easily move independently of one another. We would expect jaw movement also to affect formant frequency, because depressing the mandible would generally allow the tongue to be lowered, thus enlarging the oral cavity. In fact, theoretical and statistical models that relate

vocal tract articulatory posture to acoustic output do indeed consider jaw movement an important factor (Harshman, Ladefoged, & Goldstein, 1977; Lindblom & Sundberg, 1971). When we look at the images of Figures 7–12 and 7–14, we can see readily that in the production of a front vowel, the resonating cavities of the back of the vocal tract (the hypopharynx and oropharynx) are critical to the acoustic realization of the vowel. Similarly, a back vowel contains important resonances of the anterior mouth.

An overview of gross tongue movements for seven vowels is presented in Figure 7–16. Note that the front vowels are distinguished from two of the back vowels with a more advanced tongue position. However, it is also evident that tongue height, tongue tip advancement, and lip rounding are not the only articulatory changes occurring from one vowel to the next. The base of the tongue is changing position with the vowels to

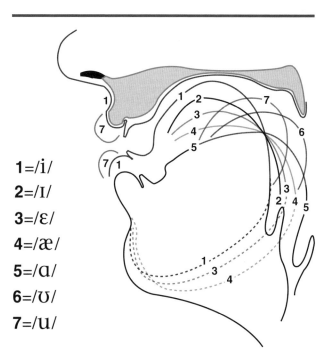

1=/i/
2=/ɪ/
3=/ɛ/
4=/æ/
5=/ɑ/
6=/ʊ/
7=/u/

Figure 7–16. Movements of the tongue create different resonating cavities for the vowels in (1) heed, (2) hid, (3) head, (4) had, (5) father, (6) good, and (7) food. Adapted from *A Course in Acoustic Phonetics*, by P. Ladefoged, 2001, Thomson Wadsworth. Reprinted with permission of Heinle, a division of Thomson Learning: http://www.thomsonrights.com.

alter the cross-sectional area of the vocal tract in the oropharynx and hypopharynx.

The movement of the articulators, most particularly of the tongue, creates somewhat distinct resonating cavities of different volumes, or sizes. Recall from Chapter 3 that the natural resonant frequencies of an acoustic resonator are specified in part by the volume of air being resonated. A smaller resonating space within the vocal tract vibrates at a higher frequency than a larger resonating space. When we considered the single-tube model of the neutral schwa vowel earlier in the chapter, we noted that as the overall length of the vocal tract shortened, the formant frequencies increased. We know, however, that the vocal tract is not a uniform tube for many vowels. Consider the production of /ɑ/, for example, as shown in Figure 7–12. A large resonating cavity is located in the oral cavity. The position of the base of the tongue creates a smaller resonating cavity in the pharynx. The vowel can therefore be modeled as two resonating tubes of different sizes (Figure 7–17). In this case, we have two tubes, each of which can be modeled as open at one end and closed at the other end. Each tube is approximately half the length of the vocal tract. The smaller resonating space of each tube means that the air inside each of those tubes would resonate at a higher frequency. In other words, the formants of each of those resonating tubes would be higher than for the longer vocal tract of the neutral schwa vowel. In reality, the oral tube is not really closed at one end but rather open at both ends, which affects the resonant frequencies by raising them

(the details of which we will not consider here). The important point to understand here is that the movement of the articulators will create different-sized resonating spaces. The larger the resonating spaces will produce the lower formant frequencies.

Avoiding a Common Misperception

The discussion of the relationship of formant frequency and articulatory position can sometimes lead to the misperception on the part of the student that formants are located at specific physical points in the vocal tract. It is important to stress that formants are not found at some numerically ordered sequence of vocal tract locations. Although constriction at a certain location of the vocal tract will raise or lower a formant, keep in mind that it is due to a change in the cross-sectional area of the vocal tract at a volume velocity minima or maxima, which in turn is a function of the standing wave resonant patterns. In fact, the horizontal and vertical tongue dimensions and lip rounding are, to a great extent, of interest to us only in that they create perturbations in the vocal tract transfer function by altering the cross-sectional area at one or more locations to create one or more resonating cavities of different volumes within the vocal tract.

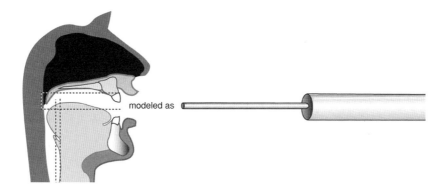

Figure 7–17. The vowel /ɑ/ modeled as two tubes.

Helmholtz Resonator

Consider the vocal tract position for the vowel /u/ in Figure 7–12. We see that the back of the tongue creates a constriction in the oral-pharyngeal cavity. The air in this posterior resonating tube behaves more as if it is enclosed in a tube closed at both ends, rather than closed at one end and open at the other. The way in which this column of air is vibrated is like the air in a bottle with a narrow neck.

The air contained in the neck of the bottle is an acoustic resonator. When air is blown across the top, it exerts a downward pressure on the air in the bottle neck. We know that air is an elastic medium, and so when the air in the neck is pushed downward, it compresses the air inside the body of the bottle. Restorative forces cause the compressed air to expand, pushing the air in the neck upward. We know from our earlier examination of oscillation that the air will move beyond equilibrium due to momentum, thus rarefying the air within the bottle, which causes the pressure to drop and sucks the air in the neck back into the bottle.

The upward and downward oscillation of the air in the bottle neck continues until frictional forces cause the oscillation to come to rest. We know that the rate of the oscillation is dependent upon the size of the resonating cavity, which can be altered by selecting different-sized bottles, or taking several similar-sized bottles and filling up each one to a different capacity with water. As the water occupies a certain amount of space in the bottle, the size of the resonating cavity of air changes, thus altering the frequency of the oscillation. Herman von Helmholtz (1821–1894) was a scientist who explored the physics of sound. He developed a method for filtering a selected frequency from a complex pressure wave, which consisted of setting the air in different-sized containers into vibration with a tuning fork. This method of identifying the resonant frequency of an acoustic resonator is called a **Helmholtz resonator**. Figure 7–1 shows an original Helmholtz resonator. The method also works well for playing in a jug band (Figure 7–18).

Figure 7–18. The Helmholtz Jug Band!

Does General American English Exist?

We know that large differences exist in the pronunciation of vowels depending upon geographic region and other demographic variables. Although we use the term General American English, it is doubtful that such a general model truly exists (Clopper, Pisoni, & de Jong, 2005). However, the topic of dialects requires an entire text unto itself. The basic science and physiology underlying the production of voice and speech is independent of the dialect.

The x-ray tracings of Figure 7–12 and the tube models of Figures 7–6 and 7–17, like most other figures attempting to show vocal tract postures, can be quite misleading because they are only two-dimensional representations of a three-dimensional phenomenon. Figure 7–19 shows three-dimensional representations of the vocal tract during phonation of four vowels derived from computerized tomography (CT) and magnetic resonance imaging (MRI) scans. These images can help us to realize that the two-dimensional line drawings leave out a considerable amount of information about resonant spaces. Clearly the one- or two-tube model of resonating spaces is too simple to fully explain the acoustics of the vocal tract: In fact, the vocal tract can be modeled

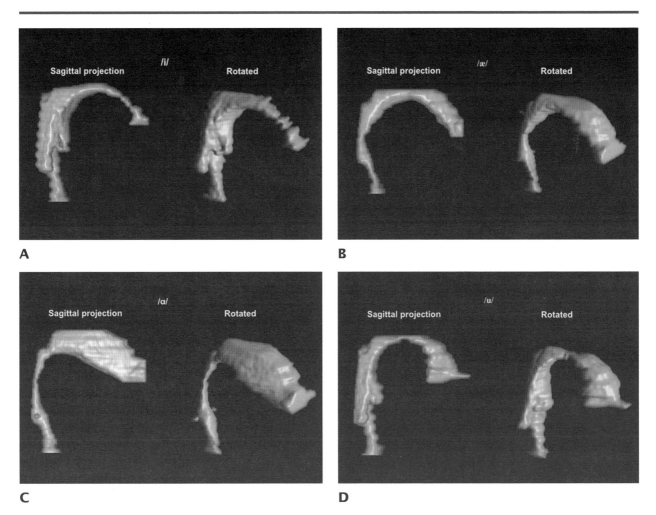

Figure 7–19. Three-dimensional representations of the vocal tract during phonation of /i/, /æ/, /ɑ/, and /u/ derived from CT and MRI imaging. Courtesy of Brad Story, Ph.D, The University of Arizona.

as a series of multiple tubes (Figure 7–20) (Titze, 1994). Although the computation of such a model is beyond our discussion, let it serve to emphasize the complexity of vocal tract acoustics and, therefore, the potential for a vast richness of sounds arising from it.

You may have noticed that we have ignored the nasal cavity in our discussion of resonating spaces of the vocal tract. The nasal cavity does introduce unique resonating characteristics, and we shall explore these features in Chapter 8.

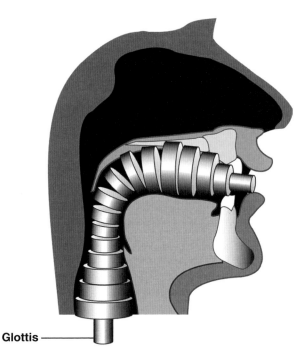

Glottis

Figure 7–20. For vowel production, the vocal tract can be modeled as a series of multiple tubes. Adapted from *Principles of Voice Production* (p. 138), by I. R. Titze, 1994, Englewood Cliffs, NJ: Prentice-Hall, Inc. Adapted with permission.

Study Questions

15. Without referring to Figures 7–13 and 7–14, draw the traditional vowel quadrilateral. Label the *x*- and *y*-axes. Place the corner vowels in the appropriate places on the chart. Indicate with arrows the direction of high to low and front to back. Indicate with another set of arrows the change in frequencies of F1 and F2.

16. What is vowel quality, and what is the relationship of articulatory posture to vowel quality?

17. How are our perceptions of vowel height and advancement governed by the relationship of F1 and F2?

18. What are resonating cavities of the vocal tract, and how do they affect vowel quality?

Vowel Formant Normative Data

In theory, an infinite number of vocal tract configurations can be achieved, each one with very slight differences in length and cross-sectional area within each resonating cavity (hypopharynx, oropharynx, and oral). Recall from our discussion of breathing in Chapter 4 that *motor equivalence* refers to the phenomenon in which individuals demonstrate different motor behav-

iors in response to the same stimulus. Rephrasing the definition, we can say that motor equivalence is the ability of the individual to assume different articulatory postures to achieve the same acoustic output. Although vocal tract posture specifies the formant frequencies, considerable variability exists among speakers for the same acoustic target, even among speakers with the same regional accents (Johnson, Ladefoged, & Lindau, 1993). Despite that variability, the rules of perturbation of standing waves, as discussed earlier in the chapter, hold for any speaker. Therefore, generalizations across speakers validly explain vocal tract posture and formant frequency (Story, 2005).

We can see now that although the vocal tract is an acoustic resonating tube, it is a variable resonator. In other words, the natural resonant frequencies of the vocal tract vary depending upon the vocal tract posture. Reflecting for a moment on the influence of both vocal tract length and size of the resonating cavities on formant frequency, it should be evident that no vowel has invariant formant frequencies. That is, one cannot specify an absolute value for F1, F2, and F3 as being the ideal or target resonant characteristics for a specific vowel. It is the relative relationship among the formants that is the critical factor. A seminal study by Peterson and Barney (1952) at Bell Laboratories provided the first such data on 10 vowels spoken by a group of men, women, and children. Hillenbrand, Getty, Clark, and Wheeler (1995) remark that the data from the Peterson and Barney (1952) study are the most widely cited in acoustics. Hillenbrand et al. (1995) replicated and added to those data, analyzing formant structure from 12 vowels spoken within an *hVd* structure, where *V* represents one of the 12 vowels (as in had, hid, hod, etc.) for men, women, and children. The authors plotted the frequencies of the first and second formants on the *x*- and *y*-axes, respectively (Figure 7–21).

Table 7–5 shows the average values for FI, F2, and F3 for 12 vowels for men, women, and children. These average values for each vowel can be referred to as their individual vowel space. That is, for each vowel, the **vowel space** is the set of F1–F2 points that specify the vowel.

Although decreasing length of the vocal tract raises all formants, the relative relationship among the formants is preserved across gender and age.

Tense-Lax Vowel Quality and Inherent Duration

Traditionally, vowels can be categorized as **tense** or **lax**. Tense vowels are sometimes defined as those produced with greater muscle contraction than lax vowels (Singh & Singh, 2006), although the physiology of this distinction is highly uncertain (Raphael & Bell-Berti, 1975). Tense vowels also have been defined as those that are produced at the extremes of articulatory posture, with the tongue higher in the oral cavity. In general, the acoustic result of the tense-lax dimension is duration, whereby tense vowels are longer and lax vowels are shorter (Pickett, 1980, p. 187). The duration of a vowel is, in part, defined by its phonetic context and by the prosody of the utterance, which we shall explore in detail further on. But duration is also an inherent characteristic of vowels. Singh and Singh (2006) identify six tense (long) vowels (/i/, /e/, /ɝ/, /u/, /o/, /ɚ/), five lax (short) vowels (/ɪ/, /ə/, /ɛ/, /ʊ/,

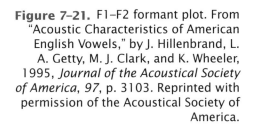

Figure 7–21. F1–F2 formant plot. From "Acoustic Characteristics of American English Vowels," by J. Hillenbrand, L. A. Getty, M. J. Clark, and K. Wheeler, 1995, *Journal of the Acoustical Society of America*, 97, p. 3103. Reprinted with permission of the Acoustical Society of America.

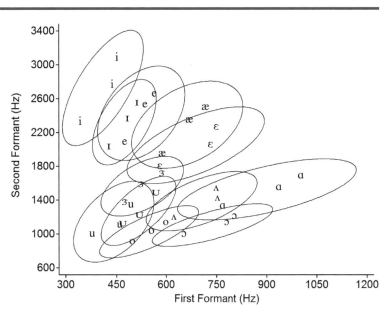

Table 7–5. Average Formant Frequencies for Men, Women, and Children[a]

Men												
	/i/	/ɪ/	/e/	/ɛ/	/æ/	/ɑ/	/ɔ/	/o/	/ʊ/	/u/	/ʌ/	/ɝ/
F0	138	135	129	127	123	123	121	129	133	143	133	130
F1	342	427	476	580	588	768	652	497	469	378	623	474
F2	2,322	2,034	2,089	1,799	1,952	1,333	977	910	1,122	997	1,200	1,379
F3	3,000	2,684	2,691	2,605	2,601	2,522	2,538	2,459	2,434	2,343	2,550	1,710

Women												
	/i/	/ɪ/	/e/	/ɛ/	/æ/	/ɑ/	/ɔ/	/o/	/ʊ/	/u/	/ʌ/	/ɝ/
F0	270	223	219	214	215	215	210	217	230	235	218	217
F1	437	483	536	731	669	936	781	555	519	459	753	523
F2	2,761	2,365	2,530	2,058	2,349	1,551	1,136	1,035	1,225	1,105	1,426	1,588
F3	3,372	3,053	3,047	2,979	2,972	2,815	2,824	2,828	2,827	2,735	2,933	1,929

Children (10-year-old boys and girls)[b]												
	/i/	/ɪ/	/e/	/ɛ/	/æ/	/ɑ/	/ɔ/	/o/	/ʊ/	/u/	/ʌ/	/ɝ/
F1	403	—	—	645	—	735	814	—	—	469	—	—
F2	3,028	—	—	2,193	—	2,255	1,336	—	—	1,351	—	—

Sources:
[a]Data from Hillenbrand, Getty, Clark, & Wheeler (1995).
[b]Data from Eguchi & Hirsh (1969).

and /ɔ/, and three vowels neutral for tenseness, /æ/, /a/, and /ɑ/. Kent, Dembowski, and Lass (1996), however, identify the tense (long) vowels as /i/, /e/, /æ/, /u/, /o/, /ɔ/, and /ɑ/ and the lax (short) vowels as /ɪ/, /ɛ/ /ʊ/, /ə/ and /ɝ/. The authors note that the central /ʌ/ is generally of longer duration and is sometimes described as a tense vowel.

Despite the lack of clarity regarding the physiology and categorization of tenseness and laxness, the **inherent duration of the vowel** is an important acoustic cue for vowel perception and appears to be governed by linguistic rules of American English. The short vowels, in general, do not appear in open syllables, which are defined as syllables ending in a vowel. So words such as *plea*, *Joe*, *you*, and *no* are open syllables with long (tense) vowels. Closed syl-

lables, those that end in a consonant, may contain either long or short vowels. So words such as *pill* and *debt* contain short vowels, but other closed syllables such as *ought* and *boot* contain long vowels.

Rhotacized Vowel Quality

The vowel /ɝ/ as in *heard* occurs as the nucleus in a stressed syllable only, whereas the vowel /ɚ/ as in the second syllable of *father* occurs as the nucleus of an unstressed syllable only. Both vowels are said to be **r-colored, or rhotic vowels** (from rho, the name of the Greek letter corresponding, sort of, to our /r/). The r-coloring of a vowel is called **rhotacization**. As with tongue height or advancement, rhotacization describes an auditory perceptual quality of a vowel associated with /r/.

Diphthongs

All the vowels discussed up to this point are **monophthongs**, or pure vowels (phthong is Greek for voiced sound). That is, the vowels are produced with a constant vocal tract posture (although not in all dialects of English). Say the words *say, tie, boy, wow, no*. Note that the vocal tract posture does not remain constant throughout the vowel in each word. In truth, each word is composed of two vowels, in which the two vowels are spoken one right after the next. Such "double" vowels are named **diphthongs**. A defining feature of diphthongs is that the articulatory posture shifts smoothly from the first vowel to the second one. If a smooth glide is not present between the two vowels, then it is not a diphthong. In general, diphthongs are wholly contained within one syllable. In American English, it is generally the rule that a consonant is placed between two vowels when both are nuclei of different syllables. For instance, in the word *coincide*, a /w/ is placed between the /o/ and the /ɪ/, and each vowel forms the nucleus for a syllable. Five common diphthongs used in American English are contained within the words *say, tie, boy, wow, no*. The diphthongs are /eɪ/, /aɪ/, /ɔɪ/, /aʊ/, and /oʊ/. (Note that some linguists represent the diphthong in words such as *say* with /e/, whereas others use /eɪ/.) The use of diphthongs, or diphthongization of vowels, is highly dependent on geographic area. Some speakers produce fewer pure vowels and more diphthongs, whereas others produce more pure vowels and fewer diphthongs.

Figure 7–22 shows the direction of vowel quality movement within the vowel quadrilateral. It is evident that certain diphthongs require greater change in articulatory posture than do others. It is also evident that the diphthongs cannot be characterized by a single tongue height or advancement or lip rounding posture. However, the diphthongs tend to move from tense (long) to lax (short). And whereas the tongue

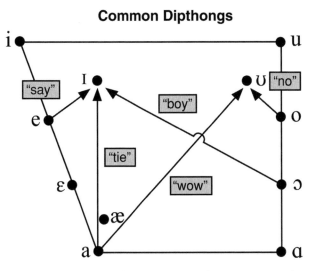

Figure 7–22. Diphthongs shown by arrows in the vowel quadrilateral. Adapted from *Phonetics: Principles and Practices*, 3rd ed., p. 102, by S. Singh and K. Singh, 2006, San Diego, CA: Plural Publishing, Inc. Adapted with permission.

height may start in a low or mid-position, the end of the diphthong is always high. The articulatory starting point for the diphthong is often called the **onglide**, and the ending articulation is called the **offglide**. Figure 7–23 shows the pattern of the onglide and offglide for the five common diphthongs. Note that each diphthong has a characteristic F1–F2 pattern, with F2 experiencing the greater change in frequency. The corresponding shifts in frequency of the first and second formants were explored by Lehiste and Peterson (1961b) and Holbrook and Fairbanks (1962). It is likely that the actual value of the formant frequencies at the onglide and offglide are subject to variability, depending upon the rate of speech and other phonetic and linguistic contextual variables. Diphthongs containing inherently long vowels have a longer duration and, furthermore, the speaker tends to undershoot, or not complete, the articulatory posture of the second vowel. Possibly, the rate of formant transition is an important perceptual cue for identification of the diphthong. We will return to the examination of diphthongs in Chapter 8 in our discussion of the consonant glides.

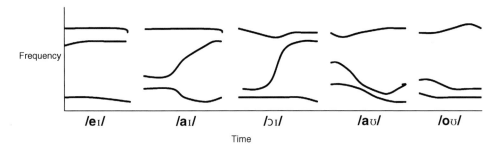

Figure 7–23. The stylized, approximate formant patterns for five American English diphthongs. The lowest black line above each vowel corresponds to F1, the middle line corresponds to F2, and the top line corresponds to F3.

Source Filter Interaction

Fant's (1960) acoustic theory of speech production presents the sound source as independent of the resonant characteristics of the vocal tract. Later work, however (Fant, 1980, 1986), demonstrates that this assumption of independence is not correct. Vocal tract resonance alters the acoustic pressure wave that is reflected back onto the vocal folds, and this alteration in turn influences the source characteristics generated by their vibration. This interaction effect is particularly relevant to the study of the singing and acting voice, as well as to therapeutic intervention for voice disorders. However, we may consider the source and filter to be distinct for this introductory exploration of normal speech and voice processes. Explore the independence that exists between the source and filter. Sustain phona-tion on a vowel. Now repeat the vowel but at a lower pitch and then at a higher pitch. Produce the same vowel softly and then loudly. In each instance, the source characteristics of the glottal volume velocity have been altered, either by shifting the fundamental and harmonic frequencies (changing pitch) or altering the relative amplitude of the frequencies (changing loudness). Yet the vowel produced was the same throughout each phonation, meaning that the vocal tract transfer function remained unchanged. Similarly, we can produce a string of different vowels all at the same pitch. In this case, the spectral characteristics of the source are constant but the resonant characteristics of the vocal tract are changed. Despite a certain degree of interaction, the source and the filter also function independently.

Why Do You Sound Like "Donald Duck" by Speaking While Breathing a Helium-Oxygen Mixture?

Helium has lower mass density of particles than air (lower than anything else except hydrogen), so sound waves travel nearly three times as fast in helium as in air. Therefore, the higher harmonics are preferentially emphasized. The frequencies at which the harmon-ics are located do not change as a result of the helium, but rather the relative amplitude of the frequencies changes. *Caution:* Inhaling helium is incredibly foolish and can cause you to suffocate and die. Don't do it!

Vowel Centralization

Stetson (1951) was one of the first speech scientists to remark upon the relationship between the spectral characteristics of vowel space and temporal aspects of speech production. Using perceptual observation, Stetson noted that in unstressed syllables in English, the vowels became centralized, moving toward a schwa-like acoustic representation. (**Vowel centralization** is also commonly referred to as **vowel reduction**.) That is, when plotting the F1 and F2 values, the space was reduced when vowels were in unstressed position. At about the same time, Fry (1955) noted that unstressed vowels were typically produced with decreased duration. Subsequently, several studies have demonstrated that vowel space decreases as the speaking rate increases (Lindblom, 1963; Tsao, Weismer, & Iqbal, 2006; Turner, Tjaden, & Weismer, 1995). Of note, some data suggest that speakers who have naturally, or habitually, faster speaking rates have not been found to have reduced vowel space on average, although the variability of the vowel space is greater for naturally slow speakers (Tsao et al., 2006).

In Chapter 9, in our discussion of prosody, we will revisit the concept of vowel reduction as an important component of speech rhythm. However, vowel reduction (and speech rhythm) are language dependent. That is, not all languages use vowel reduction as frequently as does English. And thus, languages have different perceived rhythms.

Intrinsic Pitch of Vowels

Not only do vowels have an inherent duration, but each vowel also has an **inherent or intrinsic pitch**. To explore this characteristic, say the following vowels, moving around the vowel quadrilateral from high front to low front. Say each one as a long vowel to appreciate the pitch /i, ɪ, ɛ, æ/ as in the words *heed, hid, head, had*. Now say the following back vowels, moving from low back to high back /ɑ, ɔ, ʊ, u/ as in the words *hod, hawed, hood*, and *who'd*. You might also try producing the vowels in a voiceless whisper. In both instances, you will probably hear that the pitch descends as you proceed from high front to low front, then to low back and up to high back, a characteristic confirmed by research (Lehiste & Peterson, 1961a). The perceived intrinsic pitch is tied closely to the general lowering of the second formant frequency as we move from high front to low front, then low back to high back. Look again at Figure 7–15, in which the formants are displayed as lines on a vertical frequency scale. F2 generally progresses downward, consistent with the perception of decreasing pitch.

The biomechanical coupling of the larynx and the articulators of the upper vocal tract is a popular hypothesis for the physiologic mechanism underlying intrinsic pitch. The movement of the tongue for high vowels may exert an upward pull on the hyoid bone and thereby exert a complex set of forces on the laryngeal cartilages that result in vocal fold elongation and increased pitch (Honda, 1983, 1995; Rossi & Autesserre, 1981). However, Honda (1995) reviews several other variables that may be relevant, and the theories of how these variables may contribute to intrinsic pitch. For example, EMG studies have shown that cricothyroid muscle activity correlates with vowel pitch (Honda & Fujimura, 1991; Ohala & Hirose, 1970; Vilkman, Aaltonen, Raimo, & Okasanen, 1989), suggesting a more active role of that muscle than simply passive movement due to supra- and infrahyoid muscle pull.

The Didgeridoo

The didgeridoo is an Australian instrument (Figure 7–24) that is deceptively simple in its appearance. A talented player can produce an amazing variety of sounds from this instrument, greater than that which can be produced from more commonly recognized instruments found in most orchestras. Acoustic analysis of the didgeridoo reveals that the standing waves produced in the instrument are similar to those produced in the vocal tract, and the player controls these standing waves by controlling his own source (phonatory) and filter (vocal tract) characteristics (Tarnopolsky et al., 2005). The result is a series of sounds with as great a variety as the spectrum of vowel qualities produced by the vocal tract!

Figure 7–24. The didgeridoo, an Australian woodwind instrument, has resonance properties similar to that of a vocal tract.

Study Questions

19. What did the data show from the Peterson and Barney (1952) study of vowel spaces and the replication of that study by Hillenbrand et al. (1995)?

20. To what do tense and lax vowels refer, and which vowels are generally defined as being tense or lax?

21. What is meant by the inherent duration of vowels, and how does it relate to the tense-lax feature?

22. Explain rhotacized vowel quality.

23. Define monophthong and diphthong. What are five common diphthongs in many dialects of American English?

24. What is onglide and offglide relative to diphthongs?

25. Explain the concept of intrinsic pitch of vowels.

The Most Important Articulator

Tongue Anatomy

The tongue is the most important articulatory structure of the supraglottal vocal tract, and therefore, it deserves some extra attention. It is a challenging structure to study anatomically, because it is a muscular hydrostat. That is, unlike the skeletal muscles that function like mechanical levers, a **muscular hydrostat** is composed of muscle groups that are oriented in different directions, making it hard to dissect easily for anatomical study. Thus, tongue movement is the result of a complexity of multiple muscles, or portions of muscles, at one time, with some muscles acting as agonists, others as antagonists, and still other muscles as stabilizers (Sandsers & Mu, 2013).

Anatomically, the tongue can be divided into the anterior body, contained wholly within the oral cavity, and the posterior root, contained within the oral-pharyngeal cavity. For functional purposes, the tongue is often identified by three aspects: the tip, blade (portion of the tongue immediately behind the tip that is under the alveolar ridge), and dorsum (superior surface of the tongue behind the blade yet still contained within the oral cavity). The tongue muscles are categorized as intrinsic and extrinsic (Figures 7–25 and 7–26). The intrinsic muscles of the tongue are wholly contained within the structure of the tongue, and the extrinsic

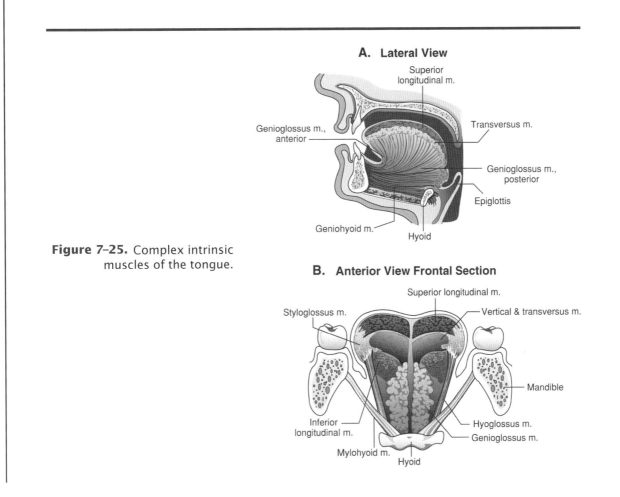

Figure 7–25. Complex intrinsic muscles of the tongue.

muscles have their origin in structures outside of the tongue. In general, the intrinsic muscles enable fine movements of the tongue, and the extrinsic muscles facilitate larger (gross) movements and provide structural support for the intrinsic muscles (Figure 7–27). Yet not every

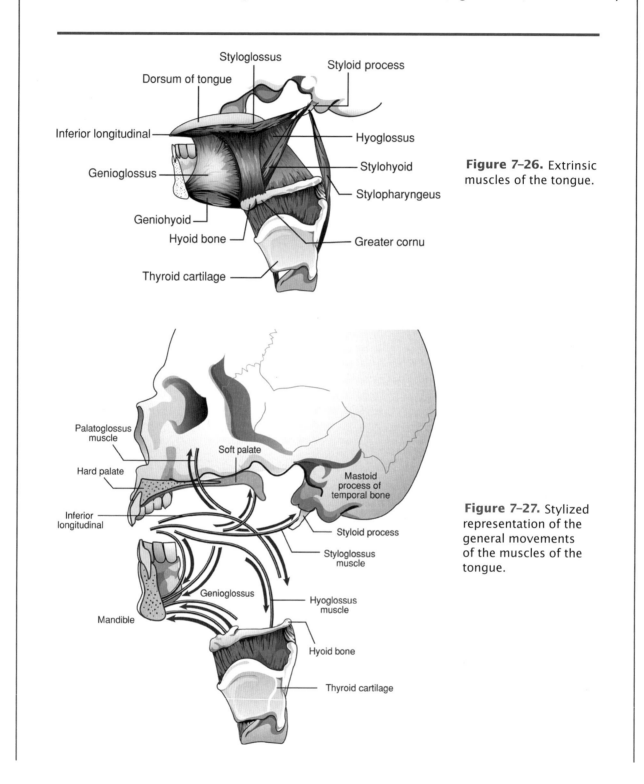

Figure 7–26. Extrinsic muscles of the tongue.

Figure 7–27. Stylized representation of the general movements of the muscles of the tongue.

anatomist agrees on which tongue muscles belong to which category!

Four paired muscles are identified as intrinsic: The superior longitudinal muscle, upon contraction, shortens the tongue and dorsiflexes the tongue tip (that is, pulls the tip and lateral margins upward). The inferior longitudinal muscle, located on the undersurface of the tongue, is responsible for retroflexion. That is, it shortens the tongue or pulls the tip and lateral margins downward when contracted. The fanlike transverse muscle, upon contraction, narrows the tongue and causes elongation of the tongue body and blade. And contraction of the vertical muscle flattens the tongue and increases its width while elongating the tongue.

Three major paired muscles are identified as extrinsic. The genioglossus forms the bulk of the tongue. Upon contraction, the posterior fibers of the genioglossus propel the tongue forward, allowing the tongue to be protruded from the mouth or to be pushed against the front teeth. Tongue retraction is achieved upon contraction of the anterior fibers of the genioglossus. When both the anterior and posterior fibers are contracted, the tongue is pulled downward. The styloglossus is an antagonist of the genioglossus. It pulls the tongue upward and backward upon contraction and elevates the lateral margins of the tongue. The hyoglossus, upon contraction, retracts and depresses the tongue. This muscle originates at the hyoid bone, and therefore, upon contraction, it may also elevate the hyoid bone and laryngeal complex. The styloglossus is responsible for retrusion (retraction) of the tongue and elevation of the lateral margins of the tongue. In addition to these three paired muscles, three smaller muscles are also considered to be extrinsic muscles by some anatomists: the palatoglossus, glossopharyngeus, and the chondroglossus muscles. Some texts do not consider these small muscles to be extrinsic or even distinct, individual muscles. Their functions specific to the tongue are

uncertain and likely work in concert with the other, larger muscles. It should be noted, however, that although the gross structures of the tongue are as described here, Miller, Watkin, and Chen (2002), in their study of variation in muscle, fat, and connective tissue, found that large differences exist across individuals.

Cranial nerve IX, the glossopharyngeal nerve, supplies general sensory innervation from the tongue root. Tactile sensation from the rest of the tongue is carried by the sensory fibers of CN XII, the hypoglossal nerve. Tongue sensation is extraordinarily refined, particularly at the tongue tip, where discrimination between points separated by less than 2 mm can be achieved. All the motor innervation to the intrinsic and extrinsic tongue muscles is provided by the hypoglossal nerve. This nerve is composed of a disproportionately large number of motoneurons, given the size of the tongue muscles, over 6,000 on each side (Atsumi & Miyatake, 1987). The exact functional significance of this arrangement is uncertain but suggests the potential for independent motor control of multiple focal areas of the tongue (Stone, Epstein, & Iskarous, 2004). (We should note, of course, that the primary purpose of the tongue is to facilitate food and liquid intake. However, swallowing function is complex and is best reserved for textbooks specifically focused on that topic.)

Understanding Tongue Movements

Although we identified the major function of each lingual muscle, in fact, no lingual gesture is achieved by contraction of only one muscle. The description of tongue movement is extraordinarily complex for several reasons. First, the arrangements of the muscles are themselves complex. Many of the muscle fibers are interwoven. For example, the fibers of the genioglossus are interlayered with the intrinsic transverse muscle fibers (Takemoto, 2001). Such interweaving makes it difficult to distinguish among the different muscles anatomically and functionally. Furthermore, tongue muscle fibers differ in size along their anterior-posterior dimension and differ in density along the medial-lateral dimension, suggesting differential function depending upon the focal area of contraction of a specific muscle. Only a few early electromyographic studies of the tongue have been conducted (Bole & Lessler, 1966; MacNeilage & Sholes, 1964; Miyawaki, 1975), perhaps because of the complexity of identification and analysis of tongue muscle movement.

Another factor contributing to the complexity of tongue movement control is the way in which tongue movement is achieved. The tongue is essentially a noncompressible structure, which means that if one area of the tongue is drawn inward (a focal compression), another area must bulge outward (a focal expansion). Constrictions in the oral and oral-pharyngeal cavities are achieved through tongue movement, which deforms the muscles of the tongue in one or more directions. Deformation is accomplished by contracting one or more muscles, resulting in a focal compression and corresponding expansion in another part of the tongue.

For any movable system, the theoretical possibilities for movement are greater than the actual movements achieved. That is, the tongue may be able to move in an almost limitless number of ways. However, in reality, not every tongue muscle movement is independent of the other tongue muscles. Contraction of certain fibers of one muscle may require contraction or passive stretch of one or more other muscles. We can say that both geometric and kinematic relationships between muscles constrain or limit the number of ways in which one or more tongue muscles can move independently. The various movements achieved by the tongue can be referred to as dimensions or **degrees of freedom**. The theoretically almost infinite number of degrees of freedom of tongue movement are reduced or constrained in number because of the kinematic and geometric relationships between groups of muscle fibers. We say, then, that the effective degrees of freedom are those that are actually usable. From a functional viewpoint, reduction in the potentially large number of degrees of freedom of a physiologic system helps to enable rapid and coordinated motor movement (Fowler, Rubin, Remez, & Turvey, 1980). As we have noted throughout our discussion of respiration, phonation, and now resonation and articulation, speech production consists of multiple synergistic muscle patterns of action. We will further explore the theories of synergy in speech production in Chapter 8. Identifying the dimensions or degrees of freedom of tongue movement is important because it can help scientists and clinicians to understand articulatory motor control for speech sounds.

Early theories of lingual motor control focused upon two degrees of freedom, the tongue tip and the body, which could then be used to describe the tongue contour or posture for different vowel sounds (Mermelstein, 1973). Subsequent mathematical analysis of tongue shapes identified only a few dimensions that could account for vowel tongue shape (Harshman, Ladefoged, & Goldstein, 1977; Kakita & Fujimura, 1977; Maeda, 1991; Stone, Goldstein, & Zhang, 1997). Most recently, however, use of sophisticated imaging techniques (described in this chapter and Chapter 8) suggests that tongue movement is considerably more complex, consisting of a greater number of degrees of freedom of the tongue than we previously thought, even for vowels (Stone, Epstein, & Iskarous, 2004; Wilhelms-Tricarico, 1995). Stone et al. (2004) developed a model of motor control in which the tongue is divided into multiple functional segments that can function in a coordinated but independent fashion, or move conjointly to achieve a given articulatory posture for sound production. Future research is needed to clarify tongue movement, how it is planned and achieved, and the resulting acoustic signal.

7.4 The Vocal Tract as a Regulator of Intensity

We have stated that formants are resonant characteristics of the vocal tract, independent of the presence or absence of a sound source. And we have stated that formants do not add energy but rather select certain frequencies to attenuate and other frequencies to radiate out of the mouth. But what happens when the glottal volume velocity is rich in harmonic energy compared to a source signal that has a lesser amount of energy? And how does the interaction of harmonic structure and formant characteristics affect the radiated intensity of the sound? We shall address these questions in order, first by comparing the vowel spectra of a low male voice and a high female voice. Then, we will revisit the voice range profile that was introduced in Chapter 6 and look more closely at the upper and lower intensity contours. Before we examine the power spectra, however, a word about energy loss is in order.

Harmonic Structure, Energy Loss, and Near-Periodicity

Our discussion of the acoustic theory of speech production assumes that no energy is lost in the vocal tract and that the voice source signal is completely periodic, but of course that is not true even in the healthiest of voice and speech production. The resonance curve of such a perfect vocal tract would look like a line spectrum, with each energy peak located at a single frequency (Figure 7–28, left). In reality, some energy is lost into the lungs through the open vocal folds, as discussed in Chapter 5; some energy is lost to the walls of the pharynx and mouth; and frictional forces result in loss of energy between the individual air particles. Furthermore, as we learned in Chapter 5, the source signal is nearly, but not perfectly, periodic. As a result, a resonance curve of the vocal tract shows peaks with a maximally resonant frequency and then gradually decreasing responsiveness (Figure 7–28, right). The shape of the resonance peaks, particularly the steepness of the slopes, is addressed further in the discussion of spectrography and acoustic filters.

In Figure 7–29, we see an idealized spectrum of the vowel /ɑ/ as it exits the vocal tract from a man phonating at a f_o of 100 Hz and woman phonating at a f_o of 200 Hz (A and B, respectively). Note that the frequency scale on the x-axis is the same for both the male and female spectrum. Immediately it is evident that the harmonics are more widely spaced in the spectrum from the woman than from that of the man. The reason is that the harmonics are integer multiples of the f_o. Therefore, only 100 Hz separate each of the harmonics in the male spectrum, whereas 200 Hz separate each of the harmonics of the female spectrum. The wider spacing of the harmonics associated with f_o means that less harmonic energy is available to be resonated by F1, F2, and F3. Compare the idealized spectra of Figure 7–29 with the actual spectra of Figure 7–30. We can distinguish still between the lower pitch (and more closely spaced harmonics) of the male voice (A) and the higher pitch (and wider spaced harmonics)

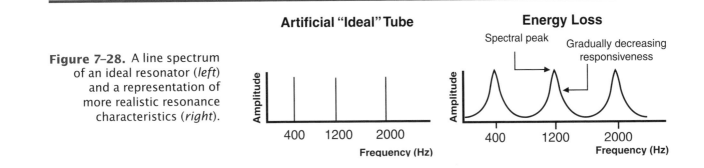

Figure 7–28. A line spectrum of an ideal resonator (*left*) and a representation of more realistic resonance characteristics (*right*).

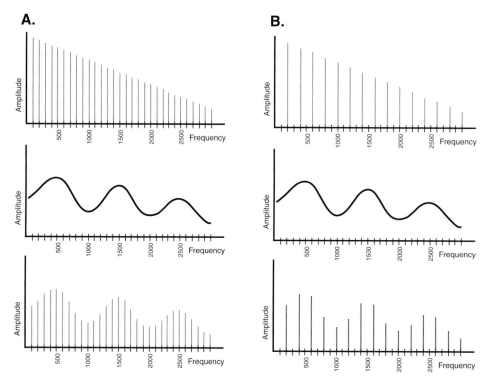

Figure 7–29. An idealized spectrum of the vowel /ɑ/ as it exits the vocal tract from a man phonating at an f_o of 100 Hz (**A**) and a woman phonating at an f_o of 200 Hz (**B**). Note that the harmonics are more widely spaced in the vowel with a higher f_o, resulting in less energy available at each formant frequency.

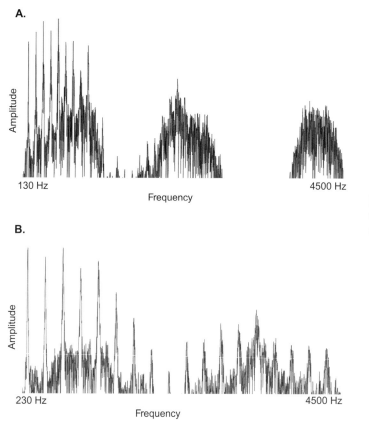

Figure 7–30. Actual power spectra of the sound wave radiated from the mouth for a man (**A**) and woman (**B**).

of the female voice (B), at least in the lower frequencies, despite the fact that these signals are not completely periodic.

Revisiting the Voice Range Profile

In Chapter 6, when we first discussed the voice range profile, it was noted that factors relating to the resonant characteristics of the vocal tract have a significant effect upon the shape of the voice range profile (VRP). Knowing now that resonant characteristics of the vocal tract attenuate certain frequencies and allow others to pass, it is reasonable to consider that formants affect the frequency intensity relationship. In particular, three vocal tract effects are noted, described in the following paragraphs.

First, examination of the upper contour of the VRP in Figure 7–31 reveals that, over most frequencies, maximal intensity increases with f_o. We had noted in Chapter 5 that this relationship was due to the fact that raising f_o is achieved by increasing vocal fold stiffness. In turn, the vocal folds offer increased glottal resistance, thereby allowing increased lung pressure with which to drive the oscillation. And recall that lung pressure is the major regulator of intensity. However, vocal tract resonance characteristics also contribute to intensity regulation. Titze (1992) demonstrates that the vocal tract radiates acoustic power more efficiently as f_o is raised. As seen in Figure 7–31, the maximum intensity contour rises as f_o is elevated. At the very highest frequencies, however, the spectral content of the voice signal contains less energy, and so less

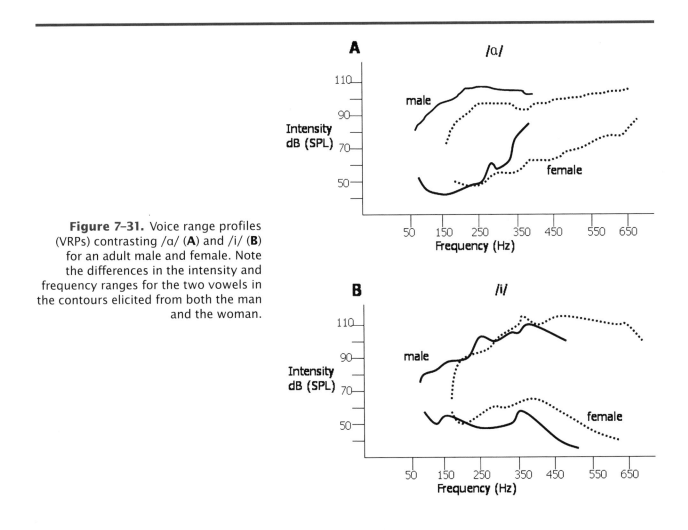

Figure 7–31. Voice range profiles (VRPs) contrasting /ɑ/ (**A**) and /i/ (**B**) for an adult male and female. Note the differences in the intensity and frequency ranges for the two vowels in the contours elicited from both the man and the woman.

incremental increase in intensity is obtained as f_o is raised further. And indeed, we note in Figure 7–31 that the upper contour ceases its steep rise and begins to flatten at the upper end of the frequency range.

A second vocal tract effect is that the vowel used to produce the VRP affects the overall contour of the plot. The use of the vowels /i/ and /ɑ/ are contrasted in Figure 7–31. We see that, in the range of the common speech frequencies, the contour is more restricted for /i/ as compared to /ɑ/. As we proceed upward into the higher frequencies, the contour for /i/ widens considerably, whereas the contour for the /ɑ/ becomes more restricted. These contrasts are due to the differences in formant frequencies for the two vowels. Recall our discussion earlier of harmonic structure and formants. We noted that when a harmonic is located far from a formant, the harmonic energy will be attenuated. The location of the harmonics depends upon the f_o, and so for any given vowel, moving the f_o will affect which harmonics are located near a formant. This same phenomenon affects the smoothness of the upper contour of the VRP.

The third vocal tract–influenced characteristic of the VRP can be seen in the slight irregularities of the upper contour, called a ripple effect (Titze, 1992). These small ripples represent fluctuations in maximal intensity due to the effect of the vocal tract filter function interacting with the f_o. The f_o and lower harmonics contain most of the energy in the sound source. As the frequency of the harmonic increases, it will intermittently match more closely the frequency of a formant. This process of increasing intensity when the f_o or one of its harmonics coincides with a formant frequency is called formant tuning. Formant tuning, also called vocal tract tuning, is what allows singers to produce sounds with great intensity and what allows some speakers, particularly actors, to "project" their voices across a large audience and helps increase overall intelligibility.

Singer's Formant and Formant Tuning

It is evident by now that the vocal tract is essential to the formulation of meaningful speech. The voice source signal provides the raw material, but the filter function of the vocal tract provides much of the meaning, without which our communication would be highly limited. Although the purpose of this text is to describe the science of speech, a moment spent examining the singing voice will help highlight the contribution of the vocal tract to sound intensity and quality.

Many trained singers can tune their vocal tract to match the f_o or one or more harmonics of the sound source with the frequency of one or more formants. The effect of formant tuning is to make the sound louder and improve certain aspects of the quality. (The quality of the singing voice is beyond the scope of our discussion here. We shall just say that certain perceptual features of the singing voice are influenced by formant tuning.) How do singers tune their vocal tract? They alter their vocal tract posture to shift the formant frequencies. These alterations are very slight but have a substantial effect. Knowing that the vowel quality is specified by the formant frequency, we would expect the vowel to change as a result of the formant tuning. In fact, the vowel quality does change, but usually so slightly that, within the song, the listener does not hear the change in vowel, only the result of greater intensity and improved quality.

One vocal tract adaptation commonly achieved by singers, particularly classical singers, is called the singer's formant. The singer's formant results in a spectral peak around 2500 to 3000 Hz, which is believed to be a clustering together of the third, fourth, and fifth formants (Sundberg, 1987, 2001). These formants may not be essential to specify vowel quality, as are the first and second formants. Therefore, the singer's formant can be achieved independently of the specific vowel being produced. The singer's formant is attributed to a lowered larynx and a widened hypopharyngeal space, which produces an enlarged resonance cavity that provides additional "carrying power" and richness to the voice. Formants can be tuned downward: that is, the frequency of the formant can be lowered, but in general formants are tuned upward so that the frequency of the spectral peak is raised.

Speaker's Formant

Although less well recognized and researched, the speaking voice also may be characterized in certain instances by notable energy in the area of the fourth and fifth harmonic. Called a speaker's formant or ring, this peak in the spectrum is not as large in amplitude as the singer's formant and is located approximately 1 kHz higher, around 3 to 4 kHz (Nawka, Anders, Cebulla, & Zurakwski, 1997; Raphael & Scherer, 1987; Sundberg, 1974). The speaker's formant is found most often in trained voices, such as those of stage actors, although not consistently (Bele, 2006). The spectral peak identified as the speaker's formant is likely a result of two factors. One is a lowered laryngeal position, which widens the hypopharyngeal space, similar to the vocal tract tuning leading to the singer's formant. However, the formant can only resonate the energy supplied to it. Thus, the second factor is adjustment of vocal fold vibration to boost the amplitude of the higher frequency harmonics. Recall our earlier discussion of the ideal 12-dB per octave roll-off. In the case of the speaker's formant, the envelope of the power spectrum of the vocal source may not fall off as steeply, thereby providing more harmonic energy in the 3- to 4-kHz region. Although our discussion focuses on the normal voice, it should be mentioned that abnormal and undesirable vocal qualities also may produce a speaker's formant (Bele, 2006). As we learned in Chapter 5, rapid and forceful closure of the vocal folds can produce greater amplitude of the harmonics. Although this spectral characteristic would then contribute to the speaker's formant, the means of achieving the increased amplitude can be traumatic to the vocal folds and generate an unpleasant-sounding voice.

Study Questions

26. What are three effects of vocal tract resonance on intensity, as reflected in the shape of the voice range profile?
27. What is the singer's formant? The speaker's formant?

7.5 Acoustic Filters

The source filter theory tells us that the vocal tract selectively resonates, or filters, a subset of harmonics of the glottal volume velocity for radiating out past the lips. When we consider formants and speak of their *location*, we really are referring to two specific characteristics of the formant, its **center frequency** and its **bandwidth**. (For our present purposes, we shall not address formant amplitude in this discussion.) Let us return for a moment to our analogy of the filters we use in the kitchen (Figure 7–32). A coffee filter is made of porous material so that the water can escape through tiny holes in the paper, whereas the coffee grounds, too large for the holes, remain trapped in the filter. We do not need to use porous paper to strain the water out of a pot of spaghetti, however. It would take too long to drain the water. Our pasta would surely become cold! The pasta is so much larger than the individual coffee grounds, it is more efficient to use a filter with much larger holes, a plastic or wire mesh strainer. The difference between the two common kitchen filters can be described by the size of the particles allowed to pass. An **acoustic filter** acts similarly, in that it selectively passes certain frequency components of

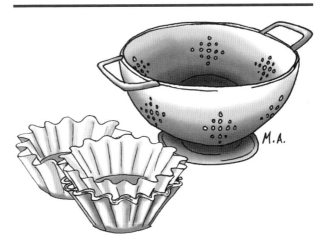

Figure 7–32. The coffee filters and strainer are size sensitive, in that they allow material to pass through depending upon its size. Acoustic filters such as the vocal tract, however, are frequency sensitive.

a complex wave. Rather than simply passing or blocking frequencies, like the kitchen strainers, it passes certain frequencies more fully, or more effectively, than other frequencies. Said another way, certain frequencies will be attenuated (decreased in amplitude) to a relatively lesser degree than other frequencies. Less **attenuation** means more of the energy of the selected frequency component is allowed to be transmitted.

Some acoustic filters are **low-pass filters**, in which case they block the high-frequency components of the wave and allow the low-frequency components to be passed. Other filters are **high-pass acoustic filters**, in which case the low-frequency components of the sound wave are blocked and the high-frequency components are passed through (Figure 7–33). The **frequency cutoff** is the delimiting frequency. In a high-pass acoustic filter, the cutoff frequency would be that frequency below which all frequencies would be damped (not allowed to pass). In a low-pass acoustic filter, the cutoff frequency would be that frequency above which all frequencies would be damped. A filter can have both a low- and a high-pass cutoff. In such case, a specified range of frequencies *between* the low- and high-pass cutoff frequencies would be filtered effectively. A filter with both a low- and a high-pass cutoff would be called a **bandpass filter** because a band of frequencies is specified that will be allowed to pass through (Figure 7–34).

Filters can have sharp or broad boundaries. You can see in Figure 7–35 that the sharp cutoff

of the filter has a very steep slope, whereas the broad boundary has a much more gradual slope. We say that the filters are **sharply or broadly tuned**. Let us say that we have a filter with a high-pass cutoff frequency of 500 Hz. In theory, any frequency above 500 Hz would be attenuated (damped) nearly completely. In reality, it is impossible to have a filter so sharply tuned. Instead, the frequencies immediately above 500 Hz are gradually attenuated as their frequencies increase. The faster the frequencies are attenuated above 500 Hz, the more sharply tuned is the filter. How much does the acoustic energy have to be attenuated in order to say that the

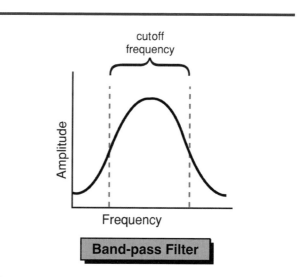

Band-pass Filter

Figure 7–34. The band-pass filter allows a range of frequencies to be passed.

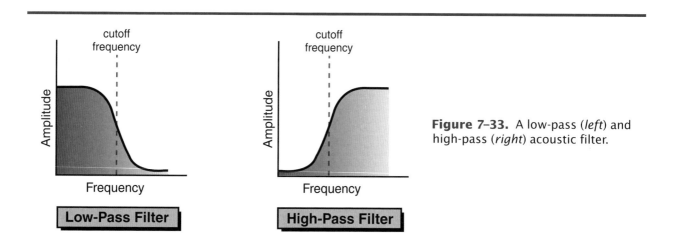

Low-Pass Filter

High-Pass Filter

Figure 7–33. A low-pass (*left*) and high-pass (*right*) acoustic filter.

filter does not allow the frequency component to pass? By convention, it is identified as the **half-power point**. That is, the cutoff frequency is defined as the frequency at which the amplitude of the frequency component is decreased by 3 dB (half of its power) (Figure 7–36). Using the "**3 dB down**" criteria, we can redefine a filter bandwidth as the frequency range between the points on the slopes of the resonance curve where the response is 3 dB lower than at the peak.

Formants act as bandpass filters, characterized by their center frequency and bandwidth. The center frequency is the midpoint or peak

of the filter. It represents the frequency that is allowed to pass with the greatest amplitude. The bandwidth is the range of frequencies between the low- and high-pass cutoff frequencies. The bandwidth specifies the range of frequencies that are allowed to pass, although with varying amounts of attenuation. For this reason, the **resonance curve** of a filter also can be referred to as the **attenuation curve**. The degree of attenuation of a given frequency component depends upon its frequency location. That is, how far it is from the center frequency (or, conversely, how close to the cutoff frequency). In other words, we can say that the bandwidth is determined by the slopes of the filter. **Bandwidth** is the width (in Hz) of the filter's peak such that half of the acoustic energy is contained within the stated bandwidth. One of the most common types of acoustic analysis, sound spectrography, requires a good understanding of filters.

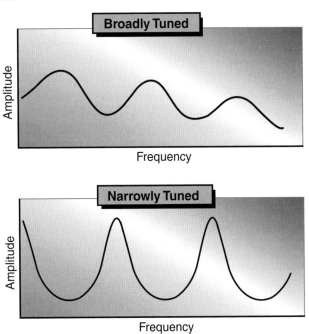

Figure 7–35. The sharply (narrowly) tuned filter is characterized by relatively steeper slopes than the more broadly tuned filter.

Study Questions

28. What are the center frequency and the bandwidth of a filter (formant)?

29. What is the effect of an acoustic filter on the frequencies of a complex sound wave?

30. What is a high-pass filter? Low-pass filter? Bandpass filter?

31. What is the difference between a sharply and a broadly tuned filter?

32. What is the half-power point on a filter?

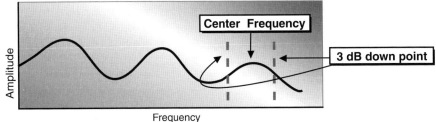

Figure 7–36. The cutoff frequencies of this bandpass filter specify the points at which the amplitude of the frequency components is decreased by 3 dB (half of its power).

7.6 Instrumentation for Measuring Vocal Tract Acoustics

Sound Spectrography

Sound spectrography (synonymously but less commonly used, sonography) is the graphic representation of the frequency and intensity of the sound pressure wave as a function of time. In the 1940s, Potter, Kopp, and Green, scientists working for Bell Laboratories in New Jersey, developed instrumentation to achieve sound spectrography. Motivated largely by World War II and the goal of identifying enemy voices, the instrumentation enabled graphic detail of short-term speech spectral information (Figure 7–37). In 1947, they published a book describing their work, *Visible Speech*, the name of which was borrowed from the title of the 1882 book by Alexander Melville Bell (1819–1905), the father of Alexander Graham Bell (1847–1922), the inventor of the telephone in 1875 (Millman, 1984). The first commercially available instrument, called a Sona-Graph, was marketed in the early 1950s by Kay Electric Company (now part of Pentax Medical, Lincoln Park, NJ). Now commonly called a spectrograph, the instrumentation has evolved over the decades with new technology, of course, and currently it is one of the most commonly used means of analyzing speech sounds. A spectrograph produces a **spectrogram**, a graphic representation of the energy of the frequency components of the speech signal as a function of time. By convention, time is plotted along the horizontal x-axis, and frequency is plotted along the vertical y-axis. The third dimension lies along the z-axis, which contains the energy or amplitude of the signal. The energy is commonly represented by the gray scale, with darker gray representing greater energy. Sometimes, energy is represented by different colors instead of shades of gray. Spectrography is a basic analytic tool of speech sounds, and therefore some time is spent here exploring this instrumentation. Additional sources of information on sound spectrography can be found in Kent and Read (1992), Baken and Orlikoff (2000), and Howard (2002).

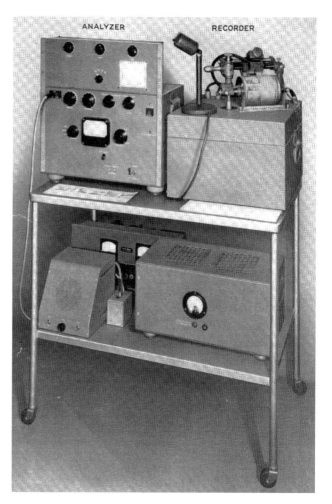

Figure 7–37. One of the earliest sound spectrographs, developed by Bell Telephone Laboratories in 1947. From *Visible Speech* by R. K. Potter, G. A. Kopp, and J. G. Green. 1947, New York: Van Nostrand. Reprinted with permission from Dover Publications, Inc.

Spectrography is based on the Fourier theorem. Recall from Chapter 3 that the Fourier theorem states that all periodic waveforms can be decomposed as the sum of a series of sine waves with frequencies in a harmonic series at specific phase relationships to one another. Fourier analysis is the process of separating a complex wave into its component sine waves. A spectrogram contains a large amount of information, not all of which can be displayed clearly at once. In creating a spectrogram, one must decide whether to display spectral information about the sound source or the filter function.

This decision is part of the time-frequency trade-off, as explained below.

Narrowband and Wideband Spectrograms

Time is the inverse of frequency. Recall the relationship of waveform period and frequency, where frequency is equal to 1/t and, inversely, the period is equal to 1/f. A spectrogram may present detailed information about the harmonic structure of the source signal or precise information about the resonant characteristics of the vocal tract. Both sets of information cannot be displayed with equal clarity at the same time because time and frequency are inversely related. A tradeoff exists in the analytic detail of the source or the filter function. The detail with which the frequency or time information is displayed is referred to as the frequency or time resolution, respectively. Most commonly, the resolution is described as the **filter bandwidth**. A narrow bandwidth resolves frequency information well but has poor time resolution. Conversely, a wide bandwidth resolves frequency information poorly but the time resolution is good.

Figure 7–38 illustrates the reasoning behind these bandwidth characteristics. The small funnel represents a narrow bandwidth filter. Individual frequencies are passed through the funnel one at a time, which means that on the output side of the funnel, each frequency remains separated. However, the small funnel size means that it will take a long time to filter all the frequencies in the speech sample. The funnel is slow. The large funnel represents a wide bandwidth filter. Several frequencies can pass through the funnel at one time. Although this means that the funneling process will be much faster, the frequencies on the output side of the funnel are clumped together and cannot be distinguished from one another. The large funnel "processes" frequencies very quickly in time but does not resolve the frequency information clearly.

In Figure 7–39, again we see that the narrowband filter setting "sees" the individual harmonics. The wideband filter setting "sees" a few harmonics at once. Thus, in spectrographic analysis, a narrow bandwidth, or simply a narrowband filter, will resolve frequency information well and time information poorly. A wideband filter will resolve time information well but frequency information poorly.

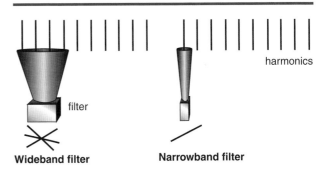

Wideband filter   **Narrowband filter**

Figure 7–38. The narrowband filter provides greater detail about the frequency information (a better frequency response) but the wideband filter is faster, providing better time resolution.

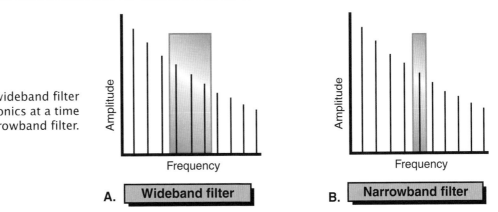

Figure 7–39. The wideband filter "sees" more harmonics at a time than does the narrowband filter.

A. **Wideband filter**   B. **Narrowband filter**

Before digital spectrography, the bandwidth of the analysis window was often set to 45 Hz to resolve frequency information and 300 Hz to resolve time information. These filters were identified as narrowband and wideband, respectively, because they are narrower or wider than the average speaking f_o of men and women. In digital spectrography, the filter is determined by the number of samples, or points, which are analyzed as a unit (Kent & Read, 1992). However, the terminology of a wideband or narrowband filter is still used generally. Digital systems allow the user to select the width of the analysis filter by window length or digital sampling points. A window length of 0.025 seconds, for example, corresponds to a narrowband filter, while a window length of 0.005 seconds corresponds to a wideband filter setting. When setting the filter using digital sampling points (50, 75, 100, 125, 200, 256, 612, 1,024), the lower number of points equates to a wideband analog filter setting and the higher number of points equates to a narrowband filter setting. (To help avoid confusion, refer to Table 7–6.) What filter setting should be used when creating a spectrogram? It depends on what information the speech pathologist wishes to examine. Let us examine several different spectrograms and the answer will become evident.

Exploring Spectrograms

Figure 7–40 displays a narrowband and wideband spectrogram of the vowel /i/. Spectral information about the source is shown clearly in the narrowband spectrogram, represented by the parallel dark lines. The lowest horizontal dark line represents the f_o and the successively higher parallel lines represent the harmonics. Recall that the gray scale represents intensity, so that the darker harmonics contain more energy. We know from our earlier examination of power spectra that the f_o and lower harmonics contain more energy than the higher harmonics. Why, then, are some of the harmonics in the middle frequencies lighter gray than the harmonics in the higher frequencies? The reason is that harmonic energy is attenuated when it does not coincide closely with a formant frequency. Note that in Table 7–5, the frequencies for the first and second formants for /i/ for women are 437 Hz and 2761 Hz, respectively. The f_o of the source signal in Figure 7–40 is approximately 230 Hz. We would expect, therefore, that the harmonics in the vicinity of F1 and F2 would be passed, whereas the harmonics far from the formant frequencies would be attenuated. Note that the spectral peaks associated with the formant frequencies are evident only by inferring their location from the relative gray scale of the harmonic lines. That is, we would infer that a formant is not located in the mid-frequencies where the harmonics are very light gray.

Examine now the wideband spectrogram in Figure 7–40. Note that the individual harmonics are not resolved clearly. Instead, we see two features. First, broader bands of energy (dark gray) are evident. These are the **spectral peaks** associated with the vocal tract formants. Note that the spectral peaks are much more clearly identifiable in the wideband spectrogram than in the narrowband spectrogram. The second notable feature is the presence of vertical striations. These striations are representative of the glot-

Table 7–6. Filter Bandwidth Settings Available in the Digital Spectrography Instrumentation by Kay/Pentax (Lincoln Park, NJ)

	Sampling Points	**Frequency**
Wideband	50	1,464.84
	75	976.56
	100	732.42
	125	585.94
	200	366.21
	256	286.10
	600	122.07
	512	143.05
Narrowband	1,024	71.53

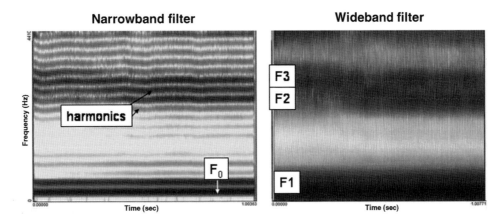

Figure 7–40. Narrow- and wideband spectrograms of the vowel /i/. The narrowband spectrogram (*left*) displays the source characteristics (the harmonics) clearly, represented by the narrow, parallel lines. The wideband spectrogram (*right*) displays the vocal tract filter function (the formants) more clearly, represented by the broad horizontal bands of dark gray. However, the effect of the formants is also evident in the narrowband spectrogram: Note that the harmonics that have frequencies close to the formants have darker gray bands (representing more energy). The harmonics whose frequencies are far from the formants frequencies have lighter gray (less energy). In the wideband spectrogram, the source characteristics are evident in the vertical striations, each of which represent one cycle of vocal fold vibration.

tal pulses, the successive opening and closing of the vocal folds. The wideband spectrogram resolves time well, and so the rapid oscillations of the vocal folds are evident, whereas the frequency information of the individual harmonics is smeared together to reveal the spectral peaks of the resonant characteristics of the formant frequencies.

Examine the wide- and narrowband spectrograms of Figure 7–41. The utterance is a sustained /i/ but the f_o is gradually raised. The narrowband spectrogram reveals an upward shift in the harmonic structure, consistent with the change in the pitch. As the f_o is raised, the harmonics similarly increase in frequency because they are integer multiples of the f_o. Observe that as the f_o is raised, some of the harmonics become lighter or dark gray. We know that gray scale represents energy, and so the change in the darkness of the harmonic lines must mean that the energy in the harmonics is changing. As the harmonic frequencies change, the harmonics move closer to or farther from the frequencies of the formants. (Recall that the vocal tract filter function and hence the formant frequencies are not changing because the vowel remains constant in this task.) We could say that the harmonics move into and out of the formants.

Now examine the wideband spectrogram of Figure 7–41. Note that, as the f_o is raised, the vertical striations move closer together. The vertical striations represent the cycles of glottal opening and closing, which proceeds at a faster rate as the f_o is elevated. Observe, however, that the location of the formants does not change. Raising the f_o does not change the vowel. The vocal tract articulatory posture remained constant, and so the formant frequencies remained unchanged. In summary, narrowband filtering provides good resolution of the harmonic (frequency) structure of the source signal, whereas wideband filtering provides good time resolution of the glottal pulses and formant structure of the vocal tract.

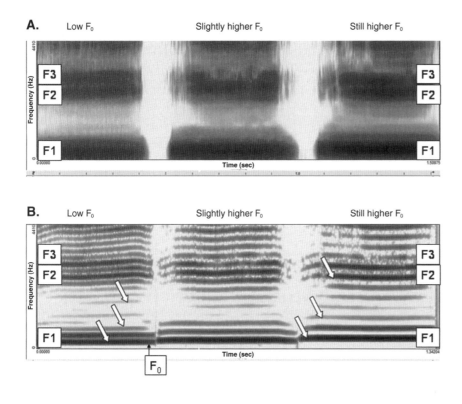

Figure 7–41. Wide- (**A**) and narrowband (**B**) spectrograms of the vowel /i/ sustained at three pitches, each pitch progressively higher than the previous pitch (*left to right*). Note that the location of the formants does not change, that is, the same vowel is produced at each pitch. Note, however, that as the pitch is increased successively, the location of the f_o and harmonics moves upward (*arrows*). The harmonics move into and out of the formants.

Linear Predictive Coding

Although spectral analysis is based upon the Fourier theorem, Fourier analysis is not the only means of decoding the spectral information in the sound pressure wave. In certain cases, another method is preferable, called **linear predictive** (or prediction) **coding (LPC)**. To understand LPC, we need to recognize that the sound pressure waveform is a time-series event. That is, the waveform represents an event, alternating compressions and rarefactions of air molecules, as it evolves over time. Both Fourier analysis and LPC transform the time-series waveform into a frequency-based spectrum, in which the frequency components of the speech signal and their respective amplitudes are represented at some window (snapshot) in time. Whereas Fourier analysis represents the amplitude of the f_o and harmonics, LPC represents the amplitude of the formant frequencies. LPC is based on the fact that the time-series speech signal is relatively predictable, meaning that from a statistical point of view, a given point or set of points in the signal can be estimated, or predicted, from the preceding point or set of points. The mathematics of LPC far exceeds the present discussion. It turns out, however, that the terms in the equation used to predict, or model, the subsequent set of points in the signal provide the frequencies and respective amplitudes of the spectral peaks, which represent the vocal tract formants (Kent & Read, 1992).

The methods of Fourier transform and LPC each have advantages and limitations (Monsen & Engebretson, 1983). Fourier analysis is based upon the assumption of a periodic signal, whereas LPC makes no such assumption. Therefore, the latter method is preferable for highly irregular voice signals. Both methods lose precision in the analysis of high f_o above

350 Hz. LPC can provide erroneous information when two formants are located very near to each other, making it appear as though only one formant exists (Ladefoged, 1996, p. 210). And LPC analysis can be inaccurate in the analysis of nasal phonemes, to be discussed in Chapter 8. However, LPC analysis can be very helpful in identifying formants when the Fourier-based spectrogram is difficult to decipher. In most instances, however, the decision of which analytic method to use is based upon the information one wants to acquire. In Figure 7–42, we can see that LPC provides a spectrum envelope from which one can measure the formants but no harmonic detail. The Fourier-based spectrum provides harmonic detail, but it is difficult to infer formant information from the spectrum. Often, both a Fourier-based and an LPC spectrum are displayed together, making it easier to interpret both vocal source and filter function information. For a more complete discussion of LPC, see Ladefoged (1996).

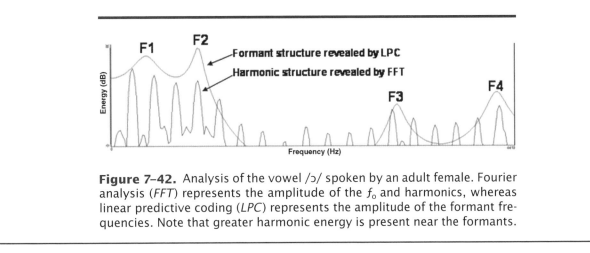

Figure 7–42. Analysis of the vowel /ɔ/ spoken by an adult female. Fourier analysis (*FFT*) represents the amplitude of the f_o and harmonics, whereas linear predictive coding (*LPC*) represents the amplitude of the formant frequencies. Note that greater harmonic energy is present near the formants.

Eight vowels are presented in the wideband spectrograms of Figure 7–43. (The LPC-generated resonance curves are represented in Figure 7–12.) Compare these figures to the stylized graphic representation of the formant frequencies of Figure 7–15. The systematic relationship of the first three formants discussed earlier is clearly evident in the spectrograms of these vowels. For the front vowels, the frequency locations of the first and second formants are generally spaced rather far apart, whereas the frequencies of the second and third formants are generally located close to each other. For the back vowels, F1 and F2 are located close to each other, whereas F2 and F3 are farther apart.

In Figure 7–44, we see the formant structure for the diphthongs. Compare their structure to that represented in the stylized spectrograms of Figure 7–23. As discussed earlier, note the presence of onglides and offglides. Also, note how it is difficult to find the steady-state portion of diphthongs, as compared to the monophthongal vowels.

Figure 7–45 presents the wideband spectrograms for the central and rhotacized vowels. In general, for the central vowels, the vocal tract more closely approximates the uniform cross-sectional tube model discussed earlier in the chapter. Recall that the values of F1, F2, and F3 for the 17.5-cm uniform tube were calculated as 500 Hz, 1500 Hz, and 2500 Hz, respectively. For the most central of the vowels, /ɔ/ and /ə/, note that the formant frequencies of these "real" vowels closely approximate this ideal vocal tract. The rhotacized vowels /ɝ/ and /ɚ/ are characterized by a very low frequency for F3, a distinguishing

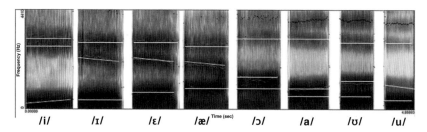

Figure 7–43. Wideband spectrograms of eight vowels. White lines have been superimposed on each vowel to indicate F1 (*bottom*), F2 (*middle*), and F3 (*top*). Compare to the stylized representation in Figure 7–15. Note once again that as the vowel quality moves from high to low front, F2 lowers, drawing F1 and F2 progressively closer together. Note also that for the back vowels, F2 and F3 are spaced relatively far apart.

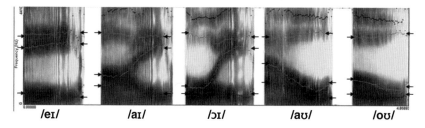

Figure 7–44. Wideband spectrograms of diphthongs.

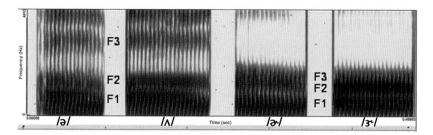

Figure 7–45. Wideband spectrograms of the central vowels /ə/ and /ʌ/, and the rhotics /ɚ/ and /ɝ/. Note that the frequency of F3 is quite low for the rhotics, making it difficult to distinguish between the second and third formants.

feature of /r/ (which we will observe in Chapter 8) and r-colored vowels.

Nearly Periodic Voice Source

Recall that the vocal source signal is nearly, but not completely, periodic. The slight jitter (cycle-to-cycle variability of the fundamental fre-quency) is clearly apparent in the narrowband spectrogram of Figure 7–40. Note that as the harmonic frequencies increase, the waviness of the harmonic lines increases. Why is that? Consider for a moment a voice source signal of 200 Hz with a normal jitter value of 0.5%. In other words, the f_o varies from cycle to cycle by 1 Hz (0.5% × 200 Hz). The fifth harmonic would therefore vary by [200 × 5] × 0.5% or 5 Hz. The tenth harmonic would vary by [200 × 10] × 0.5% or 10 Hz. Variability of 5 or 10 Hz is more visible in the spectrogram than 1-Hz variability. So, although the percentage of jitter is the same across all harmonics, it results in wider variability of the upper harmonics.

Voiceprints: Voice Science or Science Fiction?

Popular movies have often depicted sound spectrography as a method of identifying the "bad guy." The computer compares two voice samples, we see a waveform and a spectrogram displayed, and then the computer identifies the suspect with 98% accuracy. Case solved! Unfortunately, the state of the science is far removed from such science fiction. Each person does have an individual voice. And it is likely that the frequencies of the fourth and fifth formants are most sensitive to relative vocal quality (Ladefoged, 2006, p. 189), but not to the extent that a single speaker can be identified with great certainty. Spectrograms may be marked by individuality based upon the speaker's somewhat unique habits of speech, independent of phonologic and linguistic rules. For example, vowel duration and extent of aspiration may differ across individuals. As Ladefoged (1996) points out, spectral analysis might only identify that two speakers are *probably not* the same voice or *could be* the same voice. The use of phonetic sciences in the legal system is called forensic phonetics. Although forensic phoneticians apply the theories and instrumentation of speech science to various legal problems in a valid manner, the use of voice prints as a surefire method of identifying an individual remains exclusively the purview of the entertainment industry (Figure 7–46).

Quantitative Spectral Measures

Visual examination of spectrograms provides a wealth of information about the voice source and vocal tract filter characteristics of the sound pressure wave (Figure 7–47). Often, however,

Figure 7–46. Reading spectrograms is both an art and a science!

greater objectivity is needed in characterizing certain features of the spectrograms. The long-term average spectrum and the harmonics to noise ratio are two measures that offer more objective measures.

Long-Term Average Spectrum

The **long-term average spectrum (LTAS)** is an averaging of the spectral energy over a window of a specified duration of sustained vowel phonation (Löfqvist & Mandersson, 1987). The LTAS is particularly helpful when assessing features of the spectrum that are consistently present, rather than those that may be momentary phenomena. Examine the narrowband spectrogram shown in Figures 7–47 and 7–48. The left-hand portion of the spectrogram appears typical, with relatively straight and parallel dark lines

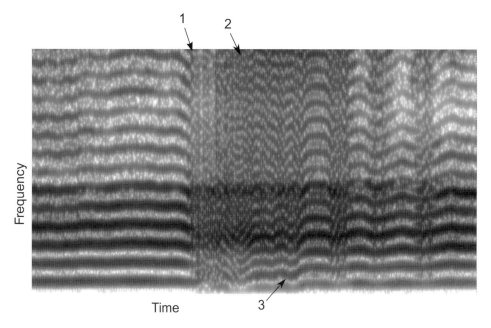

Figure 7–47. This narrowband spectrogram of sustained vowel phonation was elicited from an individual with a voice disorder. Her voice started out almost sounding normal but then changed in an irregular fashion. Note: (1) the voice break, seen as a distinct "jump" in the frequency of the harmonics, (2) the weak and noisy high-frequency harmonics, and (3) the considerable variability of the low-frequency harmonics. Compare these features to the relatively straight and parallel black lines (harmonics) on the left-hand portion of the spectrogram.

representing a consistent f_o and higher harmonics of sustained vowel phonation. As we examine the spectrogram moving forward in time, however, moving toward the right side of the figure, the harmonic structure appears less orderly. We can obtain the LTAS of different segments of the acoustic signal to compare different phonatory phenomena. Note that in this case, it makes more sense to obtain two separate LTAS rather than one LTAS of the entire sample because the voice source characteristics were changeable across the sample.

The LTAS has been used to assess overall perceived intelligibility of speakers (Hazan & Markham, 2004) and voice quality (Laukkanen, Björkner, & Sundberg, 2006). An interesting application of the LTAS is found in a study by White (2001), who had a group of listeners judge the perceived sex of a group of young children's voices.

The author found that young children whom the listeners accurately perceived to be boys had a spectral peak at 5 kHz in the LTAS, whereas those accurately perceived to be girls did not.

Harmonics to Noise Ratio

Examine again the spectrogram in Figure 7–48. The presence of noise, energy between the harmonics, is notable. Although visual inspection of narrowband spectrograms is an excellent method for analyzing voice source characteristics, it is often helpful to have a quantitative measure of the spectral noise. The **harmonics to noise ratio (H/N)** (Yanagihara, 1967; Yumoto, Gould, & Baer, 1982) is a numerical evaluation of the ratio of the energy in the fundamental and harmonics to the energy in the aperiodic, or noise component of the speech signal, averaged

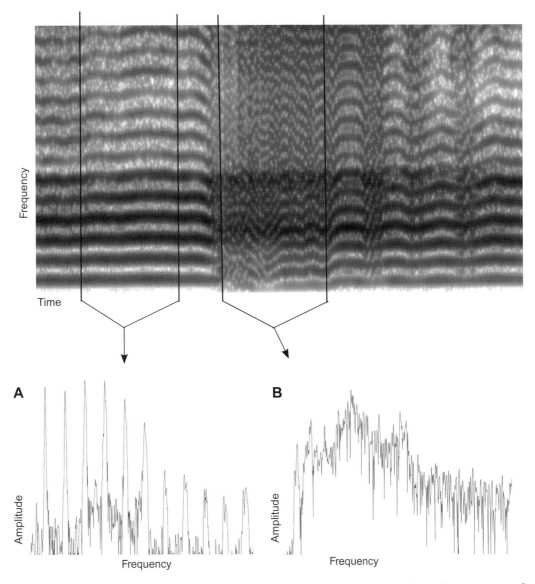

Figure 7–48. Long-term average spectra (*LTAS*) corresponding to selected segments of the narrowband spectrogram. Note that the x- and y-axes of the spectrogram correspond to time and frequency, respectively, whereas in the LTAS, the x-axis represents frequency and the y-axis represents energy. **A.** This LTAS shows well-defined harmonics and a low level of noise energy, consistent with the left-hand segment of the spectrogram. **B.** This LTAS shows poorly defined harmonics and noise throughout all frequencies. The corresponding right-hand segment of the spectrogram similarly shows less clearly defined harmonic structure.

over several cycles. Yumoto et al. (1982) found that the typical H/N from healthy speakers averaged 11.9 dB, whereas those with vocal pathologies had H/Ns well below that level. In general, the H/N correlates well with the perception of voice abnormality (de Krom, 1995). The H/Ns for the left and right segments in Figure 7–45 are 11.3 dB and 9.2 dB, respectively.

Cepstral Measures

In Chapter 6, we examined metrics that quantify the irregularity in the frequency (jitter) and intensity (shimmer) of the acoustic signal. And now we have also learned about H/N as a measure of vocal quality. These measures are time-based, meaning that they rely upon accurate identification of cycle boundaries—where a cycle begins and ends. Yet we know that, in disordered voices, vocal fold vibration can be far from periodic. In cases of irregular oscillation, identification of cycle boundaries can be unreliable. Thus, calculation of measures such as jitter, shimmer, and H/N may not be appropriate in moderate-to-severe dysphonia (Bielamowicz, Kreiman, Gerratt, Dauer, & Berke, 1996).

The spectral-based method of **cepstral analysis** (Noll, 1964) can overcome the significant weakness of time-based measures. (Note that the first four letters of cepstral are re-arranged from the word spectrum.) The cepstrum is a Fourier transform of the power spectrum that shows the extent to which the f_o and harmonic structure stand out from the background noise. The dominant cepstral peak reflects the periodicity and energy in the voice signal. The greater the periodicity and the higher the energy, the greater the amplitude of the dominant cepstral peak.

Cepstral analysis does not rely upon identification of individual vibratory cycles. Therefore, it is robust with respect to dysphonic voices. In other words, it remains valid even when the vocal signal is not periodic. Furthermore, it can be used as an "objective" measure of vocal quality. The relative amplitude of the dominant cepstral peak (the **cepstral peak prominence**, or **CPP**) has been shown to correlate well with perception of breathiness (Hillenbrand, Cleveland, & Ericson. 1994; Hillenbrand & Houde, 1996) and abnormal vocal quality (de Krom, 1995; Wolf, Martin, & Palmer, 2000). A strong advantage of using the CPP is that it can be calculated from sustained vowels or continuous speech (Heman-Ackah, Michael & Goding, 2002). In addition to the CPP, other cepstral based metrics have been explored, including the low/high spectral ratio and the standard deviation of the low/high spectral ratio. All cepstral-based measures may be sensitive to the phonemic content of the utterances upon which the metrics are based (Lowell & Hylkema, 2016). Therefore, researchers and clinicians who use these measures should document the utterances carefully.

Inverse Filtering

In the exploration of normal vocal function and the diagnosis of abnormal voice production, it can be helpful to assess the glottal volume velocity (Fritzell, 1992). We learned in Chapter 4 that the glottal volume velocity, the flow of the volume of air through the glottis, is determined by the interaction of the aerodynamic forces and the viscoelastic properties of the vocal fold tissues. However, we now know that the glottal volume velocity is not the same as the airflow exiting the oral cavity. The resonant characteristics of the vocal tract and the lip radiation characteristics have altered the glottal volume velocity. How, then, do we obtain information about the glottal volume velocity? Certainly it is not practical to measure it at the level of the glottis, for that would require a pressure transducer to be placed just above the vocal folds, something that most people could not tolerate easily. The solution is found in **inverse filtering** the speech signal at the lips.

Inverse filtering was first proposed by Miller (1959). Whereas the vocal tract filters the source signal, inverse filtering performs an inverse of the vocal tract filter, removing the filtering characteristics of the vocal tract. Recovering the acoustic pressure wave at the level of the glottis, the glottal volume velocity, is a complex task. In effect, inverse filtering is an estimate of the glottal flow signal from the speech signal. The technique currently involves capture of the airflow during speech as it exits the oral cavity using a face mask (Rothenberg, 1973, 1977). The vocal tract transfer function is estimated through complex mathematics beyond the scope of this text. Several mathematical assumptions are made in the process of inverse filtering. Exploration of the inverse filtered waveform and its spectral characteristics have been shown to relate to vocal quality, particularly breathiness and loudness (Fritzell, Hammarberg, Gauffin, Karlsson, & Sundberg, 1986). A shortcoming of inverse filtering, however, is that to some extent, the removal of the vocal tract resonance characteristics from the vocal sound source is a bit of trial and error. Instrumental controls allow the investigator to manipulate the output waveform until it appears to be free of formant influences. In this way, the process does presuppose that the investigator knows what the glottal flow waveform *should* look like. Current research continues to improve inverse filtering methodology (Alku, Story, & Airas, 2006; Lehto, Airas, Björkner, Sundberg, & Alku, 2007).

7.7 Vocal Tract Imaging: Current Research and Future Trends

Imaging vocal tract postures provides essential information about the relationships among articulatory dynamics, formant frequencies, and perceptual acoustic vowel space. Several approaches have been used over the past 80 years, each method dependent upon the state of the imaging science of the day. Early pioneering studies used x-rays (Chiba & Kajiyama, 1941; Heinz & Stevens, 1964). They provided early validation of the acoustic theory of speech production (Fant, 1960) and lay the foundation for the early seminal work on formants, such as that of Stevens and House (1955). As technology advanced, computed tomography, magnetic resonance imaging, and ultrasound imaging have been used to increase our knowledge of vocal tract dynamics. These approaches have in common the advantage of being noninvasive, meaning that the skin is not pierced or cut. A broader definition of noninvasive would include avoiding entering a body cavity to any significant extent. Placing a tongue depressor into the mouth is considered noninvasive, whereas placing an endoscope through the nose and down the throat to examine vocal fold vibration would be considered invasive (although minimally so). No technique is best for all purposes. Each technique has a set of advantages and limitations. Considerations of imaging instrumentation include subject safety (always a paramount concern!) and comfort, clarity of the images obtained, the amount of time required to obtain an image, and the ability to obtain dynamic (moving) images. We review each of the major imaging techniques below and consider the advantages and limitations of each type of instrumentation.

Conventional Radiography (x-rays)

Most people are familiar with conventional radiography, the **x-ray**. X-rays were discovered by Wilhelm Konrad von Röntgen (1845–1923) in 1895, so named because initially, their nature was unknown, and x stands for an unknown in mathematics. X-rays are a type of electromagnetic radiation, similar to radio waves, microwaves, and visible light. X-rays have a large amount of energy, sufficient to break molecular bonds and, therefore, damage the cells of living tissue. When x-rays hit a substance, some are absorbed and others pass through the substance. The ability to pass through tissue is what gives x-ray technology the advantage of "seeing inside" the body. Figure 7–12 is based upon lateral x-rays of the vocal tract, and Figure 7–49 shows an actual lateral x-ray, obtained by projecting the x-ray beam from one side of the head and throat to the other. A large amount of data about the vocal tract during speech production, some of which has been presented in this chapter, has been based upon x-ray data (Fant, 1980; Harshman, Ladefoged, & Goldstein, 1977; Hashimoto & Sasaki, 1982; Kent & Moll, 1972; Kent & Netsell, 1971; Mermelstein, 1973).

The advantage of x-ray, or conventional radiography, is its relatively low cost compared to other types of imaging that we shall discuss shortly. Some strong disadvantages exist, however, that must be considered. First, although x-ray imaging is noninvasive, it is not harmless. X-rays are damaging to human tissue and can, with sufficiently high exposure, be deadly. Second, conventional radiography takes a

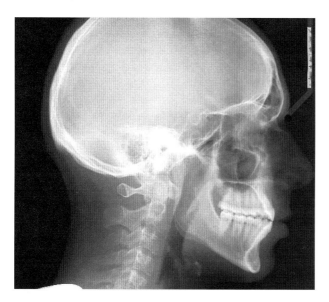

Figure 7–49. A lateral x-ray image of the head and neck. Bone (*high density*) is white and soft tissue (*low density*) is shades of gray. Air is black. The small white and light gray image under the mandible is the hyoid bone. Note the lack of depth of the image, in that all visible structures are represented on the same plane. Image courtesy of David A. Behrman, DMD, Weill Cornell Medical Center, New York, NY.

three-dimensional image and collapses it into a two-dimensional plane: It does not provide depth of image, and so overlying tissues are superimposed upon one another. An easy way to understand this phenomenon is to consider the following. Suppose you want to discover the structural contents of a chocolate layer cake without cutting into the cake. If you use conventional radiography to image the cake, it would be like taking a rolling pin and flattening the cake into a pancake. All the ingredients would be present in the image, but you would have no idea how they are arranged, and furthermore, the squishing together of icing and cake might make it difficult to understand what you are looking at. Conventional radiography works in much the same way, so that imaging of the tongue from the front or side of the face (a frontal or lateral x-ray, respectively), for example, might be obscured by bony structures such as the mandible, facial bones, and vertebrae.

Another disadvantage of conventional radiography is that different types of tissues with similar densities cannot be distinguished from one another, so different bones and cartilages might be difficult to tell apart when looking at the x-ray image. Furthermore, it is frequently difficult to distinguish between the midline and lateral edges of the tongue. Stone (1996) points out that this problem is particularly relevant for speech production, during which the tongue is frequently in a grooved posture. The use of **x-ray microbeam** overcomes the problem of delimiting tongue edge, a technique that we will explore in Chapter 8, together with other point-tracking instrumentation.

Computed Tomography (CT)

Computed tomography (CT) or, equivalently, computed axial tomography (CAT) also uses x-rays. The technology was developed independently by Drs. Alan Comack and Godfrey Hounself, for which they were awarded the Nobel Prize in 1979. Computed tomography was introduced into clinical practice by Hounsfield (1973). CT works by scanning thin sections, or slices (*tomos* is Greek for a "slice"), of the body, anywhere from 2 to 10 mm thick, using a narrow x-ray beam that rotates around the body. The digital data acquired by computed tomography are stored in the computer as a matrix of tens of thousands of pixels (tiny squares). Each pixel is assigned a number (in Hounsfield units) by the computer that is a measure of how much of the x-ray energy is absorbed by the tissues at each point in the body. Absorption is dependent upon tissue density, with denser tissue absorbing more Hounsfield units. The gray scale of the printed image is roughly proportional to the measured density of the structures being scanned. By convention, high numbers (high-density tissues) are white and low numbers (low-density tissues) are black, with shades of gray in between. The window is the range of density numbers selected for display. Multiple images from different angles are taken for each slice, and a composite image is generated. In this way, the CT image produced is a cross-section showing each of the tissues in 10-mm slices.

A strong advantage of CT imaging is that tissues of similar density can be distinguished because of the narrow x-ray beam. Bone appears bright white and air appears black (Figure 7–50). Soft tissue structures, such as the tongue, appear gray. So, unlike the squashed chocolate layer cake of conventional radiography, computed tomography would provide pictures of a series of very thin slices through the cake. By examining each of these thin slices in sequence, the structure of the cake would be revealed. However, the structure of the object being studied is still dependent upon multiple slices being taken and then reassembled. Stone (1996) uses the example of a cylinder (three-dimensional) being represented by many layered circles (two-dimensional). Another advantage is that the bor-

ders of the tongue and other tissue structures are imaged more clearly in CT than conventional x-ray because of the composite image created from multiple angles.

A disadvantage of computed tomography is the slow scanning speed, which has traditionally taken approximately 2.5 seconds per frame, clearly too slow for speech. In addition, scanning angles are limited to transverse and oblique, due to limitations in ability to angle the scanner relative to the person being scanned. Furthermore, the cost of obtaining a CT scan is much greater than conventional radiography. The most serious disadvantage by far, however, is the x-ray dosage, which is much higher than one would receive in a conventional x-ray. For example, a CT of the larynx might expose the patient to the amount of radiation received during a few hundred conventional x-rays! For that reason, the use of CT imaging for research purposes has been limited. Nevertheless, measurement of dimensions of the vocal tract based upon CT scans has been used to enhance theories of vocal tract function (Kiritani, Kakita, & Shibata, 1977; Perrier, Boe, & Sock, 1992; Sundberg, Johansson, Wilbrand, & Ytterbergh, 1987).

CT technology is dynamic with frequent new advances for both clinical and research applications. The spiral computed tomography scanner is a newer technology that obtains images as the x-ray detection equipment is rotated in a plane perpendicular to the major axis of the individual (in other words, moving in a spiral or helix around the individual). This technique allows fast and continuous acquisition of data, which reduces the amount of x-ray exposure. A safer alternative, however, is discussed below.

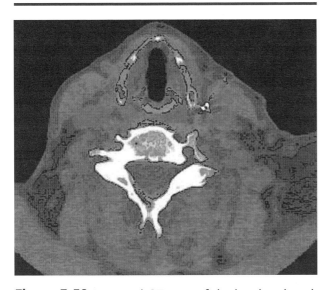

Figure 7–50. An axial CT scan of the head and neck at approximately the level of the fourth cervical vertebra. Bone (*high density*) is white and soft tissues (*low density*) are shades of gray. Air is black. Anterior is at the top of the image, and posterior is at the bottom. The white triangular-shaped structure is a vertebra. The black oblong space at the top center of the image is the airway, with the vocal folds on either side. The horseshoe-shaped crescent around the airway is the lower border of the mandible. Image courtesy of David A. Behrman, DMD, Weill Cornell Medical Center, New York, NY.

Magnetic Resonance Imaging (MRI)

Magnetic resonance imaging (MRI) is different from conventional radiography and computed tomography. MRI originated as nuclear magnetic resonance (NMR), a technique used to study the chemical and physical information about molecules in the human body. The terminology was changed in the 1970s from NMR to

MRI because of the negative association many people have with the word *nuclear*. The original NMR technology was developed in the late 1940s independently by two scientists, Felix Bloch and Edward Purcell, both of whom were awarded the Nobel Prize in 1952 for their discoveries. MRI uses radiofrequency waves and a strong magnetic field to image internal structures of the human body. (The magnetic field used in an MRI is equivalent to the strength of the magnets used to pick up cars in a junkyard!) The waves are directed at protons, the nuclei of hydrogen atoms. In the human body, protons are most abundant in water, which is distributed in different amounts in human tissue. The protons are alternately "excited" and then "relaxed," during which they emit radio signals that are processed and measured by computer. Tissues that contain substantially different amounts of water can be differentiated from one another.

Fat contains a lot of hydrogen, and bone marrow contains a lot of water (which in turn contains a lot of hydrogen). Thus, fat and bone appear white. Air contains minimal hydrogen, as does tooth enamel, so the air in the vocal tract and teeth appear black. Teeth pulp, however (the blood vessels and the nerve inside the teeth), contain significant amounts of hydrogen, and so it is white. (Teeth, therefore, can appear white with a black outline on the MRI.) Soft tissues, such as the tongue, appear gray (Figure 7–51). Similar to CT, magnetic resonance images are obtained in sequences over a number of minutes to provide images of contrasting tissues in thin planes (Figure 7–52).

MRI data have provided much information about postures of the vocal tract (Baer, Gore, Gracco, & Nye, 1991; Hasegawa-Johnson, Pizza, Alwan, Cha, & Haker, 2003) and tongue (Zheng, Hasegawa-Johnson, & Pizza, 2003). Acquisition

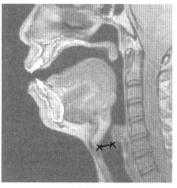

(a)

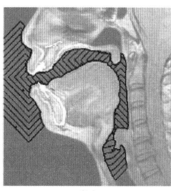

(b)

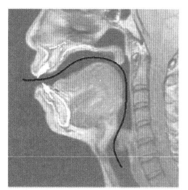

(c)

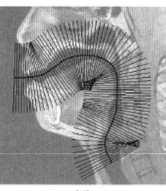

(d)

Figure 7–51. Volumetric measures of the vocal tract derived from multiple magnetic resonance images. From "Measurement of Temporal Changes in Vocal Tract Area Function From 3D Cine-MRI Data," by H. Takemoto, K. Honda, S. Masaki, Y. Shimada, and I. Fujimoto, 2006, *Journal of the Acoustical Society of America, 119,* p. 1040. Reprinted with permission from the Acoustical Society of America.

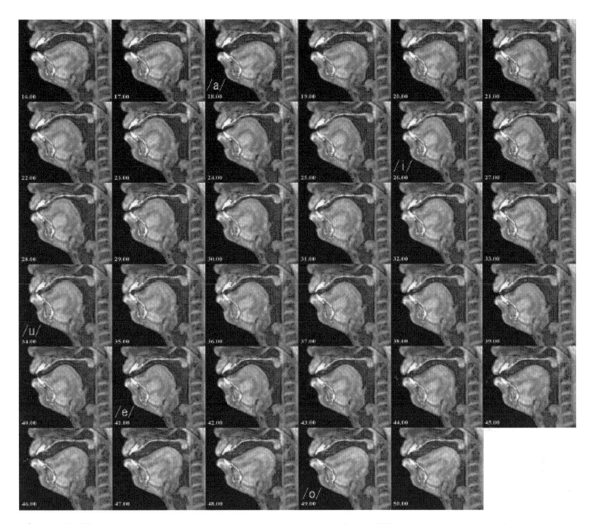

Figure 7–52. Imaging the vocal tract during production of two different Japanese vowels using cine-MRI. From "Measurement of Temporal Changes in Vocal Tract Area Function From 3D Cine-MRI Data," by H. Takemoto, K. Honda, S. Masaki, Y. Shimada, and I. Fujimoto, 2006, *Journal of the Acoustical Society of America, 119*, p. 1041. Reprinted with permission from the Acoustical Society of America.

of single slices in sagittal and coronal orientation has provided data on vocal tract postures for isolated, sustained vowels, and consonants correlated with formant frequencies measured from the acoustic signal (Moore, 1992). Midsagittal sections of the vocal tract have been used to measure vocal tract width, which is then converted to cross-sectional area (Lakshminarayanan, Lee, & McCutcheon, 1991). MRI also has been used to study the effect of vocal tract postures on voice quality (Story, Titze, & Hoffman,

2001). And MRI has been used to provide information about life span changes in vocal tract size, an important factor in defining formant frequencies (Vorperian et al., 2005).

As with all instrumentation that we have discussed, several disadvantages exist. The two main limitations of MRI are the resolution and the scan rate. The resolution of MRI is quite good, but it is not as clear as that of CT images, although as new MRI magnets increase in strength, the resolution has increased as well. (As mentioned above, tooth enamel and air, for example, both appear black in the MRI.) Scan rate, however, remains the most problematic limitation. When the technology was first developed, the original magnetic resonance images took over 5 hours to acquire. The instrumentation was nicknamed "the indomitable" because of the unflagging spirit required of the investigators and the person being scanned (Kleinfield, 1985). Currently, MRI scans take a few seconds for a single slice and a few minutes for multislice data, which is very fast compared to the original instrumentation but slow compared to speech movements. Furthermore, the individual being scanned must remain still (even holding his or her breath) during the seconds that the actual scanning is taking place. When one adds together the pauses required so that the individual can breathe together with the duration of the active scanning, the total scan time to image the entire vocal tract can become lengthy. Therefore, speech analysis is limited to study of sustainable sounds such as vowels and certain types of consonants. (Obviously, the speaker does not actually sustain the sound for minutes but rather freezes his or her vocal tract in the appropriate articulatory position.)

Like computed tomography, MRI technology has evolved over the decades and continues to benefit from technologic advances. Volumetric imaging, for example, is one development that has resulted from recent advances in image scanning rates and post-processing (computer-aided analysis of the image after it has been acquired) analytic abilities. Volumetric imaging is a reconstruction of the vocal tract in three-dimensional space. (A three-dimensional reconstruction of the vocal tract based upon measurements derived from CT and MRI is shown in Figure 7–19.) Volumetric imaging, or three-dimensional (3-D) reconstruction, using either CT or MRI scans, is based upon acquisition of sequential series of image slices through the vocal tract in one or multiple anatomic planes. First demonstrated by Baer, Gore, Gracco, and Nye (1991), 3-D reconstructions have been used to explore generation of turbulent airflow in fricatives (Alwan, Narayanan, & Haker, 1997; Narayanan, Alwan, & Haker, 1995) and vocal tract transfer function (the acoustic resonances of the vocal tract) (Story, Titze, & Hoffman, 1996, 1998).

In the late 1970s, an MRI technique called echoplanar imaging was developed and served as the basis for development of sequential MRI video imaging at the rate of approximately 30 ms per image. Some degree of image resolution is lost, however, with increased scan rate. (Recall the time-frequency tradeoff described earlier.) Long an important tool for studying static vocal tract postures, new technology allows acquisition of a series of images at fast rates, providing real-time movements of articulators (Crary, Kotzur, Gauger, Gorham, & Burton, 1996; Demolin, Hassid, Metens, & Soquet, 2002; Narayanan, Nayak, Lee, Sethy, & Byrd, 2004). Dynamic MRI, or cine-MRI, permits visualization of vocal tract dynamics by sequencing numerous images to give the impression of movement. Developed originally for imaging cardiac motion, cine-MRI is similar to stroboscopy in that the images are not acquired in real time but rather sampled intermittently. Thus, the images appear to describe articulatory movement at a rate that is slower than the true vocal tract movement. As a result of the intermittent nature of the scanned images, aligning visual images with the acoustic signal is difficult. Nevertheless, cine-MRI data are being used to develop increasingly sophisticated algorithms (mathematical formulas) for explaining the relationship of vocal tract articulatory postures and vowel quality (Takemoto, Honda, Masaki, Shimada, & Fujimoto, 2006).

Another novel technique for capturing the rapid movements of the vocal tract is the use of "spiral scanning" to provide real-time imaging (Narayanan et al., 2004). Although quite promising, currently the technology remains experimental. In most clinical and research applications, the scan rate and the inability to image vocal tract movement remain significant limitations. It is likely, however, that new technologies will overcome these limitations in the near future.

Other limitations of MRI exist. First, the MRI slices, or sections, are typically at least 5 mm wide, as compared to the CT slices, which can be as thin as 2 mm. If two structures, such as the hyoid bone and the top of the epiglottis, are separated by less than 5 mm, the two structures will appear to be flattened together in one MRI slice and appear to be in the same plane. Clearly, the narrower the section, the more accurate the representation of the relative positions of the vocal tract structures. Another limitation of MRI is that the instrumentation requires that the person being scanned lie inside a narrow-bore tube, and individuals with some claustrophobia can find the process uncomfortable, making them feel closed in. As with CT imaging, the required prone position can also influence speech data. (Lie on your back and talk. Does it feel as though the vocal tract, including the base of tongue and pharyngeal walls, is aligned slightly differently than when you speak while sitting or standing erect?)

And finally, the magnets produce a considerable amount of noise, like continual rapid hammering, as the electrical charge builds up and is opposed by the main magnetic field. One obvious difficulty in using MRI, therefore, is that obtaining the speech signal concurrent with the magnetic resonance image is quite difficult. First, the microphone cannot have any metal that might be attracted to the magnet. A bigger problem, however, is the significant noise in the MRI scanner, which distorts the signal picked up by the microphone. That latter problem is being addressed, however, with new noise-canceling microphone technology that can isolate the speech signal (Nessaiver, Stone, Parthasarathy, Kahana, & Paritsky, 2006), but nonetheless, the difficulties remain real.

Although not applicable to vocal tract imaging, as a final note, we should mention a different MRI technique that is highly relevant for understanding neural processes in speech motor production and perception. In 1994, scientists developed a technique called functional MRI (fMRI), which provided the ability to image the brain's use of oxygen during specific tasks. In combination with echoplanar techniques, fMRI provides a way to map regions of the brain involved in specific cognitive acts and motor control.

Ultrasound

Movements of the tongue have preoccupied speech scientists for decades, given the importance of tongue movement to speech production (Harshman, Ladefoged, & Goldstein, 1977). Ideally, we would want to measure tongue movement unobtrusively, without the need to place any instrumentation within the mouth and without in any way inhibiting normal articulatory movement during speech. The tongue is only intermittently visible during speech, and then only the tongue tip. The larger bulk of the tongue muscle remains hidden within the oral and oral-pharyngeal cavities. Ultrasound offers a noninvasive means of imaging the tongue during speech. Much of this discussion draws on the work of Stone (2005). **Ultrasonography** is based upon the use of extremely high-frequency sound waves, generally above 1 MHz, to detect movement of the tongue.

In Chapter 3, we learned that when a sound wave encounters a boundary and the new medium is sufficiently different from air, most of the wave will be reflected back to the sound source. The ultrasound transceiver emits and receives (hence its name: it *trans*mits and *receives* sounds) the ultra-high-frequency pressure wave. The transceiver is placed under the chin, and the pressure wave travels through the tissue of the chin and tongue until it reaches the upper surface of the tongue. At that point, depending upon its position, the surface of the tongue would be in contact with either the air in the mouth (such as for a vowel) or the hard palate (such as during production of a lingual-alveolar sound). Both air and the bony structures of the palate are sufficiently different from the muscle of the tongue to cause the ultrasonic pressure wave to be reflected back. The reflected wave, called an echo, returns to the transceiver. The speed of the sound wave is a known constant, in this case the speed of sound traveling through water (soft tissues being composed of significant amounts of water). The time it takes the echo to return to the transceiver is dependent upon the distance the wave travels. Recall from Chapter 3 that the wavelength decreases as frequency increases. The ultrasonic waves have very short wavelengths. The short wavelength allows the pressure wave to resolve (delineate) small details of tongue shape.

The image obtained from the ultrasound (Figure 7–53) consists of speckled areas and edges (Stone, 2005). The wedge-shaped image arises from the ultrasound transceiver positioned below the jaw. Ultrasound was first used in speech research by Kelsey, Minifie, and Hixon (1969) and has since been used to assess tongue dynamics in vowel and consonant production (Bressmann et al., 2005; Davidson, 2005; Watkin & Rubin, 1989). Current technologic developments include ultrasound Doppler, which is used specifically to evaluate tongue movement (Saigusa et al., 2006). An advantage of ultrasound over conventional radiography, CT, and MRI is the ability to image movement without much difficulty. Real-time ultrasound studies have contributed information on tongue movement (Stone, 2005). Current research investigates the use of ultrasound imaging as a feedback tool for articulation changes in speech therapy (Adler-Bock, Bernhardt, Gick, & Bacsfalvi, 2007).

Challenges to the use of ultrasound include the large number of data points obtained with the scan, identifying the tongue contour with clarity, identifying specific location points on the tongue, and inability to image the tongue tip. This last limitation is due to the interference of the mandible and floor of the mouth in the "line of sight" from the transceiver to the tongue tip. Similarly, the most posterior portion of the tongue can be obscured due to the hyoid bone.

Study Questions

33. What is sound spectrography?

34. What is the difference between a narrow- and wideband spectrogram? What information about the voice and speech production system does each type of filter provide?

35. How is periodicity (amount of jitter) reflected in a narrowband spectrogram?

36. Explain the long-term average spectrum and the harmonics to noise ratio.

37. What is inverse filtering?

38. What are the advantages and disadvantages of using x-rays to image the vocal tract? Computed tomography? Magnetic resonance imaging? Ultrasound?

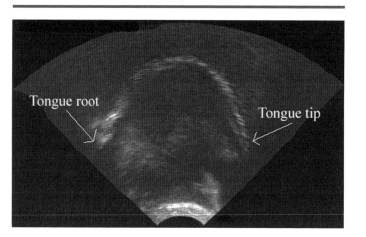

Figure 7–53. Ultrasound image of the tongue. Image courtesy of Lisa Davidson, PhD, Department of Linguistics, New York University, New York, NY.

Clinical Case 4: Ataxic Dysarthria

Clinical cases are based upon real patients whom the author has treated. Evaluation and treatment information has been edited to focus upon specific features related to the chapters. Note that clinical cases incorporate information that is covered in this and other chapters (and some information about diagnosis and therapy that you will learn in future courses). You are encouraged to review this case before you begin your study of this chapter and once again after you have completed the chapter. You may also want to revisit this case later in the semester after you have covered additional chapters.

Paul is a 30-year-old software engineer with Friedreich's ataxia, diagnosed 3 years previously. This progressive, hereditary disease causes damage to the cerebellum, spinal cord, and peripheral nerves. Paul's symptoms began with difficulty walking and progressed to slow and uncoordinated movements of the hands, muscle fatigue and weakness, and then dysarthria (neurological-based impairment speech). Paul had had a course of voice therapy when the symptoms first started. However, since that time, Paul had become very concerned about his speech. Due to the muscle weakness and incoordination of his hands, Paul relied on voice recognition software for programming, and over the past few months, the software was unable to respond accurately to his speech.

The SLP conducted an evaluation of his speech and voice. She found Paul's articulation to be characterized by significantly distorted vowels and imprecise and irregular production of consonants. Voice quality was harsh, and a vocal tremor was noted intermittently. Prosody (see Chapter 9) was characterized by excess and equal stress, limited f_o contour, excessively prolonged vowels and some consonants, and overall slow rate of speech. Overall, Paul's intelligibility was severely impaired.

The SLP knew that, due to the progressive nature of the disease and the severity of the dysarthria, speech therapy for improved articulation was not likely to produce sufficient improvement to meet Paul's work needs. The SLP recommended augmentative and alternative communication (AAC). She talked extensively with Paul about his communication needs and his daily lifestyle. Together with his brother, with whom Paul lived, they selected the AAC devices for Paul to try out. He found two devices that met his needs.

Clinical Case Discussion Questions

1. During the initial evaluation, the SLP asked Paul to sustain the vowel /a/ and /i/. During both tasks, Paul was unable to maintain consistent vowel quality. The vowel changed continually during each task. Given that Friedreich's ataxia produces uncontrolled movements, explain why the vowels changed. Include reference to resonance characteristics of the vocal tract and formant frequencies.

2. Consider the acoustic theory of speech production: How has Paul's disease affected the biomechanics of sound source production? How has it affected resonance? Could you characterize Paul's communication disorder as a voice disorder? A speech disorder? Explain.

3. After your study of Chapter 9 (Prosody), return to this case study and explain why rate, f_o contour, and syllabic stress would be impaired.

Recommended Internet Sites for Further Learning

http://www.phys.unsw.edu.au/jw/voice.html

The University of New South Wales offers good descriptions of source filter theory and resonance.

http://speech.umaryland.edu/

The Vocal Tract Visualization Laboratory of the University of Maryland, Baltimore Dental School has information about and images of the vocal tract.

http://home.cc.umanitoba.ca/~robh/howto.html

University of Manitoba Rob Hagiwara's How to read a spectrogram page. Good exploration of formant changes as viewed in spectrograms for vowels and consonants.

http://www.phon.ucl.ac.uk/resource/vtdemo/

University College London (UCL) has a fun, interactive program (unfortunately, only for Windows PC) that demonstrates how articulatory postures define vocal quality.

References

Adler-Bock, M., Bernhardt, B. M., Gick, B., & Bacsfalvi, P. (2007). The use of ultrasound in remediation of North American English /r/ in 2 adolescents. *American Journal of Speech-Language Pathology*, *16*, 128–139.

Alku, P., Story, B., & Airas, M. (2006). Estimation of the voice source from speech pressure signals: Evaluation of an inverse filtering technique using physical modeling of voice production. *Folia Phoniatrica and Logopedia*, *58*, 102–113.

Alwan, A., Narayanan, S., & Haker, K. (1997). Toward articulatory-acoustic models for liquid approximants based on MRI and EPG data. Part II. The rhotics. *Journal of the Acoustical Society of America*, *101*, 1078–1089.

Atsumi, T., & Miyatake, T. (1987). Morphometry of the degenerative process in the hypoglossal nerves in amyotrophic lateral sclerosis. *Acta Neuropathologica (Berlin)*, *73*, 25–31.

Awan, S. N., & Roy, N. (2006). Toward the development of an objective index of dysphonia severity: A four-factor acoustic model. *Clinical Linguistics and Phonetics*, *2*, 35–49.

Awan, S. N., & Roy. N. (2009). Outcomes measurement in voice disorders: application of an acoustic index of severity. *Journal of Speech-Language-Hearing Research*, *52*, 482–499.

Baer, T., Gore, J. C., Gracco, & Nye, R. W. (1991). Analysis of vocal tract shape and dimensions using magnetic resonance imaging: Vowels. *Journal of the Acoustical Society of America*, *90*, 799–828.

Baken, R. J., & Orlikoff, R. F. (2000). *Clinical measurement of speech and voice* (2nd ed.). San Diego, CA: Singular Thomson Learning.

Bele, I. V. (2006). The speaker's formant. *Journal of Voice*, *20*(4), 555–578.

Bielamowicz, S., Kreiman, J., Gerratt, B. R., Dauer, M. S., & Berke, G. S. (1996). Comparison of voice analysis systems for perturbation measurement. *Journal of Speech and Hearing Research*, *39*, 126–134.

Bole, C. T., & Lessler, M. A. (1966). Electromyography of the genioglossus muscles in man. *Journal of Applied Physiology*, *21*, 1695–1698.

Bressman, T., Thind, P., Uy, C., Bollig, C., Gilbert, R.W., & Irish, J. C. (2005). Quantitative three-dimensional ultrasound analysis of tongue protrusion, grooving and symmetry. *Clinical Linguistics and Phonetics*, *19*, 573–588.

Chiba, T., & Kajiyama, M. (1941). *The vowel, its nature and structure*. Tokyo, Japan: Tokyo-Kaiseikan.

Clopper, C. G., Pisoni, D. B., & de Jong, K. (2005). Acoustic characteristics of the vowel systems of six regional varieties of American English. *Journal of the Acoustical Society of America*, *118*, 1661–1676.

Crary, M. A., Kotzur, I. M. Gauger, J., Gorham, M., & Burton, S. (1996). Dynamic magnetic resonance imaging in the study of vocal tract configuration. *Journal of Voice*, *10*, 378–388.

Davidson, L. (2005). Addressing phonological questions with ultrasound. *Clinical Linguistics and Phonetics*, *19*, 619–633.

de Krom, G. (1995). Some spectral correlates of pathological breathy and rough voice quality for different types of vowel fragments. *Journal of Speech and Hearing Research*, *38*, 794–811.

Demolin, D., Hassid, S., Metens, T., & Soquet, A. (2002). Real-time MRI and articulatory coordination. *Comptes Rendu Biologies*, *325*, 547–556.

Fant, G. (1960). *Acoustic theory of speech production* (2nd ed.). The Hague, Netherlands: Mouton.

Fant, G. (1980). The relations between area functions and the acoustic signal. *Phonetics, 37,* 55–86.

Fant, G. (1986). Glottal flow: Models and interaction. *Journal of Phonetics, 14,* 393–399.

Fowler, C. A., Rubin, P., Remez, R. E., & Turvey, M. T. (1980). Implications for speech production of a general theory of action. In B. Butterworth (Ed.), *Language production. Vol. I. Speech and talk* (pp. 373–420). London, UK: Academic Press.

Fritzell, B. (1992). Inverse filtering. *Journal of Voice, 6,* 111–114.

Fritzell, B., Hammarberg, B., Gauffin, J., Karlsson, I., & Sundberg, J. (1986). Breathiness and insufficient vocal fold closure. *Journal of Phonetics, 14,* 549–554.

Fry, D. B. (1955). Duration and intensity as physical correlates of linguistic stress. *Journal of the Acoustical Society of America, 27,* 765–768.

Harshman, R., Ladefoged, P., & Goldstein, L. (1977). Factor analysis of tongue shapes. *Journal of the Acoustical Society of America, 62,* 693–707.

Hasegawa-Johnson, M., Pizza, S., Alwan, A., Cha, J. S., & Haker, K. (2003). Vowel category dependence of the relationship between palate height, tongue height, and oral area. *Journal of Speech, Language, and Hearing Research, 46,* 738–753.

Hashimoto, K., & Sasaki, K. (1982). On the relationship between the shape and position of the tongue for vowels. *Journal of Phonetics, 10,* 291–299.

Hazan, V., & Markham, D. (2004). Acoustic-phonetic correlates of talker intelligibility for adults and children. *Journal of the Acoustical Society of America, 116,* 3108–3118.

Heinz, J. M., & Stevens, K. N. (1964). On the derivation of area functions and acoustic spectra from cineradiographic films of speech. *Journal of the Acoustical Society of America, 36,* 1037.

Heman-Ackah, Y., Michael, D., & Goding, G. (2002). The relationship between cepstral peak prominence and selected parameters of dysphonia. *Journal of Voice, 16,* 20–27.

Hillenbrand, J., Cleveland, R. A., & Erickson, R. L. (1994). Acoustic correlates of breathy vocal quality. *Journal of Speech and Hearing Research, 37,* 769–778.

Hillenbrand, J., Getty, L. A., Clark, M. J., & Wheeler, K. (1995). Acoustic characteristics of American English vowels. *Journal of the Acoustical Society of America, 97,* 3099–3111.

Hillenbrand, J., & Houde, R. A. (1996). Acoustic correlates of breathy vocal quality: Dysphonic voices and continuous speech. *Journal of Speech and Hearing Research, 39,* 311–321.

Holbrook, A., & Fairbanks, G. (1962). Diphthong formants and their movements. *Journal of Speech and Hearing Research, 5,* 38–58.

Honda, K. (1983). Relationship between pitch control and vowel articulation. In D. M. Bless & J. H. Abbs (Eds.), *Vocal fold physiology* (pp. 286–297). San Diego, CA: College-Hill Press.

Honda, K. (1995). Laryngeal and extra-laryngeal mechanisms of F0 control. In F. Bell-Berti & L. J. Raphael (Eds.), *Producing speech: Contemporary issues* (pp. 215–232). New York, NY: American Institute of Physics.

Honda, K., & Fujimura, O. (1991). Intrinsic vowel F0 and phrase-final F0 lowering: Phonological vs. biological explanations. In J. Gauffin & B. Hammerberg (Eds.), *Vocal fold physiology* (pp.149–158). San Diego, CA: Singular.

Hounsfield, G. N. (1973). Computerized transverse axial scanning (tomography). 1. Description of system. *British Journal of Radiology, 46,* 1016–1022.

Howard, D. M. (2002). The real and the non-real in speech measurements. *Medical Engineering and Physics, 24,* 493–500.

Johnson, K., Ladefoged, P., & Lindau, M. (1993). Individual differences in vowel production. *Journal of the Acoustical Society of America, 94,* 701–714.

Kakita, Y., & Fujimura, O. (1977). A computational model of the tongue: A revised version. *Journal of the Acoustical Society of America, 62*(Suppl. 1), S15.

Kelsey, C. A., Minifie, F. D., & Hixon, T. J. (1969). Applications of ultrasound in speech research. *Journal of Speech and Hearing Research, 12,* 564–575.

Kent, R. D., Dembowski, J., & Lass, N. J. (1996). The acoustic characteristics of American English. In N. J. Lass (Ed.), *Principles of experimental phonetics.* (pp. 185–225). St Louis, MO: Mosby.

Kent, R., & Moll, K. (1972). Cinefluorographic analyses of lingual consonants. *Journal of Speech and Hearing Research, 15,* 453–473.

Kent, R., & Netsell, R. (1971). Effects of stress contrasts on certain articulatory parameters. *Phonetica, 24,* 23–44.

Kent, R. D., & Read, C. (1992). *The acoustic analysis of speech.* San Diego, CA: Singular.

Kiritani, S., Kakita, K., & Shibata, S. (1977). Dynamic palatography. In M. Sawashima & F. Cooper (Eds.), *Dynamic aspects of speech production* (pp. 159–170). Tokyo, Japan: Tokyo University Press.

Kleinfield, S. (1985). *A machine called indomitable.* New York, NY: Time Books.

Ladefoged, P. (1996). *Elements of acoustic phonetics.* Chicago, IL: University of Chicago Press.

Ladefoged, P. (2006). *A course in phonetics* (4th ed.). Sydney, Australia: Thomson-Wadsworth.

Ladefoged, P., Harshman, R., Goldstein, L., & Rice, L. (1978). Generating vocal tract shapes from formant frequencies. *Journal of the Acoustical Society of America, 64,* 1027–1035.

Lakshminarayanan, A. V., Lee, S., & McCutcheon, M. J. (1991). MR imaging of the vocal tract during vowel production. *Journal of Magnetic Resonance Imaging, 1,* 71–76.

Laukkanen, A.-M., Björkner, E., & Sundberg, J. (2006). Throaty voice quality: Subglottal pressure, voice source, and formant characteristics. *Journal of Voice, 20,* 25–37.

Lehiste, I., & Peterson, G. E. (1961a). Some basic considerations in the analysis of intonation. *Journal of the Acoustical Society of America, 33,* 419–425.

Lehiste, I., & Peterson, G. E. (1961b). Transitions, glides, and diphthongs. *Journal of the Acoustical Society of America, 33,* 268–277.

Lehto, L., Airas, M., Björkner, E., Sundberg, J., & Alku, P. (2007). Comparison of two inverse filtering methods in parameterization of the glottal closing phase characteristics in different phonation types. *Journal of Voice, 21,* 138–150.

Leong, K., Hawkshaw, M. J., Dentchev, D., Gupta, R., Lurie, D., & Sataloff, R. T. (2013). Reliability of objective voice measures of normal speaking voices. *Journal of Voice, 27,* 170–176.

Lindblom, B. F. F. (1963). Spectrographic study of vowel reduction. *Journal of the Acoustical Society of America, 36,* 1773–1781.

Lindblom, B. F. F., & Sundberg, J. E. F. (1971). Acoustical consequences of lip, tongue, jaw, and larynx movement. *Journal of the Acoustical Society of America, 50,* 1166–1179.

Löfqvist, A., & Mandersson, B. (1987). Long-time average spectrum of speech and voice analysis. *Folia Phoniatrica, 39,* 221–229.

Lowell, S. Y., & Hylkema, J. A. (2016). The effect of speaking context on spectral and cepstral-based acoustic features of normal voice. *Clinical Linguistics and Phonetics, 30,* 1–11.

MacNeilage, P. F., & Sholes, G. N. (1964). An electromyographic study of the tongue during vowel production. *Journal of Speech and Hearing Research, 7,* 209–232.

Maeda, S. (1991). On articulatory and acoustic variabilities. *Journal of Phonetics, 19,* 321–333.

Mermelstein, P. (1973). Articulatory model for the study of speech production. *Journal of the Acoustical Society of America, 53,* 1070–1082.

Miller, J. L., Watkin, K. L., & Chen, M. F. (2002). Tissues variations in intrinsic musculature of the adult human tongue. *Journal of Speech, Language, and Hearing Research, 45,* 51–65.

Miller, R. I. (1959). Nature of the vocal cord wave. *Journal of the Acoustical Society of America, 31,* 667–677.

Millman, S. (1984). *A history of engineering and science in the Bell System* (pp. 105–107). Indianapolis, IN: AT & T Bell Laboratories.

Miyawaki, K. (1975). A preliminary report on the electromyographic study of the activity of lingual muscles. *Annual Bulletin of the Research Institute of Logopedics and Phoniatrics, (University of Tokyo), 9,* 91–106.

Monsen, R. B., & Engebretson, A. M. (1983). The accuracy of formant frequency measurements: A comparison of spectrographic analysis and linear prediction. *Journal of Speech and Hearing Research, 26,* 89–97.

Moore, C. A. (1992). The correspondence of vocal tract resonance with volumes obtained from magnetic resonance images. *Journal of Speech and Hearing Research, 35,* 1009–1023.

Narayanan, S. S., Alwan, A. A., & Haker, K. (1995). An articulatory study of fricative consonants using magnetic resonance imaging. *Journal of the Acoustical Society of America, 98,* 1325–1347.

Narayanan, S. S., Nayak, K., Lee, S., Sethy, A., & Byrd, D. (2004). An approach to real-time magnetic resonance imaging for speech production. *Journal of the Acoustical Society of America, 115,* 1771–1776.

Nawka, T., Anders, L., Cebulla, M., & Zurakwski, D. (1997). The speaker's formant in male voices. *Journal of Voice, 11,* 422–428.

Nessaiver, M. S., Stone, M., Parthasarathy, V., Kahana, Y., & Paritsky, A. (2006). Recording high quality speech during tagged cine-MRI studies using a fiberoptic microphone. *Journal of Magnetic Resonance Imaging, 23,* 92–97.

Noll, A. M. (1964). Short-term spectrum and "cepstrum" techniques for vocal pitch detection. *Journal of the Acoustical Society of America, 41,* 293–309.

Ohala, J., & Hirose, H. (1970). The function of the sternohyoid muscle in speech. *Research Institute of Logopedics and Phoniatrics, Annual Bulletin, 4,* 41–44.

Perrier, P., Boe, L. J., & Sock, R. (1992). Vocal tract area function estimation from midsagittal dimensions with CT scans and a vocal tract cast: Modeling the transition with two sets of coefficients. *Journal of Speech and Hearing Research, 35,* 53–67.

Peterson, G. E., & Barney, H. E. (1952). Control methods used in a study of vowels. *Journal of the Acoustical Society of America, 24,* 176–184.

Pickett, J. M. (1980). *The sounds of speech communication.* Baltimore, MD: University Park Press.

Potter, R. K., Kopp, G. A., & Green, J. G. (1947). *Visible speech.* New York, NY: Van Nostrand.

Raphael, B. N., & Scherer, R. C. (1987). Voice modification of stage actors: Acoustic analyses. *Journal of Voice, 1,* 83–87.

Raphael, L. J., & Bell-Berti, F. (1975). Tongue musculature and the feature of tension in English vowels. *Phonetica, 32,* 61–73.

Rossi, M., & Autesserre, D. (1981). Movements of the hyoid and the larynx and the intrinsic frequency of vowels. *Journal of Phonetics, 9,* 233–249.

Rothenberg, M. (1973). A new inverse filtering technique for deriving the glottal air flow waveform during voicing. *Journal of the Acoustical Society of America, 53,* 1632–1645.

Rothenberg, M. (1977). Measurement of airflow in speech. *Journal of Speech and Hearing Research, 20,* 156–176.

Saigusa, H., Saigusa, M., Aino, I., Iwasaki, C., Li, L., & Niimi, S. (2006). M-mode color Doppler ultrasonic imaging of vertical tongue movement during articulatory movement. *Journal of Voice, 20,* 38–45.

Sanders, I., & Mu, L. (2013). A three-dimensional atlas of the human tongue muscles. *The Anatomical Record, 296,* 1102–1114.

Singh, S., & Singh, K. (2006). *Phonetics: Principles and practices* (3rd ed.). San Diego, CA: Plural.

Stetson, R. H. (1951). *Motor phonetics: A study of speech movements in action.* Amsterdam, Netherlands: North-Holland.

Stevens, K. N., & House, A. S. (1955). Development of a quantitative description of vowel articulation. *Journal of the Acoustical Society of America, 27,* 484–493.

Stevens, K. N., & House, A. S. (1961). An acoustical theory of vowel production and some of its implications. *Journal of Speech and Hearing Research, 4,* 303–320.

Stone, M. (1996). Instrumentation for the study of speech physiology. In N. J. Lass (Ed.), *Principles of experimental phonetics.* St. Louis, MO: Mosby.

Stone, M. (2005). A guide to analyzing tongue motion from ultrasound images. *Clinical Linguistics and Phonetics, 19,* 455–501.

Stone, M., Epstein, M., & Iskarous, K. (2004). Functional segments in tongue movement. *Clinical Linguistics and Phonetics, 18,* 507–521.

Stone, M., Goldstein, M., & Zhang, Y. (1997). Principal component analysis of cross-sectional tongue shapes in vowels. *Speech Communication, 22,* 173–184.

Story, B. H. (2005). Synergistic modes of vocal tract articulation for American English vowels. *Journal of the Acoustical Society of America, 118,* 3834–3859.

Story, B. H., Titze, I. R., & Hoffman, E. A. (1996). Vocal tract area functions from magnetic resonance imaging. *Journal of the Acoustical Society of America, 100,* 537–554.

Story, B. H., Titze, I. R., & Hoffman, E. A. (1998). Vocal tract area functions for an adult female speaker based upon volumetric imaging. *Journal of the Acoustical Society of America, 104,* 471–487.

Story, B. H., Titze, I. R., & Hoffman, E. A. (2001). The relationship of vocal tract shape to three voice qualities. *Journal of the Acoustical Society of America, 109,* 1651–1667.

Sundberg, J. (1974). Articulatory interpretation of the singing formant. *Journal of the Acoustical Society of America, 55,* 838–844.

Sundberg, J. (1987). *The science of the singing voice.* DeKalb, IL: Northern Illinois University Press.

Sundberg, J. (2001). Level and center frequency of the singer's formant. *Journal of Voice, 15,* 176–186.

Sundberg, J., Johansson, C., Wilbrand, H., & Ytterbergh, C. (1987). From sagittal distance to area: A study of transverse vocal tract cross-sectional area. *Phonetica, 44,* 76–90.

Takemoto, H. (2001). Morphological analyses of the human tongue musculature for three-dimensional modeling. *Journal of Speech and Hearing Research, 44,* 95–107.

Takemoto, H., Honda, K., Masaki, S., Shimada, Y., & Fujimoto, I. (2006). Measurement of temporal changes in vocal tract area function from 3D cine-MRI data. *Journal of the Acoustical Society of America, 119,* 1037–1049.

Tarnopolsky, A., Fletcher, N., Hollenberg, L., Lange, B., Smith, J., & Wolfe, J. (2005). Acoustics: The vocal tract and the sound of a didgeridoo. *Nature, 436,* 39.

Titze, I. R. (1992). Acoustic interpretation of the voice range profile (Phonetogram). *Journal of Speech and Hearing Research, 35,* 21–34.

Titze, I. R. (1994). *Principles of voice production.* Englewood Cliffs, NJ: Prentice-Hall.

Tsao, Y.-C., Weismer, G., & Iqbal, K. (2006). The effect of intertalker speech rate on acoustic vowel space. *Journal of the Acoustical Society of America, 119,* 1074–1082.

Turner, G. S., Tjaden, K., & Weismer, G. (1995). The influence of speaking rate on vowel space and speech intelligibility for individuals with amyotrophic lateral sclerosis. *Journal of Speech and Hearing Research, 38,* 1001–1003.

Vilkman, E., Aaltonen, O., Raimo, I., & Okasanen, H. (1989). Articulatory hyoid-laryngeal changes vs. cricothyroid muscle activity in the control of intrinsic F0 of vowels. *Journal of Phonetics, 17,* 193–203.

von Leden, H. (1996). A cultural history of the human voice. In R. T. Sataloff (Ed.), *Professional voice: The art and science of clinical care* (pp. 9–89). San Diego, CA: Singular.

Vorperian, H. K., Kent, R. D., Lindstrom, M. J., Kalina, C. M., Gentry, L.R., & Yandell, B. S. (2005). Development of vocal tract length during early childhood: A magnetic resonance imaging study. *Journal of the Acoustical Society of America, 117,* 338–350.

Watkin, K., & Rubin, J. (1989). Pseudo-three-dimensional reconstruction of ultrasonic images of the tongue. *Journal of the Acoustical Society of America, 85,* 496–499.

White, P. (2001). Long-term average spectrum (LTAS) analysis of sex and gender-related differences in children's voices. *Logopedics, Phoniatrics, Vocology, 26,* 97–101.

Wilhelms-Tricarico, R. (1995). Physiological modeling of speech production: Methods for modeling soft-tissue articulators. *Journal of the Acoustical Society of America, 97,* 3085–3098.

Wolfe, V. I., Martin, D. P., & Palmer, C. I. (2000). Perception of dysphonic voice quality by naïve listeners. *Journal of Speech and Hearing Research, 43,* 697–705.

Yanagihara, N. (1967). Significance of harmonic changes and noise components in hoarseness. *Journal of Speech and Hearing Research, 10,* 531–541.

Yumoto, E., Gould, W. J., & Baer, T. (1982). Harmonics-to-noise ratio as an index of the degree of hoarseness. *Journal of the Acoustical Society of America, 71,* 1544–1549.

Zemlin, W. R. (1998). *Speech and hearing science: Anatomy and physiology* (4th ed.). Needham Heights, MA: Allyn & Bacon.

Zheng, Y., Hasegawa-Johnson, M., & Pizza, S. (2003). Analysis of three-dimensional tongue shape using a three-index factor analysis model. *Journal of the Acoustical Society of America, 113,* 478–486.

8

The Production and Perception of Consonants

Figure 8–1. Pellets affixed to the tongue for imaging lingual movement during speech.

Speech is voice modulated by the throat, tongue, and the lips.

—Thomas Henry Huxley, 1872

Clinical Case 5: Facial Nerve Trauma

Clinical cases are based upon real patients whom the author has treated. Evaluation and treatment information has been edited to focus upon specific features related to the chapters. Note that these cases incorporate information that is covered in this and other chapters (and some information about diagnosis and therapy that you will learn in future courses). You are encouraged to review this case before you begin your study of this chapter and once again after you have completed the chapter. You may also want to revisit this case later in the semester after you have covered additional chapters.

Sean is a 44-year-old firefighter who suffered head trauma when, 4 months prior, a falling metal beam grazed the back of his head while he and his team were fighting to control a fire in an industrial warehouse. It knocked him to the ground face-first. However, he considered himself lucky. He never lost consciousness and ended up suffering only minor burns and cuts to his head and face, thanks to the protective clothing he wore. He was especially thankful that his eyesight wasn't damaged. However, he did have a base of skull fracture and broke numerous bones in his face. Initially, after the accident, he was unable to move the muscles of his face. With time, a small amount of movement returned, particularly the upper face. However, his lower facial muscles remained largely immobile. His neurosurgeon said that Sean's facial nerve (CN VII) was severely damaged, likely from the blow to the back of the head (the location of the nerve's nuclei in the brainstem), as well as the multiple bone fractures that damaged the nerve peripherally. He was referred to a speech-language pathologist (SLP) to improve his speech and swallowing.

The SLP conducted a thorough oral motor examination and indeed found that lip movement was severely impaired. Sean could not round, pucker, or retract his lips. His lip seal was poor and, thus, he could not puff out his cheeks and hold air within his mouth. Lingual movement (CN XII and X) and mandibular elevation and depression (CN V) were within normal limits. Sean's articulation was largely intact, except for phonemes requiring labial movement and those requiring buildup and release of intraoral pressure controlled by lip seal.

Sean's voice quality was normal, but he had limited pitch variability (that is, reduced f_o contour). Sean's wife stated that she was worried that he was depressed, because he sounded monotone and bored. However, Sean's post-trauma psychological evaluation suggested that he was dealing with the accident well. The SLP knew that, unlike disease processes, which tend to follow known courses, the neurological damage was not always known in cases of trauma. However, the abnormal prosody was puzzling to the SLP, as no damage to the larynx or vagus nerve had been reported, and no other vocal function was impaired. The SLP conducted stimulability testing to determine whether increased pitch variability was achievable. She asked Sean to read phrases with high emotional content (such as, "What a surprise!"). Sean could vary his pitch appropriately and required minimal cueing. After discussion with Sean, both he and the SLP concluded that the monotone quality was a reaction to the limited ability to use facial expressions, which seemed to "overflow" into his prosody. In addition, Sean was concentrating so hard on trying to move his lips when he spoke, he was not thinking about prosody.

Speech therapy was initiated, with the primary goal of using compensatory strategies to minimize the effect of the impaired bilabial control on phoneme production. The main adaptive strategy was increased use of mandibular movements to achieve bilabial contact (that is, exaggerated elevation and depression of the mandible). Rapid release (mandibular lowering) was used to simulate the voice bilabial plosive /b/. Simulation of the /p/ was more difficult. It tended to sound more like the voiced cognate /b/. A variety of strategies were explored to achieve a more /p/-like sound, including slowing the release of the closure or raising pitch slightly for the vowel following the /p/. A second goal for Sean was to use increased self-monitoring of his pitch to achieve appropriate prosody. After several therapy sessions, and with dedicated practice on Sean's part, he achieved clearer labial phoneme production, although they remained mildly distorted, and prosody returned to normal.

Clinical Case Discussion Questions

1. What consonants would you expect Sean to have the most difficulty producing? Think carefully—he can't contract the orbicularis oris. In addition to bilabials, could he also have difficulty producing labiodental sounds?
2. Consider the primary acoustic cues for the consonants that Sean cannot produce correctly. How might you expect those cues to be altered? What effect might those changes have upon speech perception (that is, understanding the phonemes)?
3. Consider the acoustic cues for bilabial plosives. How would exaggerated movement of the mandible and rapid release (lowering) of the mandible simulate key acoustic cues?
4. What vowels would you expect Sean to have difficulty producing accurately? Identify those phonemes on the vowel quadrilateral. Do you observe any pattern?
5. How are the formant frequencies of the vowels changed by lack of labial movement? Review Table 7–1 and Figure 7–14 to help you answer the question.
6. The listener cannot rely on the usual visual cues obtained from lip movement. How might the lack of visual cues affect listener understanding of Sean's speech? (See Chapter 11 for discussion of visual information and speech perception.)

8.1 Introduction

We turn our attention now to the production of consonants and their acoustic representation. (See Appendix D for the IPA consonant chart.) As described in Chapter 7, the production of vowels differs from consonants in two ways. Vowels are produced with a relatively open vocal tract. Consonants are produced with one or more areas of constriction, although we learn in this chapter that the constriction can be quite wide, almost open. Vowels are always voiced, whereas the sound source for consonants may be voicing, turbulent airflow, or both together. Said another way, vowels are always produced with nearly periodic airflow. Consonants can be produced with nearly periodic airflow from the vibrating vocal folds and/or aperiodic airflow arising from a constriction at the glottis or downstream in the vocal tract. A **constriction** that is closer to the mouth is said to be **downstream**, whereas a constriction closer to the vocal folds is said to be **upstream**. All the sounds in American English are **egressive**, produced on the outward flow of air from the lungs. Events that occur farther from the lungs are therefore downstream from the air source.

The relative openness of the vocal tract in the production of vowels means that vowels, in general, carry greater energy than consonants. However, the relative functional load (the contribution to meaning) of vowels and consonants is uncertain. Nearly a century ago, the experiments of Fletcher (1929) suggested that consonants carry a heavier functional load than do vowels. However, his work was based on monosyllables. More recent experimentation based upon sentences (Kewley-Port, Burkle, & Lee, 2007) suggests that vowels may carry the heavier functional load. Yet in American English, the consonants carry a heavier functional load for phonemic distinctions (that is, meaning) than do vowels.

Overview of the Pharyngeal and Velar Muscles

The Pharynx

The pharynx is the common tube that connects the nasal and oral cavities with the larynx. The pharynx is bounded by the esophagus and hypopharynx inferiorly and the cranium superiorly. From the perspective of speech production, the pharynx can be viewed as a muscular tube, the purpose of which is to resonate the sound pressure wave by variable constrictions (Figure 8–2). Three large fan-shaped muscles function primarily to constrict the pharynx and, hence, are referred to as the pharyngeal constrictors: the inferior constrictor (the largest and most powerful of this group), the middle constrictor, and the superior constrictor (the weakest of this group). Additional muscles that, on contraction, assist in pharyngeal narrowing are the following: the cricopha-

ryngeus (which encircles the opening of the esophagus), the salpingopharyngeus, and stylopharyngeus, which, upon contraction, assist in opening the pharyngeal tube by elevation of the pharyngeal wall. The stylopharyngeus also assists in laryngeal elevation.

The Velopharyngeal Port

The velum, or soft palate, contributes principally to the shape of the oropharynx and controls the velopharyngeal port, the opening between the oral and nasal cavities (Figure 8–3). The soft palate is composed of five major muscles: the levator veli palatini, tensor veli palatini, musculus uvulae, palatopharyngeal, and palatoglossal muscles. With the exception of the musculus uvulae, these are

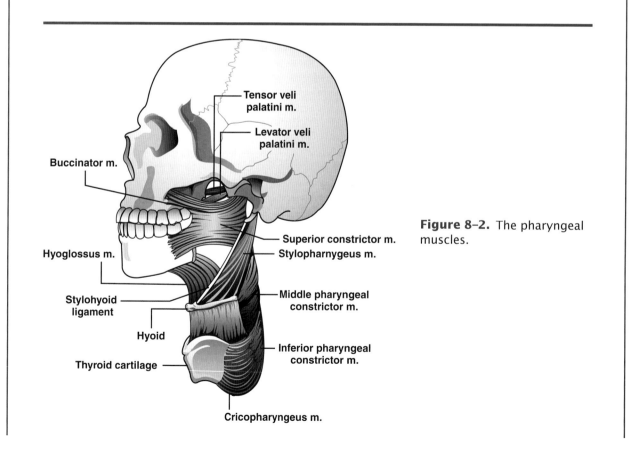

Figure 8–2. The pharyngeal muscles.

Tensor veli palatini m.

Levator veli palatini m.

Buccinator m.

Hyoglossus m.

Stylohyoid ligament

Hyoid

Thyroid cartilage

Superior constrictor m.

Stylopharnygeus m.

Middle pharyngeal constrictor m.

Inferior pharyngeal constrictor m.

Cricopharyngeus m.

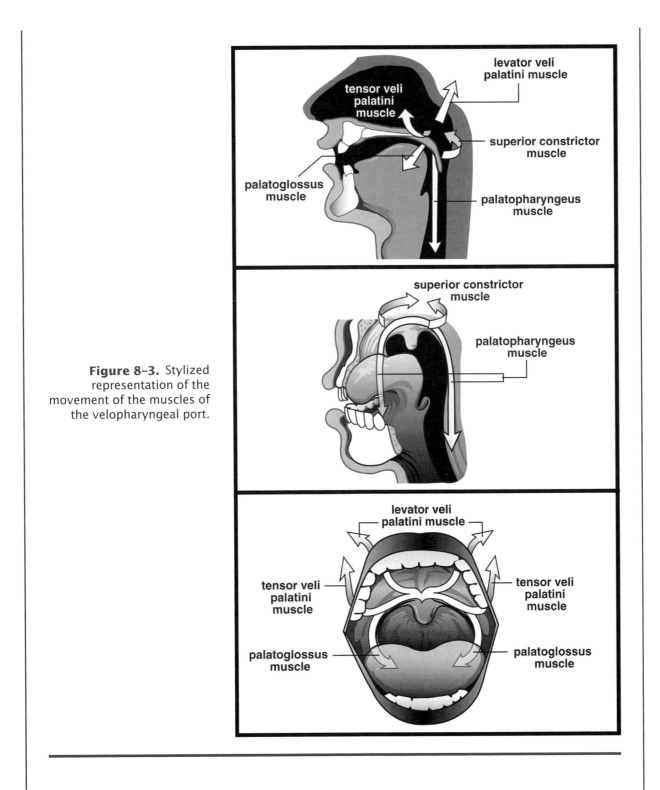

Figure 8–3. Stylized representation of the movement of the muscles of the velopharyngeal port.

extrinsic muscles of the soft palate, in that one attachment of each muscle is external to the palate. Upon contraction, the levator veli patatini and the pair of musculi uvulae elevate the soft palate and hence close the velopharyngeal port. The tensor veli palatini is responsible primarily for dilating the eustachian tube (a tube that serves to regulate pressure in the ear) but also helps to elevate the soft palate. (Sometimes this muscle is identified as a *tensor*.) The palatoglossus can be identified as a muscle of the tongue or of the pharynx. Upon contraction, it assists in elevation of the body of the tongue. The palatoglossus is not a very large or powerful muscle, but it is strategically positioned to lower the velum upon contraction, thereby opening the velopharyngeal port. The palatophayrngeal muscle also functions to lower the velum.

Innervation of the Upper Vocal Tract

The pharyngeal plexus is formed by cranial nerve XI (the accessory) and the pharyngeal branch of cranial nerve X (the vagus), which courses between the internal and external carotid arteries and enters the pharynx at the upper boundary of the middle constrictor muscle. The pharyngeal plexus supplies motor innervation to all the pharyngeal muscles, including those of the soft palate, except for the stylopharyngeus and the tensor veli palatini. The tensor veli palatini receives motor innervation from the mandibular nerve of cranial nerve V (the trigeminal). The stylopharyngeus receives motor innervation from the muscular branch of cranial nerve IX (the glossopharyngeal nerve).

Developmental Aspects of Vocal Tract Maturation

From infancy to adulthood, the vocal tract increases by more than twice its length. We know that the increased length certainly affects formant frequencies. However, in addition to overall increase in length, the relative proportions of the oral and pharyngeal cavities change, sometimes referred to as "anatomic restructuring." This restructuring includes the bending of the vocal tract to form a right angle from the nasopharyngeal to the oropharyngeal areas, descent of the hyoid bone and larynx within the vocal tract, a separation of the contact of the epiglottis from the velum, and a descent of the posterior portion of the tongue to form the anterior wall of the pharynx (Fried, Kelly, & Strome, 1982; Kent & Vorperian, 1995). All the structures that comprise the vocal tract do not grow at the same rate (Fitch & Giedd, 1999). Unique data from magnetic resonance imaging (MRI) studies (Vorperian, Kent, Lindstrom, Kalina, Gentry, & Yandell, 2005) show that growth in boys and girls is equivalent between birth and almost 7 years of age, and growth rates of the individual structures depend upon their orientation (horizontal or vertical) relative to the vocal tract. A small amount of data shows that, at the other end of the life span, senescent changes occur that result in increased vocal tract length and volume (Xue & Hao, 2003).

8.2 Three Sources of Speech Sounds

We can consider three sources of speech sounds: nearly periodic complex waves, continuous aperiodic waves, and transient aperiodic waves. One source is the vibration of the vocal folds, driven by the air pressure generated by the lungs, in which the steady flow of air is converted into a series of puffs, each of which vibrates in an alternating compression and rarefaction of air molecules. This source, as we have learned, produces a nearly periodic complex wave. Vowels are produced by this method. A second source of sound arises as the airflow is driven by the lung pressure up through the open glottis, becoming turbulent as it flows through a supraglottal constriction. Many consonants such as /s/ and /f/ are produced by this method. The sound pressure waves produced in this fashion are continuous noise, that is, aperiodic complex waves generated by turbulence. A third source of sound is transient noise, rapid pressure changes in the supraglottal vocal tract, including the pop of a /p/ and the click of a /k/. These sounds are driven not by lung pressure but by generation of pressures in the mouth.

Coarticulation

Throughout Chapter 7, we studied vowels in isolation. We know, however, that communication rarely involves production of one sound in isolation but rather is a continuous, dynamic sequencing of vocal tract movements produced in rapid succession. Let us pretend that you are sitting down at your desk reading this text and you intend to stand up and put the book away. Do you stand up completely and then reach for the book? More likely, you reach for the book as you are in the process of standing up. Not only do the two actions overlap, but they each influence the other. Adjustments are made to the standing up action to accommodate the reaching for the book action and vice versa. Sequential movements of the vocal tract in the production of speech sounds can be conceptualized similarly. For any given target sound, the phoneme immediately preceding and the one immediately following will influence the articulatory posture of the vocal tract. We make articulatory adjustments to both phonemes at the same time. In fact, we could say that we are articulating more than one phoneme at one time. This phenomenon of simultaneously articulating more than one phoneme is called **coarticulation**. We may adjust the vocal tract posture in anticipation of the next phoneme, referred to as **anticipatory or forward coarticulation**. Similarly, we may adjust the vocal tract posture because of the sound immediately preceding the phoneme, referred to as **retentive or backward coarticulation**. Throughout our discussion of consonant production, we note the effect of coarticulation. In fact, coarticulation is essential to the perception of certain consonants.

Unlike vowels, some of the consonants have virtually no distinguishing acoustic features in themselves. How, then, do we distinguish between them perceptually? The answer lies in their effect upon the vowels. In other words, the coarticulatory effect upon the vowels contributes to our discrimination of the consonants involved. The transition between the consonant and the vowel (CV) or the vowel and the consonant (VC) provides the necessary acoustic information for consonant recognition. We speak of vowel transitions as the shift in formant frequencies resulting from vocal tract dynamics in connected speech. In Chapter 7, we considered mainly the formant frequencies of the steady-state (unchanging) portion of the vowels. We examined the onset and offset, or onglide and offglide, of the vowels only in consideration of diphthongs. Now in this chapter, we examine more closely the onset and offset of the vowels as they interact with adjacent consonants.

8.3 Phonetic Description of Consonants

The phonetic description of consonants has traditionally included three features, the presence or absence of voicing, their place of constriction of the flow of air from the lungs, and their manner of articulation (Ladefoged, 2000; Pickett, 1980). For each consonant in which voicing is a distinctive feature, the voiced and voiceless cognates are considered within the description of place and manner of articulation.

Place of Articulation

The place of articulation for consonants is traditionally identified as bilabial, labiodental, (lingual) dental, (lingual) alveolar, (lingual) palatal, and (lingual) velar. Apart from the bilabial and labiodental sounds, all the other consonants are created by manipulating the airstream with the tongue against the teeth, alveolar ridge, palate, or velar area. In this chapter, we assume the prefix lingual and omit it, referring to the places of articulation as dental, alveolar, and so on. The bilabials are produced with both lips coming together to occlude the airway, as in /p, b, m/. The labiodental consonants are produced with the lower lip against the upper front teeth, as in /f, v/. The dental consonants are produced with the tongue tip or tongue blade against the upper front teeth, as in the sounds /θ, ð/. The alveolar consonants are produced with the tongue blade against the back of the alveolar ridge, as in /t, d/. Some speakers place the tip of the tongue behind the lower front teeth and others place it up near the alveolar ridge. However, the tongue blade is always placed at or behind the alveolar ridge for alveolar sounds. Palatal consonants are produced with the tongue blade against the hard palate, as in the sound /ʃ, ŋ, j/. Velar consonants are produced with the back of the tongue against the soft palate, as in /k, g/. The retroflex consonant /r/ can be produced with the back of the tongue against the alveolar ridge. A significant amount of variability, however, exists with the retroflex sound among different speakers. American English has only one pharyngeal fricative, the /h/, which is sometimes classified as a glottal sound.

Manner of Articulation

The manner of articulation refers to the degree of constriction in the vocal tract and its effect upon the airflow. The constriction may be transiently complete, in which case the airflow is fully stopped momentarily, such as occurs for **stops** (synonymously, **plosives**, in American English) and **affricates**. The constriction may be incomplete, such that the airflow is impeded to a greater or lesser extent, either for a short duration or for a relatively long period (long relative to the production of phonemes within running speech). When the constriction is incomplete and airflow continues, the consonant is said to be a **continuant**. The continuants include fricatives, glides, liquids, and nasals. Table 8–1 lists the consonants of American English by place, manner of articulation, and voicing.

Table 8–1. The Consonants of American English, Organized by Manner and Place of Articulation and Presence (+V) or Absence (−V) of Voicing

	Labial		Labiodental		Dental		Alveolar		Palatal		Velar		Pharyngeal or Glottal	
	−V	+V	−V	+V	−V	+V	−V	+V	−V	+V	−V	+V	−V	+V
Stops	p	b					t	d			k	g		
Fricatives			f	v	θ	ð	s	z	ʃ	ʒ			h	
Affricates									tʃ	dʒ	ŋ			
Nasals		m						n						
Liquids lateral								l						
Liquid retroflex								r						
Glides (semi-vowels)		w								j				

1. Distinguish an upstream constriction from a downstream constriction in the vocal tract.

2. Identify the three sources of speech sounds and the types of sound waves generated by these sources.

3. Define anticipatory and retentive coarticulation.

4 Traditionally, consonants are identified by three features. Name them.

5. What are the articulatory points of contact that identify place of articulation? Provide an example of each. Which points specify tongue contact and which do not?

6. To what does manner of articulation refer? List the seven manners of articulation and provide an example of each.

7. Which manners of articulation are considered continuants? Why?

8.4 Acoustic Representation of Consonants

Stops

In the **stop**, **or plosive**, a complete constriction of the vocal tract occurs, causing cessation of the airflow. Upon release of the constriction, the airflow resumes in a burst of sound. (Think of an explosion of escaping air; hence "plosive.") The bilabial, alveolar, and velar stops, in the voiceless and voiced cognate pairs, are /p, b/, /t, d/ and /k, g/, respectively (Figures 8–4 and 8–5). The stop consonants are complex sounds with many allophonic variations. No single, invariant

(always present) set of acoustic features exists to alert the listener to stop production. Four acoustic cues are important for perception of the stop: the silence, the burst noise, the voice onset time, and the poststop vowel formant transition. These features are each discussed below.

Stop Gap

Silence, also called the **stop gap**, occurs during production of the plosive prior to release of the airflow (Figures 8–4, 8–5, and 8–6). For the voiceless stops /p, t, k /, complete silence occurs momentarily. For the voiced stops /b, d, g/, vocal fold vibration may continue through part or all of the stop, producing a low-amplitude sound. Recall from Chapter 4 that vocal fold vibration can occur only in the presence of a transglottal pressure drop. On complete closure of the vocal tract during stop production, the supraglottal pressure will quickly equilibrate to the lung pressure, at which time phonation will cease. During running speech, the duration of the voiced stop is often short enough that the supraglottal pressure never reaches the same level as the lung pressure. In that case, the voicing continues throughout the closed portion of the voiced stop. In other cases, however, pressure equilibration occurs and the voicing ceases prior to release of the stop. The presence of voicing during the closed portion often is referred to as the **voice bar**, as indicated in the spectrogram in Figure 8–5. The voiced sound produced during the closed portion of the stop, however, is substantially damped by the vocal tract, and so it is a low-energy, soft sound. The waveforms in Figures 8–4 through 8–6 show the low-amplitude sound pressure corresponding in time to the voice bar in the spectrogram.

Release Burst

A brief transient burst noise occurs upon release of the occlusion and the impounded air. (This is the "pop" sound you often hear when someone is speaking into a microphone and has held the microphone too close to the mouth.) During

Waveform

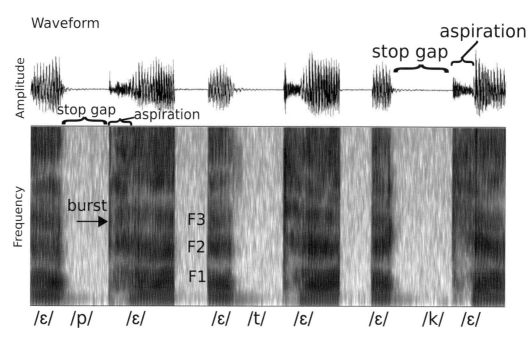

/ɛ/ /p/ /ɛ/ /ɛ/ /t/ /ɛ/ /ɛ/ /k/ /ɛ/

Wideband spectrogram

Figure 8–4. Acoustic features of the voiceless stops.

Waveform

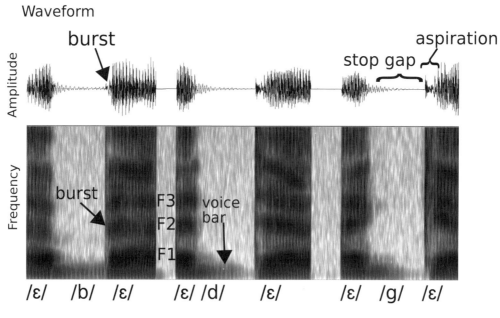

/ɛ/ /b/ /ɛ/ /ɛ/ /d/ /ɛ/ /ɛ/ /g/ /ɛ/

Wideband spectrogram

Figure 8–5. Acoustic features of the voiced stops.

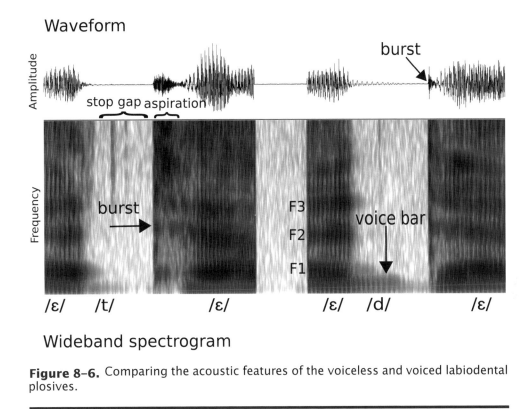

Figure 8–6. Comparing the acoustic features of the voiceless and voiced labiodental plosives.

the closed period of the plosive, the air pressure within the mouth, the intraoral pressure, is raised above atmospheric pressure. The **release burst** results from the sudden meeting of the two pressures. Duration of the burst is generally 10 to 30 ms for voiced stops and slightly longer for their voiceless cognates. The transient burst noise is seen in the waveform (see Figures 8–4 through 8–6) as a sudden change in amplitude after the flat portion of the line representing the silent closure. In the spectrogram, the burst may be seen as the sudden appearance of energy (gray) across many frequencies.

The spectral content of the burst may provide information about the place of articulation (Blumstein & Stevens, 1979; Forrest, Weismer, Milenkovic, & Douglass, 1988; Stevens & Blumstein, 1978). In the release burst of the bilabial plosives (/p, b/), the spectral envelope is generally flat to falling. That is, the energy is broadly distributed across all frequencies or, alternatively, concentrated in the lower frequencies. The alveolar plosives (/t, d/) tend to have a ris-

ing spectral envelope, meaning that the energy is concentrated in the higher harmonics. And in production of the velar plosives (/k, g/), the spectral envelope of the release burst is concentrated in the middle frequency range. You can hear the dominant frequencies of the burst by saying the voiceless plosives in a whisper. The burst of the /t/ has the highest pitch and loudest burst, followed by /k/, and then finally /p/ with the lowest pitch and softest burst (Figure 8–7).

Aspiration

Release of a voiceless stop in the initial position of a word may occur with or without aspiration (see Figures 8–4 through 8–6). The **aspiration** is like the sound produced by the voiceless fricative /h/, a bit like a rapid, brief, voiceless sigh. For example, the bilabial voiceless plosive is aspirated in "pie" [pʰai] but unaspirated in "apple" [æpəl]. A diacritic is a mark used to indicate allophonic variations. The diacritic representing aspiration is the superscript "h" because

Waveform

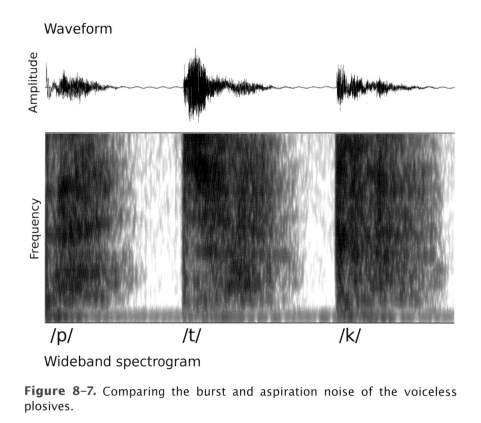

Wideband spectrogram

Figure 8–7. Comparing the burst and aspiration noise of the voiceless plosives.

the spectrum of the aspiration is like that of the /h/, with broadband noise across many frequencies. (See the discussion of /h/ in the section on fricatives.) The aspiration noise likely is a function of the transition of the vocal folds from voicing to unvoicing and back to voicing. The vocal folds are vibrating during the vowel prior to the plosive and then separate slightly during the unvoiced portion of the closed phase of the voiceless stop. Upon release of the stop, the air resumes its flow through the glottis. The turbulent airflow escaping through the narrowed vocal folds creates the aspiration noise before the vocal folds resume vibration. Aspiration does not occur in an "s"-cluster, such as /sp/ or /st/, most likely because the voiceless /s/ is produced with the vocal folds abducted, and so the vocal folds are farther apart at the release of the plosive. Aspiration does not occur after release of a voiced stop. Compare the presence or absence of aspiration noise in the three utterances "a

pair, a bear, a spare" in the waveform and spectrogram of Figure 8–8.

Voice Onset Time

The categorical perception of a voiced or a voiceless stop would appear, at first glance, to be a simple binary perception. The vocal folds are not vibrating, no laryngeal sound source is produced, and the phoneme is voiceless (p, t, k). The vocal folds vibrate to produce a phonatory sound source, and the phoneme is considered voiced (b, d, g). The acoustic representation of the voiced/voiceless contrast, however, is not straightforward. We have hinted at some complexity already in the preceding discussion of equilibration of sub- and supraglottal pressures and the resulting silence or low-amplitude voicing visualized in both the spectrogram and the waveform. The time from the release of the stop closure to the onset of voicing is called the **voice**

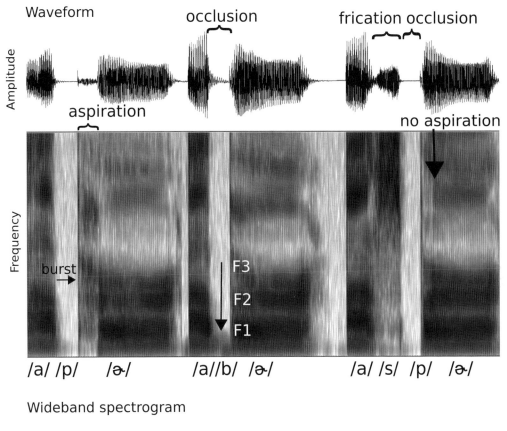

Figure 8–8. Compare the acoustic features of the plosives in "a pear, a bear, a spare." Aspiration does not occur after the voiced plosive or after the plosive in the s-cluster.

onset time **(VOT)** (Lisker & Abramson, 1964). The VOT in milliseconds (ms) can be measured from either the waveform or the spectrogram, as shown in Figure 8–9. Voicing may begin just before the release of the plosive, in which case we say that prevoicing has occurred. In prevoicing, the VOT is negative (with respect to the oral release), ranging from −75 to −25 ms (Lisker & Abramson, 1964). Voice onset may occur simultaneously with the release of the impounded (captured) air. Or voicing may begin just after the air is released, in which case the VOT is positive. Positive VOT may be short lag or long lag (McCrea & Morris, 2005). Short-lag VOTs range from 0 (no lag at all) to +25 ms after oral release (Lisker & Abramson, 1964), whereas long-lag VOTs range from 40 to 100 ms. In general, a VOT that is negative, simultaneous, or short lag, such

as /b, d, g/, is perceived as voiced, whereas long-lag VOT, such as /p, t, k/, is perceived as voiceless (Forrest, Weismer, & Turner, 1989; Klatt, 1975; Lisker & Abramson, 1964) (Figure 8–10).

It is evident that the VOT cue is a continuum, so that as the duration of the onset time approaches the 20- to 40-ms range, other cues may contribute to the voiced/voiceless perception. VOT is dependent upon speaker and phonetic context. Speaking rate, for example, influences VOT, with faster rates resulting in greater reduction in the voiced-voiceless boundary and overlap of the VOT categories (Miller, Green, & Reeves, 1986; Volaitis & Miller, 1992).

Four secondary cues supplement VOT: That is, they help the listener identify whether the VOT signifies a voiced or voiceless phoneme. One supplemental cue is the duration of the

Waveform

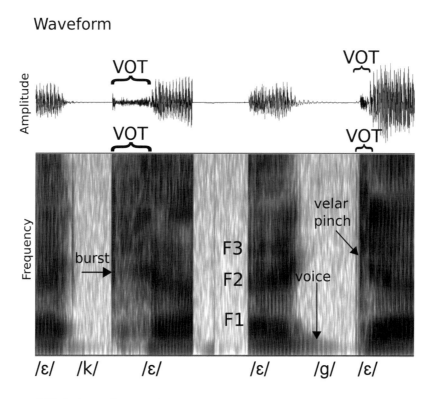

Wideband spectrogram

Figure 8–9. Note the relatively shorter VOT for the /g/ as compared with the /k/.

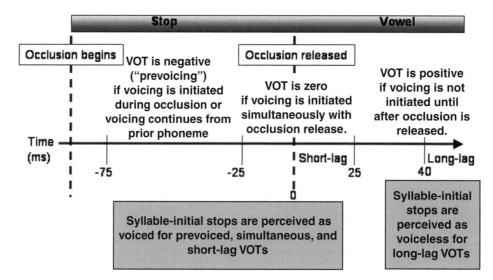

Figure 8–10. Features of voice onset time (VOT). The time line is not drawn to scale.

closure, which is generally longer for voiceless stops. A second supplemental cue is the presence of aspiration. Recall that the voiced stops are unaspirated. Aspiration by itself is not sufficient to identify the stop as voiceless, but aspiration does assist us in our identification of a voiceless stop. And a third supplemental cue of VOT is the fundamental frequency (Haggard, Summerfield, & Roberts, 1981; Kohler, 1985; Lisker & Abramson, 1971). The f_0 tends to go downward in anticipation of the closure for both the voiceless and voiced stop, a feature identified early in phonetic research (House & Fairbanks, 1953; Lehiste & Peterson, 1961). After the release burst of the voiceless stop, voicing resumes at an elevated f_0 for a moment before settling down into a stable f_0 for the steady-state portion of the vowel. In the voiced plosive, however, the f_0 for the subsequent vowel is relatively flat, whether voicing continued without interruption or with a small interruption during the closed portion of the plosive. And finally, the fourth supplemental cue to VOT is that vowels preceding voiced stops tend to be longer than those preceding voiceless stops, most likely due to anticipatory coarticulation. That is, the anticipation of cessation of vocal fold vibration for the voiceless stop likely shortens the duration of the voicing for the preceding vowel.

Some evidence suggests that VOT increases with lung volume (Hoit, Solomon, & Hixon, 1993), perhaps due to a mechanical effect of pull on the trachea exerted by the diaphragm. The pull on the trachea then may pull the larynx downward and pull the vocal folds apart, thereby delaying vocal fold vibration and increasing VOT. This theory, however, needs considerable more data for substantiation. McCrea and Morris (2005) found that VOT of voiceless stops decreased as f_0 increased. This finding contradicts earlier data, which demonstrated decreased VOT at higher frequencies. It had been hypothesized that this phenomenon may be associated with the higher supraglottal pressure associated with voiceless stops, which could maintain separation of the upper surface of the vocal folds and thereby inhibit vibration (Stevens, 1991). The reason for the decreased VOTs found by McCrea and

Developmental Aspects of VOT

Acquisition of the voicing contrast for stop consonants is a major developmental milestone. Necessary for this achievement is maturation of laryngeal control and spatial and temporal control of supraglottal articulators (Gracco & Löfqvist, 1994; Koenig, 2000, 2001; Munhall, Löfqvist, & Kelso, 1994; Warren & Hall, 1973). Very young children produce VOTs for both voiced and voiceless stops that fall only within the adult range of voiced stops. They begin to produce the voicing contrast first in syllable initial position between 15 and 30 months of age but may not attain fully mature timing contrasts until adolescence (Snow, 1997; Zlatin & Koenigsknecht, 1976). In fact, prior to achieving the contrast, young children's VOTs (for voiced and voiceless stops alike) all fall within the longer end of the adult voiced range (Macken & Barton, 1980). Not surprisingly, children demonstrate greater variability than adults in VOT in both acoustic (Kent & Forner, 1980; Ohde, 1985) and kinematic studies (Goffman & Smith, 1999). Robb and Smith (2002) compared f_0 at onset and offset of voicing surrounding voiceless stops in 4-, 8-, and 21-year-old males and females. No differences were found for f_0 offset for the vowel immediately preceding the obstruent, and this observation supports the hypotheses that this phenomenon is a result of opening the vocal folds in anticipation of the voiceless stop. For f_0 onset of the vowel immediately following the stop, however, the youngest group of children had a smaller rise in f_0, suggesting some maturational effect.

Morris (2005) is not immediately clear but may be related to complex interactions between the vocal tract and voice source.

Phonemic context also affects VOT. VOTs have been found to be longer before sonorant consonants than before vowels, and VOTs are generally longer before high vowels than before low vowels (Higgins, Netsell, & Schulte, 1998; Klatt, 1975). These differences may be due to the greater constriction of the sonorants (as compared to vowels) and high vowels (as compared to low vowels), which results in a diminished transglottal pressure drop that, if sufficient, will cause vocal fold vibration to cease. VOT is also affected by the type of utterance, that is, the speaking task. Greater speaker variability in VOT is demonstrated in running speech than in single-word utterances. One of the results of the increased variability is greater overlap in VOT for voiceless and voiced plosives. That is, they tend to converge more closely in conversation than in restricted utterances (Baran, Laufer, & Daniloff, 1977; Lisker & Abramson, 1967). It may be that suprasegmental effects related to the intent of the conversation exert an influence on VOT that is absent in the single-word test utterances (Kessinger & Blumstein, 1997).

Formant Transitions

The articulatory posture of the vocal tract shifts as the speaker moves from the stop to the vowel. For both the voiceless and voiced stops, the speaker does not wait until the vocal tract is in the optimal posture for producing the vowel, of course. Vowel production begins while the stop is still being released. The frequency of the vowel formants therefore will shift during this transition quite rapidly. The frequencies at which the formants originate are called the **locus** for that place of articulation. However, the formant structure of the vowel immediately following the stop often is obscured in the spectrogram by the burst noise. Therefore, often the locus can only be inferred. Instead, we focus upon the movement of the formants. The spectrogram in Figure 8–11 shows an upward rise of F1 in the vowel upon release of all the stop consonants. That is, vowel F1 ascends in CV position. This F1 onset occurs because the vocal tract is moving from a posture of occlusion to one of openness, as it must to release the impounded air. Similarly, for the vowel preceding the consonant, in VC position, F1 descends as the constriction is formed. We can say, therefore, that the rise in F1 in CV position and the fall in F1 in VC position is a result of the manner of articulation for the plosive. This early formant shift, although a perceptual marker for manner of articulation, is not a perceptual cue for the place of articulation. The onsets and offsets of F2 and F3 are the relevant perceptual markers for place of articulation.

Recall from Chapter 7 that constriction at the lips lowers all formants. The release of the bilabial stops, therefore, means that the following vowel will begin with narrowed lips. Therefore, F2 and F3 begin the vowel at lower frequencies, which then move upward very quickly as the lip opening is widened into the steady-state portion of the vowel. The frequencies to which the second and third formants move depend upon the vowel following the plosive. For the alveolar stops, the loci of F2 and F3 are not as low, and their movement depends on the subsequent vowel. In production of the velar stops, F2 and F3 begin close together, sometimes called the **velar pinch**, and then typically spread apart as the vowel is produced. The formant transitions that occur upon release of the voiceless stops are more difficult to observe in the spectrogram than the transitions after the voiced stops. This difficulty occurs because the transitions that occur after the voiceless stops are often obscured by the release burst noise.

The formants of the vowels immediately preceding the plosive (that is, in the VC position) also will be influenced by the movement of the vocal tract in preparation of producing the plosive. All the formant frequencies begin to drop just before the bilabial plosive because occlusion at the lips lowers all formants. Going into the dental plosive, F2 begins to rise while F3 remains steady. And approaching the velar plosive, we see the F2–F3 pinch.

Waveform

Amplitude

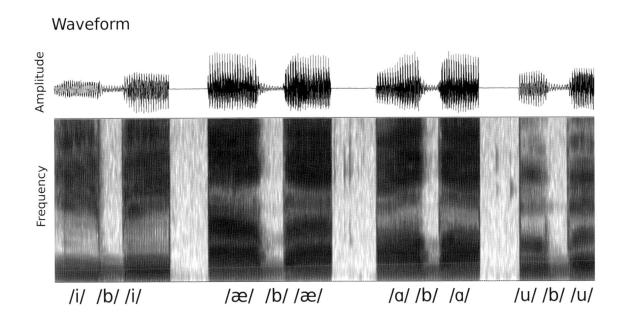

/i/ /b/ /i/   /æ/ /b/ /æ/   /ɑ/ /b/ /ɑ/   /u/ /b/ /u/

Wideband spectrogram

A

Waveform

Amplitude

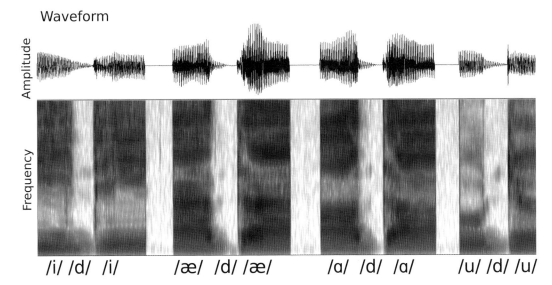

/i/ /d/ /i/   /æ/ /d/ /æ/   /ɑ/ /d/ /ɑ/   /u/ /d/ /u/

Wideband spectrogram

B

Figure 8–11. A. Formant transitions in the high and low vowels preceding and following /b/. **B.** Formant transitions in the high and low vowels preceding and following /d/. *continues*

Waveform

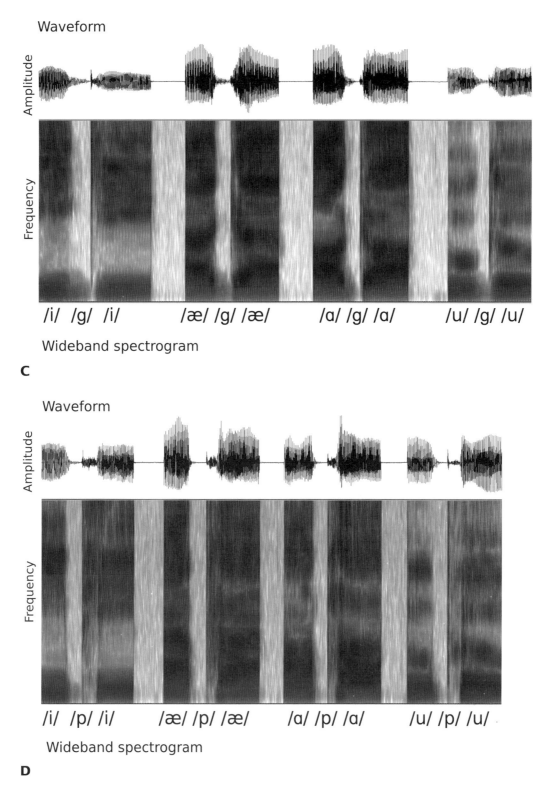

Wideband spectrogram

C

Waveform

Wideband spectrogram

D

Figure 8–11. *continued* **C.** Formant transitions in the high and low vowels preceding and following /g/. **D.** Formant transitions in the high and low vowels preceding and following /p/. *continues*

Waveform

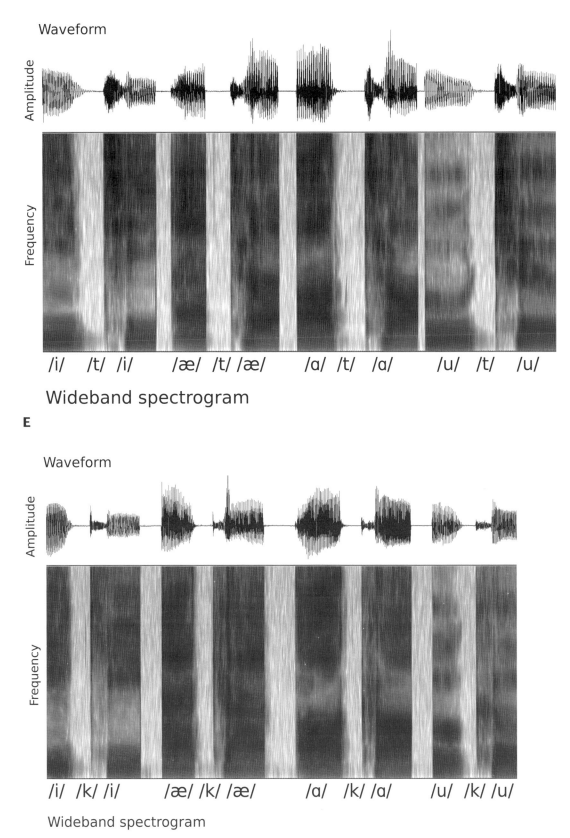

/i/ /t/ /i/   /æ/ /t/ /æ/   /ɑ/ /t/ /ɑ/   /u/ /t/ /u/

Wideband spectrogram

E

Waveform

/i/ /k/ /i/   /æ/ /k/ /æ/   /ɑ/ /k/ /ɑ/   /u/ /k/ /u/

Wideband spectrogram

F

Figure 8–11. *continued* **E.** Formant transitions in the high and low vowels preceding and following /t/. **F.** Formant transitions in the high and low vowels preceding and following /k/.

Released and Unreleased Stops

Earlier it was noted that some consonants have virtually no distinguishing acoustic features by themselves and that the consonant is identified by formant transitions of the contiguous vowels. A good example of this phenomenon is the unreleased stop. Consider the final plosives of the words "bat" and "bad" in the phrases, "He's a bat boy" and "He's a bad boy" (Figure 8–12). Although the final /t/ is released, the final /d/ is not. Is this the only feature that distinguishes the voiceless from the voiced plosive in this context? No, the perception of voicing is identified also by the duration of the vowel, which is longer before the voiced plosive by as much as one and one-half times compared to the same vowel preceding a voiceless plosive (Peterson & Lehiste, 1960).

Glottal Stop

The glottal stop /ʔ/ is achieved by rapid cessation of voicing through closure of the vocal folds. In Chapter 5, we identified hard onset of voicing as taking place when the vocal folds are firmly approximated prior to initiating phonation. Hard onset involves significant medial compression of the vocal folds, allowing a buildup of lung pressure. When the vocal folds are released, the vocal folds are blown apart and the air rushes out rapidly. The glottal stop is an allophonic variant of stops in many dialects of American English, such as when it replaces the tap (very quickly produced stop) in words such as "button" or "little." The most commonly used glottal stop, however, is in the utterance to signify negation "uh uh" (Figure 8–13). The mechanics

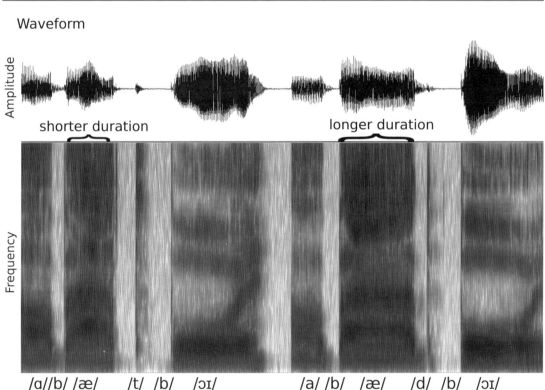

Figure 8–12. Compare the relative duration of the vowel /æ/ following the /b/ of /bæt/ and /bæd/ in the waveform and corresponding spectrogram of the sentences, "He's a bat boy. He's a bad boy." (The phrases, "a bat boy, a bad boy" have been extracted and are shown here.)

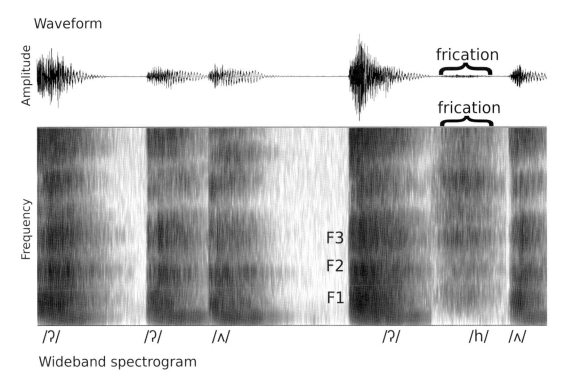

Figure 8–13. The glottal stop /ʔ/ in the common utterances that signify negation ("uh uh") and agreement ("uh huh").

and aerodynamics of the glottal stop are like the stops produced downstream in the vocal tract. The glottal stop, however, cannot be voiced because the closure for the stop gap is achieved with the vocal folds, and glottal stops are not aspirated.

Study Questions

8. Identify the four acoustic cues that contribute to our perception of a stop and describe each cue.

9. Cover the labels in the waveforms and spectrograms of Figures 8–6, 8–7, 8–8, and 8–9. Can you identify all the acoustic cues?

10. Can you draw a timeline, like Figure 8–10 (but without referring to the figure), that explains prevoicing, short-lag, and long-lag VOTs?

11. What contributes to our perception of voicing in stops, besides VOT?

12. What is the effect of lung volume and phonemic context on VOT?

13. Why do formant transitions occur before and after stop production?

14. Define locus and velar pinch.

15. What is an unreleased stop?

16. What is a glottal stop? Can you identify a common production of glottal stops?

Fricatives

In the fricative, a narrow constriction is produced by close approximation of the tongue and the teeth for the labiodentals /f, v/, between the tongue and the back of the upper front teeth for the dentals /θ, ð/, between the tongue and the alveolar ridge for the alveolars /s, z/, between the tongue and palate for the palatals /ʃ, ʒ/, and the pharyngeal or glottal /h/. It is important to note that the categorization of place of articulation can be a bit oversimplified. Lip protrusion or lip rounding occurs, particularly for the palatal fricatives and, to a lesser extent, for the alveolar fricatives.

The degree of constriction varies among the fricatives, but in all cases, it is sufficient to produce turbulent airflow. Recall the Venturi effect discussed in Chapter 5. We said that the Venturi effect is the acceleration of air through a narrowed channel. This aerodynamic phenomenon occurs when a narrow constriction is produced for the fricatives and results in frication noise. In the case of the voiceless fricatives (/f, θ, s, ʃ, h/) (Figure 8–14), the frication noise is the only sound source. The voiced cognates (/v, ð, z, ʒ/) (Figure 8–15) (/h/ having no voiced cognate in American English) are produced with two sound sources, the phonatory source and the supraglottal frication noise.

The acoustic evidence for the place of articulation is the **frication noise** generated from the turbulent airflow and the formant transitions in CV and VC contexts. The frication noise is filtered mainly by the resonating cavity downstream from the constriction. (For the voiced fricatives, the periodic sound source is filtered by the entire vocal tract, of course. The frication noise, however, is dominantly affected by the small anterior resonating space.) For the labio-

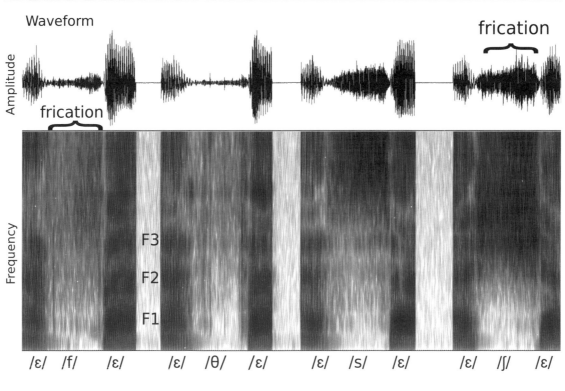

Figure 8–14. Acoustic features of the voiceless fricatives.

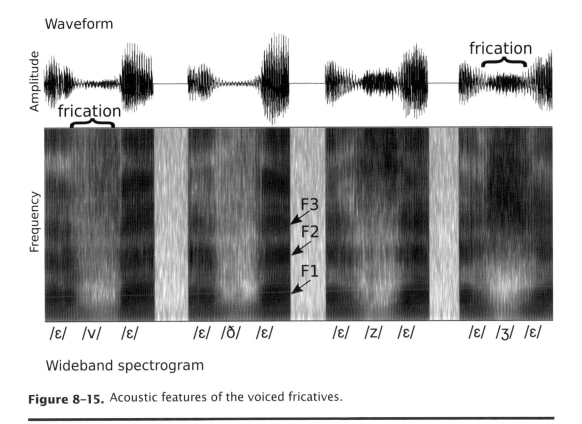

Figure 8–15. Acoustic features of the voiced fricatives.

dental and linguadental fricatives, the area of constriction is quite anterior in the oral cavity, and therefore the noise is not filtered very much by the oral cavity resonating space. Furthermore, the constriction is broad and relatively open compared to that of the other fricatives. For these reasons, the frication noise generated by these fricatives has a broad spectrum but a low level of energy. The alveolar and palatal fricatives are produced with a significantly greater degree of constriction that is more posterior in the oral cavity, providing a larger resonating space and yielding frication noise with greater energy and higher frequency. These fricatives, in particular, the voiceless cognates /s, ʃ/, are often referred to as **sibilants** because of the greater energy in the higher frequencies of the frication noise. In Figures 8–14 and 8–15, we see the greater energy in the frication noise in both the darker gray of the spectrogram and the greater amplitude of the waveform. The anterior resonating cavity downstream from the constriction emphasizes

the higher frequencies in the frication noise. For the alveolar fricatives, most of the energy is concentrated in frequencies above the average F4 value of the vowels produced by the speaker. For the palatal fricatives, most of the energy is concentrated in frequencies above the average F3 value of the speaker's vowels (Kent, Dembowski, & Lass, 1996).

The pharyngeal or glottal fricative /h/ is produced with vocal fold adduction sufficient to generate turbulent airflow but without oscillation of the mucosa. Alternatively, the pharynx is narrowed to produce the frication noise of /h/. The source of the turbulent airflow depends on both the speaker and phonetic context. In either case, most of the vocal tract is available for filtering the frication noise of /h/ because the constriction is produced far upstream. In all cases, little energy is produced. Ladefoged (2006, p. 56) describes the /h/ as a voiceless counterpart of the surrounding sound. In fact, the sound source is produced so far upstream that the /h/ takes on the spectral characteristics of the vowel following it, as shown in Figure 8–16. Furthermore, although it is classified as a voiceless fricative, in fact, the /h/ is often voiced in many speakers. In Figure 8–17, note the various degrees of voicing in the words "behind," "hello," and "huge." For some speakers, the /h/ is only completely voiceless when it precedes /j/ as in "huge."

The allophonic variations of fricatives are not nearly as complex as those of the stops. However, fricatives and stops share several common attributes, so together they are called **obstruents** (Ladefoged, 2006). Stops and fricatives are the only consonants that have a phonemic voicing distinction, and this feature influences the preceding vowel. In Chapter 7, we discussed the inherent duration of vowels, noting that contextual variables also influence vowel length. In fact, vowels are generally of longer

duration before voiced stops and fricatives than before their voiceless cognates (Figure 8–18). (Recall we noted this feature earlier when distinguishing between the unreleased stops as well as when considering a secondary cue to voicing in released stops.) Anticipatory coarticulation is likely the reason for the difference in vowel duration. That is, vocal fold vibration must stop to produce the voiceless fricative, so phonation may end a bit earlier in the preceding vowel, in anticipation of the upcoming voiceless phoneme.

Duration also varies for the consonant itself, depending upon voicing. The voiceless cognates of both stops and fricatives are of longer duration than their voiced counterparts when occurring at utterance-final position (see Figure 8–18). Again, the reason is likely due to anticipation of the upcoming cessation of voicing at the end of the

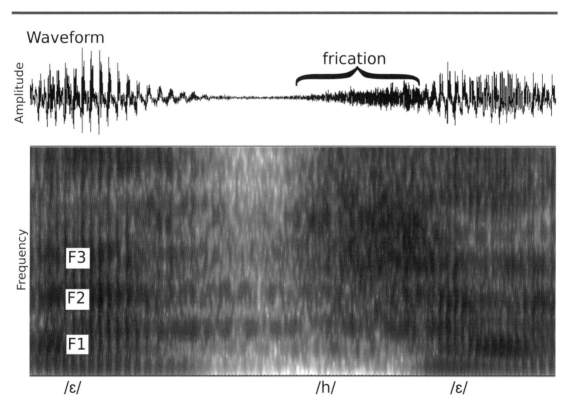

Figure 8–16. Acoustic features of the voiceless fricative /h/.

Waveform

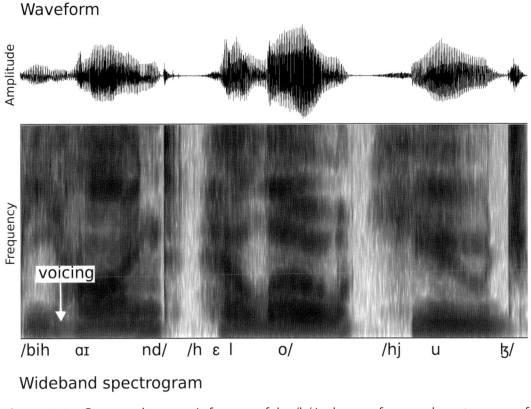

Wideband spectrogram

Figure 8–17. Compare the acoustic features of the /h/ in the waveforms and spectrograms of "behind, hello, huge." Note the presence of formant structure within the /h/ in "behind" and, to a lesser extent, in "hello" but an absence of formant structure in "huge." Note also the presence of voicing (*voice bar*) in "behind" and its absence in "hello" and "huge."

utterance. And finally, the voiced obstruents in word-final position maintain voicing throughout the full production of the consonant only if the next word begins with a voiced phoneme.

Analysis of fricatives provides a good example of anticipatory coarticulation. In Figure 8–19, we see the first formant shift position as the utterance progresses from the high front vowel quality of /i/ to the high back quality of /u/. Note that F1 transitions through production of the voiced fricative /v/. In fact, it is difficult to tell that a fricative is produced at all, if one focuses only on formant structure. Evidence of the fricative is found in the gray scale, which becomes lighter during the fricative due to the damping of sound energy by the labiodental constriction. However, it is evident that the vocal tract is mov-

ing throughout the fricative in anticipation of the postfricative vowel /u/. The tongue is not the only articulator moving during the fricative. If you say /ivu ifu/, you will note that your lips begin to protrude and round in anticipation of the /u/ before the fricative is complete. The anticipatory coarticulation is also observed in Figure 8–18 in production of the voiceless fricative /f/. The stronger frication noise and lack of voicing in the /f/ obscure observation of the formant transition. However, one still sees evidence of anticipatory coarticulation in the distinct shift in F1 from just prior to the consonant and immediately after it. Clearly the articulators are continuing to move smoothly through the fricatives despite the constriction and production of turbulent airflow. Articulator movement

Waveform

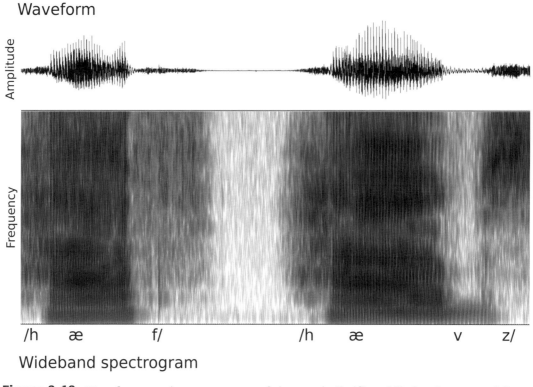

Wideband spectrogram

Figure 8–18. Waveforms and spectrograms of the words "half" and "halves" extracted from the utterances, "Cut in half. Cut in halves." Note the longer duration of the vowel preceding the voiced fricative compared to duration of the vowel preceding the voiceless fricative. Note also that the voiceless fricative in final position is of longer duration than the voiced fricative.

during the production of the other fricatives is also present, although increasingly constrained as the constriction moves farther back in the oral cavity and more of the tongue body is involved in the formation of the constriction.

Fricatives also reveal effects of coarticulation in the shift of frequency of the frication noise as a function of the adjacent vowel. The higher frequency components of the frication noise are largely unaffected by coarticulation. The low-frequency components, however, shift as a function of the frequency of the second formant of the following vowel (Olive, Greenwood, & Coleman, 1991, p. 184). In Figure 8–20, the fricatives are presented in VCV context with the four corner vowels. The upward movement of the lower border of the frication noise is evident as a function of the frequency of the second formant of the second vowel in each trio.

Study Questions

17. How is frication noise generated?

18. Define sibilant and obstruent.

19. Cover up the labels in Figures 8–14 and 8–15. Can you identify all the relevant acoustic information in the waveforms and the spectrograms?

20. Look at the waveform in Figure 8–16. What features of the amplitude and periodicity of the waveform let you know that the fricative is voiceless?

21. Examine the spectrogram in Figure 8–19. Where do you see evidence of anticipatory coarticulation?

Waveform

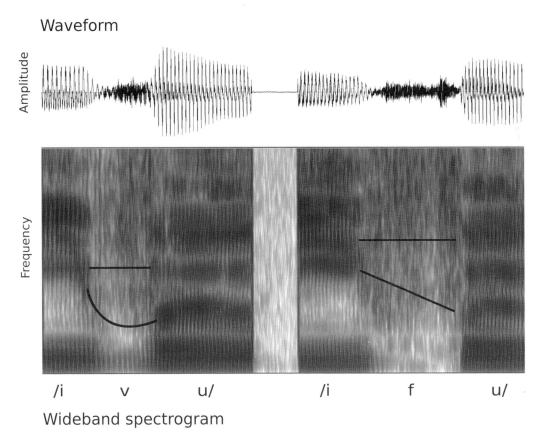

Wideband spectrogram

Figure 8–19. Note the shift of the formants through the frication noise of /f/ and /v/ so the articulatory gesture moves from the high front vowel /i/ to the high back vowel /u/.

Waveform

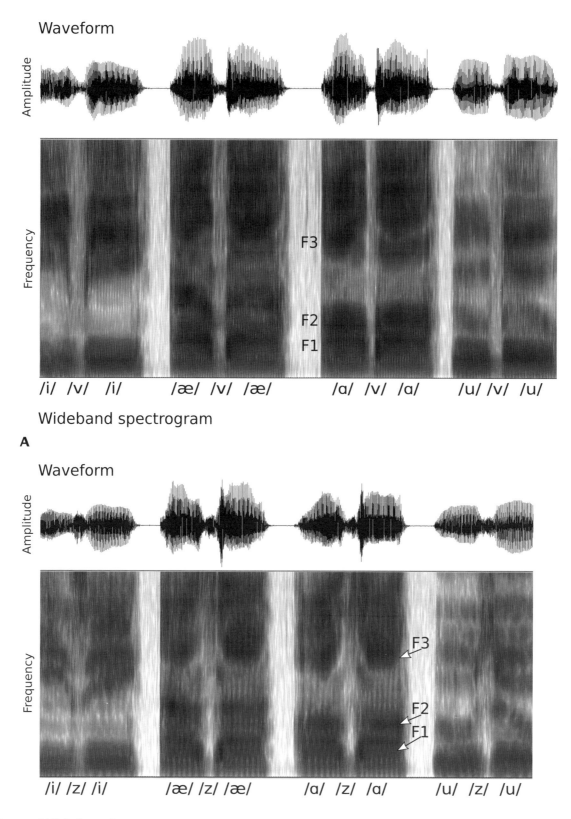

/i/ /v/ /i/   /æ/ /v/ /æ/   /ɑ/ /v/ /ɑ/   /u/ /v/ /u/

Wideband spectrogram

A

Waveform

/i/ /z/ /i/   /æ/ /z/ /æ/   /ɑ/ /z/ /ɑ/   /u/ /z/ /u/

Wideband spectrogram

B

Figure 8–20. A. Formant transitions in the high and low vowels preceding and following /v/. **B.** Formant transitions in the high and low vowels preceding and following /z/. *continues*

Waveform

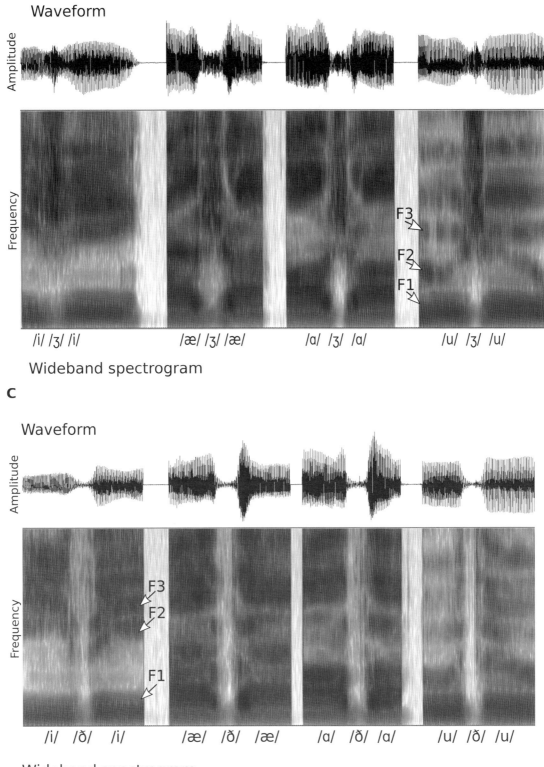

Wideband spectrogram

C

Waveform

Wideband spectrogram

D

Figure 8–20. *continued* **C.** Formant transitions in the high and low vowels preceding and following /ʒ/. **D.** Formant transitions in the high and low vowels preceding and following /ð/. *continues*

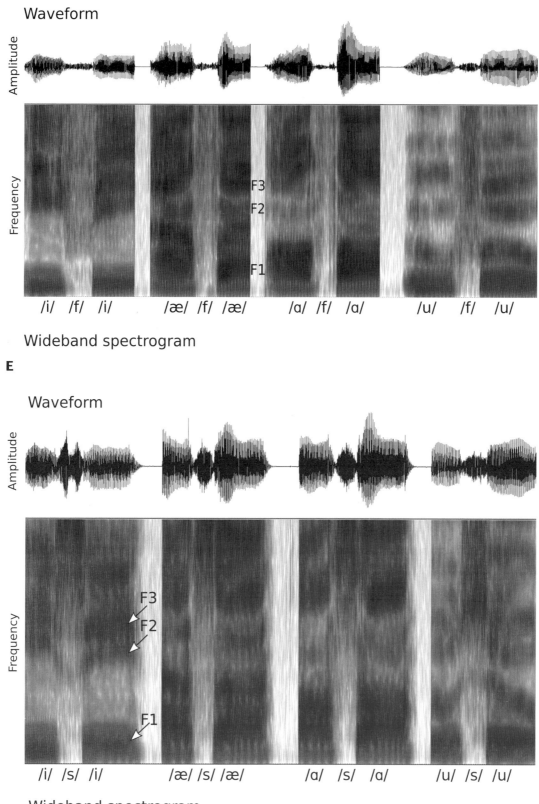

Figure 8–20. *continued* **E.** Formant transitions in the high and low vowels preceding and following /f/. **F.** Formant transitions in the high and low vowels preceding and following /s/. *continues*

Waveform

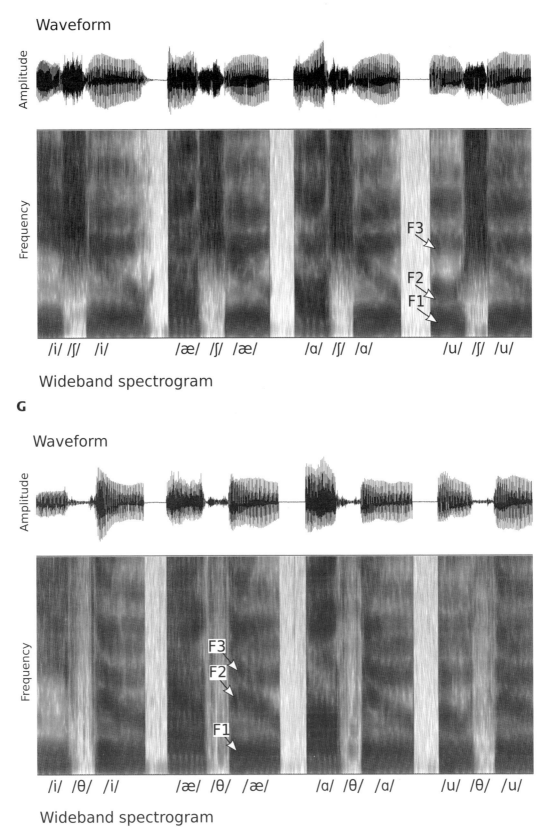

/i/ /ʃ/ /i/   /æ/ /ʃ/ /æ/   /ɑ/ /ʃ/ /ɑ/   /u/ /ʃ/ /u/

Wideband spectrogram

G

Waveform

/i/ /θ/ /i/   /æ/ /θ/ /æ/   /ɑ/ /θ/ /ɑ/   /u/ /θ/ /u/

Wideband spectrogram

H

Figure 8–20. *continued* **G.** Formant transitions in the high and low vowels preceding and following /ʃ/. **H.** Formant transitions in the high and low vowels preceding and following /θ/.

Approximants

In production of the approximants, a constriction is produced in the oral cavity, but to a lesser degree than in production of a fricative. The narrowing is not great enough to produce the Venturi effect or turbulence. Approximants include the alveolar /j/ and the bilabial /w/, both of which are also called **glides or semivowels**, and the retroflex /r/ and the alveolar /l/, the latter two of which are sometimes referred to as liquids (Figure 8–21). Despite the relatively open vocal tract in production of the approximants and the presence of formants, these phonemes are categorized as consonants largely because they do not form the nuclei of syllables.

All the approximants are produced with a central stream of airflow except the /l/, which is formed by contact of the tongue tip with the alveolar ridge, producing a lateral stream of air-

flow. As with the fricatives, lip rounding or protrusion is an important articulatory movement for some of the approximants and not just the bilabial /w/. The /j/ and, in some individuals, the /r/ are produced with lip rounding. For all approximants, the acoustic evidence for manner of production is a formant transition of approximately 75 to 250 ms, relatively slow compared to stop transitions (50 to 75 ms) but faster than diphthong transitions (approximately 350 ms). The waveform and corresponding spectrogram for the approximants are shown in Figure 8–21. Unlike the stops and fricatives, the approximants do not distinguish themselves from their neighboring vowels within the waveform. The nearly periodic sound source of the approximant flows evenly from the preceding vowel through to the following vowel. No discontinuities are found, such as the stop gap and burst of the plosive or the turbulent noise of the fricative. To

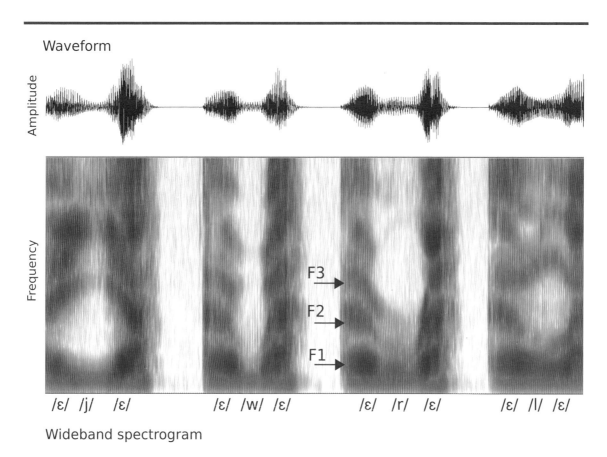

Figure 8–21. Acoustic characteristics of the glides and liquids.

understand the perceptual acoustic cues of the approximants, we must examine their spectral characteristics.

Glides (Semivowels)

The acoustic evidence for place of articulation for the approximants is the formant transition of the neighboring vowel (see Figure 8–21). For the bilabial and palatal glides (/w/ and /j/, respectively) in the CV environment, F1 rises from a low frequency up to the steady-state portion of the subsequent vowels. The reason for the upward pattern in the F1 onglide is the release of the lip rounding for both /w/ and /j/. F2 also moves upward as the /w/ is released into the following vowel. F2 moves downward, however, as the /j/ transitions to the following vowel. Recall the formant transition rule learned in Chapter 6 that a constriction in the alveolar-palatal area causes the frequency of the second formant to rise. Therefore, in the CV context, as the constriction of /j/ is released into the vowel, F2 moves downward.

Conversely, when considering the VC context, F1 moves downward from the steady-state portion of the vowel in anticipation of the glide. F2 moves downward as the vowel transitions to the /w/ and moves upward as the vowel transitions to the /j/. Movement of the formant frequencies for /w/ and /j/ in the VCV context with four diverse vowels can be observed in Figure 8–22. Note that the extent of the formant transitions is dependent upon the vowel and its characteristic formant values.

The glides are sometimes referred to as semivowels because, in the vowel-plus-glide environment, they appear quite like diphthongs. Two important acoustic differences exist, however, to distinguish the diphthong from the VC context. First, the glides are produced with greater vocal tract constriction than the vowels. Second, the formant transition from vowel to glide is faster than in that of the diphthong. Recall in Chapter 6 that we noted that the rate of formant transition from one vowel to the next is an important perceptual cue for the diphthong. Although the rate varies depending on the specific vowel com-

position of the diphthong, the transition may average approximately 350 ms in diphthongs, as compared to the VC glide transitions, which may occupy approximately 250 ms (Pickett, 1980, p. 107) or less (Olive, Greenwood, & Coleman, 1991, p. 113). However, the distinction between the two constructions is not always clear, largely due to interspeaker differences.

The lack of clarity between the diphthong and the vowel-glide environment can be revealed further by comparison of the glides with their "partner" (most similar) vowel. The glide /w/ can be compared with the vowel /u/, both of which are produced with similar, although not equivalent, vocal tract posture. The similarity of /w/ and /u/ is evident by the relative constancy of the formants in /uwu/, with little apparent change in frequency of the formants during the offglide and onglide before and after the /w/, as shown on the far right in Figure 8–22B. The movement of the formants is much less than when compared to the other VCV environments for /w/ because of the similarity in bilabial posture for the /w/ and /u/. However, the glide does differ from the /u/ in tongue position. The /w/ is formed by forward, rounded lips, but the tongue may be in any number of positions, depending on the adjacent vowel. Recall that we observed continuous anticipatory coarticulation in the case of fricatives, as demonstrated in Figure 8–18. The same phenomenon occurs with the /w/, because the tongue is not highly constrained during production of this consonant.

The glide /j/ can be compared with the vowel /i/, both of which are produced with similar although not equivalent vocal tract posture. Their similarity is evident from the relative constancy of the formants, as can be observed most particularly in the VC portion of /iji/ in Figure 8–22A. The movement of the formants is much less than when compared to the other VC environments for /j/ because of the similarity in bilabial posture for the /j/ and /i/. The difference between the two phonemes, however, is that the /i/ is produced with a more static vocal tract, and the /j/ is characterized by movement, as we noted earlier when examining the formant movements in Figures 8–21 and 8–22.

Waveform

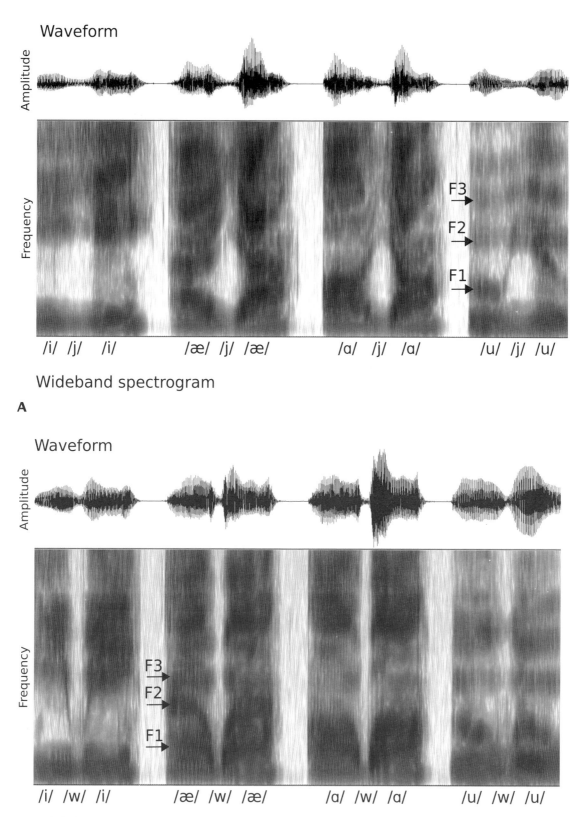

Figure 8–22. A. Formant transitions in the high and low vowels preceding and following /j/. **B.** Formant transitions in the high and low vowels preceding and following /w/.

Hydrostat Model of Tongue Articulation

Although all the articulators are critical to speech, the tongue is the most important articulator. The tongue is involved in establishing a characteristic resonance and/or directing the airflow for most sounds except [p, b, m, f, v, ʔ, h] (Stone, 1995). The tongue can function with the mandible as a unit, such as in production of /i/, or it can act independently, as in /l/. The tongue has the greatest number of degrees of freedom of all the articulators.

The movement of the tongue for vowels often is modeled as a hydrostat (Smith & Kier, 1989). A hydrostatic animal, such as the octopus, has fluid-filled sacs that function similar to the skeletal system in other animals. The octopus does not use any other type of rigid support system. The relatively open position of the vocal tract in vowel production means that the tongue frequently is moving in concert with the jaw. The tongue regulates vocal tract shape for vowels with relatively large movement patterns.

In contrast, the movement of the tongue for consonants is not typically modeled as a hydrostat. Instead, the tongue uses the hard palate, mainly, as a rigid support system. The tongue uses the hard and immobile surface as a brace against which it can push and stabilize itself. Stone (1995) explains that the tongue can take advantage of the palate in three specific ways. First, the contact helps the tongue to move independently of the mandible. For example, in the word "light," the tongue tip maintains its contact with the alveolar ridge for the /l/ even as the lateral edges are being drawn down by the lowering mandible in anticipation of the subsequent vowel. Second, the tongue-palate contact facilitates management of airflow patterns and air pressure. And third, bracing against the palate facilitates tongue shapes that might not otherwise be possible. Miller, Watkin, and Chen (2002) propose that the extracellular tissue matrix of the tongue contributes substantially to the elastic properties of muscle function. This view is consistent with Stone (1990), who models the tongue as semi-independent segments that can oppose one another when provided with an external rigid contact for stabilization, such as the palate.

Liquids

The formant pattern for the **liquids** /r/ and /l/ often can appear quite similar to the vowels in that a steady-state portion of the formant may be observed, depending on surrounding phonetic context. Both liquids are usually identified as alveolar in regard to their place of articulation, and so one would expect that F2 and F3 would rise. (Recall that a constriction in the alveolar area causes the frequencies of the second and third formant to increase.) However, features of the articulatory posture for both liquids give the acoustic evidence some unique features. These each are considered in turn.

The acoustic evidence for manner of articulation for the liquid retroflex /r/ is a low F3, an acoustic feature of all rhotic sounds (Figure 8–23). The frequencies of the first and second formants for /r/, however, are like those of the liquid /l/. Examine the formant transitions for F2 and F3 for /r/ and /w/ as the consonant moves into the subsequent vowel (see Figure 8–23). The low F3 constrains the movement of F2. We see almost a velar pinch for F2 and F3 in /r/. Now compare the location of F3 in the /r/ to that of the /w/. Although the location of F3 is not as low in the /w/ as in the /r/, it is still quite low compared to other consonants. This similarity in formant positions helps account for the relatively common articulation error of young children, in producing /w/ instead of /r/.

Two allophonic variants of the retroflex consonant are found in standard American English,

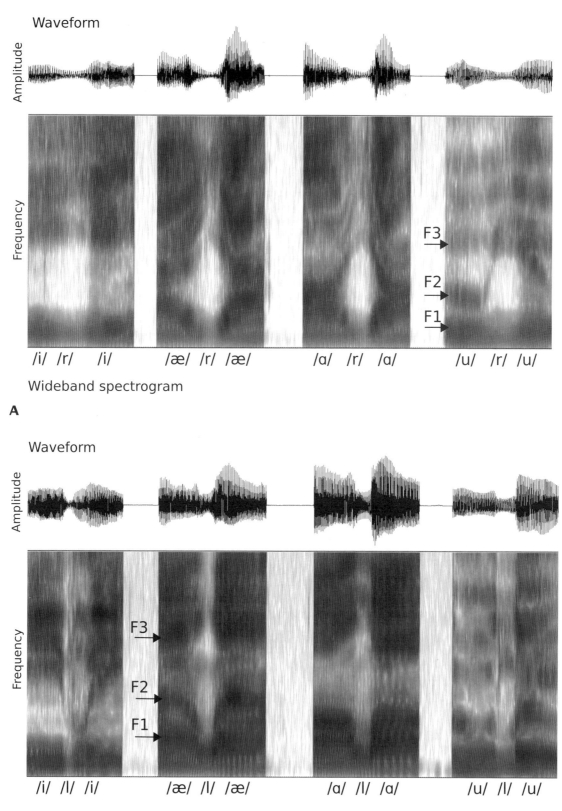

Figure 8–23. A. Formant transitions in the high and low vowels preceding and following /r/. **B.** Formant transitions in the high and low vowels preceding and following /l/.

the dark and light /r/. The dark rhotic generally occurs in the CV context, and the light rhotic occurs in the VC context. In other words, the dark /r/ comes before the vowel and the light /r/ comes after the vowel (Figure 8–24). The dark quality comes from a more posterior articulatory position of the tongue, and the light quality arises with greater tongue advancement. In the dark /r/, the tongue retracts and the back of the tongue is high, like the high, back quality vowels. In the light /r/, the tongue advances and is raised in the palatal region, like the high, front quality vowels. Recalling the formant characteristics that specify the "backness" or "frontness" of vowels, as discussed in Chapter 6, we would expect that the F1–F2 relationship would govern the quality of dark and light liquids as well. The formant structure of the /r/, however, does not

behave similarly, likely due to the very low F3 (a hallmark of the /r/), which constrains the movement of F2, as noted earlier.

In the dark /r/ (which occurs in boundary initial CV position), F3 is very low and anticipatory coarticulation does not generally occur (Figure 8–25). That is, the dark /r/ remains largely unaffected by the subsequent vowel. The velar pinch of F2 and F3 is evidence of the velarized sound of the dark /r/.

The light /r/ is preceded by a vowel within a syllable (VC) and strongly influences the preceding vowel. In fact, the vowel becomes "r-colored" (rhotacized) (Figure 8–26) as we discussed in Chapter 6. The major acoustic difference between the light and dark /r/ is that F3 is not as low for the light /r/. For many speakers, a true /r/ is only produced in boundary-initial (CV) position.

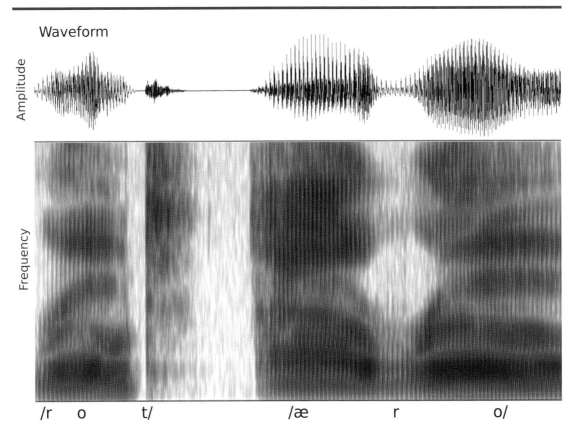

Figure 8–24. Acoustic characteristics of the "light" and "dark" /r/.

Waveform

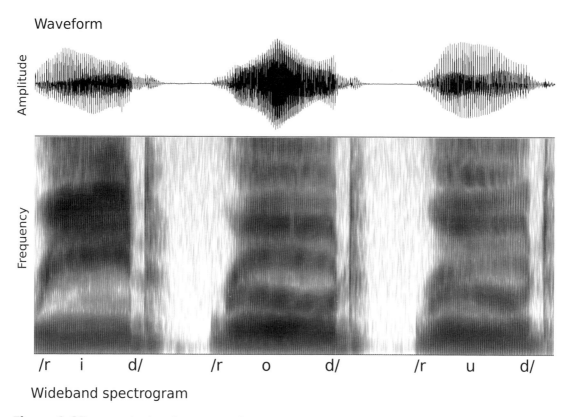

Wideband spectrogram

Figure 8–25. Note the low frequency of F3 in the dark /r/ of initial position of the words "reed, road, rude."

In those speakers, for all VC contexts, the /r/ becomes a rhotacized vowel or diphthong.

The acoustic evidence for manner of articulation for the liquid /l/ is complex due to the lateral emission of airflow. Both formants and antiformants influence the acoustic filter function. **Antiformants** are the opposite of formants. Antiformants, also called zeros, do not allow the harmonic energy to be passed well. Antiformants arise from divisions of airflow in the vocal tract, which act to capture or trap the energy rather than allow it to pass. Antiformants are a factor in production of nasal consonants, to be discussed below, because of the division of airflow from the oral to the nasal vocal tract, and in production of the lateral approximant /l/, which divides the airflow to either side of the central alveolar obstruction. The formant characteristics are similar to those of the homorganic nasal /n/ (having a similar place of articulation), with a low F1. We

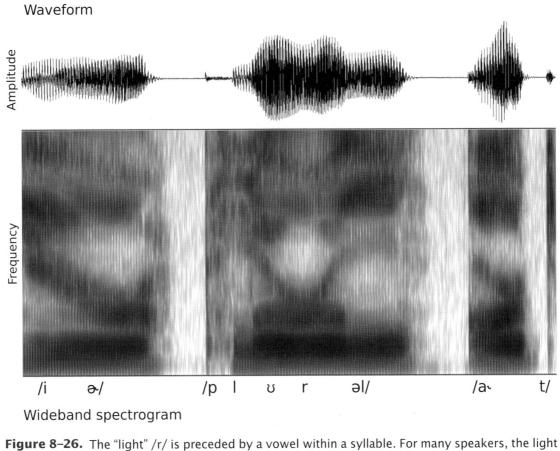

Waveform

Amplitude

Frequency

/i   ɚ/   /p   l   ʊ   r   əl/   /ɑ˞   t/

Wideband spectrogram

Figure 8–26. The "light" /r/ is preceded by a vowel within a syllable. For many speakers, the light /r/ is equivalent to a rhotacized vowel.

noted earlier that the approximants demonstrate a smooth transition with an absence of discontinuities that one sees in the stops and fricatives. That is not completely true for the /l/. A small discontinuity often can be seen in a spectrogram of the /l/ in Figures 8–21 and 8–23B, although it is much subtler than that of a stop or fricative.

The /l/ also has dark and light allophonic variants. Of note, however, the VC environment, in which /l/ follows a vowel within a syllable, results in a dark /l/. Within the CV environment, in which /l/ precedes the vowel or is in a boundary-initial position, a light /l/ occurs. These contexts are the opposite for production of the dark and light /r/. Examples of the dark /l/ following different vowels are shown in Figure 8–27. It is notable that the tongue is highly constrained in both light and dark productions, and therefore little coarticulatory

Waveform

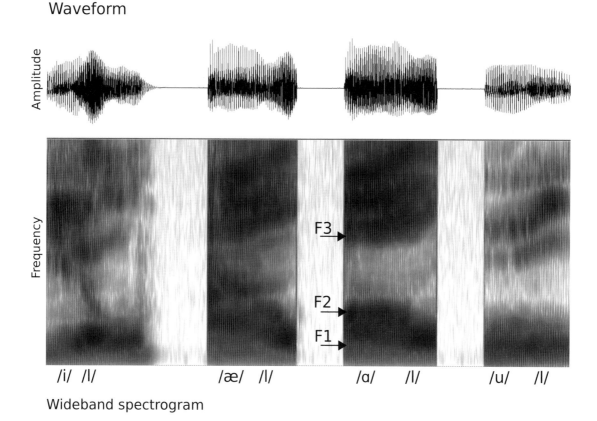

Wideband spectrogram

Figure 8–27. When /l/ occurs after the vowel within a syllable, the dark allophone is produced. The vowel followed by the /l/ is extracted from the words "eel, pal, tall, school."

effects are present in production of the /l/. We can see that, in all vowel contexts of the dark /l/, both F1 and F2 are low, resembling the glide /w/. The lateral /l/, however, has greater energy in F3 because of the more open articulatory posture. The dark /l/ is produced smoothly with no discontinuity between the vowel and the lateral. (Compare this feature to the light /l/ below.)

When /l/ occurs after the vowel and in boundary-initial position, the light allophone is produced. In Figure 8–28, the light /l/ is shown preceding four vowels of different quality embedded in words. Characteristically, we observe a low F1 and F2 for the /l/. Unlike the dark /l/, however, which is produced smoothly, the light /l/ usually has some discontinuity between the vowel and the lateral. In summary, for both dark and light productions of /l/, F1 and F2 are low, and minimal coarticulatory effects are seen. The

light /l/, however, has greater discontinuity than the dark /l/ when examined spectrographically.

Study Questions

22. Identify the glides and liquids that make up approximants. How are they like vowels?

23. In general, what are the two acoustic differences that distinguish diphthongs from glides (semivowels) within a VC context?

24. Define the dark and light /r/ and describe the acoustic features of each.

25. What are antiformants and when do they occur?

Waveform

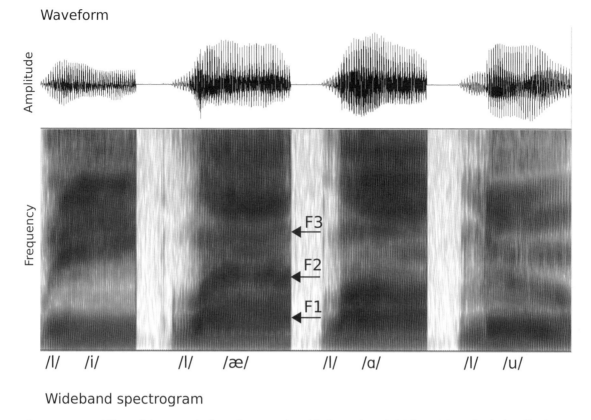

/l/ /i/   /l/ /æ/   /l/ /ɑ/   /l/ /u/

Wideband spectrogram

Figure 8–28. When /l/ occurs before the vowel and in boundary-initial position, the light allophone is produced. The initial /l/ and following vowel are extracted from the words "lead, lad, lot, loot."

Nasals

The nasals /m, n, ŋ/ are produced by occluding the oral cavity, opening the velopharyngeal port, and directing continuous airflow out through the nasal cavity. Nasals are continuants and, as such, have formant structure like vowels. The nasals can also be syllabic, occurring next to another consonant without an intervening vowel nucleus, as in "sudden" [s^dn]. Unlike vowels, however, nasals are produced with a large degree of constriction in the vocal tract, hence their classification as consonants.

The acoustic evidence for the manner of articulation for nasals is a low first formant, called a nasal murmur, and a low level of energy throughout the consonant production (Figure 8–29). All nasals are voiced. The hallmark of a nasal, however, is the faintness of the formant bands, corresponding to a marked decrease in energy when compared to the surrounding vowels. Nasally produced sounds lose energy from damping of the thick tissues and narrow nasal passages. For each of the nasal consonants, F1, the nasal murmur is generally quite low (around 250–500 Hz), resulting from the relatively large volume of the nasal passages and the very small opening of the nares to the atmosphere. F1 is associated with the resonance of the nasal cavity coupled to the pharyngeal cavity. F2 and F3 vary among the three nasal consonants, but generally a large range of frequencies above F1 contain no formant. Spectrographically (see Figures 8–29 and 8–30), one can see the low first formant and then a large area of white, where minimal harmonic energy is allowed to pass through.

The acoustic evidence for the place of articulation is not as apparent for nasals. For the vowels immediately preceding the nasal, one can

Waveform

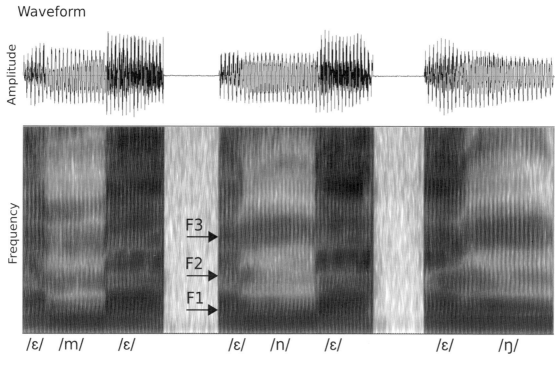

/ɛ/ /m/   /ɛ/   /ɛ/   /n/   /ɛ/   /ɛ/   /ŋ/

Wideband spectrogram

Figure 8–29. Acoustic characteristics of the nasals /m, n, ŋ /.

Waveform

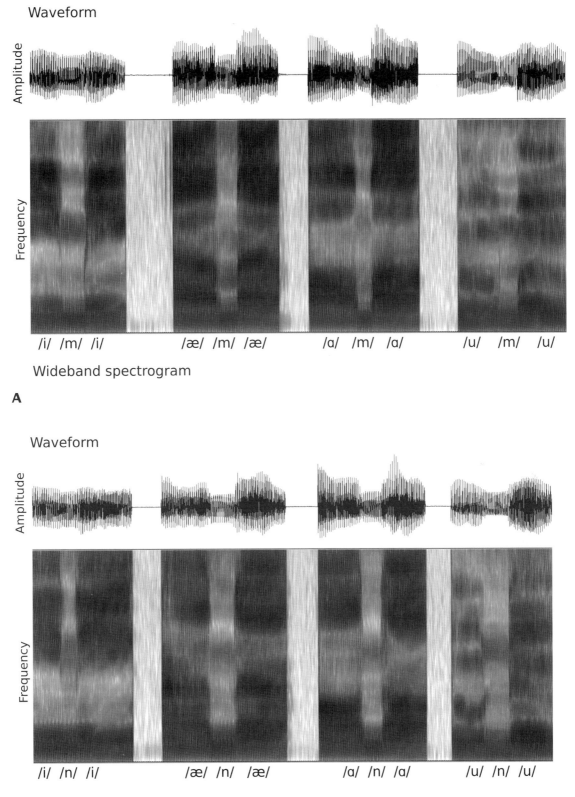

/i/ /m/ /i/   /æ/ /m/ /æ/   /ɑ/ /m/ /ɑ/   /u/ /m/ /u/

Wideband spectrogram

A

Waveform

/i/ /n/ /i/   /æ/ /n/ /æ/   /ɑ/ /n/ /ɑ/   /u/ /n/ /u/

Wideband spectrogram

B

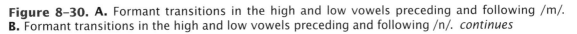

Figure 8–30. A. Formant transitions in the high and low vowels preceding and following /m/. **B.** Formant transitions in the high and low vowels preceding and following /n/. *continues*

Waveform

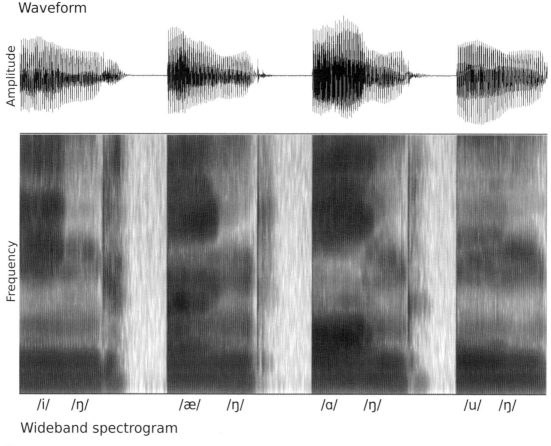

Amplitude

Frequency

/i/ /ŋ/   /æ/ /ŋ/   /ɑ/ /ŋ/   /u/ /ŋ/

Wideband spectrogram

C

Figure 8–30. *continued* **C.** Formant transitions in the high and low vowels preceding and following /ŋ/.

sometimes observe a lowering of F2 before the bilabial nasal and a velar pinch (coming together of F2 and F3) before the velar nasal. Perceptually, the distinction between the bilabial and lingua-alveolar nasals is stronger in CV than in VC syllables (Ohde, Haley, & Barnes, 2006). Although the place of oral occlusion varies for each of the nasal consonants, the nasal articulation, and hence its resulting formant structure, remains the same. In general, spectrography is not very helpful for determining the degree of nasalization.

Some linguists refer to the nasals as nasal plosives (Ladefoged, 2006). The main reason for this appellation is that the oral cavity is completely occluded for production of nasals, like the articulatory posture for plosives prior to

their release. Another related reason, however, is that the acoustic characteristics of the vowel transitions are not unlike those found in the environment of the oral plosives. Evidence of this similarity was found initially in the early high-speed motion picture studies of the vocal tract conducted by Fujimura (1961). Specifically, vowel formant onglides and offglides are similar for the bilabials /b/ and /m/, the lingual-dentals /d/ and /n/, and the velars /g/ and /ŋ/. Each stop-nasal pair is **homorganic**. That is, the place of articulation is similar. The only difference is that the velopharyngeal port is open for the nasal, so that the airflow continues to the nasal cavity, whereas for the oral stops, the airflow is halted momentarily.

Three major differences between the oral and nasal plosives may be summarized. First, oral plosives have an energy burst upon release. The buildup of intraoral pressure is not as great for the nasals because the air is continuing to exit the vocal tract through the nasal cavity. The oral opening following the release of the nasal is slower than for the oral plosive (Fujimura, 1961) because of the greater equality of pressures between the oral cavity and the atmosphere. The second major difference is the greater energy in the nasal murmur than in the voicing during the closure of the oral plosive. The sound pressure wave can exit the nasal cavity more efficiently during the nasal consonant than during the closed vocal tract of the oral plosive. And third, nasal plosives result in nasalization of the vowels adjacent to the consonant, as discussed below.

Vowel Nasalization

Nasalization of a vowel refers to the addition of nasal resonance to the vocal tract transfer function. We know that in isolation and adjacent to production of oral consonants, the vowels are produced with oral resonance. Vowel nasalization occurs because of coarticulation and was noted as early as House and Stevens in 1956. In VC combinations in which the consonant is a nasal, the velopharyngeal port is opened in anticipation of the nasal consonant while the vowel is still being articulated. Hence, the vowel preceding the consonant becomes nasalized (see Figures 8–29 and 8–30). More specifically, the portion of the vowel closest to the nasal consonant becomes nasalized. Similarly, in CV combinations in which the consonant is a nasal, the velopharyngeal port is still closing as the vowel following the nasal consonant is articulated, producing vowel nasalization of the beginning portion of the vowel. On average, the velopharyngeal port movement leads (in VC combinations) and lags (in CV combinations) the release of the oral occlusion by approximately 100 ms (Pickett, 1980).

Coupling of the nasal resonating space to the oropharyngeal cavity alters the vocal tract formants in complex ways. Nasalization adds **antiresonances** to the vocal tract transfer function, which reduces the energy of any harmonics that are near the same frequency as the antiresonance. Thus, in the spectrogram, the location of antiresonances often is reflected in a decrease or lack of visible harmonic energy. The formants are often called **poles** and the antiresonances are called **zeros** when referring to nasal resonance.

The effect of the antiresonances and zeros depends upon the degree of coupling, or amount of opening of the velopharyngeal port, as well as other factors (the mathematics of which are well beyond the scope of this discussion). However, the acoustic evidence for nasalization can be summarized as follows. First, F1 is moved to a slightly higher frequency but with lesser amplitude due to the low-frequency antiresonance. Second, higher frequency antiresonances cause dampening of F2 and F3, thereby lowering their energy (Pickett, 1980). The lower amplitude of the spectral peaks of F1, F2, and F3 can be seen in Figures 8–29 and 8–30.

Affricates

An affricate is a stop followed immediately by a homorganic fricative, as in the palatal voiceless and voiced cognates /tʃ, dʒ/ (Figure 8–31). The stop is released but the constriction remains sufficiently narrow to yield frication noise after the burst release. Note that not every instance of a stop followed by a fricative is identified as an affricate. The phonemes must be homorganic. That is, the affricate must consist of a stop and a fricative both produced in the same place of articulation. The pair must also have the same voicing. Not surprisingly, the acoustic evidence for place of articulation of the affricates is like that of both the stop and fricative. Slight alterations in duration of the stop gap or the frication noise may occur in the affricate, however. For example, it may be that the affricates contain longer duration of frication noise than the fricative alone (Kluender & Walsh, 1992). A summary of the acoustic cues for manner and place of articulation are presented in Tables 8–2 and 8–3.

Waveform

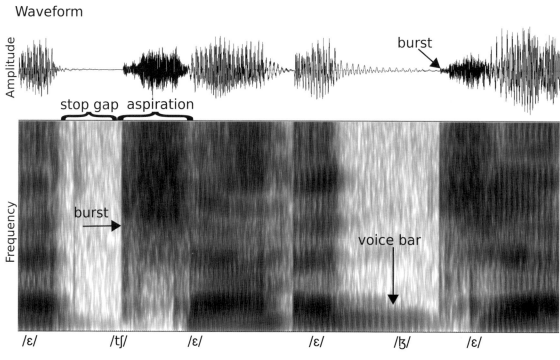

stop gap aspiration

burst

burst

voice bar

/ɛ/　　　/tʃ/　　　/ɛ/　　　　　/ɛ/　　　/ʒ/　　　/ɛ/

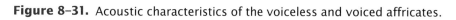

Wideband spectrogram

Figure 8–31. Acoustic characteristics of the voiceless and voiced affricates.

Table 8–2. Comparison of Acoustic Features by Manner of Production (Class of Gesture)

Acoustic Feature of Constriction	Stops		Continuants					
			Fricatives		Approximants		Nasals
	Voiceless	Voiced	Voiceless	Voiced	Glides	Liquids	
Degree	Complete	Complete	Incomplete Narrow	Incomplete Narrow	Incomplete Moderate to vowel-like	Incomplete Moderate to vowel-like	Complete Oral cavity only
Duration	Brief	Brief, but longer than voiceless	Longer	Longer, but shorter than the voiceless fricative	Moderate	Moderate	Longer
Release noise	Present, strong	Present, but weaker than voiceless stop	Absent	Absent	Absent	Absent	Moderate, but variable
Spectral energy	None	Moderate low frequency (duration depends upon VOT)	Strong mid to high frequency of frication noise	Low frequency associated with F$_0$, strong mid to high frequency of frication noise	Gradual and smooth formant movements	Gradual and smooth formant movements	Strong presence of nasal murmur

Table 8–3. Summary of Acoustic Cues by Manner of Production (Class of Gesture) and Place of Articulation for Vowel Immediately Following Consonant

Gesture Class	Bilabial	Labiodental	(Lingua) Dental	Alveolar	Palatal	Velar	Pharyngeal/Glottal
Stops	/p/ /b/			/t/ /d/		/k/ /g/	
▪ burst	Flat to falling spectrum			Rising spectrum		Middle-frequency spectrum	
▪ vowel	F1 increases F2 increases			F1 increases F2 decreases[a]		F1 increases F2[b]	
Fricatives		/f/ /v/	/θ/ /ð/	/s/ /z/	/ʃ/ /ʒ/		/h/
▪ noise spectrum		Flat, weak	Flat, weak	Strong, high frequency	Strong, high frequency	Flat, weak	
▪ vowel		F1 increases F2 increases[c]	F1 increases F2 increases[c]	F1 increases F2 decreases[d]	F1 increases F2[b]		
Glides	/w/ F1 increases F2 increases				/j/ F1 increases F2 decreases		
Liquids			/l/	/r/			
Nasals	/m/			/n/	/ŋ/		
▪ murmur	Present			Present	Present		
▪ vowel	F1 increases F2 increases			F1 increases F2 decreases[a]	F1 increases F2[b]		

[a] Except for high front vowels.

[b] May increase or decrease, depending upon vowel.

[c] Except for back vowels.

[d] Except for high front vowels.

8.5 Instrumentation and Measurement of Vocal Tract Aerodynamics

In Chapter 6, we discussed measurement of phonatory aerodynamics, including mean airflow and lung pressure, and a variety of quantitative measures that reflected phonatory dynamics from the perspective of aerodynamics, including phonation quotient, maximum sustained phonation, s/z ratio, and vocal efficiency. Now we look more closely at supraglottal air pressures, especially intraoral air pressures and nasal air pressure and flows in formation of speech sounds.

Intraoral Air Pressure

Intraoral air pressure is the pressure level in the oral cavity. When a constriction occurs in the oral cavity, the intraoral air pressure measures the pressure that builds up behind the constriction. The greater, or more complete, the constriction, the greater the intraoral air pressure, all other variables being equal. High-pressure consonants are those that are formed by relatively high levels of intraoral air pressure due to complete or very narrowed constrictions, such as those that produce plosives and fricatives.

Measurement of intraoral pressure was first introduced in Chapter 5 as a means of estimating lung pressure within carefully constructed utterances. The intraoral pressure waveform also is of interest in formation of consonants, however. During voiceless plosives, intraoral pressure rises anywhere from 3 to 7 cm of H_2O (Malécot, 1955). Voiced plosives are produced with slightly less intraoral air pressure (Arkebauer, Hixon, & Hardy, 1967). Similarly, intraoral pressure for fricatives has been measured as ranging between 3 and 8 cm of H_2O. Breathing effort for fricatives is greater, on average, than for plosives, and for voiced sounds compared to voiceless sounds (Warren, 1996), breathing effort being a general reference to the airflow and air pressure levels required for speech production. For example, the average volume of air used for voiced and voiceless fricatives has been measured at 100 and 75 mL of air, respectively, compared to 80 and 50 mL of air for voiced and voiceless plosives, respectively (Isshiki & Ringel, 1964; Warren & Wood, 1969). The greater breathing effort that is required for fricatives compared to plosives results from having to maintain sufficient pressure to drive the airflow through the narrow aperture between the tongue and the palate to generate turbulence for frication noise (Warren, 1996). The greater respiratory effort required for voiced sounds compared to voiceless consonants is related to glottal resistance. (Recall, glottal resistance is a measure of how much the vocal folds resist the airflow, measured as the ratio of the transglottal pressure to the transglottal flow.) Glottal resistance is highest in phonation of vowels, which are produced with a relatively unconstricted supraglottal vocal tract, and much lower in production of voiced fricatives because of the higher supraglottal pressure, and less still in voiceless fricatives, because of the open position of the vocal folds.

Intraoral pressure also varies as a function of intensity and phoneme position. Intensity is approximately proportional to the 1.3 power of intraoral air pressure (Hixon, Minifie, & Tait, 1967; Leeper & Noll, 1972). Phonemes in utterance-final position tend to be produced with less intraoral pressure than the same phonemes produced in initial position, particularly for voiced cognates (Stathopoulos, 1986). This difference may be due to the tendency for most speech-related variables, including f_o and intensity, to fall off at the end of an utterance.

In general, children use higher intraoral pressures than adults (Stathopoulos & Weismer, 1985; Subtelny, Worth, & Sakuda, 1966). The reason for the age difference in pressure is uncertain, although it may well be because children tend to speak more loudly than adults (Stathopoulos, 1986). Measurement of intraoral air pressure can provide information about the adequacy of breathing effort, and velopharyngeal port closure and the temporal coordination of these phenomena with movement of the articulators. A low level of breathing effort will limit the volume of air flowing through the oral cavity, and, therefore, the intraoral pressure will be lower, as compared to intraoral pressure generated during greater breathing effort. The buildup and release of intraoral pressure are closely dependent upon formation and release of vocal tract constrictions, both in the oral cavity and at the velopharyngeal port, as discussed below.

Nasal Airflow and Acoustics

Appropriate closure of the velopharyngeal port is essential for normal speech and voice production. Insufficient contact, such that a gap exists, or insufficient duration, such as premature opening of the velopharyngeal port, will result in excessive nasal airflow, the flow of air through the nares. Excessive nasal airflow results in too much nasal resonance in the acoustic signal, perceived as hypernasalization, or hypernasality. Excessive nasal airflow and nasal resonance can decrease overall intelligibility in three ways. First, the radiated acoustic signal has less energy. Recall from our discussion in Chapter 6 that

nasal antiformants dampen the acoustic radiated energy. Therefore, hypernasal speech has less intensity and may be harder for the listener to hear. Second, sometimes the emission of excessive airflow through the nose results in turbulence, which can be heard as excessive noise (sometimes referred to as nasal emission or, in more severe cases, nasal snorting). The nasally produced turbulent noise interferes with the acoustic information necessary for speech comprehension. And third, the escape of air through the open velopharyngeal port into the nasal cavity results in decreased intraoral pressure. That is, part of the airflow through the glottis is diverted to the nasal cavity, so a lesser volume of air is available to flow through the oral cavity.

Status of the velopharyngeal port can be assessed directly (relatively speaking) using imaging studies, such as endoscopy, conventional x-ray, computed tomography (CT), and MRI (Kuehn, 1976). Also possible, but less "user-friendly," is the use of **point-tracking instrumentation**, discussed later in this chapter. As you will learn, point-tracking instrumentation requires affixing sensors of some type to the articulator. It is not too difficult to imagine that many people would find the physical placement of sensors on the velum somewhat uncomfortable and certainly obtrusive when talking! Furthermore, when we consider the perception of resonance, the status of the velopharyngeal port is only indirectly related to the degree of nasality (Warren, Dalston, & Mayo, 1994). Indirect measures of velopharyngeal activity may be obtained from measures of airflow and acoustics. The topic of velopharyngeal function and dysfunction (velopharyngeal incompetence) is a large and complex topic better reserved for texts focused on speech disorders. Here we discuss very briefly the measurement of nasal airflow and then a clinical measurement of nasal acoustics.

Nasal Airflow

Recall from our discussion of aerodynamic instrumentation in Chapter 4 that airflow can be measured by having the speaker talk into a face mask. The airflow from both the nose and mouth is measured by a pneumotacho-graph (transducer that measures airflow) connected to a face mask and, ultimately, input into a computer. If we want to know how much air is being emitted from the nares, however, it is a simple task to use a smaller mask that covers only the nose (and generally secured by a strap that goes around the head). In general, nasal airflow should be minimal to zero for utterances that do not contain nasal consonants (Emanuel & Counihan, 1970; Hoit, Watson, Hixon, McMahon, & Johnson, 1994; Mueller, 1971; Thomspon & Hixon, 1979). In individuals with abnormal anatomy of the velopharyngeal port, size of the velopharyngeal opening in general correlates directly with amount of nasal opening (Warren, 1996). The relative amount of nasal airflow is dependent on intensity level, and some evidence suggests that it also is dependent upon gender (Young, Zajac, Mayo, & Hooper, 2001).

Nasalance

In general, nasal resonance can be perceived accurately, and we have discussed earlier in this chapter some of the acoustic characteristics associated with nasal resonance. However, no single invariant (unchanging) acoustic feature exists that will guarantee the perception of nasality. The perception of nasality is complex and not directly and specifically a function of nasal airflow or a single acoustic feature (Bloomer & Petersen, 1955; Stevens, Fant, & Hawkins, 1987). **Nasalance** is a ratio of the nasal energy to the overall combined nasal and oral energy as measured from the acoustic pressure waveform. An example of the instrumentation used to obtain this ratio is shown in Figure 8–32. Nasalance correlates well with perceived nasality (Dalston & Warren, 1986; Hardin, Van Demark, Morris, & Payne, 1992; Waterson, McFarlane, & Wright, 1993). Nasalance scores of necessity will be dependent upon the number of nasal phonemes within the tested utterances. Some evidence suggests that mean nasalance scores for reading of the Zoo Passage (see Appendix B for passage) should be no greater than 26% (Hardin, Van Demark, & Morris, 1990; Watterson, McFarlane, & Wright, 1993) to 32% (Dalston, Warren, & Dalston, 1991).

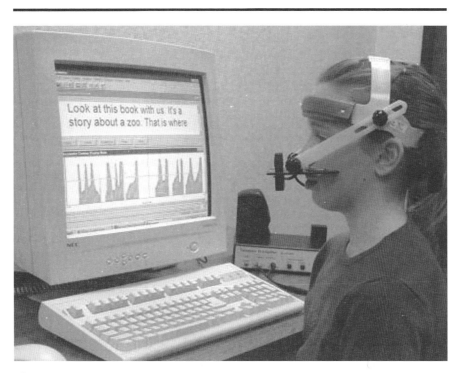

Figure 8–32. The Nasometer. Courtesy of Kay/Pentax, Lincoln Park, NJ.

Study Questions

32. What are the factors that influence the amount of intraoral air pressure used to produce speech sounds?

33. What are the three ways in which excessive nasal airflow and nasal resonance can decrease overall intelligibility?

34. Define nasalance. Look at the reading passage in Appendix B and explain why it is appropriate for measuring nasalance.

8.6 Instrumentation for Measuring Articulation

Our exploration of the instrumentation used to measure vocal tract movement began in Chapter 5 with discussion of noninvasive techniques that image large areas of the vocal tract. We continue our exploration now with a look at instruments that measure individual "flesh points," specific locations on the articulators. As a category, the data obtained from this group of instruments generally are referred to as point-tracking or pellet tracking measures.

We repeat here the now common refrain of prior sections on instrumentation from earlier chapters: No single instrument can measure everything that we are interested in observing. Two considerations particularly relevant to point-tracking instrumentation are the following: the nature of the movement of the articulators and the obtrusiveness of the sensors. Each articulator —the mandible, the lips, and the jaw—moves in a unique way and can be described by a unique set of coordinates. For example, measurement of the movement at one specific point on the jaw may be sufficient to describe opening and closing movements, whereas tracking only one point on the tongue is quite unlikely to describe

its motion fully. Therefore, the capabilities of the instrumentation with regard to tracking multiple points must be considered. A related consideration is the velocity and range of motion of a given articulator. Although mandible movement during speech may be relatively slow with large amplitude, lip movement (rounding, spread, and protrusion) is more likely to be of faster velocity with smaller amplitude. The point-tracking instrumentation selected can measure the velocity and amplitude of the relevant articulator.

A second consideration in selecting point-tracking instrumentation is its level of obtrusiveness. Although it is well recognized that the very process of scientific observation, of necessity, changes the phenomena being observed, instrumentation that impedes speech to any extent risks providing data that are not truly representative of normal speaking behaviors. All the following point-tracking instrumentation is distracting to the speaker to one extent or another. The goal, of course, is to minimize that distraction to the greatest extent possible. We discuss research relevant to this problem in the section below.

X-ray Microbeam

The use of x-rays to image the vocal tract was discussed in Chapter 7. Difficulties in delimiting tongue borders and the danger of exposure to large amounts of x-rays were noted as two significant disadvantages of its use. **X-ray microbeam** minimizes these limitations in two ways. First, the use of an extraordinarily narrow beam (approximately 0.4 mm thick) limits considerably the amount of tissue x-ray exposure (below that of standard dental x-rays, which is quite small). Second, the radiation beam is focused upon tiny gold pellets (approximately 2–3 mm in diameter) that are affixed to the articulators, which allow us to define movement of the articulators more clearly, although limited to a two-dimensional space (Figure 8–33). Gold is very dense, so the weak radiation is absorbed by the gold and can therefore be seen readily on the x-ray image. Gold is also inert, meaning that it does not react chemically in most circum-

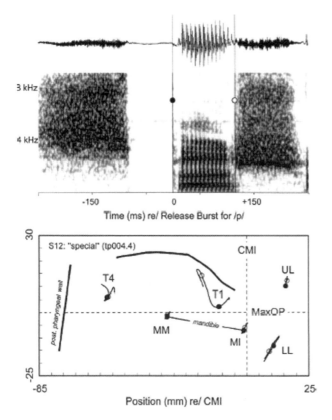

Figure 8–33. X-ray microbeam instrumentation provides information about the trajectories of articulatory movement during speech. The waveform (*top*) and corresponding wideband spectrogram (*middle*) for /spɛʃ/ extracted from the word "special." The lower panel shows the movement of the pellets placed on the upper lip (*UL*), the lower lip (*LL*), the tongue blade (*T1*), the tongue dorsum (*T4*), the border of the cheek and gum between the central incisors of the mandible (*MI*), and near the left second molar of the mandible (*MM*). The thick lines at the top and left represent the outlines of the hard palate and a portion of the posterior pharyngeal wall, respectively. The lines represent trajectories of articulator movement in the sagittal plane, viewed from the right side of the speaker's head. From "Kinematic Event Patterns in Speech: Special Problems," by J. R. Westbury, E. J. Severson, and M. J. Lindstrom, 2000, *Language and Speech, 43*, p. 410. Reprinted with permission.

stances, including when bombarded by x-rays. X-ray microbeam technology was developed by the University of Tokyo (Fujimura, 1980; Kiritani, Itoh, & Fujimura, 1975). The most comprehensive database is from research teams at the University of Wisconsin, consisting of 85 speakers over 171 experimental sessions (Westbury, 1991). The availability of the database has generated a relatively larger amount of research studies using x-ray microbeam than other point-tracking instrumentation. X-ray microbeam has been used to explore the temporal relationship of tongue tip and jaw movement in specific phonetic contexts (Nittrouer, 1991), in individuals with neurologic motor control deficits (Weismer, Yunosova, & Westbury, 2003), comparing kinematic (movement) features arising from differences in male and female vocal tract sizes (Simpson, 2001), and describing regions of the tongue that act as independent functional units during speech (Green & Wang, 2003).

A strength of x-ray microbeam instrumentation is the good temporal resolution ("scan time") to document articulatory movement. The instrumentation from the University of Wisconsin can track up to 1,000 pellet positions per second; so, for example, 10 pellets can be tracked at a rate of 100 times per second, allowing multiarticulatory tracking of tongue, lips, jaw, and soft palate at speeds appropriate for speech production. Thus, temporal coordination and coarticulation can be examined readily (Adams, Weismer, & Kent, 1993; de Jong, 1997; Nittrouer, 1991; Surpenant & Goldstein, 1998). A disadvantage is that the pellets might themselves interfere with natural tongue movement. Weismer and Bunton (1999) assessed acoustic and perceptual characteristics of speakers with and without the tracking pellets from the University of Wisconsin database. Overall, no consistent effects were found, although some individual subjects did alter articulation because of the pellets. Their data were consistent with those of Perkell and Nelson (1985), who also found little detectable interference in articulation. Another limitation is the considerable complexity and expense of x-ray microbeam instrumentation. Although availability of an excellent database helps promote research of this type, experimental design is limited by the type of data already acquired. Many research questions would, of necessity, require new acquisition of data under different test conditions. And finally, although the x-ray tissue exposure is limited, x-ray exposure for research purposes must always be acknowledged as a risk and, therefore, the risk-reward potential of the research must be considered.

Ultrasound can be combined with pellet tracking. Stainless steel pellets of 3 to 5 mm in diameter are glued to the tongue surface (using a temporary type of surgical glue) (see Figure 8–1). The pellets provide a unique echo signature that allows identification of specific points on the tongue (Stone, 1990).

Electromagnetic Midsagittal Articulography (EMMA)

EMMA (also sometimes referred to as electromagnetic articulography, or EMA) is used to track the movements of the lips, soft palate, tongue, and mandible during speech production. Developed by Schönle et al. (1987), it detects the position and orientation of articulators in the midsagittal measurement plane by measuring electromagnetically induced currents in receiver coils placed around the head (Figure 8–34). Transmitter coils are placed about the head and a constant distance is maintained from each transmitter coil to the head. Small, insulated receiver coils are attached to the articulators with temporary adhesive. The electromagnetic current is calibrated to be representative of a certain distance from the articulator to the coil. The multiple transmitter coils positioned about the head contribute to increased accuracy in location of the receiver coils. EMMA has been used to explore articulatory movement in different phonetic contexts and has contributed evidence that movement of the articulators can be recovered (assumed) from acoustic analysis (Hogden et al., 1996; Kaburagi & Honda, 2002; Kaburagi, Wakamiya, & Honda, 2005; Perkell et al., 1992; Tuller, Shao, & Kelso, 1990).

A strength of the EMMA system is that more than one articulator can be tracked simultaneously, which is very important when examining relationships among articulators. And high-velocity movements can be tracked accurately. (In Chapter 10, as we discuss theories of motor

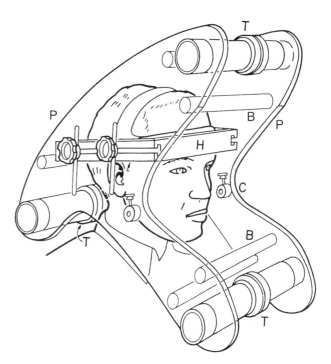

Figure 8–34. The three-transmitter version of an electromagnetic midsagittal articulometer system (EMMA). The transmitters (*T*) are secured by side plates (*P*), which are connected by spacing bars (*B*). The headmount (*H*) fits precisely between the side plates. The center of the measurement area (*C*) is positioned over the cheek. This system was built by the authors. Other systems, including a commercially available system (Carstens Medezinelektronik, GmbH, Bovenden, Germany), have slight differences but the basic principles remain the same. From "Electromagnetic Midsagittal Articulometer (EMMA) Systems for Transducing Articulatory Movements," J. S. Perkell, M. H. Cohen, M. A. Svirsky, M. L. Matthies, L. Garabieta, and M. T. T. Jackson, 1992, *Journal of the Acoustical Society of America*, *92*, p. 3084. Reprinted with permission of the Acoustical Society of America.

speech control, the importance of movement, and timing linkages between the articulators, is emphasized.) A limitation of the EMMA system is that only points are measured (unlike imaging whole structures, as we discussed in Chapter 7), a disadvantage for complex, soft tissue structures such as the tongue. Additionally, kinematic data can be obtained only from midline points on the tongue, lips, or jaw. Despite the use of multiple transmitter coils placed in different locations about the head, the best resolution (movements less than 1 mm) is located at midline. And finally, the potential negative effect to tissue health of exposure to a strong electromagnetic field is unknown but must be acknowledged.

Optoelectronic Tracking

The **optoelectronic tracking** system (Optotrak NDI Measurement Sciences, Waterloo, Canada) follows the movement of light-emitting diodes (LEDs) in three-dimensional space (side-to-side, up-down, and forward-backward) (Barlow, Cole, & Abbs, 1983). Lightweight LEDs are placed on external articulators (lips and jaw) and their movements are tracked by sensors that digitally record their positions. Amplitude and velocity movement then can be computed from the digital data. Optotrak has been used to assess stability, velocity, and displacement of articulators in children (Smith & Goffman, 1998) (see Chapter 9 for a discussion of data on speech motor control in children) and to model three-dimensional motion of the human jaw (Guiard-Marigny & Ostry, 1997; Vatikiotis-Bateson & Ostry, 1995). Lucero and Munhall (1999) presented a three-dimensional model of movement of the human face during speech based upon kinematic data obtained with the Optotrak and electromyographic data.

An advantage of the Optotrak system is the ability to record kinematic data in three-dimensional space. A limitation, however, is that the LEDs must be visible to the recording sensors, and so tongue movement cannot be measured using this instrumentation. Optotrak is useful, however, for lip and jaw movement tracking. In addition, the LEDs and their attached wires may interfere, to some extent, with speech movements.

A combination of ultrasound and the Optotrak system (Whalen et al., 2005) overcomes some of the inherent limitations of both instruments when each is employed alone. Ultrasound imaging, as discussed in Chapter 6, provides information about the pharyngeal area of the vocal tract and almost the entire tongue (except for the anterior-most tip). However, if the ultra-sound probe is allowed to move with the jaw, then the shape of the tongue can be identified (within limitations as explained in Chapter 6), but the position of the tongue relative to the vocal tract cannot be known. If the jaw is held immobile during testing, then the tongue movement can be captured relative to the vocal tract space, but the articulation is likely altered by the immobile jaw. Use of the Optotrak system simultaneously with ultrasound measurement allows clearer tracking of the outline of the tongue and allows capture of tongue movement data relative to the vocal tract (the air space above the tongue).

An optical point-tracking device specifically designed for monitoring movement of the velum is the **Velotrace**, developed by Horiguchi and Bell-Berti (1987). A lever is placed in the nasal cavity that rests on the upper, nasal surface of the velum (after topical anesthetic and decongestant have been applied inside the nose). A second lever is suspended externally to the lever inserted into the nose. A set of LEDs is positioned externally on the two levers (one to record movement and the other for reference to account for head movement). When the velum is raised or lowered, optical tracking instrumentation records the movement of the LEDs. The Velotrace, although somewhat invasive and not tolerated by all individuals, has provided unique information on the pattern and timing of velar movement during speech (Bell-Berti & Krakow, 1991; Kollia, Gracco, & Harris, 1995).

Strain Gauges

Movements of the lips and jaw also can be measured using strain gauges (Figure 8–35). The strain gauge is a sensor that measures the amount of strain (recall that strain is the change in length as a function of applied stress). The strain gauge system for measuring articulatory movement is composed of miniature strain gauges mounted on two perpendicular, thin metal strips or beams (approximately 0.13 mm in thickness) positioned parallel to each other. A rigid wire extends from the end of the outer beam and is attached to the

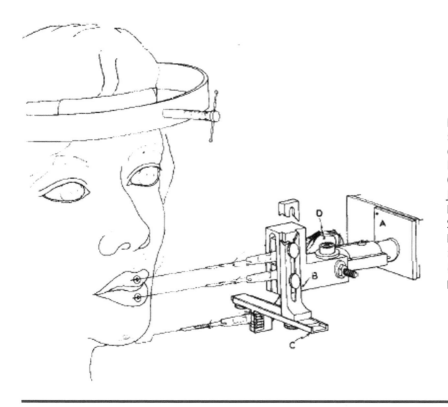

Figure 8–35. A strain-gauge system for obtaining movement data from the upper and lower lip and the jaw. From "Strain Gauge Transduction of Lip and Jaw Motion in the Midsagittal Plane: Refinement of a Prototype System," by E. M. Muller amd J. H. Abbs, pp. 198–199, *Journal of the Acoustical Society of America*, *65*, p. 484. Reprinted with permission.

midline of the lips or jaw. One beam bends when the articulator moves forward or backward, and the other beam bends when the articulator moves upward or downward. The strain gauges, attached to the beams, move in proportion to the beam movement (and, therefore, in proportion to the movement of the articulator). The movement of the strain gauge is then input into a computer (or into nondigital recorders, in the case of earlier experiments).

Strain-gauge systems have been used for decades in kinematic speech research (Abbs & Gilbert, 1973; Barlow, Cole, & Abbs, 1983). Strain gauges have been used to compare articulatory coordination of the lips and jaw in children and adults (Smith & McLean-Muse, 1987) and the effects of speaking rate on the velocity of lip movements (Shaiman & Adams, 1997). As with other point-tracking instrumentation that we have discussed, the presence of the instrumentation has the potential to alter articulator movement.

Electropalatography

Electropalatography (EPG) records the location and timing of the contact between the tongue and the palate during speech production. It consists of an array of touch-sensitive electrodes (as many as 96 electrodes) embedded in a thin acrylic palate (1 to 2.5 mm thick), called a pseudopalate. Thin wires carry the output from the pseudopalate to a computer, to provide a display of activated electrodes. The pseudopalate is custom-made for each speaker to fit as well as possible and disrupt speech as little as possible. The contact patterns of the tongue against the palate have been relatively well described in early phonetic studies (Leeper & Noll, 1972; Malécot, 1966; McGlone & Proffit, 1967; Proffit, Palmer, & Kydd, 1965). EPG is a well-established methodology used for understanding kinematics of speech production, abnormal speech production, and the effects of clinical intervention (Flege, Fletcher, & Homiedan, 1988; Fletcher &

Newman, 1991; Fletcher, McCutcheon, & Wolf, 1975; Gibbon, 2004; Gibbon & Wood, 2003; Goozée, Murdoch, & Theodoros, 2003; Hardcastle, Gibbon, & Jones, 1991). EPG has been combined with imaging instrumentation, such as ultrasound (Stone, Faber, Raphael, & Shawker, 1992), providing correlation between patterns of tongue-palate contact and tongue shape (Figure 8–36).

Advantages of EPG are the unique information it provides about articulation and its safety (particularly compared to some imaging techniques). A limitation of EPG, however, is that information is acquired only when the tongue is in contact with the palate. Therefore, EPG is particularly advantageous for providing contact information about complex consonants such as fricatives (Hoole, Ngyuen-Trong, & Hardcastle, 1993) but is not helpful for vowel analysis. The intrusiveness of the pseudopalate and contact wires also is a potential limitation. McLeod and Searl (2006) studied adaptation to the instrumentation in adults. The authors found that subjects were quite aware of the pseudopalate but that they accommodated within a few hours, and neither acoustic nor perceptual data revealed significant differences in speakers who wore the pseudopalate and those who did not. Potential changes in articulation in children, however, bear further study. Continued modification of the instrumentation has sought to minimize its obtrusiveness and may increase its utility in measurement of running speech (Murdoch, Goozée, Veidt, Scott, & Meyers, 2004) and, especially, velar movements.

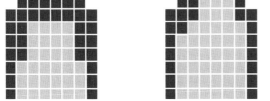

Figure 8–36. The palate used in electropalatography (*top*) and sample electropalatograms (*bottom*), in which the contact points between the tongue and palate are indicated by gray boxes.

Study Questions

35. Identify two considerations in using point-tracking instrumentation to measure articulatory movements.

36. How is x-ray microbeam technology used to explore articulation? What are its advantages and disadvantages?

37. Explain the EMMA instrumentation and identify a strength and limitation.

38. What is optoelectronic tracking? What is an advantage and limitation of this instrumentation?

39. Explain strain-gauge systems as they are used in articulation research.

40. What is electropalatography and what is an advantage and disadvantage of this instrumentation?

Clinical Case 6: Articulation Errors

Clinical cases are based upon real patients whom the author has treated. Evaluation and treatment information has been edited to focus upon specific features related to the chapters. Note that these cases incorporate information that is covered in this and other chapters (and some information about diagnosis and therapy that you will learn in future courses). You are encouraged to review this case before you begin your study of this chapter and once again after you have completed the chapter. You may also want to revisit this case later in the semester after you have covered additional chapters.

Jason is a 9-year-old boy referred to the school SLP for speech therapy due to errors in production of /s/, /r/, and the rhotics /ɚ/ and /ɝ/. The speech-language evaluation conducted by the school district revealed age-appropriate receptive and expressive language skills and appropriate pragmatic abilities. Overall intelligibility is very good. However, Jason is sometimes teased about his articulation errors by a few students, and sometimes his brother tells him that he sounds like a "baby."

The SLP noted that intermittently, /s/ was produced accurately, although usually it sounded more like /ʃ/ ("sh"). The /r/ and rhotic errors, which were produced as a /w/, were consistent and Jason was not stimulable for modification of the sounds. Therefore, the SLP decided to begin therapy by focusing upon the /s/ to help Jason achieve early success in therapy. She found that Jason could discriminate the difference between /s/ and /ʃ/, but attempts to modify lingual positioning did not meet with much success. Therefore, the SLP directed Jason's attention to the difference in pitch between /s/ and /ʃ/ (after helping him to understand the general concept of pitch and how he can make sounds with a higher or lower pitch). The SLP asked Jason him to try to make his /s/ sound higher pitched. After several tries, he did indeed produce a sound that more closely approximated /s/. With continued practice, he became consistent in his accurate productions of that phoneme.

Clinical Case Discussion Questions

1. What are the major acoustic cues of /s/ and /ʃ/?
2. Explain why a difference in pitch is perceived between /s/ and /ʃ/. That is, what is responsible for the differences in pitch? What are the articulatory postures responsible for these differences in pitch?
3. How do you explain the acoustics of fricative production to the child's parents?

Recommended Internet Sites for Further Learning

http://www.linguistics.ucla.edu/faciliti/teaching/teaching.html

The UCLA Phonetics Lab teaching page contains numerous links to tutorials and information on various topics within speech production.

http://psyc.queensu.ca/~munhallk/05_database.htm

The Speech Perception and Production Laboratory of Queen's University of Kingston, Ontario, Canada, contains videos of vocal tract imaging during speech production.

http://www.phon.ucl.ac.uk/home/johnm/siphtra/plostut2/plostut2.htm

Tutorial in voice onset time from University College London Psychology and Language Sciences.

http://home.cc.umanitoba.ca/~robh/howto.html

University of Manitoba Rob Hagiwara's How to read a spectrogram page. Good exploration of formant changes as viewed in spectrograms for vowels and consonants.

References

Abbs, J., & Gilbert, B. (1973). A strain gauge transduction system for lip and jaw motion in two dimensions: Design criteria and calibration data. *Journal of Speech and Hearing Research, 16,* 248–256.

Adams, S. G., Weismer, G., & Kent, R. D. (1993). Speaking rate and speech movement velocity profiles. *Journal of Speech and Hearing Research, 36,* 41–54.

Arkbauer, H., Hixon, T. J., & Hardy, J. (1967). Peak intraoral air pressure during speech. *Journal of Speech and Hearing Research, 10,* 196–208.

Baran, J. A., Laufer, M. Z., & Daniloff, R. (1977). Phonological contrastivity in conversation: A comparative study of voice onset time. *Journal of Phonetics, 5,* 339–350.

Barlow, S., Cole, K., & Abbs, J. (1983). A new head-mounted lip-jaw movement transducing system for the study of speech-motor disorders. *Journal of Speech and Hearing Research, 26,* 283–288.

Bell-Berti, F., & Krakow, R. A. (1991). Anticipatory velar lowering: A coproduction account. *Journal of the Acoustical Society of America, 90,* 112–123.

Bloomer, H., & Peterson, G. (1955). A spectrographic study of hypernasality. *Cleft Palate Bulletin, 5,* 5–6.

Blumstein, S. E., & Stevens, K. N. (1979). Acoustic invariance in speech production: Evidence from measurements of the spectral characteristics of stop consonants. *Journal of the Acoustical Society of America, 68,* 1001–1017.

Crystal, T. H., & House, A. S. (1988a). The duration of American-English vowels. *Journal of Phonetics, 16,* 263–284.

Crystal, T. H., & House, A. S. (1988b). Segmental duration in connected speech signals: Current results. *Journal of the Acoustical Society of America, 83,* 1553–1573.

Dalston, R. M., & Warren, D. W. (1986). Comparison of Tonar II, pressure-flow, and listener judgments of hypernasality in the assessment of velopharyngeal function. *Cleft Palate Journal, 23,* 108–115.

Dalston, R. M., Warren, D. W., & Dalston, E. T. (1991). Use of nasometry as a diagnostic tool for identifying patients with velopharyngeal impairment. *Cleft Palate–Craniofacial Journal, 28,* 184–188.

Emanuel, F. W., & Counihan, D. T. (1970). Some characteristics of oral and nasal air flow during plosive consonant production. *Cleft Palate Journal, 7,* 249–260.

Flege, J. E., Fletcher, S. G., & Homiedan, A. (1988). Compensating for /s/ and /ʃ/ production: Palatographic, acoustic and perceptual data. *Journal of the Acoustical Society of America, 83,* 212–228.

Fletcher, H. (1929). *Speech and hearing.* New York, NY: Van Nostrand.

Fletcher, S., McCutcheon, M., & Wolf, M. (1975). Dynamic palatometry. *Journal of Speech and Hearing Research, 18,* 812–819.

Fletcher, S. G., & Newman, D. G. (1991) [s] and [ʃ] as a function of linguapalatal contact place and sibilant groove width. *Journal of the Acoustical Society of America, 89,* 850–858.

Forrest, K., Weismer, G., Milenkovic, P., & Douglass, R. N. (1988). Statistical analysis of word-initial voiceless obstruents: Preliminary data. *Journal of the Acoustical Society of America, 84,* 115–123.

Forrest, K., Weismer, G., & Turner, G. S. (1989). Kinematic, acoustic, and perceptual analyses of connected speech produced by Parkinsonian and normal geriatric adults. *Journal of the Acoustical Society of America, 85,* 2608–2622.

Fried, M. P., Kelly, J. H., & Strome, M. (1982). Comparison of the adult and infant larynx. *Journal of Family Practice, 15,* 557–561.

Fujimura, O. (1961). Bilabial stop and nasal consonants: A motion picture study and its implications. *Journal of Speech and Hearing Research, 4,* 233–247.

Fujimura, O. (1980). Modern methods of investigation in speech production. *Phonetica, 37,* 38–54.

Gibbon, F. E., & Wood, S. E. (2003). Using electropalatography (EPG) to diagnose and treat articulation disorders associated with mild cerebral palsy: A case study. *Clinical Linguistics and Phonetics, 17,* 365–374.

Goffman, L., & Smith, A. (1999). Development and phonetic differentiation of speech movement patterns. *Journal of Experimental Psychology: Human Perception and Performance, 25,* 649–660.

Goozée, J. V., Murdoch, B. E., & Theodoros, D. (2003). Electropalatographic assessment of tongue-to-palate contacts exhibited in dysarthria following traumatic brain injury: Spatial characteristics. *Journal of Medical Speech-Language Pathology, 11,* 115–129.

Gracco, V. L., & Löfqvist, A. (1994). Speech motor coordination and control: Evidence from lip, jaw, and laryngeal movements. *Journal of Neuroscience, 14,* 6585–6597.

Green, J. R., & Wang, Y. T. (2003). Tongue-surface movement patterns during speech and swallowing. *Journal of the Acoustical Society of America, 113,* 2820–2833.

Guiard-Marigny, T., & Ostry, D. J. (1997). A system for three-dimensional visualization of human jaw motion in speech. *Journal of Speech, Language, and Hearing Research, 40,* 1118–1121.

Haggard, M., Summerfield, Q., & Roberts, M. (1981). Psychoacoustical and cultural determinants of phoneme boundaries: Evidence from trading F0 cues in the voiced-voiceless distinction. *Journal of Phonetics, 9,* 49–62.

Hardcastle, W. J., Gibbon, F. E., & Jones, W. (1991). Visual display of tongue-palate contact: Electropalatography in the assessment and remediation of speech disorders. *British Journal of Disorders of Communication, 26,* 41–74.

Hardin, M. A., Van Demark, D. R., & Morris, H. L. (1990). Long-term speech results of cleft palate speakers with marginal velopharyngeal competence. *Journal of Communication Disorders, 23,* 401–416.

Hardin, M. A., Van Demark, D. R., Morris, H. L., & Payne, M. (1992). Correspondence between nasalance scores and listener judgments of nasality. *Cleft Palate–Craniofacial Journal, 29,* 346–351.

Higgins, M. B., Netsell, R., & Schulte, L. (1998). Vowel-related differences in laryngeal articulatory and phonatory function. *Journal of Speech, Language, and Hearing Research, 41,* 712–724.

Hixon, T. J., Minifie, F. D., & Tait, C. A. (1967). Correlates of turbulent noise production for speech. *Journal of Speech and Hearing Research, 10,* 133–140.

Hogden, J., Löfqvist, A., Gracco, V., Zlokarnik, I., Rubin, P., & Saltzman, E. (1996). Accurate recovery of articulator positions from acoustics: New conclusions based on human data. *Journal of the Acoustical Society of America, 100,* 1819–1834.

Hoit, J. D., Solomon, N. P., & Hixon, T. J. (1993). Effect of lung volume on voice onset time (VOT). *Journal of Speech and Hearing Research, 36,* 516–520.

Hoit, J. D., Watson, P. J., Hixon, K. E., McMahon, P., & Johnson, C. L. (1994). Age and velopharyngeal function during speech production, *Journal of Speech and Hearing Research, 37,* 295–302.

Hoole, J. P., Nguyen-Trong, N., & Hardcastle, W. (1993). A comparative investigation of coarticulation in fricatives: Electropalatographic, electromagnetic, and acoustic data. *Language and Speech, 36,* 235–260.

Horiguchi, S., & Bell-Berti, F. (1987). The Velotrace: A device for monitoring velar position. *Cleft Palate Journal, 24,* 104–111.

House, A. S., & Fairbanks, G. (1953). The influence of consonant environment upon the secondary characteristics of vowels. *Journal of the Acoustical Society of America, 25,* 105–113.

House, A. S., & Stevens, K. N. (1956). Analog studies of the nasalization of vowels. *Journal of Speech and Hearing Disorders, 21,* 218–232.

Huxley, T. H., & Youmans, W. J. (1872). *The elements of physiology and hygiene: A textbook for educational institutions.* New York, NY: D. Appleton & Co.

Isshiki, N., & Ringel, R. (1964). Airflow during the production of selected consonants. *Journal of Speech and Hearing Research, 7,* 233–244.

Kaburagi, T., & Honda, M. (2002). Electromagnetic articulograph based on a nonparametric representation of the magnetic field. *Journal of the Acoustical Society of America, 111,* 1414–1421.

Kaburagi, T., Wakamiya, K., & Honda, M. (2005). Three-dimensional electromagnetic articulography: A measurement principle. *Journal of the Acoustical Society of America, 118,* 428–443.

Kent, R. D., Dembowski, J., & Lass, N. J. (1996). The acoustic characteristics of American English. In J. Lass (Ed.), *Principles of experimental phonetics* (pp. 185–225). St. Louis, MO: Mosby.

Kent, R. D., & Forner, L. L. (1980). Speech segment durations in sentence recitation between children and adults. *Journal of Phonetics, 8,* 157–168.

Kent, R. D., & Vorperian, H. K. (1995). Anatomic development of the craniofacial-oral-laryngeal systems: A review. *Journal of Medical Speech-Language Pathology, 3,* 145–190.

Kessinger, R., & Blumstein, S. (1997). Effects of speaking rate on voice-onset time and vowel production: Some implications for perception studies. *Journal of Phonetics, 26,* 117–128.

Kewley-Port, D., Burkle, T. Z., & Lee, J. H. (2007). Contribution of consonant versus vowel information to sentence intelligibility for young normal-hearing and elderly hearing-impaired listeners.

Journal of the Acoustical Society of America, 122, 2365–2375.

Kiritani, S., Itoh, K., & Fujimura, O. (1975). Tongue-pellet tracking by a computer-controlled x-ray microbeam system. *Journal of the Acoustical Society of America, 57,* 1516–1520.

Klatt, D. H. (1975). Voice onset time, frication, and aspiration in word-initial consonant clusters. *Journal of Speech and Hearing Research, 18,* 686–706.

Kluender, K. R., & Walsh, M. A. (1992). Amplitude rise time and the perception of the voiceless affricate/fricative distinction. *Perception and Psychophysics, 51,* 328–333.

Koenig, L. L. (2000). Laryngeal factors in voiceless consonant production in men, women and 5-year-olds. *Journal of Speech, Language, and Hearing Research, 43,* 1211–1228.

Koenig, L. L. (2001). Distributional characteristics of VOT in children's voiceless aspirated stops and interpretation of developmental trends. *Journal of Speech, Language, and Hearing Research, 44,* 1058–1068.

Kohler, K. J. (1985). F0 in the perception of lenis and fortis plosives. *Phonetica, 39,* 199–218.

Kollia, H. B., Gracco, V. L., & Harris, K. S. (1995). Articulatory organization of mandibular, labial, and velar movements during speech. *Journal of the Acoustical Society of America, 98,* 1313–1324.

Kuehn, D. P. (1976). A cineradiographic investigation of velar movement in two normals. *Cleft Palate Journal, 13,* 88–103.

Ladefoged, P. (2006). *A course in phonetics* (4th ed.). Sydney, Australia: Thomson-Wadsworth.

Leeper, H. A., & Noll, J. D. (1972). Pressure measurements of articulatory behavior during alterations of vocal effort. *Journal of the Acoustical Society of America, 51,* 1291–1295.

Lewis, M. M. (1951). *Infant speech: A study of the beginnings of language.* New York, NY: Humanities Press.

Lisker, L., & Abramson, H. (1964). A cross-language study of voicing in initial stops: Acoustical measurements. *Word, 20,* 384–442.

Lisker, L., & Abramson, A. (1967). Some effects of content on voice onset time in English stops. *Language and Speech, 10,* 1–28.

Lisker, L., & Abramson, H. (1971). Distinctive features and laryngeal control. *Language, 47,* 767–785.

Lucero, J. C., & Munhall, J. G. (1999). A model of facial biomechanics for speech production. *Journal of the Acoustical Society of America, 106,* 2834–2842.

Macken, M. A., & Barton, D. (1980). The acquisition of the voicing contrast in English: A study of voice onset time in word-initial stop consonants. *Journal of Child Language, 7,* 41–74.

Malécot, A. (1955). An experimental study of force of articulation. *Studia Linguistica, 9,* 35–44.

Malécot, A. (1966). Mechanical pressure as an index of "force of articulation." *Phonetica, 14,* 169–180.

McCrea, C. R., & Morris, R. J. (2005). The effects of fundamental frequency level on voice onset time in normal adult male speakers. *Journal of Speech, Language, and Hearing Research, 48,* 1013–1024.

McGlone, R. E., & Proffit, W. R. (1967). Lingual pressures associated with speaker consistency and syllable variations. *Phonetica, 17,* 176–183.

McLeod, S., & Searl, J. (2006). Adaptation to an electropalatograph palate: Acoustic, impressionistic, and perceptual data. *American Journal of Speech-Language Pathology, 15,* 192–206.

Miller, J. L., Green, K. P., & Reeves, A. (1986). Speaking rate and segments: A look at the relation between speech production and speech perception for the voicing contrast. *Phonetica, 43,* 106–115.

Miller, J. L., Watkin, K. L., & Chen, M. F. (2002). Tissues variations in intrinsic musculature of the adult human tongue. *Journal of Speech, Language, and Hearing Research, 45,* 51–65.

Mueller, P. B. (1971). Parkinson's disease: Motor-speech behavior in a selected group of patients. *Folia Phoniatrica, 23,* 333–346.

Munhall, K. G., Löfqvist, A., & Kelso, J. A. (1994). Lip-larynx coordination in speech: Effects of mechanical perturbations to the lower lip. *Journal of the Acoustical Society of America, 95,* 3605–3616.

Murdoch, B. E., Goozée, J. V., Veidt, M., Scott, D. H., & Meyers, I. A. (2004). Introducing the pressure-sensing palatography—the next frontier in electropalatography. *Clinical Linguistics and Phonetics, 18,* 433–445.

Nittrouer, S. (1991). Phase relations of jaw and tongue tip movements in the production of VCV utterances. *Journal of the Acoustical Society of America, 90,* 1806–1815.

Ohde, R. (1985). Fundamental frequency correlates of stop consonant voicing and vowel quality in the speech of preadolescent children. *Journal of the Acoustical Society of America, 78,* 1554–1561.

Ohde, R., Haley, K. L., & Barnes, C. W. (2006). Perception of the [m]-[n] distinction in consonant-vowel (CV) and vowel-consonant (VC) syllables produced by child and adult talkers. *Journal of the Acoustical Society of America, 119,* 1697–1711.

Olive, J. P., Greenwood, A., & Coleman, J. (1991). *Acoustics of American English speech: A dynamic approach.* New York, NY: Springer.

Perkell, J. S., Cohen, M. H., Svirsky, M. A., Matthies, M. L., Garabieta, I., & Jackson, M. T. T. (1992). Electromagnetic midsagittal articulometer (EMMA) systems for transducing speech articulatory movements. *Journal of the Acoustical Society of America, 92,* 3078–3096.

Perkell, J. S., & Nelson, W. L. (1985). Variability in production of the vowels /i/ and /u/. *Journal of the Acoustical Society of America, 77,* 1889–1895.

Pickett, J. M. (1980). *The sounds of speech communication.* Baltimore, MD: University Park Press.

Proffit, W. R., Palmer, J. M., & Kydd, W. L. (1965). Evaluation of tongue pressures during speech. *Folia Phoniatrica (Basel), 17,* 115–128.

Robb, M. P., & Smith, A. B. (2002). Fundamental frequency onset and offset behavior: A comparative study of children and adults. *Journal of Speech, Language, and Hearing Research, 45,* 446–456.

Schönle, P. W., Gräbe, K., Wenig, P., Höhne, J., Schrader, J., & Conrad, B. (1987). Electromagnetic articulography: Use of alternating magnetic fields for tracking movements of multiple points inside and outside the vocal tract. *Brain and Language, 31,* 26–35.

Shaiman, S., & Adams, S. (1997). Velocity profiles of lip protrusion across changes in speaking rate. *Journal of Speech, Language, and Hearing Research, 40,* 144–158.

Simpson, A. P. (2001). Dynamic consequences of differences in male and female vocal tract dimensions. *Journal of the Acoustical Society of America, 109,* 2153–2164.

Smith, A., & Goffman, L. (1998). Stability and patterning of speech movement sequences in children and adults. *Journal of Speech, Language, and Hearing Research, 41,* 18–30.

Smith, B. L., & McLean-Muse, A. (1987). An investigation of motor equivalence in the speech of children and adults. *Journal of the Acoustical Society of America, 82,* 837–842.

Smith, K. K., & Kier, W. M. (1989). Tongues, trunks, and tentacles: Moving the skeletons of muscle. *American Scientist, 77,* 28–35.

Snow, D. (1997). Children's acquisition of speech timing in English: A comparative study of voice onset time and final syllable vowel lengthening. *Journal of Child Language, 24,* 35–56.

Stathopoulos, E. T. (1986). Relationship between intraoral air pressure and vocal intensity in children and adults. *Journal of Speech and Hearing Research, 29,* 71–74.

Stathopoulos, E. T., & Weismer, G. (1985). Oral airflow and air pressure during speech production: A comparative study of children, youths, and adults. *Folia Phoniatrica, 37,* 152–159.

Stevens, K. N. (1991). Vocal fold vibration for obstruent consonants. In J. Gauffin & B. Hammarberg (Eds.), *Vocal fold physiology: Acoustic, perceptual, and physiological aspects of voice mechanisms* (pp. 29–36). San Diego, CA: Singular.

Stevens, K. N., & Blumstein, S. E. (1978). Invariant cues for place of articulation in stop consonants. *Journal of the Acoustical Society of America, 64,* 1358–1368.

Stevens, K. N., Fant, G., & Hawkings, S. (1987). Some acoustical and perceptual correlates of nasal vowels. In R. Channon & L. Shockey (Eds.), *Festschrift für Ilse Lehiste* (pp. 241–254). Dordrecht, The Netherlands: Floris.

Stone, M. (1990). A three-dimensional model of tongue movement based on ultrasound and x-ray microbeam data. *Journal of the Acoustical Society of America, 87,* 2207–2217.

Stone, M. (1995). How the tongue takes advantage of the palate during speech. In F. Bell-Berti & L. J. Raphael (Eds.), *Producing speech: Contemporary issues* (pp. 143–153). New York, NY: American Institute of Physics.

Stone, M., Faber, A., Raphael, L. J., & Shawker, T. H. (1992). Cross-sectional tongue shape and linguopalatal contact patterns in [s] and [ʃ]. *Journal of Phonetics, 20,* 253–270.

Subtelny, J. H., Worth, J. H., & Sakuda, M. (1966). Intraoral air pressure and rate of flow during speech. *Journal of Speech and Hearing Research, 9,* 498–519.

Summers, W. V. (1987). Effects of stress and final consonant voicing in vowel production: Articulatory and acoustic analyses. *Journal of the Acoustical Society of America, 82,* 847–863.

Surprenant, A. M., & Goldstein, L. (1998). The perception of speech gestures. *Journal of the Acoustical Society of America, 104,* 518–529.

Thompson, A. E., & Hixon, T. J. (1979). Nasal airflow during normal speech production. *Cleft Palate Journal, 16,* 412–420.

Tuller, B., Shao, S., & Kelso, J. A. S. (1990). An evaluation of an alternating magnetic field device for monitoring tongue movements. *Journal of the Acoustical Society of America, 88,* 674–679.

Vatikiotis-Bateson, E., & Ostry, D. J. (1995). An analysis of the dimensionality of jaw movement in speech. *Journal of Phonetics, 23,* 101–117.

Volaitis, L. E., & Miller, J. L. (1992). Phonetic prototypes: Influence of place of articulation and speaking rate in the internal structure of voicing categories. *Journal of the Acoustical Society of America, 92*, 723–735.

Vorperian, H. K., Kent, R. D., Lindstrom, M. J., Kalina, C. M., Gentry, L. R., & Yandell, B. S. (2005). Development of vocal tract length during early childhood: A magnetic resonance imaging study. *Journal of the Acoustical Society of America. 117*, 338–350.

Warren, D. W. (1996). Regulation of speech aerodynamics. In N. J. Lass (Ed.), *Principles of experimental phonetics* (pp. 46–92). St. Louis, MO: Mosby.

Warren, D. W., Dalston, R. M., & Mayo, R. (1994). Hypernasality and velopharyngeal impairment. *Cleft Palate–Craniofacial Journal, 31*, 257–262.

Warren, D. W., & Hall, D. J. (1973). Glottal activity and intraoral pressure during stop consonant production. *Folia Phoniatrica, 25*, 121–129.

Warren, D. W., & Wood, M. T. (1969). Respiratory volumes in normal speech: A possible reason for intraoral pressure differences among voiced and voiceless consonants. *Journal of the Acoustical Society of America, 45*, 466–469.

Watterson, T., McFarlane, S. C., & Wright, D. S. (1993). The relationship between nasalance and nasality in children with cleft palate. *Journal of Communication Disorders, 26*, 13–28.

Weismer, G., & Bunton, K. (1999). Influences of pellet markers on speech production behavior: Acoustical and perceptual measures. *Journal of the Acoustical Society of America, 105*, 2882–2894.

Weismer, G., Yunosova, Y., & Westbury, J.R. (2003). Interarticulator coordination in dysarthria: An x-ray microbeam study. *Journal of Speech, Language and Hearing Research, 46*, 1247–1261.

Westbury, J. R. (1991). The significance and measurement of head position during speech production experiments using the x-ray microbeam system. *Journal of the Acoustical Society of America, 89*, 1782–1791.

Whalen, D. H., Iskarous, K., Tiede, M. K., Ostry, D. J., Lehnert-Lehouillier, H., Vatikiotis-Bateson, E., & Halley, D.S. (2005). The Haskins optically corrected ultrasound system (HOCUS). *Journal of Speech, Language, and Hearing Research, 48*, 543–553.

Young, L. H. Zajac, D. J., Mayo, R., & Hooper, C. R. (2001). Effects of vowel height and vocal intensity on anticipatory nasal airflow in individuals with normal speech. *Journal of Speech, Language, and Hearing Research, 44*, 52–60.

Xue, S. A., & Hao, G. J. (2003). Changes in the human vocal tract due to aging and the acoustic correlates of speech production: A pilot study. *Journal of Speech, Language, and Hearing Research, 46*, 689–701.

Zlatin, M. A., & Koenigsknecht, R. A. (1976). Development of the voicing contrast: A comparison of voice onset time in stop perception and production. *Journal of Speech and Hearing Research, 19*, 93–111.

9

Prosody

Figure 9–1

I've always felt, even as a songwriter, that the rhythm of speech is in itself a language for me.
—Cyndi Lauper, American singer-songwriter (1953–)

Clinical Case 7: Parkinson's Disease

Clinical cases are based upon real patients whom the author has treated. Evaluation and treatment information has been edited to focus upon specific features related to the chapters. Note that clinical cases incorporate information that is covered in this and other chapters (and some information about diagnosis and therapy that you will learn in future courses). You are encouraged to review this case before you begin your study of this chapter and once again after you have completed the chapter. You may also want to revisit this case later in the semester after you have covered additional chapters.

Cheung is a 74-year-old retired lawyer. He is fully bilingual (Mandarin/English), having specialized in international Chinese American import-export law. He speaks in both Mandarin and English with his wife and adult sons. He is trying to teach his two grandchildren Mandarin, although they don't show much interest in learning it. Cheung was diagnosed with Parkinson's disease 2 years ago, a neurological disorder of the basal ganglia that causes tremors, rigidity, slowness of movement, and impaired sensory (and often cognitive) perception. He takes medication to control the symptoms, and he participates in daily physical activity (walking, riding a stationary bicycle), as recommended by his neurologist, to maintain flexibility and strength. However, recently his wife and children have complained that his speech is difficult to understand and that he mumbles and speaks too quietly. Cheung's wife reported that his speech in Mandarin was even harder to understand than his English, which she attributed to his lack of tone variation. (Mandarin is a tonal language and therefore variation in tone is essential to meaning.) Cheung's neurologist recommended a speech-voice evaluation and therapy to minimize the effects of Parkinson's disease on Cheung's speech and to maintain maximum intelligibility.

The speech-voice evaluation revealed consistently reduced intensity, delayed onset of utterances within conversational context, reduced articulatory precision, and excessive coarticulation. Prosody was moderately impaired, with decreased f_0 and intensity contours, and decreased phrasal prominence. Speech rhythm was characterized by increasing rate of speech over the course of an utterance, with increased pause time at phrase endings. Upon questioning, Cheung denied speech problems and attributed his wife and children's complaints to lack of effort to listen carefully to him. Overall, speech intelligibility was moderately impaired. Stimulability testing for increased intensity and prosodic variation revealed small improvement, but significant cueing was required.

The SLP conducting the evaluation knew that Cheung's speech deficits were characteristic of people with Parkinson's disease. Denial of speech problems was also a common occurrence associated with the neurological deficits of the disease. A course of speech-voice therapy was initiated, focusing upon increased speech intensity and articulatory precision and decreased rate of speech, together with increasing Cheung's awareness of the need to use significantly greater effort to speak loudly and clearly. Increased depth of preutterance inhalation and increased opening of the mouth during speech were used to help Cheung increase speech intensity. To help Cheung improve his prosody in English, the SLP prepared phrases that were relevant to his daily activities and asked him to select the most important word in the phrase and then use greater intensity for that word, even while maintaining increased intensity for the entire phrase. (In other words, speaking loudly for the whole phrase and even louder for the most important word.) The SLP did not know Mandarin. However, to help him increase his intelligibility in Mandarin, he invited Cheung's wife to participate in the therapy. Using a list of Mandarin words, Cheung was instructed to exaggerate tonal changes, while his wife reported on the accuracy of the words. After 1 month of twice-weekly therapy, Cheung demonstrated significantly increased self-monitoring skills, and his wife and children reported that his speech was significantly easier to understand in both languages.

Clinical Case Discussion Questions

1. What key features of prosody did the SLP address with Cheung in Mandarin and English? Which prosodic features were not addressed?
2. Explain the differences in the prosody approach used by the SLP for Mandarin and English. (Be aware of the difference between f_0 contour, word stress, and phrase prominence.)
3. What is the relationship between intensity, increased depth of inhalation, and increased mouth opening (see Chapters 5 and 7)?
4. How is the acoustic theory of speech production relevant to Cheung's speech-voice deficit?

9.1 Introduction to Prosody

Email and text are efficient methods of communication—most of the time. But we have all had the experience of being misinterpreted in both media. Humor, sarcasm, anomalous sentences, and subtleties of interpretation are difficult to transmit to the "listener" because we communicate these features beyond the phonetic level of written characters. Thus, we often resort to emoticons, the pictorial representation of a facial expression, such as the happy face or punctuation such as :). Emoticons represent not only facial expression, however; they also represent, although not always effectively, the expressiveness in our speech that transmits our intent. Such expressiveness is the topic of prosody.

The vowels and consonants that we have been considering over the course of the previous chapters are speech segments, which form the nuclei and boundaries of syllables. The syllables, in turn, are grouped together to build an utterance. The utterance can be composed of a single syllable (as in "No!") or a longer grouping that comprises a fully grammatical sentence. From an acoustic viewpoint, the meaning of the utterance is communicated at two broad levels. One level is the phoneme, the smallest meaningful segment, and the coarticulation of combinations of phonemes. The other level of meaning is carried by features that are *superimposed* upon the segments. In other words, the intent of the utterance is communicated both at the segmental and the suprasegmental level. The **suprasegmental level** or, synonymously, **prosody** is defined by Sanderman and Collier (1996) as "the ensemble of phonetic properties that do not enter into the definition of individual speech sounds" (p. 321). For ease of reference throughout this chapter, we use the term prosody.

The segmental features of vowels and consonants discussed in Chapters 7 and 8 are inherent characteristics of the phonemes, either in isolation or due to coarticulatory effects. Prosodic features, in contrast, are defined by their relative values to one another. For example, the segmental acoustic feature of voice onset time for /bit/ can be measured meaningfully without reference to the voice onset time of another voiced plosive. In contrast, the meaning, or communicative function, of the amount of stress (a prosodic feature we have yet to define) that the speaker places upon the plosive, as in, "I said beet, not Pete!" can be interpreted meaningfully only in comparison to another segment within the phrase. In this chapter, we consider the ways in which meaning is communicated through prosody and the acoustic manifestation of prosody.

9.2 Basic Building Blocks of Prosody

Prosody is a broad term that includes patterns of intonation, timing, and loudness (Cutler, Dahan, & van Donselaar, 1997). The acoustic correlates of these features are f_o contour, duration and juncture, and intensity contour, respectively. These basic building blocks are combined in a variety of ways that are both language and speaker dependent, to form syllabic stress, prominence, and rhythm. We will consider each of these basic features in turn.

Intonation (f_o Contour)

"Don't talk to me in that tone of voice!" How many of us have said that to someone at one time or another? What do we mean? Apparently, it is not the content, the actual words, to which we are objecting. Yet something about the way in which the utterance is said communicates the objectionable meaning. We learned in Chapter 3 that pitch is the perceptual correlate of frequency. We use *tone* to refer to pitch as a distinc-

tive feature at the word level, a characteristic that signifies a unique meaning, and we use *intonation* to reference utterance-level pitch contour (Lehiste, 1996, p. 232).

English is not a tonal language. That is, pitch contour is not a minimally contrastive feature. We do not have any words that are equivalent in all segmental features except for tone, as occurs in Mandarin, for example. At the prosodic level, however, intonation is important. Perhaps the most commonly recognized way in which we use intonation is the rising pitch contour that signals a question when the sentence is constructed grammatically as a statement (Figure 9–2). Questions have different intonation contours, however, depending upon whether they are closed questions (answerable only by yes or no) or open-ended questions. In Figure 9–3, we see that the yes-no question, "Did she go back?" ends with an upward rise in pitch, whereas, "Where did she go?" ends with a rise and then a fall in pitch. If the latter question ended with a rising pitch, it might be interpreted as a repetition of a question asked of the speaker.

The f_o contour contributes to our perception of emotional intent of the speaker (Monnot, Orbeo, Riccardo, Sikka, & Rosssa, 2003). In Figure 9–4,

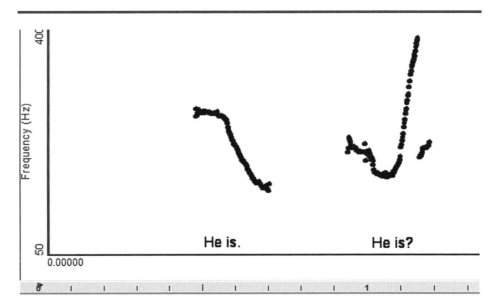

Figure 9–2. Intonation contour for the statement, "He is" and the question, "He is?" The intonation contour for the statement is flat to falling and rising for the question.

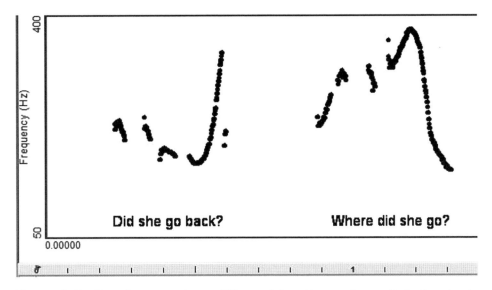

Figure 9–3. Questions may have different intonation contours. Note the rise in pitch for the first question, "Did she go back?" and a pitch rise with a final pitch fall for the second question, "Where did she go?"

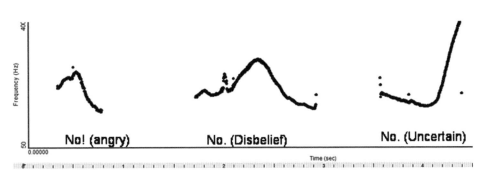

Figure 9–4. Note that the intonation contour for each of the three utterances of "No," said in anger, disbelief, and uncertainty.

the word "no" is spoken with three different emotions. Note that the f_o contours are quite distinct for each utterance. If embedded within a conversation, different responses would follow these three utterances. A response to the angry "no" might be, "Don't get mad at me." The "no" said in disbelief might elicit the response, "Really—it's true!" And a listener may respond to the uncertain "no" with "Why aren't you sure?" In other words, intonation is a powerful and necessary acoustic feature of spoken utterances.

An interesting component of intonation is f_o declination, which refers to the tendency of f_o to decrease gradually over the course of an utterance (Cohen & 't Hart, 1967). In Figure 9–5, one can observe small variations in pitch contour (to be discussed in a moment), but overall, the pitch declines from the start to the end of the sentence. Declination becomes less steep as the overall length of the utterance increases (Ohala, 1978). Is this phenomenon a result of speech physiology or linguistic factors? (Interestingly, Hauser and Fowler [1992] found that f_o declination is common in monkeys!) In short utterances, the f_o and activity of the cricothyroid muscle are strongly correlated. However, in longer utterances, the

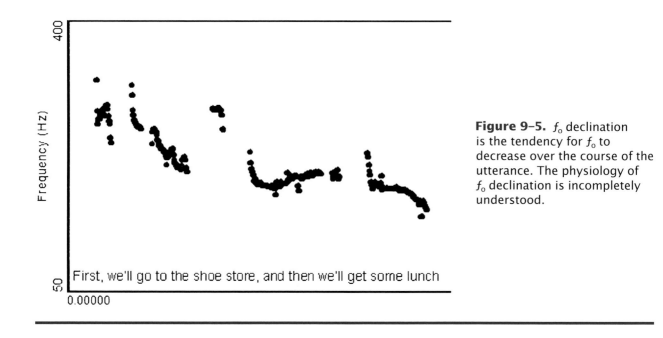

Figure 9–5. f_o declination is the tendency for f_o to decrease over the course of the utterance. The physiology of f_o declination is incompletely understood.

gradual decrease in f_o is not well correlated with muscle activity (Atkinson, 1978). The most common explanation for f_o declination has been that lung pressure slowly decreases over the length of the utterance. Thus, the vocal folds "relax" against the lowered lung pressure, causing their rate of vibration to slow (Collier, 1975; Gelfer, Harris, Collier, & Baer, 1983). However, Honda and Fujimura (1991) point out that the shift in lung pressure over the course of most utterances is insufficient to account for the declination in f_o. Interestingly, Nooteboom (1994) reports that f_o declination patterns are more marked in reading than in spontaneous speech. We might assume that in reading, visual forward scanning would help the speaker to plan for maintenance of adequate lung pressure throughout the sentence. However, it may also be that, when reading aloud in a research context, communicative intent is minimized. That is, the reader does not have the intention to communicate the information to the audience. Rather, the reader is simply performing a speaking task. Perhaps, without communicative intent directed towards a listener, f_o falls at the end of each sentence. Clearly, other factors may contribute to f_o declination.

Some evidence suggests that a decline in muscular activity occurs across the breathing, phonatory, and resonatory/articulatory subsystems. That is, declination of f_o may be part of a larger phenomenon called supralaryngeal declination (Krakow, Bell-Berti, & Wang, 1995; Vatikiotis-Bateson & Fowler, 1988). Given the interaction of the three subsystems during speech production, such a phenomenon is reasonable to hypothesize. Speakers may decrease jaw opening and centralize corner vowels (evident by changes in F1 and F2) as an utterance comes to an end. The velum also participates in declination. Krakow et al. (1995) found that velar movement amplitude decreased across utterances of eight to nine syllables that contained no nasal phonemes.

It is evident from Figures 9–2 through 9–5 that intonation contour is not a smooth function. That is, considerable pitch variability occurs within and across words as well as across the entire utterance. In fact, the intonation contour of an utterance occurs on more than one level. We shall return to this observation momentarily when we discuss syllabic stress and phrase prominence.

Study Questions

1. What is prosody?

2. What is the difference between a tonal language and intonation in a nontonal language?

3. Define intonation and provide an example of two utterances that contain the same words but have different meanings due to their different intonation contours.

4. What is f_o declination? What is the most common explanation for this phenomenon, and what are the shortcomings of that explanation? Provide an alternative hypothesis.

Timing (Duration and Juncture)

We have observed that timing at the segmental level can be an important perceptual cue, such as in the duration of the silence in voice onset time, the duration of a vowel to help identify the voiced or voiceless plosive cognates, and the duration of formant transitions to distinguish between diphthongs and a semivowel adjacent to a vowel. And the duration of labials, in general, is greater than the duration of consonants produced farther back in the oral cavity for both fricatives and stops (Peterson & Lehiste, 1960). Duration at the segmental level, therefore, is a perceptual cue to both place and manner of articulation.

At the prosodic level, however, duration can be manipulated to provide additional linguistic information. For example, duration is used to signal semantic boundaries, a phenomenon referred to as preboundary lengthening (Lehiste, 1996). Increased duration of one or more syllables in utterance-final position can signal the end of words or complete utterances (Klatt, 1976). In Figure 9–6, the word "tomorrow" is lengthened, particularly in the second syllable, when it appears in phrase-final position.

Duration is also defined by **juncture**, the pause time or separation of syllables. Juncture can influence the meaning of an utterance. A study by O'Malley, Kloker, and Dara-Abrams (1973) showed that individuals who speak algebraic equations signal the location of parentheses to their listeners using juncture by increasing pause time after a closed parenthesis. The spectrogram in Figure 9–7 shows the use of juncture to distinguish between "I'm aching a lot" and "I'm making a lot." In that example, juncture helped establish the word boundary between "I'm" and the following word. In fact, identifying distinct words from within the continuous flow of speech is an important task for the listener, and durational cues assist in that task (Cutler & Butterfield, 1990). (See Figure 9–8 for a humorous look at the effect of vowel duration on perception of word boundaries.)

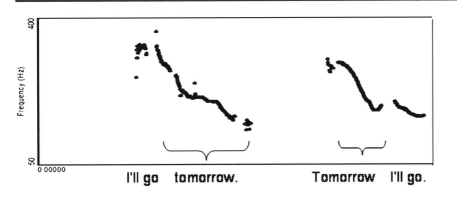

Figure 9–6. The second syllable of the word "tomorrow" is lengthened when it appears in phrase-final position.

release of the /m/

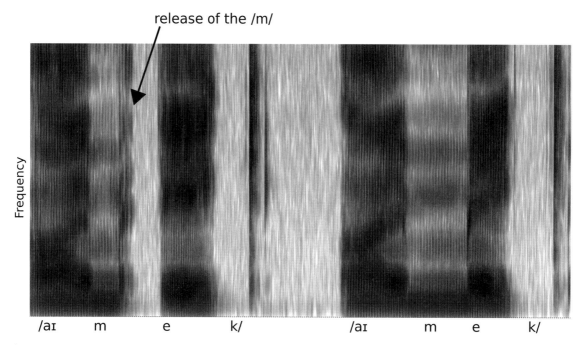

| /aɪ | m | e | k/ | /aɪ | m | e | k/ |

Figure 9–7. Juncture is used to distinguish between the utterance, "I'm aching a lot" and "I'm making a lot." The wideband spectrogram shows the first word and first syllable of the second word extracted ("I'm ach" on the left and "I'm mak" on the right) from the target utterance.

Figure 9–8. Duration is used to signal semantic boundaries, as in the preboundary lengthening of the initial diphthong /aɪ/ to change the meaning of the utterance from "white shoes" to "Why choose?" (after Peterson & Lehiste, 1960).

In Figure 9–9, we see the spectrogram of the utterances, "A bluebird's nest" and "A blue bird's nest." The meaning of the first utterance is to identify the nest of a bluebird. The meaning of the second utterance is more likely to be interpreted as the blue-hued nest of a bird. Note the duration of the pause (juncture) between the words "blue" and "bird" in the two utterances, in this case identified by the occlusion for the stop /b/ in "bird."

occlusion occlusion

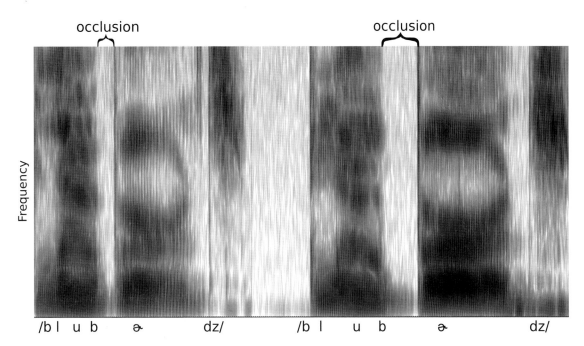

/b l u b ɚ dz/ /b l u b ɚ dz/

Figure 9–9. Juncture helps distinguish between "A bluebird's nest" and "A blue bird's nest." The wideband spectrogram shows the segment "bluebird's nest" (*left*) and "blue bird's nest" (*right*) extracted from the larger utterance.

Life Span Effects on Prosody

Prelinguistic babbling sounds like "real" speech even though it contains no "real" words. One of the reasons is that many prosodic features are similar in children and adults (Davis, Mac-Neilage, Matyear, & Powell, 2000). Smith and Robb (2006) found that children 6 years of age adjust lexical stress depending upon the location of the word in the utterance. And so, like adults, duration is longer, and both f_o and intensity are lower at utterance-final position. In fact, much evidence suggests that supra-segmental features precede the emergence of many segmental features of phonemes and may well facilitate the developmental of segmental skills (Crary & Tallman, 1993; Crystal, 1979; Menyuk & Bernholtz, 1969). At the other end of the life span, older women may use intonation differently than younger women to signal stress (Scukanec, Petrosino, & Colcord, 1996), possibly as compensation for decreased ability to increase loudness and duration.

Loudness (Intensity Contour)

In Chapter 4, lung pressure was identified as the major regulator of intensity. In Chapter 6, the vocal tract's contribution to the regulation of intensity was discussed. It was noted that vowels carry more energy than consonants because of their more open vocal tract. In addition, we noted that phonemes have intrinsic intensity characteristics, just as they have intrinsic pitch differences. **Sonority** is the loudness level of a sound relative to other sounds of similar length, pitch, and stress. We discussed how vowels and consonants have different intensity levels

Prosodic Disturbances

Dysarthria is a group of motor speech disorders that result from neurologic impairments that affect the control and execution of speech motor movements. Dysarthria often results in prosodic disturbances. Ataxic dysarthria, for example, caused by abnormal functioning of the cerebellum, results in decreased articulatory precision ("slurring"), excessive duration of vowels, and abnormal (almost "sing-song") f_o contour. Patients are often described as sounding as if they had drunk too much alcohol. Parkinson's disease, as highlighted in Clinical Case 7, often results in a monotone quality and impaired speech rate and rhythm. Cerebral palsy, caused by congenital neurological impairment, can cause decreased articulatory precision, abnormal movements that distort and prolong phoneme production, and difficulty producing accurate syllabic stress or phrase prominence. These dysarthrias are just some of the types of disorders that result in prosodic disturbances. As such, knowledge of the acoustic features that comprise prosody is important for evaluation and treatment.

depending upon the openness of the vocal tract, with greater opening generally correlating with greater intensity. In Chapter 8, we saw through examination of waveforms and spectrograms that place of articulation affects intensity level. For example, nasals have less intensity than orally produced consonants, and fricatives have variable intensity depending upon the location of the oral constriction.

At the prosodic level, intensity and f_o frequently covary. This relationship should not be surprising: Recall their covariance at the phonatory level, as discussed in Chapter 6. For example, intensity tends to decline over the course of an utterance, like f_o, although not to the same extent. The decline in intensity may be an acoustic cue that helps signal the end of the utterance to the listener (Pierrehumbert, 1979). Intensity and f_o, as well as timing, are both used to create syllabic stress and prominence.

9.3 Syllabic Stress and Prominence

Syllabic stress is the use of f_o, intensity, and/or duration to place emphasis on one or more syllables of a word. Syllabic stress is defined by the language of the speaker. Try to say the word "syllable" with the emphasis on the second instead of the first syllable. The word sounds "wrong" and may not be understood by the listener. Change the syllabic stress of the word "desert" from the second to the first syllable, and you have changed the meaning of the word from tasty treat to an expanse of sand. Stress also often distinguishes between a verb and a noun, as demonstrated in Figure 9–10. Note that duration, intensity, and f_o are used together as a stress cue. The stressed unit is often higher in pitch, louder, and of longer duration. Look again at Figure 9–9. Stress was placed on the word "blue" in the first utterance and on "bird's" in the second utterance. In Figure 9–11, the pitch tracing of the utterances of Figure 9–9 demonstrates the use of f_o contour, together with duration, in the creation of stress.

In general, the steady state of stressed vowels is longer than that of unstressed vowels, and formant frequencies are less centralized and the f_o is higher (Harris, 1978; Lehiste & Peterson, 1961). Stressed syllabic nuclei have been shown to be correlated with articulatory changes, particularly lowered jaw (independent of vowel height), and greater movement of the tongue dorsum, resulting in shifts in the F1/F2 relationship (Erickson, 2002). Recall from Chapter 7 that American English vowels become central-

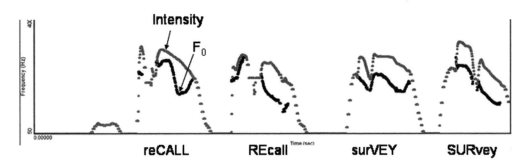

Figure 9–10. In these instances, both pitch and loudness contribute to the perception of stress. The f_o (*black lines*) is higher and the energy (*gray lines*) is greater for the stressed syllable, helping to differentiate the meaning of similar words.

Figure 9–11. f_o contour of the utterances "A bluebird's nest" and "A blue bird's nest." Note that in this utterance, f_o contributes to stress and conveyance of the meaning. However, in many cases, intensity may play a more important role than f_o in stress and prominence.

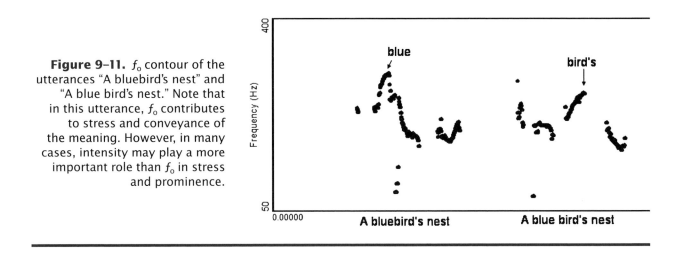

ized, or reduced, when they occur in unstressed syllables. For example, the noun recall, as in an auto recall, is pronounced /ricɔl/, while the verb recall, as in to recall a name, is pronounced /rəcɔl/ (see Figure 9–10 for the intensity and f_o tracings). In the case of the noun, the vowel of the first syllable is articulated fully, while in the verb, the vowel is reduced to a schwa.

While stress is language defined, prominence is speaker defined. **Prominence** is the amount of emphasis placed upon a syllable or group of syllables to convey meaning. Like syllabic stress, prominence is achieved through the trio of acoustic cues—f_o contour, intensity contour, and duration. However, unlike syllabic stress, prominence is not defined strictly

by the speaker's language. Rather, prominence is defined by the communicative intent of the speaker. No acoustic cue can be singled out as the major, consistent carrier of stress (Lehiste, 1996). In Figure 9–12, the utterance, "Let's go OUT tonight" might be a response to "Let's stay in tonight" whereas "Let's go out toNIGHT" might be a contrary response to "Let's go out tomorrow night." Note the peaks in both intensity and f_o on the word "out" in the first utterance and on the second syllable of "tonight" in the second utterance. Similarly, the spectrogram of Figure 9–13 reveals that the stressed syllable "night" in the second utterance has greater energy (particularly in the diphthong /aɪ/) than the parallel syllable in the first utterance.

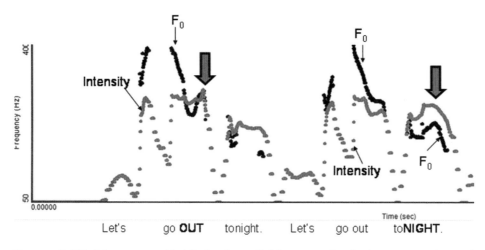

Figure 9–12. The arrows highlight the syllabic stress (and phrase prominence) placed on the word "out" and the second syllable of the word "tonight" in the first and second utterances, respectively.

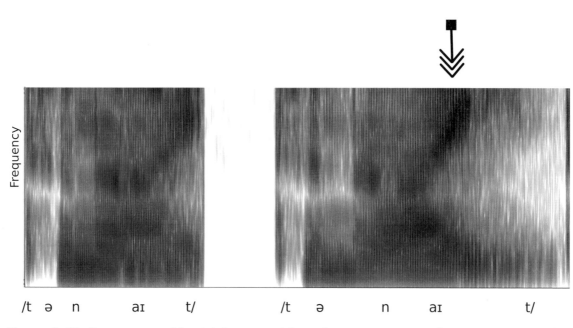

Figure 9–13. Spectrogram of "tonight" extracted from the two utterances of Figure 9–12. Note that the diphthong /aɪ/ extracted from the second utterance (*right*) contains more energy than the sample from the first utterance (*left*), consistent with the phrase prominence pattern of the two utterances.

We observed in Figures 9–2 through 9–4 that the pitch varied across even short phrases and that in Figure 9–5, the pitch moved up and down across the syllables even as it generally declined across the utterance. Below the overall utterance contour, intonation varies at the syllable level. Generally, one syllable in the utterance will receive major prominence. Depending upon

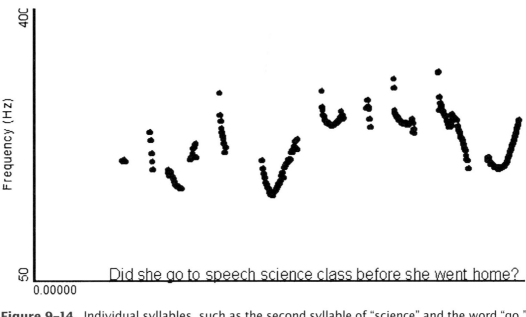

Figure 9–14. Individual syllables, such as the second syllable of "science" and the word "go," receive a slight upward inflection, whereas the overall pitch of the sentence may decline or remain relatively flat.

the length and complexity of the utterance, one or more syllables may receive secondary prominence. In Figure 9–5, "shoe" receives a strong secondary prominence after the initial pitch prominence in the beginning of the sentence. And finally, intonation contour rests upon the segmental changes in pitch. In Figure 9–14, we see that the overall pitch inflection moves upward from the beginning to the end of the question, "Did she go to speech science class before she went home?" Yet considerable variability in pitch occurs among the individual syllables within the utterance. Segmental pitch is a function of intrinsic pitch of vowels, as discussed in Chapter 7, and the pitch changes that result from coarticulatory effects of voiceless phonemes, as discussed earlier in this chapter.

Which acoustic cue is most important in signifying syllabic stress and phrase prominence—intensity, frequency, or duration? Traditionally, f_o contour has been considered the most important, but most studies suggest that a combination of cues is used (Howell, 1993; Sereno & Jongman, 1995). However, Kochanski, Grabe, Coleman, and Rosner (2005) offer evidence to suggest that intensity and, to a lesser extent, duration are more important than f_o contour in most cases. Clearly, additional research on this topic is needed.

Study Questions

5. How is duration affected by semantic boundaries?

6. What is juncture, how is it related to duration, and how does it contribute to meaning of an utterance?

7. Define stress and identify the three acoustic cues that define syllabic stress.

8. How do syllabic stress and phrase prominence differ?

Prosody Is Not Just Icing on the Linguistic Cake

Prosody is not just an extra speech feature that makes speech "interesting." While prosody is important for conveying emotional content, its linguistic role is considerably larger. Prosody has long been recognized to play a critical role in language comprehension (Cutler et al., 1997; van Els & de Bot, 1987). It assists in the expression of important information, including grammatical boundaries, discourse functions, emotional intent of the speaker, and regulation of conversational turn taking (Chun, 1988; Pierrehumbert & Hirschberg, 1990; Wennerstrom, 1994) at both the local (utterance) and global (discourse) levels (Cutler et al., 1997; Grosz & Sidner, 1986). For example, an early seminal work of Miller and Isard (1963) demonstrated improved recall of oral presentation of nonsense words or ungrammatical strings of words if the items were presented with typical sentence prosody rather than simply spoken as a list. More recently, prosody has been shown to be important in processing ambiguous sentences (Joeks, Redeker, & Hendriks, 2009; Titone et al., 2006) and processing of humorous stories and jokes (Wennerstrom, 2011). In many types of motor speech disorders, impaired prosody is a significant contributor to decreased intelligibility (see dysarthria clinical case in this chapter). And in accent management for nonnative speakers of a language, addressing prosody differences is as important as working on articulation differences (Behrman, 2014; Celce-Murcia, Brinton, & Goodwin, 1996).

9.4 Speech Rhythm

Rhythm is a perceptual phenomenon that is easy to recognize and difficult to define. We tap our foot or dance to the rhythm of music. We see the rhythm in a sequence of flashing lights in a winter holiday display. We hear the rhythm in the movement of windshield wipers on a rainy day or in a poem read aloud. Cummins (2015) highlights examples of unique but well-recognized speech rhythms, such as the auctioneer's cadence or the group recital of the American Pledge of Allegiance. When we listen to a conversation in a language that we do not know, we hear the rhythm of the language and may even correctly identify the language despite our lack of knowledge of its meaning. (We shall discuss the rhythm of different languages momentarily.)

Despite our ready awareness of both speech and nonspeech rhythms, defining and describing rhythm is not straightforward. One way to think about rhythm is by its periodicity. Something is recurring at periodic or regular intervals, with perhaps intermittent aperiodic or unexpected beats to serve as contrast to the baseline rhythm. However, in general, speech is not perceived as a periodic phenomenon (Turk & Shattuck-Hufnagel, 2013). Rhythm is a function of numerous acoustic cues. Thus, we offer a broad definition of rhythm: **Speech rhythm** is a language-dependent phenomenon that encompasses both the temporal and spectral patterned recurrence of strong and weak prosodic elements, including pitch, stress, loudness, and rate (Cummins, 2015; Fletcher, 2010; Kohler, 2009; Turk & Shattuck-Hufnagel, 2013, among many others).

We say that speech rhythm is language dependent because it has long been recognized that rhythm is perceived to differ depending upon the language spoken. Traditionally, based upon perception alone, languages have been classified as syllable timed (such as Spanish and French) or stress timed (such as English and Dutch) (Abercrombie, 1967; Pike, 1945). This rhythm typology, as it has been called, was based upon **isochronicity** of syllables. That is, syllable-timed languages contain syllables of equal duration. In contrast, stress-timed languages produce stressed units at equal intervals, such that stress-timed languages must stretch and compress units to maintain an overall equal timing of segments. The result is a predictable, yet distinct rhythm for each language group. Syllable- and stress-timed languages have been described as sounding like "machine gun" and "Morse code" styles, respectively. (This oft-used analogy has been attributed to Lloyd James [1940]) A third category, mora timed, which describes syllable weight (a descriptor that includes duration or stress), has been proposed to accommodate languages such as Japanese.

As reported by Cummins (2015), Pike's (1945) characterization of speech rhythm as stress- and syllable timed was intended to describe *transitory* stylistic differences that could exist within a *single speaker*. Abercrombie's (1967) assignation of those descriptors to classify entire languages was, in the words of Cummins, a "demonstrably false [claim that] has attracted an undue amount of attention" (p. 162). In fact, acoustic analyses (to be discussed momentarily) have failed to consistently and accurately label languages as being either wholly stress or syllable timed. Factors such as syllable type and duration of interstress intervals can influence rhythm within a given language (Bolinger, 1965; Roach, 1982).

Nevertheless, the perception of different rhythm categories persists. Thus, a modified view proposes that languages are aligned along a rhythm continuum from stress- to syllable timed (for detailed discussion on this topic, see Grabe & Low, 2002; Lehiste, 1977; Ramus, Nespor, & Mehler, 1999). Rather than explaining language rhythm based upon isochronicity, a phonological approach to language rhythm can be used (Ramus et al., 1999). In this approach, significant factors that underlie perceived distinctions in rhythm include the degree of vowel reduction in unstressed syllables (Dasher & Bolinger, 1982; Roach, 1982) and the variety of syllable structures available (Dauer, 1983). Vowel reduction in English and German, for example, is more common than in French and Spanish. And English contains more permissible syllable structures than does Spanish. However, prosodic factors also influence the perception of rhythm (Prieto, Vanrell, Astruc, Payne, & Post, 2012): The amount of syllabic stress placed on the first stressed syllables of a phrase (Beckman & Edwards, 1994) and on phrase-final syllables (Keating, Cho, Fougeron, & Hus, 2003) may influence perception of rhythm.

Temporal Measurements of Rhythm

Temporal (time-based) measures have been developed to explore speech rhythm (Dauer, 1983, 1987; Ramus et al., 1999; Roach, 1982). These measures are based upon segmentation of the speech signal into vocalic and consonantal (intervocalic) intervals. Vocalic intervals consist of vowels, as well as liquids and glides that do not have clear change in formant structure when examined spectrographically. Consonantal or intervocalic intervals consist of consonants, liquids, and glides that are clearly identifiable from vowels by change in formant structure, and segments in which vowel reduction in unstressed syllables leads to lack of clearly identifiable formant structure.

For this introductory discussion, a brief overview of the measures is provided, rather than the details of the formulas. Common measures used to analyze rhythm include %V, which captures the proportion of the total utterance that comprises vocalic intervals (Ramus et al., 1999). That is, what percentage of time is spent articulating vowels (compared to vowels + consonants)? Overall interval variability within a phrase is measured by the standard deviation of the vocalic and consonantal interval durations (ΔV and ΔC, respectively; Ramus et al., 1999). That is, measure each vocalic or consonantal interval and then determine the degree to which the intervals vary in duration. A language such as English, for example, which has variable duration of vowels (tense, lax, reduced) would be expected to demonstrate greater ΔV than Spanish, which has mainly tense vowels with little vowel reduction. Another measure, the pairwise variability index (PVI; Low, Grabe, & Nolan, 2000), compares the durations of sequential pairs of vocalic or consonantal intervals (PVI-V and PVI-C, respectively).

Dellwo and Wagner (2003) noted that both ΔV and ΔC are inversely correlated with rate of speech. Low (1998) observed a similar relationship with PVI. The rate-normalized counterparts of ∆V and ∆C are VarcoV (Ferragne & Pellegrino, 2004; White & Mattys, 2007) and VarcoC (Dellwo, 2006), respectively. Grabe and Low (2002) normalized the PVI measure for vocalic intervals (nPVI-V). However, the raw measure for consonantal segments is used (rPVI-C; Grabe & Low, 2002; Low et al., 2000) to preserve its sensitivity to phonotactic differences among languages (for example, the composition and frequency of clusters). When comparing different languages, the use of the rate-normalized metrics VarcoV, Varco C, and nPVI-V is particularly important, because speech rate varies across speakers within the same and different languages (Dellwo, Schmid, Leemann, Kolly, & Müller, 2012; Loukina, Kochanski, Rosner, & Keane, 2011; Yoon, 2010).

9.5 In Summary of Prosody

In concluding this discussion of prosody, we can emphasize the following. First, the acoustic and physiologic components of speech prosody are closely intertwined with the cognitive-linguistic components. Rules of conversational exchange are clearly achieved, in part, by the acoustic features of an utterance. Juncture, preboundary lengthening, and f_o often work in unison to signal meaning (Gussenhoven & Rietveld, 1992). This lack of independent function makes the study of prosody quite challenging. In summary, the intrinsic differences, such as inherent pitch of a vowel or comparative duration of two phonemes, and the allophonic variants of individual phonemes in themselves do not provide contrastive meaning. They are, however, critical perceptual cues used by the listener.

We can now expand upon the definition of prosody offered at the beginning of the chapter to provide more detail. Prosody is the systematic organization of various linguistic units into an utterance during the process of speech production. Its realization involves both segmental and suprasegmental features of speech, and serves to convey not only linguistic information, but also

paralinguistic and non-linguistic information. In this definition, we may consider the linguistic information to be represented by a set of discrete symbols and rules for their combination. The para- and nonlinguistic information, in contrast, is not inferable from the written counterpart but is deliberately added by the speaker to modify or supplement the linguistic information. It is important to emphasize that the dichotomy between segmental and suprasegmental features is somewhat artificial. Prosodic features such as intensity, duration, and juncture are achieved at the level of the phoneme. Although it is often necessary to segment various aspects of speech production and perception for clarity in teaching as well as research, one hopes it has become obvious to the reader that communication is a heavily interactive process among all variables.

Study Questions

9. Can you define and explain the differences between segmental and prosodic (suprasegmental) levels of speech production?

10. Define speech rhythm.

11. What is the isochrony-based typology of language rhythm? How has the theory been adapted currently?

12. What phonological features of language contribute to the perception of rhythmic differences among languages?

13. Can you provide a more complete description of prosody (compared to your response to Study Question 1) now that you have completed the chapter?

14. Why is it not entirely accurate to identify segmental and prosodic features as distinct aspects of speech?

References

Abercrombie, D. (1967). *Elements of General Phonetics.* Chicago, IL: Aldine.

Atkinson, J. E. (1978). Correlation analysis of the physiologic features controlling fundamental voice frequency. *Journal of the Acoustical Society of America, 63,* 211–222.

Beckman, M., & Edwards, J. (1994). Articulatory evidence for differentiating stress categories. In P. Keating (Ed.), *Papers in laboratory phonology III* (pp. 7–33). Cambridge, UK: Cambridge University Press.

Behrman, A. (2014). Segmental and prosodic approaches to accent management. *American Journal of Speech-Language Pathology, 23,* 546–561.

Bolinger, D. (1965). *Pitch accent and sentence rhythm, forms of English: Accent, morpheme, order.* Cambridge, MA: Harvard University Press.

Celce-Murcia, M., Brinton, D., & Goodwin, J. (1996). *Teaching pronunciation.* Cambridge, UK: Cambridge University Press.

Chun, D. (1988). The neglected role of intonation in communicative competence and proficiency. *Modern Language Journal, 72,* 295–303.

Cohen, A., & 't Hart, J. (1967). The anatomy of intonation. *Lingua, 19,* 177–192.

Collier, R. (1975). Physiological correlates of intonation patterns. *Journal of the Acoustical Society of America, 58,* 249–255.

Crary, M. A., & Tallman, V. L. (1993). Production of linguistic prosody by normal and speech-disordered children. *Journal of Communication Disorders, 26,* 245–262.

Crystal, D. (1979). Prosodic development. In P. Fletcher & M. Garman, (Eds.), *Language acquisition* (pp. 33–48). Cambridge, UK: Cambridge University Press.

Cummins, F. (2015). Rhythm and speech. In M. A. Redford (Ed.), *The handbook of speech production* (pp. 158–177). New York, NY: John Wiley.

Cutler, A., & Butterfield, S. (1990). Durational cues to word boundaries in clear speech. *Speech Communication, 9,* 485–495.

Cutler, A., Dahan, D., & van Donselaar, W. (1997). Prosody in the comprehension of spoken language: A literature review. *Language and Speech, 40,* 141–201.

Dasher, R., & Bolinger, D. (1982). On pre-accentual lengthening. *Journal of the International Phonetic Association 12,* 58–71.

Dauer, R. M. (1983). Stress-timing and syllable-timing reanalyzed. *Journal of Phonetics, 11,* 51–62.

Davis, B. L., MacNeilage, P. F., Matyear, C. L., & Powell, J. K. (2000). Prosodic correlates of stress in babbling: An acoustic study. *Child Development 71,* 1258–1270.

de Jong, K. J. (1997). Labiovelar compensation in back vowels. *Journal of the Acoustical Society of America, 101,* 2221–2233.

Dellwo, V. (2006). Rhythm and speech rate: A variation coefficient for delta C. In P. Karnowski & I. Szigeti (Eds.), *Language and language processing: Proceedings of the 38th Linguistic Colloquium, Piliscsaba 2003* (pp. 231–241). Frankfurt, Germany: Peter Lang.

Dellwo, V., Schmid, S., Leemann, A., Kolly, M. J., & Müller, M. (2012). Speaker identification based on speech rhythm: The case of bilinguals. In *Perspectives on Rhythm and Timing (PoRT)*, Glasgow, Scotland. Retrieved from http://www.isca-speech.org/archive

Dellwo, V., & Wagner, P. (2003). Relations between language rhythm and speech rate. In *Proceedings of the 15th international congress of phonetics sciences* (pp. 471–474). Barcelona, Spain.

Erickson, D. (2002). Articulation of extreme formant patterns for emphasized vowels. *Phonetica, 59,* 134–149.

Fitch, T., & Giedd, J. (1999). Morphology and development of the human vocal tract: A study using magnetic resonance imaging. *Journal of the Acoustical Society of America, 106,* 1511–1522.

Ferragne, E., & Pellegrino, F. (2004). A comparative account of the suprasegmental and rhythmic features of British English dialects. In *Proceedings of 'Modelisations pour l'Identification des Langues.* Paris, France.

Fletcher, J. (2010). The prosody of speech: Timing and rhythm. In W. J. Hardcastle, J. Laver, & F. E. Gibbon (Eds.), *The handbook of phonetic sciences* (2nd ed., pp. 521–602). West Sussex, UK: Blackwell.

Gelfer, C. E., Harris, K. S., Collier, R., & Baer, T. (1983). Is declination actively controlled? In I. Titze & R. Scherer (Eds.), *Vocal fold physiology: Biomechanics, acoustic, and phonatory control* (pp. 113–126). Denver, CO: Denver Center for the Performing Arts.

Gibbon, F. E. (2004). Abnormal patterns of tongue-palate contact in the speech of individuals with cleft palate. *Clinical Linguistics and Phonetics, 18,* 285–311.

Grabe, E., & Low, E. L. (2002). Durational variability in speech and the rhythm class hypothesis. In N.

Warner & C. Gussenhoven (Eds.), *Papers in laboratory phonology 7* (pp. 515–546). Berlin, Germany: Mouton de Gruyter.

Grosz, B., & Sidner, C. (1986). Attention, intentions, and the structure of discourse. *Computational Linguistics, 12,* 175–204.

Gussenhoven, C., & Rietveld, A. C. M. (1992). Intonation contours, prosodic structure and pre-boundary lengthening. *Journal of Phonetics, 20,* 283–303.

Harris, K. (1978). Vowel duration change and its underlying physiological mechanisms. *Language and Speech, 21,* 354–361.

Hauser, M. D., & Fowler, C. A. (1992). Fundamental frequency declination is not unique to human speech: Evidence from nonhuman primates. *Journal of the Acoustical Society of America, 91,* 363–369.

Honda K., & Fujimura, O. (1991). Intrinsic vowel F0 and phrase-final F0 lowering: Phonological vs. biological explanations. In J. Gauffin & B. Hammarberg (Eds.), *Phonatory mechanisms: Physiology, acoustics, and assessment* (pp. 57–64). San Diego, CA: Singular.

Howell, P. (1993). Cue trading in the production and perception of vowel stress. *Journal of the Acoustical Society of America, 94,* 2063–2073.

Joeks, J. C. J., Redeker, G., & Hendriks, P. (2009). Fill the gap! Combining pragmatic and prosodic information to make gapping easy. *Journal of Psycholinguistic Research, 38,* 221–235.

Keating, P., Cho, T., Fougeron, C., & Hsu, C. (2003). Domain-initial articulatory strengthening in four languages. *Papers in Laboratory Phonology, 6,* 143–161.

Klatt, D. H. (1976). Linguistic uses of segmental duration in English: Acoustic and perceptual evidence. *Journal of the Acoustical Society of America, 59,* 1208–1221.

Kochanski, G., Grabe, E., Coleman, J., & Rosner, B. (2005). Loudness predicts prominence: Fundamental frequency lends little. *Journal of the Acoustical Society of America, 118,* 1038–1054.

Kohler, K. J. (2009). Rhythm in speech and language: A new research paradigm. *Phonetica, 66,* 29-45.

Krakow, R. A., Bell-Berti, F., & Wang, Q. E. (1995). Supralaryngeal declination: Evidence from the velum. In F. Bell-Bertie & L. J. Raphael (Eds.), *Producing speech: Contemporary issues* (pp. 333–353). New York, NY: American Institute of Physics.

Lehiste, I. (1977). Isochrony revisited. *Journal of Phonetics, 5,* 253–263.

Lehiste, I. (1996). Suprasegmental features of speech. In. J. Lass (Ed.), *Principles of experimental phonetics* (pp. 226–244). St. Louis, MO: Mosby.

Lehiste, I., & Peterson, G. E. (1961). Some basic considerations in the analysis of intonation. *Journal of the Acoustical Society of America, 33,* 419–425.

Lloyd James, A. (1940). *Speech signals in telephony.* London, UK: Pitman.

Loukina, A., Kochanski, G., Rosner, B., & Keane, E. (2011). Rhythm measures and dimensions of durational variation in speech. *Journal of the Acoustical Society of America, 129,* 3258–3270.

Low, E. L. (1998). *Prosodic prominence in Singapore English* (Doctoral dissertation). University of Cambridge.

Low, E. L., Grabe, E., & Nolan, F. (2000). Quantitative characterizations of speech rhythm: "Syllable-timing" in Singapore English. *Language and Speech, 43,* 377–401.

Menyuk, P., & Bernholtz, N. (1969). Prosodic features and children's language. *Quarterly progress report of Research Laboratory of Electronics.* Cambridge, MA: MIT Press.

Miller, G., & Isard, S. (1963). Some perceptual consequence of linguistic rules. *Journal of Verbal Learning and Verbal Behavior, 2,* 217–228.

Monnot, M., Orbelo, D., Riccardo, K., Sikka, S., & Rossa E. (2003). Acoustic analyses support subjective judgments of vocal emotion. *Annals of the New York Academy of Sciences, 100,* 288–292.

Nooteboom, S. G. (1994). Limited look ahead in speech production. In F. Bell-Bertie & L. J. Raphael (Eds.), *Producing speech: Contemporary issues* (pp. 3–18). New York, NY: American Institute of Physics.

Ohala, J. J. (1978). Production of tone. In V. A. Fromkin (Ed.), *Tone: A linguistic survey.* New York, NY: Academic Press.

O'Malley, M. H., Kloker, D. R., & Dara-Abrams, B. (1973). Recovering parentheses from spoken algebraic expressions. *IEEE Transactions on Audio and Electroacoustics, AU-21,* 217–220.

Peterson, G. E., & Lehiste, I. (1960). Duration of syllable nuclei in English. *Journal of the Acoustical Society of America, 32,* 693–703.

Pierrehumbert, J. (1979). The perception of fundamental frequency declination. *Journal of the Acoustical Society of America, 66,* 363–369.

Pierrehumbert, J., & Hirschberg, J. (1990). The meaning of intonation contours in English. In P. R. Cohen, J. Morgan, & M. E. Pollack (Eds.), *Intentions in communication* (pp. 271–311). Cambridge, MA: MIT Press.

Pike, K. L. (1945.) *The intonation of American English.* Ann Arbor: University of Michigan Press.

Prieto, P., Vanrell, M. M., Astruc, L., Payne, E., & Post, B. (2012). Phonotactic and phrasal properties of speech rhythm: Evidence from Catalan, English and Spanish. *Speech Communication, 54,* 681–702.

Ramus, F., Nespor, M., & Mehler, J. (1999). Correlates of linguistic rhythm in the speech signal. *Cognition, 73,* 265–292.

Roach, P. (1982). On the distinction between "stress-timed" and "syllable-timed" languages. In D. Crystal (Ed.), *Linguistic controversies.* London, UK: Edward Arnold.

Sanderman, A., & Collier, R. (1996). Prosodic phrasing at the sentence level. In N. J. Lass (Ed.), *Principles of experimental phonetics* (pp. 321–332). St. Louis, MO: Mosby.

Scukanec, G. P., Petrosino, L. & Colcord, R. D. (1996). Age-related differences in acoustical aspects of contrastive stress in women. *Folia Phoniatrica et Logopedica, 48,* 231–239.

Sereno, J., & Jongman, A. (1995). Acoustic correlates of grammatical class. *Language and Speech, 38,* 57–76.

Smith, A. B., & Robb, M. P. (2006). The influence of utterance position on children's production of lexical stress. *Folia Phoniatrica et Logopedica, 58,* 199–206.

Titone, D. A., Koh, C. K., Kjelgaard, M. M., Bruce, S., Speer, S. R., & Wingfield, A. (2006). Age-related impairments in the revision of syntactic misanalyses: Effects of prosody. *Language and Speech, 49,* 75–99.

Turk, A., & Shattuck-Hufnagel, S. (2013). What is speech rhythm? A commentary on Arvanit and Rodriguez, Krivokapic, and Goswami and Leong. *Laboratory Phonology, 4,* 93–118.

Vatikiotis-Bateson, E., & Fowler, C. A. (1988). Kinematic analysis of articulatory declination. *Journal of the Acoustical Society of America, 84,* S128.

van Els, T., & de Bot, K. (1987). The role of intonation in foreign accent. *Modern Language Journal, 71,* 147–155.

Wennerstrom, A. (1994). Intonational meaning in English discourse: A study of nonnative speakers. *Applied Linguistics, 15,* 399–421.

Wennerstrom, A. (2011). Real pitch: The humorous effects of deaccent and L+H* pitch accent. *Pragmatics and Cognition, 19,* 310–332.

White, L., & Mattys, S. L. (2007). Calibrating rhythm: First language and second language studies. *Journal of Phonetics, 35,* 501–522.

Yoon, T. J. (2010). Capturing inter-speaker invariance using statistical measures of speech rhythm. In *Electronic proceedings of speech prosody.* Retrieved from http://www.isca-speech.org/archive

10

Theories and Models of Speech Production

Figure 10–1.

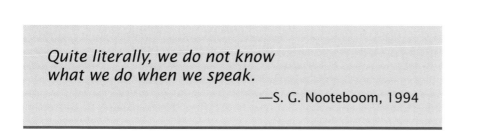

*Quite literally, we do not know
what we do when we speak.*

—S. G. Nooteboom, 1994

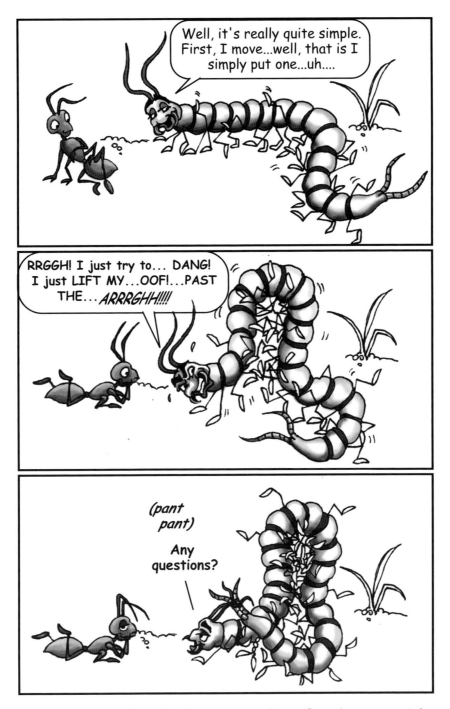

Figure 10–1. Speech production appears to be, at first glance, a straight-forward task to explain. After all, most people talk without worrying too much about the mechanics of it. But, like the centipede, we find it rather difficult to explain.

10.1 Introduction

Consider for a moment the act of reaching for a glass of water (Figure 10–2). You are motivated to reach for the glass because you are thirsty. How does your brain translate the desire for water into the motor action of reaching for the glass? How do you time the extension of your arm with the opening of your hand so that your fingers do not knock the glass over as your fingers are extended? How do you know how wide you should open your hand, so that it can encircle the glass appropriately? You don't knock into the glass and then think, "Oh, I need to open my hand wider." Do you use the visual information you obtain from your eyes to help you plan your arm and hand movements or only for correction of potential (unrealized) spatial errors of judgment? How do you judge the amount of force required to lift the glass? Likely you have had the unfortunate experience of expecting a liquid-filled container to be heavier than it actually is, and you used too much force to lift it, possibly spilling the contents in the process. What trajectory do you select to move your arm toward the glass? Most likely, you accomplish the movement in a smooth and direct fashion, but at what velocity? How do you time the deceleration of the outstretching movement so that you don't knock into the glass, but so that you don't take an overly long amount of time to reach the glass? Now repeat the gesture while looking away, as though you were reaching for the glass while focusing your attention on something else. By what motor coordinative mechanism, this time firmly planted in your memory, are you able to reach for the glass without visual feedback? Be thankful you don't need to know the answers to these questions in order to satisfy your thirst!

Figure 10–2. Many of the questions we ask about motor control of nonspeech gestures, such as arm movements, can be asked of speech motor control as well.

Each question we asked about reaching for a cup can be asked about speech production. The production of a simple utterance—for example, "Goodbye!"—is equivalent to if not more complex than the reaching activity. The utterance begins (or perhaps is preceded by) the intent to part company with a conversational partner. The contribution of the breathing subsystem must be planned. A deep breath would not be used for this utterance. In fact, we learned in Chapter 4 that initiating this short utterance with excessive lung volume would be inefficient and result in unnecessary work. The phonatory system is engaged immediately for the velar plosive /g/ that begins the utterance. This utterance is all voiced, which simplifies the contribution of the larynx to some extent, by avoiding multiple and rapid voice onsets and offsets. The resonatory/articulatory subsystem consists of multiple sequences of movements of the articulators. During the production of the initial velar, the lips round in anticipation of the vowel. To what extent is the /d/ produced? It depends upon several factors, including pragmatic features of the utterance. A more casual "g'bye" will move the initial front vowel following the voiced velar plosive to a more central quality and lip rounding will be reduced. Then, the mandible elevates to assist in the lip contact for the bilabial plosive and depresses again for the release into the final diphthong. Each phoneme requires multiple coordinated movements of all the supraglottal articulators. Each coordinated movement is controlled by multiple muscles. Each muscle contraction can result in more than one biomechanical action, depending on the level of activity of agonist and antagonist muscles and position of the other articulators.

The complex way in which we convert intention into utterance may be referred to broadly as **speech motor control**, a large and complex topic. With so many questions to ask and try to answer, it is helpful to organize our queries into categories. This organization might be nothing more than a conceptual categorization so that we might know how to think in an orderly fashion about what it is we do not know. For example, we would like to know about **spatial organization**: *where* the relevant body structures are

located in three-dimensional space at any given moment during the activity. We would like to know about **temporal organization**: *when* the separate movements occur in relation to one another. Temporal organization could include duration of events, such as the voice onset time of the bilabial plosive in *goodbye*, or the relative timing of multiple events, such as the onset of lip rounding for the /ʊ/ relative to the release of the preceding velar plosive /g/. We would like to know how the motor act is assembled and enacted. That is, what level can we identify as the basic unit targeted by the central neurologic mechanism and through what sensory modality? We also have many questions about life span. We would like to know about maturation, linguistic, cognitive, and physiologic development and growth, and its effect on motor planning and production. And we certainly would have many other questions. Our questions might best be answered through observation and experimentation. As we have learned through our review of instrumentation in Chapters 4 through 8, no single source of data can provide a complete picture of vocal tract dynamics. Therefore, our exploration of speech motor control will include numerous types of data, including acoustic, aerodynamic, visual, and kinematic information. As we progress through this chapter, it should become evident that speech production arises not only from motor control strategies at the central neurologic level but also from the physical properties of the peripheral structural anatomy—the structures of the breathing system and the vocal tract. In fact, we might hypothesize that speech motor control involves capitalizing on the biomechanical properties of the anatomy to optimize speech production within the wide array of possible speech contexts.

Traditionally, the study of speech production has addressed the subsystems in a separate and sequential order, as we have done in this text, starting with the breathing subsystem and proceeding to the phonatory, resonatory, and articulatory subsystems. Although this approach simplifies the teaching and learning of a large and complex topic, it can mislead the student into thinking that speech production is generally a sequential, linear phenomenon with independent contributions of each component to the acoustic output. Of course, we know this notion to be false and throughout the text we have hinted as much. In Chapter 4, for example, we learned that speech breathing characteristics such as the breath group are dependent upon phonatory and linguistic factors. In Chapter 5, we discussed the effects of breath pressure on frequency and intensity control. In Chapter 9, we explored the suprasegmental features of vowel and consonant production. In this chapter, we explore more fully the interactive nature of the subsystems of speech production. Just as for the glass-reaching activity, numerous theories and models have been proposed to explain the many questions and issues central to the exploration of speech motor control. We start our exploration by examining the definition of a theory and only then progress to some of the issues to be considered in a theory of speech motor control.

Study Questions

1. Broadly, what is meant by speech motor control?

2. What are some of the organizational categories of questions we might ask regarding speech motor control?

10.2 Theories and Models

A **theory** describes a phenomenon by interpreting the facts in an integrated manner. The data are explained and then the explanation can be used to predict related events. Good theories are dynamic in that new information is used to revise and update the existing theory. Theories are different from hypotheses. A **hypothesis** is a tentative theory, based on an observed phenomenon drawn from research data. Multiple hypotheses, supported by multiple research studies, coalesce to form a theory. The theory, therefore, is well substantiated, based on much research. Another way in which hypotheses are

different from theories is the relative narrowness of a hypothesis. The hypothesis is designed specifically to be a narrow statement of expectation about the behavior of a certain phenomenon so that it can be tested within a research design. A theory, however, is a set of statements that explains a relatively large phenomenon that is itself a complex relationship that guides many different events or types of behaviors. Theories are quite influential in this respect because they not only explain existing data but also help to guide the research scientist in the collection of new data and to guide the clinician in the diagnosis and treatment of speech disorders. Not only does theory inform both research and clinical practice, but clinical practice and research, in turn, also inform theory as theory grows and develops and improves through modification.

Models, on the other hand, are used as a means of simplifying complex systems or processes. Models approximate (come close to) a real-world system but include only the most essential variables of the system. In this respect, a model is a simulation, the output of which is very close to the output of the actual system. One important difference between theories and models is that, unlike theories, models are constructed to be manipulated to produce a certain output. A second important difference is that, although theories are conceptual approaches that can be supported (or refuted) by experimental data, models can take many forms. A model can be a computer simulation, a physical structure, or a theoretical construct. Models also can be based on data from animal experimentation. We noted in Chapters 4 and 5 that some of the data on breathing and phonation were derived from observation of different animals. However, animal models generally are not helpful for larger, comprehensive models of speech motor control because animals lack the capacity for human speech production.

The evolution of theories of complex processes such as speech motor control often are presented as a neat and orderly process, moving forward sequentially in time, marching ever closer to the truth. In fact, the process of developing theories and models of complex behaviors is itself a very messy business. Numerous hypotheses are proposed and tested. Discussions (often heated) ensue, either at professional scientific meetings or through letters to the editor of peer-reviewed scientific journals. Speech production is so very complex that only small parts of the entire coordinated system can be tested at any one time. And the same data set can be used to support contrary hypotheses, depending upon interpretation. Theories are put forth by one or more groups of scientists, further tested (sometimes by the same groups of scientists, sometimes by different researchers), supported, rejected, or modified, giving birth to slightly or

Occam's Razor

Pluralitas non est ponenda sine necessitate.
William of Occam

In the 14th century, William of Occam (about 1285–1349), a medieval monk of the Franciscan Order and an English philosopher, said, "Plurality should not be posited without necessity." It means, in a nutshell, that the least complex theory that can best explain an observed phenomenon, or set of phenomena, and its output shall be the best theory (Figure 10–3). Also referred to as the *principle of parsimony*, it is used generally to guide sci-entists away from creating overly complex theories. Being a monk, William advocated minimalism in all aspects of life, including leading a life of poverty. He was excommunicated by Pope John XXII, largely because William spoke out against the wealth of the papacy. Although the quotation is attributed to William, the concept was common among philosophers of the time (and has since become known as **Occam's razor**). The theory arose from weighty issues of theology that we will not address here (speech communication being a sufficiently weighty topic for this text).

Figure 10–3. Occam's razor advises us to avoid unnecessary complexity to our theories.

greatly revised or completely new theories, and the cycle continues.

Throughout this process, technologic advances influence the shaping of new theories and models. Advances in computed tomography (CT) and magnetic resonance imaging (MRI), for example, as discussed in Chapter 7, provide new insights into vocal tract configuration which, in turn, contribute to modifications of theories of vocal tract control. Certainly, increased computational power has greatly influenced the ability of all scientists to manage large amounts of data and perform complex calculations that previously would have been impractical or even impossible to accomplish. Finally, it is important for students to realize that theories, models, and the research designs used to gather supporting data are not immune to popular theoretical trends. The *zeitgeist*, or spirit of the times, represents the intellectual culture at a given moment in a given place and usually transcends a single field. For example, the focus on nonlinear dynamical systems theory, a complex and theoretical branch of mathematics, became popularized as *chaos theory* (Gleick, 1987) and spawned novel directions in speech production research (some of which are discussed further on).

Numerous theories have been developed to explain speech communication. Traditionally, these theories have been divided into those that address primarily speech production (speech motor control) and those that address primarily speech perception. We explore the theories of speech production in this chapter and those of speech perception in Chapter 11. We begin our discussion by highlighting some questions, framed as theoretical issues, that every theory must address either directly or indirectly.

Study Questions

3. What are the differences between a theory and a hypothesis?

4. What is a model and what forms can a model take?

10.3 Theoretical Issues for Consideration

Theories of speech motor control may differ substantially in fundamental ways or only finely in the small details and subtle interpretations. Some theories are mutually exclusive but most are not, and most speech scientists share more commonalities than differences in their approaches. No theory addresses every speech phenomenon to yield a comprehensive explanation of the entire system of speech motor control. The ways in which we can discuss these theories are as diverse as the theories themselves. But all theories must address some basic questions about how the vast complexity of the speech production system is controlled and adapted to meet the many demands of communication. We consider briefly some of these larger questions.

Degrees of Freedom

A fundamental issue that needs to be addressed by any theory of speech motor control is the way in which the multiple *potential* degrees of freedom of the vocal tract are constrained to a lesser number of *effective* degrees of freedom. Recall from Chapter 7 that we first defined degrees of freedom as the possible ways in which the tongue muscles can move. We can examine degrees of freedom in the larger context of speech motor control. Each of the many muscles involved in producing an utterance must be coordinated with some other muscle or muscles relative to speed, range of motion, direction of movement, force of movement, and duration of movement. We know that production of a syllable or even a single phoneme requires activation of more than one muscle. And we know from discussion of motor equivalence in earlier chapters that a single articulatory gesture can sometimes be achieved with different patterns of muscle activation. Generally, the degrees of freedom of an articulator are fewer than the number of muscles used to move the articulator, because not every muscle can achieve a unique movement of an articulator (Laboissière, Ostry, & Feldman, 1996; Stone, 1991; Wilhelm-Tricarico, 1996). We could say, then, that each potential movement of each muscle represents a degree of freedom. And we could describe an *articulatory space* by the coordinates that correspond to the effective degrees of freedom of an articulator, the ways in which the articulator can move (Mermelstein, 1973; Rubin, Baer, & Mermelstein, 1981). How, then, do we control these many degrees of freedom to produce an organized set of gestures that yield a coherent utterance?

The reduction and organization of degrees of freedom of the speech production system are addressed by many different but highly interrelated approaches. Theories may focus on target output of the system as a means of control. A different approach, based on dynamic systems theory, posits that muscles are combined into functional groupings that work in coordination. Alternatively, theories may focus on control achieved by a hierarchical organization in which higher levels of control by the cerebral cortex govern lower neurologic levels, such as the brainstem, using sensory feedback and feedforward control. Some theories posit a motor program of one type or another that serves to organize the potential degrees of freedom. Each of these approaches is examined in turn.

Output Targets

One way to conceptualize speech motor control is as a targeted plan of action. That is, perhaps the central nervous system has some goal or target output for which it controls muscle activity. Some of the proposed variables which may function as the output goal and through which feedback is regulated, include articulatory gestures, acoustic targets, and aerodynamic pressures (Kent, 2000). We consider each of these briefly.

One group of theories proposes that acoustic targets and perceptual accuracy are the control variables during speech (Guenther, 1995; Guenther, Hampson, & Johnson, 1998; Houde & Jordan, 1998; Perkell et al., 1997; Perkell, Mat-thies, Svirsky, & Jordan, 1996; Savariaux, Perrier, & Orliaguet, 1995). In other words, the goal of articulator movement may be a specific acoustic event. The output, then, is the acoustic consequences of the movements of the articulators. The internal program used to move the articulators also contains information about the acoustic consequences, which is factored into the timing of the articulatory gestures. Information from auditory and somatosensory feedback is used to create and update the internal model. Some evidence to support this theory comes from the speech of individuals with hearing impairment. Limitations in auditory feedback typically result in distortions in speech production, suggesting that the acoustic signal is of primary importance in targeting articulator movement. The concept of motor equivalence also is used to support this theory. That is, the gestures used to produce a sound, the acoustic event, may vary, depending upon coarticulatory, suprasegmental, and speaker variability. That variability is not disruptive if the output target—the acoustic signal—remains mostly preserved.

Another possible output target is the articulatory gesture, the movement of the articulators themselves (Lindblom, Lubker, & Gay, 1979; MacNeilage, 1970; Saltzman & Munhall, 1989). Within this model, the speaker has a sequence of targets that correspond to specific sounds, so that speech production is organized by control signals that guide articulator movement and associated vocal tract configuration. The speaker has an internal cognitive map composed of spatial targets of the vocal tract that guides the articulators in achieving the gestures. The cognitive map therefore equates an auditory goal with one or more vocal tract gestures. The cognitive map contains flexibility in that articulator gestures may originate from any starting point. This approach has been used to develop artificial speech, demonstrating that a set of preprogrammed gestures can have sufficient flexibility to meet conversational demands. However, a disadvantage is that a very large number of gestures would have to be stored in the brain and readily accessed.

A third potential output target might be stable aerodynamic variables (Warren, 1986; Warren, Dalston, & Dalston, 1990; Warren, Dalston, Morr, Hairfeld, & Smith, 1989), with resistance to the airflow a key factor in muscular control. In other words, to what extent does the speech production system seek to maintain a stable (or target) air pressure? We learned in Chapter 4 that mechanoreceptors are located throughout the vocal tract and that breathing is regulated, in part, by sensory feedback from pressure receptors. Therefore, it is reasonable to ask whether pressure regulation contributes to speech motor control. It has long been hypothesized that sensory information from pressure receptors is used in the production of high-pressure consonants (those that require increased intraoral pressure, as we discussed in Chapter 8) (Prosek & House, 1975). Data from typical subjects and those with velopharyngeal incompetence support the hypothesis that the speech production system seeks to maintain stable air pressure and resistance in production of high-pressure consonants. Moon and colleagues (Moon & Folkins, 1991; Moon, Folkins, Smith, & Luschei, 1993) examined data from individuals with cleft palate. Their theories focused on regulation of air pressure as an inherent physiologic property of the respiratory system. The authors hypothesized that both perceptual accuracy and aerodynamic stability are important regulators of speech motor control.

In contrast, Huber, Stathopolous, and Sussman (2004), in assessment of healthy subjects, hypothesized that the goal of the aerodynamic adaptation was maintenance of the correct acoustic-perceptual target, not the air pressure and vocal tract resistance targets in themselves. The mechanisms of regulation of intraoral air pressure for consonant production in speakers who do not have intact vocal tract structures provide insight into the possible mechanisms of speech motor control in speakers with intact vocal tract structures. Individuals with velopharyngeal incompetence (VPI) are unable to close the velopharyngeal port completely during speech, due to neurologic deficits, cleft palate, or other anatomic anomalies. Speakers with VPI

therefore have impaired ability to regulate intraoral pressure during high-pressure consonants such as plosives and fricatives. Glottal stops and pharyngeal fricatives are sometimes used as an alternative, to compensate for the lack of intraoral pressure. Warren (1986) hypothesized that these consonant replacements increase airway resistance and minimize the pressure loss. Alternatively, a *nasal grimace* (constriction of the nasal passages) can supply increased resistance to the airflow, particularly when the cross-sectional area of the velopharyngeal gap exceeds the cross-sectional area of the nasal passages (Warren, 1986). Moon et al. (1993) noted that the inherent physiologic characteristics of the respiratory system, coupled to the vocal tract, make it likely that both passive elastic recoil and active muscle contraction forces are used to maintain the target pressure. Finnegan and Hoffman (2000) hypothesized that these passive aeromechanical forces may be sufficient to maintain target consonant pressures. Warren (1986) also noted that sensory feedback may contribute to maintenance of a stable pressure. Kim, Zajac, Warren, Mayo, and Esseck (1997) hypothesized that active muscle control may be obtained from expiratory muscle activity to increase lung pressure or inhibition of postinspiratory muscle activity to increase elastic recoil. In other words, both volitional, passive aeromechanical factors and reflexive control may contribute to aerodynamic stability in the vocal tract.

Study Questions

5. Explain the difference between potential and actual degrees of freedom of the vocal tract.

6. What is an output target, relative to theories of speech production? Can you name three possible output targets? What evidence has been cited to support the theories for each of these three output targets?

Motor Programs

A **motor program** is a prestructured set of central commands capable of carrying out a movement (Sternberg, Knoll, Monsell, & Wright, 1988). Sensory feedback is used prior to the movement for initial position and tuning, during the movement for monitoring and adjustments, and following the movement for assessment. However, the many stages of central processing are too slow for online control of rapid movements and for moment-to-moment movement modifications. Therefore, two levels of the motor system are proposed. At the executive level, the information-processing stage, complex movements are selected, organized, and initiated. At the effector level, the motor programs are enacted through the neuromuscular system for controlling and executing movements as they unfold. Motor program errors can occur at the executive level. Errors of program selection can include the wrong action, or inaction, for a given environment or the wrong spatiotemporal action pattern, such as where and when to act. Errors in program execution can occur at the effector level also. The intended action or movement pattern may be correct, but an unexpected change in the environment during execution may occur, for which compensation must then be made.

Some problems with motor program theory exist. One is the storage problem. Tens of thousands of motor control programs would be necessary for achieving speech motor control of sounds within all the different environments. Second, the motor program theory does not account very well for novel gestures. However, an argument in support of the theory of motor programs is that, for rapid movements, feedback processing may be too slow. A "preprogrammed" (or "hard-wired") set of instructions would explain the ability to circumvent sensory feedback. It would also explain the preservation of stable and accurate articulatory gestures within variable contexts. Furthermore, reaction time often increases with movement complexity, implying that a larger or more complex motor program must be accessed, which inherently takes more time than a simpler program (Kent, Adams, & Turner, 1996).

Dynamic Systems

Nonlinear dynamics is a theoretical approach that has strongly influenced theories and models of speech production over the past few decades. In the models based on dynamic systems, the primary objective is to explain a mechanism that would reduce or constrain the potentially infinite number of degrees of freedom of the speech production system to a few effective, or useful, degrees of freedom. In this approach, groups of muscles work together synergistically to achieve a target gesture (Kelso, Saltzman, & Tuller, 1986). The timing of the movements is not an absolute or inherent property of an articulator but rather an intrinsic characteristic of the relationship among the different muscles for a given movement. For example, a group of lingual and mandibular muscles may work together to achieve lingual-alveolar contact for a target consonant. The set of muscles engaged is called a coordinative structure. The coordinative structure is fluid, however, in that the muscles that comprise the set will change depending on the target. In other words, a muscle can belong to more than one structure and work synergistically with different groups of other muscles. This fluidity enables the speech production system to adapt to different suprasegmental and coarticulatory conditions. The strength of modeling synergistic movements of the articulators within a framework based on dynamic systems is that it accounts for both the biomechanical properties of the different articulators and the different possible combinations of muscle activation patterns. At the same time, however, it constrains the degrees of freedom for any given articulatory gesture.

Serial Ordering and Sensory Feedback

Sensory feedback is a transfer of a portion of the system's output back to the input for regulation and error correction. Sensory information is essential to all aspects of human activity, no less so in regard to speech production. Different types of sensory modalities may contribute to speech motor control. Most likely, the visual modality has a lesser role, given that we do not watch ourselves speak, whereas the auditory and somatosensory modalities play more featured roles. Does speech motor control reflect a predominantly motor organization or does somatic sensory information modulate or gate motor movement sufficiently that motor planning reflects a predominant sensorimotor control system? Information about muscle length and velocity of muscle fiber shortening is provided by muscle spindles throughout the vocal tract. Tactile feedback is gained from mechanoreceptors that provide information about contact between articulator surfaces. Pressure receptors, located throughout the vocal tract, provide information about pressures within the oral and pharyngeal cavities. Our auditory perception of the acoustic output provides the feedback that informs the speaker regarding accuracy of the gestural targets. Certainly, no one would deny the overall importance of sensory feedback in motor speech control. But the specific role it plays is complex and much remains uncertain.

The concept of a feedback loop is a central theme of sensorimotor control theory. Two kinds of feedback loops need to be considered, open and closed. Gracco (1995) provides a delightful example of an open feedback loop—the toaster. The duration of activity (the toasting) is controlled by a timer, which is set externally by the person hungry for toast. Once the timer is set, the toasting is independent of the person who set the timer. Stated more generally, in an **open feedback loop**, the mechanism that controls the action is not a central part of the activity itself but rather an outside agent (Figure 10–4). The control is independent of the action. And this outside agent can only control the activity in the future, not at the present time while the activity is occurring. In effect, no direct feedback is available during the target activity. In a **closed feedback loop**, the controlling action is dependent upon the output. The feedback is a portion of the output, which is returned to the system and becomes part of the input. The output of the system, therefore, is modulated by the system's response to what it produces.

The degree to which sensory feedback contributes to speech motor control is unclear, and its contribution may not be the same throughout the life span. That is, sensory feedback may contribute substantially to the formation of gestures and motor programs, but once acquired, its contribution may be less significant (Borden, 1979; Lane & Tranel, 1971). Some support for that

Figure 10–4. In an open feedback loop, the mechanism that controls the action is an outside agent and not part of the mechanism itself. We may set the timer on the toaster, but once set, the toasting proceeds without our intervention.

theory is found in the experiments of altered feedback, including oral anesthesia (Gammon, Smith, Daniloff, & Kim, 1971) and reduced auditory feedback (Kelso & Tuller, 1983), in which only a limited negative effect on speech has been obtained. However, another group of data suggests that altered sensory input results in mechanical compensation to motor output (Putnam & Ringel, 1972; Scott & Ringel, 1971). Those data are from **perturbation studies**, a study design that we will examine shortly. In contrast, a phenomenon that weakens the potential role of sensory feedback in speech motor control is the mismatch in speed between neural signals and some speech movements. The sensorimotor feedback loops are often slower than the ballistic (rapid burst or explosive) movements that comprise speech (Kent & Moll, 1975). Gracco (1995), however, notes that, given the density of sensory receptors in the vocal tract in general and the lips and tongue in particular, it is difficult to imagine that sensory information is not a critical part of speech motor control.

In contrast to the feedback models, the **feedforward models** propose that adjustments in speech production are made at the periphery of the system, that is, to the actual articulatory gestures. In this way, the voice production system is said to be primed to move in a coordinated and efficient manner. A feed-forward system would,

in theory, respond more quickly to errors than a feedback system because the speaker would not have to wait until a gesture was completed to receive information about its accuracy (Lane et al., 2005). The feed-forward model would also account for the lack of significant error in speech production when the feedback channels are disrupted, such as cited above. Perhaps a combination of both feed-forward and feedback information is used to minimize errors and allow for rapid corrections.

Spatiotemporal Organization

Another issue to be considered by theories of speech motor control is an explanation of how the articulators move in space and time. The movement of the articulators relative to some *frame of reference* often is referred to as the spatiotemporal dynamics of articulator movement. Spatiotemporal dynamics references the spatial dimension, or the path of an articulator, and the temporal (time) dimension. The path is the sequence of positions in space occupied by an object or articulator (Munhall & Jones, 1995, p. 522). The temporal component of the movement is included in the trajectory. The trajectory references the timing of the sequence of positions. The following example will help to clarify the distinction. Draw an imaginary circle on this page with your fingertip and repeat the motion several times. The path followed by your fingertip is described as a circle. Your finger can follow that path at different velocities, slowly or quickly, accelerating and decelerating as you chose. The trajectories are different, but in theory, the path remains the same. However, observe what happens as you accelerate the movement of your finger. Does the path remain the same? Most likely, the circle changes shape a bit. The path does not remain constant as the trajectory is altered. In theory, the path and the trajectory are independent. In fact, however, they are not independent of each other.

Although articulator movement occurs in a three-dimensional space, much of the research in motor speech control has explored trajecto-

---

Study Questions

7. What are motor programs? What are the two proposed levels of motor programs? Discuss two weaknesses of motor program theory and a theoretical response to those weaknesses.

8. What are dynamic systems? What are the advantages of a theory based on nonlinear dynamic systems?

9. Explain serial ordering and sensory feedback. What are open and closed feedback loops?

ries of a single articulator in one or two dimensions (Figure 10–5). That is, the amplitude of movement of the lower lip or jaw, for example, is plotted as a function of time. One of the reasons for this simplification is limitations of the instrumentation used to measure articulatory movement. As reviewed in Chapters 7 and 8, most instrumentation provides information about the evolution, or change over time, in a single dimension. A second reason is the difficulty in conceptualization of the evolution of more than one or two spatial dimension simultaneously. Munhall and Jones (1995) examine some of the specific problems one encounters in such an attempt. We can summarize the problem, however, by noting that the complexity of movement grows exponentially (nonlinearly) as the dimensions increase.

Finally, a third difficulty in describing the spatiotemporal characteristics of movements of the vocal tract is that articulators move in different ways. The tongue and mandible, for example, as we have discussed previously, have different mechanical restrictions, and so their movements are dissimilar (see Understanding Tongue Movements [Chapter 7] and Movements of the Mandible [later in this chapter]). Let us assume for the moment that the brain directs articulator movement through a set of directions that we will call a motor program. (Whether we conceive this program as neurally "hard-wired" or as an abstract conceptual organization of synergistic oscillators is irrelevant for purposes of this discussion.) The motor program might encompass directions to move the tongue tip upward, for example. Up and down and right

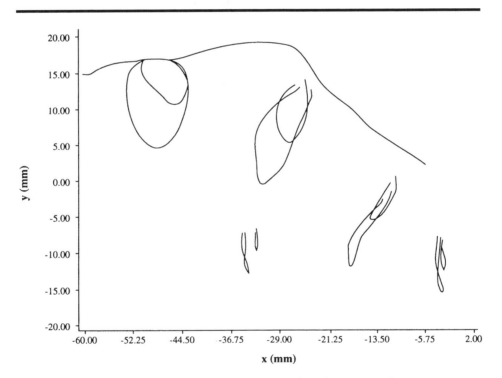

Figure 10–5. X-ray microbeam data show the paths of tongue and jaw movements in the production of a nonsense utterance /kcek/ in normal and loud speech. The upper trace represents the midsagittal contour of the palate. The top three pairs of paths are from the motion of the tongue tip, blade, and dorsum. The bottom two pairs of paths represent jaw movement taken from mandibular teeth. From "The Spatial Control of Speech Movements," by K. G. Munhall and J. A. Jones, in *Producing Speech: Contemporary Issues.* (p. 528) by F. Bell-Berti and L. J. Raphael, Eds., 1995, New York: American Institute of Physics. Reprinted with permission.

Spatiotemporal Index

The **spatiotemporal index (STI)** is an index of the consistency of movement across 10 repetitions of an utterance (Smith, Goffman, Zelaznik, Ying, & McGillem, 1995). Obtain the displacement of a point as a function of time. The time series is then time and amplitude normalized. Amplitude normalization is accomplished by subtracting the average value (over some preselected number of data points) and dividing by the standard deviation of every data point. The standard deviation is calculated for the displacement of 10 data points at 50 equally spaced points along the time-series record. The sum of those 50 standard deviations is the STI. Time normalization is performed by the technique of Kleinow and Smith (2000). The STI does not differentiate between temporal and spatial variability but rather gives an overall measure of the degree to which multiple repetitions of an utterance are the same or different. In this way, STI provides a quantitative measure that allows comparison across individuals and research studies. A limitation of the STI is that the measure involves linear normalization (Lucero, Munhall, Gracco, & Ramsay, 1997). Natural modifications in an utterance, including adjustment in speaking rate or clarity, may result in nonlinear changes (Cutler & Butterfield, 1991; Flege, 1988).

and left, therefore, could be considered a spatial *frame of reference*. But the motor program may use a different set of directions, or reference frames. Perhaps the program directs the tongue to elongate specific muscles in a certain trajectory, using sensory feedback from muscle spindle activity as the frame of reference. Therefore, one spatial reference frame might be muscle fiber length, whereas another might be action around a joint, such as the mandibular joints. A tactile reference frame might use the response from mechanoreceptors on the articulator's surfaces. A constriction reference frame might describe sound production using coordinates that specify the locations and degrees of constriction in the vocal tract (Browman & Goldstein, 1992; Saltzman & Munhall, 1989). An acoustic or auditory perceptual reference frame may use the spectral features of the acoustic signal (Perkell et al., 1997; Savariaux et al., 1995). It has been theorized that central neural programming uses more than one spatial frame of reference during production of an utterance (Guenther et al., 1998; MacNeilage, 1970; Munhall & Jones, 1995). A theory of speech motor control must consider carefully the frame of reference when describing articulator movement.

Unit of Analysis

Another issue that needs to be addressed by a theory of speech motor control is specification of the basic unit to be coordinated and controlled. Units may be sounds, syllables, words, or gestures, for example. How these units are coordinated and sequenced over time has been the topic of decades of research (Fowler, 1980; Kent & Minifie, 1977; MacNeilage, 1970). Analysis of the spectrograms in Chapters 7 and 8 reveals abrupt changes that demarcate transitions from one sound to the next. We know from analysis of kinematic data, however, that multiple gestures occur simultaneously, such as lip rounding and tongue advancement, to produce a given spectral result. What then do we define as the basic unit of speech for analysis of motor control? Scientists do not agree upon one single unit of measurement for speech motor control (Fowler, 1980; MacNeilage, 1970). It is generally assumed, however, that because coarticulatory effects extend across the segmental level, units greater than the phoneme must be considered, such as the phrase level (Smith, 1992) or even longer. Figure 10–6 shows the underlying kinematic activity of just a single point on

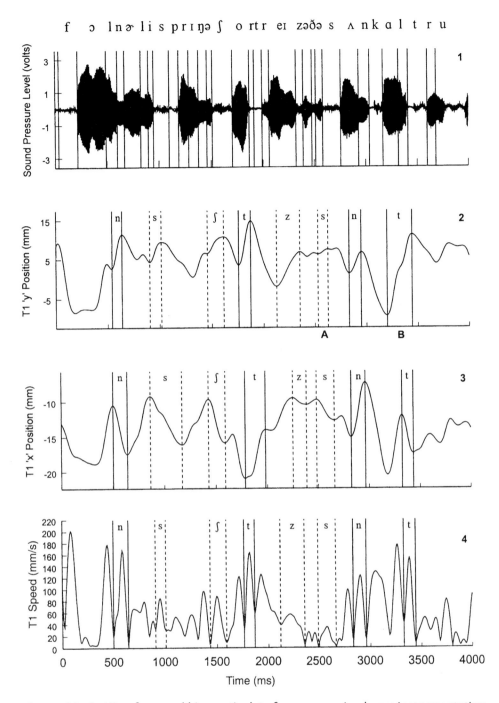

Figure 10–6. Waveform and kinematic data from x-ray microbeam instrumentation are segmented into "units," demonstrating the underlying kinematic activity of just a single point on the tongue and how the movement does not closely correspond to the segmentation of the waveform. The top panel is the sound pressure level waveform of a male speaker reading "fall and early spring, the short rays of the sun call a true." The vertical lines represent partitioning of the signal into phonetic segments. Panel 2 plots the vertical trajectory of a marker on the tongue blade (T1). Panel 3 plots the horizontal trajectory of the same marker, and the bottom panel plots the speed of the marker. Reprinted with permission from Tasko, S. M., and Westbury, J. R. (2002). Defining and Measuring Speech Movement Events. *Journal of Speech, Language, and Hearing Research, 45,* p. 129. Copyright 2002 by American Speech-Language-Hearing Association. All rights reserved.

the tongue and how the movement does not closely correspond to the segmentation of the waveform. The waveforms emphasize the continuity of movement underlying the segmentation of the acoustic signal. Kinematic data often are parsed into units by defining the articulatory movement along a single dimension. Tasko and Westbury (2002) provide a nice overview of the ways in which that dimension may be characterized. The dimension is often a specific anatomic point, such as the movements of a specific location selected on the tongue body, lip, or jaw (Löfqvist & Gracco, 1994, 1997), or a complex statistical analysis (Adams, Weismer, & Kent, 1993; Hertrich & Ackerman, 2000). Alternatively, the reference for the dimension may be the orientation of the measurement instrumentation (Kelso, Vatikiotis-Bateson, Saltzman, & Kay, 1985; Ostry & Munhall, 1985). Once the units have been selected, however, then the relevant features of those units must be identified, such as the peak velocity, amplitude, and duration and the temporal relationship among the different units. Tasko and Westbury (2002) propose that, for kinematic data, the basic unit should contain one acceleration and one deceleration, a single stroke, as it were, of the specific point or points being tracked. The authors note that this definition has the advantage of being intuitively appealing and, furthermore, it can be defined without reference to other units such as the phoneme or syllable. Additionally, their method is independent of assumptions about the temporal organization of gestural movements. A disadvantage, however, is that such a system would work only for single points of articulation. The tongue, for example, cannot be defined by a single acceleration and deceleration.

Movements of the Mandible

Movement of the mandible and its role in the regulation of speech motor control has been of recurring interest to the speech science community. This interest may be due in part to the role of the mandible as a major regulator of oral cavity opening during speech. This role may place it at great risk as a source of breakdown in speech motor control, both developmentally and in cases of mechanical or neurologic injury in adults (Dworkin, Meleca, & Stachler, 2003; Green, Moore, & Reilly, 2002).

The mandible articulates with the cranium via the bilateral temporomandibular (TM) joint (Figure 10–7). The TM joint is the only movable joint in the skull (the others being skull sutures). The TM joint is a synovial condyloid joint, which means that a meniscus (cartilaginous disk) lies within the synovial capsule between the condyle (the upper arm of the mandible) and the mandibular fossa (indentation in the cranium into which the condyle fits).

The TM joint has three ligaments (Figure 10–8): the temporomandibular, spheno-mandibular, and stylomandibular ligaments. The muscles of the mandible (Figures 10–9, 10–10, and 10–11), also referred to sometimes as the muscles of mastication, can be divided into the elevators, which act to close the mouth, and the depressors, which open the mouth. The elevators include the temporalis, the masseter, and the internal or medial pterygoid. The depressors include the external or lateral pterygoid and three suprahyoid muscles, the anterior belly of the digastric, the mylohyoid, and the geniohyoid muscles. During soft to moderate-intensity routine-type conversation, however, only the lateral and the medial pterygoid muscles and the anterior belly of the digastric muscles are active (Tuller, Harris, & Gross, 1979). The muscles that elevate (close) the jaw are stronger than those that open the jaw, enabling the jaw to close with tremendous force, a requirement for chewing more so than for speech. Although only certain muscles are listed here as being responsible for jaw elevation and depres-

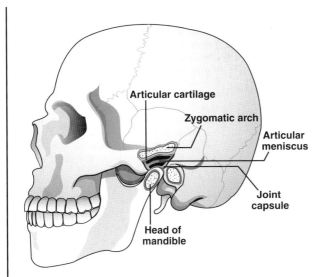

Figure 10–7. The temporomandibular joint.

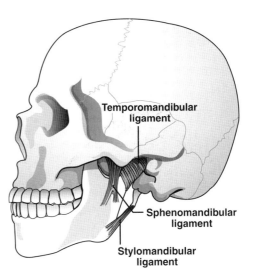

Figure 10–8. Ligaments of the temporomandibular joint.

Figure 10–9. Muscles that depress the mandible.

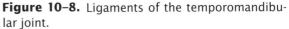
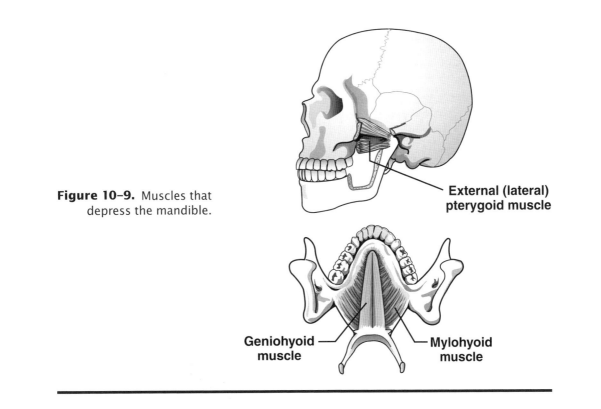

sion, these muscles do not work in isolation. Muscles of the tongue as well as many of the supra- and infrahyoid muscles become active to some degree during mandible movement.

During mouth opening (Figure 10–12), the jaw rotates downward and translates both downward and forward. Translation is a linear movement forward (for opening) or backward

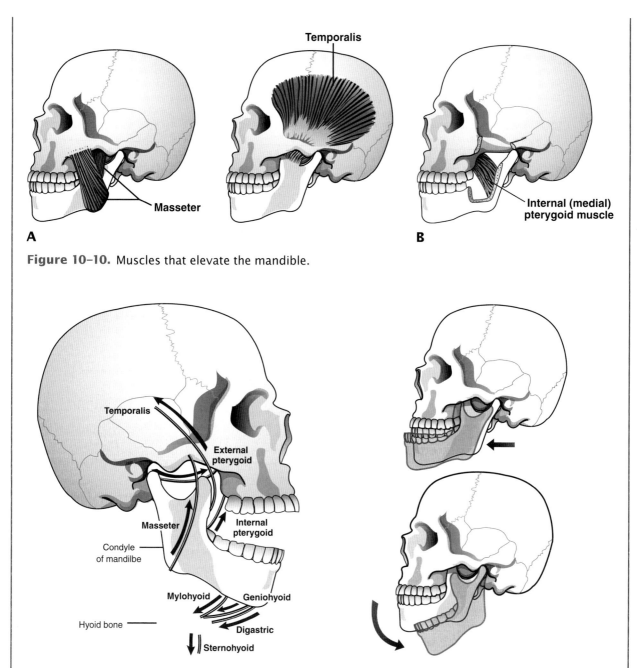

Figure 10–10. Muscles that elevate the mandible.

Figure 10–11. Schematic of muscle activity of the mandible.

Figure 10–12. Movements of the mandible.

(for closing) in the horizontal plane and downward (for opening) or upward (for closing) in the vertical plane. Rotation represents an angular movement upon opening and closing. Only approximately half of the opening of the mouth is achieved by depression (downward rotation) of the mandible. The remainder of the opening is achieved by forward translation of the mandible in the TM joint. The reverse occurs during closure of the mouth, with rearward and upward translation and upward rotation. Although the layperson might think of

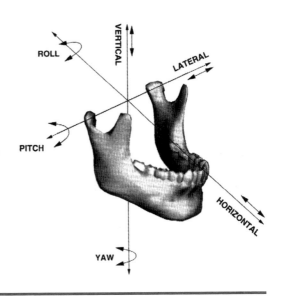

Figure 10–13. Mandibular movements. Reprinted by permission from "An Examination of the Degrees of Freedom of Human Jaw Motion in Speech and Mastication," by D. J. Ostry, E. Vatikiotis-Bateson, and P. L. Gribble, 1997, *Journal of Speech, Language, and Hearing Research*, 40, p. 1342. Copyright 1997 by American Speech-Language-Hearing Association. All rights reserved.

jaw motion as a simple up and down motion, its kinematics during speech are quite complex. Chewing tends to require relatively slow movements in which the mandibular depressors are active only during mouth opening and the jaw elevators are active only during mouth closing. In contrast, during speech, coactivation of both sets of muscles occurs and jaw movement is much faster (Luschei & Goldberg, 1981; Ostry & Munhall, 1994). Jaw kinematics have been analyzed using x-ray microbeam (Ostry & Munhall, 1994) and the optoelectronic position-measuring system (Optotrak) (Ostry, Vatikiotis-Bateson, & Gribble, 1997; Vatikiotis-Bateson & Ostry, 1995). The following discussion is based on their work.

Jaw movement can be analyzed as six degrees of freedom, represented by six dimensions, three rotational and three translational, which provide a complete description of the mechanics of jaw motion (see Figure 10–13). All the jaw muscles contribute to both rotation and translation (Laboissière et al., 1996), and therefore "the mapping between the jaw muscle actions and the mechanical degrees of freedom of jaw motion is complex" (Ostry et al., 1997, p. 1342). The sagittal plane (pitch), vertical and horizontal jaw positions, and coronal plane (yaw) may be independently controlled

during speech. (Think of "pitching" forward and "rolling" to the side. Yaw would be equivalent to spinning around.) In other words, the six potential degrees of freedom of the mandible are constrained to four actual, or effective, degrees of freedom during speech, with the first three dimensions explaining most of the movements.

Green, Moore, and Reilly (2002) note that both Mysak (1968) and Dworkin (1978) addressed the stabilization of the mandible as a clinical approach to improving articulation in children with abnormal or excessive mandibular movements during speech. As discussed later in this chapter, a common strategy in speech research has been the use of a bite-block for either stabilizing or disrupting jaw movements, depending on the research focus (Dworkin, 1996; Netsell, 1985). Shiller, Laboissière, and Ostry (2002) explored mandible stiffness and its relationship to kinematics. They found that automatic stiffness adjustments in response to a jaw perturbation contributed to kinematic control. In a later study (Shiller, Guillaume, & Ostry, 2005), the authors found that speakers voluntarily can control mandible stiffness, which the authors posited may contribute to stabilization of orofacial kinematics.

Study Questions

10. Explain frame of reference, path, and trajectory relative to spatio-temporal organization. What are three difficulties in describing spatiotemporal organization of articulatory movements?

11. Why is it challenging to determine the basic unit of analysis for speech motor control?

Coarticulation

Another basic question to be addressed by theories of speech motor control is the complex issue of coarticulation. Coarticulation, as discussed in Chapter 7, is the adjustment of articulator movements to target more than one speech sound simultaneously. Hence, it reflects the influence of contiguous speech sounds upon each other (Kent & Moll, 1972) and the temporal coordination of multiple articulators (Caruso, Abbs, & Gracco, 1988; Gracco & Abbs, 1986; Westbury, Severson, & Lindstrom, 2000). The adjacent speech sounds exert influence upon each other due to acoustic-phonetic requirements and biomechanical connections (Perkell & Matthies, 1992). As Bell-Berti, Krakow, Gelfer, and Boyce (1994, p. 78) state, coarticulation is a "blurring of the edges" of segmental articulations.

In Chapter 6, we discussed the concept of phonatory efficiency, in which the efficiency of vocal fold vibration is an interaction between the biomechanical characteristics of the vocal folds and the aerodynamic forces. The phenomenon of coarticulation also may be viewed as an interaction of efficiency. In this case, the interaction is between the biomechanical characteristics of the articulators and the acoustic output. Lindblom (1990) theorized that the speaker operates under two opposite efforts, the requirement that speech be produced clearly so that it is intelligible to the listener and the "default" level of operating at a low cost in terms of effort output. Energy may be conserved, therefore, by coarticulation in lieu of preservation of "canonical" (ideal) phonemic forms.

The biomechanical properties of the articulators also constrain movement velocities, amplitudes, and coordination of timing (Bell-Berti & Harris, 1981; Ostry, Gribble, & Gracco, 1995; Payan & Perrier, 1997; Perrier, Ostry, & Laboissière, 1996). The tongue (see Understanding Tongue Movements in Chapter 7) and mandible (see Movements of the Mandible in this chapter) are good examples of how their respective biomechanical properties define their re-spective movements. The data from several kinematic studies show that the position of an articulator during production of a given consonant is inversely related to the amplitude of the movement immediately before and after that consonant. That is, the larger the amplitude of movement of an articulator for a given phoneme, the less the amplitude of movement for the adjacent phoneme (Ostry, Gribble, & Gracco, 1995). In other words, some portion of the variability in coarticulation may be due to muscle mechanics and jaw dynamics, not necessarily to central neural control. Perkell and Matthies (1992) review three broad theories that have been put forth to explain coarticulation: the "look-ahead" model of anticipatory coarticulation (Ohman, 1967), the "frame theory" (Bell-Berti & Harris, 1982; Gelfer, Bell-Berti, & Harris, 1989), and the "hybrid model" (Bladon & Al-Barnerni, 1982; Perkell & Matthies, 1992). We review each of these models briefly.

Motor Planning: How Far Ahead?

Where does one look when driving a car? Although it depends on the road conditions and speed (sunshine or rain, busy pedestrian thoroughfare or interstate highway), in general we monitor activity a few cars ahead of our own. If we stared only at the taillights of the car right in front of us, it is more likely that unexpected events would cause us to react inefficiently or incorrectly. To a certain extent, looking ahead enables us to drive more smoothly and diminishes our errors. Does the analogy hold for speech motor control as well? One unsolved question is the extent to which we plan ahead when speaking.

In the look-ahead model of anticipatory coarticulation (Ohman, 1967), the degree and timing of coarticulation are regulated by the need to preserve accurate acoustic representation of the sounds. For example, in the word "eon," lip spreading for the /i/ is allowed to be released and mandible lowering is allowed to begin only when these movements will not distort the formant patterns of the initial vowel, which could render the vowel unintelligible. (Another commonly cited example of forward motor planning is the speech error, as discussed further on in the section Language and Speech.)

Frame Theory

The **frame theory** is based on the concept that the infant's babbling consists of a cyclic alternating opening and closing of the mouth arising from the movement of the mandible (the "frame") superimposed upon vowel and consonant production (the "content") (Davis & McNeilage, 1995; Redford, MacNeilage, & Davis, 1997; Shattuck-Hufnagel, 1979). In this theory, the opening and closing movements of the mandible are grounded in rhythmic oscillatory movement. With maturation, the cyclic opening and closing evolves into the syllable structure (the frame) and the segmental articulation of phonemes (the content). According to this theory,

therefore, the syllable is rooted in a rhythmic stress pattern, which originates in an area of the brain different from where phonemic content originates. According to Vilain, Abry, Badin, and Brosda (1999), the development of coarticulation proceeds in three stages. First, the oscillatory opening and closing of the mandible accompanied by phonation yields a "protosyllabic frame" that provides the speech rhythm. The slots or frames are the specific positions in the syllable to which the fillers or content can be placed, or to which they can be assigned. Next, as independent control of articulator movement is achieved through cognitive and physiologic maturation, segmental content (the vowels and consonants) emerges. And, finally, as maturation progresses, global control of the vocal tract allows the adult-like coarticulation patterns to emerge.

In the frame theory of anticipatory coarticulation (Bell-Berti & Harris, 1982; Gelfer et al., 1989), the timing of the onset of the cessation of lip spread and onset of mandible lowering are not the critical factors. The gestural kinematics for these sounds are relatively invariant, and, therefore, the movements are initiated in a relatively fixed moment in time. Perkell and Matthies (1992) note that the frame theory is consistent with the concept of task dynamics theory, in which the kinematic features of articulation are a direct consequence of the intrinsic features of underlying abstract gestures (Bell-Berti & Krakow, 1991; Fowler, 1980; Saltzman & Munhall, 1989).

Developmental Aspects of Speech Motor Control

Much research has been devoted to studying the maturation of speech motor control in children. Commonly, these studies compare acoustic and kinematic variables in children and adults. Children under 12 demonstrate developmental patterns approaching mature spatiotemporal patterns, but the patterns are not as stable as those of the adult (Smith & Goffman, 1998). For example, in general, one finds greater variability of lip muscle activity within and across children for both kinematic and acoustic analyses (Wohlert & Smith, 2002). Although articulator movement becomes increasingly stable with maturity, the stability may vary with age as new lexical and motor skills are learned (Green et al., 2002). Studies show that maturation of both temporal and spatial accuracy of articulatory gestures occurs well into adolescence (Eguchi & Hirsch, 1969; Goffman & Smith, 1999;

Green, Moore, Higashikawa, & Steeve, 2000; Green et al., 2002; Grigos, Saxman, & Gordon, 2005; Kent, 1976; Kent & Forner, 1980; Ohde, 1985; Sharkey & Folkins, 1985; Smith & Gartenberg, 1984; Smith & Goffman, 1998; Smith & McLean-Muse, 1986; Tingley & Allen, 1975; Walsh & Smith, 2002; Watkin & Fromm, 1984). Using the spatiotemporal index (see the Spatiotemporal Index earlier in this chapter), Maner, Smith, and Grayson (2000) found that stability of lip movement was greater in adults than in young children and that the complexity of the utterance in children was directly correlated with lip movement stability. It could be said that children retain a greater number of degrees of freedom of articulator movement than adults.

Schmidt (1975) proposed that children, as well as adults, learn novel sound production through motor programs composed of schemata, which are learned relationships between articulator movements, feedback information, and acoustic outcomes. Schemata are enhanced through repetition, particularly practice within different phonemic environments. A clinical parallel of the schemata theory is that training new speech behaviors within a therapy session is accomplished by practicing the target motor behavior within different phonemic and semantic contexts.

One interesting parameter of developmental research is the inquiry into scaling of articulator movement in children compared to such scaling in adults. That is, do children move their articulators over a relatively smaller distance for the same gesture as compared to adults, given, or course, that the size of their articulators is smaller? The relationship between movement amplitude and structural size may appear straightforward and directly linear. We can refer to this component as the biomechanical factor. However, a potentially competing factor is the maturation of the child. Handwriting, for example, is generally larger in children than in adults, despite their substantially smaller hand size (Hamstra-Ble-

tze & Blote, 1990). Data from a small sample study found a positive relationship between orofacial structure size, displacement, and velocity in adults (Kuehn & Moll, 1976). In a small study comparing children and adults, however, no relationship between structural size, amplitude of movement, and peak velocity was found (Smith & McLean-Muse, 1986). In a larger study of children and adults, however, Riely and Smith (2003) found that the amplitude of articulatory movements in 5-year-old children does not adhere to a linear size-scaling principle. That is, the children produced speech movement amplitudes equivalent to those of adults. Their peak movement velocities, however, were significantly lower. Children's movements, therefore, appeared to be of relatively larger amplitude (given the structural size of the articulators) and slower than those of adults. The authors concluded that speech motor control is more like handwriting in that case than gross motor behavior such as walking. The authors hypothesized that perhaps that strategy allowed children to have more time to plan motor sequencing and to process sensory feedback for error correction. Of note, adult women in their study had smaller articulatory structures than adult men, but their amplitude and velocity data were not different from those of adult men.

Sensory information is of critical importance in the acquisition of speech motor control, although the specifics are not completely understood. Some gross level of motor control for oral vegetative functions, such as swallowing, and for prespeech behaviors is present at birth, and increasingly fine motor control is achieved as maturation progresses. For mature speech to evolve, the child must be able to manipulate and coordinate vocal tract articulatory gestures and also be able to discriminate the acoustic characteristics of speech (Gracco, 1995). Acquisition of speech sounds then progresses generally in an orderly fashion, with more complex articulatory gestures acquired more slowly (Kent, 1992).

Hybrid Model

The **hybrid model** of anticipatory coarticulation (Bladon & Al-Barnerni, 1982; Perkell & Matthies, 1992), as its name implies, is a combination of the look-ahead and frame theories. The articulatory gesture, however, is divided into two phases: an initial low-velocity movement, followed by a second, higher velocity movement, which is the most prominent feature of the sound production.

Velar Coarticulation

In contrast to the numerous kinematic studies of the oral articulators (jaw, lips, and tongue), less data have been generated on velar movement. Studies of nasal coarticulation show that the velum is influenced by movement of the other articulators and by syllabic structure (McClean, 1973). The velum demonstrates greater displacement and movement velocity when a nasal consonant is followed by a high vowel as compared to a low vowel (Kent, Carney, & Severeid, 1974; Moll, 1962). Likely, the velum participates actively in prosodic stress (Krakow, 1993). Kollia, Gracco, and Harris (1992) found that, in general, the movement and timing characteristics of the velum were similar to those of the lips and jaw, although closing of the velum was not as strongly linked to movement of the other articulators as was the opening.

Influences of Speech Motor Control Theory on Clinical Practice

Lest you think that theories of speech motor control are of academic interest only, with no practical application to clinical situations, we raise here a controversial topic that is quite relevant to clinical practice. The issue, articulated clearly by Weismer (2006), addresses the theoretical basis for the use of nonverbal assessment of oral motor function in patients with dysarthrias (motor speech disorders). Gerratt, Till, Rosenbek, Wertz, and Boysen (1991), in a survey of speech-language pathologists affiliated with the American Veterans Administration Hospital system, found that oromotor, nonverbal evaluations were used more frequently and found to be more valuable than auditory-perceptual measures in the diagnosis of motor speech disorders. Weismer (2006) posits that this common clinical practice arises from the popular Mayo Clinic perspective of motor speech disorders (Darley, Aronson, & Brown, 1996), in which motor speech disorders are a direct manifestation of the neuropathologic signs of the underlying disease. Clinical diagnostic testing, therefore, is based heavily on perceptual and instrumental assessment of oromotor function within nonspeech contexts. Weismer (2006) points out that this approach does not appear to be grounded directly in one or more theories of motor speech control. For example, if the acoustic output (Guenther et al., 1998) or the articulatory gesture (Saltzman & Munhall, 1989) is the primary goal of the speech motor act, then nonspeech oromotor tasks would not tap into the appropriate motor control system. Weismer (2006) argues that motor control processes are task specific. In other words, articulatory movement in the absence of linguistically based utterances does not reflect motor control used in speech. This task-specificity approach is consistent with general theories of motor control of other complex systems of the human body, such as the hand (Wilson, 1998). The take-home message here is that diagnostic and therapeutic methods used by a clinician should be driven by an underlying, coherent theory of speech motor control.

Thus, in the word "eon," the second vowel has a relatively slow-velocity initial formant transition from the high front vowel, during which time the coarticulatory effect is most dominant. This movement is less prominent, acoustically, than the subsequent higher velocity formant transition that signals the more open vowel. Coarticulatory features such as lip rounding (Boyce, Krakow, Bell-Berti, & Gelfer, 1990) and nasalization (Gelfer et al., 1989) may be examples of this two-phase hybrid model.

Study Questions

12. Define coarticulation.
13. Briefly describe the three theories of coarticulation.

10.4 Investigational Considerations

Systematic gathering of copious amounts of research data is required to understand the speech production system (Fujimura, 1980). Just as we considered issues central to theories of speech motor control, we may also consider issues central to the *research*, or testing, of those theories. Briefly, we consider three issues: the nature of the utterances used to test theories within experimental designs, a type of experimentation called perturbation studies, and the search for **invariant features** of speech under conditions of altered rate.

Speaking Task

Most research in speech motor control seeks to vary one feature systematically while holding the others constant. In this way, the effect of changing a parameter can be observed more easily, without confounding effects of other changes

that might obscure the main effect. This control is achieved often by selecting a specific utterance to be spoken by all subjects multiple times. But what are the subjects asked to say? The task may be repetition of a CVC (consonant-vowel-consonant) construction, reading, or spontaneous monologue, for example. Typically, the speaking tasks are defined narrowly to specify phonetic context. That is, the utterance is constructed carefully to reveal (one hopes) the specific features of interest to the investigators. Often, the formant structure of specific vowels is investigated because, as we learned in Chapter 7, formants are specified by vocal tract posture. When movement of the lips or mandible is of interest, for example, utterances would be constructed to emphasize labial and mandible movements. Some of the many possibilities include repetitions of a target phonetic environment embedded in a "carrier phrase," such as the well-known carrier phrase of Peterson and Barney's (1952), *I see a hVd* in which the V represents different vowels tested. Other test utterances may include isolated CVC or VCV (or more complex) nonsense words, such as *sapapple* (Caruso, Abbs, & Gracco, 1988), or a short utterance, such as *Buy Bobby a poppy* (Max & Caruso, 1997).

Although short carefully constructed utterances allow for clearer interpretation of the data, how well do the kinematics that underlie these relatively simple utterances reflect the more complex articulatory gestures of discursive speech? Only a few studies have examined articulatory dynamics outside of simple stimulus material (Tasko & McClean, 2004; Tasko & Westbury, 2002). The weakness of running speech is the variability across subjects in phonemic environment. This variability introduces an unknown factor that may influence findings. Yet a strength of running speech is that certain features of equivalent motor responses and gestural invariance may only be revealed within a complex linguistic and motor environment (Dworkin, Meleca, & Stachler, 2003). As noted by Adams et al. (1993), although substantially greater control can be achieved in assessing a single gesture type or articulator, such an approach may be "inadequate for characterizing general organizational principles of speech production" (p. 50).

Even within a narrowly defined speech task, however, an important consideration in research results is the issue of speaker variability. Each speaker can vary considerably in his or her motor behavior when producing the same utterance. A seminal study by Hughes and Abbs (1976) explored the subject variability of displacement of articulators and muscle activity over repeated productions of the same utterance. Perkell, Matthies, Svirsky, and Jordan (1996) comment that this variability may be due to individual differences in vocal tract geometry or, alternatively, to differences in strategies of motor control. Recall our definition of motor equivalence, first introduced in Chapter 4, in which we said that it is a phenomenon in which individuals demonstrate different motor behaviors in response to the same stimulus (Hughes & Abbs, 1976). Motor equivalence applies to task repetition within individuals, also. In other words, the movements of the articulators that are used to produce a given utterance may well be variable upon repetition of the utterance. The variability may occur because multiple sets of synergistic muscle fibers can accomplish the same task (Abbs, Gracco, & Blair, 1984; Perkell et al., 1996; Sharkey & Folkins, 1985). Although motor equivalence helps preserve normal articulatory function (think of it almost like having "backup" systems), it complicates the process of determining which sets of muscles or portions of muscles specifically contribute to a gesture.

Perturbation Studies

One strategy used in research on speech motor control is the use of a disturbance, sometimes unanticipated, to the speaker's vocal tract. The disturbance is referred to as a perturbation. The ways in which the individual compensates for the perturbation is often referred to as an adaptive response. Adaptation to perturbations during the speech act can be viewed as an "online" compensation. The compensation may reflect

the mechanism used to overcome the disruption, thereby providing insight into important variables in speech motor control (Folkins & Abbs, 1975; Huber, Stathopoulos, & Sussman, 2004; Kelso, Tuller, Vatikiotis-Bateson, & Fowler, 1984; Lindblom, Lubker, & Gay, 1979; MacFarland, Baum, & Cabot, 1996; Munhall, Löfqvist, & Kelso, 1994; Putnam, Shelton, & Kastner, 1986). Perturbations may take the form of a physical or biomechanical disruption or an acoustic or aerodynamic alteration.

Perturbations may be static, such as placing a foreign object in the mouth to alter the contour of the mouth or the ability of the mouth to close. Examples of static perturbation include the artificial palate and the bite-block. An **artificial palate** is an appliance, inserted into the mouth and attached to the upper teeth, that changes the contour of the palate (Baum & McFarland, 2000; Hamlet, Cullison, & Stone, 1979; McFarland, Baum, & Chabot, 1996). These studies provide information about how the articulation of an individual phoneme may be disrupted, as well as information about how a speaker might adapt to or learn to compensate for the impediment and what, if any, carryover might occur once the impediment is removed (Aasland, Baum, & McFarland, 2006; Baum & McFarland, 1997).

Another means of perturbing the speech production system is with use of a bite-block. The **bite-block** is typically a semi-rigid material made from a dental molding impression placed in a frontolateral position between the upper and lower central incisor teeth. It is kept in place during utterance production. It has been shown that normal speech is not adversely affected by fixation of the mandible with a bite-block (Abbs & Kennedy, 1982; Fowler & Turbey, 1980; Gay, Lindblom, & Lubker, 1981). Recall our discussion earlier of reference frames in the production of articulatory gestures. Muscle length may be one reference frame used by the nervous system to regulate gestures. Use of a bite-block changes the target muscle lengths for the mandible and lips. Of interest, data show that speakers adapt to or compensate for the bite-block immediately (Lindblom, Lubker, & Gay, 1979), providing evidence that the speech production system can adapt to different reference frames to produce a given phoneme under different conditions.

Perturbations may be dynamic, such as an unanticipated rapid tap on the lip or jaw (Abbs & Gracco, 1984; Gracco & Abbs, 1985; Shaiman & Gracco, 2002) or the release of air pressure from a face mask (Zajac & Weissler, 2004). Together, these studies have shown that both the perturbed and the nonperturbed articulators demonstrate rapid compensatory changes, suggesting that novel articulatory patterns are developed to compensate for the obstruction. These changes occur very quickly, suggesting that somatosensory information contributes nonvolitional control of motor output. Of note, the studies of lip perturbation show that the response is task specific. In production of /f/, for example, perturbations to the lower lip or mandible produce no upper lip response (Gracco & Abbs, 1985; Shaiman, 1989), and in lingual articulation, an unanticipated jaw perturbation produces tongue and mandible response but no upper lip response (Kelso et al., 1984).

The data from perturbation studies may be offered as evidence to support the theory that articulatory gestures and their associated somatosensory inputs comprise a goal that is related to but distinct from the acoustic output (Tremblay, Shiller, & Ostry, 2003). Of interest, Tremblay et al. (2003) altered the movement path of the mandible without altering the acoustic output by having subjects "mouth" movements without producing voice ("silent speech"). Subjects adapted jaw movements to correct for the perturbation, even in the absence of acoustic output. The authors interpreted this as evidence that somatosensory information is, by itself, an invariant component of speech motor control, that "the somatosensory goal is pursued independent of the acoustics" (p. 868).

Perturbation studies also have been used to explore the contribution of aerodynamic regulation to speech motor control. This question is most relevant for high-pressure sounds, and therefore, perturbation studies in this area have focused upon plosive production. The discussion regarding maintenance of stable aerodynamic

values earlier in the chapter under the section Motor Programs included perturbation research designs in which compensation for rapid and unexpected air pressure changes was evaluated (Huber, Stathopolous, & Sussman, 2004; Moon, Folkins, Smith, & Luschei, 1993; Warren, 1986). Zajac and Weissler (2004) use a perturbation design to explore regulation of air pressure in speakers with intact vocal tracts. These perturbation experiments contributed to the understanding of how the vocal tract maintains aerodynamic stability under conditions of rapidly varying air pressures and flows that result from articulatory activity during running speech.

Perturbation also can be achieved by altering perceptual feedback, which can result in compensatory changes that persist once the altered feedback is removed (Jones & Munhall, 2000). Delayed auditory feedback (presenting the speaker's voice back to him or her through headphones but at a few milliseconds' delay) causes marked changes in speech fluency (Howell, El Yaniv, & Powell, 1987). Altering the frequency content of the auditory feedback causes the speaker to distort f_o and intonation contour (Elman, 1981) and can change kinematics of lip, jaw, and tongue movement (Forrest, Abbas, & Zimmermann, 1986). In summary, analysis of the adaptations to perturbations to the articulators during speech (that is, self-equilibration of the articulators) may be representative of the inherent flexibility of the speech motor control system (Kelso & Tuller, 1983) or provide information about the role of sensory feedback in motor control (Löfqvist, 1997; Tremblay et al., 2003).

Rate

Inferences of neural control of speech production may be made from observing how the coordination of articulatory dynamics changes with speech rate. Numerous studies have demonstrated the tendency for increased speech rate to have a direct correlation with movement velocity of orofacial structure (Adams et al., 1993; Gay, Ushijima, Hirose, & Cooper, 1974; Kuehn & Moll, 1976; McClean, 2000; McClean & Clay, 1996; Ostry

& Munhall, 1985; Shaiman, Adams, & Kimelman, 1997; Vatikiotis-Bateson & Kelso, 1993).

Although many studies have found increased rate of speech to directly affect speech kinematics, the findings do not all agree. Some studies show that increased rate of speech results in decreased amplitude in the movement (displacement) of the articulators, whereas others suggest that displacement actually increases or does not change consistently in all subjects (Dromey & Ramig, 1998; Gay et al., 1974; Gracco & Abbs, 1985; Kuehn & Moll, 1976; Lindblom, 1963; McClean, 2000; Ostry, Vatikiotis-Basteson, & Gribble, 1997; Ostry & Munhall, 1985; Shaiman et al., 1997; Vatikiotis-Bateson & Kelso, 1993). Corresponding changes in the spectral characteristics of the acoustic signal accompany changes in speech rate (Ostry & Munhall, 1985; Vatikiotis-Bateson & Kelso, 1993). McClean and Tasko (2003) found that the speed of jaw movement during a simple utterance was correlated strongly with speaking fundamental frequency and intensity. However, the relationship is not straightforward and is dependent on factors such as extent of articulator displacement. That is, displacement is highly dependent upon segmental and suprasegmental features as well as individual differences in structural size. Speaking rate may influence transglottal pressure drop in the control of vocal fold vibration for stop consonants (Boucher & Lamontagne, 2001). These studies suggest that activation of the muscles that control articulator movement is not independent of the respiratory and laryngeal systems.

Several factors may contribute to the contradictory findings in regard to speaking rate and articulator movement. Variability may increase as a speaker moves away from his or her preferred speaking rate (Smith et al., 1995). Slowing speech increases irregularity of gestural movements (Adams et al., 1993). The amount of force may affect displacement velocities and amplitudes (Adams et al., 1993). Articulatory strategies used to achieve increased rate of speech may change with increasing age (Goozée, Stephenson, Murdoch, Darnell, & Lapointe, 2005). A variety of patterns of anticipatory coar-

ticulation (Perkell & Matthies, 1992) and articulatory strategies may be used to achieve changes in speaking rate (Adams et al., 1993; Matthies, Perrier, Perkell, & Zandipour, 2001; Shaiman et al., 1997). And, finally, speech motor control strategies may be different for decreasing compared to increasing rate of speech (Adams et al., 1993).

Recall our example at the beginning of this chapter about reaching for a glass. Scientists who study the spatiotemporal movement of our limbs might analyze the trajectory with variables such as the distance from the hand at its starting position to the cup (the target), the size of the target, and the biomechanical constraints of the arm and hand joints with their tendinous and muscular connections. In this way, the relationship between speed and accuracy, for example, could be analyzed. In speech, however, we are at the disadvantage of not having exact targets. (Recall our discussion earlier about not having single, isolated articulatory targets for each gesture.) How, then, can we analyze the speed-accuracy aspect of the spatiotemporal relationship? Research has examined the difference between typical "conversational-style" speech and that which is often referred to as **clear speech**, in which the subjects are instructed to speak as clearly or precisely as possible (Ferguson, 2004; Hargus Ferguson & Kewley-Port, 2002; Picheny, Durlanch, & Braida, 1986, 1989; Schum, 1996). Most of the research in this area has been motivated by assessing speech intelligibility for individuals with hearing impairments, although it has also been explored in cases of speech disorders (Goberman & Elmer, 2005). Clear speech is characterized in general by decreased speech rate. The decrease in rate is achieved by increased use of pausing and increased duration of pauses, as well as increased mean speaking f_o, increased f_o variability, and increased intensity of selected consonants, with less vowel reduction (Bradlow, Kraus, & Hayes, 2003; Krause & Braida, 2002; Picheny et al., 1986; Uchanski, Choi, Braida, Reed, & Durlach, 1996).

It has been hypothesized that global objectives such as "loud," "clear speech," "ease," or "economy of effort" may exert an overall influence on kinematics (Dromey & Ramig, 1998; Lindblom, 1990; Perkell, Zandipour, Matthies, & Lane, 2002). In the literature about speech disorders, it has been shown that this task can be useful in the discrimination between different types of disorders (Roy, Gouse, Mauszycki, Merrill, & Smith, 2005) and can increase the prominence of specific features of a disorder (Kent & Kent, 2000; Kent, Kent, Rosenbek, Vorperian, & Weismer; 1997). Tasko and McClean (2004) found that a variety of different utterance contexts may be important for revealing underlying patterns of speech motor control.

Study Questions

14. What are some of the relevant factors in the discussion of speaking task in speech motor control research?

15. How are adaptations to perturbation explored in speech motor control? Include expected and unexpected perturbations, as well as transient and static disruptions.

16. How have the data from perturbation studies been used to support different theories of speech motor control?

17. How is variability of articulator movement influenced by speaking rate?

18. Define "clear speech" and describe its acoustic features.

10.5 Influences From Connectionist Models

Unlike the serial models presented earlier, the **connectionist models** propose a nonlinear, or nonhierarchical, set of components. Linguistic processing is the result of a vast network of elements that are connected in different ways. The various elements, therefore, process information simultaneously and interact with one another. In

---

Gestural Phonology

Whereas articulation is concerned with the motor aspect of sound production, phonology describes the patterns of sounds used in a language and is firmly anchored within the domain of linguistics. However, as Kent (1992) emphasizes, physiologic maturation and sensorimotor coordination cannot be ignored within a theory of phonology. Issues of speech motor control do intertwine with phonology, perhaps nowhere more so than in the theoretical approach called *articulatory phonology*. Also referred to as *gestural phonology*, this theory holds that the basic unit of phonology is the articulatory gesture (Browman & Goldstein, 1992, 1994). An utterance, therefore, can be decomposed into smaller units of gestures, each having a specific spatiotemporal configuration. The emphasis of articulatory phonology is that the basic unit of speech is not a static articulatory posture but rather a dynamic articulatory gesture. The reference frame for the articulatory gesture is a vocal tract constriction. The gesture can be described by specific values (Saltzman & Munhall, 1989) and is composed of individual overlapping units. Each formation and release of a constriction is considered a gesture. For example, the word "bat" begins with a gesture whose task is lip closure. Specific biomechanical characteristics of the lips (e.g., their mass and stiffness) define the velocity of the gesture. Gestural phonology is primarily a linguistic gestural model, but it is consistent with a major motor speech production model called the task dynamic model (Saltzman & Munhall, 1989).

the terminology of the connection models, each input layer node represents a feature, activation of the node represents a value of the feature, and a pattern of node activations represents a higher level entity. For example, flowers could be described as a pattern of node activations, where each node represents a distinctive feature that might be used to describe the flower, such as five petals, yellow in color, single bud, and so on. Each node has an activation value of one (presence) or zero (absence) for a specific feature. Each node can participate in several input patterns, and so we say that the input patterns have distributed representations.

Related to the connectionist models are the parallel-distribution processing (PDP) models, in which information processing is modeled on brain activity. The PDP models propose that a parallel array of neural connections supplements the serial pathways. Mental processing is distributed throughout a highly complex neural network, in which a multitude of inhibitory and excitatory neural signals work in coordinated units to produce a series of muscle contractions that will achieve the target articulatory gestures. Connectionist and PDP theories have been used heavily in computational models of speech production and perception with considerable success. Frequently termed **neural networks**, these complex computer programs are hypothesized to model central and peripheral nervous system activity in speech motor control (Guenther, Ghosh, & Tourville, 2006).

10.6 Language and Speech

This text does not address language science, but certainly we must acknowledge that the acoustics of speech production occur within the intention of language. The two are wholly integrated with regard to neurologic processes (Dromey & Benson, 2003), and the need to study the effects of language on speech motor control is well recognized (Maner et al., 2000; Strand, 1992; Strand & McNeil, 1996). The motor and cogni-

tive demands of speech communication require an individual to allocate attention to the performance of multiple tasks simultaneously. In the case of increased complexity of utterance and language-processing demands, spatiotemporal variability increases (Maner et al., 2000). Two major views exist that describe how increased processing complexity is managed by the speech production system. One view is that a limiting factor exists, which might be considered a limitation of resources. That is, an individual has finite resources that must be allocated appropriately. The other view is that each component of the multiple tasks must be processed serially, and so a potential "bottleneck" can occur as each component is processed individually (Dromey & Benson, 2003). In either theory, individuals with normal and fully developed speech and language skills compensate appropriately. Individuals with immature skills, as in the case of a child, or abnormal skills, as in the case of a language delay or speech motor control problem, however, cannot compensate appropriately. Some studies have found that motor distractors alter speech (Chang & Hammond, 1987; Dromey & Benson, 2003; Kelso, Tuller, & Harris, 1983). For example, distracting motor tasks such as finger tapping have been found to cause changes in speech rate (LaBarba, Bowes, Kingsberg, & Freeman, 1987). Smith, McFarland, and Weber (1986) did not find any such effect, although the authors did find a reverse effect, in that alterations in speech showed parallel changes in finger movements. In one view (LaBarba, Bowers, Kinsberg, & Freeman, 1987), the functional distance between simultaneous tasks influences level of interference. That is, the more similar the neural circuitry for central processing of tasks, the greater the chance of interference. Linguistic distractors increased spatiotemporal variability (Dromey & Benson, 2003; Maner et al., 2000).

So-called *speech errors* are another example of the interplay between the linguistic and the motor levels of speech production (Brown, 2004). Speech errors may be the result of errors at any number of stages of speech production, including syntactic (grammatic structure), semantic (word meaning), or sensorimotor levels. In examination of speech motor control, we mainly concern ourselves with the errors within a sensorimotor context. Shattuck-Hufnagel (1979) used the **slot-and-filler model** to ac-count for sound errors in word initial position, similar to the **frame and content theory** (MacNeilage, 1970). The slot, or frame, is the syllable, which contains the suprasegmental information of stress pattern. The filler is the phonetic information assigned to the slot or frame. Speech errors are thought to occur in marked or stressed segments (Brown, 2004; Fromkin, 1973; Levelt, Roelofs, & Meyer, 1999). As addressed earlier in the chapter, however, identification of the relevant size of the segment—phoneme, syllable, or suprasegmental stress unit—remains an unresolved problem. Common categories of speech errors include the phonetic feature and the syllable (Figure 10–14). Errors of speech may provide information about different levels, or stages, of speech encoding, depending on whether the error is one of semantics or phonemics.

Study Questions

19. What are the two views of how the speech production system adapts to increases in processing complexity?
20. Briefly explain how the slot-and-filler model and the frame and content theory account for speech production errors.

Recommended Internet Sites for Further Learning

http://www.uiowa.edu/~acadtech/phonetics/english/frameset.html

The University of Iowa phonetics tutorial. This is a terrific website for learning the different features of the consonants. Provides IPA symbol, audio sample of consonants, graphical display of oral cavity during production, and video of actual production. Highly recommended.

Figure 10–14. Errors in speech may be revelatory of the mechanisms by which we encode speech. Errors in speech may occur at several levels, including (**A**) the feature level, where *big* and *fat* becomes *pig* and *vat* (Fromkin, 1973), and (**B**) the syllable level, where the *heater switch* becomes the *sweeter hitch* (Fromkin, 1973).

References

Aasland, W. A., Baum, S. R., & McFarland, D. H. (2006). Electropalatographic, acoustic, and perceptual data on adaptation to a palatal perturbation. *Journal of the Acoustical Society of America, 119,* 2372–2381.

Abbs, J. H., & Gracco, V. L. (1984). Control of complex motor gestures: Orofacial muscle responses to load perturbations of the lip during speech. *Journal of Neurophysiology, 51,* 705–723.

Abbs, J. H., Gracco, V. L., & Blair, C. (1984). Functional muscle partitioning during voluntary movement: Facial muscle activity for speech. *Experimental Neurology, 85,* 469–479.

Abbs, J. H., & Kennedy, J. G. (1982). Neurophysiological processes of speech movement control. In N. Lass, L. McReynolds, J. Northern, & D. Yoder (Eds.), *Speech, language, and hearing: Normal processes* (pp. 84–108). Philadelphia, PA: W. B. Saunders.

Adams, S. G., Weismer, G., & Kent, R. D. (1993). Speaking rate and speech movement velocity profiles. *Journal of Speech and Hearing Research, 36,* 41–54.

Baum, S., & McFarland, D. (1997). The development of speech adaptation to an artificial palate. *Journal of the Acoustical Society of America, 102,* 2353–2359.

Baum, S., & McFarland, D. (2000). Individual differences in speech adaptation to an artificial palate. *Journal of the Acoustical Society of America, 107,* 3572–3575.

Bell-Berti, F., & Harris, K. S. (1981). A temporal model of speech production. *Phonetica, 38,* 9–20.

Bell-Berti, F., & Harris, K. S. (1982). Temporal patterns of coarticulation. *Journal of the Acoustical Society of America, 65,* 1268–1270.

Bell-Berti, F., & Krakow, R. A. (1991). Anticipatory velar lowering: A coproduction account. *Journal of the Acoustical Society of America, 90,* 112–123.

Bell-Berti, F., Krakow, R. A., Gelfer, C. E., & Boyce, S. E. (1994). Anticipatory and carryover effects: Implications for models of speech production. In F. Bell-Berti & L. J. Raphael (Eds.), *Producing speech: Contemporary issues* (pp. 77–97). New York, NY: American Institute of Physics.

Bladon, A., & Al-Bamerni, A. (1982). One-stage and two-stage temporal patterns of velar coarticulation. *Journal of the Acoustical Society of America, 72*(Suppl. 1), S104.

Borden, G. J. (1979). An interpretation of research on feedback interruption in speech. *Brain and Language, 7,* 307–319.

Boucher, V., & Lamontagne, M. (2001). Clinical implications of active and passive aspects of devoicing. *Journal of Speech, Language, Hearing Research, 44,* 1005–1014.

Boyce, S. E., Krakow, R. A., Bell-Berti, F., & Gelfer, C. E. (1990). Converging sources of evidence for dissecting articulatory movements into core gestures. *Journal of Phonetics, 18,* 173–188.

Bradlow, A., Kraus, N., & Hayes, E. (2003). Speaking clearly for children with learning disabilities: Sentence perception in noise. *Journal of Speech, Language, and Hearing Research, 46,* 80–97.

Browman, C. P., & Goldstein, L. (1992). Articulatory phonology: An overview. *Phonetica, 49,* 155–180.

Browman, C. P., & Goldstein, L. (1994). Gestural syllable position effects in American English. In F. Bell-Bertie & L. J. Raphael (Eds.), *Producing speech: Contemporary issues* (pp. 19–33). New York, NY: American Institute of Physics.

Brown, J. C. (2004). Eliminating the segmental tier: Evidence from speech errors. *Journal of Psycholinguistic Research, 33,* 97–101.

Caruso, A. J., Abbs, J. H., & Gracco, V. L. (1988). Kinematic analysis of multiple movement coordination during speech in stutterers. *Brain, 111,* 439–456.

Chang, P., & Hammond, G. R. (1987). Mutual interactions between speech and finger movements. *Journal of Motor Behavior, 19,* 265–274.

Cutler, A., & Butterfield, S. (1991). Word boundary cues in clear speech: A supplementary report. *Speech Communication, 10,* 335–353.

Darley, F. L., Aronson, A. E., & Brown. J. R. (1996). Differential diagnosis patterns of dysarthria. *Journal of Speech and Hearing Research, 12,* 246–269.

Davis, B. L., & MacNeilage, P. F. (1995). The articulatory basis of babbling. *Journal of Speech and Hearing Research, 38,* 1199–1211.

Dromey, C., & Benson, A. (2003). Effects of concurrent motor, linguistic, or cognitive tasks on speech motor performance. *Journal of Speech, Language, and Hearing Research, 46,* 1234–1246.

Dromey, C., & Ramig, I. O. (1998). Intentional changes in sound pressure level and rate: Their impact on measures of respiration, phonation, and articulation. *Journal of Speech, Language, and Hearing Research, 41,* 1003–1018.

Dworkin, J. P. (1996). Bite-block therapy for oromandibular dystonia. *Journal of Medical Speech-Language Pathology, 4,* 47–56.

Dworkin, J. P., Meleca, R. J., & Stachler, R. J. (2003). Moore on the role of the mandible in speech production: Clinical correlates of Green, Moore, &

Reilly's (2002) findings (Letter). *Journal of Speech, Language, and Hearing Research*, *46*, 1016–1021.

Eguchi, S., & Hirsch, I. J. (1969). Development of speech sounds in children. *Acta Otolaryngologica Suppl.*, *257*, 1–51.

Elman, J. (1981). Effects of frequency-shifted feedback on the pitch of vocal productions. *Journal of the Acoustical Society of America*, *79*, 45–50.

Ferguson, S. H. (2004). Talker differences in clear and conversational speech: Vowel intelligibility for normal-hearing listeners. *Journal of the Acoustical Society of America*, *116*, 2365–2373.

Ferguson, S. H., & Kewley-Port, D. (2002). Vowel intelligibility in clear and conversational speech for normal-hearing and hearing-impaired listeners. *Journal of the Acoustical Society of America*, *112*, 259–271.

Finnegan, E. M., & Hoffman, H. T. (2000). Response to Zajac and Warren. *Journal of Speech, Language, and Hearing Research*, *43*, 1534.

Flege, J. E. (1988). Effects of speaking rate on tongue position and velocity of movement in vowel production. *Journal of the Acoustical Society of America*, *84*, 901–916.

Folkins, J. W., & Abbs, J. H. (1975). Lip and jaw motor control during speech: Responses to resistive loading of the jaw. *Journal of Speech and Hearing Research*, *18*, 207–220.

Forrest, K., Abbas, P. J., & Zimmerman, G. N. (1986). Effects of white noise masking and low-pass filtering on speech kinematics. *Journal of Speech and Hearing Research*, *29*, 549–562.

Fowler, C. A. (1980). Coarticulation and theories of extrinsic timing control. *Journal of Phonetics*, *8*, 113–133.

Fowler, C. A., & Turvey, M. T. (1980). Immediate compensation in bite-block speech. *Phonetica*, *37*, 306–325.

Fromkin, V. A. (1973). *Speech errors as linguistic evidence*. The Hague, Netherlands: Mouton.

Fujimura, O. (1980). Modern methods of investigation in speech production. *Phonetica*, *37*, 38–54.

Gammon, S. A., Smith, P. J., Daniloff, R. G., & Kim, C. W. (1971). Articulation and stress/juncture production under oral anesthetization and masking. *Journal of Speech and Hearing Research*, *14*, 271–282.

Gay, T. J., Lindblom, B., & Lubker, J. (1981). Production of bite-block vowels: Acoustic equivalence by selective compensation. *Journal of the Acoustical Society of America*, *64*, 802–810.

Gay, T., Ushijima, T., Hirose, H., & Cooper, F. S. (1974). Effects of speaking rate on labial consonant-vowel articulation. *Journal of Phonetics*, *2*, 1627–1637.

Gelfer, C. E., Bell-Berti, F., & Harris, K. S. (1989). Determining the extent of anticipatory coarticulation: Effects of experimental design. *Journal of the Acoustical Society of America*, *86*, 2443–2445.

Gerratt, B. R., Till, J. A., Rosenbek, J. C., Wertz, R. T., & Boysen, A. E. (1991). Use and perceived value of perceptual and instrumental measures in dysarthria management. In C. A. Moore, K. M. Yorkston, & D. R. Beukelman (Eds.), *Dysarthria and apraxia of speech: Perspectives on management* (pp. 77–93). Baltimore, MD: Paul H. Brookes.

Gleick, J. (1987). *Chaos: Making a new science*. New York, NY: Viking Press.

Goberman, A. M., & Elmer, L. W. (2005). Acoustic analysis of clear versus conversational speech in individuals with Parkinson disease. *Journal of Communication Disorders*, *38*, 215–230.

Goffman, L., & Smith, A. (1999). Development and phonetic differentiation of speech movement patterns. *Journal of Experimental Psychology: Human Perception and Performance*, *25*, 649–660.

Goozée, J. V., Stephenson, D. K., Murdoch, B. E., Darnell, R. E., & Lapointe, L. L. (2005). Lingual kinematic strategies used to increase speech rate: Comparison between younger and older adults. *Clinical Linguistics and Phonetics*, *19*, 319–334.

Gracco, V. L. (1995). Central and peripheral components in the control of speech movements. In F. Bell-Bertie & L. J. Raphael (Eds.), *Producing speech: Contemporary issues* (pp. 417–431). New York, NY: American Institute of Physics.

Gracco, V. L., & Abbs, J. H. (1985). Dynamic control of the perioral system during speech: Kinematic analyses of autogenic and nonautogenic sensorimotor processes. *Journal of Neurophysiology*, *54*, 418–432.

Gracco, V. L., & Abbs, J. H. (1986). Variant and invariant characteristics of speech movements. *Experimental Brain Research*, *65*, 156–166.

Green, J. R., Moore, C. A., Higashikawa, M., & Steeve, R. W. (2000). The physiologic development of speech motor control: Lip and jaw coordination. *Journal of Speech, Language, and Hearing Research*, *43*, 239–256.

Green, J. R., Moore, C. A., & Reilly, K. J. (2002). The sequential development of jaw and lip control for speech. *Journal of Speech, Language, and Hearing Research*, *45*, 66–79.

Grigos, M. I., Saxman, J. H., & Gordon, A. M. (2005). Speech motor development during acquisition of the voicing contrast. *Journal of Speech, Language, and Hearing Research, 48,* 739–752.

Guenther, F. H. (1995). Speech sound acquisition, coarticulation, and rate effects in a neural network model of speech production. *Psychological Review, 102,* 594–621.

Guenther, F. H., Ghosh, S. S., & Tourville, J. A. (2006). Neural modeling and imaging of the cortical interactions underlying syllable production. *Brain and Language, 96,* 280–301.

Guenther, F. H., Hampson, M., & Johnson, D. (1998). A theoretical investigation of reference frames for the planning of speech movements. *Psychological Review, 105,* 611–633.

Hamlet, S., Cullison, B., & Stone, M. (1979). Physiological control of sibilant duration: Insights afforded by speech compensation to dental prostheses. *Journal of the Acoustical Society of America, 65,* 1276–1285.

Hamstra-Bletze, L., & Blote, A. W. (1990). Development of handwriting in primary school: A longitudinal study. *Perceptual Motor Skills, 70,* 759–770.

Hertrich, I., & Ackermann, H. (2000). Lip-jaw and tongue-jaw coordination during rate-controlled syllable repetitions. *Journal of the Acoustical Society of America, 107,* 2236–2247.

Houde, J. F., & Jordan, M. I. (1998). Sensorimotor adaptation in speech production. *Science, 279,* 1213–1216.

Howell, P., El Yaniv, N., & Powell, D. J. (1987). Factors affecting fluency in stutterers. In H. F. M. Peters & W. Julstijn (Eds.), *Speech motor dynamics in stuttering* (pp. 361–369). New York, NY: Springer-Verlag.

Huber, J. E., Stathopoulos, E. T., & Sussman, J. E. (2004). The control of aerodynamics, acoustics, and perceptual characteristics during speech production. *Journal of the Acoustical Society of America, 116,* 2345–2353.

Hughes, O. M., & Abbs, J. H. (1976). Labial-mandibular coordination in the production of speech: Implications for the operation of motor equivalence. *Phonetica, 33,* 199–221.

Jones, J. A., & Munhall, K. G. (2000). Perceptual calibration of F0 production: Evidence from feedback perturbation. *Journal of the Acoustical Society of America, 108,* 1246–1251.

Kelso, J. A. S., Saltzman, E. L., & Tuller, B. (1986). The dynamical perspective on speech production: Data and theory. *Journal of Phonetics, 14,* 29–59.

Kelso, J. A. S., & Tuller, B. (1983). Compensatory articulation under conditions of reduced afferent information: A dynamic formulation. *Journal of Speech and Hearing Research, 26,* 217–224.

Kelso, J. A. S., Tuller, B., & Harris, K. S. (1983). A "dynamic pattern" perspective on the control and coordination of movement. In P. F. MacNeilage (Ed.), *The production of speech* (pp. 137–173). New York, NY: Springer-Verlag.

Kelso, J. A. S., Tuller, B., Vatikiotis-Bateson, E., & Fowler, C. A. (1984). Functionally specific articulatory cooperation following jaw perturbations during speech: Evidence for coordinative structures. *Journal of Experimental Psychology and Human Perceptual Performance, 10,* 812–832.

Kelso, J. A. S., Vatikiotis-Bateson, E., Saltzman, E., & Kay, B. (1985). A qualitative dynamic analysis of reiterant speech production: Phase portraits, kinematics and dynamic modeling. *Journal of the Acoustical Society of America, 77,* 266–280.

Kent, R. D. (1976). Anatomical and neuromuscular maturation of the speech mechanism: Evidence from acoustic studies. *Journal of Speech and Hearing Research, 19,* 421–447.

Kent, R. D. (1992). The biology of phonological development. In C. A. Ferguson, L. Menn, & C. Stoel-Gammon (Eds.), *Phonological development: Models, research, implications* (pp. 65–90). Timonium, MD: York Press.

Kent, R. D. (2000). Research on speech motor control and its disorders: A review and prospective. *Journal of Communication Disorders, 33,* 391–428.

Kent, R. D., Adams, S. G., & Turner, G. S. (1996). Models of speech production. In N. J. Lass (Ed.), *Principles of experimental phonetics* (pp. 3–45). St. Louis, MO: Mosby.

Kent, R. D., Carney, P. J., & Severeid, L. R. (1974). Velar movement and timing: Evaluation of a model for binary control. *Journal of Speech and Hearing Research, 17,* 470–488.

Kent, R. D., & Forner, L. L. (1980). Speech segment durations in sentence recitations between children and adults. *Journal of Phonetics, 8,* 157–168.

Kent, R. D., & Kent, J. F. (2000). Task-based profiles of the dysarthrias. *Folia Phoniatrica and Logopaedica, 52,* 48–53.

Kent, R. D., Kent, J. F., Rosenbek, J. C., Vorperian, H. K., & Weismer, G. (1997). A speaking task analysis of the dysarthria in cerebellar disease. *Folia Phoniatrica and Logopaedica, 49,* 63–82.

Kent, R. D., & Minifie, F. D. (1977). Coarticulation in recent speech production models. *Journal of Phonetics, 5,* 115–133.

Kent, R. D., & Moll, K. L. (1972) Tongue body articulation during vowel and diphthong gestures. *Journal of Speech and Hearing Research, 15,* 453–473.

Kent, R. D., & Moll, K. (1975). Articulatory timing in selected consonant sequences. *Brain and Language, 2,* 304–323.

Kim, J. R., Zajac, D. J., Warren, D. W., Mayo, R., & Essick, G. (1997). The response to sudden change in vocal tract resistance during stop consonant production. *Journal of Speech, Language, and Hearing Research, 40,* 848–857.

Kleinow, J., & Smith, A. (2000). Influences of length and syntactic complexity on the speech motor stability of the fluent speech of adults who stutter. *Journal of Speech, Language, and Hearing Research, 43,* 548–559.

Kollia, H. B., Gracco, V. L., Harris, K. S., (1992). Functional organization of velar movements following jaw perturbation. *Journal of the Acoustical Society of America, 92,* 474.

Krakow, R. A. (1993). Nonsegmental influences on velum movement patterns: Syllables, sentence, stress and speaking rate. In M. K. Huffman & R. A. Krakow (Eds.), *Phonetics and phonology: Vol. 5. Nasals, nasalization, and the velum* (pp. 87–116). New York, NY: Academic Press.

Krause, J., & Braida, L. (2002). Investigating alternative forms of clear speech: The effects of speaking rate and speaking mode on intelligibility. *Journal of the Acoustical Society of America, 112,* 2165–2172.

Kuehn, D. P., & Moll, K. L. (1976). A cineradiographic study of VC and CV articulatory velocities. *Journal of Phonetics, 4,* 303–320.

LaBarba, R. C., Bowers, C. A., Kinsberg, S. A., & Freeman, G. (1987). The effects of concurrent vocalization on foot and hand motor performance: A test of the functional distance hypothesis. *Cortex, 23,* 301–308.

Laboissière, R., Ostry, D. J., & Feldman, A. G. (1996). Control of multi-muscle systems: Human jaw and hyoid movements. *Biological Cybernetics, 74,* 373–384.

Lane, H., Denny, M., Guenther, F. H., Matthies, M. L., Menard, L., Perkell, J. S., . . . Zandipour, M. (2005). Effects of biteblocks and hearing status on vowel production. *Journal of the Acoustical Society of America, 118,* 1636–1646.

Lane, H. L., & Tranel, B. (1971). The Lombard sign and the role of hearing in speech. *Journal of Speech and Hearing Research, 14,* 677–709.

Levelt, W. J. M., Roelofs, A., & Meyer, A. S. (1999). A theory of lexical access in speech production. *Behavioral and Brain Sciences, 22,* 1–75.

Lindblom, B. (1963). Spectrographic study of vowel reduction. *Journal of the Acoustical Society of America, 35,* 1773–1781.

Lindblom, B. (1990). Explaining phonetic variations: A sketch of the H & H theory. In W. J. Hardcastle & A. Marchal (Eds.), *Speech production and speech modeling* (pp. 403–440). Dordrecht, Netherlands: Kluwer.

Lindblom, B., Lubker, J., & Gay, T. (1979). Formant frequencies of some fixed-mandible vowels and a model of speech motor programming by predictive simulation. *Journal of Phonetics, 7,* 147–161.

Löfqvist, A. (1997). Theories and models of speech production. In W. J. Hardcastle & J. Laver (Eds.), *The handbook of phonetic sciences.* Cambridge, MA: Blackwell.

Löfqvist, A., & Gracco, V. L. (1994). Tongue body kinematics in velar stop production: Influences of consonant voicing and vowel context. *Phonetica, 51,* 52–67.

Löfqvist, A., & Gracco, V. L. (1997). Lip and jaw kinematics in bilabial stop consonant production. *Journal of Speech, Language, and Hearing Research, 40,* 877–893.

Lucero, J. C., Munhall, K. G., Gracco, V. L., & Ramsey, L. O. (1997). On the registration of time and patterning of speech movements. *Journal of Speech, Language and Hearing Research, 40,* 1111–1117.

Luschei, E. S., & Goldbeg, L. J. (1981). Neural mechanisms of mandibular control: Mastication and voluntary biting. In V. B. Brooks (Ed.), *Handbook of physiology: The nervous system.* (Vol. 11, pp. 1237–1274). Bethesda, MD: American Physiological Society.

MacNeilage, P. F. (1970). Motor control of serial ordering in speech. *Psychological Review, 77,* 182–196.

Maner, K. J., Smith, A., & Grayson, L. (2000). Influences of utterance length and complexity on speech motor performance in children and adults. *Journal of Speech, Language, and Hearing Research, 43,* 560–573.

Matthies, M. L., Perrier, P., Perkell, J. S., & Zandipour, M. (2001). Variation in speech movement kinematics and temporal patterns of coarticulation with changes in clarity and rate. *Journal of Speech, Language, and Hearing Research, 44,* 552–563.

Max, L., & Caruso, A. J. (1997). Acoustic measures of temporal intervals across speaking rates: Variability of syllable- and phrase-level relative timing. *Journal of Speech, Language, and Hearing Research, 40,* 1097–1110.

McClean, M. D. (1973). Forward coarticulation of velar movement at marked junctural boundaries. *Journal of Speech and Hearing Research, 16,* 286–296.

McClean, M. D. (2000). Patterns of orofacial movement velocity across variations in speech rate. *Journal of Speech, Language, and Hearing Research, 43,* 205–216.

McClean, M. D., & Clay, J. L. (1996). Simulation of lower-lip motor unit activity and movements in speech. *Journal of the Acoustical Society of America, 99,* 3249–3252.

McClean, M. D., & Tasko, S. M. (2003). Association of orofacial muscle activity and movement during changes in speech rate and intensity. *Journal of Speech, Language, and Hearing Research, 46,* 1387–1400.

McFarland, D., Baum, S., & Cabot, C. (1996). Speech compensation to structural modifications of the oral cavity. *Journal of the Acoustical Society of America, 100,* 1093–1104.

Mermelstein, P. (1973). Articulatory model for the study of speech production. *Journal of the Acoustical Society of America, 53,* 1070–1082.

Moll, K. I. (1962). Velopharyngeal closure of vowels. *Journal of Speech and Hearing Research, 5,* 30–77.

Moon, J. B., & Folkins, J. W. (1991). The effects of auditory feedback on the regulation of intraoral air pressure during speech. *Journal of the Acoustical Society of America, 90,* 2992–2999.

Moon, J. B., Folkins, J. W., Smith, A. E., & Luschei, E. S. (1993). Air pressure regulation during speech production. *Journal of the Acoustical Society of America, 94,* 54–63.

Munhall, K. G., & Jones, J. A. (1995). The spatial control of speech movements. In F. Bell-Berti & L. J. Raphael (Eds.), *Producing speech: Contemporary issues* (pp. 521–537). New York, NY: American Institute of Physics.

Munhall, K. G., Löfqvist, A., & Kelso, J. A. S. (1994). Liplarynx coordination in speech: Effects of mechanical perturbation to the lower lip. *Journal of the Acoustical Society of America, 95,* 3605–3616.

Mysak, E. D. (1968). *Neuroevolutional approach to cerebral palsy and speech.* New York, NY: Teachers College Press.

Netsell, R. (1985). Construction and use of a bite-block for the evaluation and treatment of speech disorders. *Journal of Speech and Hearing Disorders, 50,* 103–106.

Nooteboom, S. G. (1994). Limited lookahead in speech production. In F. Bell-Bertie & L. J. Raphael (Eds.), *Producing speech: Contemporary issues* (pp. 3–18). New York, NY: American Institute of Physics.

Ohde, R. N. (1985). Fundamental frequency correlates of stop consonant voicing and vowel quality in the speech of preadolescent children. *Journal of the Acoustical Society of America, 78,* 1554–1561.

Ohman, S. E. G. (1967). Numerical models of coarticulation. *Journal of the Acoustical Society of America, 41,* 310–320.

Ostry, D. J., Gribble, P. L., & Gracco, V. L. (1995). Coarticulation in jaw movements in speech production: Is context sensitivity in speech kinematics centrally planned? *Journal of Neuroscience, 16,* 1570–1579.

Ostry, D. J., & Munhall, K. G. (1985). Control of rate and duration of speech movements. *Journal of the Acoustical Society of America, 77,* 640–648.

Ostry, D. J., & Munhall, K. G. (1994). Control of jaw orientation and position in mastication and speech. *Journal of Neurophysiology, 71,* 1528–1545.

Ostry, D. J., Vatikiotis-Bateson, E., & Gribble, P. L. (1997). An examination of the degrees of freedom of human jaw motion in speech and mastication. *Journal of Speech, Language, and Hearing Research, 40,* 1341–1351.

Payan, Y., & Perrier, P. (1997). Synthesis of V-V sequences with a 2D biomechanical tongue model controlled by the equilibrium point hypothesis. *Speech Communication, 22,* 185–205.

Perkell, J. S., & Matthies, M. L. (1992). Temporal measures of anticipatory labial coarticulation for the vowel /u/. Within- and cross-subject variability. *Journal of the Acoustical Society of America, 91,* 2911–2925.

Perkell, J. S. Matthies, M. L., Lane, H., Guenther, F., Wilhelm-Tricarico, R., Wozniak, J., & Peter, G. (1997). Speech motor control: Acoustic goals, saturation effects, auditory feedback and internal models. *Speech Communication, 22,* 227–250.

Perkell, J. S., Matthies, M. L., Svirsky, M. A., & Jordan, M. I. (1996). Perspectives on normal motor speech control. In D. Roin, K. Yorkston, & D. Beukelman

(Eds.), *Disorders of motor speech* (pp. 27–43). Baltimore, MD: Paul H. Brookes.

Perkell, J. S., Zandipour, M., Matthies, M. L., & Lane, H. (2002). Economy of effort in different speaking conditions. I. A preliminary study of intersubject differences and modeling issues. *Journal of the Acoustical Society of America, 112,* 1627–1641.

Perrier, P., Ostry, D. J., & Laboissière, R. (1996). The equilibrium point hypothesis and its application to speech motor control. *Journal of Speech and Hearing Research, 39,* 365–378.

Peterson, G. E., & Barney, H. E. (1952). Control methods used in a study of vowels. *Journal of the Acoustical Society of America, 24,* 176–184.

Picheny, M., Durlach, N. & Braida, L. (1986). Speaking clearly for the hard of hearing II: Acoustic characteristics of clear and conversational speech. *Journal of Speech and Hearing Research, 29,* 434–446.

Picheny, M., Durlach, N. & Braida, L. (1989). Speaking clearly for the hard of hearing III: An attempt to determine the contribution of speaking rate to difference in intelligibility between clear and conversational speech. *Journal of Speech and Hearing Research, 32,* 600–603.

Prosek, R. A., & House, A. S. (1975). Intraoral air pressure as a feedback cue in consonant production. *Journal of Speech and Hearing Research, 18,* 133–147.

Putnam, A. H. B., & Ringel, R. L. (1972). Some observations of articulation during labial sensory deprivation. *Journal of Speech and Hearing Research, 15,* 529–542.

Putnam, A. H. B., Shelton, R. L., & Kastner, C. U. (1986). Intraoral air pressure and oral airflow under different bleed and bite-block conditions. *Journal of Speech and Hearing Research, 29,* 37–49.

Redford, M. A., MacNeilage, P. F., & Davis, B. L. (1997). Production constraints on utterance-final consonant characteristics in babbling. *Phonetica, 5,* 172–186.

Riely, R. R., & Smith, A. (2003). Speech movements do not scale by orofacial structure size. *Journal of Applied Physiology, 94,* 2119–2126.

Roy, N., Gouse, M., Mauszycki, S. C., Merrill, R. M., & Smith M. E. (2005). Task specificity in adductor spasmodic dysphonia versus muscle tension dysphonia. *Laryngoscope, 1215,* 311–316.

Rubin, P. E., Baer, T., & Mermelstein, P. (1981). An articulatory synthesizer for perceptual research. *Journal of the Acoustical Society of America, 70,* 321–328.

Saltzman, E. L. (1991). The task dynamic model in speech production. In H. F. M. Peters, W. Hustjin, & C. W. Starkweather (Eds.), *Speech motor control and stuttering* (pp. 37–53). Amsterdam, Netherlands: Elsevier Science.

Saltzman, E. L., & Munhall, K. G. (1989). A dynamical approach to gestural patterning in speech production. *Ecological Psychology, 1,* 333–382.

Savariaux, C., Perrier, P., & Orliaguet, J. P. (1995). Compensation strategies for the perturbation of the rounded [u] vowel using a lip tube: A study of the control space in speech production. *Journal of the Acoustical Society of America, 98,* 2428–2442.

Schmidt, R. A. (1975). A schema theory of discrete motor learning. *Psychological Review, 82,* 225–260.

Schulman, R. (1989). Articulatory dynamics of loud and normal speech. *Journal of the Acoustical Society of America, 85,* 295–312.

Schum, D. (1996). Intelligibility of clear and conversational speech of young and elderly talkers. *Journal of the American Academy of Audiology, 7,* 212–218.

Scott, C. M., & Ringel, R. L. (1971). Articulation without oral sensory control. *Journal of Speech and Hearing Research, 14,* 804–818.

Shaiman, S. (1989). Kinematic and electromyographic responses to perturbation of the jaw. *Journal of the Acoustical Society of America, 86,* 78–88.

Shaiman, S., Adams, S. G., & Kimelman, M. D. (1997). Velocity profiles of lip protrusion across changes in speaking rate. *Journal of Speech, Language, and Hearing Research, 40,* 144–158.

Shaiman, S., & Gracco, V. L. (2002). Task-specific sensorimotor interactions in speech production. *Experimental Brain Research, 146,* 411–418.

Sharkey, S. G., & Folkins, J. W. (1985). Variability of lip and jaw movements in children and adults: Implications for the development of speech motor control. *Journal of Speech and Hearing Research, 28,* 8–15.

Shattuck-Hufnagel, S. (1979). Speech errors as evidence for a serial-ordering mechanism in sentence production. In W. Cooper & E. Walker (Eds.), *Sentence processing* (pp. 100–136). New York, NY: Springer-Verlag.

Shiller, D. M., Guillaume, H., & Ostry, D. J. (2005). Voluntary control of human jaw stiffness. *Journal of Neurophysiology, 94,* 2207–2217.

Shiller, D. M., Laboissière, R., & Ostry, D. J. (2002). Relationship between jaw stiffness and kinematic variability in speech. *Journal of Neurophysiology, 88,* 2329–2340.

Smith, A. (1992). The control of orofacial movements in speech. *Critical Reviews in Oral Biology and Medicine, 3,* 233–267.

Smith, A., & Goffman, L. (1998). Stability and patterning of speech movement sequences in children and adults. *Journal of Speech, Language, and Hearing Research, 41,* 18–30.

Smith, A., Goffman, L., Zelaznik, H. N., Ying, G., & McGillem, C. (1995). Spatiotemporal stability and patterning of speech movement sequences. *Experimental Brain Research, 104,* 493–501.

Smith, A., & Kleinow, J. (2000). Influences of length and syntactic complexity on the speech motor stability of adults who stutter. *Journal of Speech, Language, and Hearing Research, 43,* 513–520.

Smith, A., McFarland, D. H., & Weber, C. M. (1986). Interactions between speech and finger movements: An exploration of the dynamic pattern perspective. *Journal of Speech and Hearing Research, 29,* 471–480.

Smith, B. L. & Gartenberg, T. E. (1984). Initial observations concerning developmental characteristics of labiomandibular kinematics. *Journal of the Acoustical Society of America, 75,* 1599–1605.

Smith, B. L., & McLean-Muse, A. (1986). Articulatory movement characteristics of labial consonant productions in children and adults. *Journal of the Acoustical Society of America, 80,* 1321–1328.

Sternberg, S., Knoll, R. L., Monsell, S., & Wright, C. E. (1988). Motor programs and hierarchical organization in the control of rapid speech. *Phonetica, 45,* 175–197.

Stone, M. (1991). Imaging the tongue and vocal tract. *British Journal of Disorders of Communication, 26,* 11–23.

Strand, E. A. (1992). The integration of speech motor control and language formulation in process models of acquisition. In R. Chapman (Ed.), *Processes in language acquisition and disorders* (pp. 86–107). St. Louis, MO: Mosby-Yearbook.

Strand, E. A., & McNeil, M. R. (1996). Effects of length and linguistic complexity on temporal acoustic measures in apraxia of speech. *Journal of Speech, Language, and Hearing Research, 39,* 1018–1033.

Tasko, S. M., & McClean, M. D. (2004). Variations in articulatory movement with changes in speech task. *Journal of Speech, Language, and Hearing Research, 47,* 85–100.

Tasko, S. M., & Westbury, J. R. (2002). Defining and measuring speech movement events. *Journal of Speech, Language, and Hearing Research, 45,* 127–142.

Tingley, B. M., & Allen, G. D. (1975). Development of speech timing control in children. *Child Development, 46,* 186–194.

Tremblay, S., Shiller, D. M., & Ostry, D. J. (2003). Somatosensory basis of speech production. *Nature, 423,* 866–869.

Tuller, B., Harris, K. S., & Gross, B. (1979). Electromyographic study of the jaw muscles during speech. *Haskins Lab Status Report on Speech Research, 56,* 83–102.

Uchanski, R., Choi, S., Braida, L., Reed, C., & Durlach, N. (1996). Speaking clearly for the hard of hearing IV: Further studies of the role of speaking rate. *Journal of Speech and Hearing Research, 39,* 494–509.

Vatikiotis-Bateson, E., & Kelso, J. A. (1993). Rhythm type and articulatory dynamics in English, French and Japanese. *Journal of Phonetics, 21,* 231–265.

Vatikiotis-Bateson, E., & Ostry, D. J. (1995). An analysis of the dimensionality of jaw movement in speech. *Journal of Phonetics, 23,* 101–117.

Vilain, A., Abry, C., Badin, P., & Brosda, S. (1999). *From idiosyncratic pure frames to variegated babbling: Evidence from articulatory modeling.* San Francisco, CA: International Congress of Phonetic Sciences.

Walsh, B., & Smith, A. (2002). Articulatory movements in adolescents: Evidence for protracted development of speech motor control processes. *Journal of Speech, Language, and Hearing Research, 45,* 1119–1133.

Warren, D. W. (1986). Compensatory speech behaviors in individuals with cleft palate: A regulation/control phenomenon? *Cleft Palate Journal, 23,* 251–260.

Warren, D. W., Dalston, R. M., & Dalston, E. T. (1990). Maintaining speech pressure in the presence of velopharyngeal impairment. *Cleft Palate Journal, 27,* 53–58.

Warren, D. W., Dalston, R. M., Morr, K. E., Hairfield, W. M., & Smith, L. R. (1989). The speech regulating system: Temporal and aerodynamic responses to velopharyngeal inadequacy. *Journal of Speech and Hearing Research, 32,* 566–575.

Watkin, K. L., & Fromm, D. (1984). Labial coordination in children: Preliminary considerations. *Journal of the Acoustical Society of America, 75,* 629–632.

Weismer, G. (2006). Philosophy of research in motor speech disorders. *Clinical Linguistics and Phonetics*, *20*, 315–349.

Westbury, J. R., Severson, E. J., & Lindstrom, M. J. (2000). Kinematic event patterns in speech: Special problems. *Language and Speech*, *43*, 403–428.

Wilhelm-Tricarico, R. (1996). A biomechanical and physiologically-based vocal tract model and its control. *Journal of Phonetics*, *24*, 23–28.

Wilson, F. R. (1998). *The hand.* New York, NY: Vintage Books.

Wohlert, A. B., & Smith, A. (2002). Developmental change in variability of lip muscle activity during speech. *Journal of Speech, Language, and Hearing Research*, *45*, 1077–1087.

Zajac, D. J., & Weissler, M. C. (2004). Air pressure responses to sudden vocal tract pressure bleeds during production of stop consonants: New evidence of aeromechanical regulation. *Journal of Speech, Language, and Hearing Research*, *47*, 784–801.

11

Theories of Speech Perception

Figure 11–1. Direct connections between the input and the output are not always evident! The activity can be initiated from any point in the sequence.

Sometimes I am not so sure of what I absolutely know!

—King Mongkut of Siam to Anna Leonowens in Rodgers and Hammerstein's *The King and I*

11.1 Introduction

Imagine being in another country where your native language is not spoken, and you don't understand the language spoken there. Everyone speaks so quickly. Even the animals seem to understand what is said in this other language! We may think that this "foreign" language (foreign at least to *our* ears) is spoken at a much faster rate than our native language is spoken, which we perceive at a much slower rate, with clear periods of silence to differentiate the words and sentences. (All languages are spoken at about the same rate—between 8 and 12 phonemes per second.) How do we attend to and understand the rapidly incoming speech signal? What are the elements that allow us to perceive speech and do so in a seemingly effortless manner?

Speech is produced through the continuous sequencing of articulatory vocal tract gestures from one segment to the next, almost like little "beads on a string," but the listener must perceive discontinuities in the flow of speech sounds to make sense of the utterance. How do we reconcile the underlying continuity with the perceptual discontinuities or distinctive features of the auditory signal?

11.2 The Perception of Sound Waves

Our *perception* of the frequency of a sound is not equal to the measured frequency of the pressure wave, nor is our perception of its intensity equivalent to the measured intensity of the wave. Each perceptual construct depends on how well our brain analyzes sounds for frequency and intensity. **Pitch** is the perceptual correlate of frequency and **loudness** is the perceptual correlate of intensity. Pitch and loudness are subjective human judgments based upon a complex interplay of factors. While our perception of pitch is based strongly on the frequency of the sound wave, it is also influenced by the intensity of the sound. Similarly, our perception of loudness, although based primarily on intensity, is also strongly influenced by the frequency. **Psychophysics** is the study of the relationship between the physical properties of a stimulus and our subjective experience of the stimulus. The German experimental psychologist Gustav Fechner (1801–1887), a pioneer in experimental psychology, is credited with noting that the relationship between stimulus intensity and perception of the strength of the stimulus are nonlinear. In other words, the perception of the sound increases as the logarithm of the stimulus. So, to perceive a series of sounds as increasing in loudness with equal increments, the actual intensity of the sounds would have to increase logarithmically. (This information has been recognized since the 1800s. The logarithmic scale corresponds well to perceived intensity differences in the human ear. The human ear is designed to perceive the middle frequencies comprising speech with much less intensity than is needed for very high or very low frequencies.) The psychoacoustic phenomenon of loudness can be measured using the phon or sone scale. Two popular methods that measure the psychoacoustic phenomenon of pitch are the musical semitone scale and the Bark scale.

Perception of Intensity

Loudness refers to how the intensity of the sound is perceived by an individual. As with all perceptions, loudness is a subjective assessment dependent on a variety of factors, including some that can be measured, such as the frequency of the sound and other psychoacoustic phenomena that are not easily measurable. We will return to the topic of loudness and psychoacoustic measurement later in this chapter. Volume is a term commonly used by the layperson to describe loudness. The speech-language pathologist should avoid using volume to refer to intensity or its perceptual correlate, loudness.

The **difference limen** or "just noticeable difference" (often abbreviated JND) is the minimal difference between two sounds that can be perceived as having different loudness levels.

Commonly, the difference limen is 1 dB. However, for very loud sounds, the JND drops to approximately one-third to one-half dB.

The sensitivity of the human ear is highly dependent on frequency. Therefore, two pressure waves of different frequencies, both at 60 dB SPL, will not be perceived as having equal loudness. A psychoacoustic scale for intensity, the **phon scale**, uses a 1,000-Hz pure tone as the reference frequency and is measured in **phons**, the unit of equal loudness. If a given sound is perceived to be equal in loudness to a 60-dB sound at 1,000 Hz, then it is said to have a loudness of 60 phons. If a sound is 60 phons, that means it is as loud as a 1,000-Hz tone produced at 60 dB.

Figure 11–2 displays the variation in the perception of intensity for the average human ear. The very lowest curve (known as the **minimum audibility curve**) represents the intensities that are at the absolute threshold of hearing for young people (as hearing acuity decreases with age) and is also considered to be what is called **audiometric zero** (0 dB HL, measured in units of hearing level). Note the vertical line intersecting 1000 Hz on the *x*-axis. Now look at each of the phon curves (labeled from 0–120) and observe where each curve intercepts the 1000-Hz line. The 10-phon line intercepts the 1000-Hz line at 10 dB, the 20-phon curve intercepts the 1000-Hz line at 20 dB, and so on up to 120 phon, which intercepts the 1000-Hz line at 120 dB. Each curve represents the equivalent loudness level of a 1000-Hz tone across frequencies. For example, the 30-phon line is equally loud at all frequencies as a 1000-Hz tone at 30

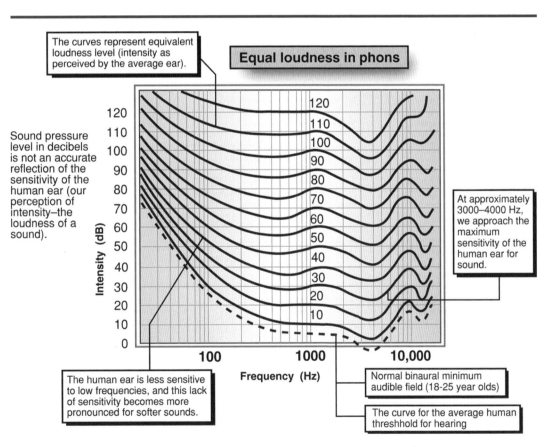

Figure 11–2. Equal loudness curves. Adapted from "Loudness: Its Definition, Measurement, and Calculation," by H. Fletcher and W. A. Munson, 1933, *Journal of the Acoustical Society of America, 5,* p. 90. Reprinted with permission.

dB, and the 50-phon line is equally loud at all frequencies as a 1000-Hz tone produced at 50 dB. In another example, a 100-Hz tone produced at 60 dB would sound as loud as a 1000-Hz tone produced at 50 dB (the 50-phon line). The human voice, as we learned in Chapter 5, is complex, with periodic and aperiodic speech sounds, which means that our perception of its loudness will be different than that of a pure tone. A basic rule of thumb for estimating the loudness of a sound is that the intensity must increase by a factor of 10 for the sound to be perceived as twice as loud. In other words, loudness doubles for every 10-phon increase.

While the phon scale is very useful, especially in the field of audiology, we cannot compare across each phon line to relate the loudness of two sounds of different frequencies. Therefore, another psychoacoustic scale for intensity, the **sone scale**, was created as a linear scale of loudness and derives from orchestral music. It is presumed that the typical range of loudness for an orchestra is 40 to 100 phons. The sone scale was developed by asking individuals to judge when a sound had doubled in loudness relative to a 1000-Hz reference tone produced at 40 dB, which was assigned a value of 1 sone, an arbitrary unit of loudness. For example, 50 phons equal 2 sones, 60 phons equals 4 sones, 70 phons equals 8 sones, and so on. Every 10-dB increase in sound pressure corresponds to an increase of 1 sone.

Perception of Frequency

Our ear is not equally sensitive to frequency change at all intensity levels. Typically, we can hear smaller differences between two lower frequencies than between two higher frequencies. Human auditory perceptual sensitivity to smaller frequency differences means that we can perceive the 100-Hz difference in fundamental frequency between male (f_o = 120 Hz) and female (f_o = 220 Hz) voices very well, but we have considerable difficulty perceiving the 100-Hz difference between 1000 Hz and 1100 Hz.

Many people who sing, play a musical instrument, or read musical notation are familiar with the musical semitone (ST) scale. A scale is simply a series of notes that progress stepwise upward and downward. The **semitone scale** is a chromatic scale, a Western cultural musical scale that consists of 12 tones. Each tone, or pitch, is separated from its neighbor by a semitone, the interval of one half-step. (Play any 12 consecutive keys on the piano, including both the white and black keys, and you have played a chromatic scale [Figure 11–3].) The distance between two frequencies or two pitches is called an interval. A semitone is the smallest distance between two pitches. An octave is 12 semitones. (See Appendix C for a listing of notes and their equivalent frequencies in the musical chromatic scale.) The semitone scale reflects our nonlinear perception of pitch. For example, "middle C" on the piano (designated C4) is equal to 261.63 Hz, and one octave above that (C above middle C, designated C5) is equal to 523.25 Hz, a difference of 261.62 Hz. Go up one more octave to C6, and the difference between 1,046.50 Hz (C6) and 523.25 Hz (C5) is 523.25 Hz. Note that the difference in frequency between octaves increases with increasing pitch. This nonlinear difference accounts for our greater sensitivity to differences between

Figure 11–3. The musical scale.

lower pitches compared to higher pitches. Note also that the difference between each octave is equal to the frequency of the lower pitch. In fact, an octave is equivalent to a doubling of frequency. We can measure the distance between the frequencies of two sounds by dividing the frequency of one sound by the frequency of the second sound.

To determine the semitone difference between two frequencies (that is, to convert a frequency range to a semitone range), use the following formula:

Difference in ST between two frequencies
$$= 39.86 \times \log_{10}(f_{higher}/f_{lower})$$

For example, the difference between average male speech (120 Hz) and female speech (220 Hz) of 100 Hz can be converted to semitones as follows:

$$\text{Difference in ST} = 39.86 \times \log_{10}(200/100)$$
$$= 39.86 \times 2 = 79.72$$

Thus, the difference between the two speakers is approximately 80 semitones. The semitone scale is often used in both research and clinical applications when investigating speaking pitch.

The Bark scale is a mathematically derived scale that converts the acoustic phenomenon of frequency into the psychoacoustic phenomenon of pitch (Miller, 1989). The Bark scale is a *nonlinear transformation* of the frequency scale. In other words, the Bark scale changes, or transforms, our nonlinear perception of pitch into a scale where equal distances on the Bark scale correspond to equal distances in pitch.

Study Questions

1. How does pitch relate to f_o?

2. How does loudness relate to intensity?

3. What is the semitone scale? What is the difference, in semitones, between 392 Hz and 440 Hz?

11.3 Topics in Speech Perception

Theories of speech perception, like theories of speech production, contain both overlapping and distinct aspects. Many of the perception theories are not highly explicit regarding all aspects of speech perception and, thus, experimental testing of these theories is not always an easy matter, nor is it always successful. And, like theories of speech production, the same data can be used to support different perception theories. In general, theories of perception specify the objects of perception and the mapping from sound to object. Many factors complicate the explanation (and, hence, the theories) of our ability to perceive speech in all its varying contexts: lack of invariance, the relevant unit of perceptual analysis, lack of segmentation, perceptual normalization, the degree to which perception of speech is a specialized mechanism, and contextual effects. We consider each of these in turn.

Lack of Invariance

Recall, in Chapter 8, we said that when something is invariant, it does not change. An entire system may be invariant, or one or more features of the system may be invariant. If a feature is invariant, then it does not change even within the context of different operations. We noted that one way of gaining insight into speech motor control is to examine the "sameness" or invariance of articulator movement trajectories. So, too, in the exploration of speech perception, the search for invariant features has contributed to theories of speech perception.

Research data have shown, in general, a lack of acoustic-phonetic invariance. That is, a specific set of acoustic features is not always present for a given phoneme every time the phoneme is produced, regardless of the phonetic context. We saw in Chapters 8 and 9 that the formant patterns and other acoustic features of consonants will change, depending on coarticulatory and prosodic effects. Examine the location and direction of the formants in Figure 11–4. All three formant patterns would result in the

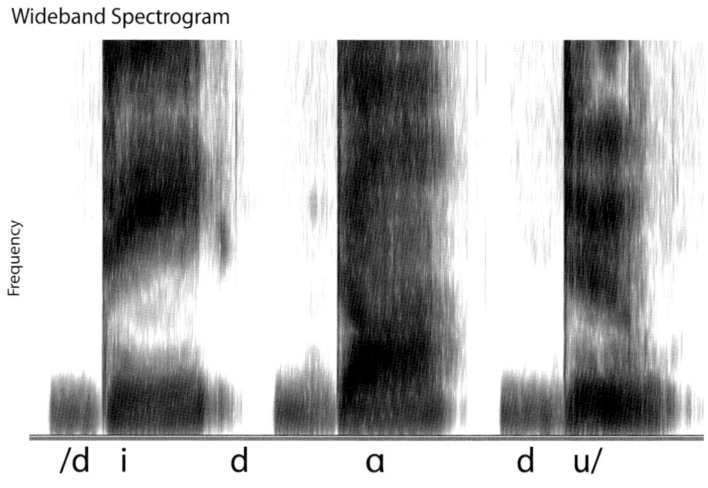

Wideband Spectrogram

Figure 11–4. Wideband spectrogram of /di dɑ du/. Note that the onglide formant pattern is unique for each vowel, and the voice onset time (observe the voice bar) is different for each of the three plosives. Yet each plosive is perceived as /d/. What acoustic cues cause us to perceive the /d/?

perception of the voiced plosive /d/, yet all three formant patterns differ. No one-to-one relationship exists between the formant transitions and the perceived consonant.

The speech signal itself is not linear. If speech were truly linear, then for each phoneme perceived, an invariant corresponding segment of sound would exist within the utterance (Chomsky & Miller, 1963). But we have learned that such a relationship does not exist. Coarticulation, prosody, rate, and effort all result in a lack of invariance and linearity in the speech signal. The lack of invariance and linearity has long been recognized (Delattre, Liberman, & Cooper, 1955) and has been a significant issue, if not the most significant issue, that theories of speech perception must address (Fowler, 1994; Kewly-Port & Luce, 1984; Liberman & Mattingly 1985; Stevens, 1981; Sussman, Hoemeke, & Ahmed, 1993).

Speech and Language Perception

The study of speech perception is generally focused upon the perception of phonemes rather than the perception of syllables, words, or phrases. We rarely notice the specific phoneme unless it is produced inaccurately. Instead, we focus on the utterance. Yet much of the research in speech science in perception is focused at the phonetic level. Although a large body of research has explored word and utterance perception, that research is generally regarded as belonging to language science.

Pattern Playback

A seminal study in the history of research on speech perception is that of Liberman, Delattre, and Cooper (1952) using a machine the authors created called the **Pattern Playback**. This early "talking" machine was built by Cooper at Haskins Laboratories (see Haskins Laboratories later in this chapter) just after World War II. The machine converted spectrographic pictures into sound. The spectrograms were based either upon machine-made sine waves or hand-painted copies of spectrogram segments. The Pattern Playback machine was used throughout the following two decades to learn more about underlying acoustic cues in the perception of speech. Kiefte and Kluender (2005) replicated the original study of Liberman et al. (1952) and, although their findings differed somewhat in details, their data did not challenge the main observations of the researchers using the original Pattern Playback machine.

Unit of Analysis Revisited

In Chapter 10, we noted that determination of the minimum meaningful unit of speech was one major problem that must be considered in theories of speech production. This issue is no less important in theories of speech perception. Consider speech communication as the transfer of bits of information from speaker to listener. Each bit could represent a feature of a phoneme, such as voicing, release burst, or nasal murmur. It has been estimated that this transfer rate occurs at speeds ranging from 40 to 4,000 bits per second (Liberman, Mattingly, & Turvey, 1972). Clearly, some means of chunking, or encoding, bits or features during the transfer of information would greatly increase the efficiency of perception. For example, the features might be encoded into phonemes, which are further encoded into syllables (Pitt & Samuel, 1993), or the features might be encoded directly into the syllable (Massaro & Oden, 1980; Studdert-Kennedy, 1980), into context-sensitive allophones (Wickelgren, 1976) and into context-sensitive spectra (Klatt, 1979).

Lack of Segmentation

In Chapters 7 and 8, we segmented the acoustic signal into events, such as formant transitions and burst noise, to describe vowels and consonants. We also learned that certain features identify the different consonants. One would expect, therefore, that the acoustic signal could be divided into segments that, in isolation, would be perceived as a single consonant. In fact, although we may perceive an utterance as being composed of a series of distinct phonemes, clear boundaries between phonemes cannot be identified to any reliable extent. This lack of clear boundaries between phonemes may be somewhat confusing at first glance. After all, in Chapters 7 and 8, we discussed the features of many different spectrograms that served to identify vowels and consonants. Was this not segmentation of the acoustic waveform? The answer is a qualified "yes." We can segment the acoustic waveform using purely acoustic criteria, which, in fact, we did using the many spectrograms pre-sented earlier. But (and here is the important qualifier) those segmentations frequently do not correspond to the segmentation perceived by the listener (Fant, 1980). If a direct correspondence between acoustic features and perception did exist, then it would be a simpler matter to achieve nearly complete accuracy of computerized speech recognition systems (Goldinger, Pisoni, & Luce, 1996).

Perceptual Normalization

Underlying much of the research on speech perception is the assumption that, as listeners, we convert the acoustic signal into a linear sequence of phonemes. To accomplish this process, the large amount of variability within an utterance and among different utterances must somehow be normalized. **Normalization** refers to the process of simplification by smoothing out variability or "noise" and the unnecessary or superfluous variability to capture better the essence of a signal. Variability between speakers may arise from differences in the physical properties of the larynx and vocal tract, age and gender of a speaker, habits of articulation (including regional differences and accents), and suprasegmental features such as speaking rate. Because we are human beings and not computers, within a given speaker, a significant amount of variability may be expected to occur, driven by linguistic content as well as other variables that are independent of the linguistic content, such as the emotional state of the speaker at one moment in time.

Perceptual normalization implies a simplification of the acoustic signal leading to more efficient comprehension by removing speaker idiosyncrasies (Eisner & McQueen, 2006; Ladefoged, 1989; Ladefoged & Broadbent, 1957). Several factors can assist in normalization, one factor being lexical information. That is, selecting the correct phoneme based upon which word was most likely to have been spoken, given the content of the utterance (Norris, McQueen, & Cutler, 2003). In such a case, familiarity with a speaker's voice can aid in the process of normalization (Nygaard & Pisoni, 1998).

Although most research on speech perception has been focused at the segmental level, suprasegmental information also is important in the process of normalization. Goldinger, Pisoni, and Luce (1996) point out an interesting dichotomy. Listeners can identify an individual known to the listener just from the sound of the speaker's voice alone (Van Lancker, Kreiman, & Emmorey, 1985), and we can identify age (broadly) and gender of the speaker (Abercrombie, 1967). Evidence suggests that suprasegmental features do assist in speech perception, guiding the listener to focus on the parts of the utterance that are semantically most important (Cooper & Sorenson, 1977; Cutler & Fodor, 1979; Darwin, 1975; Studdert-Kennedy, 1980). Therefore, listeners do pay attention to the variability in the speech signal, both using it and ignoring it at the same time.

Study Questions

4. How does the general lack of invariance in the speech signal present a problem for theories of speech perception?

5. How is the problem of unit of analysis, which we addressed in Chapter 10 on Speech Production, relevant to theories of perception?

6. What is segmentation, relative to speech perception?

7. Define normalization and briefly explain its importance in speech perception theories.

Specialized Perception of Speech

Under certain circumstances, if we are told that what we are hearing is not speech, we likely will not perceive speech sounds. Yet if we are told that what we are hearing is speech, then we will likely perceive speech sounds (Remez, Rubin, Pisoni, & Carrell, 1981). Why is that? Is there a uniquely human mechanism for the perceptual

recognition of speech sounds? Or can the perception of speech be explained by general theories of perception used to explain human recognition of other sensory phenomena, such as the perception of visual stimuli or sounds of animals and machines and things like the wind and waves that are sounds but not speech sounds? A large body of research has explored the potential specialization of perception of speech, much of it based on ambiguous stimuli, that is, sounds that may or may not come from the speech signal. A few examples of such research will clarify what is meant by ambiguous stimuli.

Liberman and Mattingly (1985) and Studdert-Kennedy (1980) have proposed that speech perception involves specialized, uniquely human, neural processes. This theory arises largely from a seminal study by Liberman, Harris, Hoffman, and Griffith (1957), in which a continuum of synthetically produced consonant-vowel (CV) syllables from /b/ to /d/ to /g/ were generated by changing the transition of the second formant in small, graded increments. Listeners perceived sharp discontinuities in sounds, despite the small, gradual changes in formant transitions. That is, in listening to each slightly altered syllable in sequential order, a sudden shift in plosive was perceived. Listeners categorized the syllables into three distinct categories, identifying /b/, /d/, or /g/.

In Chapter 6, we noted that the abrupt transition from one state to another due to a continuously changing variable is called a quantal change (Stevens, 1972). In **categorical perception**, stimuli that vary along some continuously changing dimension are perceived as belonging to two or more discrete categories. That is, people will "chunk" stimuli into categories to facilitate understanding of the utterance, based on exemplars of those stimuli (Kuhl, 1991). Those stimuli that are perceived as belonging to the same category can be quite difficult to discriminate, leading to errors in speech perception. The phenomenon of discontinuous, categorical perception is an example of the **quantal perception** of speech sounds. Quantal perception does not occur with nonspeech sounds (Kewley-Port & Luce, 1984), hence leading some researcher to propose a specialized mechanism for speech perception (Repp, 1982). The **motor theory of speech perception**, described later in this chapter, is based on quantal change in perception.

Other researchers, however, propose that the data from Liberman et al. (1957) do not support a unique mechanism for speech perception. Further, quantal perception does not necessarily occur in a continuum of changing vowels (Fry, Abramson, Eimas, & Liberman, 1962), contributing a further question to the position of specialized speech processing. Miller, Wier, Pastore, Kelley, and Dooling (1976) used nonspeech stimuli to simulate different durations of voice onset time (VOT). (Recall that VOT is the duration between the release of the closed portion of the plosive and the onset of voicing.) An aperiodic noise burst was followed by a periodic buzz-like sound. Subjects were asked to distinguish between the "noise" and the "no-noise" stimuli. The researchers found that participants could—and did—identify the two phenomena correctly, suggesting categorical perception for nonspeech stimuli. Other researchers (Eimas & Miller, 1980; Jusczyk, Pisoni, Walley, & Murray, 1980; Pisoni, 1977; Pisoni, Carrell, & Gans, 1983)

Talking With the Animals

Animal research in speech perception adds a unique perspective on the debate regarding a uniquely human mechanism for speech perception. Kuhl (1987) found that chinchillas demonstrate categorical perception of speech, yet obviously these animals have no specialized speech-processing mechanism. Some evidence exists for categorical perception for place of articulation in primates (Morse & Snowdon, 1975) and Japanese quail (Kluender, Diehl, & Killeen, 1987). The problem with these types of data, however, is pointed out very well by Goldinger, Pisoni, and Luce (1996) and Repp (1983), who note that the fact that animal behaviors may resemble those of human beings does not in any way mean that animal and human behaviors derive from a similar underlying mechanism.

had similar findings with other types of synthetic stimuli. Just as we found in Chapter 10, research data can be used as "evidence" for theories that are direct opposites of each other.

Duplex Perception

The phenomenon known as *duplex perception* also has been cited as evidence both for (Repp, 1982; Whalen & Liberman, 1987) and against (Fowler & Rosenblum, 1990; Pastore, Schmeckler, Rosenblum, & Szczesiul, 1983) the theory of a specialized perceptual mechanism for speech. **Duplex perception**, first described by Rand (1974), is the simultaneous perception of nonspeech and speech stimuli extracted from segments of the speech signal. A common example is two syllables that differ only by a single acoustic cue are divided into two parts, such as /da/ and /ga/, which differ critically in the transition of the third formant. The remainder of the syllable, called the base, is the same for both syllables. In isolation, the F3 transitions are perceived as whistle-like, called chirps. The base is perceived as an ambiguous syllable. When the base is presented to a listener through one earphone of a headset, and the chirp is presented through the other headphone (called a dichotic listening task), the listener hears simultaneously the chirp and either the syllable /da/ or /ga/, depending upon the onset frequency of the F3 transition. The perception of a completed syllable has been interpreted to mean that speech perception takes precedence over nonspeech perception. Fowler and Rosenblum (1990), on the other hand, suggest that this phenomenon indicates only that meaningful sounds (such as speech, as compared to a formant chirp) take precedence over nonmeaningful sounds. This position is part of Fowler's **direct-realist theory** of speech perception, discussed later in this chapter.

The McGurk Effect

Additional evidence used to support the theory of a unique mechanism for the perception of speech is a perceptual illusion known as the **McGurk effect** (McGurk & McDonald, 1976; Roberts & Summerfield, 1981). McGurk and

McDonald (1976) created a film in which a speaker produced the syllable /ga/ but the syllable /ba/ was dubbed into the soundtrack, so the viewer observed the lip gesture for /ga/ but heard /ba/. Surprisingly, the researchers found that the subjects, and even they themselves, heard neither /ga/ nor /ba/ but rather /da/! The articulatory information from both the auditory and visual perceptions was combined to yield a different phoneme. In other words, given an incongruity in aurally and visually presented stimuli, a third and unique stimulus is perceived. Although the McGurk effect has been cited as evidence of unique perception for speech (Liberman & Mattingly, 1985), others (Massaro & Cohen, 1993) hold that the illusion does not indicate any uniqueness in speech perception.

Contextual Effect

Perception of speech can be influenced by contextual information, such as the semantic meaning of an utterance. In a seminal study, Remez, Rubin, Pisoni, and Carrell (1981) demonstrated the critical importance of contextual cues upon perception with the use of "sinewave speech." **Sinewave speech** is composed of sine waves that track the center frequencies of F1, F2, and F3 of a naturally produced sentence. In other words, a "real" sentence, as spoken by a human being, is recorded. Next, the center frequencies of the first three formants are identified. Then, the spectral content of the signal is removed and replaced with sine waves, the frequencies of which are located along the frequencies of the formants previously identified. The "voice" quality of the resulting acoustic signal is quite unnatural, to be sure. However, when listeners are told that they are listening to actual speech, they could understand the sentences correctly with a high degree of accuracy. This study had a strong impact on the field of speech perception, shifting some of the research emphasis away from identifying underlying phonetic perceptual cues and toward more global features. It has been argued that sinewave speech provides evidence for the uniqueness of speech perception (Carrell & Opie, 1992).

Warren and Warren (1970) tested the effect of semantic meaning on speech perception with simple sentences, such as, "It was found that the wheel was on the shoe." They replaced the /w/ in "wheel" with a cough. Subjects perceived the sentence accurately and did not perceive that the /w/ was missing. A task used to demonstrate the effect of context on perceptual recognition of words is called the gating task (Grossjean, 1980). Listeners are presented with a sequence of fragments of a word. The fragments become progressively longer. For example, t-tr-tre-tres-tresp-trespa-trespass. Generally, the fragments are increased in increments of 50 ms. The listeners try to identify the word after the presentation of each successive fragment. This process is called gating. It takes approximately one-third of a second to identify the word within a gating task, whereas it takes only approximately one-fifth of a second to identify the word within a semantically meaningful context correctly.

Study Questions

8. Can you describe the seminal study that led to the theory that humans have specialized neural mechanisms for the perception of speech?

9. Define categorical and quantal perception and the motor theory of speech perception.

10. Define duplex perception and briefly describe the research study that describes this phenomenon.

11. What is the McGurk effect?

12. How does context affect speech perception?

11.4 Theories of Speech Perception

Theories of speech perception are many and complex, some with overlapping features and others with highly disparate approaches. Categorizing the theories into larger groups can be advantageous because it helps us to understand the broad viewpoints of each theory. Yet such categorization is problematic in that theories rarely fit neatly into a single category. We review briefly two influential approaches to categorizing theories of speech perception, those of Kent (1997) and those of Goldinger, Pisoni, and Luce (1996).

Kent (1997) organizes an approach to theories of speech perception by grouping their general attributes: bottom-up/top-down, active/passive, and autonomous/interactive. The bottom-up theories are those in which the acoustic signal provides essential and sufficient information for perceptual recognition. In this approach, the link between the information received and the perceptual recognition is direct, with no or minimal intervening stage. This approach is also referred to as *data driven*, precisely because the data obtained from the acoustic signal drive or direct, the listener's perception of speech. In the top-down approach, the information from the acoustic signal is not sufficient for perceptual recognition. Higher level information from contextual, linguistic, and cognitive cues is necessary for accurate speech perception. Kent does acknowledge that no theory is completely bottom-up or top-down and that, certainly, all theories must rely, to some extent, on the acoustic signal. Rather, theories might emphasize more the

direct connection to the underlying acoustic signal (bottom-up) or the need for additional information processing from other cues (top-down).

The active/passive grouping of general attributes of theories of speech perception addresses a related concept—the degree to which information in addition to the acoustic signal is necessary. Active theories emphasize the cognitive role in perception, including the formation and testing of hypotheses about the phonetic or linguistic interpretation of the information in the acoustic signal. In contrast, passive theories postulate a smaller role for cognitive processing and presume a more automatic perceptual response.

And finally, Kent (1997) identifies the autonomous/interactive features of theories of perception. An autonomous theory posits that perceptual processing occurs in the absence of external data, such as communicative context or general knowledge. In other words, perception occurs within a closed system. In contrast, interactive theories are open systems, in which the stages of perceptual processing access data external to that which is contained within the acoustic signal. Certainly, no theory of speech perception is wholly active or wholly autonomous, just as no theory is wholly passive or wholly interactive. Rather, these categorizations are simply one tool that can be applied to the analysis of an otherwise highly complex set of theories of speech perception.

Haskins Laboratories

Outstanding research is conducted by numerous scientists throughout the world on many aspects of speech perception. Haskins Laboratories, originally located in New York City and now in New Haven, Connecticut, has produced a large amount of remarkable research. Haskins Laboratories is a private, nonprofit research laboratory founded in 1935 and named after its founder, Dr. Caryl P. Haskins. The current and past presidents of Haskins Laboratories were major research scientists, all of whom you have met in the pages of this textbook, Dr. Franklin Cooper (president 1955–1975), Dr. Alvin Liberman (president 1975–1986), Dr. Michael Studdert-Kennedy (president 1986–1992), Dr. Carol Fowler (1992–2008), and, currently, Dr. Ken Pugh. Research on human communication at Haskins Laboratories has provided groundbreaking work in diverse areas of human communication, including speech production and motor behavior; speech perception, synthesis, and analysis; nonlinear dynamics; and complexity theory, as well as linguistics and phonetics.

Goldinger et al. (1996) use a different approach to grouping theories of speech perception. They divide the theories into those that specifically address speech perception and those that address word recognition. Speech perception theories (most theories on the general topic of perception of the acoustic signal) focus on identification of phonemes within the speech signal. Word recognition theories focus on the process by which a sequence of phonemes is transferred to lexical representations held in the memory of the listener. Some of the theories of both speech perception and word recognition are presented in a brief overview. We turn now to a brief review of individual theories. All these theories are highly complex, and the interested reader is directed to Goldinger et al. (1996) as well as the original research, cited throughout the following discussion.

Motor Theory

The well-known motor theory of speech perception (Liberman, Cooper, Shankweiler, & Studdert-Kennedy, 1967; Liberman & Mattingly, 1985) posits that speech perception is based on invariant articulatory gestures. That is, speech perception uses the motor commands of the speech production system as the units of perception. The listener accesses his or her own knowledge of how sounds are produced and then uses that reference to process the perception of sounds produced by another individual.

Three key features describe the motor theory: the biological specialization of perception for speech, analysis by synthesis, and the lack of invariant aspects of the acoustic signal. Earlier in this chapter, we discussed the concept of a specialized mechanism for the perception of speech and the arguments that are used to support and refute that position. In analysis by synthesis (Liberman & Mattingly, 1985), the auditory patterns, or features, are mapped onto a language-specific representation, such as phonemes or gestures. The mapping is accomplished by means of a mechanism that takes the basic unit, such as

the syllable, and generates the equivalent auditory pattern and matches it against the input. The extent to which the auditory pattern and the input match each other serves as the feedback, which then acts to correct the proposed unit. The process repeats itself until a sufficiently accurate match has been achieved. Analysis by synthesis, therefore, refers to perception as an iterative process in which the iterations involve articulation. The third major premise of motor theory is that invariant features are not attributes of the acoustic signal but rather are attributes of the perception itself. That is, the units of perception that provide the phonetic information for the listener are the underlying, *intended* articulatory gestures and not the actual physical movements of the articulators themselves.

One of the criticisms of the motor theory is that categorical perception does not necessarily mean that motor theory is correct and that some of the assumptions about perception upon which motor theory rests have little empirical foundation. Furthermore, the specific mechanism for analysis by synthesis and for linking intended gesture to perception has not been clearly described. And finally, iterative computations are inherently inefficient and slow and may not be realistic for "online" monitoring. Echoing the general discussion about theories, models, and parsimony in the beginning of Chapter 10, Klatt (1989) notes that the vagueness of the motor theory makes it more of a philosophy than a theory or model.

Direct-Realist Theory

The direct-realist theory is based on the work of Fowler (Fowler, 1986, 1990; Fowler & Dekle, 1991), which derives from the theories of visual perception by Gibson (1966) and the concept of a percept. A **percept** is that which the listener hears—the "object"—as contrasted with the actual acoustic event. (Recall that perception is a subjective occurrence that rarely, if ever, matches exactly the actual physical event being perceived.) The direct-realist theory presumes a direct mapping from acoustic qualities to the gestures that produce them. That is, perception consists of a single step from the acoustic signal to the percept. An example commonly used from general perception theory is that of looking at a chair. We perceive the chair by recognizing the object as a whole. This direct link contrasts with the analysis-by-synthesis premise of the motor theory, in which we recognize the chair by processing the individual parts and then building that into a percept of a chair.

A strength of the direct-realist theory is that it places speech perception within the larger context of general theories of event perception. Furthermore, the proposed lack of cognitive mediation of the acoustic signal would allow for faster perceptual processing than that proposed by the motor theory. However, a major criticism of the direct-realist theory is that it heavily underestimates the computational complexity of perception. In addition, considerable additional empirical support is needed to validate this theory.

Native Language Magnet Theory

The **native language magnet theory** (Frieda, Walley, Flege, & Sloane, 1999, 2000; Kuhl, 1991; Kuhl & Meltzoff, 1996) holds that the phonetic categories of one's native language are organized as prototypes, which begin in infancy by attracting or assimilating nearby members of the same phonetic category. Such prototypes are called "perceptual magnets." They facilitate processing of speech information that is linguistically relevant by distinguishing irrelevant distinctions close to the prototype from important distinctions near category boundaries. In this way, the perceptual magnets enhance the differences between distinct phonemes. Kuhl and Meltzoff (1996) propose that the infant's exposure to his or her native language results in the organization of native vowels into these prototypes, which form the basis not only of his or her perception but also the production of his or her native language. One of the weaknesses of

this theory is the lack of a generic prototype, given the variability of vowel production across speakers of the same language (Frieda, Walley, Flege, & Sloane, 1999).

Acoustic Landmarks and Distinctive Features

Stevens (2002) proposed a model of speech perception in which words are represented in memory as a sequence of segments, each of which consists of a bundle of binary (on or off) distinctive features. Perception is based on landmark detection, using points of minimal and maximal change. Acoustic correlates are measured near landmarks, and estimation is made of distinctive features and syllable structure. A match to lexicon is conducted, using lexical information to synthesize a set of landmarks and cues, which is then compared to the acoustics correlated in the vicinity of the landmarks, and error correction is made. Analysis is based on a process of segmentation and landmark identification. The landmarks are driven by articulatory considerations. Only one underlying representation for each lexical item is presented.

In Stevens' model, three sets of landmarks are used: vocalic, glide, and consonantal. In the vocalic landmark, the targets are the frequency and amplitude of F1 in the vowel in an area in which no spectral discontinuities are present. For glides, the targets are the F1 profile and the reduction in amplitude, again limited to a region in which no spectral discontinuities exist. For consonants, the target is the point of abrupt spectral discontinuity. Consonants are classified further as continuant, sonorant, and strident, based on closure, and the distribution of energy at the higher frequencies. This spectral information of the landmarks is considered "articulator free." In contrast, "articulator-bound" features would be spectral information around the landmarks that specify the features related to the position and movement of the articulators. Relative to vowels, such features would include high, low, back, and forward, for example. For consonants, such features would include constriction location, such as the lips, and vocal fold activity (voiced or not). In this theory, each articulator bound feature is a module represented in the brain, which in turn is a genetic endowment for language.

TRACE

The premise of the **TRACE model** (Elman & McClellan, 1988; McClelland & Elman, 1986) is that speech units are arranged into three interactive levels: features, phonemes, and words. Each level comprises nodes, or processing units. For example, at the feature level, one node would detect voicing, and another would detect lip rounding. Certain groups of nodes share excitatory activation. For example, in the word "pat," the phoneme /p/ would share excitatory connections with features corresponding to the voiceless bilabial plosive. Other nodes would share inhibitory links, such as those features associated with the vowel following the plosive. In theory, these excitatory and inhibitory links would preserve the listener's ability to discriminate among different phonemes. To perceive continuous speech, according to the TRACE model, initial activation of the feature nodes is followed by activation of the phoneme nodes and then finally the word nodes. In other words, activation occurs from the bottom upward. Activation can also spread from the top downward, which in theory would account for contextual influence upon perception of individual phonemes.

A major premise of the TRACE model is that perception is represented as a process of multiple stages involving a one-to-many and a many-to-one mapping. Feedback and competition among nodes at the same level are used to stabilize perception. In summary, the TRACE model consists of an auditory front end (the ear), auditory feature extraction, a phonetic level, and a lexical level. TRACE is implemented within a connectionist architecture and has both feedforward and feedback connections within and between each level.

A criticism of TRACE theory is that only a limited set of features is implemented: phonemes

and words. It remains uncertain whether such a limited set of features can be used to account for all the different types of voices, speaking rates, and variability of a given language.

The Cohort Theory

Goldinger et al. (1996) identify the **cohort theory** as a word recognition theory. Kent (1997) identifies this theory as emphasizing a passive, bottom-up, autonomous approach. In the cohort theory (Marslen-Wilson, 1987; Marslen-Wilson & Tyler, 1975), the beginning of a word is perceived and then all words that have that beginning—the cohort—are reviewed, from which the correct word is selected. The cohort is formed based only on similar acoustic features. Only after the initial cohort is selected are semantic and grammatic features considered to narrow the selection process.

Study Questions

13. Briefly review the approaches to categorization of speech perception theories by Kent (1997) and Goldinger et al. (1996).

14. Explain the three key features that describe the motor theory of speech perception.

15. What is a percept and how is it relevant to the direct-realist theory of speech perception?

16. What are the three sets of landmarks used in Stevens' (2002) model of speech perception?

17. What is the major premise of the TRACE model of speech perception?

18. Briefly define the cohort theory of speech perception.

Teaching Computers to Talk

In a scene from a 1986 science-fiction movie, *Star Trek IV: The Voyage Home*, in which the crew of a futuristic space ship travels back in time to the 1980s, two of the crew members are faced with a computer of the time. Trying to communicate with it, one of the crew members says, "Computer. Computer?" Obtaining no response, he tries again by talking into the mouse. When advised that he should use the keyboard, the crew member responds, "Keyboard. How quaint."

When the movie first came out, the scene was amusing because, of course, we knew that computers could not understand speech. Thirty years later, however, the scene is not as funny, because computers can understand speech—to an extent.

What does it mean that a computer can "understand" speech? It means that the computer can convert an acoustic signal that it receives into written text or respond by generating its own acoustic signal. The computer program must be provided with the meaning and pronunciation of some basic words and commonly appearing word sequences. The programs will perform best if they are provided with a period of training in which they can learn the pronunciations and word sequences of an individual. For those programs that must respond to hundreds of individuals, such as those used to respond to customer services calls, the human speaker is constrained to use a much smaller set of words. In that way, the computer can handle the large variability in speaking style. In addition to learning the lexicon, the grammar, and the pronunciation, computers must also learn how to converse. Prosodic features are used to train computers to learn conversational rules, so that the computer "knows" when it is its turn to speak (Edlung & Heldern, 2005). Speech recognition by computers is important in the field of speech-language pathology, with the potential for significant clinical application for patients with motor speech problems (Parker, Cunningham, Enderby, Hawley, & Green, 2006).

11.5 What Babies Can Tell Us About Perception

The exploration of the mechanics of speech perception has included study of infants for a few reasons. Adults are likely to rely on their knowledge base of syntax, semantics, and pragmatics in the perceptual process, rather than rely only on the acoustic signal. This multilevel coding makes it much more complicated to understand specific perceptual processes within an experimental design. In addition, the perceptual experiences of an adult are extensive and not completely known. These unknown experiences likely influence speech perception in complex ways. Research with infants may limit, to some extent, this confounding variable. However, this approach is based upon the assumption that the infant perceptual system is, mechanistically, like that of the adult, an assumption that may not be true. The infant's perceptual system is immaturely developed and may well function differently than an adult's. Eliminating perceptual experience may yield only a different system of perception, rather than some type of core system untarnished by experience. Nevertheless, research on infant perception has yielded important information.

Methodology in infant research can be grouped broadly into two strategies. First, much of infant research involves assessing reaction to auditory stimuli. If two different auditory stimuli are presented to an infant, and the infant reacts uniquely and consistently to each one, then we presume that the infant detected a difference between the two stimuli (Eimas, 1975; Moffit, 1971). Alternatively, the infant can be trained to react in certain ways to different stimuli. Then, on presentation of a novel (new) stimulus, if the infant reacts in one of the manners previously trained, the assumption is made that the infant somehow identifies or categorizes the new stimulus with one of the prior groups of sounds.

The motor theory, which emphasizes articulatory knowledge as a basis for speech perception, would lead one to expect that an infant might have a different mechanism of speech perception than that of an adult. Eimas, Siqueland, Jusczyk, and Vigorito (1971) provided the first set of data to suggest that infants as young as 1 month old could perceive differences between speech sounds. Subsequently, additional studies confirmed their findings (Moffitt, 1971; Trehub & Rabinovitch, 1972). This information leads naturally to additional studies to determine what contrasts in phonemes and phonemic features are distinguishable by infants, focusing particularly on consonants rather than vowels (Aslin & Pisoni, 1980; Eimas & Miller, 1980; Hillenbrand, Minifie, & Edwards, 1979). In general, these research data show that by 4 months of age, infants can discriminate basic contrasts in their native language.

The ability of infants to discriminate such basic native contrasts suggested that certain speech perception capacities represent innate mechanisms, which led to further questions regarding whether such capacities were specific to speech in general and to the infant's native language specifically (Jusczyk, 1996, p. 334). Although methodologic issues are not insignificant in infant research, much of the early data suggested that infants have the capacity to discriminate, with little training, between nonnative phonemic features and, furthermore, that continued exposure to a dominant language decreases that ability (Eilers, Wilson, & Moore, 1979; Eimas, Miller, & Jusczyk, 1987; Trehub, 1976; Werker & Lalonde, 1988).

The question of a specialized mechanism for speech perception is pondered equally in infants as in adults. Early exploration documented the differences in discrimination of speech and nonspeech stimuli in infants (Eimas,

1974), but other research demonstrated infants' abilities to discriminate nonspeech contrasting stimuli (Jusczyk, Pisoni, Walley, & Murray, 1980; Jusczyk, Rosner, Reed, & Kennedy, 1989). Such studies with infants are methodologically challenging and therefore available data are limited. Nevertheless, these studies do provide equivocal evidence for specialized processing of speech information. Clearly, additional research data are needed to clarify this topic.

Like the question about the perception of language by adults, the question of perceptual normalization in infants—how infants learn to understand words despite the variability within and between speakers—is an important area of research (Kuhl, 1979). Evidence from several studies (Jusczyk, Pisoni, & Mullennix, 1992; Kuhl & Miller, 1982; Miller & Eimas, 1983) suggests that infants can manage the inherent variability in the speech signal, including changes in pitch contour and voice quality (Jusczyk, Pisoni, & Mullennix, 1992; Kuhl, 1983) and rate (Eimas & Miller, 1980), although at some cost to speech processing. That is, compensation for rate and pitch variations do occur but may interfere with comprehension to some extent.

Speech perception is not, of course, an isolated phenomenon in the maturation of infants. Factors such as memory and attention (Jusczyk, Bertoncini, Bijeljac-Babic, Kennedy, & Mehler, 1990; Kuhl, 1987) and language acquisition (Gleitman & Wanner, 1982; Morgan, 1986) interact with speech perception. Although these topics are well beyond the scope of this textbook, currently they provide some of the most fertile areas in research on the development of perception in infants.

Study Questions

19. What are the two broad strategies used in research studies on infant perception of speech?

20. Can you briefly review some of the findings of studies on infant speech perception?

Teaching Old Dogs New Tricks

As adults, we lose the ability to discriminate between phonemes that are not phonemically contrastive in our native language (Aslin & Pisoni, 1980; Lisker & Abramson, 1964; Polka, 1992). In fact, some evidence suggests that adults require extensive training to be able to discriminate reliably among phonemes of a nonnative language (Strange & Dittmann, 1984), which can be measured electrophysiologically (Tremblay, Kraus, Carrell, & McGee, 1997). Eimas (1975) posited that phonetic categories are a function of neural connections that are plastic (alterable) in youth but become less flexible as adults (which harkens to the old saw "You can't teach an old dog new tricks!"). Other research, however, suggests that, with appropriately targeted teaching stimuli and methodology, adults can learn to discriminate nonnative phonemic contrasts well (Logan, Lively, & Pisoni, 1991). (There may be hope for old dogs yet!)

Recommended Internet Sites for Further Learning

http://clsp.jhu.edu/

The Center for Language and Speech Processing at Johns Hopkins University has several interesting videos of seminars on various topics of speech perception. Many are rather advanced. Examples include:

Temporal primitives in auditory cognition and speech perception. David Poeppel, University of Maryland, December 2, 2008.

Detecting Deceptive Speech, Julia Hirschberg, Columbia University, October 2, 2007.

http://www.youtube.com/watch?v=73LE1vKG fy4&NR=1

Video demonstrating the McGurk effect.

http://www.phon.ucl.ac.uk/cgi-bin/wtutor?tutorial=pitch

The University College London pitch tutorial by Mark Huckvale provides much high-quality information on psychoacoustics.

References

Abercrombie, D. (1967). *Elements of general phonetics*. Chicago, IL: Aldine.

Aslin, R. N., & Pisoni, D. B. (1980). Some developmental processes in speech perception. In G. Yeni-Komshian, J. F. Kavanagh, & C. A. Ferguson (Eds.), *Child phonology: Perception and production* (pp. 67–96). New York, NY: Academic Press.

Carrell, T. D., & Opie, J. M. (1992). The effect of amplitude comodulation on auditory object formation in sentence perception. *Perception and Psychophysics, 52,* 437–445.

Chomsky, N., & Miller, G. A. (1963). Introduction to the formal analysis of natural language. In R. D. Luce, R. Bush, & E. Galanter (Eds.), *Handbook of mathematical psychology* (Vol. 2, pp. 269–321). New York, NY: Wiley.

Cooper, W. E., & Sorenson, J. (1977). Fundamental frequency contours at syntactic boundaries. *Journal of the Acoustical Society of America, 62,* 683–692.

Cutler, A., & Fodor, J. A. (1979). Semantic focus and sentence comprehension. *Cognition, 7,* 49–59.

Darwin, C. J. (1975). On the dynamic use of prosody in speech perception. In A. Cohen & S. G. Nooteboom (Eds.), *Structure and process in speech perception* (pp. 178–194). Heidelberg, Germany: Springer-Verlag.

Delattre, P. C., Liberman, A. M., & Cooper, F. S. (1955). Acoustic loci and transitional cues for consonants. *Journal of the Acoustical Society of America, 27,* 769–773.

Edlung, J., & Heldner, M. (2005). Exploring prosody in interaction control. *Phonetica, 62,* 215–226.

Eilers, R. E., Wilson, W. R., & Moore, J. M. (1979). Speech discrimination in the language-innocent and language-wise: A study in the perception of voice onset time. *Journal of Child Language, 6,* 1–18.

Eimas, P. D. (1974). Auditory and linguistic units of processing of cues for place of articulation by infants. *Perception and Psychophysics, 16,* 513–521.

Eimas, P. D. (1975). Auditory and phonetic coding of the cues for speech: Discrimination of the [r-l] distinction by young infants. *Perception and Psychophysics, 18,* 341–347.

Eimas, P. D., & Miller, J. L. (1980). Contextual effects in infant speech perception. *Science, 209,* 1140–1141.

Eimas, P. D., Miller, J. L., & Jusczyk, P. W. (1987). On infant speech perception and the acquisition of language. In S. Harnad (Ed.), *Categorical perception* (pp. 178–194). New York, NY: Cambridge University Press.

Eimas, P. D., Siqueland, E. R., Jusczyk, P., & Vigorito, J. (1971). Speech perception in infants. *Science, 171,* 303–306.

Eisner, F., & McQueen, J. (2006). Perceptual learning in speech: Stability over time. *Journal of the Acoustical Society of America, 119,* 1950–1953.

Elman, J. L., & McClelland, J. L. (1988). Cognitive penetration of the mechanisms of perception: Compensation for co-articulation of lexically restored phonemes. *Journal of Memory and Language, 27,* 143–165.

Fant, G. (1980). The relations between area functions and the acoustic signal. *Phonetics, 37,* 55–86.

Fowler, C. A. (1986). An event approach to the study of speech perception from a direct-realist perspective. *Journal of Phonetics, 14,* 3–28.

Fowler, C. A. (1990). Sound-producing sources as objects of perception: Rate normalization and nonspeech perception. *Journal of the Acoustical Society of America, 88,* 1236–1249.

Fowler, C. A. (1994). Invariants, specifiers, cues: An investigation of locus equations as information for place of articulation. *Perception and Psychophysics, 55,* 597–610.

Fowler, C. A., & Dekle, D. J. (1991). Listening with eye and hand: Cross-modal contributions to speech perception. *Journal of Experimental Psychology: Human Perception and Performance, 17,* 816–828.

Fowler, C. A., & Rosenblum, L. D. (1990). Duplex perception: A comparison of monosyllables and slamming of doors. *Journal of Experimental Psychology: Human Perception and Performance, 16,* 742–754.

Frieda, E. M., Walley, A. C., Flege, J. E., & Sloane, M. E. (1999). Adults' perception of native and nonnative vowels: Implications for the perceptual magnet effect. *Perception and Psychophysics, 61,* 561–577.

Frieda, E. M., Walley, A. C., Flege, J. E., & Sloane, M. E. (2000). Adults' perception and production of the English vowel /i/. *Journal of Speech, Language, and Hearing Research, 43,* 129–143.

Fry, D. B., Abramson, A. S., Eimas, P. D., & Liberman, A. M. (1962). The identification and discrimination of synthetic vowels. *Language and Speech, 5,* 171–189.

Gibson, J. J. (1966). *The senses considered as perceptual systems.* Boston, MA: Houghton-Mifflin.

Gleitman, L., & Wanner, E. (1982). The state of the state of the art. In E. Wanner & L. Gleitman (Eds.), *Language acquisition: The state of the art* (pp. 3–48). Cambridge, UK: Cambridge University Press.

Goldinger, S. D., Pisoni, D. B., & Logan, J. S. (1991). The nature of talker variability effects on recall of spoken word lists. *Journal of Experimental Psychology: Learning, Memory, and Cognition, 17,* 152–162.

Goldinger, S. D., Pisoni, D. B., & Luce, P. A. (1996). Speech perception and spoken word recognition: Research and theory. In N. J. Lass (Ed.), *Principles of experimental phonetics* (pp. 3–48). St. Louis, MO: Mosby.

Grosjean, F. (1980). Spoken word recognition processes and the gating paradigm. *Perception and Psychophysics, 28,* 267–283.

Hillenbrand, J., Minifie, F. D., & Edwards, T. J. (1979). Tempo of spectrum change as a cue in speech sound discrimination by infants. *Journal of Speech and Hearing Research, 22,* 147–165.

Jusczyk, P. W. (1996). Developmental speech perception. In N. J. Lass (Ed.), *Principles of experimental phonetics* (pp. 328–361). St. Louis, MO: Mosby.

Jusczyk, P. W., Bertoncini, J., Bijeljac-Babic, R., Kennedy, L. J., & Mehler, J. (1990). The role of attention in speech perception by young infants. *Cognitive Development, 5,* 265–286.

Jusczyk, P. W., Pisoni, D. B., & Mullennix, J. (1992). Some consequences of stimulus variability on speech processing by 2-month-old infants. *Cognition, 43,* 253–291.

Jusczyk, P. W., Pisoni, D. B., Walley, A. C., & Murray, J. (1980). Discrimination of relative onset time of two-component tones by infants. *Journal of the Acoustical Society of America, 67,* 262–270.

Jusczyk, P. W., Rosner, B. S., Reed, M., & Kennedy, L. J. (1989). Could temporal order differences underlie 2-month-olds' discrimination of English voicing contrasts? *Journal of the Acoustical Society of America, 85,* 1741–1749.

Kent, R. D. (1997). *The speech sciences.* San Diego, CA: Singular.

Kewley-Port, D., & Luce, P. A. (1984). Time-varying features of initial stop consonants in auditory running spectra: A first report. *Perception and Psychophysics, 35*, 353–360.

Kiefte, M., & Kluender, K. R. (2005). Pattern playback revisited: Unvoiced stop consonant perception. *Journal of the Acoustical Society of America, 118*, 2599–2606.

Klatt, D. H. (1979). Speech perception: A model of acoustic-phonetic analysis and lexical access. *Journal of Phonetics, 7*, 279–312.

Klatt, D. H. (1989). Review of selected models of speech perception. In W. D. Marslen-Wilson (Ed.), *Lexical representation and process* (pp. 159–226). Cambridge, MA: MIT Press.

Kluender, K. R., Diehl, R. L., & Killeen, P. R. (1987). Japanese quail can learn phonetic categories. *Science, 237*, 1195–1197.

Kuhl, P. K. (1979). Speech perception in early infancy. Perceptual constancy for spectrally dissimilar vowel categories. *Journal of the Acoustical Society of America, 66*, 1668–1679.

Kuhl, P. K. (1983). Perception of auditory equivalent classes for speech in early infancy. *Infant Behavior and Development, 6*, 263–285.

Kuhl, P. K. (1987). The special mechanisms debate in speech research: Categorization tests on animals and infants. In S. Harnad (Ed.), *Categorical per-ception: The groundwork of cognition* (pp. 355–386). Cambridge, UK: Cambridge University Press.

Kuhl, P. K. (1991). Human adults and infants show a "perceptual magnet effect" for prototypes of speech categories, monkeys do not. *Perception and Psychophysics, 50*, 93–107.

Kuhl, P. K., & Meltzoff, A. N. (1996) Infant vocalizations in response to speech: Vocal imitation and developmental change. *Journal of the Acoustical Society of America, 100*, 2425–2438.

Kuhl, P. K., & Miller, J. D. (1982). Discrimination of auditory target dimensions in the presence or absence of variation of a second dimension by infants. *Perception and Psychophysics, 31*, 279–292.

Ladefoged, P. (1989). A note on "Information conveyed by vowels." *Journal of the Acoustical Society of America, 75*, 2223–2224.

Ladefoged, P., & Broadbent, D. E. (1957). Information conveyed by vowels. *Journal of the Acoustical Society of America, 29*, 98–104.

Liberman, A. M., Cooper, F. S., Shankweiler, D. P., & Studdert-Kennedy, M. (1967). Perception of the speech code. *Psychological Review, 74*, 431–461.

Liberman, A. M., Delattre, P. C., & Cooper, F. S. (1952). The role of selected stimulus-variables in the perception of the unvoiced stop consonants. *American Journal of Psychology, 54*, 497–516.

Liberman, A. M., Harris, K. S., Hoffman, H. A., & Griffith, B. C. (1957). The discrimination of speech sounds within and across phoneme boundaries. *Journal of Experimental Psychology, 43*, 358–368.

Liberman, A. M., & Mattingly, I. G. (1985). The motor theory of speech revisited. *Cognition, 21*, 1–36.

Liberman, A. M., Mattingly, I. G., & Turvey, M. T. (1972). Language codes and memory codes. In A. W. Melton & E. Martin (Eds.), *Coding processes in human memory* (pp. 307–334). New York, NY: Winston.

Lisker, L., & Abramson, A. S. (1967). The voicing dimension: Some experiments in comparative phonetics. In *Proceedings of the Sixth International Congress of Phonetic Sciences*. Prague, Czech Republic: Academia.

Logan, J. S., Lively, S. E., & Pisoni, D. B. (1991). Training Japanese listeners to identify /r/ and /l/: A first report. *Journal of the Acoustical Society of America, 89*, 874–886.

Marslen-Wilson, W. D. (1987). Functional parallelism in spoken word recognition. *Cognition, 25*, 75–102.

Marslen-Wilson, W. D., & Tyler, L. K. (1975). Processing structure of sentence perception. *Nature, 257*, 784–785.

Massaro, D. W., & Cohen, M. M. (1993). The paradigm and the fuzzy logical model of perception are alive and well. *Journal of Experimental Psychology: General, 1221*, 115–124.

Massaro, D. W., & Oden, G. C. (1980). Speech perception: A framework for research and theory. In N. J. Lass (Ed.), *Speech and language: Advances in basic research and practice* (Vol. 3, pp. 129–165). New York, NY: Academic Press.

McClelland, J. L., & Elman, J. L. (1986). The TRACE model of speech perception. *Cognitive Psychology, 18*, 1–86.

McGurk, H., & MacDonald, J. (1976). Hearing lips and seeing voices. *Nature, 264*, 746–748.

Miller, J. D., & Eimas, P. D. (1983). Studies on the categorization of speech by infants. *Cognition, 13*, 135–165.

Miller, J. D., Wier, C. C., Pastore, R. E., Kelley, W. J., & Dooling, R. J. (1976). Discrimination and labeling of noise-buzz sequences with varying noise-lead times: An example of categorical perception. *Journal of the Acoustical Society of America, 60*, 410–417.

Moffitt, A. R. (1971). Consonant cue perception by 20- to 24-week-old infants. *Child Development, 42,* 717–731.

Morgan, J. L. (1986). *From simple input to complex grammar.* Cambridge, MA: MIT Press.

Morse, P. A., & Snowdon, C. T. (1975). An investigation of categorical speech discrimination by rhesus monkeys. *Perception and Psychophysics, 17,* 9–16.

Norris, D., McQueen, J. M., & Cutler, A. (2003). Perceptual learning in speech. *Cognitive Psychology, 47,* 204–238.

Nygaard, L. C., & Pisoni, D. B. (1998). Talker-specific learning in speech perception. *Perceptual Psychophysics, 60,* 355–376.

Parker, M., Cunningham, S., Enderby, P., Hawley, M., & Green, P. (2006). Automatic speech recognition and training for severely dysarthric users of assistive technology: The STARDUST project. *Clinical Linguistics and Phonetics, 20,* 149–156.

Pastore, R. E., Schmeckler, M. A., Rosenblum, L., & Szczesiul, R. (1983). Duplex perception with musical stimuli. *Perception and Psychophysics, 33,* 469–474.

Pisoni, D. B. (1977). Identification and discrimination of the relative onset of two component tones: Implications for voicing perception in stops. *Journal of the Acoustical Society of America, 61,* 1352–1361.

Pisoni, D. B., Carrell, T. D., & Gans, S. J. (1983). Perception of the duration of rapid spectrum changes in speech and nonspeech signals. *Perception and Psychophysics, 34,* 314–322.

Pitt, M. A., & Samuel, A. G. (1993). An empirical and meta-analytic evaluation of the phoneme identification task. *Journal of Experimental Psychology: Human Perception and Performance, 19,* 699–725.

Polka, L. (1992). Characterizing the influence of native language experience on adult speech perception. *Perception and Psychophysics, 52,* 37–52.

Rand, T. C. (1974). Dichotic release from masking. *Journal of the Acoustical Society of America, 55,* 678–680.

Remez, R. E., Rubin, P. E., Pisoni, D. B., & Carrell, T. D. (1981). Speech perception without traditional speech cues. *Science, 212,* 947–950.

Repp, B. H. (1982). Phonetic trading relations and context effect: New experimental evidence for a speech mode of perception. *Psychological Bulletin, 92,* 81–110.

Repp, B. H. (1983). Categorical perception: Issues, methods, findings. In N. J. Lass (Ed.), *Speech and language: Advances in basic research and practice*

(Vol. 10, pp. 243–335). New York, NY: Academic Press.

Roberts, M., & Summerfield, Q. (1981). Audio-visual adaptation in speech perception. *Perception and Psychophysics, 30,* 309–314.

Roberts, J., Hunter, L., Gravel, J., Rosenfeld, R., Berman, S., Haggard, M., . . . Wallace, I. (2004). Otitis media, hearing loss, and language learning: controversies and current research. *Journal of Developmental and Behavioral Pediatrics, 25,* 110–122.

Stevens, K. N. (1972). The quantal nature of speech: Evidence from articulatory-acoustic data. In E. E. David Jr. & P. B. Denes (Eds.), *Human communication: A unified view* (pp. 51–66). New York, NY: McGraw-Hill.

Stevens, K. N. (2002). Toward a model for lexical access based on acoustic landmarks and distinctive features. *Journal of the Acoustical Society of America, 111,* 1872–1891.

Stevens, K. N., & Blumstein, S. E. (1981). The search for invariant acoustic correlates of phonetic features. In P. D. Eimas & J. L. Miller (Eds.), *Perspectives on the study of speech* (pp. 1–38). Hillsdale, NJ: Erlbaum.

Strange, W., & Dittmann, S. (1984). Effects of discrimination training on the perception of /r-l/ by Japanese adults learning English. *Perception and Psychophysics, 36,* 131–145.

Studdert-Kennedy, M. (1980). Speech perception. *Language and Speech, 23,* 45–66.

Sussman, H. M., Hoemeke, K., & Ahmed, F. (1993). A cross-linguistic investigation of locus equations as a phonetic descriptor for place of articulation. *Journal of the Acoustical Society of America, 94,* 1256–1268.

Trehub, S. E. (1976). The discrimination of foreign speech contrasts by infants and adults. *Child Development, 47,* 466–472.

Trehub, S. E., & Rabinovitch, M. S. (1972). Auditory-linguistic sensitivity in early infancy. *Developmental Psychology, 6,* 74–77.

Tremblay, K., Kraus, N., Carrell, T. D., & McGee, T. (1997). Central auditory system plasticity: Generalization to novel stimuli following listening training. *Journal of the Acoustical Society of America, 102*(6), 3762–3773.

Van Lancker, D., Kreiman, J., & Emmorey, K. (1985). Familiar voice recognition: Patterns and parameters: Part I. *Journal of Phonetics, 13,* 19–38.

Warren, R. M., & Warren, R. P. (1970). Auditory illusions and confusions. *Scientific American, 223,* 30–36.

Werker, J. F., & Lalonde, C. E. (1988). Cross-language speech perception: Initial capabilities and developmental change. *Developmental Psychology, 24,* 672–683.

Whalen, D., & Liberman, A. M. (1987). Speech perception takes precedence over nonspeech perception. *Science, 237,* 169–171.

Wickelgren, W. A. (1976). Phonetic coding and serial order. In E. C. Carterette & M. P. Friedman (Eds.), *Handbook of perception* (Vol. 7, pp. 227–264). New York, NY: Academic Press.

12

Instrumentation

Donald Finan

Figure 12–1

There are two possible outcomes. If the result confirms the hypothesis, you've made a measurement. If the result contradicts the hypothesis, you've made a discovery.

—Enrico Fermi, physicist (1901–1954)

12.1 Introduction to Measurement

How many hours a day do you spend speaking or listening to someone speak? We do these things so often that it's easy to take for granted the astonishing complexity of the processes of speech production and perception. As you have learned throughout the preceding chapters, the production of speech involves elegant and intricate biomechanical processes that yield a continually varying and highly complex acoustical output. Our auditory systems are uniquely qualified for decoding the speech waveform, allowing us to not only identify the phonemes but also analyze perceptually speech intensity, vocal f_o, nasal resonance, and voice quality. You likely use your perceptual skills constantly to assess a speaker's gender, emotional state, and even health. Yet even in the case of the most highly trained individual, perception is a subjective assessment, subject to the biases and inaccuracies of measurement common to every human perception.

To obtain objective data on speech production and to perform complex analyses beyond the capacity of human perception, instrumented measures must be used. Currently, the term "instrumentation" means "computerized recording and/or analysis," as older, analog devices, such as tape recorders, are rarely used anymore. The focus of this chapter is to explore the basics of digital (computerized) signal acquisition for analysis of speech production. Emphasis will be placed on instrumentation for capturing and recording acoustic signals, but selected instrumentation systems for capturing physiologic signals related to speech production will be highlighted throughout.

Instrumentation systems are not constrained to the research laboratory setting. Indeed, the proliferation of economical yet powerful, and often portable, computer systems has broadened the access to objective measures of speech to include any number of clinical settings. Instrumentation systems will never completely replace a clinician's perceptual abilities and clinical expertise, but the objective data obtained by using instrumentation can provide unique insight of

Boring

Perhaps the topic of instrumentation seems insanely boring. Perhaps the last thing you want to think about are details of how a microphone works or why computers use the binary system to count instead of the decimal system like us humans. Actually, this material can be quite exciting. Think about it this way: Making accurate measurements of speech (arguably the most complex motor behavior that humans do) is quite a challenge. The challenge is to capture the characteristics of speech so that your measurements are valid and are as accurate as possible. Quality data can be directly compared to those of another clinician or researcher and can guide therapeutic approaches and lead to new research directions. It is not an easy task, once you think about it a bit. Well, keep thinking about it as you explore this topic. Perhaps you'll be the one who comes up with a novel strategy to make the task a bit more accurate, a bit easier, and a bit less boring.

speech function that can enhance and guide clinical decision making (Behrman & Orlikoff, 1997; Mehta & Hillman, 2007). Further, instrumental data may be used in the clinical setting to provide evidence of therapeutic progress as well as for immediate biofeedback of patient performance. It is essential that instrumentation be used correctly, however, as even the highest quality musical instrument will only produce noise if used improperly.

12.2 Basic Principles of Measurement

If you've used a digital recording device such as a laptop computer, portable digital recorder, or cell phone, you know how easy it can be make a sound recording. For many devices, a single button press (or mouse click) is all that it takes for the system to acquire data. But how valid and useful are the data that you've acquired with so little effort? Well, that depends. Many variables can cause your recording to be inaccurate, misleading, and, ultimately, unusable. Understanding and controlling these variables is key to obtaining a valid recording that is suitable for analysis.

When we are acquiring speech data (acoustic, aerodynamic, or physiologic, for example), we are making a measurement of some aspect of speech production. Obtaining valid, accurate, and reliable measurements is tricky stuff. In fact, there is an entire science of measurement called "metrology." With the advent of "single-click" recording devices, the procedures required to obtain valid measurements can all too easily be overlooked. All measurements have a level of uncertainty to them, but it is essential to minimize that uncertainty.

To minimize measurement uncertainty (in other words, to increase the validity of your measurement), we'll need to keep in mind some basic principles of measurement.

First, we need to determine what we want to measure. If we are interested in measuring the formants of the vowels, for example, we will need to acquire the acoustic waveform for speech. Assessing the function of the velopharyngeal port during speech may entail acquiring an acoustic waveform in order to calculate nasal resonance, aerodynamic data to assess airflow through the velopharyngeal port, or even electromyographic data directly from the muscles that move the velum, among other potential techniques. Determining the **measurand** (the physical quantity being measured) also involves the careful selection of the speech and/or movement task to be performed by the speaker.

Second, we must choose the correct instrumentation based on the desired measurand.

For example, appropriate instrumentation for obtaining acoustic data would include a high-quality microphone, microphone preamplifier, and a recording system with adequate performance specifications.

Third, the instruments used must be calibrated to ensure that our measurements are accurate, reliable, and comparable to measurements made by others. **Calibration** is a process in which the output of a measurement system is compared to a known standard so that we can report our data in standard units of measure. As a simple example, we all know that a foot consists of 12 inches in length. An inch (as defined in the medieval English statute *Composition of Yards and Perches*) measures exactly 3 barleycorns in length. Those barleycorns do need to be round and dry, however. So, if we go about finding three round and dry barleycorns, we have our standard for the inch measurement. Simple! These procedures clearly won't yield a very accurate or repeatable measurement, though, as round dry barleycorns likely differ quite a bit in size from each other. This is indeed an example of calibration, however, using round dry barleycorns as the "known standard." Luckily, the standards we use today for calibration are a great deal more accurate.[1] (See History of Measurement in Chapter 2 for more details.)

Finally, appropriate measurement procedures need to be followed. Specifically, we must choose the speech or movement task carefully, perform that task consistently, and use the instrumentation correctly in order to maximize accuracy. When measuring human behavior, it can be tempting to allow for deviations from the specified speech or movement task, as we often want to help someone who may be experiencing frustration or difficulty with the task. However, accurately capturing the person's actual performance of the task is the true goal!

---

[1]How accurate are today's known standards? The most recent specification for the standard that defines the meter is based on the distance light can travel (in a vacuum) in $1/299,792,458$ of a second. This method yields an accuracy of 0.0000000001 meters (0.1 nanometers) for the meter standard, which is just a bit more accurate than what can be achieved by lining up (round and dry!) barleycorns (Cardarelli, 2012).

Error in Measurement

Error may be defined as "a deviation from accuracy or correctness; a mistake" and a "belief in something untrue" (Dictionary, n.d.). This website further states that error can be a "moral offense; wrongdoing; sin." Although that's a bit extreme for our purposes, errors in measurement can certainly lead to a deviation from accuracy, and that deviation may even cause us to believe data that are untrue. Remember, the goal of measurement is to obtain valid, objective data.

Measurement error can occur due to deviations from best practices for each of the four measurement principles listed above, all of which are under our control. Error can also occur due to instances beyond our control, however, and we need to be aware of all potential sources of error. Electronic instruments all have inherent error. No matter what manufacturers say, no microphone is perfectly able to capture sound, and no analysis system (hardware, software, or app) is able to analyze the sound wave without error. All electronic instruments generate their own error, called "self-noise," due to the physical properties of the electronic components. This internal or self-noise of an electronic system is typically very small in magnitude, and it forms the basis for that instrument's **noise floor**. If appropriate measurement procedures are followed, the noise floor will be of an extraordinarily small magnitude as compared to the signal that you

---

Noise Isn't Always a Bad Thing

Recall from our discussion in Chapter 3—noise is not always a bad thing—it's not necessarily error. Here we consider several different types of noise. Self-noise is a type of noise that produces undesirable changes to the captured signal by introducing noise generated by the instrument's own electronic circuits. The amount of self-noise generated is called the instrument's noise floor. Signals that are the same magnitude (a signal to noise ratio of 1.0) or lower than the instrument's noise floor (a signal to noise ratio of <1) will be indistinguishable from the noise. Self-noise IS a bad thing. It's a fact of electronic life, however, and it must be monitored (and potentially addressed) when making sensitive recordings and measurements.

Measurement error can also be considered a type of noise, as it also yields undesirable changes to the captured signal. If a ruler's markings are not accurate, for example, the resulting measurements will be in error. For speech analysis purposes, a microphone that is best suited (due to its performance characteristics) to capture the sound of a bass drum would likely introduce substantial measurement error if used to capture the high-frequency sounds of a fricative. (More on microphones in a bit.) Environmental or ambient sound can be undesirable noise. Unless the goal is to record environmental or ambient sound, the intrusion of such sound energy into a desired recording of speech would result in the speech signal becoming compromised.

Sometimes, however, noise is the desired signal. In fact, aeroacoustics is a branch of acoustics that studies the noise generated by airflow. As we discussed in Chapter 8, turbulent airflow generates frication noise for fricative, affricate, and aspirated stop-plosive phonemes, and each phoneme is characterized by distinctive acoustic characteristics of the frication noise. Further, as we discussed in Chapters 5 and 6, noise is a consequence of the process of phonation, and the analysis of this noise may lead to a better understanding of not only normal phonation but also the effects of pathology on the production of voice. So, if the goal is to analyze the aeroacoustics of speech in order to better understand the processes involved in producing phonemes and phonation, noise is indeed a good thing!

are capturing, and it will not negatively affect our desired signal.

Another way of describing this relationship is to say that the target signal is captured with a high signal to noise ratio. The signal to noise ratio describes the magnitude of the signal that you are capturing as compared to the amount of the noise (a type of error) in the system. A high signal to noise ratio means that there is a large amount of signal (e.g., an acoustic speech waveform) as compared to the noise floor of that instrument. Other factors beyond an instrument's self-noise (for example, environmental sounds that can be picked up by a microphone just as easily as a speech waveform, distortion or alteration of the signal's original characteristics due to incorrect use of an instrument) can negatively affect the signal to noise ratio and the integrity of the captured signal as well, and we'll describe them in later sections in this chapter.

It is important to keep in mind that inherent error always exists when making any measurement. Thus, we need to be cognizant of the factors that can lead to error. For most cases, if the appropriate procedures are followed, instruments are in good working condition, and the instruments are used within their operating range, self-noise will not be a significant source of error that will affect your measurement. In some situations, such as using a sound level meter to measure the ambient sound pressure level (SPL) in a very quiet room, however, the instrument's self-noise may need to be taken into consideration. Using an instrument beyond its operating range, taking measurements in adverse environments (such as capturing speech acoustics in the presence of background sound), or selecting inappropriate operating settings for instruments can all result in significant measurement error. Reduction of error is accomplished by identifying the potential sources of error and by adhering to the principles of measurement.

Study Questions

1. List physical events generated by the process of speech production.

2. Describe the four general principles that should be followed when taking measurements of speech.

3. Define measurement, calibration, measurement error, noise, and noise floor.

4. What information does the "signal to noise ratio" provide?

5. What's the difference between subjective and objective measures of speech?

Transduction

Transduction means the process of changing energy from one form to another. Instruments that we use to capture and measure speech employ this process as they change a speech signal into an electronic signal that can be captured by a recording system such as a computer. A microphone is an example of such a transducer, converting the acoustic energy (sound) of speech into electrical energy. A microphone is a special type of transducer, however, known as a sensor.[2] A sensor is a transducer device that specifically detects some form of energy (such as a physical quantity) and produces an output that is proportional to the magnitude of that energy. The microphone produces electricity (or a change in electricity) as its output, and the amount of change in the electrical output of the microphone is directly due to the amount (and change) of acoustic energy that it transduces.

[2]Not all transducers are sensors. For example, loudspeakers (or headphones or earbuds) are types of transducers that produce acoustic energy (sound) when electrical signals are sent to them. In contrast, microphones respond to acoustic energy and generate corresponding electrical signals. Therefore, the loudspeaker transduces electrical energy into sound energy, while the microphone transduces sound energy into electrical energy.

Other sensors respond to different types of physical energy. For example, the thermostat in your house contains a temperature sensor that transduces changes in ambient temperature. Other sensors respond to changes in air pressure, airflow, light, movement, and other physical quantities. Many of these sensors can be used to capture and measure the behaviors of speech production. For example, pressure sensors can be used to measure the air pressure inside a speaker's mouth as he or she produces phonemes that require the generation of significant amounts of air pressure, such as plosives, as we learned in Chapter 8.

Perhaps we can consider the electrical signal generated by the microphone as a type of simulacrum—a representation or superficial likeness of something. In our example, the electric signal generated by a microphone is a representation, but only a likeness of the original speech acoustic signal and, therefore, a simulacrum (Figure 12–2). In reality, the microphone has imparted a small amount of error to the signal due to its internal self-noise as well as its performance character-

istics. Therefore, the electrical signal from the microphone is not an exact representation of the original speech signal. Recall we acknowledged earlier that no "perfect" microphone exists, as all of them will introduce a certain level of self-noise and signal distortion.

The change in the signal from the original to the electrical representation is due to the microphone's transfer function, like the transfer function of the vocal tract we studied in Chapter 7. All instruments that we use to capture and measure signals have their own transfer function, in that the signal that they capture will be changed (hopefully very slightly) as compared to the original signal.

Some electronic devices, such as amplifiers and filters, have desirable transfer functions by design, while the transfer function of other devices (for example, microphones) is largely a product of the physical characteristics of the instrument. Certain microphones have transfer functions that are designed for specific conditions, however the transfer function may result in undesirable changes to the signal if used in

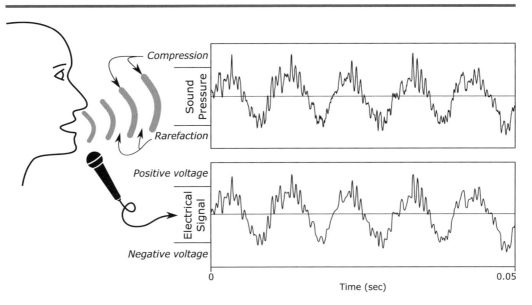

Figure 12–2. Sound pressure waveform (*top panel*) of the vowel /a/ and electrical representation in volts (*bottom panel*) generated by a microphone. Note that the two representations are highly similar but not identical. The electric and physical properties of the microphone have produced a signal that differs slightly from the original signal's acoustic sound pressure wave. The goal in selecting and using a microphone is to yield an electrical representation that is as close to the original acoustic waveform as possible.

Transfer Function

Technically, the transfer function is a representation of how the output of some instrument is different than the input. The difference between the output and the input is known as that instrument's transfer function, which can be described by a mathematical equation. An amplifier's transfer function would show that the output signal is greater in magnitude than the input signal, for example, and the mathematical function may be as simple as a multiplication factor in this case. If the output magnitude was twice the level of the magnitude of the input signal, the equation would be

"Output = 2 × Input."

In this chapter, the term "transfer function" is used to represent the concept that devices such as microphones and other sensors, amplifiers, filters, and data recorders will all yield an output signal that is in some way different than the original input signal.

other situations. For example, a microphone designed to capture the voice signal may be desirable when capturing live singing performance but unsuitable for use in a laboratory or clinical setting when capturing speech for analysis. Devices with desirable transfer functions change the input signal in a predictable way for specific purposes. Let's come back to this topic in a bit, however, as perhaps first we should consider how instruments work in general.

It's Electric!

The terms "electrical" and "electronic" have made their way into several of the previous paragraphs, and rightfully so. If we're trying to understand instrumentation, we will need to cover a bit of the basics of electricity. Electronic devices (instruments) rely on the ability of elec-

trons to be pushed around. Don't worry, they don't mind. Let's revisit our microphone example. As a transducer, the microphone changes acoustic energy into electrical energy. Specifically, the microphone responds to changes in air pressure of the sound wave by causing electrons to be pushed through the microphone's connecting wires. These wires connect to the next device in the instrumentation chain, typically a device called a microphone preamplifier. The pattern of movement of the electrons in the wire is a simulacrum (or representation) of the original acoustic energy signal. If a high-quality microphone is used, that electrical representation may be similar to the original signal, whereas a low-quality microphone may yield an electrical signal that deviates greatly from the original signal. In other words, the transfer function of a low-quality microphone may yield an electrical signal that is fraught with error.

Electricity can be measured in terms of potential energy and kinetic energy (recall our discussion in Chapter 2 of energy). The term "volts" refers to the potential energy in an electrical system (how much "push" is applied to the electrons), and the term "current" refers to that system's kinetic energy (the actual movement of electrons in wires and circuits). A signal displayed as an electrical waveform (as in Figure 12–2 and all the waveforms shown in Chapter 8) is typically represented as variations in voltage.

12.3 Sensors for Capturing Speech

The microphone is a sensor device that transduces some of the physical events of speech into electrical signals that we can analyze with a computer. Microphones are used to capture sound; technically they are responding to the associated minute fluctuations of air pressure termed compressions and rarefactions that we studied in Chapter 3. However, for the measurement of speech production, we can employ other types of sensors as well, as we learned in earlier chapters. In addition to pressure sensors, airflow sensors are another type of specialized sensor device that responds to the aerodynamics of speech (Zajac, Warren, & Hinton, 2009). The most common type of airflow sensor used for the measurement of speech production is called a pneumotachometer, more commonly called a "pneumotach" (see Chapter 6). The initial part of that word, "pneumo," refers to air, "tach" refers to speed (or more precisely, velocity), and "meter" refers to measurement. So, a pneumotachometer measures airflow as the rate (velocity) of movement of air, specifically. For speech, a pneumotach can be used to measure a person's transoral (through the oral cavity), transnasal (through the nasal cavity specifically), and translaryngeal airflow (through the larynx and trachea, equaling transoral + transnasal airflow). In terms of the electrical signal generated by the pneumotach, a displayed positive voltage indicates outward (exhalation) airflow, while voltage of a negative value indicates inward (inhalation) airflow (Figure 12–3). As with other sensors, the magnitude of the voltage reflects the intensity of the signal, which in this case is the rate of airflow.

In combination with a pressure sensor, a pneumotach device can allow for the calculation of velopharyngeal or laryngeal resistance, measurements of how easily air flows through the velopharyngeal port or the vocal folds during phonation, respectively. (See discussion in Chapters 6 and 8, respectively.) For the velopharyngeal port, a high level of resistance to airflow (as indicated by very low transnasal airflow) should be evident during the production of nonnasal phonemes, while production of nasal phonemes is associated with low levels of velopharyngeal port airflow resistance due to the opening of the velopharyngeal port. A similar measurement of airflow through the larynx during phonation may show a lower than normal laryngeal resis-

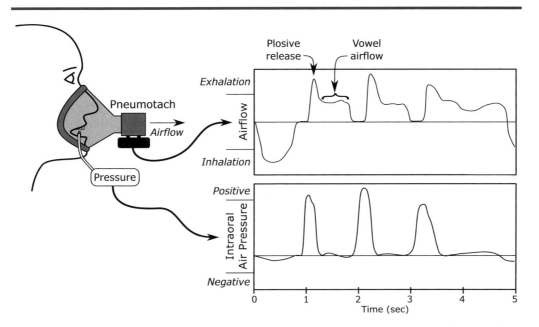

Figure 12–3. Pneumotachometer and pressure sensor used to capture translaryngeal airflow (the combination of nasal and oral airflow) and intraoral pressure level during speech production. Shown here is a stylized representation of inward airflow (0 to 1 second), three repetitions of the syllable /pa/ (1 to 4 seconds), and brief exhalation prior to the initiation of another inhalation (4 to 5 seconds). The second repetition of /pa/ yielded the highest intraoral pressure peak. The brief peaks in the airflow signal represent the sudden outflow of air upon release of the plosive /p/, and the relatively steady airflow that immediately follows is due to the vowel production. The buildup of air pressure for the plosive is accompanied by cessation of airflow because the lips and velopharyngeal port are closed.

tance (as characterized by high levels of trans-laryngeal airflow) due to pathology that limits closure of the vocal folds.

Electromyographic (EMG) sensors are used to capture the electrical activity of muscles. (Refer to Chapter 4 for discussion of EMG and muscle activity.) When a muscle contracts, its biologically generated electrical activity increases. EMG sensors, or electrodes, may be attached to the surface of the skin over the muscle (surface electrodes) or they may be intramuscular ("needle") type. Electrocardiography (ECG) is a comparable process that uses surface electrode sensors attached to the skin of the chest to capture the electrical activity of the heart. Electroencephalography (EEG) and auditory brainstem response (ABR) techniques are conceptually like EMG and ECG, but they use surface electrodes to capture electrical activity from neurons in the brain (EEG) and brainstem (ABR). As is the case for other types of sensors, the magnitude of the captured signal's voltage reflects the intensity of activation of the muscle fibers (EMG and ECG) or neural circuits (EEG and ABR), and the rate at which the signal's voltage varies in a cyclic pattern reflects the frequency.

In addition to the sensors presented above, there are many other types of sensors used to capture specific aspects of speech (Barlow, Finan, Andreatta, & Boliek, 2009). For example, force sensors may be used to measure the amount of lip, tongue, or jaw force generated during speech or during selected nonspeech movements, several different types of sensors are used to transduce movements of the chest wall and abdomen during respiratory movements, articulography instruments employ position sensors to measure movements of the tongue, jaw, and lips. and specialized cameras use light sensors to examine the vocal tract, such as the stroboscopic and videokymographic instrumentation we studied in Chapter 6. The technique of electropalatography (or palatometry) utilizes sensors that detect contact with the tongue to determine tongue to palate contact shapes for different phonemes. One relatively recent development is the use of ultrasound sensors to produce an image of the tongue. This technique has proven useful in providing real-time feedback to clients as they produce speech (Bernhardt, Gick, Bacsfalvi, & Adler-Bock, 2005).

These and other specialized sensors are components in instrumentation chains designed to capture and measure muscle and neural activity, muscle contraction patterns, forces generated by muscle contraction, movement of speech structures, air pressures and airflows, and the resulting acoustic waveform of speech. These objective data may be used for basic and clinical research purposes as well as to provide real-time or delayed feedback to clients. As technology progresses, the challenge to scientists, clinicians, and students is to explore how emerging sensor devices can be used to obtain novel and valuable data on the production of speech.

12.4 Microphones

The most commonly used sensor for capturing speech is the microphone. Any electronic device that is used to capture sound (such as cell phones, laptop computers, portable sound recorders, and hearing aids) employs one or more microphones. Unfortunately, most of those devices use microphones that are not capable of capturing a speech signal suitable for careful measurement and analysis. (Recall our discussion on measurement error.) Different types of microphones are designed for different sources of sound, varied acoustic environments, and physical forms. And each type of microphone has different performance capabilities, such as how the microphone will respond to very low-intensity or high-intensity sounds. These performance capabilities are collectively called specifications. Some microphone specifications are suitable for capturing speech for analysis while others are inadequate.

Microphone Designs

There are three main types of microphone designs: handheld, lavalier, and head-worn (sometimes called headset). A handheld microphone may be held or mounted to a microphone stand that may be on the floor or a table. Lavalier (or lapel) microphones are hands-free types of microphones that are unobtrusively attached to the front of an individual's shirt or jacket. Lavalier and head-worn microphones are commonly used by lecturers, public speakers, and television broadcasters. For speech capturing and analysis purposes, head-worn microphones are preferred because the relative position of the speaker to the microphone needs to be maintained precisely for measures related to sound intensity. Because a head-worn microphone is referenced to that person's own head, the mouth-to-microphone distance will remain constant throughout the captured speech sample.

Microphone Transducer Types

There are two main microphone transducer types, termed dynamic and condenser, and they respond in similar ways when exposed to sound waves in the air. Other types of microphones are available that are similar in function to dynamic and condenser models, but these two designs are most commonly used. For both dynamic and condenser microphones, the compressions and rarefactions of sound waves produce slight inward and outward movement of a small, thin plastic membrane called the microphone's diaphragm. The movement of this membrane is analogous to how the eardrum moves when exposed to sound.

A dynamic microphone relies on the principle of inductance to transduce that sound wave into an electrical signal. Specifically, the moving diaphragm membrane is connected to a coil of extremely thin wire that surrounds (but does not touch) a small magnet. When that coil of wire is pushed around by the moving diaphragm, the magnetic field causes electrons in the wire to be pushed around as well. This process is called electromagnetic induction, and as you recall, the pushing around of electrons in wires is the basis of electricity. The larger the push on the dia-

phragm (due to a more intense sound wave), the greater the push on the electrons and therefore the greater the resulting voltage in the wires.

Condenser microphones work a bit differently than dynamic microphones, as they don't rely on the principle of electromagnetic induction. Instead, inside the condenser microphone is a small device called a capacitor that can hold and release an electrical charge (analogous to voltage in this instance) that mirrors the movement of the diaphragm. (The term "condenser" is a historic term for the term "capacitor," which is more commonly used today.) Unlike the dynamic microphone, however, the condenser microphone requires some external source of power. Typically, condenser microphones may be powered by a small battery that may be in the handle of the microphone (or in a separate battery compartment) or by power (called phantom power) supplied by the preamplifier device to which the microphone is connected. Without such a source of external power, the condenser microphone will not function.

One subtype of condenser microphones is the electret microphone. Unlike true condenser microphones that typically require phantom power of 10 volts to 48 volts, electret condenser microphones only require a small bias voltage of approximately 2 volts (easily supplied by a battery). For this reason, electret condenser microphones are commonly found in battery-powered devices such as laptop computers, cell phones, and portable voice recorders. However, the performance of electret microphones is typically inferior to high-quality condenser microphones.

For both dynamic and condenser types of microphones, greater movement of the diaphragm due to a greater sound intensity results in a greater electrical charge, as represented by an increase of voltage in the wires of the microphone. Also, the compression component of the sound wave will typically produce a positive voltage, while the rarefaction phase will produce a negative voltage. Referring back to Figure 12–2, the electrical (voltage) waveform could have been produced by either a dynamic or a condenser microphone.

Microphone Performance Characteristics

Directionality

The purpose of a microphone is to capture sound. Depending on the microphone's directional response pattern, it may preferentially capture sound coming from a specific direction relative to the microphone or it may capture sounds that emanate from all directions. A microphone that captures sound equally well from all directions (in front, in back, or from the sides of the microphone) has a directional response pattern (or polar pattern) that is termed omnidirectional. Some microphones respond better to sounds that are coming from directly in front of the microphone. These types are described as having a cardioid or unidirectional polar pattern (Figure 12–4). Microphones with cardioid response patterns are better at reducing ambient noise if the microphone is pointed directly at the sound source of interest.

It should be noted, however, that microphones with cardioid (unidirectional) response patterns suffer from a phenomenon termed the proximity effect. Simply put, if the sound source becomes close to the unidirectional microphone, the low frequencies in that sound will become increased in amplitude. Thus, the microphone's transfer function (see below discussion on Frequency Response) will be altered to have a greater emphasis on the low frequencies than it would if the sound source was farther from the sensor element.

Optimally, we want to capture sound from the sound source of interest without capturing sounds that are not of interest, such as ambient noise. For this reason, an omnidirectional microphone is often used in a recording environment that exhibits very low levels of ambient noise. In the absence of such a low-noise environment, a unidirectional (cardioid) microphone may be substituted, keeping in mind the fact that the microphone must not be positioned close to the sound source (the speaker's mouth) to avoid

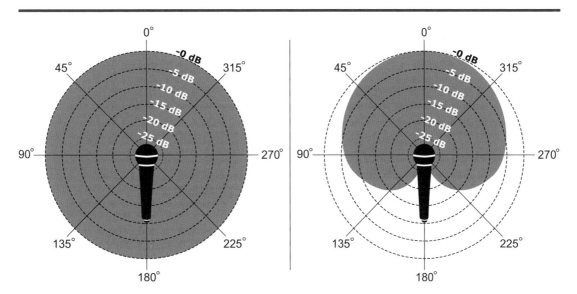

Figure 12–4. Polar plots showing the directional response pattern (*shaded*) of an omnidirectional (*left*) and cardioid (*right*) microphone. Note the substantial attenuation of sound (over 15 dB at 135° and 225° with increasing attenuation when approaching 180°) that will occur to the sides and especially to the rear of the cardioid microphone. The cardioid response pattern can be used to reduce the capture of undesired ambient noise if the sound source of interest is oriented near 0° relative to the front of the microphone.

the proximity effect. The distance from the mouth to the microphone that yields the flattest frequency response will differ depending on whether a handheld or head-worn unidirectional microphone is used. The manufacturer's specifications should indicate the reference distance necessary for attaining a flat frequency response (that is, minimizing the proximity effect) for the specific microphone.

Frequency Response

Optimally, a microphone will respond equally to sounds of low frequency and of high frequency. However, this is not always the case. Some microphones are designed to respond best only to low-frequency sounds and, thus, are used to capture sounds that are primarily of lower frequencies (think of a bass drum or a tuba, for example). Some microphones respond best to high-frequency sounds and, therefore, are better suited to capturing sounds produced by piccolos, birds, and clanging cymbals. The range of frequencies that a microphone can respond to is most commonly displayed as a frequency response plot (Figure 12–5). The pattern displayed by the frequency response plot represents the microphone's transfer function. No microphone will respond equally to all frequencies, but many will have a relatively uniform response over a range of frequencies.

For analysis of speech and voice production, a flat (uniform) frequency response pattern is optimal. Recently proposed standards for instrumental assessment of voice production recommend utilizing microphones with less than 2 dB fluctuation of microphone response across the frequency range of speech (Awan et al., 2015; Svec & Granqvist, 2010).

The frequency response plot is a graphic representation of the microphone's transfer function, and it illustrates how the microphone itself will change the captured signal as compared to the original sound waveform. For the microphone shown in Figure 12–5, the transfer function will result in slight attenuation of the captured signal at frequencies below 50 Hz and a relative increase in the amplitude of frequencies between 4 kHz and approximately 18 kHz. A microphone with a very different frequency response pattern is shown in Figure 12–6. For this microphone, signals of 100 Hz and less will be attenuated (by approximately −7 dB at 50 Hz), and frequencies from approximately 2 to 10 kHz will be increased in amplitude (by up to 5 dB at 5 kHz) as compared to a reference level at 1 kHz.

Recall that the goal of capturing the speech signal for analysis is to obtain as close to the original acoustic signal as possible. Microphones with frequency response patterns such as displayed in Figure 12–6 are commonly used to

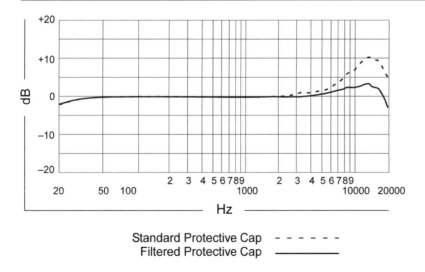

Standard Protective Cap - - - - - -
Filtered Protective Cap ——————

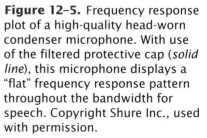

Figure 12–5. Frequency response plot of a high-quality head-worn condenser microphone. With use of the filtered protective cap (*solid line*), this microphone displays a "flat" frequency response pattern throughout the bandwidth for speech. Copyright Shure Inc., used with permission.

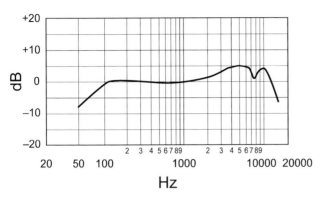

Figure 12–6. Frequency response plot of a commonly used dynamic "vocal" microphone. Note the prominent peaks in response above 2 kHz. The highest peak is centered at 5 kHz with a signal increase of approximately +5 dB in magnitude as compared to the reference frequency of 1 kHz. This type of "performance" microphone is often used in live vocal situations where the transfer function (the boost in higher frequencies) yields a signal that is considered to be aesthetically pleasing to listeners. Copyright Shure Inc., used with permission.

Acoustic Magicians

Selecting a microphone for vocal or instrument use is an art practiced by acoustic magicians called audio technicians, who are walking encyclopedias of microphone specifications. These mysterious yet highly skilled individuals live behind specialized devices called mixing boards and are masters at identifying which microphone is best suited to an individual's voice or instrument type. Consequently, they are also able to identify which microphones will make an individual sound terrible. If you are a recording or performing artist, it is wise to keep the audio technicians happy.

Feedback

If you've ever been to a concert with an amplified band, you may have heard a loud and high-pitched squealing noise that unexpectedly emanated from the speakers. This unpleasant noise is the result of acoustic feedback. When utilizing microphones and amplified loudspeakers, the potential exists for the sound projecting from the speakers to be picked up by the microphone and reamplified. That signal will quickly be produced by the speakers, once again picked up by the microphone, and reamplified in a self-perpetuating loop called feedback.

Feedback can occur if the amplifier's output level through the loudspeakers is too high or the microphone is positioned too closely to the loudspeakers. Both situations can cause sound from the speakers to "bleed" into the microphone's input, initiating the feedback loop. Strategies to eliminate feedback include reducing amplifier gain, utilization of a cardioid pattern microphone (if possible), and signal-processing techniques used to attenuate the specific frequency generated by the feedback loop.

In addition to live amplified sound systems, hearing aids are susceptible to feedback due to the proximity of the loudspeaker element and the microphone sensor. Systems used to capture and record signals with a microphone, however, are not susceptible to feedback as they do not incorporate loudspeakers into the instrumentation chain.

---

capture singing as their transfer functions (frequency response curves) yield a waveform that is aesthetically pleasing to listeners. A microphone's transfer function characterized by non-uniform (nonflat) response across the frequency range may compromise certain types of analyses (such as inverse filtering of voice) performed on the captured signal (Svec & Granqvist, 2010).

Sensitivity and Dynamic Range

Like the frequency response range, microphones have a range of sound intensities for which they can respond. This range of intensities is called the microphone's dynamic range, and it reflects the difference between the highest intensity and lowest intensity sound that the microphone can capture without significantly distorting (adding noise to) the captured signal. A microphone's dynamic range is defined by the microphone's maximum sound pressure level minus its self-noise.

For example, consider a microphone with the maximum sound pressure level specified at 150.5 dB and self-noise at 42.5 dB. The resulting dynamic range will be 108 dB (150.5 dB − 42.5 dB = 108 dB). Note that this microphone's noise floor is 42.5 dB. Therefore, this microphone cannot capture sounds that are lower in intensity than 42.5 dB, and it will not do a great job at levels that are near to that. Given this dynamic range, this particular microphone is best suited to capture sounds that are higher in intensity, with a maximum limit of 150.5 dB. Considering that this microphone is a head-worn type and will be located very close to the source of sound (the mouth) where intensity is high suggests that its dynamic range (and maximum limit) will be suitable for capturing speech. The dynamic range of speech is approximately 40 to 130 dBA (for shouting) as measured at a distance of 30 cm from the speaker's mouth, with the levels being an additional 15 dB higher if the distance to the microphone is only 5 cm as would occur with a head-worn microphone (Svec & Granqvist, 2010). (The term "dBA" refers to the sound pressure level in decibels as measured using an "A" weighting scale that simulates the sensitivity of human hearing.)

A microphone's sensitivity is defined by the voltage level that it produces upon presentation of a sound. For practical purposes, a microphone that has greater sensitivity will be able to respond to lower intensity sounds. A microphone of lower sensitivity requires a larger sound intensity for it to respond. A sound level meter used to measure low levels of ambient noise in a room, for example, requires a highly sensitive microphone. High sensitivity, however, comes with a tradeoff. In general, the higher the sensitivity, the lower the maximum sound pressure level for which that microphone can respond without distorting, that is, altering the original characteristics of the captured signal.

Adequate Microphone Performance for Speech Analysis

For capturing a speech signal that is suitable for analysis, care needs to be taken to ensure that a microphone with adequate performance characteristics is selected. The microphone's frequency range and dynamic range (Figure 12–7) should be substantially wider than the physiologic range of speech to ensure that the performance specifications are not exceeded.

The microphone's dynamic range minima (noise floor) should be at least 15 dB lower than the lowest expected speech sound pressure level (i.e., a 15-dB signal to noise ratio) in order to minimize contribution of the microphone's self-noise to the captured speech signal (Awan et al., 2015; Svec & Granqvist, 2010). For some analyses (e.g., perturbation measures of voice), a signal to noise ratio of at least 30 dB may be necessary (Svec & Granqvist, 2010).

The microphone's frequency range should optimally be "flat" (i.e., variation of 2 dB or less) throughout the frequency range of speech frequencies. The minimum range of speech frequencies recommended for speech analysis is 50 Hz to 8 kHz (Awan et al., 2015). Such a frequency range will allow for analysis of fundamental frequency, the first four vowel formants, and most acoustic energy from fricatives, but analysis of very low (possibly pathological) fundamental frequencies and high components of vowels and fricatives necessitates a wider frequency range of <50 Hz to at least 16 kHz (Svec & Granqvist, 2010). Although condenser microphones require an external source of power, they typically have frequency response characteristics that are flatter than dynamic microphones (Svec & Granqvist, 2010; Titze & Winholtz, 1993). No matter the type of microphone, it is essential that the performance capabilities of the microphone exceed the dynamic and frequency ranges of speech production to capture a signal with an adequate signal to noise ratio and without significant waveform distortion.

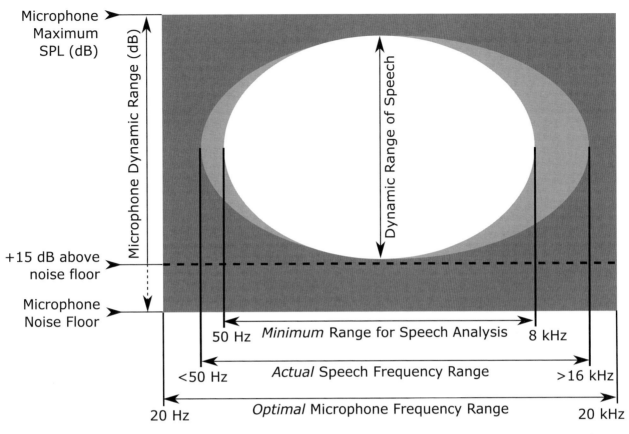

Figure 12–7. Frequency range and dynamic range of speech shown as a subset of the performance characteristics range of a hypothetical microphone. The microphone's frequency range and dynamic range should be substantially greater than the physiologic range of speech.

Study Questions

6. Define "transfer function" and provide an example of a system with a transfer function.

7. How is a sensor a transducer, but not all transducers are sensors?

8. What sensors are commonly used to measure speech?

9. Why can the electrical signal generated by a microphone be considered a "simulacrum" of the original acoustic waveform?

10. How can an electrical signal represent the amplitude and frequency components of a sound?

11. What are the two main types of microphone transducers?

12. Describe frequency range, dynamic range, directionality, and sensitivity in terms of microphone performance characteristics.

13. What's the frequency range for speech?

12.5 Amplification

Sensors such as microphones are the initial links in a signal capture instrumentation chain. As the transducer, the sensor changes the physical event (such as the acoustic pressure wave) to an electrical signal. That sensor-generated electrical signal, however, is typically of an extremely low voltage. To utilize that small signal, typically the next link in the instrumentation chain is a stage of amplification.

The output of a sensor is typically connected to the input of a device called a preamplifier that increases the amplitude (or magnitude) of the signal's voltage to a level that can be utilized by other instrumentation devices, including signal recorders and computers. Many types of amplifiers exist, including microphone preamplifiers and biopotential, power, and video amplifiers. Here, we present only microphone preamplifiers and biopotential amplifiers (a type of preamplifier).

The amount of increase in amplitude, the amplifier's transfer function, is termed gain. To achieve gain (which results in an increase in the signal's power), amplifiers require an external source of electrical power. Often that power comes from an electrical outlet, but some amplifiers are battery powered. Condenser microphones and other active sensors (including electronic pressure sensors) require power to function. In these cases, the preamplifier may supply the requisite voltage to the sensor. As previously described, this supply voltage is typically called phantom power when used with condenser microphones, but it may be called bias or excitation voltage for electret microphones and other active sensors.

The amplifier type used with microphones is typically just called a microphone preamplifier. This instrument will have an input that is matched to the electrical properties (specifically the impedance) of the microphone and to the physical properties of the microphone's connector. A microphone's impedance is typically rated as low, medium, or high (often reported as Low-Z, Medium-Z, and High-Z), and high-quality microphones are typically rated as having low impedance. Roughly, impedance refers to the ease at which electricity will flow through the microphone's circuit.

Specialized preamplifiers are used with sensors that capture bioelectric signals such as those produced by muscle activation. Such devices are termed biopotential amplifiers (or just bioamplifiers), as they have specialized components and circuitry to optimize their response to biologically generated electrical activity. The input to the biopotential amplifier is also matched to the electrical properties of the associated sensor. Among other biological events, biopotential amplifiers are used with EMG (electromyographic) electrode sensors to capture muscle activity and ABR (auditory brainstem response) electrode sensors to capture neuronal activity in the brainstem related to central auditory pathway function.

Amplifier Performance Characteristics

Although there are numerous performance characteristics that reflect how an amplifier will function, three specifications are universal across amplifier types: gain, frequency response, and dynamic range.

Gain

Amplifiers are used to increase the amplitude of a signal (in terms of electrical voltage for a preamplifier and often in terms of electrical current for a power amplifier used to drive loudspeakers), and the amount of the increase in amplitude is termed the amplifier's gain. Each amplifier will have a range of gain levels that it can produce. Amplifiers used with sensors that produce very low amplitude signals, such as dynamic microphones or EEG sensors, may produce voltage gain of 100,000 times or more. When selecting a gain level for an amplifier, caution must be taken so that the amplified signal does not exceed the input dynamic range of the next instrument in the signal chain.

Frequency Response

As is the case for microphones, the frequency response of an amplifier reflects the range of low to high frequencies for which that amplifier can respond. Typical audio amplifiers can respond to the frequency range of 20 Hz to 20 kHz (or higher), equivalent to the average range of human hearing.

Amplifiers that are used with certain transducers such as pressure, force, or displacement (position and movement) sensors will typically have a frequency range that starts as low as 0 Hz, as such devices may need to capture signals that do not change or change very slowly. For example, airflow through the mouth to produce /pɑ/ is nearly constant (0 Hz or close) throughout the vowel (see Figure 12–3), and thus both the airflow sensor (pneumotachometer) and the associated instrumentation preamplifier must be able to respond to frequencies as low as 0 Hz.

Dynamic Range

Amplifiers will also have a dynamic range specification. Instead of reflecting the range of sound pressure level that the microphone can respond to, the amplifier's dynamic range equals the lowest to highest output level of the amplifier. The lowest output level is limited by the amplifier's own noise floor, while the highest level is dictated by where the amplifier starts to significantly distort the signal. At the high end of the dynamic range, the amplifier will add significantly more

---

Peak Clipping

Peak clipping is a form of waveform distortion that occurs when a signal's amplitude exceeds the dynamic range of an instrument. It results in the removal of the peaks (maxima) and valleys (minima) of the signal, as though they had been clipped by a pair of electronic scissors (Figure 12–8). It is critical to understand that once the signal has been clipped, the waveform has been distorted and the clean (nonclipped) original signal cannot be restored.

Sensors (microphones, pressure sensors, etc.), amplifiers of any type, and even recording devices such as analog-to-digital converters can all produce clipping if the amplitude of the captured signal exceeds the instrument's dynamic range. Note that amplifiers may have a dynamic range specification for both the input (connection from the sensor) and output (connection to a recording device) stages. A signal that exceeds the dynamic range of the input stage of the amplifier will experience peak clipping independent of the amplifier's gain setting, while a signal that is clipped at the amplifier's output stage will show increasing distortion with increased amplifier gain settings.

Interestingly, peak clipping is a common and desirable feature of electric guitar amplifiers, where it is termed overdrive or distortion. But in the case of capturing a speech signal, clipping is a type of noise that must be avoided.

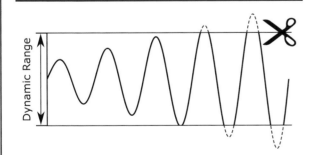

Figure 12–8. Example of a clipped sine wave. The signal peaks and valleys that exceed the instrument's dynamic range have been "clipped" (*solid line*), as if by an electronic scissors. Once clipping has occurred, the signal has been distorted and the original form cannot be restored.

A Special Consideration: Electrical Safety

Electrical safety is paramount when using instrumentation. If the electrical voltage is high enough, electricity can pass through the human body in the form of electrical current. Even a very small amount of current passing through your heart can be sufficient to negatively affect its function. Clearly, this would be a bad thing. Considering that all amplifiers require a source of electrical power to function, amplifiers that may be directly coupled to the body (in the form of connection with skin-mounted EMG or ABR sensors or the like) present a risk of electrical shock or worse.

Unlike preamplifiers used with microphones, biopotential amplifiers are required to be electrically isolated from the individual for safety purposes. Sensors used to capture biologically generated electrical activity are physically connected to the individual and by wires to the biopotential amplifier. Because of this, there is a risk of electrical shock or electrocution if something were to go wrong with the electronic circuits of the amplifier or with the electrical wiring that powers the amplifier. Biopotential amplifiers minimize that risk by physically isolating the wires connected to the individual from any circuitry in the amplifier that could potentially be connected to the hazardous electrical supply from the wall outlet.

noise (termed total harmonic distortion, or THD) to the signal, and it may even "clip" the signal (see Peak Clipping). As is the case for microphones, maintaining a signal within the amplifier's functional operating parameters for frequency and dynamic range is essential to capture a signal accurately.

Amplifier Compatibility

So, can a microphone preamplifier be used with biopotential sensors? No. Microphone preamplifiers are not electrically isolated from the individual, and thus there is a small risk of electrical shock if something were to go wrong with the circuit (see A Special Consideration: Electrical Safety). Fortunately, considering that microphones should not be electrically coupled to the body, this risk is very slight. However, "very slight" is not good enough in terms of sensors directly attached (i.e., electrically coupled) to the body, and thus the risk of electrical shock with bioamplifiers is minimized due to the physical and electronic design of such amplifiers.

Additionally, the frequency range, dynamic range, gain range, and even the connector types and impedance rating are not compatible between biologic sensors and microphone preamplifiers. They just won't work. Similarly, a microphone can't be connected to a biopotential amplifier.

Study Questions

14. Define gain and phantom power.

15. Explain the similarities and differences of microphone preamplifiers and bioamplifiers.

16. Why must only bioamplifiers be used with physiologic sensors attached to the body?

17. How do the performance characteristics of frequency range and dynamic range apply to amplifiers?

18. What is peak clipping and how can it be avoided?

12.6 Making the Connection

To connect microphones to preamplifiers or other sensors to appropriate amplifiers, specialized electrical plugs and matching sockets are used. (In common parlance, an electrical plug is known as the male connector, while the socket is called the female connector, collectively referred to as connector gender.) A myriad of connector types may be used with the various types of sensors used to capture speech, but microphones typically use variations of only two types: XLR and TRS (or phone) connectors.

High-quality microphones typically utilize XLR-type connectors. A microphone cable with both a female and a male XLR connector will connect to the microphone and preamplifier, respectively (Figure 12–9). A XLR cable contains three separate wires, or conductors, carrying electrical signals between the connected devices. In addition to the full-size XLR connectors shown in Figure 12–9, some devices such as some head-worn microphones may use a smaller "mini-XLR" connector. Further, there are other types of XLR connectors that have more than three individual connectors each (pins or sockets), but these types are uncommon in audio applications.

A second commonly used type of connector for audio systems is the phone connector. More accurately called the TS or TRS connector, this type of plug and socket has been used for many years in countless audio applications. Yes, phone does refer to telephone. These types of connectors have been in use since the late 1800s, originally in telephone switchboards. Interestingly, most cell phones still use a phone connector as the headphone jack. The phone connector should not be confused with the "phono"-type audio connector (also called "RCA" or "A/V" connector), as the two are mechanically incompatible.

The most common sizes of phone connectors are 1/8 inch and 1/4 inch, with the specific label denoting the diameter of the plug. Phone connectors may have two, three, or four individual connections, with the connections listed as tip, ring, or sleeve, based on their location on the plug (Figure 12–10). Consequently, a two-conductor phone connector is labeled a TS (for tip, sleeve) connector, one with three conductors is listed as TRS (for tip, ring, sleeve), and one with four conductors is termed TRRS (for tip, ring, ring, sleeve). While it is unusual for high-quality microphones to utilize phone connectors rather than XLR connectors, it is quite common to find low-cost microphones with phone connector types.

TRS connectors and cables contain three individual conductors and can carry two independent signals. Consequently, such connectors are commonly used on headphones and earbuds to allow for stereo audio signals where the right ear and the left ear receive slightly different audio signals. A TS connector and cable only contains two individual conductors and can therefore only carry one signal. The more

Figure 12–9. A balanced microphone cable with male (*left*) and female XLR connectors. The three conductor pins and associated receptacles can be seen in the male and female connectors, respectively.

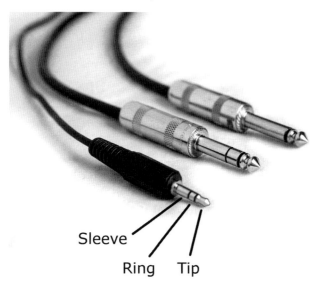

Sleeve

Ring   Tip

Figure 12–10. Three examples of phone connector plugs. The left connector is a TRS (Tip, Ring, Sleeve) type of size 1/8 inch (or 3.5 mm), commonly used as a connector for headphones or earbuds. Some microphones use this type of connector, as most laptop computers (as well as cell phones) have compatible jacks. The center and right connectors are both 1/4 inch (7 mm) in diameter. The middle connector is also a TRS type, while the right connector is a two-conductor TS (Tip, Sleeve) type. Some headphones, earbuds, and microphones use 1/4-inch connectors, but it is increasingly common that only the 1/8-inch size is used for headphones and earbuds to facilitate connection to smartphones and tablets.

complex TRRS connector can carry three distinct signals and is therefore often used to carry stereo audio in addition to a microphone signal. You may find a TRRS connector on headphones or earbuds that you use with your smartphone.

Standard XLR connectors contain three connecting pins (or sockets, on the female XLR connectors), and they are typically configured so that the microphone and preamplifier are linked using balanced wiring. A balanced configuration includes two signal conductors that are out of phase with each other and a third conductor that acts as an electrical shield. This special configuration makes the microphone's cable less susceptible to the ingress of external electrical (electromagnetic) noise that could otherwise alter the captured signal. Microphones config-

ured with balanced wiring have been found to perform better on some speech analyses than microphones with unbalanced outputs (Titze & Winholtz, 1993). A TRS connector may also be connected for balanced microphone wiring in a manner equivalent to a XLR connector. Note that a microphone with a connector type of three (or more) conductors may be configured with a balanced wiring scheme, but the mere presence of at least three conductors does not necessarily ensure that this is the case. Therefore, a microphone that utilizes a TS connector (or other connectors with only two conductors) cannot be configured for balanced wiring.

Devices such as EMG or ABR electrodes, airflow and pressure transducers, and various other sensors utilize specialized connector types, some of which may be proprietary to the device's manufacturer. As is the case for microphones, the purpose of the cables and connectors is to carry the electrical signal that originated at the sensor to the next stage of instrumentation while maintaining signal integrity.

Study Questions

19. What type of connectors is commonly used with microphones?

20. What is "balanced wiring" and for what purpose is it used?

21. Which specific types of microphone connectors may be used with a balanced wiring configuration?

22. What is the ultimate purpose of cables and connectors used to join sensors and amplifiers?

12.7 Recording Environment

Along with the performance specifications of microphones, amplifiers, and other instruments, the environment in which you choose to capture your signal plays an important role. Additive noise in the form of acoustic room (ambient) sound as well as electromagnetic interference can negatively affect the accuracy of the captured signal.

Ambient Acoustic Noise

Ambient or room acoustic noise may be generated by ventilation systems, speech from passersby, and fans that are internal to instruments themselves, among other sources. Often, the ambient acoustic noise generated by ventilation systems may be of low frequency. Given the auditory system's poor sensitivity to low-frequency sound, you may not even be aware of the presence (or magnitude) of such noise. However, additive acoustic noise has been shown to have a detrimental effect on the reliability and validity of acoustic voice analyses (Deliyski, Shaw, & Evans, 2005a).

If an acoustically treated room (such as a sound isolated booth) is not available, a sound level meter can be used to assess the ambient sound level of the room to determine its suitability for recording purposes. The use of octave band filtering can provide detail on the frequency of the noise, which may help to identify and eliminate the source of the offending noise. If a sound level meter with octave band filtering is not available, a standard sound level meter may be used as well. The presence of very low-frequency noise may be assessed by measuring the ambient sound level with the meter set on an A weighting scale as compared to the same measurement using a C (or linear, if possible) weighting scale. With this strategy, a higher ambient sound pressure level reading for the C weighting scale would indicate the presence of low-frequency noise. Simple but effective strategies for reducing ambient sound interference include turning off equipment that is not in use (to eliminate internal fan noise), moving noisy equipment to a location distant to the microphone, or employing a microphone with a cardioid response pattern. If the source of the noise can't be eliminated or controlled (which may be the case for ventilation noise), you should consider a different recording environment.

Electromagnetic Interference

Electromagnetic interference may be another source of noise present in a recording environment. This type of noise may be generated by electromagnetic induction from varying electrical voltages and currents present in power cords, signal cables, computer monitors, and many other electrical devices. Cell phones and other wireless communication devices generate high-frequency electromagnetic (radio) waves that also are potential sources of electromagnetic interference. For recording of speech acoustic and nonacoustic signals, any of these sources may generate additive noise in the captured signal.

Identifying the presence of electromagnetic interference can be challenging. An oscilloscope may be used at various locations along the instrumentation chain to display the electrical waveform of the desired signal and to identify the presence of electromagnetic noise. In the United States, the alternating current (AC) from electrical outlets that powers electrical instruments (besides battery-powered devices) cycles at 60 Hz. Electromagnetic interference from power cords that may be laying alongside a microphone or other signal cable may therefore yield an additive 60-Hz waveform (and harmonics above 60 Hz) to the captured signal. The amplitude of this additive 60-Hz noise waveform can be comparable to a microphone signal's electrical voltage level, potentially yielding a very low signal to noise ratio. Radio frequency signals (such as cell phone transmission) are of much higher frequency and are typically very low in amplitude. The signal generated by a microphone would likely be much greater in magnitude than radio frequency noise, but signals from EMG and other physiologic sensors may be of low enough amplitude that they are susceptible to significant interference from radio frequency electromagnetic noise.

As is the case for reducing ambient acoustic noise, eliminating or reducing the source of electromagnetic noise should be attempted. Electromagnetic noise from power sources (60-Hz noise) is often due to inductance from signal cables that lie parallel with power cables connected to wall outlets. Physically separating signal and power cables (or aligning them at right angles) may be enough to reduce the interference of the 60-Hz noise. Signal cables should be of shielded construction to be less susceptible to electromagnetic noise. Note that shielding is not the same as the cable's insulation. The plastic coating on the outer surfaces of cables is the insulation that prevents electrical current from passing to you should you touch the cable. Shielding is a conductive layer inside of the signal cable that is used to reduce susceptibility to electromagnetic interference. Microphone and other specialized signal cables will typically be shielded. In addition, microphone cables configured with "balanced" wiring are less susceptible to electromagnetic noise. As you recall, microphone cables with XLR connectors are typically configured with balanced wiring, but lower quality microphones and cables may not be configured with balanced wiring.

The recording environment should be selected with the goals of reducing both the ambient acoustic and electromagnetic noise. The presence of high levels of either (or both) types of environmental noise can have a detrimental effect on your captured waveform as reflected in a low signal to noise ratio. Sound-isolated rooms are optimal environments for capturing speech acoustics, but even quiet clinical rooms may be acceptable if the ambient noise level is low enough (Maryn & Zarowski, 2015).

Study Questions

23. Define ambient and electromagnetic noise.

24. How may a sound level meter be used to assess the presence of ambient (room) noise?

25. What is the source of 60-Hz electromagnetic noise?

26. What is the goal for selecting an appropriate recording environment?

27. What is the advantage of using balanced wiring with microphones in terms of environmental noise?

28. List strategies for reducing ambient (room) noise.

29. List strategies for reducing electromagnetic interference.

12.8 Data Acquisition: Let's Get Digital

We've traveled quite a distance down the instrumentation path from the sensor to the amplification stage, but now what? At this point, we have captured an electrical signal whose amplitude varies continuously over time as an analog representation (albeit a simulacrum) of the original physical event of interest. But if we want to view, analyze, and save that electrical signal, we'll need to transfer it to a computerized recording device. This process is termed data acquisition (often abbreviated as DAQ), and it requires a dramatic transformation to take place. Our time-varying electrical signal must be converted to a sequence of numbers that the computer can, well, compute. Once this conversion has occurred, the signal is now in digital form.

Even though we subdivide our day into discrete hours, minutes, seconds, or even smaller units, time is a continuous phenomenon and any physical events that occur in the real world are therefore continuous events as well. Similarly, the electrical representations of physical events generated by sensors such as microphones and pressure transducers are also continuous in terms of time. These representations are termed "analog" signals. In addition to microphones and other sensors, instruments such as microphone preamplifiers and biopotential amplifiers are also analog devices as both the input and output signals are continuous representations in time. Tape recorders and turntables (record players) are analog recording and playback devices. Analog recording and playback devices are still used today, primarily for music, but such devices are not suitable or practical for modern recording and analysis of speech signals. Computerized (digital) recording devices allow for efficient signal capture and essentially unlimited strategies for signal analysis.

Computers are digital devices and as such cannot directly make use of analog signals. Instead, the computer requires that an analog signal be converted to a digital form. The term "digital" implies two things: a computerized system and sequences of numbers represented in binary notation (Figure 12–11).

Digital devices such as laptop computers, tablets, smartphones, hearing aids, cochlear implants, high-definition televisions, DVD and Blu-ray disk players, voice recorders, and many other devices all function by manipulating sequences of numbers. These numbers may represent the colors displayed on the computer's screen, the letters you type into a word processing program, or the waveform of a sound captured by a microphone. What is common across all digital devices, however, is that the numbers are represented in binary notation. Binary notation is a system for representing numbers based on the digits 0 and 1, unlike decimal notation

that we're used to using where numbers are represented using the digits 0 through 9.

When you think about it, computers are not terribly smart. They can only follow explicit instructions, and they can only count to one due to limitations of their electronic components. Further, they can't represent events in a continuous (analog) format, as computer circuitry necessitates subdividing continuous events into discrete segments. As real-world events (and their electrical representations) are continuous in time (in other words, analog), the computer must convert continuous analog signals into representations that are sequences of discrete (yet related) binary numbers.

The process of transforming an analog signal to a digital (or "digitized") representation is called "analog-to-digital conversion," "data acquisition," or just "digitization" (Figure 12–12). The device used to digitize a signal, an analog-to-digital converter (ADC), may be integrated with a laptop or desktop computer (as an integral component of the computer's soundcard), tablets, smartphones, portable digital voice recorders, and other specialized instruments.

Analog-to-digital conversion involves segmenting an electrical signal into discrete time intervals, with a measurement of the signal at each time interval termed a sample. The number of samples of the signal taken per second is termed the sampling frequency (or sampling rate). The amplitude level of the signal at each sample is segmented as well in a process called quantization. By these means, the signal can be captured by the computer in digital format with representation in terms of time (discrete samples) and amplitude (quantization levels) (Figure 12–13).

Sampling: Time Representation

The process of sampling involves taking a series of measurements of the signal to be digitized at discrete (and equal) time intervals. For data acquisition, several standard sampling rates have been established. For example, the sampling frequency of 44.1 kHz (44,100 samples per second)

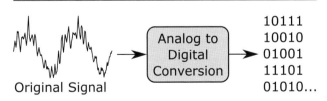

Figure 12–11. Computers "see" real-world (analog) signals as patterns of individual numbers. The process of data acquisition involves converting analog signals to a sequence of numbers using the binary counting system that is limited to the digits "0" and "1."

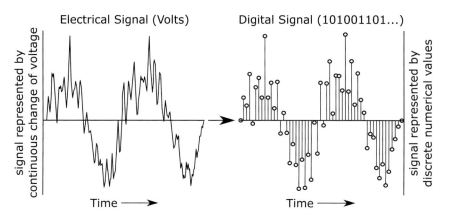

Figure 12–12. Analog-to-digital conversion is the process of transforming an analog electrical signal into a corresponding digital representation that can be processed by a computerized device. Here, the open circles on the right panel represent individual measurements called "samples" taken at discrete time intervals. Computers use binary notation (limited to the digits "0" and "1") to represent the measured values of the discrete samples.

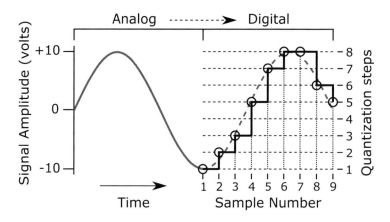

Figure 12–13. The process of data acquisition involves converting an analog signal into a digital representation. Time is represented by discrete samples (open circles; a total of nine samples are shown here) separated by fixed time intervals, while amplitude is represented by discrete "quantization steps" or levels. Technically, there is no representation of the signal within the gaps of time and amplitude in between the samples and quantization steps, respectively. Note that the digitized signal (*solid line on right*) is not smooth (continuous) like the original analog signal. Instead, the discrete steps deviate from the original waveform (*dashed line*).

is used to encode audio tracks onto compact discs, and sampling frequencies of 48 kHz, 96 kHz, and higher are commonly used in modern recording studios. Higher sampling frequencies produce a greater number of samples per waveform cycle, yielding a digitized signal that is closer in representation to the original analog signal than would be obtained with a lower sampling rate (Figure 12–14). However, higher sampling frequencies result in greater amounts of data to be stored. For example, a 30-second signal digitized with a sampling rate of 10 kHz

4 samples/cycle   11 samples/cycle

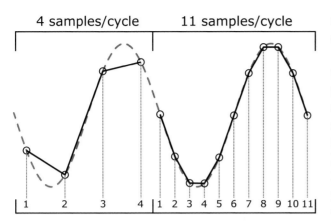

Figure 12–14. The effect of low and high sampling rates. The sine wave cycle (*dashed line*) on the left has been sampled at a rate of four equally spaced (in terms of time) samples per cycle, while the cycle on the right has been represented by 11 samples. The "reconstructed" signal shape is illustrated by solid lines connecting the successive samples. Increasing the numbers of samples taken per cycle yields greater accuracy of the captured signal as evidenced by the increased overlap with the original waveform.

(and a bit depth of 16 bits, see below) yields a file that is 600 kB in size, while the use of a 20-kHz sampling rate will produce a data file that is twice as large. Modern computers typically have adequate storage space for even relatively lengthy signals digitized at high sample rates, but file storage space can be an issue if many recordings are archived.

Back in Chapter 3, we learned the inherent relationship between time and frequency. Recall that frequency is the number of cycles (repetitions) of an event per second. Consequently, knowledge of the duration of an individual cycle (or repeated event) can be used to calculate that event's frequency, by using the formula $f = 1/T$, where "T" reflects the period, or duration in time of one cycle and "f" refers to the calculated frequency. Conversely, the cycle, period can be calculated by taking the reciprocal of frequency, or $T = 1/f$. These formulas can be used to describe parameters related to sampling frequency for data acquisition. As described above, the sampling frequency (the number of samples taken per second) equals $1/T$, where "T" reflects the

time interval between consecutive samples, called the sampling interval.

The sampling frequency expressly limits the maximum frequency of a captured signal as each complete cycle of the signal must be sampled at least twice for it to be represented in digital form. Therefore, the sampling frequency for data acquisition must be at least twice as high as the highest frequency in the original analog signal (that is, yielding at least two samples per cycle) (Nyquist, 1928; Shannon, 1949). This concept, called the Nyquist-Shannon sampling theorem, (or, equivalently, the Nyquist theorem) forms the basis for determining the minimum sampling frequency required when converting a signal from analog-to-digital format. The Nyquist frequency is the highest frequency that an analog-to-digital converter can capture and is equal to exactly half of the sampling frequency. The Nyquist rate is the sampling frequency that will yield two samples per cycle of the waveform. In other words, to capture a signal that contains frequencies up to 10 kHz, a sampling rate of *at least* 20 kHz (the Nyquist rate) must be used. The 44.1-kHz compact disc standard sampling rate can therefore be used to digitize signals that contain frequencies up to 22,050 Hz.

For speech, relevant acoustic energy can range from approximately 50 Hz to over 16 kHz, but most energy is below 10 kHz (Baken & Orlikoff, 2000; Monson, Hunter, Lotto, & Story, 2014; Svec, Schutte, & Miller, 1996). To adequately sample speech signals of up to 10 kHz, a sampling frequency of at least 20 kHz is required, and capturing signals that may contain frequencies of up to 16 kHz requires a sampling rate of at least 32 kHz. Note that these sampling rates will produce only two samples per cycle for the highest frequencies, but the use of even higher sampling rates will result in additional samples per cycle of the signal. Digitizing a signal by using a sampling rate substantially higher than the Nyquist (minimum) rate, termed **oversampling**, results in a digitized signal that is closer in shape to the original signal at the expense of increased data file size (see Figure 12–14).

The sampling rate may be selected by the user of the computer as data acquisition software (or apps) will typically list a series of predeter-min-ed sampling rates to choose from. Common sampling frequencies include 8,000 Hz, 11,025 Hz, 22,050 Hz, 24 kHz, 44.1 kHz (CD quality rate), 48 kHz, and 96 kHz. The reason for the some-what odd numbers is 44.1 kHz is the industry standard sampling frequency for music CDs, and 11,025 is one-quarter of 44.1 kHz and 22,050 is one-half of 44.1 kHz. Sampling rates greater than 40 kHz would be considered an oversampling rate for signals up to 20 kHz. The maximum sampling rate for any computer is limited by the performance characteristics of the analog-to-digital converter. High-quality laboratory or recording studio data acquisition systems may be able to sample at extremely high rates, while laptop computers, smartphones, and tablets may be limited to 96 kHz or less. Although the sampling rate of 26 kHz appears to be adequate for analyzing many parameters of speech, includ-ing fundamental frequency, jitter, and shimmer (Deliyski, Shaw, & Evans, 2005b), oversampling by digitizing using higher rates (such as the "CD standard" of 44.1 kHz) is recommended to increase the accuracy of the captured signal and to allow for analysis of higher frequency com-ponents of speech (Monson et al., 2014; Svec & Granqvist, 2010; Vogel & Morgan, 2009).

Quantization: Amplitude Representation

The second process required to convert an ana-log electrical signal to digital form is quantiza-tion. The process of sampling involves taking a series of measurements of a signal at discrete time intervals to obtain a time-based representa-tion of the signal. Quantization creates a repre-sentation of amplitude by mapping the original signal's electrical voltage level at each sample to a series of discrete numerical values called quan-tization levels (see Figure 12–13). Recall that the original physical event and the captured (as by a microphone) electrical simulacrum are analog signals and are thus continuous in terms of time and amplitude. As computers cannot represent continuously changing events, the continuous

amplitude values of the signal must be con-verted to a predetermined amount of discrete digital number values, or quantization levels.

The number of mapped quantization levels relates directly to the accuracy of the digitized signal's representation in a manner that is con-ceptually similar to variations in sampling rate. Thus, a higher number of quantization levels will produce a more accurate digitized signal in terms of the amplitude representation. As for sampling rate, the number of total quantization levels is limited by the performance characteris-tics of the analog-to-digital converter.

Without delving too far into computer theory, the number of quantization levels ("bit depth") is equal to 2^b, where "b" typically equals 8, 16, or 24 "bits." Thus, an 8-bit analog-to-digital converter has 2^8 (or 256) quantization levels, while a 16-bit digitizer has 2^{16} (or 65,536) dis-crete quantization levels. A 24-bit analog-to-digital converter has an astounding 16,777,216 discrete quantization levels! A 24-bit ADC, there-fore, will yield a digitized waveform with much higher accuracy in terms of amplitude represen-tation than an 8-bit ADC (Figure 12–15).

Frequency-Based Error: Aliasing

Similar to what we've seen for sensors and ampli-fiers, digital error can include added noise or waveform distortion. However, the cause of the error is specific to the process of digitization. As described previously, the sampling rate directly limits the highest frequency that can be captured.

Therefore, the frequency range of the ADC is limited by the sampling rate. If the signal con-tains frequencies higher than the Nyquist fre-quency, a unique type of digital error termed "aliasing" can occur. Aliasing is the result of undersampling: sampling at a rate that is less than twice the highest frequency in the signal (i.e., sampling at less than the Nyquist rate). With less than two samples captured per wave-form cycle, an errant lower frequency "aliased" waveform will be created in the digitized signal (Figure 12–16).

To prevent aliasing, frequencies in the orig-inal signal above the Nyquist frequency must

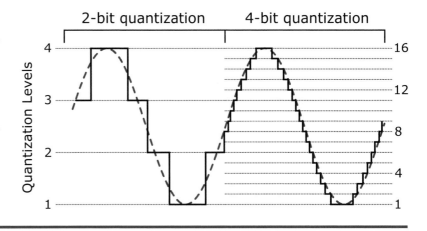

Figure 12–15. The effect of increasing quantization bit depth on quantization error. The digital representation (*solid line*) produced with 4-bit quantization (i.e., 16 amplitude levels or "steps") follows the original analog signal (*dashed line*) much more closely than the digital representation resulting from 2-bit quantization.

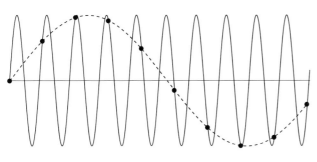

Figure 12–16. A waveform sampled at a rate below the Nyquist frequency will yield an "aliased" signal (*dashed line*). This process, called "temporal aliasing," yields a novel (and undesired) low frequency that is added to the captured signal; thus it results in distortion of the original waveform. Here, the original high-frequency waveform (*solid line*) will not be captured as the sampling rate only yields one sample per waveform cycle (i.e., "undersampling"). Consequently, the errant lower frequency aliased waveform will be added to the digital representation.

be eliminated by filtering them out. Recall our discussion of low- and high-pass filtering from Chapter 7. Anti-aliasing filters are low-pass (that is, they attenuate high frequencies) analog filters that attenuate frequencies above the Nyquist frequency. Many ADC systems incorporate anti-aliasing filters in their circuitry, and they are automatically engaged during digitization. Some analog-to-digital conversion systems, however, do not have integrated anti-aliasing filters. In this case, the signal to be captured must be conditioned by a separate anti-aliasing filter device

connected prior to the input of the ADC. (Interestingly, the process of aliasing forms the basis for stroboscopy, the technique we learned about in Chapter 6 to visualize vocal fold oscillation.)

Amplitude-Based Error: Quantization Noise and Peak Clipping

A second type of digitization error is quantization noise (or error). Recall that an ADC will have a limited number of quantization steps for which to represent a signal's amplitude. The dynamic range of the ADC is limited to the voltage range that can be input, and the quantization levels are spread equally throughout the ADC's dynamic range. The difference between the original signal and the digitized representation is termed **quantization error** or quantization noise (see Figure 12–15). An ADC with greater bit depth (number of quantization levels) will yield a lower amount of quantization error for a given signal amplitude. If only a small portion of the ADC's dynamic range is taken up by the signal's amplitude, however, only a fraction of the available quantization levels will be used. This situation is essentially like employing a digitizer with a lower bit depth. Laboratory-type ADC systems may have an input voltage range of ±5 volts or even ±10 volts. Computer soundcards and smartphone microphone inputs are designed to accept very low line level (output of a preamplifier) or microphone level (output directly from a microphone) signals. These ADC systems will likely have an input voltage range of only about ±1 volt.

For example, let's assume that the signal from a microphone's preamplifier has a maximum amplitude of ±1 volt, and the ADC has a dynamic range of ±10 volts. Your signal's amplitude will be filling only 10% of the ADC's dynamic range, and thus only 10% of the available quantization levels will be used. A 16-bit ADC will have 65,536 available quantization levels, but utilizing only 10% of the available levels will yield only 6,553 amplitude steps applied to the captured signal. This reduction in applied amplitude levels will result in an increase in quantization error as compared to using the full dynamic range of the ADC.

An analog-to-digital converter with greater bit depth (such as a 24-bit digitizer as compared to a 16-bit system) will yield a lower amount of quantization error if the signal's amplitude comprises most of the dynamic range of the ADC without exceeding its limits. In fact, you should use as much of the ADC's dynamic range as possible without exceeding the limits, as exceeding the dynamic range will result in peak clipping (see Peak Clipping).

With all other factors being equal, an ADC with greater bit depth will yield less quantization error than one with lower bit depth (that is, a 24-bit ADC compared to a 16-bit system). However, even with an extremely large number of quantization levels (such as with a 24-bit digitizer), a signal that is very low in input voltage amplitude will be digitized with greater quantization error than one in which the maximum amplitude voltage is closer to the limits of the ADC's input dynamic range. This is because a very low-input amplitude voltage (relative to the input dynamic range) will be mapped to just a fraction of the total quantization levels.

On the other hand, a signal that is greater in amplitude than the input dynamic range of the ADC system will be clipped. Therefore, the gain of the preamplifier connected to the ADC should be adjusted such that the signal fills up as much of the ADC's dynamic range quantization space as possible without exceeding the input voltage limits.

Study Questions

30. Define digitization, sampling, quantization, and ADC.

31. What is aliasing and how can it be prevented?

32. What does the Nyquist rate have to do with the maximum frequency of a digitized signal?

33. What is quantization error and how can it be minimized?

34. How is an ADC with 24-bit quantization depth better than one with 16-bit quantization depth?

35. Why is it important to "fill up" the quantization space?

36. Contrast undersampling and oversampling.

12.9 Data Storage

Unless your goal is only to temporarily display a waveform on a computer screen, data storage is necessary. Digitized signals may be stored in a variety of distinct data file types. However, all data files are of either compressed or uncompressed format. Uncompressed data files store all discrete data values generated during digitization. For example, a single signal (or a mono audio signal) digitized at a 44.1-kHz sampling rate and 16-bit resolution will necessitate storage of 705,600 bits[3] per second, or a file that

---

[3] A "bit" equals a single "0" or "1" digit, and a "byte" equals eight bits. As you know, sometimes a bite is just too much, therefore a "nibble" equals half of a byte, or four bits. Seriously. For further reference, a "kilobyte" (kB) equals 1,000 bytes, and a "megabyte" equals 1,000,000 bytes (or 1,000 kB).

is 5.3 MB (megabytes) in size for every minute of digitized data. If two signals were digitized simultaneously (as for a stereo audio file), the resulting file would be twice this size. Common types of uncompressed file formats are WAV (file extension .wav; typically associated with computers running the MS-Windows operating system) and AIFF (file extension .aiff; typically associated with computers running Mac OS).

Data files are compressed to reduce the size of the stored file. Compression strategies can be categorized as lossy or lossless, with the former being associated quite literally with a loss or discard of some of the data in the captured signal to produce the file size reduction. You are likely quite familiar with the lossy data compression formats MP3, WMA, and AAC that are commonly used to reduce the size of audio files. Data digitized at high sample rates and bit depths yield correspondingly large data file sizes. Lossy data compression techniques reduce file size by essentially eliminating data values that may not be perceptually salient to most listeners. Lossy data compression strategies can reduce the file size by 90% or more, but the consequence is that 90% (or more) of the data will have literally been eliminated. This loss of data does certainly impact the quality of the recorded signal and may negatively affect the validity of subsequent speech or voice analyses (Vogel & Morgan, 2009). The amount of data compression is reflected in the file's bit rate, which is equal to the number of encoded data bits stored per second. As described above, a signal digitized at 44.1 kHz at a 16-bit quantization depth will produce a bit rate of 705,600 bits per second (or 705.6 kilobits per second, abbreviated kbps). The lower the bit rate (due to encoding with a lossy compression strategy), the smaller the file size and the greater the loss of signal quality. Once the signal's quality (accuracy) has been lost, it cannot be recovered. Converting from a compressed (such as MP3)

format to an uncompressed file format will not restore the signal's quality.

Lossless data compression techniques do exist, however, and such techniques can be used to reduce the size of the data file without any loss of signal integrity. Some common lossless formats include Apple Lossless (ALAC), WMA (Windows Media Audio) Lossless, and Free Lossless Audio Codec (FLAC). Due to their method of compression, these lossless compression techniques cannot reduce the size of files as much as lossy compression techniques can. Unlike lossy techniques, however, lossless compression techniques are not commonly used.

While speech signals stored in compressed files may be suitable for certain purposes that don't require high signal accuracy (such as when transcribing a language sample), detailed speech analyses may be negatively affected by the reduction in signal quality inherent to data compression (Vogel & Morgan, 2009). Further, many speech analysis applications do not support opening and analysis of data files of some compressed formats. Given the relatively low cost of data storage for today's computer systems and the potential for data quality reduction during compression, the best way to store data files for speech analysis is in an uncompressed file format.

Study Questions

37. Compare and contrast lossy versus lossless compression.

38. Why should data file compression not be used when recording (and storing) signals for analysis?

39. How does a file's "bit rate" tell you about the quality of the signal?

Digital-to-Analog Conversion

We live in the analog domain, so if we want to listen to an audio signal that has been digitized, we'll have to convert the digital signal to an analog form. The process of converting a digital signal to an analog signal is simply termed "digital-to-analog conversion" (abbreviated D-to-A or DAC), and various interpolation techniques are used to fill in the gaps between discrete digital samples. The DAC output will consist of a continuously varying voltage waveform or, in other words, essentially a re-creation of the predigitized electrical signal but with the addition of associated digitization error. The process of digital-to-analog conversion is required to play a digital sound file through analog devices such as loudspeakers, headphones, or earbuds.

The transducers that change electrical signals to sound in headphones, earbuds, and loudspeakers are analog devices, even if the devices are advertised as digital or digital ready. Most laptop computers, smartphones, and other digital music players output an analog signal directly to the headphones or earbuds. In contrast, some new types of earbuds utilize an integrated digital-to-analog converter to produce an analog waveform from a digital signal output by the smartphone. So, even though a digital signal is produced by the smartphone, an analog waveform signal is still delivered to analog transducers that produce the sound wave that you hear.

Interestingly, if we tried to directly listen to a digital audio data file without first converting to an analog form, all we would hear would be unpleasant static, no matter how beautiful the original sound. I don't recommend this unless you are a fan of the genre of "noise music" or of the musical futurist Luigi Russolo, who wrote the book, *L'Arte dei Rumori* or *The Art of Noises*. A 1917 performance of Russolo's Gran Concerto Futuristico apparently engendered violent disapproval from his audience in the form of thrown rotten fruit accompanied by enthusiastic shouting and jeering (Goldsmith, 2012).

Study Questions

40. Why would we need to convert signals from digital to analog form?

41. Why do devices such as headphones and earbuds require an analog signal?

12.10 Balancing Cost, Complexity, and Accuracy in Digital Data Acquisition

Several factors must be taken into consideration when capturing and recording a speech signal. In addition to the issues raised previously about microphone performance specifications, amplifier gain, and ADC settings, we must also take into consideration the recording environment and the spending limit of your credit card. Reference-grade instrumentation systems that incorporate "measurement standard" microphones or other specialized sensors, low-noise preamplifiers, and high-precision ADC systems can be prohibitively expensive for many clinics and laboratories. On the other end of the cost spectrum for data acquisition devices are smartphones, tablets, and laptop computers.

It's certainly the case that portable electronic devices have been increasing in quality while not necessarily increasing in price with each new model year, but it is not clear whether the performance of portable devices with integrated sound capture hardware (such as smartphones, tablets, digital voice recorders, and even laptop computers) is adequate for the capture and analysis of speech. These digital devices utilize an internal soundcard that contains integrated preamplifiers, anti-aliasing filters, and analog-to-digital converters, and most will also have at least one built-in microphone. As for any type of instrumentation, the performance specifications of the instrument's components (that is, integrated soundcards and internal microphones) will have a direct impact on the quality of the captured and recorded signal.

Typically, soundcards will have a frequency range of 20 Hz to 20 kHz and will support several common sampling rates such as 22.05 kHz, 44.1 kHz, 48 kHz, and perhaps even higher. Sampling rates of 44.1 kHz or higher are adequate for digitizing acoustic speech signals, and even rates as low as 26 kHz may be used for signals subject to certain voice analyses (Deliyski, Shaw, & Evans, 2005b). The performance specifications of internal (built-in) microphones are not easy to determine. Many smartphones and tablets contain more than one internal microphone, sometimes on different sides of the device, with the combination of microphones often used as a strategy for reducing ambient noise to increase the quality of the speech signal (such as the increase the signal to noise ratio) for telephony applications (DeCanne, 2013). The performance specifications of frequency range, sensitivity, dynamic range, and directionality may be different for the various microphones on the device, and manufacturers may use different microphones (with differing performance characteristics) across device models. However, most smartphones, tablets, and laptops will support the connection of an external microphone through a 1/8-inch TRS or TRRS port, and many of these devices can even supply requisite power sufficient for operation of condenser microphones (likely electret condenser types) that only require a supply voltage of approximately 2 volts. An external microphone may have superior (and documented) performance characteristics to the internal microphone(s).

To prevent peak clipping, some portable recording devices utilize a strategy called automatic gain control (AGC). This process auto-matically reduces the gain of the preamplifier if the signal approaches the limit of the system's dynamic range. Thus, the amplitude of the recorded signal will remain nearly constant, reducing or eliminating the amplitude variation present in the original signal. Given that measurements of the sound pressure level of speech as well as of speech amplitude variation (shimmer) are central to numerous assessment and therapeutic protocols (for example, Fox et al., 2006), automatic gain control processes must be disabled.

Strong interest exists in utilizing such low-cost portable devices for the acquisition of speech and other acoustic signals. Recent studies have investigated the suitability of smartphones for acquiring high-quality recordings of speech acoustics (Oliveira, Fava, Baglione, & Pimpinella, 2016; Uloza et al., 2015; Vogel, Rosen, Morgan, & Reilly, 2014) and for obtaining accurate measurements of sound pressure levels (Fava et al., 2016; Kardous & Shaw, 2014). Smartphones and tablets may support adequate sampling rates for capturing acoustic speech signals, but the performance of internal versus external microphones, automatic gain control processes, the quality of the microphone preamplifier, adequacy of anti-aliasing filtering, and the dynamic and frequency ranges of the systems is not clear, especially when considering devices with hardware and application software produced by different manufacturers. Although more research clearly needs to be done in this area, results from these preliminary studies on smartphones are promising.

Another portable recording platform is the ubiquitous laptop computer. These devices typically incorporate a soundcard that will support standard (and adequate) sampling rates (e.g., 44.1 kHz, 48 kHz, etc.) and a quantization resolution of at least 16 bits. As for smartphones and tablets, the soundcard of a laptop computer will typically supply a relatively low level (approximately 2 volts) of power through a 1/8-inch TRS input jack, sufficient for operation of many external electret condenser microphones. Condenser microphones that require a higher level of power (perhaps up to 48 volts of phantom power) for their operation would require the

A Special Case: External ADC Systems

In recent years, a new category of microphone has emerged: the USB microphone (Figure 12–17). Unlike conventional microphones that consist of a sensor that requires separate stages of preamplification and subsequent analog-to-digital conversion, USB microphones incorporate both preamplification and digitization stages into the microphone itself in addition to the sensor element. Similarly, there are external ADC interfaces for use with standard analog microphones. These devices integrate preamplification, anti-alias filtering, and analog-to-digital conversion into a single instrument that is designed to interface seamlessly with a computer by means of a digital (typically USB) connection.

The output of a USB microphone or an external ADC interface is a digital signal (remember our 1s and 0s?) that can be stored directly to a computer file. The quality of USB microphones ranges from low to high, and the same performance issues regarding frequency range, dynamic range, and directionality apply as for conventional analog microphones. Because the analog-to-digital converter is a component of the USB microphone and external ADC interface, issues regarding digitization performance (sampling rate, bit depth, anti-alias filtering, dynamic range) apply to these devices as well. As for complementary analog instruments, exceeding the dynamic range of the USB microphone or external ADC interface will result in clipping of the captured signal. Capture/recording software that is compatible with the USB microphone or external ADC interface will typically support various standard sampling rates.

As for many devices, you often get what you pay for. Low-cost USB microphones or external ADC interfaces may be associated with inadequate performance specifications and/or inclusion of excessive digitization and self-noise. You should be able to obtain documentation of performance specifications for higher quality USB microphones and external ADC interfaces. If documentation is not available, you should be wary of using any device, be it a USB microphone, external ADC interface, or traditional analog microphones and preamplifiers.

Figure 12–17. A handheld style dynamic microphone (*left*) with XLR connector for connection to a microphone preamplifier and a studio-style USB condenser microphone (*right*) with a USB type "A" (full-sized) plug for direct connection to a computer.

use of an external microphone preamplifier, and any microphone that utilizes an XLR connector would either require an external preamplifier or a specialized XLR to 1/8-inch TRS adaptor for coupling to the laptop's soundcard input. With an appropriate external microphone and preamplifier (if required) and in an appropriate recording environment, a laptop computer may prove to be a suitable choice for capturing and analyzing speech acoustics for clinical purposes.

What about capturing and recording physiologic signals like intraoral air pressure or tongue elevation force? Computer soundcards typically have a frequency response range from 20 Hz to 20 kHz, and thus signals that vary slowly (less than 20 Hz) cannot be captured. Signals such as intraoral pressure, oral or nasal airflow, and lip, tongue, or jaw movement vary in a frequency range of 0 Hz to much less than 20 Hz, and thus a device with a standard audio-based soundcard (e.g., computers, smartphones, tablets) will not be able to capture such signals. The alternative is to use a general-purpose laboratory data acquisition (or ADC) system that will have a frequency range that goes all the way down to 0 Hz. Such a system would prove adequate for capturing speech acoustic signals as well, however, as laboratory data acquisition hardware typically support sampling rates of well over 40 kHz (i.e., an upper frequency range of greater than 20 kHz).

A general-purpose laboratory data acquisition system may not be in the budget for many clinics and even some research labs, however. For clinical purposes of recording speech acoustics, a suitable laptop computer with an integrated soundcard coupled to a microphone with adequate performance specifications may be adequate (Neel, 2010), but for purposes of capturing low-frequency signals or for performing fine-grained analyses of speech acoustics that require high precision of measurement (e.g., perturbation analyses), an instrumentation system that consists of a high-quality microphone (or other physiologic sensors as required), preamplifier, and laboratory-type analog-to-digital converter is required (Awan et al., 2015; Deliyski, Evans, & Shaw, 2005; Svec & Granqvist, 2010; Titze, 1995).

Study Questions

42. Why is it difficult to know the actual performance characteristics of portable digital recording devices such as smartphones, tablets, laptop computers, and portable voice recorders?

43. What are the performance characteristics of a typical computer soundcard?

44. How may external microphones be connected to portable digital recording devices?

45. How are USB microphones different from standard analog microphones?

46. Why can't computer soundcards be used with signals that have frequencies less than 20 Hz?

12.11 Best Practices for the Use of Instrumentation

The goal for data acquisition is to obtain the highest quality (i.e., most accurate) representation of the speech signal. When approaching this task, guidelines of best practice for instrument performance and use should be considered. For each stage of the instrumentation chain, there are numerous factors that can potentially limit the quality and accuracy of the captured signal (Figure 12–18).

Sensor Performance and Use

For both acoustic (microphone) and nonacoustic sensors, performance specifications for frequency range and dynamic range must meet or exceed the expected maxima for the signal being captured. Further, the response should be relatively even (flat) throughout the frequency range of the signal to be captured in order to

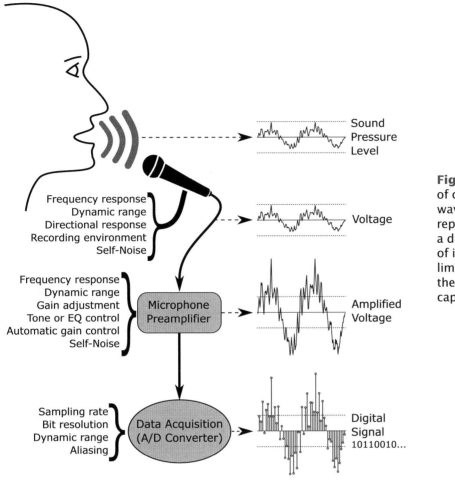

Figure 12–18. The process of capturing a speech acoustic waveform from transducer to representation on a computer as a digital signal. For each stage of instrumentation, the potential limiting factors that may affect the integrity and accuracy of the captured signal are displayed.

minimize the potential for waveform distortion. The noise floor of the sensor (including self-noise and environmental noise) must be low enough relative to the magnitude of the signal to be captured in order to provide an adequate signal-to-noise ratio. For microphones, the noise floor should be at least 15 dB (optimally 30 dB) lower than the lowest expected speech intensity. Head-worn microphones are preferred to handheld types in order to maintain the consistent mouth-to-microphone distance required for obtaining measures of speech sound pressure level with a calibrated microphone as well as for performing amplitude perturbation (shimmer) analysis (Maryn & Zarowski, 2015; Svec & Granqvist, 2010; Winholtz & Titze, 1997). Head-worn microphones should be of omnidirectional type and positioned at an angle of 45 degrees

and at a distance of 4 cm relative to the lips (Figure 12–19) (Awan et al., 2015; Deliyski, Shaw, & Evans, 2005a; Svec & Granqvist, 2010; Titze, 1995).

The recording environment should be selected with the goal of reducing the potential for ambient noise (acoustic and/or electromagnetic) to be picked up by the sensor or associated instrumentation. This may be as simple as moving the sensor away from a noise source or as complex as capturing the signals within a specialized room that incorporates extra electromagnetic shielding via a "Faraday Cage." For microphones and vibration sensors (e.g., accelerometers), ambient noise may include environmental acoustic sound (potentially including subsonic vibration) as well as electromagnetic interference, while other nonacoustic sensors may only be susceptible to electromagnetic

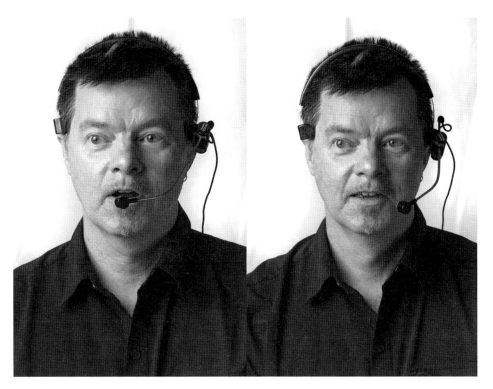

Figure 12–19. Use of a head-worn microphone showing incorrect placement of the sensor element (*left*) directly in line with the breath stream. Such placement will yield "pops" and turbulent noise in the captured signal upon production of plosives, affricates, and sibilants due to interaction with the breath stream. Placement of the microphone element shown in the right panel (45° from the breath stream with a 3- to 4-cm distance to the mouth) is recommended to minimize such artifacts (Awan et al., 2015; Titze, 1995).

interference. In some cases, the use of a cardioid microphone will aid in the suppression of ambient acoustic noise, but it must be positioned at a distance that will eliminate the proximity effect (Svec & Granqvist, 2010). Shielded instrument (signal) cables must be used throughout the instrumentation chain, including balanced wiring for microphone connections.

Note that the above recommendations are for signal capture with optimum accuracy. For acoustic signals, such performance likely requires the use of a laboratory standard "measurement" type of microphone, a high-precision preamplifier, and a sound-isolated booth. While certain precise measurements necessitate such equipment, adequate accuracy and repeatability of captured signals may be attained with instruments that are more readily available (and easier

on your credit card) such as many studio-grade "performance" microphones and preamplifiers.

Preamplifier Performance and Use

Preamplifiers should exhibit low self-noise and have dynamic and frequency ranges that exceed those of the connected sensor. For microphone preamplifiers, automatic gain control, frequency equalization (i.e., "tone" or bass and treble controls), and noise cancellation processes must be disabled (Awan et al., 2015). Further, the gain of the preamplifier should be adjusted to yield an output signal that fills the quantization space (dynamic range) of the analog-to-digital converter but is below the level that would produce clipping. Note that the microphone preamplifier may be an integral component to a computer's soundcard (via the "microphone input" port), but the above recommendations still apply.

Data Acquisition System Performance and Use

An optimal data acquisition system for capturing acoustic signals from microphones will have capabilities of high sampling rates (at least 44.1 kHz) and bit depth of at least 16-bit quantization (Awan et al., 2015). For certain nonacoustic signals that may be generated by force sensors, airflow sensors, and so on, the ADC must be able to capture signals of frequency as low as 0 Hz. Typically, computer soundcards are designed to capture only audio signals (i.e., in the range of 20 Hz to 20 kHz), and thus a laboratory-type ADC is required to capture low-frequency nonacoustic signals. Anti-aliasing filters (integrated with the digitizer or soundcard or external if necessary) must be used to eliminate the potential of aliasing artifact. The signal that is input to the data acquisition system should fill but not exceed the dynamic range of the ADC. In this regard, a 24-bit digitizer is preferential to a 16-bit system due to the increased dynamic range and reduced quantization error. The recorded file should be saved in a noncompressed format.

Study Questions

47. For optimal signal capture performance, what are the recommended microphone specifications?

48. What is the recommended sampling frequency and bit depth for capturing speech signals?

49. Why is a head-mounted microphone recommended for capturing speech?

50. Describe lower cost instrumentation that would be adequate for capturing speech in a clinical setting.

12.12 Let's Wrap This Thing Up!

Instrumentation systems do not replace a clinician's perceptual abilities. Indeed, the objective data obtained can support and guide the clinician's expert judgement. Appropriate use of instrumentation to obtain an accurate representation of the original speech signal yields objective data that can provide unique and valuable insight into the underlying movements, aerodynamics, and acoustics of speech production.

It is imperative that instrumentation systems be used properly, as the computer's analysis and your subsequent interpretation of the data will be negatively affected by an inaccurate recording. Neither the instruments nor the computer will tell you if you've captured a signal that is inaccurate and invalid. It is up to you to be able to identify error in recording that may occur at any point along the instrumentation chain.

Following guidelines of best measurement practices will lead you toward the goal of obtaining the most accurate representation possible of the captured speech signal. As you work with instrumentation systems, you will become more familiar with their performance abilities and limitations. With such knowledge, you will become more adept at utilizing instrumentation to make objective measures, and perhaps you will even work toward developing new and improved methods of capturing even more accurate representations of speech.

If you've made it this far through this chapter, bravo to you! You've likely learned some things along the way, and hopefully you found the material to be a bit more interesting than you might have originally suspected. On the other hand, if you made your way back here by skipping ahead because you couldn't wait to read the exciting conclusion, make sure you go back as there's some really interesting stuff in the middle bits of this chapter. Happy learning!

References

Awan, S., Barkmeier-Kraemer, J., Courey, M., Deliyski, D., Eadie, T., Hillman, R., et al. (2015). *Rec-*

ommended protocol for instrumental assessment of voice. Unpublished manuscript, American Speech-Language-Hearing Association: Ad hoc Committee on Instrumental Voice Assessment Protocols.

Baken, R. J., & Orlikoff, R. F. (2000). *Clinical measurement of speech and voice* (2nd ed.). San Diego, CA: Singular Thomson Learning.

Barlow, S. M., Finan, D. S., Andreatta, R. D., & Boliek, C. (2009). Kinematic measurement of speech and early orofacial movements. In M. R. McNeil (Ed.), *Clinical measurement of sensorimotor speech disorders* (pp. 80–99). New York, NY: Thieme Medical.

Behrman, A., & Orlikoff, R. F. (1997). Instrumentation in voice assessment and treatment. *American Journal of Speech-Language Pathology, 6*(4), 9.

Bernhardt, B., Gick, B., Bacsfalvi, P., & Adler-Bock, M. (2005). Ultrasound in speech therapy with adolescents and adults. *Clinical Linguistics and Phonetics, 19*(6–7), 605–617.

Cardarelli, F. (2012). *Encyclopaedia of scientific units, weights and measures: Their SI equivalences and origins.* London, UK: Springer London.

DeCanne, B. (2013, September 9). *Achieving better voice quality: Why smartphones need 3 microphones.* Retrieved September 12, 2016, from http://www.embedded.com/design/real-world-applications/4420680/Achieving-better-voice-quality--why-smartphones-need-3-microphones

Deliyski, D. D., Evans, M. K., & Shaw, H. S. (2005). Influence of data acquisition environment on accuracy of acoustic voice quality measurements. *Journal of Voice, 19*(2), 176–186.

Deliyski, D. D., Shaw, H. S., & Evans, M. K. (2005a). Adverse effects of environmental noise on acoustic voice quality measurements. *Journal of Voice, 19*(1), 15–28.

Deliyski, D. D., Shaw, H. S., & Evans, M. K. (2005b). Influence of sampling rate on accuracy and reliability of acoustic voice analysis. *Logopedics Phoniatrics Vocology, 30*(2), 55–62.

Dictionary (n.d.). In. Dictionary.com. Retrieved from http://www.dictionary.com/browse/error

Fava, G., Oliveira, G., Baglione, M., Pimpinella, M., & Spitzer, J. B. (2016). The use of sound level meter apps in the clinical setting. *American Journal of Speech-Language Pathology, 25*(1), 14.

Fox, C. M., Ramig, L. O., Ciucci, M. R., Sapir, S., McFarland, D. H., & Farley, B. G. (2006). The science and practice of LSVT/LOUD: Neural plasticity-principled approach to treating individuals with Parkinson disease and other neurological disorders. *Seminars in Speech and Language, 27*(4), 283–299.

Goldsmith, M. (2012). *Discord: The story of noise.* Oxford, UK: Oxford University Press.

Kardous, C. A., & Shaw, P. B. (2014). Evaluation of smartphone sound measurement applications. *Journal of the Acoustical Society of America, 135*(4), 186–192.

Maryn, Y., & Zarowski, A. (2015). Calibration of clinical audio recording and analysis systems for sound intensity measurement. *American Journal of Speech-Language Pathology, 24*(4), 608.

Mehta, D., & Hillman, R. E. (2007). Use of aerodynamic measures in clinical voice assessment. *SIG 3 Perspectives on Voice and Voice Disorders, 17*, 14–18.

Monson, B. B., Hunter, E. J., Lotto, A. J., & Story, B. H. (2014). The perceptual significance of high-frequency energy in the human voice. *Frontiers in Psychology, 5*, 587.

Neel, A. T. (2010). Using acoustic phonetics in clinical practice. *SIG 5 Perspectives on Speech Science and Orofacial Disorders, 20*, 14–24.

Nyquist, H. (1928). Certain topics in telegraph transmission theory. *Transactions of the American Institute of Electrical Engineers, 47*(2), 617–644.

Oliveira, G., Fava, G., Baglione, M., & Pimpinella, M. (2016). Mobile digital recording: Adequacy of the iRig and iOS device for acoustic and perceptual analysis of normal voice. *Journal of Voice, 31*(2), 236–242.

Shannon, C. E. (1949). Communication in the presence of noise. *Proceedings of the IRE, 37*(1), 10–21.

Svec, J. G., & Granqvist, S. (2010). Guidelines for selecting microphones for human voice production research. *American Journal of Speech-Language Pathology, 19*(4), 356–368.

Svec, J. G., Schutte, H. K., & Miller, D. G. (1996). A subharmonic vibratory pattern in normal vocal folds. *Journal of Speech Language and Hearing Research, 39*(1), 135.

Titze, I. R. (1995). *Workshop on acoustic voice analysis: Summary statement.* Iowa City, IA: National Center for Voice and Speech.

Titze, I. R., & Winholtz, W. S. (1993). Effect of microphone type and placement on voice perturbation measurements. *Journal of Speech, Language, and Hearing Research, 36*(6), 1177–1190.

Uloza, V., Padervinskis, E., Vegiene, A., Pribuisiene, R., Saferis, V., Vaiciukynas, E., . . . Verikas, A. (2015). Exploring the feasibility of smartphone microphone for measurement of acoustic voice parameters and voice pathology screening. *European Archives of Oto-Rhino-Laryngology, 272*(11), 3391–3399.

Vogel, A., & Morgan, A. (2009). Factors affecting the quality of sound recording for speech and voice analysis. *International Journal of Speech-Language Pathology, 11*(6), 431–437.

Vogel, A. P., Rosen, K. M., Morgan, A. T., & Reilly, S. (2014). Comparability of modern recording devices for speech analysis: Smartphone, landline, laptop, and hard disc recorder. *Folia Phoniatrica et Logopaedica, 66,* 244–250.

Winholtz, W. S., & Titze, I. R. (1997). Conversion of a head-mounted microphone signal into calibrated SPL units. *Journal of Voice, 11*(4), 417–421.

Zajac, D. J., Warren, D. W., & Hinton, V. A. (2009). Aerodynamic assessment of motor speech disorders. In M. R. McNeil (Ed.), *Clinical measurement of sensorimotor speech disorders* (pp. 64–79). New York, NY: Thieme Medical.

Measurement Conversions

Metric System to U.S. (English System) Measurement

Prefix	Multiply by:	Factor	Example, With Abbreviations
terra-	trillion	10^{12}	terrameter, Tm
giga-	billion	10^9	gigameter, Gm
mega-	million	10^5	megameter, Mg
kilo-	thousand	10^3	kilometer, km
hecto-	hundred	10^2	hectrogram, hg
deca-	ten	10^1	decameter, dm

Prefix	Divide by:	Factor	Example, With Abbreviations
deci-	ten	10^{-1}	nonagram, ng
centi-	hundred	10^{-2}	micrometer, μm
milli-	thousand	10^{-3}	millimeter, mm
micro-	million	10^{-6}	centimeter, cm
nano-	billion	10^{-9}	decigram, dg
pico-	trillion	10^{-12}	picogram, pg

Reading Passages

The Rainbow Passage

When the sunlight strikes raindrops in the air, they act like a prism and form a rainbow. The rainbow is a division of white light into many beautiful colors. These take the shape of a long round arch, with its path high above and its two ends apparently beyond the horizon. There is, according to legend, a boiling pot of gold at one end. People look, but no one ever finds it. When a man looks for something beyond his reach, his friends say he is looking for a pot of gold at the end of the rainbow.

Throughout the centuries, men have explained the rainbow in various ways. Some have accepted it as a miracle without physical explanation. To the Hebrews, it was a token that there would be no more universal floods. The Greeks used to imagine that it was a sign from the gods to foretell war or heavy rain. The Norsemen considered the rainbow as a bridge over which the gods passed from Earth to their home in the sky. Other men have tried to explain the phenomenon physically. Aristotle thought that the rainbow was caused by reflection of the sun's rays by the rain. Since then, physicists have found that it is not reflection, but refraction by the raindrops which causes the rainbow. Many complicated ideas about the rainbow have been formed. The difference in the rainbow depends considerably upon the size of the water drops, and the width of the colored band increases as the size of the drops increase. The actual primary rainbow observed is said to be the effect of superposition of a number of bows. If the red of the second bow falls upon the green of the first, the result is to give a bow with an abnormally wide yellow band, since red and green lights, when mixed, form yellow. This is a very common type of bow—one showing mainly red and yellow, with little or no green or blue.

Comments

This reading passage is from Fairbanks, G. (1960). *Voice and articulation drillbook* (2nd ed.) New York: Harper and Brothers, p. 127. A common misconception is that this passage is "phonetically balanced," meaning that the frequency of occurrence of the phonemes in the passage is equivalent to that of general American English. Given that the passage was written in 1960, it is highly unlikely that conversational English has remained the same for the past 45 years.

The Farm Passage

John and I went to the farm in June. The sun shone all day, and wind waved the grass in wide fields that ran by the road. Most birds had left on their trek south, but old friends were there to greet us. Piles of wood had been stacked by the door, left there by the man who lives twelve miles down the road. The stove would not last till dawn on what he had cut, so I went and chopped more till the sun set. The sky stays light quite late as far north as that, but I knew it would be a cold night. The car seat was piled high with stuff, but it would have to stay there for the night. It was too far to go to take it all out now. Food was the next thing. John had lit the stove, so I cooked up some hash and beans, which was what was in the cans that I could reach with least work. My box with most of the food was deep in the car, and it was too dark now to dig my way down to it. When served hot, hash and beans taste quite good if it's been a long time since you last ate. We had some bread, of a sort that you find in small stores far from the towns, where the new ways to make bread, and the new types of flour have not yet reached. We had passed such a place on the road, and had stocked up with some things that can't be bought in a town. Things like home baked bread; and real cheese made from cow's milk; jam with real fruit in it; and fresh milk with rich deep cream on top. We shall not have a chance to buy these in the cold months that are to come

Comments

The Farm Passage (Crystal & House, 1982). Segmental durations in connected speech signals:

Preliminary results. *Journal of the Acoustical Society of America, 72*, 705–716. consists of 313 monosyllabic words, comprising 553 consonants and 327 vowels in various classes of speech sounds according to their frequency of occurrence in conversational English.

The Grandfather Passage

You wish to know all about my grandfather. Well, he is nearly 93 years old, yet he still thinks as swiftly as ever. He dresses himself in an ancient black frock coat, usually missing several buttons. A long beard clings to his chin, giving those who observe him a pronounced feeling of the utmost respect. When he speaks, his voice is just a bit cracked and quivers a bit. Twice each day, he plays skillfully and with zest upon a small organ. Except in winter, when the snow or ice prevents, he slowly takes a short walk in the open air each day. We have often urged him to walk more and smoke less, but he always answers "Banana Oil." Grandfather likes to be modern in his language.

Comments

This reading passage is from Darley, Aronson, and Brown (1975). The colorful history of this passage can be found in Reilly and Fisher (2012). Reilly, J., and Fisher, J. L. (2012). Sherlock Holmes and the strange case of the missing attribution: A historical note on *"The Grandfather Passage." Journal of Speech Language, and Hearing Research, 55*, 84–88.

The Zoo Passage

Look at this book with us. It's a story about a zoo. That is where bears go. Today it's very cold out of doors, but we see a cloud overhead that's a pretty, white fluffy shape. We hear that straw covers the floor of cages to keep the chill away; yet a deer walks through the trees with her head high. They feed seeds to birds so they're able to fly. Everybody

Comments

This passage is from Fletcher, S. G. (1972). Contingencies for bioelectronic modification of nasality. *Journal of Speech and Hearing Disorders, 37*, 329–346. This passage contains no nasal consonants.

The Towne-Heuer Passage

If I take a trip this August, I will probably go to Austria. Or I could go to Italy. All of the places of Europe are easy to get to by air, rail, ship, or auto. Everybody I have talked to says he would like to go to Europe also.

Every year there are varieties of festivals or fairs at a lot of places. All sorts of activities, such as foods to eat, sights to see, occur. Oh, I love to eat ices seated outdoors! The people of each area are reported to like us—the people of the U.S.A. It is said that that is true except in Paris.

Aid is easy to get because the officials are helpful. Aid is always available if trouble arises. It helps to have with you a list of offices or officials to call if you do require aid. If you are lost, you will always be helped to locate your route or hotel. The local police will assist you, if they are able to speak as you do. Otherwise, a phrase book is useful.

I have had to have help of this sort each trip abroad. However, it was always easy to locate. Happily, I hope, less help will be required this trip. Last trip every hotel was occupied. I had to ask everywhere for flats. Two earlier trips were hard because of heat or lack of heat at hotels.

On second thought, I may want to travel in autumn instead of in August. Many countries can be expensive in the summer months and much less so in autumn. November and December can make fine months for entertainment in many European countries. There may be concerts and musical events more often than during the summer. Milan, Rome, and Hamburg, not to mention Berlin, Vienna, and Madrid, are most often mentioned for music.

Most of my friends and I wouldn't miss the chance to try the exciting, interesting, and appetizing menus at most continental restaurants. In many European countries, food is inexpensive and interestingly prepared. Servings may be small but meals are taken more often so that there is no need to go hungry.

Maritime countries make many meals of seafood such as mussels, clams, shrimp, flounder, and salmon or herring. Planning and making your own meals cannot be done even in most small, inexpensive hotels. One must eat in the dining room or in restaurants. Much fun can be had meeting the local natives during mealtimes. Many of them can tell you where to find amusing and interesting shops and sights not mentioned in tour manuals.

Comments

This passage comes from Heuer, R., Towne, C., Hockstein, N. E., Andrade, D. F., and Sataloff, R.vT. (2000). The Towne-Heuer Reading Passage—A reliable aid to the evaluation of voice. *Journal of Voice, 14*, 236–239. The authors note that it was written intentionally to have awkward phrasing, to test the abilities of the speaker to manage voice and speech production under a variety of linguistic demands. Within the first four paragraphs, there are 100 potential juncture-vowel occurrences with which to test the phonation onset style of the reader (particularly the presence of hard glottal attacks). The first four paragraphs do not include any nasal sounds, whereas the last three paragraphs have 183 such occurrences.

The Caterpillar

Do you like amusement parks? Well, I sure do. To amuse myself, I went twice last spring. My most MEMORABLE moment was riding on the Caterpillar, which is a gigantic rollercoaster high above the ground. When I saw how high the Caterpillar rose into the bright blue sky I knew it was for me. After waiting in line for thirty minutes, I made it to the front where the man measured my height to see if I was tall enough. I gave the man my coins, asked for change, and jumped on the cart. Tick, tick, tick, the Caterpillar climbed slowly up the tracks. It went SO high I could see the parking lot. Boy was I SCARED! I thought to myself, "There's no turning back now." People were so scared they screamed as we swiftly zoomed fast, fast, and faster along the tracks. As quickly as it started, the Caterpillar came to a stop. Unfortunately, it was time to pack the car and drive home. That night I dreamt of the wild ride on the Caterpillar. Taking a trip to the amusement park and riding on the Caterpillar was my MOST memorable moment ever!

Comments

This passage is from Patel, R., Connaghan, K., Franco, D., Edsall, E., Forgit, D., Olsen, L. et al. (2013). "The Caterpillar": A novel reading passage for assessment of motor speech disorders. *American Journal of Speech-Language Pathology, 22*, 1–9. This passage was designed to provide a contemporary, easily read, contextual speech sample at Grade level 5.0, containing prosodic contrasts and words of increasing length and complexity. It contains 197 words and 261 syllables; 64% of words are "high frequency" based on Fry (2000). *1000 instant words.* Westminster, CA: Teacher Created Resources.

The Marvin Williams Passage

Marvin Williams is only nine. Marvin lives with his mother on Monroe Avenue in Vernon Valley. Marvin loves all movies, even eerie ones with evil villains in them. Whenever a new movie is in the area, Marvin is usually an early arrival. Nearly every evening, Marvin is in row one, along the aisle.

Comments

This passage was written by Professor Robert F. Orlikoff when he was a speech-language pathology student at Teachers College, Columbia University. It contains many nasal sounds and few voiceless sounds, resulting in *few* voice onsets and offsets.

The Christopher Cook Passage

Twelve or thirteen minutes ago, I had a highly respected and prosperous person visit my toy store on Thomas Street. Called Christopher Cook, he is an important official in the town. His daughter Tessie is studying calculus at the local university. She is, perhaps, the smartest and prettiest girl in the country. It must be close to her birthday, because her father purchased a very expensive toy carousel. He had me gift wrap it for him using the most colorful paper I have in the entire store.

Comments

This passage was written by Professor F. Robert Orlikoff when he was a speech-language pathology student at Teachers College, Columbia University. It contains many voiceless sounds, resulting in *frequent* voice onsets and offsets.

Frequencies of the Musical Scale (A_4 = 440 Hz)

Musical Note	Frequency	Musical Note	Frequency	Musical Note	Frequency	Musical Note	Frequency	Musical Note	Frequency
C_0	16.35	C_1	32.70	C_2	65.41	C_3	130.81	C_4	261.63
$C_0\# (D_b)$	17.32	$C_1\# (D_b)$	34.65	$C_2\# (D_b)$	60.20	$C_3\# (D_b)$	138.59	$C_4\# (D_b)$	277.18
D_0	18.35	D_1	36.71	D_2	73.42	D_3	146.83	D_4	293.66
$D_0\# (E_b)$	19.45	$D_1\# (E_b)$	38.89	$D_2\# (E_b)$	77.78	$D_3\# (E_b)$	155.56	$D_4\# (E_b)$	311.13
E_0	20.60	E_1	41.20	E_2	82.41	E_3	164.91	E_4	320.63
F_0	21.83	F_1	43.65	F_2	87.31	F_3	174.61	F_4	349.23
$F_0\# (G_b)$	23.13	$F_1\# (G_b)$	46.25	$F_2\# (G_b)$	92.50	$F_3\# (G_b)$	185.00	$F_4\# (G_b)$	369.99
G_0	24.50	G_1	48.99	G_2	97.99	G_3	196.00	G_4	392.00
$G_0\# (A_b)$	25.96	$G_1\# (A_b)$	51.91	$G_2\# (A_b)$	103.83	$G_3\# (A_b)$	207.00	$G_4\# (A_b)$	415.30
A_0	27.50	A_1	55.00	A_2	110.00	A_3	220.00	A_4	440.00
$A_0\# (B_b)$	29.14	$A_1\# (B_b)$	58.27	$A_2\# (B_b)$	116.54	$A_3\# (B_b)$	233.08	$A_4\# (B_b)$	466.16
B_0	30.87	B_1	61.74	B_2	123.47	B_3	246.94	B_4	493.88

Musical Note	Frequency
C_5	523.25
$C_5\# (D_b)$	554.37
D_5	598.33
$D_5\# (E_b)$	622.25
E_5	659.26
F_5	698.46
$F_5\# (G_b)$	739.00
G_5	783.99
$G_5\# (A_b)$	830.61
A_5	880.00
$A_5\# (B_b)$	932.33
B_5	987.77

The International Phonetic Alphabet

THE INTERNATIONAL PHONETIC ALPHABET (revised to 2015)

CONSONANTS (PULMONIC)

	Bilabial	Labiodental	Dental	Alveolar	Postalveolar	Retroflex	Palatal	Velar	Uvular	Pharyngeal	Glottal
Plosive	p b			t d		ʈ ɖ	c ɟ	k ɡ	q ɢ		ʔ
Nasal	m	ɱ		n		ɳ	ɲ	ŋ	N		
Trill	ʙ			r					R		
Tap or Flap		ⱱ		ɾ		ɽ					
Fricative	ɸ β	f v	θ ð	s z	ʃ ʒ	ʂ ʐ	ç ʝ	x ɣ	χ ʁ	ħ ʕ	h ɦ
Lateral fricative				ɬ ɮ							
Approximant		ʋ		ɹ		ɻ	j	ɰ			
Lateral approximant				l		ɭ	ʎ	L			

Symbols to the right in a cell are voiced, to the left are voiceless. Shaded areas denote articulations judged impossible.

CONSONANTS (NON-PULMONIC)

Clicks	Voiced implosives	Ejectives
⊙ Bilabial	ɓ Bilabial	ʼ Examples:
ǀ Dental	ɗ Dental/alveolar	pʼ Bilabial
ǃ (Post)alveolar	ʄ Palatal	tʼ Dental/alveolar
ǂ Palatoalveolar	ɠ Velar	kʼ Velar
ǁ Alveolar lateral	ʛ Uvular	sʼ Alveolar fricative

OTHER SYMBOLS

ʍ Voiceless labial-velar fricative

w Voiced labial-velar approximant

ɥ Voiced labial-palatal approximant

ʜ Voiceless epiglottal fricative

ʢ Voiced epiglottal fricative

ʡ Epiglottal plosive

ɕ ʑ Alveolo-palatal fricatives

ɺ Voiced alveolar lateral flap

ɧ Simultaneous ʃ and x

Affricates and double articulations can be represented by two symbols joined by a tie bar if necessary.

t͡s k͡p

VOWELS

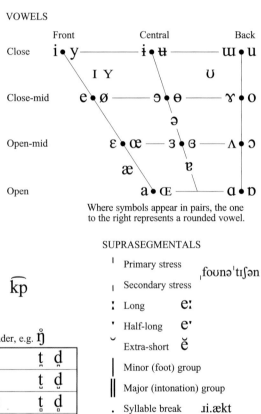

Where symbols appear in pairs, the one to the right represents a rounded vowel.

SUPRASEGMENTALS

ˈ Primary stress

ˌ Secondary stress   ˌfoʊnəˈtɪʃən

ː Long   eː

ˑ Half-long   eˑ

˘ Extra-short   ĕ

| Minor (foot) group

‖ Major (intonation) group

. Syllable break   ɹi.ækt

‿ Linking (absence of a break)

TONES AND WORD ACCENTS

LEVEL		CONTOUR	
e̋ or ˥ Extra high		ě or ˩˥ Rising	
é ˦ High		ê ˥˩ Falling	
ē ˧ Mid		e᷄ ˦˥ High rising	
è ˨ Low		e᷅ ˩˨ Low rising	
ȅ ˩ Extra low		e᷈ ˧˦˧ Rising-falling	
ꜜ Downstep		↗ Global rise	
ꜛ Upstep		↘ Global fall	

DIACRITICS Some diacritics may be placed above a symbol with a descender, e.g. ŋ̊

̥ Voiceless	n̥ d̥	̤ Breathy voiced	b̤ a̤	̪ Dental	t̪ d̪		
̬ Voiced	s̬ t̬	̰ Creaky voiced	b̰ a̰	̺ Apical	t̺ d̺		
ʰ Aspirated	tʰ dʰ	̼ Linguolabial	t̼ d̼	̻ Laminal	t̻ d̻		
̹ More rounded	ɔ̹	ʷ Labialized	tʷ dʷ	̃ Nasalized	ẽ		
̜ Less rounded	ɔ̜	ʲ Palatalized	tʲ dʲ	ⁿ Nasal release	dⁿ		
̟ Advanced	u̟	ˠ Velarized	tˠ dˠ	ˡ Lateral release	dˡ		
̠ Retracted	e̠	ˤ Pharyngealized	tˤ dˤ	̚ No audible release	d̚		
̈ Centralized	ë	̴ Velarized or pharyngealized	ɫ				
̽ Mid-centralized	e̽	̝ Raised	e̝ (ɹ̝ = voiced alveolar fricative)				
̩ Syllabic	n̩	̞ Lowered	e̞ (β̞ = voiced bilabial approximant)				
̯ Non-syllabic	e̯	̘ Advanced Tongue Root	e̘				
˞ Rhoticity	ɚ a˞	̙ Retracted Tongue Root	e̙				

470

Index